Simply Blessed

D1302178

Simply Blessed

Finding Joy in the Little Things

KIM CHAFFIN

BroadStreet
PUBLISHING

BroadStreet Publishing Group, LLC
Racine, Wisconsin, USA
BroadStreetPublishing.com

Simply Blessed: Finding Joy in the Little Things

Stock or custom editions of BroadStreet Publishing titles may be purchased in bulk for educational, business, ministry, fundraising, or sales promotional use. For information, please e-mail info@broadstreetpublishing.com.

Cover design by Chris Garborg at garborgdesign.com
Typesetting by Katherine Lloyd at theDESKonline.com

Printed in the United States of America

18 19 20 21 22 5 4 3 2 1

To my daughter, Hanna.
She is the strongest person I know because
she has found her strength in her weakness.

"That is why, for Christ's sake, I delight in weaknesses,
in insults, in hardships, in persecutions, in difficulties.
For when I am weak, then I am strong."
(2 Corinthians 12:10)

I would like to acknowledge Barb Hollace
for her prayers, wisdom, and editing.
This book could not have been written without her.
She is to me like Aaron was to Moses.

CONTENTS

STANDING FIRM

IT'S MORE THAN A BUILDING

GETTING STARTED

God does not call the qualified; he qualifies the called. For me, writing a book is the perfect example of this. Spelling and proper grammar are not my strong suits. I once wrote a phone message to my dad from a man who wanted a quote on some "rough castings," and I wrote "ruff castings." My dad called me into his office and began barking like a dog when he saw the way I had spelled "rough."

Even with the "ruff" beginning, I was excited about the joy I found in writing. Now what was I to do with it? God often gives me great ideas while I'm in the shower. One day in the shower, as I prayed for clarity about what to do with my writing, I felt him speaking to my heart to write a blog. He dropped the name of it into my head and my heart as I washed the shampoo out of my hair: *Heartfelt Ramblings of a Midlife Domestic Goddess*. I laughed out loud!

"Domestic goddess" is what I called myself for years because I thought it sounded more exciting than "stay-at-home mom," "homemaker," or "taxicab driver." And it was much more professional when I cleaned spit-up off my shirt, picked a horse hoof out of the dryer (courtesy of my daughter), and cleaned up a rotting cow's head my dogs had dragged into the driveway from a nearby field. My husband laughed so hard when I called him and said, "Can you tell me where in the *Domestic Goddess Handbook* it says, 'Cow's head cleanup'?" Despite the repulsiveness of those chores, it was in those moments that I learned to laugh and give thanks to God, because in him we can find joy in all things.

My heartfelt ramblings within the pages of *Simply Blessed* are not deep theology, and I have a few reasons that I wrote the book the way I did. When I was a new believer, I was filled with so many questions. Sitting in my first Bible study, I remember feeling overwhelmed by the fact that everyone else seemed to know who the patriarchs were, while I was not even sure if I was really saved or if there was some special way I should be praying. I learned so much from Beth Moore's beautifully written *The Patriarchs*, but I still walked away wishing there was a book that covered the basics, the nuts and bolts, to help me understand. I felt like a kid who was pushed into the deep end of the pool with those who already knew how to swim. As they enjoyed their time in the water, I was frantically dog-paddling, trying to keep up. I needed a foundation I could set my feet on.

In this thirty-one-day collection of short devotional stories that go back to the nuts and bolts of Christianity, I hope you see God for who he is: God. He is not a religion like the one we have made him into. He is the God of relationship. He is comfortable, like your favorite Saturday sweatpants.

The second reason I wrote this book the way I did is because even the most expert swimmer can use a refresher course from time to time. There is something about being in the presence of a new believer that renews you. To see the newfound joy in them is exhilarating. This thirty-one-day jaunt with God is meant to bring the most seasoned believer back to the shallow end of the pool for a bit and give someone who is just coming to know God a firm foundation to stand on.

Please do not rush through this book. Take one day at a time and complete the simple "Pray It," "Do It," "Write It," "Think About It," or similarly named tasks at the end of each day. You will also find a journal page at the end of each day for any other thoughts you want to write down. Feel free to use it in addition to the journal/notepad I ask you to buy in the following pages. If you miss a day because life gets crazy, don't try to cram in two days. Just pick up where you left off and keep moving forward. Enjoy your journey with God!

Finding God in the Mundane

We can easily get so wrapped up in religion that we forget to look for God in everything, even the little things. Often, it is the littlest things that show us the true character of God. In the everyday moments (as well as in times of heartache), I think we can find joy if we are willing to look for it. God is never too busy for us. In the funny, painful, and even mundane moments, he is waiting to pour out his love and forgiveness on each of us.

For years, I believed there was a God—but I lived under the misconception that he was this unapproachable, almighty, and powerful heavenly being that you prayed to only if something was wrong. I treated him like he was the all-powerful Wizard of Oz, and I laid my requests before him with the same uneasiness Dorothy felt before the wizard.

When my son was in kindergarten, I knew something needed to change in my life. It was as if something was missing. I found myself thinking a lot about God. I started feeling that maybe *he* was what was missing from my life.

One particular Friday afternoon, I had to make a parenting decision and stick to it. I told my son that if he did not stop misbehaving, he would not get to go to the lake for the weekend with the rest of the family. He was warned that the two of us would stay home. My son was five years old and did not think I would really do that. He was wrong.

That weekend, while we were home alone, God continued to convict me about going to church. He put a particular little church on my mind and reminded me that several years ago, I had met a woman who attended there. I checked the service time and on Sunday, my son and I went to church. Much to my surprise, the woman God had reminded me of still went there. That Sunday morning, as the pastor gave his sermon, my heart began to feel so much love. There was an altar call, and I went forward and told God I needed him in my life.

That day, in that little church, God changed me. That was the moment I let go of my Wizard of Oz misconception and God began to show me he wanted to be involved in all parts of my life. I began to see him in even the most mundane things.

God is with us in everything, even our daily tasks—the everyday, often boring or trivial things of life that we take for granted. For example, I saw God in my pile of ironing one day. Okay, not literally, but figuratively.

As I stood at the ironing board with a huge pile of my husband's button-downs and a sour attitude, God showed me how blessed I was to have a husband. Not only did I have a husband, but I had a husband who had a job that allowed me to stay home and take care of our family. In that pile of ironing, something so little in the scheme of life, I found happiness. All of a sudden, what felt like a bothersome job became a joy to me, and I prayed for my husband as I ironed that pile of shirts. God is with us in everything, even the mundane things of life. Look around you— he is there.

Pray It

Today, say a prayer asking God to guide you as you do this study. If you are not sure how to pray, I will get you started and you can finish in your own words:

> *Dear Lord, please help me find joy in all things. I want to know you better, Lord.*

Do It

Think about your normal day. What is going to be the best time for you to read this book without interruption? Make a game plan and do your best to stick with it. I know life happens, so be intentional about taking each day to seek God.

If you don't have a Bible, please go to your local Christian bookstore and get one. I love the NIV translation, but there are so many good translations to choose from. Don't be afraid to ask for help at the store when picking out your Bible.

Grab a notebook or a journal while you are out today or tomorrow. It doesn't need to be fancy. A spiral notebook will work just fine.

Blessings

You are on your way to a new habit, a new place with God. Look for him today. He is there in the little things: the spilled milk, the dirty laundry, the sound of silence. From the most mundane things to the most painful things, you can find unexpected joy if you take the time to look for it. I'm looking forward to joining you tomorrow.

A Penny for Your Thoughts

REDEEMED

In Christ, we are made new. We are clothed in his righteousness (Isaiah 61:10); the sin-stained rags from our past are gone. The enemy (satan) wants nothing more than to trip us up with lies, which cause us to stumble. If we believe the lie that we are not worthy of God's love and compassion, we may pursue things that are not in our best interest.

The readings in this section give us a glimpse of how we can overcome any obstacle with God. The short lessons will give you hope and remind you how much God loves you while showing you that God has much better things planned for you than what the world offers. I pray that after reading these short lessons, you will have the courage to tell the enemy to take a hike when he comes knocking at your door.

Day 2

Off-Road Driving

*W*e dipped our toes in the water yesterday, and today we're going to get all the way into the proverbial pool I talked about in my introduction. God has some awesome things for us, so what are you waiting for? Jump in, the water is perfect.

I live in the Pacific Northwest, and it is common to see big trucks or Jeeps covered in mud from a day of off-road driving. Much of the area where I live has not been touched by the development of homes or strip malls, so it's the perfect place to have some fun.

One day I saw a Jeep with the doors off. The driver as well as the Jeep was covered with mud. My daughter and I both had a good laugh when we saw him. What a joy it must be to play in the mud, to have the freedom to just get dirty, laugh, and enjoy the thrill of the ride.

A short time after seeing that Jeep, my husband and I took his truck into the mountains of Idaho for a hike to Hunt Lake. In order to get to the trailhead, we had to take a logging road up the mountain. I was thankful that my husband was behind the wheel, because I was in a bit of a panic about how narrow the road was and how steep the drop-off was at times. (When it comes to panic, I am an expert.)

On those rough logging roads, the Forest Service makes "kelly humps," which are drainage ditches big enough to swallow a little car. At one point during our ride, we hit a bump that bounced my

11

husband so hard, he hit the ignition with his leg and turned the truck off. At first we didn't realize what had happened. I had the "What now?" feeling in my stomach. We were in the mountains with no cell service and a broken-down truck. We had a good laugh once we figured out what had happened.

We didn't find any mud pits that day, but the truck was dirty and I had one of the best days ever with my husband as we drove over a few trees and through the kelly humps.

There is a different kind of off-road driving that seems exhilarating at first—but the excitement doesn't last long. We go off-road driving when we let sin take hold of the wheel and we just roll with it. Eventually, sin takes us right down into the biggest kelly humps ever. We are stuck in a giant pit, and it seems like there is no way to get out.

Unlike the mud that flies from the tires of the trucks and Jeeps that go off-road driving, it is shame, a feeling of unworthiness and helplessness, that is kicked up when we let sin drive us off the road. Temptation grabs the wheel and pushes us out of the driver's seat, and we find ourselves broken, covered in the dirtiness of our sin, lost, and alone. You can bet that the sin that drove us there is not going to help us out of the kelly hump. As a matter of fact, it is going to stand there and kick dirt on us, laughing like the bully on the playground. If we look back, it is often clear to us where we took a wrong turn and went off the road we were supposed to stay on. When that happens, it is time to ask God to take the wheel. Only God can get us out of the mud pit of sin and shame.

Think of God as a powerful car wash. Let him wash you clean: "Generous in love—God, give grace! Huge in mercy—wipe out my bad record. Scrub away my guilt, soak out my sins in your laundry" (Psalm 51:1–2 MSG)."

When we leave a car wash, we leave the dirt and grime behind.

We can do the same with our mistakes and poor choices when we bring them to God. The road is going to be bumpy from time to time, but with God in the driver's seat, you'll always stay on the right road. Someday, I hope to get real dirty when mud flies from the wheels of my Jeep as I am safely buckled in—but in my day-to-day life, I'll keep my eyes focused on Jesus and let God take the wheel.

Will I get off on the wrong road from time to time? Yes, I will—and so will you, because we are not perfect. We all fall short from time to time, and we need to remember that our repentance washes us clean. Given God's forgiveness, we go from our dirty rags to his glorious riches.

Pray It

I invite you to say a simple prayer asking God to show you what needs to be washed away from your life. Don't rush your prayer. Take some time to sit quietly and let God show you what he wants to wash away. If you are not sure how to start a prayer, I will get you started and you can finish in your own words:

> *Father, I am not perfect. I know there have been times I have gone off the course you have set for me. Please take the wheel and steer me back to the road that you have chosen for me, because I know it is good. I have sinned and I need you to wash me from the inside out. Lord, you are generous in love, full of grace, and huge in mercy, so I am asking that you would scrub away my guilt and soak me in your forgiveness.*

Think About It

Take some time to think about what you just read. Did God show you any areas in your life that need to be washed clean?

Write It

Please turn to the next page and take a moment to write what is on your heart. What is it you need washed out of your life? I believe that when we have been cleansed of a spiritual stain, the enemy loses control over it.

A Penny for Your Thoughts

Rags to Riches

*Y*esterday we looked at how we can get off the road—or course—that God has planned for us and how he is like our spiritual "car wash." God doesn't stop there. That is just the beginning of our journey with him. Today I want to look at the story of a young girl named Annie. This story will help paint a picture of what God has for each of us.

Annie is a Broadway musical based on the popular Harold Gray comic strip *Little Orphan Annie*. It is the story of a little orphan girl who is desperately looking for her parents. After running away from the orphanage to find them, she is brought back. Luckily for Annie, she finds herself in the right place at the right time and ends up in the home of billionaire Daddy Warbucks for Christmas. As the story unfolds, you see a bond forming between them. The little girl captures the heart of Daddy Warbucks, and he opens his home and his heart to her.

Many of us can relate to this story. We often see ourselves as worthy of only rags, when God wants to pour his riches—his love, mercy, grace, and forgiveness—on us. God, through his forgiveness, wants to remove the rags of our past and clothe us in something new. When we repent of our sins and believe in our hearts that Christ died for our sins, we are made new. Our rags are gone.

"Therefore, if anyone is in Christ, the new creation has come:

The old has gone, the new is here!" (2 Corinthians 5:17). Seems simple, right? Confess, believe, throw out our rags, and move on to a life of spiritual riches in Christ. For many, that is exactly what happens—but some of us find ourselves putting our rags back on again, doubting that we are really forgiven. You may believe there is no way God can actually forgive you. Maybe you have heard countless times that you are useless and unworthy. Maybe that is what you believe God sees when he looks at you.

God doesn't dangle forgiveness in front of us like we might dangle a carrot in front of a horse. It is not something he puts just out of our reach and only offers to a few lucky people. It is freely given to all of us. When we don't believe that we are truly forgiven, we continue to wear the rags of our past. It is like saying, "God, I don't believe you are big enough."

In Christ, you can move from rags to riches if you simply accept the forgiveness he freely offers. Isaiah 61:10 tells us that God wants to dress us in his finest:

> I will rejoice greatly in the LORD,
> My soul will exult in my God;
> For He has clothed me with garments of salvation,
> He has wrapped me with a robe of righteousness,
> As a bridegroom decks himself with a garland,
> And as a bride adorns herself with her jewels. (NASB)

Read that again. He has clothed you in "garments of salvation." He has wrapped you in a "robe of righteousness." You are compared to a bridegroom and a bride. A bridegroom looks his best on his wedding day, and his bride is glowing and radiant. This is what God wants for you.

I heard an amazing woman of God named Jan speak at a women's retreat in May 2014. She said, "Stop wearing the rags of this world when you are clothed in righteousness." She was saying that we have been forgiven, redeemed, and made righteous in the eyes of God. We are spiritually new, yet we continue to pick up the hurt, sin, and shame of our old life and put it back on.

If you had your choice between crisp, clean, white socks and smelly, dirty socks that have walked through all manner of mud and filth, you would choose the clean ones, right? It is an easy choice when it's about socks. But for some reason, when it comes to receiving all that God has for us, we find ourselves reaching for the past, no matter how dirty it is.

We can't keep dressing ourselves in our sins and guilt because our past is familiar to us and the world tells us it is what we deserve. We need to look to God, who sees beyond our mistakes. He *wants* to clothe us in righteousness.

God has given you a new wardrobe, so what are you waiting for? Throw out the rags and clothe yourself in the riches of his love, mercy, grace, and forgiveness. Take some time today to let the love of God fill your heart. Just sit with God for a moment before you move on to the tasks that I have for you today.

Think About It

Take a moment to read today's Scriptures again: 2 Corinthians 5:17 and Isaiah 61:10. Think about what they are saying. It is so important that you believe them to be true about you.

Write It and Pray It

Write your own prayer today. I encourage you to use the Scriptures I have given you as part of your prayer, because praying Scripture will help you see the truth of God in your own life: the truth that you can be clothed in righteousness. Use the next page to write your prayer.

A Penny for Your Thoughts

You Are More Than the Choices You Make

D o you remember the question I asked you yesterday? "If you had your choice between crisp, clean, white socks and smelly, dirty socks that have walked through all manner of mud and filth, you would choose the clean ones, right?" It is an easy choice when it's about socks. But for some reason, when it comes to receiving all that God has for us, we can get all tripped up because our past has a way of putting what feels like a permanent mark or label on us.

A few years ago, there was a quiz on Facebook where, if you got the wrong answer, you were required to turn your profile picture into a photo of a giraffe. There were giraffes all over Facebook. Of course, no one really turned into a giraffe, but I remember laughing for three days that I was one of the losers with a giraffe for a profile picture. It showed everyone that I made the "wrong choice."

Often, people allow the choices they make to define how they see themselves. Instead of a goofy giraffe, they see a big scarlet letter, a label that can be a self-fulfilling prophecy. Those unhealthy labels are lies the enemy wants us to never let go of. As I am writing this, the words to the song "You Are More" by Tenth Avenue North are playing in my head. The song talks about how we are more than the choices we make. Because of God's love, we are remade and are no longer labeled by our past mistakes.

With God, we can find our real identity. I have seen women move from lives of sorrow to lives of joy when they opened their hearts to receive his love and forgiveness. In him, they were truly remade. They tossed away any labels the enemy had them believing and raised their eyes to the Lord for a true picture of who they are!

Scripture has a lot to say about who we are in Christ, and when we dig in to find the truth, we can expose the lies we have believed about who we are. If you have never looked at the Bible, knowing where to start may feel a bit overwhelming. Don't worry—I've got you covered. In today's tasks, I have included some Scriptures that will show you how God feels about you.

Read It and Think About It

Take some time to read the following verses and let them sink in. Roll them around in your head and your heart. If one of them really jumps out at you, write it down and keep it where you will see it each day. I have Scriptures on sticky notes that I see every morning when I open my cupboard to get a coffee cup. I encourage you to do the same thing.

- God loves you: "But God is so rich in mercy, and he loved us so much, that even though we were dead because of our sins, he gave us life when he raised Christ from the dead. (It is only by God's grace that you have been saved!)" (Ephesians 2:4–5 NLT). God's love is enormous. You can find your identity in him, not in your mistakes.
- You are God's masterpiece: "For we are God's masterpiece. He has created us anew in Christ Jesus, so we can do the good things he planned for us long ago" (Ephesians 2:10 NLT). God created you and has a plan

for you. You need to understand that, no matter what lies you have believed. God sees you as his beloved daughter.

- You are without blame: "Even before he made the world, God loved us and chose us in Christ to be holy and without fault in his eyes" (Ephesians 1:4 NLT). When you allow God to erase the lies you carry from your past, you will begin to see yourself as he sees you: without blame.

Write It

I believe at least one of the preceding verses really spoke to you. Write it down on a sticky note and put it where you can see it. Every time you see it, read it. Let it be a reminder to you that there is nothing you have done that God cannot forgive.

Pray It

Take the simple truth of the preceding Scriptures and write your own prayer today on the next page. It doesn't need to be long or fancy. Who cares if your spelling is not perfect? God is not concerned about your grammar. He is concerned about the heart behind the words. This is between you and God, so be honest.

Listen to It

If you have access to the Internet, look up the song "You Are More" by Tenth Avenue North and listen to it before the end of the day. Let the words speak to your heart.

A Penny for Your Thoughts

God Loves Even Pigpen

In yesterday's lesson, we looked at the choices we make and the labels those choices can put on us. This is such an important idea that I want to camp on it a little longer in today's lesson. Being a picture person, I can relate to the cartoon character Pigpen from the *Peanuts* comic strip by Charles M. Schulz. Pigpen is a cute little boy who is always surrounded by a little whirlwind of dust and grime. It reminds me of the days my children would come in from playing and strip down in the laundry room to prevent the dirt from being dragged throughout the house.

As their parent, I stood there with a smile on my face, listening to them carry on about the fun they had, and knowing that under all the dirt were my perfect and beautiful children. No amount of dirt, grime, or naughty behavior could ever make me love them less. With each passing year, I have prayed for their safety, their futures, and their spouses. My children are now adults, and I have not stopped praying for them. I want them to have lives of abundant love, laughter, and joy. I pray for blessings for each of them and that they will achieve all their dreams.

When God looks down on us, his children, do we look a little like Pigpen? Are we going through life covered in lies that make us feel dirty? The enemy wants nothing more than to make us feel that we are unworthy and unlovable and that we will never deserve happiness. With shovelfuls of lies, the enemy will continue to pile his garbage on each of us.

This must break God's heart. As a parent, he loves each of us. Jeremiah 29:11 says, "'For I know the plans I have for you,' declares the LORD, 'plans to prosper you and not to harm you, plans to give you hope and a future.'"

God wants the best for each of us. As I'm writing this, I'm looking out my back window and across the field at a big pile of horse manure that my neighbor is cleaning up. I believe that God wants to pull us out of the pile of manure that the enemy has shoveled on us. He wants to pull us out of it and give us a new life—a life that is more than we could ever ask for.

Is the enemy shoveling lie after lie on top of you? Is he making you feel dirty, unworthy, and completely unlovable? I'm here to tell you that you don't have to take it anymore. You can tell the enemy to take a hike. When he comes at you with those lies, you need to hold tight to the truth of God and speak it back to the enemy: "In the name of Jesus, get away from me, satan. I'm not going to listen to you or believe anything you have to say to me." I say this quite often when I am praying.

Set your eyes on the Lord and ask him to remove all the lies the enemy has heaped on you. You are more than the choices you have made. Pigpen is a cute cartoon character, but we shouldn't look like him. God wants us clothed in his love and righteousness and living a healthy life, not one that is filled with dirty lies.

If this book is in your hands, I believe it's because you want something more than this world has to offer you. If that is the case, you can take the first step into a new life by saying this simple prayer. If you are already living life with God but the lies of the enemy have you believing something that is not true, this applies to you as well.

Pray It

A simple prayer is all it takes. Today I would like to offer you a prayer of salvation. It is freely given to all by Jesus Christ. Scripture says, "If you declare with your mouth, 'Jesus is Lord,' and believe in your heart that God raised him from the dead, you will be saved" (Romans 10:9).

If you are not sure if you are ready to ask God into your life right now, that is okay. Keep reading this book daily. You can move along to the "Do It" task for today; you can return to the following prayer any day or at any hour. You don't even need to use the prayer I have given you. You just need to ask God to forgive you of your sins, ask him to be your friend, and confess that you believe Jesus died for your sins. There are no right or wrong words. If you have already given your heart to the Lord, you are welcome to pray this prayer and ask God to continue working in you. It is up to you, but I can assure you that life is amazing when you do it with God by your side.

> *Dear Lord, I'm tired of believing the lies. I know you want so much more for me. Your Word says that you have plans to prosper me, and I believe that to be true. Lord, I don't want to do this anymore on my own. I'm asking that you reach down and pull me out from under the lies the enemy has heaped on me. Father, I want to know you and know your Son. I want a life full of joy. Please forgive me of my sins. I declare today that Jesus is Lord, and I believe that he was raised from the dead. Thank you for sending your Son to die for me so that I could live. Amen.*

Welcome to the family. Inviting God into your life is a huge thing, and you may find that there are some tears of joy. I felt so good in the moment that I wanted to shout it out for all to hear!

Today is a special day, so enjoy it. I have two simple things for you to do today if you are not too filled with joy to concentrate.

Do It

If you have not bought a Bible or a notepad or journal yet, please do so because you are going to need them.

Think About It

When I gave my life to the Lord, I wish that someone had explained two things to me. First, that the guilt I had carried from past sins was gone. (I talk about that in the lesson for Day 3.) As a new believer, I kept turning back to the feeling of guilt I had from my past mistakes, and I began to doubt that I was saved. I would pray over and over things like, "Please, God, forgive me. I mean this with my whole heart. I am sorry, I want you in my life, and I hope you know I mean it." I also prayed that when my time came to die, God would not turn me away from salvation. I was a hot mess. I am here to say that when you ask God into your life, he forgives and empties the trash. He doesn't want you digging your guilt back out of the dumpster.

Second, giving your heart to the Lord is not a ticket to a smooth-sailing life. You will experience troubles—but with God, you will be able to face them head-on. Before I began my friendship with the Lord, I was not a worry to the enemy. After I gave my life to God, the enemy began to look for cracks in my armor. I have learned that I need to be on guard and in prayer to withstand his schemes. Later in the book, we will talk about taking your battle stance to withstand the sucker punches life tends to throw at you.

If I had known these two truths, I would not have doubted my salvation and gone dumpster diving for my past guilt. I also would have been more prepared when the trials came.

What about you? What kind of future do you envision as you get to know God?

A Penny for Your Thoughts

God Is the Gardener of Our Hearts

 ne thing I have learned in my journey with God is that I am
a continual work in progress. The same is true for you. God
is shaping you daily, and it is a process that will continue until
you stand before him in heaven. It is easy to fall into the trap of,
"I am forgiven and now I can go on with my life as usual." That is
not how it works. Yes, we are forgiven, but God doesn't want us
stepping backward into the muck. He will gently begin to prune
us and reshape us. Let me explain.

In 2011, we had a slow start to spring where I live. Snow
and dark, gloomy days had overstayed their welcome, and it was
wearing on everyone. I am a winter girl, but even I was thinking,
Enough already.

During that so-called spring, my husband, in his message for
a communion service at our church, talked about how the trees
shed their leaves in the fall in preparation for the spring, when
there is new birth. He related the idea that all of us need to die to
ourselves and shed our sins so that we can be born again just like
the trees in the spring. I love this analogy.

When we are made new in the love of Christ, we are born
again. We are full of new growth and new life. One of the things
my husband said that hit me was that some trees hang on to some

of their leaves, refusing to drop them—in a sense, they refuse to die to the fall to be reborn again in the spring. Like the trees, we have things we won't let go of—no matter how unhealthy they are, we cling to them.

That Sunday after church, I found myself thinking back to the fall of 2009. Each fall, a company comes and prunes our trees. That particular fall, God demonstrated to me what it looks like to be pruned. The young man responsible for trimming the beautiful tree at the end of my driveway went from branch to branch. As he worked away at the tree, it was like a haircut gone bad. If you have ever tried to trim your own hair, you know what I mean. You try so hard to get the longer side even with the shorter side. And before you know it, your hair is way shorter than you wanted and totally uneven. The poor guy tried to even out the tree, and before long, there was the ugliest excuse for a tree where there had once been a beautiful one.

He rang my doorbell and stood on my step, asking me to forgive him for what he had done to our tree. I hope that the look on my face was not one of total horror as he pointed to my tree. On one hand, I wanted to raise my voice and ask him, "What were you thinking?" He had mangled my favorite tree! On the other hand, it hit me that I had a chance to be Christlike.

I took a deep breath, put a smile on my face, and got control of my words before they came spilling out. I said to him, "Wow, you really got at it. Sometimes God has to prune us to take away the bad growth so that we can grow stronger. You may have just done that to our tree. Thank you for being honest." I closed the door and stood in the entry, looking out my window and trying desperately not to be upset over a tree.

I was thankful I had not blown up at the young man. When the owner of the company heard about it, he apologized. He promised to replace it if didn't grow back. God nudged my heart. He showed me that he also prunes us. I knew I had to let go of the tree and wait until the spring to see what would happen.

As spring approached, we began to see new growth on our tree. It has become a stronger and even more beautiful tree than before. We have joked many times about having that young man come over and do the same to all our other trees.

God has a long list of skills. One of them is that he is like a gardener who prunes each of us to grow stronger and more beautiful in the likeness of his Son. When we first find him, we shed our old life like the trees in the fall (we did this in the last two lessons). And in the spring, we experience new growth. It is because God loves us that he comes alongside us and prunes away what is keeping us from really growing. Like a master gardener trims and shapes his masterpiece, God is shaping us. It may be uncomfortable, but the result is perfect. The new growth makes us stronger and healthier.

Just as the pruning is an ongoing process with my trees, God's pruning continues throughout our lives. Jesus teaches us in John 15:1–8:

> "I am the true vine, and my Father is the gardener. He cuts off every branch in me that bears no fruit, while every branch that does bear fruit he prunes so that it will be even more fruitful. You are already clean because of the word I have spoken to you. Remain in me, as I also remain in you. No branch can bear fruit by itself; it must remain in the vine. Neither can you bear fruit unless you remain in me.
>
> "I am the vine; you are the branches. If you remain in me and I in you, you will bear much fruit; apart from

me you can do nothing. If you do not remain in me, you are like a branch that is thrown away and withers; such branches are picked up, thrown into the fire and burned. If you remain in me and my words remain in you, ask whatever you wish, and it will be done for you. This is to my Father's glory, that you bear much fruit, showing yourselves to be my disciples."

We are all works in progress. If we want to see growth, God must have his way in us. I have had some ugly things pruned from me. With each cut, I have grown closer to God and more beautiful in the image of Christ. Whether you're a new believer or someone who's been walking with the Lord for years, pruning is an important part of your relationship with him. As he prunes you, you will become even more beautiful than you already are. I am not saying it is not going to hurt a little. God might cut some relationships out of your life. Or maybe there is an idol—something that you esteem more than God—that you cling to as your comforter. Maybe the very thing you crave for comfort is what is holding you back from living a happy and healthy life.

Pray It

Grab your journal and write a prayer asking God to prune you. Ask him to cut off what is keeping you from really growing and producing spiritual fruit. It may hurt or feel a little uncomfortable. Let him prune from your life the things or relationships that are keeping you from living a happy, healthy, and victorious life. Trust him, because there is new fruit in your future. Throughout the day, keep asking him to prune you, and be open to what he shows you.

Do It

On days three and four, you wrote your own prayers in this book. Today, grab your notebook or journal and copy the prayers you wrote from days three and four. Having a prayer journal is very important. It is good to able to go back and read the prayers you have written when you are struggling with something. You can also use your prayer journal to record the things God has shown when you are praying or studying his Word. Make it a habit to record the prayers I ask you to write over the next twenty-six days in the journal. When you are finished with this book, you can continue your studies and prayers using the same journal. It's very special to be able to look back at your prayers and see how they have been answered and how much you have grown in your walk—your friendship—with God.

A Penny for Your Thoughts

Profitable Living

With every good partnership, both parties must be willing to put in the effort. Our relationship with God is a partnership. He prunes us so that we will bear fruit, but we also have to be willing to make an effort on our end. God can move heaven and earth, but if we are not willing to make some changes and choose what is the most beneficial for our lives, we will find it hard to get ahead. In the business world, we would be stuck in the "red," never making a profit. Any business owner will tell you: it's all about being in the black and making a profit. A profitable business is a good business. It succeeds, while a business that shows no profit fails. (Let me clarify that I am not lumping nonprofit businesses into this category.)

A coffee shop is not going to sell its product without taking into account the cost of everything, including the cost of the beans, rent, wages, and so on. It is all calculated into the equation to determine the cost of your coffee so that the business can make a profit from it.

You are probably wondering where I am going with this. *Profitable* may seem like a strange word to focus on—but trust me, it's not. Profitable seemed to be the word that God wanted to stick into my head and my heart because he had a lesson for me, and I want to share it with you.

The same day I started thinking about the word *profitable*, I was heading out of town for my son's baseball tournament. With my bags packed, I jumped into my daughter's car because my husband was using my car to transport our daughter and a few other softball players to a tournament. My daughter had taken her iPod connection out of her car and forgotten to turn the radio volume down. I turned the car key, and the speakers boomed with static. Being the easily scared Midlife Domestic Goddess I am, I was lucky I didn't hit the gas and run the car through the wall of the garage. With a shaking hand, I reached for the volume and then for the tuner knob to get something besides static. The first station it picked up was Moody Radio. God had something to tell me on my road trip that day.

On Moody Radio, they were having a discussion about a politician who had recently stumbled. I am not going to go into who it was or what he did, because that's not the point I am trying to make. What the woman on the radio said that struck me was that this politician didn't make a choice that was "profitable" for him. *Profitable*. There was the word that God had put on my heart earlier that day.

As the radio host talked about the situation, I started thinking. Did the politician gain anything from his choice? Better yet, when we choose to do something, do we take the time to think if it is profitable for us? Will it be beneficial for us? Will we gain from it, or will there be loss from it?

The radio host went on to explain that when we choose to look at porn, take part in sexting, or any other number of worldly things, we are not doing anything illegal. There is no law against it, and people think because it is not illegal, it is all good. That is when we need to make the profitable choice. We need to realize just because something is legal doesn't mean it is right and profitable for us. This is where our side of the partnership comes into play. When we choose to cross that moral line, we dishonor God and ourselves. How can we gain in doing that?

When I woke up the next day, *profitable* was still at the forefront of my mind. I knew God was trying to get me to see something. If a business chooses to do things that don't bring them a profit, they will go bankrupt and end up shutting their doors. We are much the same. If we don't choose things that are spiritually profitable, we will not gain anything. For that matter, if we choose to live our lives according to what feels good and ignore God's principles, we will find ourselves in a place of spiritual bankruptcy.

When we honor God, our bodies, our parents, our spouse, and our neighbors, we are being profitable. As we esteem God in all those ways, press into his Word, and spend time in prayer, the reward is eternal life. All of that is profitable. When we choose to say no to sin and do what is morally right, we honor God. When we take a moment to stop and think about what Jesus would do, and we choose to do what honors God (whether or not that decision is socially acceptable), we are living a profitable life.

In 1 Corinthians 10:23, Paul says, "All things are lawful, but not all things are profitable. All things are lawful, but not all things edify" (NASB). That Scripture makes you think, doesn't it? We need to be careful about the choices we make, because they can lead to profitable living or spiritual bankruptcy. Which one do you choose?

Think About It

Today, make it a point to really think about the choices you are making. Are they wise choices? Are they things that will leave you with regret? Are they profitable choices, or are they leaving you feeling bankrupt?

Pray It

Ask God to expose any areas in your life that you need to step away from. I am not going to give you a prayer today. I want you to do this on your own and write it in your journal. Remember, your words do not need to be eloquent; they just need to be from your heart.

Do It

Look up 1 Corinthians 10:23 in your Bible. Circle it and date it. Make a note in the margin that says, "Today I am going to choose what is profitable for me."

Also, look up and read Matthew 6:33, Philippians 4:8, and 2 Timothy 3:16. If any of them stand out to you, circle them in your Bible and write them in your journal, on the "Penny for Your Thoughts" page, or on a sticky note and place it where you will see it as a reminder to choose the best for your life.

A Penny for Your Thoughts

Gossip Is Like a Drain

*K*eeping in step with the idea of profitable living, let's take a look at gossip. I struggle with this one from time to time, and it is not a profitable choice. I know what God has done for me and I want to honor him in all I do; but occasionally, I have to ask God to forgive me for my big mouth. Gossip can be so easy to fall into, and we all do it. *Just one little tidbit won't hurt anyone*, we think. The problem is one tidbit can lead to one more and before we know it, we are discussing the personal lives of others, which need not be talked about.

"Did you hear so-and-so got a divorce?"

"Did you hear he had an affair?"

"Did you hear they are broke and that their kids are out of control?"

We have all been there. Why is it that someone else's pain can give us such joy when we talk about it? I am not perfect in any way, so let me be honest: gossip is one area of my life where God is really working on me.

I have had to ask God to convict me when this ugly side of me tries to pull me down the drain. As I have taken this to God for help, I am getting better in this area. Sometimes I feel like God is putting his hand over my mouth to keep it shut. Other times I have to remove myself from conversations when I see a door opening to gossip. It feels so much better in my heart when I avoid talking about someone else's pain and personal matters.

What about you? Do you find yourself sitting with a group of friends, talking about the pain of someone's divorce or how they got themselves into some kind of trouble? Do you also get sucked down the gossip drain?

Gossip has a way of making us feel better about ourselves by highlighting how someone else has messed things up worse than we have in our own lives. Gossip is a double-edged sword—on the other side of that good feeling we seem to get when we gossip, we dishonor both God and ourselves by doing the opposite of what he instructs. How can that make us feel good at all?

Gossip is frowned upon by God. Scripture warns us about it. Ephesians 4:29 really hits home with me: "Do not let any unwholesome talk come out of your mouths, but only what is helpful for building others up according to their needs, that it may benefit those who listen." Our speech needs to build others up and benefit those who listen. Gossip does the opposite.

It is wrong, yet we all seem to take part in it. It is as if we rank our sins and put gossip at the bottom of the "sin list." We think it is not all that bad, so we justify it. That is not the case; a sin is a sin. The tongue is a sharp knife that can deeply cut the person on the other end of your words. Here are a few more Scriptures that warn about gossip and its consequences:

- A gossip betrays a confidence,
     but a trustworthy person keeps a secret. (Proverbs 11:13)
- A perverse person stirs up conflict,
     and a gossip separates close friends. (Proverbs 16:28)
- The words of a gossip are like choice morsels;
     they go down to the inmost parts. (Proverbs 18:8)
- "It's your heart, not the dictionary, that gives meaning to your words. A good person produces good deeds and words season after season. An evil person is a

blight on the orchard. Let me tell you something: Every one of these careless words is going to come back to haunt you. There will be a time of Reckoning. Words are powerful; take them seriously. Words can be your salvation. Words can also be your damnation." (Matthew 12:34–37 MSG)

We all have the option to choose what is good and stop ourselves from being sucked down the gossip drain. If you want to move from rags to riches, you need to make a conscious choice to turn away from gossip. Put the plug in the drain by asking God to convict you when you feel yourself being sucked in.

Pray It

Ask God to convict you when gossip begins to rear its ugly head. You can also pray that he will help you choose your words and that you will be an example to others. If gossip is something you struggle with, be sure to record your prayer in your journal or write it on a sticky note where you will see it. Don't forget, you can also pray Scripture. Psalm 141:3 is perfect: "Set a guard over my mouth, LORD; keep watch over the door of my lips."

Do It

Make today a gossip-free day. If you stumble, ask God to forgive you and try it again. Do the same thing tomorrow and the day after that. Try to make a gossip-free life part of who you are. Don't beat yourself up when you stumble. I know I blow it from time to time. Thankfully, God forgives us and he continues to grow us. It is a process and we are not perfect. If we were perfect, we would not need Christ.

Give yourself a little extra time to complete tomorrow's reading and tasks.

A Penny for Your Thoughts

In God's Eyes, I Am ...

*T*oday I am going to change things up a little, and it will require a bit more time. Please try to make sure this time won't be interrupted. Grab your Bible and read Proverbs 31 before you read any further in today's lesson.

God has a sense of humor! He woke me up one morning with, "She gets up while it is still night" (Proverbs 31:15). As I lay in bed, bits and pieces of Proverbs 31 were rolling through my head. I tried to close my eyes and ignore them, but God was persistent. I climbed out of bed, let the dogs out and fed them, got a coffee cup for myself, grabbed my husband's hot chocolate, and had it waiting by the coffee pot with a cup for him. A warm blanket was beckoning me from the couch, so I grabbed my Bible and my Bible study and dug into the Word.

When my husband came out of the bedroom to grab his coffee, I laughed as I said, "God woke me up and told me that I am a Proverbs 31 woman." I said this not to reference a specific ministry but to articulate that God wanted me to understand how the concepts of this chapter applied to my life. I shared my rationale with my husband: I was up before my family, and I had his coffee cup all ready for his mocha.

For years, I have felt inferior to the Proverbs 31 woman. If I could get a show of hands, I wonder how many other women feel the same way. I'm sure I am not the only woman who has thought,

Me? The woman in Proverbs 31? Yeah, right. For example, I am sometimes a train wreck in the kitchen. (I once had a Thanksgiving mishap and my turkey ended up being steamed, baked, and barbecued before it made it to the table.) After a day of cooking with my grown son, we were cleaning up when I noticed that the dishtowel he was holding had a pair of my undies stuck to it, thanks to static cling. Thankfully, my son did not see the undies in the towel. The woman described in Proverbs 31 would never have her unmentionables in the kitchen!

For a whole week, God continued to wake me up early, speaking the words of Proverbs 31 to my spirit. Yet I tried to avoid reading the chapter. I found it easy to believe that I was redeemed in Christ, adopted into the family of God, and a needed part of the body of Christ. But for some reason, I continued to feel that I was inadequate compared to the Proverbs 31 woman. She seemed to be everything I was not.

One morning after my study, I was feeling a bit defeated because I could not get that perfect lady out of my head. God began to push back with his Word. Bits and pieces of the chapter I had been avoiding for years came to mind. God showed me that what is written in Proverbs 31 doesn't just describe one woman. The woman in Proverbs 31 is every woman who walks with the Lord. She is every woman who puts God first. In my heart, God was showing me the qualities of many godly women. Being the kind of godly woman described in that chapter may look different for each of us based on where we live in the world, whether we work outside the home or at home, or if we are married or single. What each of us has in common is the desire to bring honor to God in all we do.

I began to realize why God brought me to Proverbs 31. I was studying who I am in Christ, and God was trying to show me that he sees me as someone I never thought I could be. For years, I thought the woman of Proverbs 31 was some superwoman I could never hold a candle to. That week, however, I decided to read the chapter with an open heart, and God showed me that I am "worth far more than rubies" (Proverbs 31:10). I have virtue and a huge heart filled with his love, which I want to share with others. He showed me that I am choosing to honor him in my life. As I read further, I was reminded that I have a healthy fear of him and that I seek his wisdom and wait on his timing.

I *am* like the woman in Proverbs 31. Yes, I make mistakes. My house is not always perfectly clean. I order pizza at times because my day was crazy, but my life honors God. My works are for him and are done because of his love in me.

God looks at your heart, not the dinner you put on the table. He would rather have you serve a peanut butter and jelly sandwich made from a heart of love than a gourmet dinner made from a place of bitterness or obligation. My hope is that you will see who you are in God and never compare yourself to someone else like I did.

God loves you, and you are worth more than rubies. You were bought with a price, and it is the blood of Christ. You belong to the body of Christ and you matter. You, my sister, are "fearfully and wonderfully made" (Psalm 139:14)—and if you struggle with seeing yourself as God sees you, I hope you press into the Word of God and find his truth.

Think About It

Are there things you have believed about yourself that are destructive?

Do It

God's Word contains so many verses about our identity in Christ. Spend some time in your Bible today, and look up the following Scriptures:

- Genesis 1:27 – You were created in God's image.
- 1 Peter 2:9 – You are chosen by God, made royal though him, and you are God's possession.
- John 1:12 – You have been given the right to become a child of God.
- Ephesians 2:10 – You are God's handiwork, created in Christ.
- Galatians 3:26 – You are a child of God.

Pray It

God, please show me the beauty you see in me. Show me who I am in your eyes. Remove the destructive lies I have believed about myself. Lord, in your eyes I am _____. Today, I say no to these destructive things, and I know you will help me to no longer go back to them. Thank you, Lord, for helping me find my true beauty in you. Amen.

A Penny for Your Thoughts

WHERE
THE
HEALING
BEGINS

I have never met a person who has not walked through some kind of pain. Life seems to have a way of landing a sucker punch from time to time. Sometimes the pain comes from choices we make, and sometimes the pain is caused by others.

Abuse in all forms wreaks havoc in the lives of many. Broken homes, sexual abuse, drug use, and alcohol abuse are just a few of the things that leave deep scars on us. In God, healing can be found. There is no pain too big for God to take it from us.

This section takes a look at the amazing healing that can be found when we let go and let God take control.

Check Your Burdens at the Cross

Sometimes I think it helps to step back from our own lives for a minute and take a look at God from a different perspective. Today is going to have a different feel to it. I'm going to share a fictional story I wrote that shows the forgiveness that was offered to us all on the cross. I was honored to have this also run on *Living Better50* magazine before it made it into the pages of this book.

Tonight was her Christmas party—an elegant ballroom party, it was a dream come true. The last two months at this job had made her feel like her past was finally behind her. The dress and shoes she had borrowed fit her perfectly. However, as she slipped on her tattered winter coat, feelings of sadness and shame came over her.

Upon arriving at the party, she noticed a coat check. What would they think when they saw her dirty coat? She turned away and rolled her coat over her arm. Inside out, no one would see the stains from her past life. The coat told the story of many wild nights partying and waking up in drug houses and hotel rooms that were rented by the hour. Past memories followed her to the food table.

Walking around the room, she carried the coat and balanced her plate of delicious-looking hors d'oeuvres. Every few minutes she would try to shift her coat to the other arm without spilling her food. It was a burden to carry her coat, but it was nothing compared to the burden she carried in her heart. The mistakes of her past were so heavy—but she just couldn't let them go.

The guy from accounting was on his way over to her, and she had nowhere to run and hide. He was probably going to ask her to church again. Like any church would want her, she thought. Besides, he was an accountant and he would have a heyday tallying up all her mistakes. He reached out and said, "Let me check that coat for you; it looks like a burden."

As he took the coat from her, he noticed the stains. *Here comes judgment*, she thought. But instead he looked at her with the most amazing kindness and said, "This coat looks like it has known its share of heartache. It reminds me of my life before Christ. I dragged my shame around with me wherever I went. It kept me from enjoying life. One day I found myself wanting to end it all, but something pulled at my heart. Before I realized what I was doing, I walked into a church. I guess I wanted to see if God was real. I opened a Bible, and I will never forget what I read. 'Come to me, all you who are weary and burdened, and I will give you rest. Take my yoke upon you and learn from me, for I am gentle and humble in heart, and you will find rest for your souls. For my yoke is easy and my burden is light.' It was at that moment I realized I could leave my burdens with Christ. Finally, I had found rest and peace."

There was no judgment in his eyes. Instead, there was a joy that seemed so different from anything she had ever seen. He walked away with her coat, and she stood there for a moment, thinking about how good it felt to no longer be carrying it. With tear-filled eyes, she wondered if there was any truth in what he said. Could she find rest and peace too? Right there, in the middle of the party, she said, "God, if you are real, can you give me rest? I am tired and I hurt so badly from carrying all my mistakes. I want to live my life differently. Can you take my burdens and give me rest?" In that moment, she found peace that she had never felt before.

Just as in the story you just read, Christ wants to give you rest. If you are carrying burdens that are weighing you down, Christ is waiting to take them from you. He wants you to check your burdens at the cross and enjoy a life free of shame. You simply need to ask him. He is not concerned with how you word it—it doesn't have to be fancy. He is looking at your heart.

Pray It

Check your burdens at the cross. Let them go and let Jesus give you rest. In one simple prayer, you can find new joy. Pray what's on your heart and don't hold back! Let go of your burdens and let the healing begin. Feel free to speak your prayer aloud or write it out in your journal or on the page at the end of this devotional:

> God, I need you. I am weary and I don't want to continue on the same path.

Think About It

Just sit for a bit and let God's love surround you. Rest in him and take comfort in him.

Do It

Take time today to write in your journal or on the next page. Write what is on your heart. Tell God what it is that you need from him. Do not worry about spelling and grammar—just write whatever comes to you.

A Penny for Your Thoughts

Clean Out the Cushions

I asked you to check your burdens at the cross yesterday. It is the first step to healing. In order to really heal, we need to dig deeper to discover what may be harming us that we may not even know about. All of us, no matter where we are in our walk with the Lord, have a tendency to let things bottle up inside us. Occasionally, we need to do some spiritual and emotional deep cleaning, just as we do physically in our homes.

Have you ever lifted the cushions off your couch? If you have, you know that a lot of junk gets lost within the cushions. Sometimes we can find a treasure in there: maybe some money or something we have been looking for and thought would never be found. Most of what we find, however, is garbage. Old food, paper, and sometimes things we are not sure we even want to touch. God continues to show himself to me in the day-to-day things, and he showed me something very important in the cushions of my friend's couch.

One night, I was sitting on my friend's couch with my daughter, my exchange student, and my friend's daughter. We were all talking about how comfortable the couch was and how we could go to sleep. As my exchange student ran her hand between the cushions to feel how thick they were, she got the most surprised look on her face as she pulled out a steak knife. Yep, a *steak knife*. Tucked into those comfy cushions was something harmful. We

are a lot like those couch cushions. Over time, we can collect a lot
of things that are harmful to us. We often stuff the pain from our
past deep down into the caverns of our hearts like the things that
are hidden in the cushions of our couches. Sometimes, we may
not even be aware of the harmful things within us. Then again,
maybe we know they are there—just like we know there's stuff in
our couch cushions—but we avoid deep cleaning.

As I sat on that couch, God showed me that we all have to
clean out the garbage we collect within us, just as we need to do
with our couch. Sometimes, to clean out our hearts, we need to
repent from our sins. Other times, the cleaning is done by letting
God remove any pain we are holding from our past hurts. Many of
us carry things within us that can truly cause us harm—much like
the steak knife we found between the cushions that night.

Psalm 51 is David's prayer to God for forgiveness and cleans-
ing. We can all learn a lesson from David's words:

> Have mercy on me, O God,
>   according to your unfailing love;
> according to your great compassion
>   blot out my transgressions.
> Wash away all my iniquity
>   and cleanse me from my sin.
> (Psalm 51:1–2)

I hope as you read this, you will want to do some deep cleaning not just between your couch cushions but also within yourself
by asking God to transform you, as David did. He goes on to pray:
"Create in me a pure heart, O God, and renew a steadfast spirit
within me" (Psalm 51:10).

My challenge for you today is to take the time to do some
"deep heart cleaning." Clean out the things that could be causing

you pain. Make this a time to dump out the lies, shame, and regrets you may be harboring. You don't have to do it by yourself. Ask God to show you what you have deep within you that may be hurting you. You can take the same words David prayed and put them in prayer for yourself. Praying Scripture is powerful because you are praying the words of God. As he reveals what you need to let go of, ask him to clean it out for good and make room for more of him. Make today a cleaning day! Clean out your heart first, then go peek under the cushions of your couch—you might be surprised what you find in both places.

Pray It

I will get your prayer started today, but then pray your own words and ask God to show you what deep cleaning needs to be done in your heart. I encourage you to write this prayer in your journal so you can go back to it when you feel like you need a good deep cleaning:

> God, today I want to do some deep cleaning. Show me what is tucked deep within me that I am unaware of and that is causing harm.

Do It

I was not kidding about checking under your couch cushions. As you do the deep cleaning in your heart, take the time to also clean out your couch cushions. Truth be told, I am writing this in true Midlife Domestic Goddess style, which means I am in my pajamas with my hair a mess and drinking coffee from my "He Makes All Things New" coffee cup, but my couch cushions are clean. I checked them this morning.

A Penny for Your Thoughts

Failure to Thrive

A green thumb I have not. I can't even keep a cactus alive. With a stroke of luck, I have kept a violet alive for just over four years. I keep it in my kitchen by my sink in hopes that I'll remember to water it now and then.

Just like my violet needs to flourish and thrive, so do we. There is a condition called "failure to thrive." Failure to thrive refers to children who have a weight gain that is lower than the weight of other children their same age. It can be caused by environmental factors and the health of the child. One of the environmental factors that can lead to failure to thrive is the loss of the emotional bond between parent and child. No matter how old we get, we are still children of God—and without a strong emotional bond with our heavenly Father, how can we expect to thrive?

Many days, my violet is left thirsty for a drink of water that will bring it life. Without water, it will surely wither and die. We need to be watered if we want to flourish and thrive. To thrive, we must go beyond laying our burdens down and doing deep cleaning. We need to be watered to really flourish. Jesus is the way to a life that thrives. He is living water. "On the last and greatest day of the festival, Jesus stood and said in a loud voice, 'Let anyone who is thirsty come to me and drink. Whoever believes in me, as Scripture has said, rivers of living water will flow from within them'" (John 7:37–38).

It is Jesus who gives us life, and it is through Jesus that we can grow into a deep emotional connection with our heavenly Father: "Jesus answered, 'I am the way and the truth and the life. No one comes to the Father except through me. If you really know me, you will know my Father as well. From now on, you do know him and have seen him.'" (John 14:6–7).

Are you thriving, or are you struggling to survive, like my violet? If you find yourself in a state of "failure to thrive," cry out to Jesus. Tell him you are thirsty and that you need to know his Father. No matter how old you are, you are still a child of the one true God, and you need to have a strong connection with him. Stop trying to make it day by day. Jesus came to give you life. You were made to thrive. God doesn't want you to just survive.

Listen to It

Casting Crowns sings a song called "Thrive," and the words of the song are perfect for today. If you have access to the Internet, please look up the song and listen to it before moving on in today's lesson.

Pray It

Say a prayer telling God that you are tired of just trying to survive and that you want to really thrive. Ask him to fill your heart with his love, hope, strength, and joy. Don't forget to also write it in your journal.

Do It

Take some time to look back at what we have covered so far in this book. Next, grab your journal and write what is on your heart about what we have covered so far. Journaling is a wonderful way to communicate to God what you are feeling, and it is a great way to look back and see all that God has done for you. You can also use the next page to record your thoughts if you prefer.

Listen

Today, when you are out and about, look for a Christian music station in your car or find one to listen to at home. I love to listen to worship music while I putter around my house or drive in my car. Playing worship music is one more way to make God a part of your day.

A Penny for Your Thoughts

Shhh ... Daddy Is Here

*T*here is no limit to the healing that can be found with God. As we look at healing, I want to take some time to focus on something that affects many people: abuse. Abuse comes in all forms. I believe that physical, mental, and sexual abuse affects more people than we may know. It is something that people don't want to talk about. With it comes a sense of shame that is heaped upon the victim of the abuse. Many who are abused never come forward (especially after sexual abuse, because they feel it is somehow their fault). That false sense of guilt can really hurt the person who is holding it in. For me, the molestation I experienced as a child had a huge hold on me for many years. I want to share with you a powerful thing I witnessed one night, and I hope it speaks to your heart the way it did to mine.

My husband and I made the decision to get another dog. We chose to go to the humane society and adopt. Wow, were we in for a surprise. Little did we know the dog we took into our home had been neglected and abused. Thirty-six hours into his time with us, Rudy had worn out his welcome and I was a wreck.

We believe that Rudy was locked for hours and hours at a time in a crate and possibly left in his urine and feces. Rudy was not happy with the idea of going into a crate at night, and it took two of us to get him in. He would slam his body into our doors and scratch them. He was even able to get our doors open, and it would take two of us to drag him back outside. He felt he was to be in the house with us at all times. When he wasn't slamming into our doors trying to break into the house, he was howling nonstop for no reason. He refused to eat, he didn't know how to fetch a ball, and he would become so scared and his heart would beat so fast we thought he would have a heart attack. The poor dog couldn't be still. I won't go into detail about what came from Rudy's body the first couple of weeks while he detoxed.

At one point, my husband was out of town and I was on my own with Rudy. After lots of tears and phone calls to my husband, who felt bad that I was dealing with Rudy on my own, I started looking for a trainer. I was thrilled to find a trainer on my second call. He came to our home to evaluate Rudy, and he ended up taking him for three weeks. I got to see Rudy and work with the trainer a few times. Each time there was a positive change in Rudy.

When Rudy came back to live with us, we sent our other dog away to live with the trainer for one week. Our other dog would learn some new things, and Rudy would have a chance to learn the rules of his new home without any distractions. The trainer told us that Rudy was like working with someone who was high on crack. That didn't leave us with the greatest feeling, but we were determined as a family to make it work.

That first night with Rudy back home was not an easy night. We couldn't get him to go into his crate, so we thought he would be okay in our shed. Boy, were we wrong. Rudy somehow was able to turn the doorknob, pull the door in, and escape. (Did you catch that? He pulled the door *in*; he didn't push it open. Steve McQueen might have been a better name for him.) We heard him in our yard howling at 2 a.m. We rolled out of bed, headed outside, and tried to get him back into the shed and calm him down. Rudy was a maniac.

I watched my husband gently pet Rudy and softly tell him, "It's okay, calm down, I am your daddy. Shhh ... Daddy is here and you are okay." I listened to my husband with tears streaming down my cheeks. I thought of how God often has to do the same with his children.

Many of us have been mistreated and neglected in one way or another. We are hurt and scared. Some of us have been molested, others beaten or verbally abused. For some of us, fear has so much control that we can hardly function in our daily routine. When we decide to draw near to God for his help, he responds to us in the same way my husband calmed our hurting dog. God longs to comfort his children. He wants each of his children to feel his presence and know that it is going to be okay.

As I stood in my shed that night, I remembered a few years prior when I had cried out to God as I dealt with the sexual abuse I had experienced as a child. I remember praying in a way I had never prayed. Instead of saying, "Lord," I said, "Abba, Father, Daddy, why did you let this happen to me?" When I prayed that prayer, I felt the deep love of my heavenly Father. In my heart, I heard him say, "It's okay, I am here. Let me take your pain." I knew at that moment that for every tear I had cried because of that experience, my Father in heaven had cried one right along with me. I also knew at that moment that God did not want harm to come to me. It was not his fault. He wants what is good for me, and he wants that for all his children.

We live in such a broken world—the enemy comes to kill and destroy, but God never forsakes us. I also believe that God can and will take our pain and use it for good. I have been able to minister to others who have been harmed sexually.

Just like my husband calmed and loved our dog that night, God wants to do the same to anyone who has been hurt. If you are hurting, God can handle it. Psalm 18:16 reminds us that God can and will help you: "He reached down from on high and took hold of me; he drew me out of deep waters."

Let him reach down and pull you out of whatever pain is drowning you. Let him be there for you; cry out to him about all your hurts and fears. Tell him that you need him. Let him gently speak to you in your heart. Who knows—maybe in your heart you will hear him say, "Shhh, it's okay, Daddy is here." Trust God and let the healing begin.

If you have been hurt by any form of abuse, I encourage you to talk to someone. There is nothing wrong with seeing a counselor. I believe with my whole heart that there is healing in God, but I also feel that having access to a counselor is very important. I saw a counselor about my abuse and I took it to God. Please do the same.

Do It

If you have suffered from any form of abuse, please seek help if you have not. Seek prayer from others also. Do not let the sun go down on another day without dealing with your pain. It may take a while, and the healing may even hurt a little, but the results are worth it.

If you have not suffered abuse, give thanks and say a prayer for those who are hurting. Chances are there are people in your life who are carrying the pain of sexual abuse and you are not even aware of it. Many others may have been physically, mentally, or verbally abused; the pain from any form of abuse can feel debilitating. You can pray your own prayer or use the prayer I have written in the following section.

Pray It

Pray for those who have been hurt by abuse. If that is you, I am sorry for the pain you have been through. Join me in prayer:

Lord, today I lift up all those who have known the pain of sexual, physical, mental, or verbal abuse. Lord, please reach down from on high and draw them out of the painful waters they may feel they are drowning in. Please let today be the start of healing. Bring them peace and comfort. Hold them close to you and let them know they are safe in your arms. Take from them the pain they have been carrying and replace it with joy. I pray that you give them beauty for ashes and the oil of joy in place of their pain and mourning. Father, please show them the people in their lives they can go to and trust, because getting it out takes it out of the enemy's hands and puts it in yours. Please, Lord, I pray that they would find a Christian counselor to talk to and that you would provide a way for them to get out of an abusive situation that may be currently happening. In Jesus' name, amen.

Resources

If you are a victim of abuse, please reach out to the following organizations:

- National Domestic Violence Hotline: 1-800-799-7233 or 1-800-787-3224 (TTY)
- National Sexual Assault Telephone Hotline: 1-800-656-4673
- American Association of Christian Counselors: www.aacc.net

A Penny for Your Thoughts

God Is Like an All-You-Can-Eat Buffet

*Y*esterday, I talked about the pain of abuse. Abuse is not the only thing that can hurt us. Life is full of all kinds of hurts, but we have a big God who has just what we need for whatever we are facing each and every day. As I mentioned in Day 1, I see God in the everyday, mundane things, which means I see him in some very unexpected places—even all-you-can-eat buffets.

Every once in a while, my dad likes to take us all to the local buffet for an all-you-can-eat dinner. He loves it because the grandkids can get whatever they want, it makes for a fast meal, and everyone leaves full. (We laugh about wearing our loose-fitting "buffet pants" so we can get our money's worth.)

The hot, fresh rolls are my favorite on the buffet, along with a little mashed potatoes and gravy. Talk about blowing my calorie intake for the whole week. Oh, and did I forget to mention the yummy sweets to wrap up the meal? I often think I'll need to run a half marathon to burn those extra calories. But the meal is always a fun family time, so it is worth it.

Sitting in church one week, I got the picture of God being much like a buffet. At the buffet, we step up to a whole assortment of food with an empty plate and fill it with anything we want. We can also approach God and fill our souls with a never-ending supply of exactly what we need. The best thing about God's buffet is that it's free. One day we may need a serving of grace with a double helping of forgiveness. The next day we might need strength, peace, and comfort. When we belly up to God's buffet, we will not need to go looking to the world to fulfill our hunger and thirst.

Just think of all the wonderful things God offers us to partake in when we go to his buffet. There you and I can pick from joy, wisdom, understanding, compassion, kindness, love, forgiveness, comfort, strength, peace, gentleness, patience, clarity, rest, grace, and healing, just to name a few of the wonderful things he offers.

There is no limit on the serving sizes you can take. You can come as often as you need and want. There is no guilt when you eat all you want from his buffet—there is no shame, and you always feel satisfied. Psalm 34:8 tells us to experience the delicious things God has for us: "Taste and see that the LORD is good. Oh, the joys of those who take refuge in him!" (NLT).

Don't you think it is time to step up to the buffet and start loading your plate with what you need? There is never a line and it is always open. God can give you exactly what you need, unlike the world, which will continue to leave you feeling empty. What are you waiting for? Go and get your fill. One simple prayer is all it takes to fill your plate.

I often pray breath prayers (short prayers that I can say within one breath) throughout the day because there is no limit to how many times I can go back to the Lord to dish up what I need. Those simple prayers continue to keep me in step with God. Each prayer I end with "thank you" or "amen." Simple breath prayers are perfect if you are still getting comfortable with the process of praying. It is important that we each have a few minutes set aside daily for prayer time. Breath prayers not only help us grow in our prayer life but they also help us grow in a deeper relationship with the Lord, because we are checking in with him throughout the day.

Pray It

Throughout your day, please be intentional about saying some breath prayers. If someone cuts you off while you're driving your car, pray for their safety or ask God to keep your anger in check. No prayer is ever too small; and when you make breath prayers an important part of your day, your prayer life will grow.

Here are some examples of breath prayers to get you started today:

- *Father, I need your strength today because I am hurting. Amen.*
- *Lord, I am having a hard day and I am seeking comfort in you. Amen.*
- *Father, please give me a double portion of grace today when I handle problems at work. Amen.*
- *Lord, give me patience and gentleness with my children today. Amen.*
- *Father, fill me with your joy so that others see you in me today. Amen.*
- *I need your forgiveness, Lord. My pride got in the way. Amen.*
- *Father, I need wisdom and clarity in what I should do next. Amen.*
- *I am tired. Lord, today I need rest. Amen.*
- *I want more of you, Lord. Fill me. Amen.*

I have found that when I am really hurting, just saying, "Jesus, I need you" is enough to help me be more aware of his presence in my life. Please be intentional about this today.

A Penny for Your Thoughts

You Can't Control Everything

I hope you enjoyed using the breath prayers yesterday. They are a simple way to stay in touch with God throughout the day. When God becomes a part of every day, we learn something very important: *We can't control everything, but God is always in control.*

I have met only one woman who seems to be okay with not trying to control things: my friend Krista. I don't know how she does it, but she is always calm and can just let things go. I, on the other hand, need to be reminded on a regular basis to "Let go and let God."

Control is a big thing for most women. We can easily slip into the trap of trying to control everything. Because of past hurts, we can go through life trying to control everything as a way of protecting ourselves. We attempt to micromanage, direct, and sway those in our lives. The need to control can cause a sense of panic when we are faced with something that we *can't* control. This is an unhealthy place to be. If the need to be in control is controlling you, it is time to make a change. God can help you, but he needs you to be willing to let go.

My hair is a funny reminder that I am not the one in charge. I have short hair, and sometimes I wake up with it going everywhere. It is my "Flock of Seagulls" hair (if you are a product of the '80s, you will know what I mean). On those days, my hair is a simple reminder that I can't control everything. It has a mind of its own and there is nothing I can do about it. Life can be the same way—no matter how hard we try to control it, we can't.

God is the only one who is in control at all times. He is the only constant that we can count on. When I let go of things I had no control over and gave them to God, I began living in victory and not panic. The same can be true for you.

Nothing happens in the universe that is not in God's control. He has no limitations. Psalm 62:11 says it well: "Once God has spoken; twice have I heard this: that power belongs to God" (ESV).

To keep trying to control what you can't is just going to waste your time. If you can't control your hair on a bad hair day, what makes you think you can control life better than God himself? Let go and let God have control.

Do It

What areas in your life are you still trying to control even though you can't? In the space provided, list the things you need to let go of trying to control and trust God to handle.

_____

_____

_____

_____

_____

_____

_____

Pray It

Now take the things you wrote above and add them into the prayer I have provided (or feel free to write your own prayer). Whether you use my prayer or your own prayer, write it in your journal.

Also, you may need to pray this prayer or your own prayer about control many times. It is very easy to slip back into our old habits. I have prayed a lot of prayers when the issue of control has reared its ugly head in my life. It will most likely be the same for you.

> *Father, I can so easily slip into the trap of trying to control everything. I micromanage, direct, and try to sway people in my life. I don't want to feel a sense of panic when something comes up that I have no control over. Instead, Lord, I ask that you fill me with your peace and help me to take a deep breath and fully let go of these things: _____*
>
> _____
>
> _____
>
> _____.
>
> *Today, I am taking my first step out of the unhealthy place of allowing the need to control to control me. Father, in the days to come, when I feel the sense of needing to control something I can't, please remind me that you have got this. Let me feel your presence near me so that I can let go. With you, I know I can do this. Amen.*

Don't Forget

Use breath prayers like those we talked about yesterday. This prayer is a simple reminder to let go and let God: *You have got this, God. Amen.*

A Penny for Your Thoughts

From Zero to Irrational
in Less Than Three Seconds

*L*etting go of control and trusting God was our focus yesterday. Today I want to look at fear. Fear can easily control us if we are not careful. Fear can be crippling. I have been in that dark place. You lose all sense of rational thinking. One evening, I unloaded on my husband out of fear. I wish I could take those words back.

World travel is not at the top of my comfort list. We were discussing going to South Korea for tae kwon do training. Our destination was the demilitarized zone in South Korea. At the time, tensions were high in South Korea because the citizens did not agree with their military's involvement in Afghanistan. I was in full freak-out mode.

I just knew we were going to die. Scenario after scenario went through my mind. If we did not die, surely World War III was going to break out and we would be stuck there. If that didn't play out, there was still the demilitarized zone with men in full riot gear and guns and lots of protesters—a scary place, even on a good day.

My husband was trying to book our plane tickets when I came storming into the office. If I had been a cartoon character, smoke would have been spewing from my nose and ears. I was a maniac. I told my husband, "It's not safe! If you even think of taking my kids out of the country, I am going to get a lawyer and fight you." My fear was uncorked, and I went from zero to irrational in less than three seconds. That kind of speed is great if you are a racecar driver, but it set me up for one major wreck.

Thankfully, I have an amazingly gracious husband who would never put any of us in harm's way. He told me we could try the trip another time. Then we had an honest discussion about fear. Lovingly, he told me, "It is not healthy to live life in fear." Those words stung. He was right. But how could I get past my fear? Maybe you are also wondering how you can get past your fears.

First, I needed to go to God. I started praying and telling him the things I feared about the trip. Peace began to settle over me. I was even calm enough to look at the trip again. This time, as the trip approached, I was in a better place. However, the demilitarized zone still did not feel right to me. The only thing I could do was put it in God's hands and trust him completely.

God has a way of getting our attention. A few days before we left, our pastor gave a sermon on fear and shared Psalm 34:4: "I sought the LORD, and he answered me; he delivered me from all my fears."

That was the first verse I ever memorized—and I had forgotten it.

As I sat in church, God's living and breathing Word spoke to me loud and clear: he tossed me a rope and pulled me out of the darkness. All I had to do was seek him when fear tried to creep in. He would answer me. He could and would deliver me from my fear.

The trip was awesome, and God was with me every moment. As it turned out, the visit to the demilitarized zone was canceled. There were some big safety issues, and my uneasy feelings were confirmed. I learned in that moment that God was in control and he had all things covered. Looking back, if I had let fear win, I would have missed out on a great time with my family.

If you are struggling with fear, take it to the Lord right now. Do it before you find yourself where I was.

Do It

The Bible is full of verses about fear. Here are a few for you to look up. Write the Scriptures in the spaces provided or in your journal:

- Philippians 4:6–7
- Psalm 56:3
- Psalm 34:4

Pray It

Say a prayer today asking God to help you remove any fear you are holding onto. There is power in praying Scripture, and you can make any of the verses you just looked up into a prayer. Here is a simple example based on Psalm 34:4 to get you started:

> *Father God, I am struggling with fear regarding _____. I believe that your Word is true. The Bible says, "I sought the Lord and ... he delivered me from all my fears." Lord, I am seeking you now, and I am asking and believing that you will deliver me from all my fears. I ask this in the name of Jesus. Amen.*

Write It

Now, take at least one of the other Scriptures you looked up, record it in your journal, and write about what it means to you. Really be honest with God as you journal today. If you are really feeling motivated, you can do this with all the Scriptures I gave you. You can also write your own prayer using any of these Scriptures. When fear tries to creep in, grab your prayer journal and tell the enemy to take a hike. You don't have to live life in bondage; with God on your side, fear has no power over you.

A Penny for Your Thoughts

Fear Is Not from God

*Y*ou read yesterday about how irrational I became when I let fear take control. I feel fear can be a big issue for a lot of us, so I want to visit it one more time. Fear can have a tight hold on us, and it can keep us from really experiencing all that God has for us.

Fear is not from God, but you should have a reverent fear of the Lord, in the sense that you are in awe of him. There is also the fear that makes the hair on the back of your neck stand up. That kind of fear is a warning, telling you to avoid danger.

The kind of fear I am talking about is fear the enemy sends our way. Once we let that kind of fear take root, it can become the default mode in which we operate. My fear caused by a childhood trauma caused me to parent from a place of fear more than once. With God, I have been able to overcome it—and you can overcome your fears too.

Fear is one of the most powerful weapons the enemy tries to use against us, but with faith, we can overcome fear. If you are operating out of a mode of fear, you don't have to anymore. Go to the Lord, tell him your fears, and ask him to take them away. Rely on the truth of God's Word. Fear that cripples us, that takes us away from living life victoriously, is not from God. "Be strong and of good courage, do not fear nor be afraid of them; for the LORD your God, He is the One who goes with you. He will not leave you nor forsake you," declares Deuteronomy 31:6 (NKJV).

The enemy wants to see God's plans for our lives fail. He loads up a big flaming arrow of fear and fires it into our camp. All it takes is one little spark to start a raging fire of fear in our hearts. If you have a hurt from your childhood, shame from a past mistake, or fear of rejection, the enemy is going to look for a crack in your armor and he is going to fire right at it. God, however, has given us the ability to extinguish all those flaming arrows. He has given us the most powerful weapon, faith. Ephesians 6:16 says, "In addition to all this, take up the shield of faith, with which you can extinguish all the flaming arrows of the evil one."

When you raise your shield of faith, you can extinguish the flaming arrows. There may be times when you feel you need help holding up your shield of faith. If you find yourself in a place where you feel too worn out to fight, you can ask others to pray with you and for you. Don't ever think you are weak because you ask for prayer. Calling in reinforcements that can raise their shields of faith around you is a strategic move. A good soldier never goes into battle alone, and you don't have to either. When the arrows come flying at you, raise your shield and call in reinforcements. Stand strong with your feet planted on the Word of God, and you will extinguish the flaming arrows of the enemy.

You can claim Scripture for yourself in a prayer. Remember the prayers I had you write yesterday using Scripture? Deuteronomy 31:6 can be put into a prayer like this:

> *Lord, your Word tells us to be strong and of good courage. I need you to give me that strength and courage. I no longer want to be afraid, and Lord, I believe you are the one who goes with me. I believe you will not leave me or forsake me. I give you my fear, Lord, because with you, I do not need to fear. Thank you, God, for being here for me always. Amen.*

Think About It

A soldier never walks into battle alone, and neither should you. It is so important to have a prayer partner or two. I have a few close friends that I call on for prayer, and they can count on me when they need prayer. None of us can go through life on our own—we need to support each other in prayer.

Suzanne is one of the women I can turn to for prayer. She is the coauthor of a book called *Fast Friends: The Amazing Power of Friendship, Fasting, and Prayer.* Suzanne and her coauthor, Wendy, encourage you to find a sister in Christ to be your prayer partner. They want you to find someone who "will pray with fervor for your requests as you pray for hers. A friend who will intercede when you are too weak or tired to pray anymore for your own burdens."*

It is so important to have a friend or two that you can count on.

Pray It

Today your assignment is to pray about whom you can ask to be your prayer partner. Make sure they are walking with the Lord and that you can trust them to keep your prayer requests to themselves. Make sure that both of you agree that you will pray for each other. Promise to be honest with each other and to always encourage each other.

Do It

Today, go back over what we have covered so far. Is there anything you did not finish? Look over the prayers you have written and take some time to journal, listen to worship music, read from your Bible, or spend a little extra time in prayer. It doesn't matter which of these you choose. Just choose to make time with God.

---

* Suzanne Niles and Wendy Simpson Little, *Fast Friends: The Amazing Power of Friendship, Fasting, and Prayer* (Racine, WI: BroadStreet Publishing Group, 2015), 32.

A Penny for Your Thoughts

The Blessing Box

I am sure you have heard the expression "Count your blessings." In our deepest pain, our blessings may be hard to find because it is difficult to see past our present circumstances. When we choose to walk with God, there is no guarantee that there won't be struggles. By acknowledging our blessings and worshiping God in the storm, we not only honor him, but it opens heaven's floodgates of strength and comfort to carry us through whatever we are facing. The times when we feel like we have nothing in us are the times we need to praise him all the more.

In the summer of 2011, we walked through a painful time when our daughter was harmed in an act of violence. More than once, I thanked God that there were only twenty-four hours in a day, because with each morning, his mercies were new (Lamentations 3:22–23). At one point during that hard time, my friend Lori took my hands and raised them to the Lord and said, "Thank God for the blessings you can see." At first, I looked at her like she was crazy and I thought, *How can there be anything to be thankful for in this nightmare?* As I sat on the floor with tears streaming down my cheeks, my friend held my hands up to the Lord, and I said, "Thank you, Lord, that they did not kill my daughter." In that moment, one of the most painful in my life, I felt a sense of joy. My daughter was alive! I had missed that in my cloud of pain. With my hands still held up by my friend, I began to thank God for the blessings I had not noticed in my pain.

Suddenly, I realized my friend had let go of my hands and I was holding them up on my own. I was still hurt by what had happened to my daughter and concerned about what lay ahead of us, but I had new strength. For the first time in more than a month, I was able to sleep through the night. The next day, I added a night of sleep to my list of blessings.

Several years later, while thanking God for a new blessing in my life, I got the idea of making a blessing box for my husband and myself. It sits in the area where we spend time in study and prayer. On hard days when we struggle to find the words to pray, my husband and I can dump out the blessings in the box and read them one at a time. It is very powerful. I can start on empty and when I am done reading them, I am running on a full tank of joy.

When we praise God in the middle of the storms, we find the strength to keep treading water and stay afloat while the waves crash around us. Giving God thanks allows him to turn our sorrows into joy. And as Scripture says, "A joyful heart is good medicine" (Proverbs 17:22 NASB).

Do It

Stir up the creativity within yourself today and make a blessing box. Have fun with it. I found a cool wooden box, printed the words "Blessing Box" in bright colors, and attached them to the box. I keep different colors of construction paper and a pair of scissors with the blessing box. The blessing box sits next to the chair where my husband and I have our quiet time, and we write our blessings down and drop them in the box.

If you'd like to include the whole family, get some fun things with which to decorate a blessing box and invite everyone to help with the decorating. Set aside time each week to share your blessings with each other and add them to your blessing box. If you have small children, they may be thankful that they got a cookie, and that is just fine. Encouraging your children to be thankful for the little things is so important. Once or twice a year, dump the box out as a family and look back at your blessings. You can keep those blessings or start over and fill the box up again. And, of course, when you are having a tough day, you can empty the blessing box and give thanks to God for each blessing. Taking time to do this fun task will give you so much joy.

Pray It

Today as you make your blessing box, don't forget to spend some time in prayer. Let your prayer focus be on giving thanks for your blessings. Giving God praise for what he has done is so important.

A Penny for Your Thoughts

STANDING FIRM

When we ask God into our lives, he wants more than just us going through the motions. He wants a relationship with us. He wants us to hunger for him, to seek him in everything.

I have heard my husband say more than once that when we walk with God, it is not all butterflies and rainbows. There are going to be storms—and if we are not anchored securely to the Lord, we can be shipwrecked. This section is meant to help you see the importance of prayer, worship, and study. My hope is that you will plant your feet even more securely in God's truth.

What Are You Plugged Into?

*I*n this age of technology, I find myself having to make room in my carry-on bag or my purse for all my chargers. I have two phone chargers: one for the car and one for the wall outlet. My computer and charger take up space, but how could I even think of traveling without them? I am typing this on a plane as I'm heading to Reno to watch my daughter play in the softball world series. Besides the charger cords I have already mentioned, we have the camera charger, my husband's iPad charger, his cell phone charger, my daughter's computer charger, and her cell phone charger. The number of chargers the three of us carried on this trip got me to thinking about how much importance we put on being plugged in and fully charged when it comes to our electronics.

Airports are now set up with charging stations for all electronic equipment. In my hometown, the police have actually been called because people are plugging their electrical equipment into private commercial power sources. Heaven forbid we should let our batteries die. Thankfully, all the devices have a warning on them to tell us we are running on empty. I will admit I have found myself in a bit of a panic when my phone was about to die. I plug it in each night before I go to bed so it is fully charged and ready to go in the morning.

Wouldn't it be great if people made it as much of a priority to recharge their souls—by plugging into God's Word, prayer, and church—as they do to recharge their electronics? We can be running on empty, yet we choose to overlook the warnings. Our lives can be falling apart, but we are more concerned about Facebook, the next tweet, or what is on TV. We plug into the things of the world rather than what is healthy for our souls, only to find ourselves emptier than we were in the beginning.

Often, we go through our days looking like we have it together on the outside, yet on the inside we are running on empty. It is as if our souls are flashing the red warning light, trying to tell us that we are running on empty. I wish I could understand why we are so quick to keep all our devices charged while we move through life on empty. The Word of God is full of so much wisdom and hope. Just opening a Bible, plugging into God, is a surefire way to get recharged. Jesus knew this when he said, "Come to me, all you who are weary and burdened, and I will give you rest. Take my yoke upon you and learn from me, for I am gentle and humble in heart, and you will find rest for your souls" (Matthew 11:28–29). And Paul knew the benefit of staying connected to God: "May the God of hope fill you with all joy and peace as you trust in him, so that you may overflow with hope by the power of the Holy Spirit" (Romans 15:13).

Just as we have to rely on our chargers to keep our favorite electronic gadgets running, we need to be relying on God, his Word, and prayer to keep our souls fully charged. What are you plugging into? Is it really working for you, or are you just going through the motions, the bare minimum, so you don't completely shut down? Giving God a few minutes each day is important; I want to encourage you to take a look at your past few days. Have you made time to pray? Have you opened a Bible, done some kind of a Bible study, or have you applied any of the lessons in this book to your life over the past week? We often think we don't have time for God, and that is a destructive train of thought. God would never say he doesn't have time for us. If we have time to check Facebook, tweet, watch TV, work out, read a magazine, and visit with friends, we have time for God. My sweet friend Erin, who started the Whatever Girls Ministry, has a favorite word: *intentional*. In all we do, we need to be intentional—we need to act with purpose and deliberateness. Just as we are intentional at plugging in our phones, we need to be intentional at plugging into God through prayer and study.

Think About It

What are you plugging into? Are you running on empty while your phone is fully charged? Take a look at your day today. Are you taking time to read your Bible and plug into God on a regular basis (not including the time you are taking to read this book)? Mark your answer below.

Yes_____ No_____

If you are already making God a significant part of your day, keep at it. If you answered no to the above question, are you willing to commit to spending some time plugging into God with five minutes a day for five days (besides the time spent reading this book)? Let's call this a "five-for-five challenge." Mark your answer below.

Yes_____ No_____

If you answered yes to the five-for-five challenge, read from the book of Psalms over the next five days, starting today. Take your time when you read the Scriptures. You may only be able to read a couple of verses in five minutes if you spend time really digging into the meaning of them. Many Bibles offer commentary, which will also help you understand more about the verses you are reading. If your Bible does not provide this feature, biblestudy tools.com is another option you can use.

Do It

Plan on tomorrow's lesson taking longer than normal—I will give you more tips on studying the Bible. Also, you may want to grab an extra bookmark to mark this section of your book so you can come back to it easily over the next five days.

Following is your five-for-five challenge (record your answers in the spaces provided):

Day 1. Scripture passage or passages:

What did you take from what you read today?

Day 2. Scripture passage or passages:

What did you take from what you read today?

Day 3. Scripture passage or passages:

What did you take from what you read today?

Day 4. Scripture passage or passages:

What did you take from what you read today?

Day 5. Scripture passage or passages:

What did you take from what you read today?

A Penny for Your Thoughts

Foggles

*M*y husband got his private pilot's license in 2013. During his training, he had to fly wearing something called foggles. Foggles are glasses that simulate foggy conditions, low-ceiling clouds, and nighttime conditions. They are frosted on the top half to limit the pilot's field of vision and force them to use only the flight instruments. While wearing foggles, pilots must fly according to instrument flight rules rather than visual flight rules.

This training equips the pilot to be ready for real-life situations when there is little to no visibility. In a situation like that, the pilot must rely on two things: their instruments and the air traffic controller. A pilot who isn't knowledgeable in instrument flight rules can find himself in a very dangerous situation.

Many times, life can be hard for us to navigate. It can leave us standing in what feels like a fog. Like a pilot, we, too, need to train. Setting aside time to study God's Word prepares us for those times when we find ourselves in turbulence. Pilots rely on their instruments for guidance, and we can rely on God's instrument: his Word, the Bible.

"All Scripture is God-breathed and is useful for teaching, rebuking, correcting and training in righteousness," says 2 Timothy 3:16. The Word of God can guide us step-by-step when we feel like we are not sure what's in front of us. Take a look at what Psalm 119:105 says: "Your word is a lamp for my feet, a light on my path."

Just as a pilot counts on the air traffic controller, we can count on God. Prayer gives us a direct line to God. No need to find the correct frequency for prayer—we just need to speak. God is waiting to hear us:

Then they cried to the Lord in their trouble,
    and he delivered them from their distress.
He made the storm be still,
    and the waves of the sea were hushed.
Then they were glad that the waters were quiet,
    and he brought them to their desired haven.
(Psalm 107:28–30 ESV)

God wants to be more than the "Mayday call" that we make in our time of need. He wants us to be in prayer to him daily, about everything, so that when the turbulences of life come at us, we can ride them out in the security of his presence. God wants us to pray always and do it with thanksgiving. The New Testament makes these two recommendations regarding prayer:

- [Pray] at all times in the Spirit, with all prayer and supplication. To that end, keep alert with all perseverance, making supplication for all the saints. (Ephesians 6:18 ESV)
- Do not be anxious about anything, but in everything by prayer and supplication with thanksgiving let your requests be made known to God. And the peace of God, which surpasses all understanding, will guard your hearts and your minds in Christ Jesus. (Philippians 4:6–7 ESV)

Life is going to get bumpy. At times, you are going to feel like you are wearing foggles—but when you study the Bible regularly and have a strong prayer life, you can navigate your way safely through whatever lies ahead of you.

How To

Today we are going to do things a little differently. I have been asking you to look up Scriptures, write prayers, and so on, but today I want to show you how to really dig in and study the Word of God. Follow these ten tips:

1. If you want to study a book of the Bible, I suggest using a Life Application Study Bible. It provides commentary so that you can better understand the meaning of the Scriptures.

2. Read the introduction to the book of the Bible you choose to study. It helps to understand the context of the book you are reading. Here are some things to look for in the introduction:
   - Who wrote it?
   - Who is the audience?
   - Where is it taking place?
   - Was there anything special about the culture in the introduction?
   - Why was the book written? (For example, it may be instruction addressed to a certain group of people.)

3. Once you have read the introduction, begin by reading the whole section of Scripture you want to study one time all the way through. Then go back and reread it slowly. If something jumps out at you, write it down in your journal and take some time writing what it means to you. If you are not sure what something is saying, read the commentary and look at the cross-references that are given.

4. Don't rush. Take your time. I have found so much information in just a couple of verses.

5. Underline the things that really stand out to you. This makes it easier to find later.

6. Do a word study. If a word jumps out at you, chances are God has something he wants to show you. I did a word study on "stagnant," and what I found studying just that one word was amazing.

7. Biblehub.com is a great website where you can compare several translations of Scripture at once. But don't rely only on the online stuff, or you will miss one of my favorite sounds: the sound that the pages of your Bible make as you turn them.

8. Logos software is also a wonderful program for insight into the Scriptures. They offer several package options. You can look at a verse in several translations and find several Bible commentaries. The basic package would be the best way to start if you are interested (but it is a little expensive).

9. Join a Bible study group so that as you dig into the Word, you can glean from what others have learned. Additionally, a group study holds you accountable if you are struggling to make daily Bible study a habit.

Do It

Let's dig in. Go to Ephesians 2:1–10 and apply the tips for studying the Bible I gave you earlier.

1. Read the introduction of Ephesians and answer the following questions. I suggest recording your answers in your journal:

   • Who wrote it?

- Who is the audience?
- Where is it taking place?

10. Now, read the whole section slowly and underline things that stand out to you.
    - What is this section of Scripture about?
    - Which verses stood out to you? Write them in your journal.

11. Read the commentary on those verses and look up the cross-references. You can use biblehub.com to look at them in another translation, if you want. Record your cross-references in your journal.

12. Now, take a moment to write down what you learned from the truth of God's Word and how it applies to you.

Remember, God wants to hear from you daily, not just when you have a "Mayday" prayer. How scary it would be to have the pilot frantically looking through the pages of the flight-training book to get you through the fog. Please don't wait until you are in the middle of the fog to grab your Bible.

Don't Forget

Complete day 2 of the five-for-five challenge. I know today was a long lesson, but try to finish day 2 of the challenge before the end of the day.

A Penny for Your Thoughts

Cottonwood Christianity

I used the analogy of my husband's foggles in yesterday's lesson to show the importance of prayer and study. Because these are such important elements for "standing firm" (the title of this section), we are going to continue to focus on prayer and study.

We have a family lake cabin in Idaho, and in the seventy-plus years our family has owned the property, we have had a lot of cottonwood trees torn out of the ground during big storms. Some of the cedars and other trees take damage, but for the most part they stay in the ground.

When the cottonwoods grow, their roots tend to stay near the surface; in other words, they are shallow. They grow out sideways and don't have a good foundation. That is why they tip over in the storms. The cedars and other trees possess a root system that presses deeper and deeper into the ground, building a good foundation.

We have removed several cottonwoods over the years to protect our cabin, cars, and other buildings, because we get some powerful storms. Their root system seems to have a never-ending supply of new growth that continues to grow out and not down, leaving us with lots of new, weak trees. I've heard that some neighborhoods have banned the planting of cottonwoods because of the damage caused by their aggressive roots and falling trees.

Just as there are two kinds of trees—those that grow deep roots and those that grow shallow roots—there are also two kinds of Christians: the ones with deep roots that can withstand a storm and the ones with shallow roots that get knocked over by the storm. In Luke 6:46–49, Jesus explained it this way:

> "Why do you call Me, 'Lord, Lord,' and do not do what I say? Everyone who comes to Me and hears My words and acts on them, I will show you whom he is like: he is like a man building a house, who dug deep and laid a foundation on the rock; and when a flood occurred, the torrent burst against that house and could not shake it, because it had been well built. But the one who has heard and has not acted accordingly, is like a man who built a house on the ground without any foundation; and the torrent burst against it and immediately it collapsed, and the ruin of that house was great." (NASB)

Jesus' parable about the two houses shows us that we need a strong foundation—we need to have deep roots. This parable illustrates the difference between faith that can withstand a storm and faith that cannot. Both the men heard what Jesus said. However, only one of them put what Jesus said into practice. Are you regularly getting into God's Word on your own? In your everyday life, do you act on what you read, or do you just skim over it and take nothing with you, like the man who built his house without a foundation?

When you are rooted in the Bible on a daily basis, your roots grow deeper and your faith grows stronger. Just going to prayer meetings won't do it. Just going to church won't do it. And just hanging out with Christians won't do it. We need to be in the Word too.

Since I started my friendship with God, I have come to see the importance of being in the Word and letting my roots grow deep in the Lord. I am not perfect. There are days I pray but I don't open my Bible. When I don't take time to read a little from my Bible, I miss some special time with the Lord. It is something I have had to really change in my life. I want to have roots that will hold strong in the storms of life.

God wants all of us to put into action what Jesus said. We all need to make it a priority to read and study the Bible. He will change all of us through his Word, a little bit each day. If you feel you are firmly planted and your roots are deep, it doesn't mean you get a free pass and can skip time with the Lord in prayer and study. It should become a part of your ongoing walk. I like to think of study as fertilizer (and any gardener knows the importance of feeding their plants in order to keep them healthy).

Think About It

Take a moment and honestly answer these questions (write your answers in your journal):

- Are you deeply rooted, or are your roots shallow, like a cottonwood's?
- When the storms of life hit, will you be torn out of the ground, or do you have the kinds of roots that will leave you standing strong no matter how fierce the storm gets?

Do It

Take some time to be with God and water your roots with his presence. Take all the time you want. You can choose any or all of the following ways to spend time with him today:

- Spend time in prayer, followed by a time of silence so that you can listen to what he speaks to your heart.
- Write in your journal.
- Put on some worship music and give thanks to him for all he is doing in your life. Worshiping the Lord through music and praise is a way of saying that God is worthy, and it declares our devotion to him.
- Take time to read more in your Bible.

Stay rooted in the Word, and you will withstand life's storms.

Don't Forget

Remember to complete day 3 of the five-for-five challenge.

A Penny for Your Thoughts

He Is the God of Constant Opposites

In the spring of 2016, I had a day that was horrendously bad. I was overwhelmed with pain and confusion, and I did not know what to do. Exhausted and drained, I felt like I was being buried under a growing pile of something nasty and stinky—and I couldn't get out of it no matter what I did. I am thankful that I had a firm foundation, or I would have been taken out like the cottonwoods I wrote about in yesterday's chapter.

In my fifty years, I have learned that life is hard from time to time, but in the middle of everything, there is one constant I can count on: God. No matter how deeply I may feel buried in a pile of something that stinks, he is "the same yesterday, today, and forever" (Hebrews 13:8 NKJV).

In Revelation 22:13, God says this about himself: "I am the Alpha and the Omega, the First and the Last, the Beginning and the End." God uses three comparisons to describe himself. Notice each one is the opposite of the other. God says he is "the Alpha and the Omega." These are the opposite ends of the Greek alphabet. He says he is "the First and the Last." He is before all others and after all others. Finally, he says he is "the Beginning and the End." Everything begins and ends with him.

What I mean by God being the God of "constant opposites" is

that he is the opposite of our painful circumstances. He is constant, and we can always count on him, no matter how badly our circumstances may stink. We can also count on him because he is the God of "opposites." It may seem strange to think that the God who is constant could be the God of opposites, but it's true. In order to understand this, I think the best thing to do is just dig into the Word.

Do It

Look up the following Scriptures, write them in the space provided, and you will see exactly what I mean by "constant opposite":

- **2 Corinthians 12:9.** In our weakness, he is the constant opposite—he makes us strong.

  _____

  _____

  _____

- **Psalm 147:3.** In our brokenness, he is the constant opposite—he brings us healing.

  _____

  _____

  _____

- **Ephesians 1:7.** In our sin, he is the constant opposite—he offers redemption.

  _____

  _____

  _____

- **Isaiah 61:3.** In our sorrow, he is the constant opposite—he brings us joy.

_____

_____

_____

- **Luke 19:10.** When we are lost, he is the constant opposite—he will find us and save us.

_____

_____

_____

- **Matthew 11:28.** When we are tired and weary, he is the constant opposite—he will give us rest.

_____

_____

_____

See what I mean? He is the God of constant opposites. On those days when we feel overwhelmed by heaping shovelfuls of something stinky being dumped on us, we can count on God to be not only our constant but also our constant opposite. When we reach out to him, he is waiting to pull us out of it. He will clean us up, set our feet on something firm, and give us strength to keep going.

I mentioned in the introduction to this section that my husband always says, "There is no guarantee that walking with Jesus means everything is going to be butterflies and rainbows." He is right (and now he gets to see it in print that I admitted he was right). There are going to be hard times, but no matter what happens, you can count on God to be your constant opposite. In your weakness, he will give you strength. In your brokenness, he will give you healing. When you are caught in sin, he offers redemption. In your sorrow, he brings joy. When you are lost, through him, you are found. When you are weary, he alone can bring you rest.

God is the beginning, the end, and the constant opposite in all of our painful circumstances. When we have a clear understanding of who God is, we will be able to stand firm in even the most painful times.

Think About It

Do you see any other areas where God is the constant opposite in your life?

Pray It

Write a simple prayer of thanks in your journal. Thank God for being the God of constant opposites that you can always count on.

Don't Forget

Remember that today is day 4 of the five-for-five challenge.

A Penny for Your Thoughts

Don't Bite into the Apple

*A*nother thing we need to be able to stand firm against is lies. By that I mean the lies that the enemy (satan) tries to feed us. Some of the biggest lies we believe start with a little bit of truth. If you don't believe me, just take a look at Eve. Thanks to the serpent, Eve bit into one of the biggest lies in the history of the world.

In the middle of the garden of Eden was a fruit-bearing tree, the tree of the knowledge of good and evil. God instructed Adam and Eve not to eat its fruit—the consequence of disobedience would be mortality (Genesis 2:17). However, the serpent questioned God's instructions as well as his loving intentions. Genesis 3 records the serpent's lie: "He said to the woman, 'Did God really say, "You must not eat from any tree in the garden"?' ... 'You will not certainly die,' the serpent said to the woman. 'For God knows that when you eat from it your eyes will be opened, and you will be like God, knowing good and evil'" (vv. 1, 4–5).

The cunning lie began when the serpent said to Eve, "Did God really say ..." He questioned the truth of what God had said. He introduced doubt. Then he went on to say, "You will not certainly die. ... For God knows that when you eat from it your eyes will be opened, and you will be like God, knowing good and evil" (Genesis 3:4–5).

The enemy took the instructions that God had given to Adam

and Eve and told them that if they ate of the fruit they would know "good and evil." He offered them wisdom. Unfortunately for Eve, he left out the part about dying. Instead, he got Eve to focus on the fact that she could be like God. He tempted Eve by getting her to look at something God clearly said was off-limits, the forbidden tree, and convinced her it was something she should be allowed to enjoy.

Satan is the prince of deceit. Lying is his primary weapon. In John 8:44, Jesus referred to satan as the "father of lies" when talking to the Pharisees. I love how he held nothing back in this Scripture: "You belong to your father, the devil, and you want to carry out your father's desires. He was a murderer from the beginning, not holding to the truth, for there is no truth in him. When he lies, he speaks his native language, for he is a liar and the father of lies" (John 8:44).

Satan's goal is to get us to believe that "feeling good" is better than the truth of God's Word. God wants me to be happy, right? Certainly, this must be from God. The enemy wants you to entertain the idea that God's Word must be wrong because of how happy you feel after biting into the proverbial apple. Getting us to doubt God's Word is his mode of operation. He is clearly no match for God, so his only way to hurt God is to cause his children pain. Greed, anger, sexual sin, and pride are just some of the things he can use to pull us away from the truth of God's Word.

If you find yourself in a place where you justify your choices based on the belief that God's Word is unfair, prohibitive, or no longer applicable to the times, you have bitten into a lie. In Christ, you have the authority to rebuke the enemy. Tell him to take a hike because you are not going to believe the lie he has fed you. Drop the apple and step back. Ask God to forgive you and don't look back.

Think About It

Have you bitten into the apple? Are you justifying your particular sin by assuming that "everyone does it"? Do you find yourself thinking, *What I am doing was wrong at the time it was written, but it doesn't apply now*? If you have taken bites out of the apple, what are they? There is no shame in writing your honest answers here; you don't need to share it with anyone except God. Getting it out takes it out of the enemy's hands and puts it into God's. Please use the space on the "Penny for Your Thoughts" page to record your answer.

Pray It

Now, take some time and pray. Ask God to forgive you for those bites out of the apple, and ask him to show you any other lies you may have bitten into that you are not even aware of. I want this to be from your heart, not mine, so I am not going to start the prayer. There is no need to write it down. Just spend time with God and be totally honest with him.

Don't Forget

How's the five-for-five challenge going? Today should be the last day. If you are behind, don't beat yourself up. Just pick up where you left off and keep going until you are done.

A Penny for Your Thoughts

Never Leave Wiggle Room for Doubt

*B*esides being the father of lies, satan loves to trip us up in many other ways. One of the things he uses is doubt. Left alone, doubt can get us so discombobulated that we can begin to second-guess God and his plan for our life.

When my daughter was little, she had a knack for wiggling herself right in between my husband and me. Whether we were sitting, standing, or lying in bed, she would wiggle herself right in. It became a joke with us. We would sit as close as we could on the couch, and in no time she would be on our laps. Then it started, her famous wiggle. It was such a subtle movement, and before long she would be sitting between us. Every time she accomplished this, she would look up at us with her big brown eyes and a little wry smile, as if to say, "Look what I just did."

With our daughter, we could let our guard down. We could leave her wiggle room. There are some areas of our lives where we cannot let our guard down. Doubt is one of them. If we give doubt any wiggle room, it *will* wiggle its way in. Trust me, when doubt wiggles in, it won't be looking up at you with big brown eyes like those of my little girl. On the contrary, it will sit there with an Eddie Haskell-like smile, the kind of look that says, "Trust me, I would never lead you astray." The truth is, doubt wants nothing more than to lead you so far off track that you no longer believe what is true to be true.

As I was offered several new writing opportunities, doubt began to creep in. It pulled up a seat next to me with its Eddie Haskell smile, and it tried to take me off track. Doubt tried to make me believe there was no way I would be able to do the one thing I had prayed God would open the door for me to do. I had prayed about writing for a ministry serving mothers and daughters, about writing for a magazine, and about eventually writing a book. Yet as God began to open the doors, I began to doubt I had the ability to do it. Maybe he had called the wrong person.

Yep, doubt had snuggled in between God's promises and me. I had to get it out of the way, so I did the one thing I knew would work: I gave my doubt to God. Raising my shield of faith, I prayed, "God, you opened this door, so I trust you will give me what I need to write about. Please give me the words and the topics, and take my pride out of the way so that my words are your words. Please, God, remove the doubt."

I told God that I felt like Moses, who did not have the words prior to approaching Pharaoh (Exodus 3 and Exodus 4:1–17). I knew God sent Aaron, Moses' brother, to be his helper, and I asked him to give me a helper too. That night, as I slept, God sent me a helper. He sent the Holy Spirit to help me. I woke up singing this Scripture: "Seek ye first the kingdom of God, and his righteousness; and all these things shall be added unto you" (Matthew 6:33 KJV).

God showed me that night if I seek him first and trust him with my writing, he would give me just what I needed. In that moment, doubt was kicked out of the comfortable seat it had made next to me. God had opened the door for my writing, and I had to trust that he would not open the door and leave me standing there with nothing to say.

If you find yourself doubting what God has for you, the best thing you can do is to take that doubt right back to him in prayer and ask him to show you his truth. You need to believe that God is not going to open a door and then leave you standing there with nothing but doubt in front of you. If God has called you to do something and you feel he has called the wrong person, think again. It is most often the person who seems the least qualified that God chooses. Remember, with him anything is possible (Matthew 19:26).

Our daughter is an adult now, and if she ever wants to wiggle in between us, you better believe we will give her all the room she needs. As far as doubt goes, I've learned an important lesson, and I hope my lesson speaks to your heart too. Never leave wiggle room for doubt. If it creeps in, tell it to take a hike and have faith. Faith causes doubt to turn and run.

Think About It

Take some time to think about where you have felt doubt in your life. If you find there is some doubt holding you back, what is it?

Do It

Look up the following Scriptures and circle them in your Bible. Next to them, write today's date and "With faith, I will not let doubt win."

- Philippians 4:13
- Matthew 14:31
- Matthew 21:21
- James 1:6

Pray About It

Write a prayer in your journal asking God to remove any doubt you may have. The enemy loves to make us think we are not worthy, capable, or deserving of our dreams. He loves to use doubt as a way to trip us up, but we can counter with prayer and the truth of God's Word. Remember, there is no "proper prayer formula." Just pray from your heart.

A Penny for Your Thoughts

Let No Ivy Take Root

*A*s we continue our journey in learning to stand firm, I want to share something that a friend of mine taught me. One night at Bible study, the group members were talking about spiritual battles, and my much younger but very wise friend Nina gave a great analogy of what can happen when we let our guard down. Being a picture person, it came through loud and clear to me. I became fixated on the picture painted in my mind by her words. In my heart, I knew there was a lesson in it. She said, "When we let our guard down, the enemy and sin have a way of creeping in like ivy on a house."

Ivy is beautiful to the onlooker, but it is damaging to the structure underneath. Ivy starts from one little root and grows slowly. It creeps and wraps itself around trees, fences, and buildings. Sound familiar?

The enemy sits patiently, waiting for his chance to plant that one little root that in time will grow and slowly begin to take over. As it grows, it tears away at whatever it has attached itself to. Many things that the world sees as perfectly acceptable are sin in God's eyes and can take over a person.

As I researched ivy, I discovered that as it wraps its way around a tree, for example, it sucks the life out of it. What looks beautiful from the outside is actually killing the tree. Even a tree with deep roots will be harmed when the root of an ivy plant takes hold.

On buildings that have any cracks, ivy grows into the cracks and causes harmful structural damage. Moisture also gets into those damaged areas that the ivy has made bigger, becoming the perfect breeding ground for mold and fungus.

How easily we can become like those homes covered in ivy, beautiful on the outside and falling apart inside because of the damage caused by the roots of sin, shame, and lies from the enemy. Just like the tree that is slowly dying, the life is being sucked out of us. Something foul, like mold or fungus in a house, can be growing in us where the root of evil has broken into old wounds.

God's Word tells us to "be alert and of sober mind. Your enemy the devil prowls around like a roaring lion looking for someone to devour" (1 Peter 5:8). We need to be on guard as believers. "For our struggle is not against flesh and blood, but against the rulers, against the authorities, against the powers of this dark world and against the spiritual forces of evil in the heavenly realms," writes Paul in Ephesians 6:12. Daily, we need to be putting on the armor of God and digging in deep to tear out any roots the enemy is trying to plant in our heads and our hearts.

As you read this, I hope you will look hard at yourself. Is there ivy in your life that needs to be torn out before it slowly sucks the life out of you? Ask God to search your heart and bring to your attention any strongholds that have taken root. Then ask God to use his mighty hand to tear out the ivy in your life.

Something important that you need to know is that when ivy is pulled off a building, parts of the building come with it. Ask God to be the life-giving "spackle" that fills in those holes where the ivy has been pulled out from you personally. God can rebuild what was meant for harm. You just need to stand firm and let God tear out any ivy that has taken root.

Think About It

Today, take some time to seek God and see if there is anything you need to have removed from you. Are anger, hurt, resentment, or past mistakes eating away at you? God is bigger than any mistakes you have made. He is bigger than your pain and any anger you may have. It might hurt a little as the ivy comes out, but God will fill in the holes with healing.

Pray It

Today, ask God to remove anything that has taken root. I will get you started, and you can continue praying as you are led:

Dear God, I have something within me: _____. It is slowly eating away at me. I need you to pull it out and fill it in with your goodness, God. I want to live a life of victory.

Do It

In the story about the ivy, I mentioned that we should be putting on the armor of God daily. Take some time for the following activities related to our spiritual armor:

- Read Ephesians 6:10–16 and, in the space provided, list the different parts of the armor and the purpose of each.

_____

_____

_____

- On a sticky note or piece of paper, write a short prayer about putting on the armor of God and place it where you will see it when you pick out your clothes each morning. Let it be a reminder to you each day that there are more important things than your shoes, accessories, and so on.

A Penny for Your Thoughts

You Can't Be in Two Places at Once

$\mathcal{W}$elcome back. I hope you remembered to put on your armor as we discussed yesterday. Before we move on to today's lesson, see if you can remember one piece of armor and why it is important. No need to write it down; this is just a quick review from yesterday.

Now, let's dig in to today's lesson. As a child, I always wanted to stand on the spot called the Four Corners, where Colorado, Arizona, New Mexico, and Utah come together. How cool I thought it would be to put a hand in one state, my other hand in another state, and a foot in each of the two other states. I guess you could say I wanted to be in four places at once. The idea of being in more than one place at once stayed with me all through my childhood, and I admit that every time we drive across a state line, I wonder just where I would need to stand to be in two places at once.

In the summer of 2012, while having some much-needed quiet time, I watched a storm roll in over Priest Lake, Idaho. I could see the dark clouds in the distance, but what really caught my eye was the lake water. I could see a distinct line where the edge of the storm was. On the north side of the line, the water was choppy, but on the other side of the line, the water was perfectly calm. I found myself thinking, *Cool—you could be in the storm with one half of your body and in the calm with the other.* Not a good idea. Who wants to be caught standing in the water in a lightning storm? The way the storm was coming in, it would have been only a matter of a few minutes before I would have been fully covered by the storm with no calm waters left to protect me.

As I looked at that stormy lake, I knew again that God was talking to me. I love the way he shows me what he needs me to see in the world around me. I think he wants to show all of us his glory in the world around us; we just have to open our eyes and our hearts to him.

As the storm rolled in that day, God was trying to show me the importance of not living a double-minded life. If I had walked into the lake to stand in the calm water and in the stormy water, I would have been like a double-minded person with one foot in the Word and one foot in the world. (When I say, "in the world," I mean living a lifestyle of doing whatever makes me happy and giving no thought to what God would think about it.) Before long, the storm would have overtaken me, just like the world can pull us down when we live with double-mindedness. James 4:7–8 tells us: "Submit yourselves, then, to God. Resist the devil, and he will flee from you. Come near to God and he will come near to you. Wash your hands, you sinners, and purify your hearts, you double-minded."

How easy it is to dip our feet into the world. We tell ourselves, *It's okay if I do this or that as long as I am doing this over here for God. I'll be okay. I am not hurting anyone.* That is what the enemy wants us to think. He waits for us to let our guard down. And before we know it, we can be over our heads in sin and shame from doing what felt good or putting false gods, such as money, toys, and ourselves, before the one true God.

As God's children, we are not of this world—yet the things of this world often look so good to us that we find ourselves listening to the voice of the enemy: "Come on in, the water feels great. You know you deserve this, and it won't hurt to take a quick plunge." Before we know it, we are drowning and we find ourselves fighting against the waves to get back to the safety of the calm water.

The Bible clearly lays out for us what we are to avoid:

> Put to death, therefore, whatever belongs to your earthly nature: sexual immorality, impurity, lust, evil desires and greed, which is idolatry. Because of these, the wrath of God is coming. You used to walk in these ways, in the life you once lived. But now you must also rid yourselves of all such things as these: anger, rage, malice, slander, and filthy language from your lips. Do not lie to each other, since you have taken off your old self with its practices and have put on the new self, which is being renewed in knowledge in the image of its Creator. (Colossians 3:5–10)

Similarly, the Bible also outlines what we should seek out: "Therefore, as God's chosen people, holy and dearly loved, clothe yourselves with compassion, kindness, humility, gentleness and patience" (Colossians 3:12).

I still want to put my hands and feet in those four states at once, but as far as being a child of God and being in the world at the same time, I choose to be in one place only. My hope is that you will choose to do the same.

We need to be on our guard and careful not to step into what the world sees as good. It is so important that we are in the Word (the Bible) and seeking God's direction in all areas of our lives. We can't be in two places at once. Being a child of God means we are no longer of this world, and we need to do our best to stay clear of what is not from God.

God offers so much more than the world offers, and if you want to find healing and live a life in victory, you can't be in two places at once.

Do It

- Look up the definition of double-mindedness. Write it here:

  _____

  _____

- What does 1 Corinthians 10:21 say? Write your answer here:

  _____

  _____

- What does 1 John 2:15 say? Write your answer here:

  _____

  _____

- What does James 4:7–8 say? Write your answer here:_

  _____

  _____

Pray It

Take a moment to think about the lesson on double-mindedness and read the Scriptures you just wrote down. Really search your heart and be honest with yourself. Is there anything you need to turn from? If you want to heal from the pains of your past, you can no longer be in a place of double-mindedness. Spend some time with God in prayer today, and don't forget the power of praying Scripture. Ask God to reveal any double-mindedness in your life. Also, feel free to journal about anything that is on your heart.

A Penny for Your Thoughts

Take Your Battle Stance

*T*oday we will bring this section to a close, and I want to end with what I feel is the most important thing we can do when it comes to "standing firm." We need to take our battle stance.

Several years ago, my family trained in tae kwon do. Wearing a helmet and chest protector, we would face our opponents. With hands held up, ready to block a blow from our opponent, and our feet firmly planted, we took our battle stance. Every attack our opponent launched was countered with a block or advance from us. We practiced all kinds of blocks and footwork to be prepared to defend ourselves during a sparring match. Hours of training were required for us to develop our skills and be able to successfully spar against someone.

The analogy of tae kwon do sparring is the perfect way to look at prayer. Life has a way of serving up a lot of heartache. The loss of a job, a broken marriage, sickness, and unexpected deaths are just a few of the things we face. The most effective way to defend ourselves is to assume a battle stance. In other words, just as we were wearing protective head and chest gear, with our hands up ready to block and our feet firmly planted, we need to be ready to counter with prayer at all times and for all things. When we counter with a prayer of praise in the middle of a battle, we blindside the enemy with our faith. It is like a perfectly landed uppercut.

A few days ago, I asked you to write down the different pieces of the armor of God; let's revisit Ephesians 6:13–18:

> Therefore take up the whole armor of God, that you may be able to withstand in the evil day, and having done all, to stand firm. Stand therefore, having fastened on the belt of truth, and having put on the breastplate of righteousness, and, as shoes for your feet, having put on the readiness given by the gospel of peace. In all circumstances take up the shield of faith, with which you can extinguish all the flaming darts of the evil one; and take the helmet of salvation, and the sword of the Spirit, which is the word of God, praying at all times in the Spirit, with all prayer and supplication. To that end, keep alert with all perseverance, making supplication for all the saints. (ESV)

The most powerful weapon we have is prayer. I mentioned in an earlier chapter that we walked through something painful with one of our children. It was one of the worst nightmares we could have ever imagined as parents. My husband and I took it head-on in our battle stance: hands folded, we dropped to our knees, and we cried out to God to help us, to heal our child, and to carry us in our weakness. We have come out of the hardest thing we have ever been through stronger in our faith.

I have learned to pray big and have seen big things come to be. I often laugh because I have said, "Here I am, God, the persistent lady who is going to keep at it just like the persistent widow." The persistent widow is from a parable that Jesus taught in Luke 18:2–8:

> He said, "In a certain city there was a judge who neither feared God nor respected man. And there was a widow in that city who kept coming to him and saying, 'Give me

justice against my adversary.' For a while he refused, but afterward he said to himself, 'Though I neither fear God nor respect man, yet because this widow keeps bothering me, I will give her justice, so that she will not beat me down by her continual coming.'" And the Lord said, "Hear what the unrighteous judge says. And will not God give justice to his elect, who cry to him day and night? Will he delay long over them? I tell you, he will give justice to them speedily. Nevertheless, when the Son of Man comes, will he find faith on earth?" (ESV)

We need to be persistent in prayer just like the widow was with the judge. Jesus used that parable to show his disciples the importance of prayer, and it applies to us today. I have been ending a lot of the chapters in this book with prayers. Why? Because I want you to understand the importance of making prayer as much a part of your day as you make working, eating, and sleeping. Knowing God goes beyond just saying, "I believe." God wants to be more than your acquaintance. He wants to have a deep and personal relationship with us, and prayer is the most effective way to do that.

The more you pray, the more you will hear God. Now, I am not saying it will be an audible voice. It is in my spirit that I feel him nudge me to pray for someone or something. What used to be a one-way street, me praying to God, has now become a two-way street—I pray to him, and he leads me to pray more by laying things on my heart. He woke me up one night from a sound sleep to pray for a young woman in her travels. The next day, on Facebook, I discovered that Rachel and her group had been trying to get home from a mission and were asking for prayer because they were running into all kinds of things that were keeping them from getting home. I am so thankful I listened to the feeling in my heart and prayed for them. Never ignore those promptings from God.

Not only has God shown me how to pray for someone, but he has also prompted others to pray for me. I have had more than one phone call from a friend when I am having a tough day, and they say, "You are on my heart, so I have been praying for you."

I cannot stress this enough. To really stand strong in our faith, we cannot forget to take our battle stance. Don't wait until you are in the middle of something painful to pray. "Do not be anxious about anything, but in every situation, by prayer and petition, with thanksgiving, present your requests to God" (Philippians 4:6). Just like my family and I trained for tae kwon do, we can train ourselves in prayer. The more we pray, the stronger our prayer life becomes.

Pray It

Close this book and take your battle stance. Take some time to pray. You can get down on your knees if you feel led to do so. Pray from the caverns of your heart. Pray big. Pray honestly. And with thanksgiving, present your prayers to the Lord. Make today a day of prayer. We can get back to the other busywork tomorrow.

A Penny for Your Thoughts

IT'S MORE THAN A BUILDING

I have learned valuable lessons about the importance of being plugged in to a church. I think many people are missing out on the support, spiritual growth, and friendships that come from a church community.

I feel that having the support of a church during trials is an essential part of overcoming the painful things that happen in this life. A soldier never goes into battle alone, and we are not meant to go through the everyday battles of life alone. A church is more than a building. It is about relationships, finding support when you need it, and having others who hold you accountable.

This section is an assortment of things I have learned about why it is important to be a part of a church, including discipleship, finding your gifts, and dealing with offenses.

Why Church?

There is strength in numbers. When we are plugged in to a church body, we find that strength in difficult times. I hear so many people say they know God but don't feel they need to go to church. My response is that a soldier would not go into battle alone, and neither should we. As I mentioned in previous chapters, in 2011 my family walked through a violent storm. As the storm raged around us, we rode it out in the safety and security of our church. God used our church as his hands and feet.

Ecclesiastes 4:9–12 teaches us that there is value in people coming together to support each other:

> Two are better than one,
>> because they have a good return for their labor:
> If either of them falls down,
>> one can help the other up.
> But pity anyone who falls
>> and has no one to help them up.
> Also, if two lie down together, they will keep warm.
>> But how can one keep warm alone?
> Though one may be overpowered,
>> two can defend themselves.
> A cord of three strands is not quickly broken.

If you are not attending a church, I strongly urge you to find a church where you are comfortable and can go to services on a regular basis. There is so much to be gained by having a church that you call your own. If you are already plugged in to a church, I still want you to finish this lesson, because it may speak to you in a new way about just how important church really is.

In the middle of our storm, it was an outpouring of love and support from our church that sustained us. Both the prayers that we heard and the unspoken prayers members of our church sent to God on our behalf were like a healing ointment to our wounds. The arms that held us were like the arms of Christ himself. When I could not sleep because the pain was so deep, my sweet friend sat and prayed over me so I could sleep. During that prayer, she took my hands and held them up for me and said, "I want you to praise God. Until you can hold your hands up on your own, I will do it for you." Just like Moses needed help holding his hands up (Exodus 17:10–13), she helped me. Meals were delivered, grocery runs were made, and phone calls filled with love were spoken to our hurting hearts.

I heard a story about a man who said he needed to get home for church over the Easter holiday. He said he was a CEO and needed to be at the church. Sadly, what he meant was that he only went to church on Christmas, Easter, and Other times (like weddings and funerals). I admit when I heard what he called himself, I chuckled, but it is sad when you really think about it. He knows enough about God that he chooses to go to church to celebrate the birth and the resurrection of Jesus, God's Son. Otherwise, he only shows up for weddings and funerals.

He is not alone. Maybe you do the same thing. I am not trying to make you feel bad. My goal is for you to understand how much more you will receive from God when you are attending church.

Let me share more of my family's story to illustrate my point. One day when we were in the middle of our storm, I sat on the floor in tears, praying for strength, when something amazing happened. As I prayed, I saw a picture of a soldier in full combat gear. As I continued to pray, I felt that I needed to ask a man in our church, who was a soldier himself, to pray for us. When I called him and told him I was struggling and needed him to pray, he said something I will never forget. He said, "When we go out, we go in groups of thirteen—and when one is injured, two drop back to pick up the injured soldier." He went on to say that our child was the injured soldier and that my husband and I needed to pick her up. He said, "She is weak right now, and you need to carry her armor. Carry her armor until she can carry it on her own. You also need to trust that we are your church and we will stand in front of you and fight for you." That is exactly what our church did. While we carried our daughter, our church took a protective stance around us. They also continued to do what they were called to do—take the love of Christ to the world—but they never once left us unattended. If we only attended church on a "CEO" basis, we wouldn't have survived our storm the way we did.

Scripture shows us the importance of church. I could give you a few Scriptures and do the work for you, but as we come to the end of this book, I want you to finish strong—so grab your Bible, look up the following verses, and write them in the space provided or in your journal. I hope they speak to your heart about the importance of why we should go to church:

- Matthew 18:20
- Hebrews 10:25
- Colossians 3:16

Finding a church can be an adventure. Talk to friends about where they go. Make sure there is a good leadership team and that the pastor is accountable to others. Pick a church that offers worship music you enjoy. If you have children, look at the programs they offer. Ask if they have small groups available, because those are a great way to meet people and connect to the church. After you attend a church, talk openly as a family about your experience. Give your kids a chance to tell you what they liked and disliked about the church. Sometimes you need to visit a church a few times to really know if it is the right fit for you. Don't be afraid to ask questions. Most importantly, you need to make sure the church is biblically sound. Look for a church that believes that Jesus is the Son of God and that God sent him to die for your sins. Look for a church that believes in water baptism, the Holy Spirit, and all the gifts that are given by God.

When we felt God moving us to a new church, we asked to see the youth room and meet the youth leaders, and we asked some of the kids what they loved about their church. Finding a church is a very personal decision. Don't be discouraged if it takes a while to find the right fit. I can't tell you how many churches you will need to visit before you find the right fit, but I can say it takes lying on several mattresses when looking for a new one—so don't stop looking until you find the place you are most comfortable. It is worth the effort.

So, why church? Because we were never meant to go through life alone, and that includes the Christian life. In fact, if we are to grow up in the faith, we need God, of course, but we also need each other. As Van Bradeen says in his book *Live Love*: "even though Jesus is [our] savior and his perfect word transforms us, Christian life is not complete without other believers. Jesus designed his church to be devoted to each other's spiritual maturity."*

---

* *Live Love* (CreateSpace, 2017), 21.

Do It

- If you don't have a church, start looking for one. Do you have friends who are plugged in to a church? Start asking them where they go. Look up the churches near you and read their belief statements. You can also call a church if you are interested in it and ask to talk to the pastor. If you work on Sunday mornings, look for a church that offers a Sunday evening service or a weeknight service.
- Make a list of things you want in a church. Here are some things to think about: What service times will work for you? Do you have children? If your children are younger, does the church offer Sunday school? If they are older, is there a youth group? Are small groups offered, and are there times that work for you? If you are single, you may want to find a church that has a singles group or a young adults group. What is the worship style of the church? Some people like a more traditional style of worship while others may want a more contemporary style.

These are just some things to get you started on your list. You may find that some of the things are an absolute must and others are optional.

After you attend a church, think about these things. If you are married, talk with your spouse about how they felt at the church. If you have kids who are old enough to give input, listen to their thoughts. You want to find a church where your whole family is happy.

Pray It

Pray for God's guidance about where you should go. On day 1 of this devotional, I talked about when I found my way to a little church. That church was put on my heart after I said a simple prayer: "God, I think maybe I need you, and I don't know where to go to church." Start praying for God's guidance.

A Penny for Your Thoughts

You Can't Build a House Without Nails

$\mathcal{W}$e looked at the importance of belonging to a church in the last chapter. I want to take it one step further. There is more than just belonging to a church. (If you started the process of finding a church, I know it may take you a while to find the right one, but I want to keep moving forward—so keep reading, and when you find the church that fits you, you'll be ahead of the game.)

Attending church is important, but I believe with my whole heart that God wants more than just warm bodies in church. I believe he wants us all to be taking an active role so that the church can function successfully. Let me explain.

We built our home in 2000, and I remember going by each day to see it coming together. As the framing of the house went up, I was filled with anticipation as to what it would look like finished and with a fresh coat of paint on the walls. I would lie awake at night wondering how my furniture would look and what color carpet I would choose. The framing was the most exciting part for me. So much time went into cutting each board to the exact length and then, piece by piece, the boards were fit together to build the frame that holds our home together. During that time, nails were everywhere.

Those nails were an important piece of the puzzle. Each one of those nails plays a special part in holding our home together. Over the years, it is within the walls of our house that I have watched my family grow and mature in the Lord. It is within those walls that my husband and I grow older together. If the walls could talk, they would tell of both laughter and heartache.

Within those sturdy walls, we have held Bible studies, hosted youth events, fed sports teams, and spent time with the Lord. We have walked through joy and pain as a family. We have cried out to God to hold us in the storm. Inside those walls are the nails that hold them together, and someday, if God is willing, I will rock my grandbabies within them also.

Just as nails need to be hammered into just the right spot to hold the frame of a house together, we, the body of Christ, each need to be functioning in the right area so that our church body can stand strong.

As the body of Christ, we are alive in Him, and each member of the body—no matter our age, color, sex, or background—has been given gifts from God for the good of the body. Romans 12:4–8 couldn't say it more clearly:

> For just as each of us has one body with many members, and these members do not all have the same function, so in Christ we, though many, form one body, and each member belongs to all the others. We have different gifts, according to the grace given to each of us. If your gift is prophesying, then prophesy in accordance with your faith; if it is serving, then serve; if it is teaching, then teach; if it is to encourage, then give encouragement; if it is giving, then give generously; if it is to lead, do it diligently; if it is to show mercy, do it cheerfully.

Sadly, many people find a church, but they do not feel like they are an important part of the body—that they have anything to offer and would be missed. I felt like that when I was a new believer. I didn't know how to play an instrument, and I always felt sorry for the person who was standing in front of me during worship because of how poorly I sing. As I would sit in church and listen to people who could pray the most amazing prayers, recite a Scripture from memory, and give a talk, I became discouraged. I remember thinking that the people who could lead a study had something I did not. Those that could pray with eloquence were certainly needed more than me. What did I have to offer?

I had fallen into the trap that many do. We can't forget that the little toe has an important job. Without it, the body has a hard time standing. Or the elbow: without it, the hand could not get food to the mouth. Over time, I began to see that being part of the body was more than just the gifts in the Scripture I shared a moment ago.

Some of us have the gift of a smile that can encourage the sad. Just because you don't hear someone praying beautiful prayers over people doesn't mean that in their quiet time they are not powerful prayer warriors. Maybe you are a prayer warrior. Your gift could be hospitality, because you make people feel welcome when they are with you. We can't forget about those who have the heart of a servant. They have the most important job, working behind the scenes and often getting no thanks for the time they put in.

Each of us matters. If you feel you have no gifts to offer the church, I want to challenge you to find your gift. I am not asking you to take a specific spiritual gifts test like I did. The test made me feel worse. Many times, the test tries to fit a square peg into a round hole. Rather, prayer is the first (and best) place to start. Ask God to show you how he can use you in your church. I would love to help you get started with a prayer. I have written a prayer for you at the end of this chapter. You are welcome to use it or pray on your own.

Second, ask those you know best what gifts they see in you. Our friends see things in us that we often don't. You may be surprised to learn that your friends see more than one gift in you. Use the space at the end of today's lesson to write down the feedback you get from your friends.

Lastly, think outside the box. If you love to cook, then you could ask if there is a need to cook dinners from time to time for those that are sick or recovering from surgery. Stacie, a very dear friend of mine, is a financial advisor, so she uses her talents to teach a class that shows Christians how to better steward their financial resources. My sweet friend Traci has a way of making women's retreats so special with handmade gifts. Another woman I recently met has the gift of writing. Diane as offered to use her gift to send handwritten cards of encouragement to the people God puts on her heart. She is also part of the first-impressions team at church, and whenever there is a visitor, Diane is ready to send them a handwritten follow-up note. There are countless ways you can serve your church—and no matter what you do, it is important to the body as a whole.

A house will not stand without the nails hammered securely in place, and a church is the same. Without each member securely in place and serving how they have been built to serve, our churches cannot function to their fullest ability. My hope is that you would want to be hammered into the church to help it stand.

Pray It

Where can you serve in the church? The best place to start is with prayer. Ask God to show you where you can best serve or what would be a good fit for you. Ask him not to limit you to just one thing but to show you how your talents and abilities can be used wherever there is a need.

Think About It

What are your talents and the things you enjoy doing the most? Often, you can find a way to serve using your hobbies. Complete the following exercises, writing your answers in the space provided or in your journal:

- List your talents and hobbies:

_____

_____

_____

_____

- Is there a way you can see yourself using one of your gifts to serve? For example, maybe you enjoy working out. You could start a walking group and encourage others to get out and be active. You could use it as a time of fellowship, and it would be a great way for newcomers to meet the people in your church.

Do It

In the near future, complete the following steps:

- Ask your friends what gifts and strengths they see in you. They may see something you don't see in yourself.
- Set a meeting with your pastor or women's ministry leader and ask them how you can serve.

Every nail counts, so find out where you best fit and allow yourself to be hammered into the framework of your church.

A Penny for Your Thoughts

Day 30

What's Really Behind Your Smile?

 $\mathcal{W}$ e are so close to the end of this thirty-one day journey. I want to touch on two more things: hiding your hurt behind your smile, and lastly, the occasional offense that will happen from time to time. Today let's look at what is behind that smile.

We should feel that we can be honest about our hurts at church, but for some reason that is not always the case. I have a friend named Cassie who has a huge heart for the Lord. When her busy life allows, she shares a word of wisdom on my blog under "Cassie's Corner." I cannot take full credit for this day's reading because I got the idea from her. She is full of "Cassie-isms," as I like to call them.

Cassie wrote an article for my blog called "My Church Lady 'Smile' Mask," and in it she says this about her "Church Lady Smile": "Come on now, you know what I'm talking about. The smile on your face you wear on Sundays at church whether you realize you do or whether you adorn yourself with it right before you walk in the door. My mask looks confident, happy and sounds cheerful and loving. I place this mask on every time I feel like I am going to emotionally lose it at church."*

---

* http://heartfeltramblings.com/2014/05/19/my-church-lady-smile-mask.

I am sure that every one of us knows what it's like to put a smile on our face when inside we are falling apart. Unfortunately, I think this is an issue in our churches today. In the one place we can be vulnerable, real, and lay all our problems out, we clam up and paint a smile on our face. I wish I knew where that comes from.

While at a leadership meeting for church, my husband expressed something that lines up with Cassie's article. What he really liked about our church was that he could be real. If he was having a hard time, he could be honest about it. There was a time in our past when we would go to church and everyone seemed to be smiling, like everything was perfect. He always wondered how they could all be so happy when there were times he was hurting so deeply. Those smiles and the "we have got it all together" attitude made him feel there must be something wrong with him.

We need to be able to drop the smile that covers our pain and let what is really behind the smile come out in our churches. When we are hurting, God calls the rest of the body (our church) to be there for us. How can they help us if we don't speak up? In 1 Corinthians 12:25–26, Paul writes, "So that there should be no division in the body, but that its parts should have equal concern for each other. If one part suffers, every part suffers with it; if one part is honored, every part rejoices with it." And in his letter to the Ephesians, Paul reminds us that "from him [Jesus] the whole body, joined and held together by every supporting ligament, grows and builds itself up in love" (Ephesians 4:16).

It is clearly spelled out for us in that Scripture that we need to be there for one another in the good times and the bad. I am going to go out on a limb and say that most of us would be there for someone who was hurting without hesitation, but when it comes to saying we are hurting, we sidestep the issue. It seems much easier to give comfort than to receive it.

The smiles on our faces should not be there to cover up the pain inside. Your smile should be there because you know that you have a church body that takes you as you are.

I encourage you to open up with a pastor or a friend in your church if you are carrying a burden. Don't be afraid to say, "I need prayer." If you are hurting, wipe off the smile that covers your pain and be honest. When you hang on to your pain in silence, the enemy is given power that really is not his to have. Letting it out brings it into the light, and the enemy loses his grip. Who knows—your honesty may inspire someone else to open up, and it may start a domino effect that is greatly needed in our churches. When you go to church, be real, be honest, and let others see that they can be real too. Also, be available to pray and talk with others who are being real about their troubles.

Pray It

Today, get real with God and tell him about the burdens that are on your heart. You can journal if that works for you. Do not rush this—be totally honest with God.

Think About It

Is there an area that you just prayed about that you are keeping to yourself?

Do It

Reread the Scriptures from today: 1 Corinthians 12:25–26 and Ephesians 4:16.

Simply put, these verses are advising us that we are to be there for one another at all times. I asked you to think about whether there are any areas of your life in which you are burdened. If there are, please talk with a pastor or a friend that you can trust. You don't need to be hiding behind a Church Lady Smile when inside you are crying in pain. If you are in the process of looking for a church and do not have a pastor to speak to, please go to a friend who will be happy to pray with you and support you.

A Penny for Your Thoughts

Let Go of the Offense

*T*oday we bring things to a close, and I want to finish with something that happens to all of us. Offenses. None of us are immune to them, and left unaddressed, they can leave deep wounds and tear relationships apart. Siblings have a way of rubbing each other the wrong way. "Squeal like a pig" was what my brother would say as he pulled the very short hair on the back of my neck upward to bug me. I would get so mad at him for that. Yes, we made each other mad from time to time—but no matter how big the offense, we would work it out because we were family and loved each other.

Offenses are part of life. We are occasionally going to rub one another the wrong way at work, at school, in our families, and in church. As new parents, we thought we would try out a church and see what it was all about. We began to make connections and felt like the church was where we wanted to be—until we got offended. Rather than working it out, we refused to go anymore. It would be another five years before we went to *any* church. We let an offense keep us away.

Thankfully, God continued to tug on our hearts to bring us back. We found a church that we called home for many years. We served and grew in the Lord at that little church until our children needed a church with an active youth group. We found a new church with a youth group that would meet our new need.

After a few years in our church, there was a problem with the handling of our tithing. Rather than leaving and giving up on the church, we worked it out and continued to attend the church until we felt God leading us in a new direction. We followed God's leading, and he brought us to a newly planted church, not because we had been offended but because it was where God needed us to be.

We lost five years in our walk with God because of an offense, and we could have walked away a second time if we had not understood the importance of working things out with our church. I know my family is not the only family to become offended by something in church. I have heard many people say that they no longer go to church because they were offended in some way by someone in their church. Can you imagine if we quit our job, quit school, or left our home every time we got offended?

We can take a different approach. Here's what my friend, Joe Duenich, said in one of his sermons:

When you're family, you love each other and you work things out. You don't just decide that you're going to leave the family.

Now have you ever wanted to run away from church? Have you ever been hurt or disappointed by someone in the church? I think if we are all honest, we all have been disappointed or maybe disillusioned in the church, maybe had some unmet expectations. But at the end of the day, when it is all said and done, we have to stick it out and continue to work things out.

The reality is that we are going to rub each other wrong from time to time, even in our churches. One day we may be the offended and the next day we may be the offender. Even among our closest friends in church, there may be offenses. Let's take a look at Psalm 55:13–14: "But it is you, a man, my equal, my companion, my familiar friend. We used to take sweet counsel together; within God's house we walked in the throng" (ESV).

How sad it is that people who used to consider themselves equals, companions, and familiar friends no longer counsel together in the house of God. How many more today have walked away from church, ended friendships, and missed out on the fellowship when they "walked in the throng" (i.e., the church body)?

As a church body, we must expect that from time to time there will be trials, even among our true friends. When those times come, they will be painful because we are friends and because we are united in Christ. Most conflicts can be solved if we sit down with the person who offended us and talk about it. Sometimes it is just a simple misunderstanding.

When we turn and run from a church because of an offense, we give the enemy the victory. Please do not get me wrong—some offenses may be of such concern that after you talk about it, you may need to find a new church. If we had continued to see the misuse of our tithing, we would have changed churches.

Before you leave a church because you were hurt, talk with the person who offended you. If, after talking with the person, you still feel you have not gotten things rectified, your next step is to ask your pastor or another member of your church to step in and go back to the person who caused the offense. Do your best to try to work things out between those involved before you leave the church. If things still continue to cause hurt, don't stop going to church altogether. Find a new church and stay plugged in. We missed several years because we let an offense that could have been worked out run us completely out of any church. Thankfully, my husband and I have now learned to face the offenses head-on and with love. We have also had to say, "I am sorry," because we have accidentally offended someone. There have also been times when we have had to forgive an offense knowing that we may never get an apology—but in those moments, God has done a mighty work in us.

In the book of Matthew, Jesus gave clear instructions about how to handle an offense: "If your brother sins against you, go and tell him his fault, between you and him alone. If he listens to you, you have gained your brother. But if he does not listen, take one or two others along with you, that every charge may be established by the evidence of two or three witnesses. If he refuses to listen to them, tell it to the church. And if he refuses to listen even to the church, let him be to you as a Gentile and a tax collector'" (Matthew 18:15–17 ESV). *Gentile* and *tax collector* were terms that were used when speaking to those of that culture and time. Though those words may not apply now, the way to handle the offense has not changed. Most offenses are a simple misunderstanding, and there will be no need to involve anyone else.

I can't stress enough the importance of this principle. Do not let an offense drive you away from the church. Don't let an offense sit and fester until you explode in anger toward the person who offended you. Let nothing get in the way of your relationship with God!

Think About It

Is there is an offense either in church or in your personal life that needs to be addressed? What is it?

_____

_____

_____

Pray It

Please pray and ask God to help you with the correct words to say to the person with whom you have the offense. Also, pray that God would prepare the other person's heart and that he will show you if you need to apologize for something you've done.

Do It

Follow the instructions in Matthew 18:15–17 and don't let the sun set on another day without dealing with the offense. Don't give the enemy the victory. Christ extended his forgiveness to you, and in handling offenses, you are given the opportunity to extend forgiveness too.

A Penny for Your Thoughts

Epilogue

In closing, I pray that my heartfelt ramblings have led you to look for God in the day-to-day, mundane moments of your life. My hope is that you also feel "Simply Blessed" by the love of Jesus and that you always remember to look for joy in the little things. As you close this book, do not stop—continue to grow deeper in your relationship with God through study, prayer, fellowship, serving, worship, and other Christian books. God should be your source always.

Blessings to you from the Midlife Domestic Goddess and "may the God of hope fill you with all joy and peace as you trust in him, so that you may overflow with hope by the power of the Holy Spirit" (Romans 15:13).

About the Author

God is in the everyday moments that many people overlook. This is where **Kim Chaffin** finds lessons from God, practical lessons that find their way from her heart to her keyboard. Kim created *Heartfelt Ramblings of a Midlife Domestic Goddess*® to help people see that God doesn't ask us to be religious, but he wants to have a relationship with you and me. He is comfortable, like a pair of fuzzy socks or pajamas that feel so good after a long day.

Priest Lake, Idaho, is Kim's favorite place to write. She cherishes summer days spent at the lake. Beyond the pages of *Simply Blessed*, Kim is a contributor for the Whatever Girls Ministry (thewhatevergirls.com) and *LivingBetter50* magazine (livingbetter50.com).

God has not only given Kim a passion to write but also the desire to speak. She finds joy in sharing the Lord at women's events, weekend retreats, and sermons at church.

Kim is a wife of twenty-eight years and a mother of two. She is also a graduate of Eastern Washington University, where she earned a degree in sociology with an emphasis in crime corrections. Kim believes we must never stop growing and learning, which is why she is taking online classes through Portland Bible College.

Her sense of humor and heart for the Lord can be found at her website, heartfeltramblings.com, on Facebook at facebook.com /HeartfeltRamblingsOfAMidlifeDomesticGoddess, Instagram @ heartfelt_ramblings, and on Twitter at @Mom4Godalways.

A Penny for Your Thoughts

A Penny for Your Thoughts

A Penny for Your Thoughts

A Penny for Your Thoughts

Animals and World Religions

LISA KEMMERER

OXFORD
UNIVERSITY PRESS

OXFORD
UNIVERSITY PRESS

Oxford University Press, Inc., publishes works that further
Oxford University's objective of excellence
in research, scholarship, and education.

Oxford   New York

Auckland   Cape Town   Dar es Salaam   Hong Kong   Karachi
Kuala Lumpur   Madrid   Melbourne   Mexico City   Nairobi
New Delhi   Shanghai   Taipei   Toronto

With offices in

Argentina   Austria   Brazil   Chile   Czech Republic   France   Greece
Guatemala   Hungary   Italy   Japan   Poland   Portugal   Singapore
South Korea   Switzerland   Thailand   Turkey   Ukraine   Vietnam

Published by Oxford University Press, Inc.
198 Madison Avenue, New York, New York 10016

www.oup.com

Oxford is a registered trademark of Oxford University Press

Library of Congress Cataloging-in-Publication Data
Kemmerer, Lisa.
Animals and world religions / Lisa Kemmerer.
p.   cm.
Includes bibliographical references.
ISBN 978-0-19-979067-8 (hardcover : alk. paper)—
ISBN 978-0-19-979068-5 (pbk. : alk. paper)
1. Animals—Religious aspects.
2. Human-animal relationships—Religious aspects.
3. Religions.   I. Title.   II. Title: Rightful relations.
BL439.K46 2011 205'.693—dc22
2011005863

Verse by Meng Haoran and Sikong Tu reprinted from *The Columbia Anthology of Traditional
Chinese Literature* edited by Victor A. Mair. Copyright ©1994 Columbia University Press. Reprinted with
permisssion of the publisher. Verse from the *Acaranga Sutra and the Sutrakrtanga* reprinted from *Sources
of Indian Tradition: From the Beginning to 1800* edited by Ainslee T. Embree. Copyright © 1998
Columbia University Press. Reprinted with permission of the publisher. Verse from *The Teachings of the
Compassionate Buddha*, edited by E. A. Burtt, reprinted with the permission of Winifred Burtt Brinster.
Verse from "Ahimsa in the Mahabharata" reprinted with the permission of Chris Chapple. Verse reprinted from *Chinese
Religion: An Anthology of Sources* translated by Deborah Sommer, from Han-shan Tzu shih-chi (Collected poems of
Master Han-shan), Ssu-pu ts'ung-k'an edition. By permission of Oxford University Press, Inc.

1 3 5 7 9 8 6 4 2

Printed in the United States of America
on acid-free paper

This book is dedicated to fostering a deep, pervasive, and all-inclusive compassion, as indicated by core teachings in the world's dominant religious traditions.

Proceeds will be redirected back to animal advocacy.

CONTENTS

ACKNOWLEDGMENTS

Special thanks to Tom Regan for his ongoing willingness to offer expert comment, and to Norm Phelps for writing a foreword for this volume—and to both of them for all that they do to change the plight of nonhuman animals.

Many thanks to those within various religious traditions who read and commented on chapters, including Christopher Key Chapple (Buddhism), Louis Komjathy (Chinese religions), Richard Schwartz (Judaism), Stephen Kaufman (Christianity), Richard Foltz (Islam), and two unknown reviewers. Thank you to Stella Zhou (as well as some of the previously mentioned individuals) for assistance with activist contacts (and translations).

Finally, thank you to all who exemplify religious commitment through animal advocacy, and my deepest thanks to animal activists everywhere.

FOREWORD

If organized religions were to include animals fully within the scope of their compassionate ministries, the benefit to the animals would be tremendous. In the United States alone, the disappearance of fried chicken and spaghetti with meatballs from church suppers would save millions of animals every year. And if Jews, Christians, and Muslims declined to include the slaughtered bodies of God's most helpless children in any meal on which they asked God's blessing, the number would reach far higher.

What has been less obvious to most observers is that religious practitioners—and religion itself—would benefit spiritually as much as animals would benefit physically and emotionally.

Charles Darwin provided an irrefutable case demonstrating that evolution by natural selection makes it impossible to plausibly deny our fundamental physical, mental, and emotional similarity to nonhuman animals. In *Animals and World Religions*, philosopher Lisa Kemmerer makes an equally irrefutable case that the foundational teachings of the world's most ancient, widespread, and influential religions (which henceforward I shall, solely for convenience, call the "major religions") recognize the same profound physical, mental, and emotional similarity that Darwin described.

Every aspect of Darwin's theory has been accepted by mainstream science *except* his claim that we are fundamentally similar to nonhuman animals. Yet his claim has never been refuted—it has simply been ignored... until recently. Ethologists such as Jane Goodall, Marc Bekoff, and a host of others at universities and field stations around the world are now affirming and extending what Darwin indicated. Likewise, far too many religious practitioners, including clergy and theologians, have simply ignored the foundational teachings of their faith regarding our fundamental similarity to nonhuman animals.

This fundamental similarity, Kemmerer points out (buttressing her claims with an impressive array of citations from the world's great religious traditions), brings animals fully within the protective circle of the call of religious traditions for universal, unbounded compassion. Our religions cannot be fully realized until practitioners grant animals equal protection universally indicated by religious teachings, and this requires people to refuse to be complicit in the exploitation, abuse, and slaughter of our nonhuman family members. Religion needs animals to be protected as much as the animals need religion to protect them, because religion that fails to protect animals fails to keep its own promise.

A "dominionistic" outlook is at least partly responsible for our abuse of animals. The failures of religion with regard to animals—as with regard to human beings—are many and obvious. Consider the Inquisition, the Crusades, the conquest of the Western hemisphere, the Salem witch trials, and the religious wars that devastated Europe for centuries, and of which the Balkans and Northern Ireland are the last exhausted spasms (one hopes!). Yet most of us do not blame religion for our inhumanity to one another (for very good reason). Our savagery is widespread; the faithful have no monopoly on violence and greed, which is prevalent with or without religion. Atheists can be as cruel as believers, and on occasion, perhaps more so. Most of us recognize that inhumanity is caused by forces that act on and within us universally, and into which religion is dragged after the fact, so to speak, as a justification. In its true form, religion conquers these forces; it does not serve as their bodyguard.

The same is true of our savagery toward animals; it arises from causes other than religion—our fears and appetites, for the most part—and we commandeer religion into its service as an after-the-fact justification. Religious rationales for the enslavement, abuse, and slaughter of animals are as much a betrayal of true religion as are religious justifications for the enslavement, abuse, and slaughter of human beings. Those who have enlisted religion in the service of cruelty, callousness, and killing have gone astray from religious teachings and expectations, regardless of the victim's species. They have grafted the branch of religion onto alien roots.

Lisa Kemmerer has written *Animals and World Religions* to remind us of this, and to direct our attention back to the true—and universally compassionate—roots of religious traditions around the world. Doctor Kemmerer believes—rightly, in my opinion—that it is time for the defenders of animals, both religious and secular, to turn their attention from the failures of religion and redirect energy toward foundational teachings that call us to compassion, nurturance, and service toward those whose lives depend on our mercy. We cannot summon religion home simply by shouting that it has lost its way. We must make positive steps to bring change.

Isaac Bashevis Singer, Nobel laureate in literature and compassionate vegetarian for the last half century of his life, noted that scriptures include animals within the injunction to love your neighbor as yourself. Lisa Kemmerer shows us that these teachings of compassion toward all living beings spring directly from the ancient, essential heart of all major religions. The problem is that we have become accustomed to seeing our scriptures through the lens of tradition and custom, and that lens has been clouded by millennia of animal enslavement and slaughter.

At one level, *Animals and World Religions* is a solidly grounded, scholarly survey of a set of teachings common to the world's major religions. On another level, it is an inspiring and eloquent call for a fresh look at what we thought we knew about the tenets of our faiths. If I may be permitted to echo, with all respect, the words that led Saint Augustine to a new and life-changing understanding of religion: *Tolle, lege,* "Pick it up and read it." This book will leave you with a new—and hopefully life-changing—understanding of the profound message of compassion that is as unrestricted by species as it is by nationality, race, and gender, and which lies at the heart of the world's religious traditions.

—Norm Phelps

(Author of *The Dominion of Love: Animal Rights According to the Bible, The Great Compassion: Buddhism and Animal Rights,* and *The Longest Struggle: Animal Advocacy from Pythagoras to PETA*)

Animals and World Religions

Introduction

From the standpoint of religious traditions, what is our rightful role with regard to red-winged blackbirds and short-eared lizards? What do sacred teachings tell us about our responsibilities to bluefin tuna and Black Angus cattle?

Humans often dominate and exploit other creatures. Contemporary factory farming, for example, causes acute suffering, prolonged misery, and premature death to billions of nonhuman animals every year, across continents, on behalf of those who choose to eat animal products. From factory farms to medical laboratories, individuals from nonhuman species have become objects for our purposes, and means to human ends. Technology, mass production, and the sheer number of flesh-eating humans crowded onto this planet have increased the volume and intensity of nonhuman animal exploitation exponentially. Most of us never see the creatures whom we dominate and exploit, their dark eyes and steamy breath, wavy hair or intricate feathers, swaying tails or shiny beaks. We do not have the chance to know them as individuals—their preferences and fears, affections and curiosities—we see only a slab of flesh wrapped in cellophane, a bit of dairy in a plastic container, with an obscure label that fails to mention the truth: This that you eat is part of someone else's body.

In the seventies and eighties, philosophers Tom Regan and Peter Singer exposed the horrors of the slaughterhouse and the cruelty of animal laboratories, noting that humans could get along quite well without these cruel animal exploiting institutions. Using carefully considered philosophical arguments, Regan and Singer demonstrated that our exploitation of other creatures is morally/ethically inadmissible.

Forty years later, there is much greater awareness of nonhuman animal exploitation, but little has changed in the food, fur, and research industries. In fact, the number of factory-farmed creatures has increased exponentially—we are consuming even more animal products. Why have people failed to respond to philosophical truths, to carefully consider moral imperatives presented by learned contemporary ethicists? Why have institutions of cruelty thrived in spite of increased exposure and consequently, a growing voice of moral condemnation?

Unfortunately, human beings "have been slow to pick up on the logic-based arguments provided by philosophy" (Foltz, *Animals*, 1). Perhaps many people have not responded because they are motivated more by faith, spirituality, and/or religious convictions than by logic or moral philosophy. For people, who focus primarily on religions beliefs, "an argument based on the sources of religious tradition will be more convincing than one that is not" (Foltz, *Animals*, 3).

As it turns out, the world's great religious teachings concur with Regan and Singer—we ought not to be exploiting nonhumans as we do in our animal industries. Unfortunately, "people are usually only partially aware of what is taught" by their inherited religious traditions, and we tend to be "highly selective" as to which aspects of our sacred teachings and writings we are familiar with—and those that we practice (Foltz, *Animals*, 4). Reading sacred literature, examining spiritual teachings, and pondering the lives of great religious adepts can remind people of time-honored spiritual principles and provide insights into the human being's proper place in the universe.

Karl Jaspers referred to the great religious awakenings that took place in various places around the world in the first millennium BCE[1] as the Axial Age. At this time, the world's largest contemporary religions were formed, and morality—how we behave—was placed "at the heart of the spiritual life" in the religions that originated in India, China, and the Middle East (Armstrong, xii, xiv). The taproot of this religious/moral framework is compassion; compassionate action became the *essence* of religious practice during the Axial Age (Armstrong, xiv). The great sages of that time, who formed each of today's major religions, placed compassion, generosity, kindness, charity, benevolence, inclusiveness—the empathic life—at the core of religious teachings and practice. These sages taught that respect for the lives of all beings was the *essence* of religion (Armstrong, xiv–xv).

Scholar and author Kimberley Patton (Harvard Divinity), when asked in a recent interview, commented that "religious traditions contain extremely long and rich and ancient commentaries on the topic of animals. They are very interested in animals as existential beings. And this goes back centuries, millennia even" (Patton, 30). She notes that every religious tradition provides followers with "very rich resources for seeing animals more as theological subjects than as objects," and that contemporary mainstream responses, which ignore the desperate plight of non-human animals,[2] "are largely ignoring their own heritages" (Patton, 30). Author,

---

[1] BCE indicates "before the common era"; CE indicates "of the common era." While this time reference is synonymous with the Christian calendar, these terms are at least a small attempt to honor the world's many religions, cultures, and calendars, while remaining intelligible to a largely English-speaking readership.

[2] To understand the moral and spiritual importance of nonhuman animal exploitation, it is imperative that readers see what happens behind the scenes in animal industries. Such information can be found on many websites, including Vegan Outreach (http://www.veganoutreach.org/whyvegan/animals.html), Farm Sanctuary (http://www.farmsanctuary.org/mediacenter/videos.html), VIVA! USA (http://www.vivausa.org/visualmedia/index.html), VIVA! in the United Kingdom (http://www.viva.org.uk/), People for the Ethical Treatment of Animals (http://www.petatv.com/), the Humane Society (http://www.humanesociety.org/news/multimedia/, and Physicians Committee for Responsible Medicine (http://www.pcrm.org/resources/).

scholar, and activist Paul Waldau, when asked, "Which religions are the most animal-friendly?" replied without pause: "All the ones that are listening to their heart" (Waldau, "Animal," 31).

Waldau notes that religions sometimes move in directions that prompt and motivate the masses toward a great "expansion of justice and ethics" (Waldau, "Guest," 238). While religions have different worldviews, different prophets and saints, and different conceptions of the spiritual forces of the universe, religions tend to share core *moral* ideals—core conceptions of what is right and wrong, good and bad behavior. This is not surprising given that peoples around the world cannot live in community if they murder, steal, and lie—certain core moral ideals must be upheld in order to maintain social structures (Rachels, 26). Consequently, religions tend to foster moral principles that allow us to live comfortably and peacefully with one another. Whether termed *ahimsa, metta, karuna, ci,* or love, for example, the world's largest and oldest religious traditions teach people that we must protect the weak and needy from cruelty, exploitation, and indifference. Most of us are aware of these core spiritual teachings and their application with regard to human beings (though we often fail to put this knowledge into action), but few people seem to understand the application of such pervasive religious moral injunctions with regard to fishes and mice, hogs and horses, turkeys and elephants.

Intent and Focus

There is no *one* Buddhism, and there is no *one* Christianity. There are hundreds of Christian churches, each with its own particular creed, interpretations, traditions, practices, and leaders. First-century Indian Buddhism differs radically from twenty-first-century Japanese Buddhism. Neo-Confucian religious traditions, which began to take shape around 1000 CE, permanently altered the Confucian tradition; Buddhism permanently altered Daoism. Every religious tradition changes across time and place, and so every great religious tradition is rich with diversity.

Religions are notoriously complicated, necessarily so because they endure over vast time periods, travel expansive continents, are transplanted onto distant but well-developed cultures in varied climes, and endure through extensive cultural and political changes. In light of texts and teachings, in light of interpretations and commentaries accumulated over centuries, there is an overwhelming array of attitudes and responses surrounding any given topic among religious traditions. Paul Waldau notes that

> over the millennia of their existence, [religious] traditions have provided
> an astonishing array of views and materials, some of which are in significant
> tension with each other. Since such diversity leads to challenging problems
> on virtually any subject...it also affects significantly many issues that arise

when one seeks to describe each tradition's views of animals. (Waldau, *Specter*, 3)

In light of this diversity, almost any religious practice or belief might be defended and/or sanctioned by a particular phrase, sentence, isolated story, or obscure document within a given religious tradition's accumulated stories and literature. Given this, how can we reach any worthy conclusions concerning our rightful relations with nonhumans?

In spite of this diversity of accumulated religious lore, it is possible to locate a preponderance of core teachings that point to a particular moral outlook, which can be discerned by examining texts, the lives of moral exemplars, and long-standing, deep-rooted, foundational religious ideals. Sometimes the sheer volume of teachings on a given viewpoint will seal the debate. Sometimes *who* offers the moral teachings, or *where* the teachings are recorded, will carry the weight of authority. For example, in the world of Islam, the Qur'an carries more weight than any other text, and words attributed to Muhammad carry more weight than words attributed to any other individual. Though a variety of contending views clutter the airways, some views inevitably prove obscure, or of little importance, because they are found in secondary texts, because they are credited to an individual who carries comparatively less esteem in the religious tradition, or because such a view is an anomaly in a tradition that overwhelmingly supports an opposing point of view. If we are diligent in examining available information, we can reach dependable conclusions regarding core moral teachings.

This book examines a host of indigenous religious traditions and seven of the world's most prosperous and well-represented religions (the Hindu, Buddhist, Confucian, Daoist, Jewish, Christian, and Islamic traditions). (When I use the term *religions* in this book, I refer specifically to these religions.) This volume does not focus on the many differences *among* branches of a given religion, such as that of Mahayana and Theravada Buddhists, Sunni or Shi'a Muslims, Orthodox or Reform Judaism, or that of Protestant and Catholic Christians. Rather, this work focuses on *core* teachings within each religious tradition that reach across sectarian boundaries, like *ahimsa* in Buddhist traditions or *love* in Christian traditions.

Each chapter of this book is divided into a series of sections. Section headings are not identical across chapters (for example, interpenetrability) because, despite remarkable similarities that lie at the core of religious traditions, each religion is distinct and unique.

"Sacred Nature, Sacred Anymals" (the "y" will soon be explained), focuses on nature generally, exploring religious teachings that instruct people on rightful relations with trees, mountains, soil, and water—ecosystems and the environment—which are essential habitats for nonhuman animals. "Philosophy and Morality" explores specific, core religious teachings that establish rightful relations between humans and all other creatures. Subsequent sections focus on religiously sanctioned relationships between the divine and nonhumans, and relations that are outlined in sacred texts and teachings between humans and nonhumans. The latter topic is further divided into two categories: nonhumans as individuals in their own right, and spiritual and physical kinship between humans and nonhuman animals.

"Interpenetrability" is particularly important to religious traditions that offer a cyclical vision of life, such as reincarnation/transmigration. In traditions in which individuals might be reborn as an indigo bunting or the tiny, South American Robinson's mouse opossum, there is no definitive line between Italians, indigo buntings, and mouse opossums—there is no eternal or ultimate distinction between humans and the rest of the animate world. In contrast, religions that do not hold a cyclical vision of life do not generally include species interpenetrability. Consequently, this section is included only in the first four chapters.

"Anymal Powers" examines special abilities that are attributed to nonhumans in sacred stories and literature, including creative powers, spiritual devotion, and special knowledge, such as the ability to assist and teach human beings.

The final section of each chapter focuses on animal activists who are motivated by religious belief. These activists are driven by religious commitments, by their spiritual understanding of what constitutes rightful relations between humans and other creatures, and by their knowledge of how contemporary flesh, entertainment, "lab" animal, and clothing industries violate religiously prescribed rightful relations between humans and nonhuman animals.

Positive Presentation

This book focuses on religious teachings that are relevant to animal advocacy.

In keeping with the moral outlook established in the Axial Age, the time period during which the texts of today's great religions were formed, today's major religions continue to be, overall, radically friendly toward nonhuman animals. This book reflects this strong religious/moral tendency without presenting opposing arguments. I do not offer opposing arguments for three reasons.

First, arguments against animal advocacy are easy to come by. Most of us grow up believing that human exploitation of other creatures is religiously sanctioned, and most religious people (whether Buddhist or Christian, Jew or Indigenous) will therefore readily defend their tendency to exploit nonhuman animals, as well as in their community and culture—especially dietary preferences. This tendency is also encouraged and perpetuated by religious leaders. Religious leaders generally share and defend the larger community's exploitative habits. I do not offer arguments in favor of animal exploitation because others can and will do so; such arguments are easy to come by.

This tendency should neither surprise us nor affect our point of view:

> As has happened so often in history when the religious imagination has been
> called upon to support racist, sexist, and other exclusivism that obviously
> harmed marginalized humans, religious themes can lend themselves to

obscuring and justifying the marginalization of nonhuman lives. (Waldau, "Guest," 237).

People tend to defend the status quo—their way of life—*whatever* their way of life might be, even when their religion is rich with teachings that convey the importance of radical social change. Force of habit and personal investment in the status quo combine to encourage humanity to turn a blind eye to animal-friendly scriptures. Nonetheless, "religious traditions offer plenty of 'resources' for countering such trends" (Waldau, "Guest," 237). Therefore, the abundant but often ignored resources that lie within each of the world's great religions, which have the power to transform our relations with nonhumans and the earth itself, are rightly the focus of this book.

Second, religious arguments that are commonly posed in favor of exploiting nonhumans are unconvincing in light of a richer understanding of religious teachings, writings, ideals, and exemplars. Such arguments are, generally, both shallow and specific; they run counter to the deepest moral convictions of religious traditions, as this book amply demonstrates. Thankfully, core religious teachings speak against factory farming, and cruel exploitation in general. I encourage readers to ponder what religious arguments might be posed to defend factory farming or animal experimentation in light of the information provided herein. I also encourage readers not to draw any conclusions until they have read the entire book, *including the appendix.*

Third, to include even the most common religious justifications and rationalizations for the exploitation of nonhuman animals in each religious tradition would expand this text considerably. This book is quite long enough—testimony to a rich diversity of animal-friendly teachings from each of the world's most popular religious traditions.

Ideals, Not Actions

This book presents religious ideals; this volume does not attempt to explain how people within each religious tradition actually behave, or what they actually believe.

Compassion is a central teaching of every major religion, but, most people are unaware of how animal industries operate, of how our economic choices either do or do not contribute to intense suffering and uncounted premature deaths. Consequently, religious teachings too often fail to affect what people actually do— what they purchase or consume.

Sacred teachings are no more effective than the knowledge and religious commitment of practitioners. Humans can have an endless supply of noble thoughts, but if they are not accompanied by a call to action, then the ideas themselves are of little value. As it turns out, many religious people proudly claim the idealistic spiritual teachings of their faith, yet simultaneously deny that these teachings apply to their personal choice of foods, clothing, entertainment, or pharmaceuticals. For example, religious people are likely to agree that compassion is a central tenet of their religious ethics, but that there is nothing cruel about the production and consumption of milk or cottage cheese. Dairy products, they assert, do not require the taking of life, and are therefore neither cruel nor against core religious teachings. Of course it is possible to feed and tend a nursing cow and calf without cruelty and without taking life (by simply sharing a cow's nursing milk with her calf), but this mere possibility has nothing to do with the actual production of cow's milk on dairy farms. Consequently, this possibility cannot justify the consumption of yogurt, cheese, or milk purchased from local grocery stores.

Although most religious people confirm core animal-friendly teachings in their particular religious tradition, even grant that such teachings are foundational, they tend to simultaneously offer a host of reasons to explain why they need not live by these teachings—why they can continue to eat blueberry yogurt and poached cod yet remain consistent with core religious teachings.

Dietary habits are the basis of most arguments posed in defense of animal exploitation. This means that religious arguments in favor of animal exploitation generally have nothing to do with religious convictions or the realities of animal exploitation. Such arguments are almost always rooted in a desire for meaty lasagna or shrimp salad, for example. Furthermore, those who pose such arguments have long believed, without actually looking into the matter, that their religion actually supports their consumption of vanilla yogurt and flounder fillets. This misconception is bolstered by common consensus: Pretty much everyone else in their religious community thinks and behaves similarly, consuming flesh, eggs, and dairy products, and believing that their diet is religiously sanctioned.

In contrast, other some religious adherents openly admit that they are unwilling to honor core, animal-friendly religious teachings in their daily lives, usually with regard to diet. Such people admit that they are unwilling to implement religious ideals at the expense of treasured dietary preferences, and because the vast majority of their peers are doing the same, there is little incentive for change.

Martin Luther King Jr. asked whether organized religion was "too inextricably bound to the status quo to save our nation and the world" (King, 409). Is organized religion too inextricably bound to the status quo to offer any meaningful response to the ongoing, egregious exploitation of billions of nonhuman animals? As long as a significant majority continues to support animal exploitation regardless of core religious ideals, most religious people are unlikely to change. As long as few people are willing to challenge common practices, the majority tends to feel free to continue in their habitual way, oblivious of the myriad, devastating affects of their actions. Not one major religion has thus far forcefully challenged *any* factory farming practice (Waldau, "Guest," 234). If religious traditions cannot offer a meaningful response to contemporary moral issues such as that of animal exploitation, they risk being "dismissed as an irrelevant social club with no meaning for the twentieth century" (King, 409). In the words of Paul Waldau, "Mainline cultural and intellectual traditions have debased all other animals" and in the process, we have forsaken our religious obligations and debased ourselves (Waldau, "Guest," 238).

One need only look to the writings of Christians during the Crusades, or to the practice of slavery, to witness the human tendency to justify cruelty in the name of faith—even while continuing to assert that religion is rooted in kindness and generosity (Regan, 106–38). Martin Luther King lamented, "I see the church as the body of Christ. But, oh! How we have blemished and scarred that body through social neglect and through fear of being nonconformists" (King, 408). It is highly likely that future generations will view factory farms and animal experimentation as we now view the Crusades and slavery—as cruel acts committed by those of faith, even in the name of faith, out of ignorance, selfishness, and indifference.

Religions exist, and can only exist, within cultures, in a specific time and place. Racist, sexist, and speciesist tendencies and practices do not indicate a divine sanction of, or the karmic irrelevance of, racism, sexism, or speciesism. Although scriptures have been widely used to justify cruel practices across religious traditions, a preponderance of *core* teachings in every major religious tradition speak against exploitation and cruel domination of any kind. Though this book highlights animal-friendly teachings, it is important to note that the discrepancy between religious teachings and actual practice is often disappointing.

Therefore, *this book can make no claim about actual behavior*—about religious practice—but makes claims only about religious ideals. These chapters do not demonstrate that religious adherents, whether indigenous or Jew, actually *live* in ways that work toward the liberation of nonhuman animals, or even in ways that are sensitive to the lives of other living beings. Yet, ironically, almost all religious people, whether Buddhist or Daoist, Christian or Muslim, are likely to agree that the animal-friendly teachings gathered in this book are central to their religion. How are we to understand this phenomenon of affirmation *and* denial, of granting the truth of religious ideals while shirking responsibility for implementation?

This book is about what religions teach, not about how religious people live. In truth, there appears to be embarrassingly little correlation between the two.

Things We Tend Not to Know

Most of us believe that core teachings in our religion (and religions more generally) do not align with the agenda of animal activists, that religions do not require adherents to rethink their meaty diet. But in reality, religious traditions offer a wealth of moral teachings and spiritual ideals that *surpass animal welfare to align with animal rights and animal liberation,* that reach beyond a vegetarian diet and require adherents to adopt a *vegan* diet. Those who believe otherwise tend to lack information in three critical areas.

First, such people often have no idea what goes on in breeding facilities, on factory farms, in feedlots, on transport trucks, or in slaughterhouses. (This is why it is critical to read the appendix of this book before drawing any conclusions: Please see the appendix to explore factory farming and the fishing industry.) Most of us do not know what sorts of creatures are used in animal labs, how many non-humans are used, in what ways, or to what end. Collectively, we do not know about the lives and deaths of fox, chinchilla, or mink on fur farms or in leghold traps. We have not seen how pet mills, zoos, or circuses cage, feed, or train nonhuman animals.

To understand the extent of the problem—to understand the moral and spiritual importance of this subject—is it essential to view undercover footage of what happens behind the scenes, of what happens behind the closed doors of factory farms. I encourage readers to explore undercover footage taken in all of these industries, which can be accessed online on many websites, including the following:

- For U.S. footage, visit Mercy for Animals (http://www.mercyforanimals.org/) and Compassion Over Killing (http://www.cok.net/).
- For Canadian footage, see Canadians for Ethical Treatment of Farm Animals (http://www.cetfa.com).
- For Australian footage, visit Animals Australia (http://www.animalsaustralia. org/).
- For European footage, see Vief Pfoten (Four Paws) (http://www.vier-pfoten. org/website/output.php).
- For footage from France, see Éthique Animaux (http://www.l214.com/), Eyes on Animals (http://eyesonanimals.com/) and Varkens in Nood (Pigs in Peril) (http://www.varkensinnood.nl/english_.htm).
- For excellent footage from the Netherlands (and for an overall view), see Compassion in World Farming (http://www.ciwf.org.uk/).

I also highly recommend these two short online videos:

- *Do They Know It's Christmas?* (http://www.youtube.com/watch?v=vCX7f_s1CA4)
- *Alec Baldwin Narrates Revised "Eat Your Meat"* (http://www.petatv.com/tvpopup/ Prefs.asp?video=mym2002)

For more general information about factory farming, also visit these sites:

- Farm Sanctuary (http://www.farmsanctuary.org/mediacenter/videos.html)
- HSUS (http://video.hsus.org/)
- PCRM (http://www.pcrm.org/resources/)
- PETA (http://www.petatv.com/)
- Vegan Outreach (http://www.veganoutreach.org/whyvegan/animals.html)
- VIVA! USA (http://www.vivausa.org/visualmedia/index.html) or VIVA! UK (http://www.viva.org.uk/)

Sometimes when people view undercover footage they imagine that these cases are extreme—that they are certainly not representative of the industry more generally. Nothing could be farther from the truth. For example, any time undercover investigators penetrated the locked doors of factory farming they have come away with similar footage. Only when animal industries are prepared for visitors does the footage look different. Even then, it is shocking to watch: Slaughter is inevitably and few industries will allow visitors to witness this process. Slaughter is always more drawn out and riddled with uncertainties than one likes to imagine.

Second, people lack an understanding of—have often not even heard about—speciesism. To fail to notice structurally induced sufferings of Latinos and African-Americans is racist. To be indifferent to white male domination in the U.S. political system is both racist and sexist. Similarly, to turn a blind eye to factory farming is speciesist.

Many societies have progressed in their understanding of how religious teachings inform and guide human relations across races, ages, and sexes, for example, because we understand that racism, ageism, and sexism are extremely hurtful and are therefore morally and spiritually objectionable. Unfortunately, few people understand how religious teachings inform and guide human relations with other species and speak against speciesism. In fact, few people are even aware of the cruel exploitation that stems from our domination of and indifference to other creatures.

Third, we often fail to critically examine conventional spiritual teachings, which we tend to learn young and accept without challenge, even without examination. Those who believe that a particular religion supports the status quo with regard to nonhuman animals have often neglected to examine sacred texts, core teachings, and/or the practical application of religious ideals to assess our current treatment of nonhuman animals.

Foundational religious teachings indicate that our relations with other creatures ought to be compassionate and nonexploitative. Is this overwhelmingly protective, compassionate religious outlook toward nonhumans surprising? Is there a religion that encourages painful and life-destroying exploitation of sentient beings for such paltry reasons as palate or publications, curiosity or convenience? No, and no. Yet people from almost every major religion lack an understanding of contemporary animal industries and animal exploitation; we know little or nothing of speciesism, and precious little about what sacred teachings actually say regarding rightful relations between humans and nonhumans, and so we tend to cite passages from sacred texts, or refer to conventional religious teachings, to support contemporary animal exploitation. Understanding core religious teachings *and* contemporary animal exploitation is critical to grasping why this issue is spiritually important, and why we are compelled to change some of our most basic habits if we adhere to one of the world's most represented religions.

This book specifically focuses on aspects of religious traditions that protect and value other animals because teachings of compassion are prevalent in all dominant religions, because people tend to be ignorant of the implications of these prevalent teachings with regard to non-human animals, and because this spiritual ignorance causes egregious and ongoing suffering and billions of premature deaths. I hope that this book offers a deeper, richer understanding of sacred writings and of core religious principles concerning our rightful relations with other creatures. Ultimately, I hope that this book brings positive changes for nonhuman animals. But the reader must ultimately judge: Do the world's most commonly claimed religions support contemporary animal exploitation, or do they not?

Acceptance, Reform, or Liberation?

There are various ways one might react to ongoing, prevalent animal exploitation (see appendix). In fact, most people react in various ways, and our reactions tend to change as we collect more information, as the weight of new information penetrates and settles into our spiritual consciousness.

One common reaction to new information on the topic of animal exploitation is to simply reaffirm the status quo, to believe—in spite of evidence to the contrary—that all is well on our farms and in our slaughterhouses. Such denial is becoming more difficult as information about factory farming reaches mainstream conscience, as undercover footage finds its way into mainstream media, exposing the horrible truths lurking behind closed doors.

A second common reaction is to admit that there are moral problems inherent in contemporary animal industries, while asserting that exploiting animals is not itself irreligious. Such welfarists often emphasize the need for reform. They may seek larger farrowing crates or a ban on battery hen cages, more fishing regulations or improved fishing technology, and/or an end to particularly painful practices such as debeaking and dehorning. Welfarists look to updated laws and new technology to improve the lives and deaths of exploited animals; they seek to reform animal exploitation.

Still others, on learning about animal exploitation, decide that other creatures do not exist for our purposes, that there is something inherently irreligious about exploiting other sentient beings—especially given that such exploitation is unnecessary to our survival and has even proven to be harmful to our health (as our diet currently is, and as animal experimentation has proven to be) (Anderegg, 18). People who find animal exploitation unacceptable, and who consequently wish to end such practices, are "liberationists" (or "abolitionists"). Liberationists do not want larger farrowing crates, but empty farrowing crates. They do not want fewer trawlers pulling sea life from the seas, but no trawlers pulling sea life from the seas. They do not want an end to debeaking and dehorning, but an end to factory farming. Liberationists often argue that animals do not exist for our purposes, and that it is therefore morally and spiritually wrong for us to use them for our ends, as if they were tools, or a medium of exchange.

If contemporary factory farming runs contrary to spiritual obligation, contrary to scriptures, and contrary to examples set by the world's most frequently claimed religions and their affiliated moral and spiritual exemplars, then people committed to any one of these religious traditions are obligated, at a minimum, to stop supporting factory farming—to stop buying their products. Denial will not suffice; religious adherents must first and foremost *cease to support these industries*. Alternatively, religious adherents can admit that they are not particularly religious—that they really don't care what their religion teaches, and that they therefore have no intention of changing their way of life based on core religious teachings.

Atheists and Agnostics

Even an atheist or agnostic is likely to be interested in discovering moral teachings that are remarkably consistent across religious traditions. Even someone who self-defines as entirely outside all religious traditions is likely to be fascinated by the prodigious power that lies behind such consistent moral convictions across time and place, and might therein find reason to ponder human obligations toward, and treatment of, nonhuman animals. When the world's largest and oldest religions come together on a single point of morality, it is likely that we have struck upon something that human beings cannot afford to ignore, something to which we might all aspire, something that is central to who we all aspire to be more generally, whether or not we adhere to any of the world's many religions.

Words and Social Change

Words help to shape our understanding of the world. Language legitimizes and is made legitimate by those in power, and is therefore rife with "political and ideological investment" (Fairclough, *Critical*, 7). Consequently, language supports and contributes to domination, and is an important medium for social control and a viable method of bringing social change (Fairclough, *Language*, 2–3).

Ludwig Wittgenstein, an influential Austrian philosopher who died in 1951, noted that language is a moral matter, "an activity, or a form of life," the importance of which should not be overlooked (Wittgenstein, 23). Wittgenstein believed that the job of philosophy is to sort out conceptual confusions that arise when we use language carelessly, or without reflection. He considered the problems that arise from language to be "deep disquietudes," and philosophy as "a battle against the bewitchment of our intelligence by means of language" (Wittgenstein, 111, 109). He noted that communication, the use of language in a meaningful manner, is a "speech *act*"; language "is not simply a mirror of life, it is the doing of life itself" (Gergen, 35).

Wittgenstein recognized language as a human creation. Wittgenstein therefore also recognized language as arbitrary, as an imperfect reflection of reality, not an inherent phenomenon of the universe.

A popular introductory text for linguistics includes "a cartoon in which two disgruntled cavemen are attempting to converse. One says to the other: 'f w wnt tlk rlly gd, w'll hv t nvnt vwls'" (Cameron, 1). This comic reminds readers that people do not just *use* language; "they comment on the language they use. Frequently they find it wanting and, like the cavemen, propose to improve it" (Cameron, 1). Language is not static; it is created and recreated by those who speak and write. New terms such as *quark* or *black hole* describe a more recent human understanding of the universe. Fifty years ago *Internet* and *megabyte* were not part of our vocabulary. Meanwhile, *whither, nigh,* and *thee* have become obsolete.

Humans need never be stymied by a lack of words; we simply create what we need. But through our created words, language reflects culture and society, and simultaneously maintains a particular, established way of thinking. Our choice of words is an active process, and the words we choose make a statement beyond surface meanings. *We* produce language, *we* give it meaning, and *we* affirm or challenge each word by accepting or rejecting that word. Consequently, our use of language can either aid or hinder change.

Because words carry more than surface meaning, choosing new words is an important tool in the process of changing thought (Fairclough, *Critical*, 3). Someone—or likely many people—were behind the purposeful selection of *African American* as a group indicator. *Darkie, Pickinini,* and *colored* are obsolete. *Nigger* has shifted from common use to either rare and extremely contentious, or friendly insider jargon, like *queer*. Feminists have also employed verbal activism. Most contemporary textbooks from Western nations no longer refer only to men, but use both feminine and masculine pronouns. Feminists continue to put pressure on those speaking in public to think about the meanings and affects of words. Sexist labels, like *chick* or *broad*, are more and more apt to turn heads, or to illicit a negative or questioning response. In many contemporary social circles, sexist words bring on confrontation and/or alienation.

Words are a form of activism. A speaker or writer who chooses words carefully can bring listeners and readers to ponder the words they read or hear.

By calling traditional usages into question, reformers effectively force everyone who uses a particular language to declare a position in respect of sexism, racism, speciesism, and so on. Language reformers provide a new array of word options: For example, a speaker can say, "Ms. A. is the chair(person)" and convey approval of language that is sex-inclusive, or a speaker can say "Miss A. is the chairman" and convey a more conservative attitude about language and sex. What a speaker can no longer do is to select either alternative and convey by it nothing more than "a certain woman holds a particular office." *Choices* as to how we word such sentences have removed the option of political neutrality (Cameron, 119). One either conveys ignorance, indifference, or conservatism, or an acceptance of sex-inclusive language.

When confronted with a new term, we are simultaneously confronted with the *reason* for that term, and we must decide whether or not we will accept or reject this new word. We *must* choose. And in the process, we are confronted with social justice issues. Consequently, the success of a new word is not measured by its frequency of use, but by its ability to bring people to question conventional language. A new word elicits dialogue whether or not it is widely accepted into a community's vocabulary.

The words we choose are morally important; careless use of words is therefore morally objectionable. Intellectual and moral progress can be aided by thoughtful, accurate word choices, and by challenging words and the way others use language (Rorty, 9).

Consequently, I have chosen to alter a few common English language practices throughout this book. For example, I do not refer to nonhuman animals as "that" or "it" any more than I would do so in reference to a human being. Nor do I use the word "animal" as if it excluded *Homo sapiens*.

Lexical Gaps

The "highest value to which language-users can aspire is accuracy" (Cameron, 135). *Lexical gaps* are concepts or concrete items in our world that do not have adequate (or any) verbal representation. Lexical gaps hinder effective communication: How will we talk about poodles if we do not have the word *poodle*? Linguistic accuracy is therefore dependent on word availability, on an accumulation of words that *say* what we *mean*.

There is no word in the English language to describe the category "every animal outside of the speaker's species." For scholars and activists involved in animal rights, animal ethics, and animal liberation, this lexical gap is problematic. The use of *animals* as if it referred only to nonhumans is inappropriate because humans are animals—primates, mammals. As a result, several word combinations have emerged to fill this lexical gap, including *nonhuman animal, other animals*, other-than-human animals, and *animals other than humans*, but when writing or speaking specifically about nonhuman animals, such terms quickly become cumbersome. Nonetheless, authors and lecturers currently speaking and writing on subjects such as animal law or animal minds must use these cumbersome concoctions if they are to remain accurate in their speech and writing.

Dualism

Makeshift word combinations (like *nonhuman animal*) are inadequate not only because they are cumbersome, but also because they are dualistic. *Nonhuman*, for example, artificially divides animals "into two seemingly opposed categories: humans and everyone else" (Adams, *Pornography*, 39–40).

Dualism encourages people to assume that one category is the norm (white, male, human, or Christian, for example), while opposites (brown, female, animal, non-Christian) are assumed to be inferior and less desirable (Adams, *Pornography* 50). Dualistic thinking stirs up division and competition, contention and malevolence, and is therefore proven to be problematic racially, sexually, environmentally, and religiously.

Although this may not be a *necessary* outcome of dualism, it has been a very *real* outcome. Whichever sex, religion, race, or species has not been envisioned as the norm—at the top of the hierarchy—has too often been considered lesser, even exploitable, whether for free labor or scientific experimentation. Consequently, dualistic terms such as *nonhuman animal, other-than-human animals,* and *other animals* are likely to perpetuate Western dualisms, hierarchies, and exploitation, and are therefore undesirable both morally and linguistically.

"Anymal"

As a means of simultaneously filling a lexical gap and avoiding cumbersome, dualistic, or speciesist language, I use the word *anymal* throughout this text. *Anymal* (pronounced "enē-məl") is a contraction of *any* and *animal*, and is pronounced just as the words *any* and *mal* (in *animal*) are pronounced.

Anymal refers to *all* animals, unique and diverse, marvelous and complex, colorful and common, who do not happen to be the same species as the speaker—whatever species the speaker may be. *Anymal* is therefore a shortened version of "any animal that does not happen to be the species that I am." In this book, the speaker/author is a human being, so *anymal* refers to any animal who is not a human being. Similarly, if a chimp signs *anymal,* all human beings will be included in this term, but she and the rest of her species will not.

Anymal is short and simple, easy to pronounce, easy to remember, and is neither speciesist (placing humans in a separate category from all other animals) nor dualistic (employing the fundamentally dualistic terms *non* and *other*).

Anymal provides an alternative referent that is consistent with biology; people *are* animals—mammals and primates. We have fallen into the speciesist habit of thinking that we are not animals, perhaps in part due to a prejudiced and ill-informed view of other creatures as savage beasts combined with an inflated sense of humans as uniquely civilized. This situation is, no doubt, made worse by our lack of a simple word to convey the category "all other animals." We are in need of a word to talk about rabbits and rattlesnakes, gophers and grackles—all species of the world excluding the speaker or author.

As Wittgenstein noted, language effects actions. How we *label* other living beings affects our relationship with other creatures (Rorty, 192). In short, how "we speak about other animals is inseparable from the way we treat them" (Dunayer, 9). Using *animal* incorrectly—using *animal* to refer only to "other" species—ignores shared similarities and falsely distances people from bald uakaris and Chinese crocodile lizards. By distancing ourselves, we allow ourselves to imagine that unnecessary suffering and forced premature death—though recognized as dreadful among human beings—is somehow just and right for Amazon River Salmon and krsko-polje pigs. In this way, linguistic dishonesty helps to enable human disregard for the suffering that we cause nonhuman animals (Adams, "Foreword," x), and has encouraged us to treat other creatures as commodities, spare parts, Petri dishes—things expendable for human ends.

Language ought to reflect the truth—humans are animals. *Anymal* does so while simultaneously opening dialogue, encouraging each of us to think about how we use *animal*, and *why* we often and unknowingly use this word as if it did not include humanity. Misusing *animal* in this way perpetuates exploitation and abuse of anymals because it helps humanity to imagine that we are not *animals* who are similar to pigs and turkeys in morally relevant ways—most specifically in our ability to suffer and our desire to be left alone to live our own lives. When we speak honestly, when we use appropriate terms, when we speak in a way that reflects what is true biologically, we are more apt to see ourselves as individual animals, and we can then understand that the green acouchi, spot-crowned barbet, and metallic blue guppy are also individuals.

Using language correctly—acknowledging that we are included in the scientific definition of what it is to be an animal—reminds us of morally relevant similarities across species and thereby helps us to maintain rightful relations with gorky geese, southern Viscachas, northern water snakes, and Azores cattle—the larger animal world. *Anymal* forces speakers to choose—or reveal their ignorance—regarding word choice and speciesism. In the process, dialogue is sparked on the subject of animal exploitation. This topic, in turn, will help us to rethink our religious commitments, our rightful place as animals among animals.

Indigenous Traditions

We are as one: earth, sky, all living things, the two-legged, the four-legged, the winged ones, the trees, the grasses.
— Sioux myth of White Buffalo Woman

Quetzalcoatl became famous for his moral principles. He had great respect for all forms of life. He did not believe in killing flowers by picking them, or killing any of the animals of the forest.
— Aztec myth of Quetzalcoatl

Unlike other chapters in this book, the present chapter does not deal with one particular religious tradition. Unlike religions discussed in subsequent chapters, indigenous religious traditions do not share a founder (as do Buddhists, and Muslims, for example); nor do they share a particular body of sacred texts (as do Hindus and Jews, for example). Indigenous religious traditions tend to be similar in critical ways, but each tradition is distinct and separate. I use the term "indigenous traditions" throughout this chapter, but I use the term only as a generalization. While most indigenous religious traditions will fit within the patterns mentioned herein—the vast majority, in fact—it is always likely that there is an exception to the rule.

"Indigenous"

It is difficult to determine exactly what *indigenous* means. What if a newborn Inuit, born in the Arctic, is adopted by French parents living in Paris? What does it mean for that individual to be indigenous to the Arctic if, as an adult, she is French in language, custom, and nationality? Is a German boy, adopted into a traditional Inuit tribe at birth, more "indigenous" than the Inuit adopted by a French couple? What about an Inuit who lives in the Arctic, works as a chiropractor, wears denim, drives a snowmobile, lives on fast-food fries, attends a Protestant church, and hunts seals with high-powered guns from fast-moving boats? Is she indigenous? What of human immigrants who left the land of their grandmothers in the eighteenth century—who were forced to do so because more recent human immigrants arrived from Europe?

Before Caucasians arrived in the Americas, it was easier for earlier immigrants—for "indigenous" peoples—to avoid upsetting the ecological balance, largely because of their small numbers and a dearth of technology. This is no longer the case. Many earlier immigrants in Western nations now live just like other Westerners, with ready access to medical care, electricity in their homes, and well-stocked grocery stores. Most contemporary "indigenous" people, like the rest of us, would struggle mightily if deprived of manufactured clothing, bags of flour and sugar, and gasoline-powered transport. Many earlier immigrants who continue to hunt and fish now use high-powered guns, fast-moving boats, plastic nets, steel traps, snowmobiles, and all-terrain vehicles. The Makah of northwestern Washington State recently hunted whales, presumably reenacting ancient "traditions," with the aid of U.S. government-funded helicopters. Can such methods legitimately be considered part of an ancient "hunting and gathering" tradition? Is such a hunt "indigenous," as some claimed?

Is *indigenous* a matter of birth, a matter of location, or a matter of lifestyle? Is *indigenous* rooted in ways of believing, thinking, and living, or is *indigenous* a matter of genetics?

Indigenous literally means "native." If we take this term literally, evidence suggests that *all* human beings are indigenous to Africa. There are no "native" humans in the Americas, Russia, or Japan. There are no "indigenous" Brazilians, Indonesians, or Chinese. We are all immigrants, except humans living in Africa; whether yellow, red, or white—humans are native *only* to Africa. Some of us have arrived in Europe, New Zealand, or Canada more recently, whereas others migrated long ago; each group of people has changed somewhat physically due to centuries of genetic isolation, but *when* we arrived in our current location is not important with regard to the term *indigenous*.

Though all humans are indigenous only to Africa—or perhaps certain regions of Africa—most of us use this term to mean something quite different. For the purposes of this chapter, *indigenous religious traditions* refer to spiritual beliefs and practices that existed before the advent of Jewish, Confucian, Daoist, or Hindu traditions (which means that they also existed before Buddhist, Christian, and Islamic beliefs and practices). These ancient belief systems and their associated lifeways have, of course, changed across centuries, but there has been much more continuity than change, particularly in their mythology, which I will turn to shortly. The beliefs and lifeways of indigenous peoples persisted as identifiable religious traditions for centuries—most often until they were damaged or destroyed by Western influence—and each indigenous religious tradition is unique.

It is important to remember that indigenous religious traditions in contrast to religious traditions discussed in subsequent chapters, each have their own distinctive history, beliefs, and practices. The vast majority of indigenous religious traditions share no common root, whether through a particular founder or through a shared text. Nonetheless, there are considerable similarities with regard to indigenous teachings concerning human relations with animals and the rest of the natural world.

For the purposes of this chapter, *indigenous* religious traditions are discussed in the *present* tense—without assessing whether or not the particular groups of indigenous peoples mentioned continue to honor ancient beliefs and lifeways. As with other chapters in this book, religious teachings and practices are presented without attempting to assess whether or not a particular spiritual tradition is honored. As noted in the introduction, *this book focuses on religious ideals rather than actual beliefs and practices.*

This chapter explores beliefs, myths, and practices from a plethora of indigenous peoples around the world. This kaleidoscope of indigenous religious beliefs and practices demonstrates that despite a lack of shared origins and texts, indigenous religious traditions tend to share important similarities concerning rightful relations between humans and nonhumans.

Myth

Myth, perhaps most appropriately described as sacred wisdom, is critical to understanding religions. Myths contain a people's worldview; they "encapsulate and condense...views of the world, of ultimate reality, and of the relationships between the Creator, the universe, and humanity" (Henare, 201–2). For example, sub-Saharan African mythology answers "questions of meaning and value" about a people's place, and relations with the larger world (Opoku, 351). Maori (New Zealand) myths contain a people's worldview and spiritual vision (Henare, 202). Myths of the Koyukon (interior Alaska), called Distant Time stories, contain the sacred word of the Koyukon and are best understood in relation to the historic position of the Bible in Western societies (Jette, "On Ten'a"). Similarly, Koyukon myths provide people "with a foundation for understanding the natural world" (R. Nelson, *Make*, 18, 227).

Myths are a living reality intended to guide daily life. Stories told through myths are "believed to have occurred in remote times" but are also believed to affect "daily life and human destiny" (Silva, 307). Myth is not about the past, ultimately, but about the present. For instance, the Nahua (Mesoamericans dwelling in the mountains of Mexico, near Mexico City), describe myth as an ever-present truth (Silva, 307). In the Arctic, myth is believed to tie traditional Koyukon people to their past while governing daily life (C. Thompson). Mayans (northern Central American region, including present-day nations of Guatemala, Belize, western Honduras, El Salvador, and southern Mexico) continue to use myth to teach children (Montejo, 177). Myths tell people who they are and how to live.

Sacred Nature, Sacred Anymals

Indigenous peoples do not generally hold an idea of "nature" separate and apart from humanity or from the spirit world. Instead, they most often view the supernatural world as here, among us, and they tend to view humans as just one part of a perpetual sacred life that encompasses the entire cosmos (Prabhu, 58): "For indigenous people, the environment and the supernatural realm are interconnected" (Montejo, 176–77). Indigenous peoples in India, for example, generally accept that "there is no distinction between the sacred and the profane or even between nature and humans" (Prabhu, 58). The Arapaho (South/Central America) view creation as an ongoing process in which the sacred is ever-present in the natural world. Melanesian indigenous people believe that humans, plants, and animals are all infused with spirit, and "the environment is a place of worship" that sustains all forms of life (Namunu, 251). Melanesian indigenous people teach their young that we are all "surrounded with creative energies flowing through trees, grasses, streams, and rivers, mountains, sea, sky and all the galaxies, animals, birds, and humans. . . . The ecosystem [is] viewed with awe" (Namunu, 251).

Myths teach humanity to find the sacred in and through all aspects of the natural world (J. Brown, 26), and expose humanity as just one part of an ongoing sacred life that includes the entire cosmos. For example, indigenous peoples in India feel that humans, "nature, and the supernatural are all bound in a mutual relationship" (Prabhu, 57).

Supernatural and natural become one in the indigenous worldview, and mythology invariably provides a spiritual outlook of admiration and respect for the natural world *in and of itself* (Clark, 124). For indigenous peoples, nature is often viewed as a "temple, and within this sanctuary [people ought to show] great respect to every form, function, and power. . . . [R]everence for nature and for life is *central* to their religion" (J. Brown, 37). Humans must show respect to iguanas and eels (as well as rivers and trees), and respect is built into many indigenous religious beliefs and practices (Kwiatkowska-Szatzscheider, 268, 271). Koyukon Distant Time stories, for example, teach people to *serve* nature—all of nature— the dominant force (Jette, "On Superstitions," 88). The West African term *Nyam* refers to "an enduring power and energy" that is within all life forms, such that "all forms of life are deemed to possess certain rights, which cannot be violated" (Riley, 479).

The Western dualistic division of nature and humanity, or nature and civilization, stands in stark contrast to the indigenous view, in which humans are part of the world around them, and in which the entirety of the natural world shares in the powers of the spiritual world. Whether birch tree or lilac, Mexican long-tongued bat or Chinese paddlefish, cliff or beach—everything that indigenous people find in the world around them is considered sacred.

Indigenous Philosophy and Morality
Oneness and Interdependence

Just as indigenous peoples tend to view the earthly and the sacred as one, so they tend to recognize their own villages as part of a larger community that includes *all* of the natural world—poplar trees, minke whales (further endangered by plastics in our oceans), red-billed tropicbirds, geraniums, Tasmanian devils (the world's largest marsupial carnivore, currently endangered), sword ferns, and rugged mountains. Traditional Melanesians, for example, view the entire world, animate and inanimate, as part of their community (Namunu, 251). Haida people (western Canada) feel that their identity is "based on the land, the trees, and the whole of life within" (Suzuki, xxxiv); the land and all creatures "represent their history, their culture, their meaning, their very identity" (Suzuki and Knudtson, xxxi).

Indigenous peoples also tend to understand their expansive community is interdependent. Indigenous myths generally "illustrate the fact that all living things and natural entities, have a role to play in maintaining the web of life," whether grass snake or raccoon dog, human or grape vine (Cajete, 629). All beings are equal, and balance is essential. Myths of the Koyukon (interior Alaska) explain how Raven created a harmonious universe in which all beings both control and are controlled in equal measure. A Warao hunter (Orinoco Delta, Venezuela) "expects to be hunted" by others, such as boa constrictors and jaguars, even as he hunts (Wilbert, 396–97).

Indigenous peoples often feel a sense of responsibility to maintain the "continuity and balance of the cosmos" (Kwiatkowska-Szatzschneider, 271). The Cree (North Dakota, Montana, and north into Canada) note that "when humans live in balanced reciprocity with animals, each creates the continued conditions for the survival of the other as members of a society" (Feit, 423). When people do not live in a respectful and reasonable way, the web of life is shaken, endangering the existence of all who live in the extended community. The Nahua (near Mexico City) understand that their surroundings (*cemanahuac*, "that which surrounds us") are not only essential for their survival, but for the survival of all that dwell therein (Silva, 303, 319): All of nature is "important for the existence of any one being" (Silva, 303, 319).

Mayan *Popol Vuh* creation stories, for instance, highlight interconnections between humans, anymals, plants, and the land. Mayan myths remind that "the lives of humans, plants, animals, and the supernatural world" are interconnected in a deep kinship (Montejo, 180). Their creation stories tell humans that they have been placed into, and are dependent on, a larger, preexistent world. In the *Popol Vuh* there is a

> collective survival that must exist between humans, plants, and animals. Humans are not separate ... [because] according to Mayan creation myths,

corn... entered into the body and became the flesh of human beings. This, in turn, explains the profound respect, appreciation, and compassion that Mayans feel for trees and animals for whom they pray during the cyclical ceremonies of the Mayan new year. (Montejo, 177–78)

Human bodies are formed with corn, symbolic of the reality that humans cannot live without plant life. In the *Popol Vuh*, anymals of the earth—and the plants and land itself—do not belong to people; "rather, people belong to the earth" (Henare, 202).

Similarly, one of the "cardinal beliefs in the traditional religious heritage of Africa is the interconnectedness [and interdependence] of all that exists" (Opoku, 353). Indigenous sub-Saharan Africans understand humans to be "an inextricable part of the environment" and find "themselves to be in a neighborly relationship with... earth, trees, animals and spirits" (Opoku, 351). They do not see themselves as separate and distinct from nuguni cattle or Africana sheep, "but rather as beings in relation with the world around them" (Opoku, 353).

The Warao people (Orinoco Delta, Venezuela) also have no sense of separation between humanity and the rest of the living world. They "identify all animals (including themselves) by the root form 'arao,' meaning 'life'" (Wilbert, 393). Their own name entails the word for all life: *W-arao*. Their species classification system categorizes humans *with* other species, neither distinct nor separate.

The Warao classify species according to eco-niches (water, land, trees, or air), according to where they *sleep* (Wilbert, 393). They categorize species according to those who sleep *in* the ground, *on* the ground (terrestrial), in flood-forest pools and channels or swamp streams (aquatic), in tree trunks, or in tree overstories (arboreal) (Wilbert, 394). Life forms are thus viewed as aquatic, terrestrial, or aerial (including arboreal); humans belong in the category of *terrestrial animals* along with two-toed ungulates like the Chacoan peccary and the southern pudu.

Interestingly, according to Warao species categorization, one species can fit into more than one category, and individuals from one species can also be put in two different categories. For example, human communities that dwell and sleep in trees would fall into a different category from human communities that live and sleep on the ground. Given the interconnected nature of indigenous understandings, this makes perfect sense.

Warao cosmology is based on a vertical slice of the earth's surface, but their understanding of community is horizontal: "Hierarchical station and inborn advantage" are irrelevant (Wilbert, 394). While Warao categories differentiate according to ecological zones, those who rest in trees are not better than water sleepers or land nappers. For the Warao, "merit for all is vested in balanced complementary diversity," through a dynamic of reciprocity (Wilbert, 394).

Ayllu is an Andean, Quechua word that refers to one's extended family, their larger community, including the feathered Peruvian booby, the wooly Bolivian ram, and the slick new Peru blue tetra—all protected by Quechua morality. For the Quechua, "it is not only that everything is alive, but that everything is a person with whom one converses and shares, equally" (Valladolid, 655).

> In this worldview humans are the equals of the maise, the llama, the mountains, the stars, rocks, lakes, the departed who are also alive, and so on. All are nature; humans do not feel alienated from her, nor superior to her. Humans are not distant from nature, they are part of nature. Humans feel that all are their *ayllu*, a Quechua word that in its broadest sense refers to the family that extends beyond just the human relatives. The rocks, the rivers, the sun, the moon, the plants, the animals are all members of the *ayllu*. All those that are found in the territory where they live in community are their *ayllu*. (Valladolid, 656)

Anymals, and the lands on which they depend, have their respected place in the *ayllu*. From the smallest beetle to the majestic mountain protector, *Apu Huanshan*— "all are important," and all are one community (Valladolid, 657–58).

Respect, Responsibility, and Compassion

Because indigenous peoples consider anymals (and often plants and earth as well) to be part of their community, indigenous peoples tend to respect the totality of the natural world (VanStone, 122). Kinship entails certain proper and required behaviors (McLuhan, 56, 99), whether one is dealing with a transparent sea cucumber (recently "discovered" deep in the ocean) or the United Kingdom's great crested newt (which stands dangerously close to extinction because of human population expansion and agricultural development).

Waswanipi people (Canadian subarctic) recognize that all creatures are "bound together," not only through "common mythic origins," but also by their "kindred 'human' qualities, their capacity for consciousness, [and] their inherent and unquestioned 'social' worth" (Suzuki, 68). This recognition of anymals as inherently valuable entails human responsibilities. Consequently, indigenous ethics do not generally focus only on (or apply only to) human beings. Instead, they teach interspecies moral codes that help humans to live harmoniously and peacefully among other animal communities. Because anymals and humans are kin, because anymals are recognized as *people*, indigenous myths frequently teach human responsibilities with regard to the extended family of beings (Noske, 185; Kinsley, *Ecology*, 33).

The Yup'ik people of northwestern Alaska consider anymals—from polar bears to ring seals (once endangered by hunting, now endangered by global climate change)— to be part of their moral community (Feinup-Riordan, 543). In the Yup'ik understanding, part of maturity as members of an interdependent, interrelated, interspecies community is to learn how to behave in the context of *shared cultures*, that is, to learn how to behave compatibly and respectfully within the diverse cultures of a myriad beings and communities. Similarly, the Koyukon (interior Alaska) uphold "a code of moral and social etiquette" that extends to all creatures (R. Nelson, *Make*, 228; Kwiatkowska-Szatzscheider, 268, 271). Indigenous peoples in western Canada speak of anymals "with the same respect [they] have for humans," insisting that the forests be protected because anymals "have a right" to the forests on which they depend for survival (Suzuki, xxxv). As individuals of one community among many, Australian Aborigines (Northern Territory), have a "moral obligation to learn to understand, to pay attention, and to respond" to other individuals and communities, whether wallaby or wombats (Suzuki, 47, italics removed). The peoples of the great plains of North America also felt it necessary to uphold a host of moral obligations across species, including polite communication and "truthful speech, generosity, kindness, and bravery" (Harrod, 91). The moral obligations of peoples of the Great Plains extend to all "beings whom humans meet in their everyday life—the animals, plants," and nature more generally (Harrod, 91).

Myths that convey a moral message often remind indigenous peoples to respect every aspect of the natural world, and to show compassion for other members of their extended community, including anymals and plants. Mayan myths, contained in the *Popol Vuh*, "ensure respect and compassion for other living beings" (Montejo, 177) and obligate people to show "understanding, respect, and compassion" for all of creation (Montejo, 183). While some myths offer rewards, others use threats to encourage humans to follow the moral path laid out by ancestors. Mayan myths, for example, warn against abuse and destruction of any aspect of the natural world, and reinforce these teachings with stories of a horrible fate that awaits those who fail to show compassion and respect for the surrounding landscape and other living beings (Montejo, 183).

Indigenous ethics generally require human beings to treat anymals with great respect. For example, before clearing a new patch of ground, the Bhima Saoras of central and southeast India show respect and compassion by offering a prayer to acknowledge that they are "robbing" wild creatures of their homes, and thereby endangering the lives of these members of their extended community. In that same prayer, they ask "creatures big and small" to "go away with their children," so that people might cultivate the land without causing harm to Indian game chickens or gaur (ox family) (Prabhu, 57). The Bhima Saoras recognize clearing

> a patch of forest for cultivation as an encroachment on the right to life of the other creatures of the forest. Not wanting to clash with them, they ask the animals to move away with their children. The terms they use, such as 'children,' reveal their belief that the animals of the forest have the same status [as human beings]. (Prabhu, 57)

For the Bhima Saoras, Bengal tigers, dawn bats, jambu fruit doves, and the slender loris are part of their moral community. They deserve respect, and human relations with anymals entail moral and spiritual obligations. The Bhima Saoras view themselves as but one species among many living in the same interspecies community, all of which depend on the land for survival. Their broad-minded attitude restricts the amount of land that they are willing to take for crops, even though many of their own children die of starvation each year. The Bhima Saoras' spiritual understanding of their rightful place in the natural world prevents them from contributing to the massive human overpopulation problem that has devastated landscapes and destroyed anymal communities throughout most of the world, too often driving anymals to extinction (Prabhu, 57).

The Nicobarese (Nicobar Islands, east of mainland India) also view the entirety of the natural world as part of their sacred moral community. They talk to plants while they gather leaves, begging forgiveness for taking the plant's leaves and explaining why they have done so. "For the Nicobarese, there is animate life even in plants and trees," and they must maintain polite and respectful relations with these green and growing beings (Prabhu, 57–58). Their conversations with plants reveal humility—a recognition that they do not own other living entities—and that they cause harm by taking plants' leaves. Their words are directed to the leaves and the plants, but their conversation is an ongoing dialogue with the cosmos, a conversation that is fundamentally spiritual in nature. The indigenous people of the Nicobar Islands, through this ongoing communication, are reminded that they cannot take perpetually. The plants need their leaves, and there is a limit to that which humans may take and legitimately ask forgiveness.

The Nahua (near Mexico City) consider all that dwell in the *cemanahuac* ("that which surrounds") to be included in their moral sphere (Silva, 319). They see power in the world around them, and believe that the forest can bring harm to those who overexploit, or who lack reverence. Like the Nicobarese, the Nahua ask permission before taking anything from the trees. "Everything that exists in nature has its limits, can be exhausted, and is invaluable" (Silva, 319). The Nahua know that they cannot live without their ecosystem, and they view everything within the natural world as worthy of respect.

As part of a larger, mutually dependent community with a shared morality, the Nahua expect that other creatures will also take from human beings. For example, the Nahua do not seek to eliminate "competitive" species, but expect other anymals to eat part of their crops and food stores (Silva, 319–20). When they see a Mexican jay enjoying a few of their freshly planted seeds, or a field mouse seeking sustenance in their food stores, they are neither surprised nor moved to deadly violence. For the Nahua, sharing is common sense: How could any reasonable human being thrive while forcing others to starve?

Sharing is a compassionate act, and interspecies indigenous ethics require compassion: Humans are to be compassionate toward anymals, and anymals, in their turn, will then show compassion for needy and dependent human beings. (The topic of anymals' compassion is covered in the section on hunting.) Given that anymals and humans are considered to be part of one and the same community, an ethic of compassion is consistent with community moral expectations around the world. Compassion is praised and encouraged, and selfish or cruel behaviors are discouraged. For instance, an Iroquois myth records how a man, in his time of need and desperation, was saved by anymals because they "remembered his kindness to them in former days, how he had never slain an animal unless he really needed it for food or clothing, how he had loved and protected the trees and the flowers" (Spence, 259).

The Aztec myth of Quetzalcoatl explains how a great hero, the son of a union between a goddess and the sun, taught humanity the art of being human. In this myth, compassion and respect for life—all life—are central to what it means to be human. Quetzalcoatl taught the Aztec people

> how to raise corn and cotton, weave cloth, work with gold, jade, feathers, wood, and stone, and write, paint, and dance. Quetzalcoatl became famous for his moral principles. He had a great respect for all forms of life. He did not believe in killing flowers by picking them, or killing any of the animals of the forest. (Rosenberg, 494)

Andean cultivation is a ritual infused with love "not only for their plants and animals, but also for the whole landscape that accompanies them in the nurturance of their fields, or 'chacras,' which they consider to be members of their family, or *ayllu*" (Valladolid, 651–52). Andean peasants willingly share with their *ayllu*, their extended family—nature. They expect natural elements and wild creatures to share what they cultivate, so these experienced agriculturalists plant

> a furrow for the hail, another one for the frost, another for insects, because they recognize all of these realities of nature as members of their *ayllu*. They do not worry when the frost lightly burns the leaves of their crops; they say, "The frost has come to take its portion." (Valladolid, 657)

When the snow comes late in spring and destroys leafy vegetables, when a busy mole uproots growing greens, Andean peasants recognize that the whole family, the larger community, has come to the table. With such an outlook there is little room for anger or disappointment when a deer mouse or silvery-throated jay shares in the bounty; there is no incentive to eradicate other species or prevent anymals from taking what they need to live—even if they take that which humans have cultivated.

Autonomy

Australian Aborigine (Northern Territory) codes of behavior require that humans respect the autonomy of individual creatures, whether sea eagle, numbat, yabby, brolga, goanna, Australian fur seal, koala, or little lesser bilby (who has not been sighted since the 1960s, and is likely extinct). Australian Aborigines do not consider it their rightful role to control or manipulate other species; each anymal community is autonomous: "No species, no group or country is 'boss' for another; each adheres to its own Law. Authority and dependence are necessary within parts, but not between parts" (Suzuki, 47, italics removed).

Chewong (Malaysia) morality also requires humans to respect the autonomy of other creatures. A Chewong story tells of two young people who suffered for failing to respect a squirrel's autonomy. The young couple did not intend to be cruel: They captured a squirrel and kept her as a much-loved pet, robbing her of individual freedom, as well as her proper place in the wilds. As a result, the "guardian of all animals... went into a fury at the plight of a single, tiny squirrel" (Suzuki, 43–44). The anymal guardian brought a raging storm down on the couple, snuffing out not only their lives, but their souls, for such a "grave offense" against the squirrel (Suzuki, 43–44). In the Chewong worldview, each creature has a role to play, "and proper behavior on the part of humans vis-à-vis [anymals] must be observed" (Suzuki, 44, italics removed). For example, as this story demonstrates, wild anymals must not be trapped and detained, or domesticated.

The Desana (northwestern Amazon, in Colombia) also respect the autonomy of anymals by giving a wide berth to critical wild habitat—places frequented by anymals. They hold particular water holes and wallows as sacred sanctuaries for wildlife alone, protected from human meddling by Vai-mahse, the great protector of anymals. Humans are expected to scrupulously avoid such places, and if they pass close by, they must pass in silence. Humans are not to disturb the ocelot or anaconda who come for a drink or a bath (Suzuki, 117).

Humans must respect anymals, and to respect anymals, they must respect their autonomy. Indigenous myths teach people to leave anymals free and in the wild, and to avoid interfering with the lives of these myriad independent individuals.

Great Peace

In the process of living among and pursuing blue grouse and herring, indigenous peoples often come to know anymals—their kin—intimately. Consequently, there is considerable dissonance between the closeness they often come to feel for anymals and any necessity they might have to kill anymals for food or clothing. The Makah (western Washington State), once dependent on whales, often commented on the terribly sad cry of a dying whale. Indigenous hunters in India, anticipating the horrors of death, ask forgiveness before an arrow leaves their bow, and simultaneously reiterate that "the arrow is supposed to be a messenger of remorse" (Prabhu, 58). Myths indicate that the tension of killing one's kin is as old as human-anymal relations.

Many indigenous creation stories tell of a time when there was no bloodshed (Harrod, 44), a time when animals lived peacefully in community with one another, sharing one language and one culture. A Hopi myth recalls a time when "many Hopis lived at Oraibi, with birds and animals living as equals among them" (D. Brown, 14). The Cherokee remember a time of universal peace, when "humans and animals freely communicated," including hoary marmot and human and great blue heron (Bierlein, 115). The Cheyenne of the Great Plains remember the original creation, a world where "people and animals lived in peace. None, neither people nor animals, ate flesh" (Erdoes, 390). A Navajo (North America) myth recalls a time when there was plenty of food for everyone and all creatures "spoke the same language, and they all had the teeth, claws, feet, and wings of insects" (Rosenberg, 499). Navajo people remember that these early humans could remove their wings, they lived in caves, and humans "ate only what food they could gather and eat raw, such as nuts, seeds, roots, and berries"—they were vegan, holding to a completely plant-based diet (Rosenberg, 499).

Indigenous myths also record how "the interrelatedness of the creation is disturbed"—why and how killing and predation broke the original great peace (Harrod, 44). Cherokee myths recall that humans greedily began to kill anymals for fur and food: "It was easy to do at this time, as the animals were completely unprepared to be hunted and they walked up to human beings, trusting them. Then the animals became angry" (Bierlein, 115). The bears met in council, and committed to open warfare (Spence, 249). Then the deer met in council, then fish and reptiles, and finally birds and insects. They were all angry with humans, and decided to inflict humans with various punishments, such as nightmares and disease (Bierlein, 115).

Maori mythology (New Zealand) holds Tane as the father and protector of forests, birds, and insects, and Tangaroa as the father and protector of fish and reptiles (Rosenberg, 388). When the gods squabbled, Tu (the god of humans) attacked Tane's children by hanging nooses to trap birds. "Once caught, he defiled them" by cooking and eating them (Rosenberg, 390). He then attacked Tangaroa's children by weaving nets, and pulling fishes from the sea. "These too he defiled by cooking them, and [eating] them" (Rosenberg, 390).

This Maori myth explains why people eat other creatures, why "the warrior god and his human children have dominated and eaten the children of [the] gods of earth and sea" (Rosenberg, 390). The explanation portrays flesh eating as a cruel aberration. In this myth human predation began when the gods squabbled, when the god Tu conquered the anymals' protector deities and proceeded to destroy and defile anymals, taunting those who had been conquered. Humans are cast as warlike and deadly in Maori mythology, consuming fish and birds as their vicious god taught them. And their deadly diet assures that there will be no peace on Earth: Angry seas and wild storms pound and threaten human villages (Rosenberg, 390). Maori myths explain how the original peace was broken, and how this has made life more difficult, and more tragic, for all.

Cheyenne myths (North America, Great Plains region) speak of a long-ago world that was created as an interrelated whole, where all beings shared kinship: Minnows, black-capped chickadees, and people "lived together as friends" (Harrod, 49). In a fascinating turn of events (that looks much like projection), Buffalo People begin to feel superior (being large and powerful), and come to believe that they are entitled to kill and eat Human People. In response, Humans remind Buffalo that all creatures have been created equally—one should not eat the other. Yet they also assert that, if one creature *is* to reign supreme, it ought to be Humans. At an impasse, Human People and Buffalo People decide to have a contest—a race—to determine who will be the dominant species. Interestingly, humans admit that they are slower—that they would lose the contest they have chosen (an admittance of inferiority even before the contest begins!)—so birds are pitted against buffalo *on behalf of humans*.

On the day of the great race, Slim Buffalo Woman lines up next to hummingbird, meadowlark, hawk, and magpie—four against one, and not one human at the starting line, not one human fast enough to join the contest. At the end of the race, only magpie remains, defeating Slim Buffalo Woman by a mere hair—or perhaps a feather. As a result, "people became more powerful than the buffalo and all the other animals"—even the birds, who raced for physically challenged humans (Erdoes, 390–92).

While the race itself is a marvel of revealing details, human domination is somehow thought to be justified by this myth—perhaps because the story reveals the arbitrary nature of human power and the injustice that lies at the core of our reign of terror. In any event, the myth describes how the community of beings was broken, at which point Humans eat flesh, and Buffalo must live in fear and terror (Harrod, 50).

Indigenous myths that remember a Great Peace, a vegan world where all species consumed only plants and plant products, and shared space peacefully, invariably remember this vegan world as superior. Indigenous myths portray the present state of perpetual violence, of predation and consumption, as inferior to the original great peace. Interspecies violence—eating one another—is identified as a great loss for all involved.

Afterlife

Most indigenous peoples think it obvious that all creatures share an ongoing spirit life that entails anymal souls—something by which individual anymal spirits endure after the destruction of the physical body. The Cree and Koyukon hold a cyclical view of life in which the spirits of anymals are reborn. Inuit peoples of north-central Canada believe that no soul is ever extinguished, that spirits resurface in other organisms; "life goes on without end" (Suzuki, 49–50, italics removed).

A central feature of Igorot (Philippines) belief is that every living creature has a soul (Tauli-Corpuz, 286). Yup'ik people also believe that mortal flesh belies the immortal soul; all living beings have souls that are part of "an endless cycle of birth and rebirth" (Feinup-Riordan, 543).

Mayans anticipate sharing the afterlife with anymals. Most likely, they would be appalled at the thought of an afterlife devoid of agouti, spider monkeys, dogs, owl's eye butterflies, marine toads, tarantulas, singing quail, and nurse sharks. The *Popol Vuh* contains a wonderful Mayan description of "crossing over" to a world beyond, in which dogs help their people to make the transition. In this story, a great "river of tears" must be crossed between this life and the next. A dog will help the "human soul to pass across the great river of tears into the underworld only if [he or she] is treated kindly on earth.... [T]his river is said to be full of big alligators, and it is impossible for the souls to cross without the help of their dogs" (Montejo, 185). In this Mayan spiritual vision, the "relationship between humans and animals transcends" life on Earth, and how we treat dogs holds critical "importance in the afterlife" (Montejo, 185–86). This myth emphasizes responsibility, and the moral imperative of compassion, as well as retribution for cruelty or indifference to anymals. For Mayans, our relationship with canine companions reaches beyond the grave and carries the weight of the eternal.

Hunting

Indigenous hunters who do not use mechanized transport or modern weapons must live and work close to anymals whom they kill for food. Indigenous hunters, to be successful, must discover the sleeping places of the hooded skunk, know what the mountain beaver prefers to eat, learn the quirks and habits of the river otter, yet ultimately kill these familiar members of their extended family. For indigenous peoples, who view all creatures as kin, who recognize anymals as "creatures who possess consciousness and life," the necessity of hunting, fishing, and trapping creates a "moral dilemma" (Harrod, 45). The Inuit hunter, for example, can experience "considerable psychological pain in the process of slaying [anymals] that he believes are endowed with the vitality, sentience, and sacredness inherent in his own human kin" (Suzuki, 104).

Not surprisingly, many indigenous myths reveal the troubled conscience of indigenous hunters (Serpell, 29).

> Native American tribal cultures experienced feelings of ambivalence and guilt about the killing of animals. One of the ways some native cultures seem to have dealt with their uneasy feelings is by developing a mythology or worldview according to which it was believed that the animals "gave" her or his life as a "gift." (Kheel, 101)

Indeed, indigenous peoples sometimes hold a cyclical view of life in which anymals willingly give their temporary bodies to become human food, and then return to be born again. The Cree and Koyukon hold this point of view, believing that caribou and spruce grouse have the power to decide whether or not to be captured or killed.

Indigenous peoples who believe that brush rabbits and ruffed grouse *choose* to die to feed and clothe humans also believe that they will make this compassionate and generous choice only if people maintain proper, respectful behavior and attitudes toward those they hunt. Those who do not wish to die for humans will not do so. Those who do not wish to return to woodlands or prairies near a particular village will not do so. Humans must show extreme respect for anymals on which they depend for survival if they are to be successful in their hunt or when fishing.

Respect requires balance, not taking more than is needed, and treating the lives of sentient individuals with respect. Many indigenous myths explain human moral obligations with regard to anymals—what they must do to respect and preserve natural ecosystems (Opoku, 357). Koyukon Distant Time stories, for example, include many myths that explain how people ought to relate to nature in order to maintain balance and harmony (VanStone, 61). Indigenous myths are filled with stories that offer "a complex of metaphors that teach…proper relationship[s] and respect for the natural world" (Cajete, 628). Not surprisingly, indigenous religious beliefs and practices limit what hunters might legitimately do to gorillas and pythons, wildebeests and black-bellied whistling-ducks. "When humans live in balanced reciprocity with animals, each creates the continued conditions for the survival of the other as members of a society" (Feit, 423).

Victoria Tauli-Corpuz, who grew up among the Igorot, in a small community in the northern Philippines, remembers an important indigenous concept that means something like "'exercise caution,' 'don't do it,' or 'have limits,'" which guides human relations with "other human beings, other creations (animal, plant, microorganism), the spirit world, and nature in general" (Tauli-Corpuz, 281). She also remembers a closely related concept that specifically restricts what humans may do to anymals; this understanding is best translated as "taboo, forbidden, holy, or sacred" (Tauli-Corpuz, 281). These restricting forces are central to Igorot life. For the Igorot people, these two concepts are "fundamental principles which underpin the traditional religion of the Igorots and by which every Igorot should live" (Tauli-Corpuz, 281). In their understanding, humans must use restraint if they are to stay within the bounds of that which is morally acceptable and they must always maintain respectful relations with the natural world.

Indigenous hunting is rooted in necessity, and limiting what humans may do to yellow-rumped warblers, long-eared jerboa, snubfin dolphin, and Caribbean monk seals (pronounced extinct in 2008) is central to indigenous morality. Hunting without necessity is *contrary* to indigenous spiritual beliefs and practices; such killing is dangerous, taboo, and contrary to ancient lifeways. A Waswanipi Cree hunter (Canadian subarctic), while noting that technology and modern techniques allow humans to take life beyond what is necessary, cautions against doing so. He notes that killing anymals "for fun or self-aggrandizement" demonstrates "the ultimate disdain" for other creatures (Suzuki, 106, italics removed). The Cree believe that anymals decide whether or not to be hunted, and such disdain would surely lead to starvation; no anymal would return to give his or her life to such a hunter.

Divine-Anymal Relations

In some instances, indigenous myths teach of a higher power that protects anymals, a power that expects human beings to show tremendous respect for anymals. In this worldview, anymals are not envisioned as gifts from god for our purposes: They are not ours to use and exploit—they are independent and have their own relationship with the Creator. Mythology indicates that the Higher Power creates a world for all living beings in which each anymal is "precious" and is entitled to live peacefully and prosperously as suits his or her nature. In these creation stories, it is made clear that the Creator continues to care deeply about the well-being of the myriad creatures. Mayan myths remind people that the Creator has a specific intent for anymals:

> You the deer: sleep along the rivers, in the canyons. Be here in the meadows, in the thickets, in the forests, multiply yourselves.... You precious birds: your nests, your houses are in the trees, in the bushes. Multiply there, scatter there, in the branches of trees, the branches of bushes. (Montejo, 183)

This Mayan creation story explains that the Creator intended anymals to prosper in their native habitat. "The fact that the Creator and Shaper provided each animal with its own habitat means that each has the right to a place and the right to live without being exterminated" (Montejo, 183).

In other instances, indigenous peoples do not have a Creator and Shaper, but see anymals as sacred in and of themselves (also see the section in this chapter titled "Sacred Nature, Sacred Anymals"). Indigenous peoples who hold this view speak of nature as divine in and of itself; to these indigenous peoples, anymals *are* divine. The Koyukon, for example, associate with anymals *as spiritual powers* (VanStone, 65). There is no human ruler in Koyukon communities, reflecting their larger vision of a world without any one almighty ruler (Jette, "On Superstitions," 97). Instead, anymals, plants, and the natural world are "endowed with spirits and with spiritually based power" (R. Nelson, *Make*, 228). "Nature is not governed by God, nature *is* God" (R. Nelson, "Passage").

Similarly, the Ainu of northern Japan view anymals as gods in disguise, bringing the gift of food to human beings (Kinsley, *Ecology*, 35, 36). For the Ainu, killer whales, Japanese deer, and the endangered Japanese crane are "powerful spirits involved in elaborate and intricate relations" with human beings (Kinsley, *Ecology*, 37).

Whether indigenous peoples recognize a Creator who continues to care about the well-being of anymals, or recognize anymals as sacred in their own right, the sacred is never distinct and separate from anymals. Consequently, indigenous peoples invariably hold a respect for anymals that entails reverence.

Anymals as Creators

Many indigenous peoples hold that the universe was created by an anymal or anymals (Harrod, 162). For the Lengua of Gran Chaco (northern Argentina, Paraguay, and southeast Bolivia), Beetle is the Creator (Bierhorst, 133). For the San (Southern Africa), the praying mantis is an incarnation of the Creator, Kaggen, who takes the form of many creatures, including human beings (Opoku, 356). Myths from the Great Plains teach that Coyote was self-creating, but humans were created by anymals (Harrod, 161). Myths from the White River Sioux (North America: Dakotas, Minnesota, Nebraska, and north into Canada) recall a "lively, playful, good-hearted rabbit," who created, loved, and raised a human being (Erdoes, 5–6).

In the mythology of the Yaruro (northwestern South America), the original ancestors and clan guardians—the Creators—are Jaguar and Snake (Bierhorst, 182). Jaguar created water. Snake, often considered the first person, created the earth. Snake Person then placed a rope into the hole where human beings were dwelling, and they climbed up to reach the world (Bierhorst, 182).

South American mythology remembers how the giggling Ovenbird, who was one of the First People, enraged Fire, who then scorched the bird community (Bierhorst, 139). One survivor, Tus, searched until he discovered another survivor, Sparrow. They traveled together until they found where People had dug into the earth to survive Fire. They asked Tapir to dig down and release the buried humans from the earth. Sparrow danced and beat charcoal until sprouts appeared, and continued to dance trees into the world, providing food and shade. Sparrow threw rocks up into the trees to break off branches, each of which became a different type of tree, bringing variety to the forests. Sparrow thereby "planted the algarroba tree that saved the world" (Bierhorst, 145).

Arapaho (south-central North America) myths teach that gentle and willing anymals, pure of motive, make great sacrifice to bring about creation and maintain species. For example, Turtle offers his body as a symbol of the world yet to come, Eagle gives feathers, Garter Snake provides the circumference of the globe, and White Buffalo Woman willingly provides food (Harrod, 51). Creation happened only due to the generous effort of anymals.

Other indigenous myths tell of an overarching Creator, who is dependent on the help of anymals. In the Central Andes (South America), a feline deity (who is a monster slayer), requires the help of anymals, including Dog, Falcon, Eagle, and Lizard (Bierhorst, 221). The Dunne-za (western Canadian subarctic) remember how the Creator sent diving animals such as Beaver and Muskrat deep under their watery home to retrieve a clump of silt with which to create the world. In this lively story, all of the anymals attempted to dive to the bottom of the water, but it was too deep. Finally, the earth was formed from the lump of silt brought to the surface by Muskrat (Suzuki, 38).

In the Mayan *Popol Vuh*, plants and anymals were created first, and they helped the Creators to bring humanity into existence. Mountain Cat, Coyote, Crow, and Parrot told the Creators where they could find abundant corn to accomplish their creative task. The Creators "took the road the animals showed them," and thereby found the corn, which they ground up to create human beings (Rosenberg, 482). Anymals then helped to gather food for the newly created and very dependent humans. The food that they were given "entered into the flesh and blood of the first human beings" (Montejo, 177). In this story, anymals are critical to the formation and survival of humanity.

Yoruba (Nigeria, Africa) mythology records how a chicken and cat were essential to the creation of the world. A young, discontented god, Obatala, wished to create land in a world that had only sky and water. He also wanted to create people to build villages and raise crops. With help from the god of prophecy, he sets out to accomplish his dream with a chain, some sand, a chicken, a palm nut, and a cat. As Obatala climbed down the chain toward the water, he threw down the sand, followed by the hen, who scratched the sand with her feet, spreading the earth out to become land. He then planted the palm nut on the newly created continent and settled in with the cat as his companion. Obatala eventually decided to fashion humans, but he was drunk at the time, and botched the job. Yoruba mythology reminds people that we are not essential to the workings of the world, and we were created with many noteworthy imperfections (Rosenberg, 403–6).

Indigenous peoples tend to view anymals as Creators, whether they work alone, in groups, or in tandem with a divine Creator.

Human-Anymal Relations

Indigenous belief systems tend to hold that the surrounding natural world is spiritually powerful and that a social and spiritual relationship exists between *all* creatures (Gill, *Native American Traditions*, 121). Furthermore, they tend to each believe that any "spiritual connection to the Creator [Great Mystery, Cause without Cause, etc.] happens in this life, in this place, in this moment" (Gonzales, 499). Therefore, how humans treat nature in day-to-day life—how we treat anymals—is crucial spiritually.

Anymals as Individuals

As noted, indigenous peoples tended to live close to anymals. Myths demonstrate that indigenous peoples observe anymals closely; their stories contain rich details from the personal lives of Moose and Skunk, Falcon and Trout—all of whom are understood to be "people" in their own right, living with others of their kind just as humans live in families and communities. These detailed observations of anymals are often mixed with philosophical reflections that "reveal an absorbing and seemingly inexhaustible fascination with animals," who are most often portrayed as "behaving, talking, and thinking like humans" (Opoku, 353).

Indigenous peoples tend to view human traits as universal—anymals share all that we experience. Many indigenous myths mention commonalities shared across species lines (Opoku, 357), of trans-species "shared aspects of personhood" (Feinup-Riordan, 545). For example, indigenous religious traditions tend to hold that *all* creatures share communication, similar patterns of thought, that Namdapha flying squirrels, markhor (goat family), human beings, piraya piranha, and Enderby Island cattle share similar, basic feelings. Fear and anger are not believed to be unique to humanity. The protective nature of motherhood is understood to be equally strong in spectacled bears, singing quail, Scandinavian *Homo sapiens,* and "dairy cattle" (whose newborns are immediately and routinely stolen and sold to the veal industry). Many indigenous myths also reveal an understanding that "animals have religious natures" (Kinsley, *Ecology,* 38). As noted, anymals are thought to be not only spiritual beings, but also moral agents. For example, Cree (North American Plains) recognize white-tailed prairie dogs and short-horned lizards as persons with individual personalities, volition, and responsibilities: "Cree hunters say that many kinds of animals have distinct families such as beaver colonies and geese mates, and are capable of willful action and responsibility for things they do" (Feit, 421).

One oft-mentioned trait shared across species is communication, but this trait is simply one of many fundamental interspecies similarities. Anymals in Yup'ik myths speak freely not only to one another, but also to humans (Erdoes, 389), and share a variety of individual personality traits, creating common ground for human-anymal interactions and communications. Sub-Saharan Africans not only communicate with other species, but also understand that turacos, Grevy's zebras (endangered due to habitat loss, poaching, and competition with domestic grazing animals reared for slaughter), and skinks are "just like" human beings (Opoku, 351). Andeans can and do converse with other species (along with plants and the very earth itself), who "speak, cry, dance" (Valladolid, 655). In the Koyukon (interior Alaska) worldview, Arctic hares and suckerfish, long-tailed weasels and black-footed ferrets "talk to each other, and understand human language and behavior" and also share a variety of emotions and hold a range of individual personal traits familiar to humans (Kinsley, *Ecology,* 38). For the Waswanipi people (Canadian subarctic), all creatures "act intelligently and have wills and idiosyncrasies, and understand and are understood" by human beings (Suzuki, 68, italics removed).

Through close observation and reflection, indigenous peoples come to see how similar they are to other creatures. Seeing themselves in other creatures, humans who reflect on the Indonesian Smokey honeyeater (only recently "discovered" by humanity), or the now very rare Madagascar tomato frog (recently destroyed by humanity), are thereby able to "meditate on themselves" (Opoku,

353). Knowledge of anymals enhanced indigenous people's understandings of their own life and their own family relations.

Indigenous peoples, in keeping with their understanding that all animals share fundamental similarities, acknowledge self-awareness in anymals. The Yup'ik worldview, for example, grants arctic fox and whooping cranes an awareness of themselves as individual living entities amid many living entities (Feinup-Riordan, 543). Yup'ik people also recognize every creature as a unique individual who experiences the world from his or her own point of view. They consider each anymal, from "the powerful bear to the small, apparently insignificant tundra lemming," to be a "thinking, feeling being" (Feinup-Riordan, 543). They ponder not only how humans view anymals, but also how anymals view humans (Feinup-Riordan, 541).

Indigenous peoples generally recognize individual anymals, like individual human beings, as unique. A Sioux elder (plains and prairies between the Rocky Mountains and the Great Lakes in the Missouri River basin) comments that the great spiritual power, Wakan Tanka (Great Mystery), taught each individual being different ways of accomplishing the same feat—each individual is therefore one of a kind. For those who are observant, each Bailey's pocket mouse and every whooper swan creates personalized nests; every pink fairy armadillo and burrowing owl creates a personalized burrow; each anymal moves, sleeps, and approaches life in a unique fashion, as does every human being (Forbes, 120–21).

The Chewong (Malaysia) took this idea of the unique individual to extraordinary heights. Focusing on the unique traits of individuals and species, they developed a highly sophisticated understanding of relativity of perception (Suzuki, 109). Chewong understand that each species has its own worldview—a particular perception of reality just as surely as each conscious being has his or her own "eyes." There is a golden lion tamarin way of perceiving matter, a tufted duck way of seeing objects in light, a polar bear way of viewing life, a side-blotched lizard way of knowing, a cave swift way of thinking, a water snail way of understanding birth and death, and a Javan rhinoceros way of comprehending reality (which we are in danger of losing because only about sixty Javan rhinoceros remain).

For the Chewong, there is no "correct" way of perceiving reality; in order to understand a Panamanian night monkey or a blue chin triggerfish, one must endeavor to see the world through his or her eyes. Such an attempt lends one to compassion and grants "enormous freedom for each species to pursue its own peculiar strategy for survival" (Suzuki, 110–11). The empathic Chewong worldview, while granting basic similarities across species, honors the distinctive nature of each species.

Kinship and Community

Indigenous peoples generally recognize humanity as just one form of life amid many forms of life—one community of animals amid many communities of animals. Each community, and each being, is unique but fundamentally similar; each community and each being is important in its own right and to the larger whole. Additionally, there is no conception of the autonomous individual, free to do as he or she chooses. Nor is there any single community more important than all others. Indigenous people tend to be keenly aware of their debt and dependence in relation to the larger whole. For most indigenous peoples, there is no such thing as a "species barrier"; in the indigenous understanding, species are interdependent, fluid, and interconnected, and this understanding is reflected in their language and their morality.

The central feature of proper interspecies relations in nearly every indigenous culture is to view every other individual, whether Nicaraguan seed-finch or tiger salamander, as part of self and community. In keeping with other indigenous peoples, for example, the Chewong do not have a word for humans as separate from anymals. Similarly, the Haida include anymals in the language they use to refer to their personal family members, referring "to whales and ravens as 'brothers' and 'sisters' (Suzuki, xxxii). The Haida also recognize other communities as composed of individuals of a particular type, just like human communities: They refer to "fish and trees as the finned and tree people" (Suzuki, xxxii). These various peoples are not understood to be separate and distinct, but are viewed as part of a larger family and community of beings. Like human races, the various living beings look different but are fundamentally similar. Jenny Leading Cloud of the White River Sioux (Dakotas, Minnesota, Nebraska, and north into Canada) comments:

> Man is just another animal. The buffalo and the coyote are our brothers; the birds, our cousins. Even the tiniest ant, even a louse, even the smallest flower you can find—they are all relatives. We end our prayers with the words *mitakuye oyasin*—"all my relations"—and that includes everything that grows, crawls, runs, creeps, hops, and flies on this continent. (Erdoes, 5)

Similarly, Cree (North American Plains) recognize coyotes, magpies—all creatures—as members of communities in a world rich with communities of every stripe and speckle (Feit, 428). In the traditional Cree worldview, anymals are understood to be part of the same larger community to which humans belong:

> The animal world is a part of the same kind of social world that humans inhabit, and in much conversation a social metaphor serves to talk about the whole world.... [M]any of the actions of animals are intelligible and predictable. The whole world is therefore a socially informed world, in which habit and learning rather than natural law explain the actions of animals and other nonhuman persons. As a result, communication between all beings is possible, and animals can in their turn interpret and understand the actions and needs of humans. (Feit, 421)

The Cree therefore believe that anymals decide whether or not to allow a hunter to eat; muskrats and snow geese willingly give themselves to a morally worthy hunter, as a generous gift (Kinsley, *Ecology*, 13). When asked why animals permit themselves to be killed, the Cree response is similar to how we might explain sharing food with the poor in our own communities: Deer and geese are aware of the needs of hungry fellow creatures, and share accordingly. The implication is that offering your body to those who have nothing else to eat "is a responsible thing to do as a moral social being"—as a member of a larger, interdependent community of beings (Feit, 421). The gift of food and life, given to those who are dependent and at their mercy, further demonstrates to the Cree, and many other indigenous communities, that rainbow trout, Gunnison sage-grouse, and antelope are compassionate, generous, upstanding members of the larger community, and are therefore greatly deserving of respect.

Indigenous myths sometimes describe an ancestral line that begins with a reptile, bird, fish, or xenarthra (anteaters, armadillos, and sloths), for example, enhancing their sense of kin with anymals, and their sense of membership in a larger community of beings. Some indigenous peoples understand that their community shares a particular animal as an ancestor, from which they have descended. This anymal is sometimes a community's totem, viewed as a close member of their extended community. Totems carry a community's identity outside of the human community (Vecsey, 51).

Many indigenous peoples believe that all living beings share one common ancestor, whether human, anymal, or some distinct combination, clearly creating a *family* of animals. For example, South American mythology teaches that the first people were bird people (Bierhorst, 139); all beings stem from this original, feathered community. Okanogan (northern Washington State and British Columbia) people believe that "the ancients," those who lived at the beginning of time, were of many species, including human beings (Erdoes, 14). Navajo myth explains how land animals (including humans) who did not flee from the great flood became "water people, such as fish and seals" (Rosenberg, 502). Australian Dreamtime myths record how people and other beings are "derived from the same stock, that was neither one nor the other," neither anymal nor human (Noske, 184).

Some stories tell how one species or group of individuals emerged from an individual or group of individuals from another species. An Inuit (Arctic) story begins with "a small group of Inuit children" who were engrossed in play. When the children were frightened by the clapping of hands, "they grew wings and rose up from the ground and turned into *nikjatut* (willow grouse) and flew away" (Suzuki, 103, italics removed). This enchanting story reminds children that willow grouse have descended from young Inuits like themselves (Suzuki, 103). Adults and children alike are reminded that willow grouse are their kin—descendants of Inuit children. They are reminded that willow grouse are fundamentally similar to human beings.

A South American (Argentina, Selk'nam, and Yamana) myth explains how the women of a particular community became animals of various types; their distinctive, colorful body paint created the distinctive colors of the many different species. In this story, Squid Woman ran into the sea without taking off her conical dancing hat. Two women washing on the shore of a lake became ducks, while a plump mother became a loggerhead duck, incapable of flight (Bierhorst, 167–68). This myth demonstrates how indigenous people behold anymals and see humanity.

A Toba (also South American) myth remembers an ice age that froze all people, at which time a Toba hero created birds from the frozen bodies of the dead, turning old men into yulo birds, adolescents into ducks and herons, and middle-aged people into vultures. He also turned mothers into anteaters, and one old man into an alligator (Bierhorst, 143–44).

Indigenous human primates who live among other types of primates often have a store of myths that account for the undeniable, remarkable similarities that they share with neighboring primate communities. An African story in Matabeleland teaches that baboon communities were formed by humans who moved up into the hills, forgetting human language over time, abandoning human clothing, and growing body hair (A. Smith, 109). In the Mayan *Popol Vuh*, monkeys are leftover human beings from an earlier creation, a creation that existed prior to the great flood (Rosenberg, 482).

But, as noted, appearances are not generally thought to be critical to kinship in the indigenous worldview. Some myths teach of shared ancestry not only for animals, but also for plants, minerals, and natural features. For example, Australian Aborigines recognize human beings as animals *and* plants because "all three have identical ancestors" (Kinsley, *Ecology*, 33). The Koyukon believe that all beings "are connected by a common ancestry; everything that exists on Earth—whether it be human beings, animals or plants; rocks or rivers or snowflakes—shares a spiritual kinship arising from shared origins" (Suzuki, 34).

Indigenous myths remind human beings that they are neither separate nor distinct in a handful of different ways. Another way in which they remind humans of their links with anymals is through myths that tell of interspecies marriages, offspring, and adoptions. These myths can also describe a people's origins. For example, Inuit mythology teaches that "humans and animals alike originated from the copulation of a woman and an animal" (Noske, 185). In a Maina (Central Andes) story, a young man who survives the great flood takes Parrot woman for his bride, from which the Maina community springs (Bierhorst, 217).

Other myths describe interspecies marriage without reference to creation, simply assuming that such marriages are natural among kin. A Passamaquoddy (North America) myth explains how Owl claimed a beautiful human bride (Erdoes, 399–402); an Algonquin myth tells of a man who marries a beaver (Spence, 169–70). A bear fathers two children with a human being in Haida mythology (Erdoes, 419–421). In the African myths of Matabeleland, a woman is fooled into marrying a handsome man (who is actually a lion), bearing children who are human (A. Smith, 87–90). In Guiana (South America), Yekuana lore tells of one mythic hero who marries a fish, and a great hero who marries the daughter of a vulture king. He is able to accomplish this marriage only with the aid of anymals, given the great risks and difficult trials that this particular marriage entails (Bierhorst, 71–72).

The North American Pomo people remember a rattlesnake who courted and won a Pomo maiden; she raised four sons with her snake husband, and taught her children not to bite their human relatives. At some point she voluntarily made a complete transition from human to snake, opting out of her human community altogether (Erdoes, 397–98).

A myth from the Central Andes describes a woman who had an affair with a duck, resulting in the birth of twins. This marriage did not work out so well, and her controlling husband kills her. He then finds two eggs in her womb, producing twins. When the time is right, a dove explains to the offspring how their father killed their mother. One of the twins, the hero of the story, avenges his mother's death (Bierhorst, 216).

In another story about a less-than-perfect marriage, a Sioux myth recalls a chief who arranged a contest whereby any one of his many anymal kin might win his beautiful daughter as a bride. "Snail, Squirrel, Otter, Beaver, Wolf, Bear, and Panther" try first, but fail (Spence, 282). "Next came the birds," but they also failed (Spence, 282). Salmon was the final suitor, and though the humans thought that he was ugly, he succeeded. Salmon claimed his prize, but the Sioux people decided not to leave their princess among the fish, so Coyote and Badger led the charge, shot an arrow, and killed Salmon. The daughter then became the wife of one of the wolves, who were apparently more attractive to this particular community.

Indigenous myths also include stories of anymals adopted into human families and communities, and of humans adopted by anymals. A Guiana (South American) myth explains how a toad adopted two boys when their mother was poisoned (Bierhorst, 83). An African story (Matabeleland) tells of a woman who adopted a brave and protective guinea fowl (A. Smith, 7–10). In a Brazilian Highland myth, Jaguar adopts and raises a human child (Bierhorst, 101).

A particularly interesting Mistassini Cree story reminds human beings that an individual's sense of community has more to do with association than genetics, more to do with perception than with external distinction. This understanding is foundational to indigenous cultures, but seems to be lost on industrialized human beings. This Cree myth describes a hunter who comes upon a caribou community and sees them as a human community, including a beautiful young woman caribou, whom he marries. After they are married, "all the caribou appear to him as humans who have a society" just like human societies (Kinsley, *Ecology*, 17).

Indigenous languages and myths remind human beings of their connection with the Earth and anymals. Indigenous peoples acknowledge both the "shared origins of all life" and "ancient bonds of kinship between human beings and other species"

(Suzuki, 5). For indigenous peoples, who view all anymals as kin, family life and community include sea lions and wildebeests, grey pelicans and Australian dingoes, as well as buzzards, ermine, and the Baiji dolphin (the first cetacean to go extinct in recent history).

Interpenetrability

As noted, indigenous cultures have a strong tendency to understand that "humans share an essential identity with other forms of life" (Kinsley, *Ecology*, 33). This understanding is manifest in language, morality, and myth. Myths in particular help human beings to remember that there is more of similarity than difference between the Pampas cat of South America (endangered by farming, ranching, and hunting) and the Shasta ground sloth. In fact, indigenous myths generally offer no separation between human, silky anteater, pinnated bittern, and horned toad; "the division between subject and object, between landscape and people, does not exist" (Kwiatkowska-Szatzscheider, 276).

This unique vision might best be described as "interpenetrability" (Valladolid, 658). Anymals take on human form, and humans take anymal forms. Myths indicate that indigenous peoples "see no division between the animal and human spheres; each takes the other's clothing, shifting appearances at will" (Erdoes, 389). Myths often recall a time when birds, fish, reptiles, and mammals moved easily across species boundaries, and conversed at will (Erdoes, 5). For example, White Buffalo Woman is both human and buffalo (Erdoes, 48). Haida (British Columbia, Canada) mythology explains how a young woman who loved to swim gradually morphed into the first beaver (Erdoes, 392). In the Gran Chaco (Paraguay region), a woman turns into a jaguar (Bierhorst, 129). A Cherokee myth describes a man who moves in with bears, learning to live as they live and growing thick body hair, though he continues to walk upright. When hunters kill his bear friend, he returns to his human community and wife, but soon dies because he "still had a bear's nature and could not live like a man" (D. Brown, 22). Yup'ik myths tell of times long ago, when anymals "often lifted up their beaks or muzzles, transforming themselves" into human beings (Feinup-Riordan, 545). A Yup'ik boy who lived among the geese flew away with the geese-people when autumn migration began; a female goose came to live with humans for a short time, staying out late in the spring and returning home with mud smeared on her face from eating grasses in the marshlands (Feinup-Riordan, 545).

Snakes tend to take a prominent place in many religious traditions, no less so in myths of species interpenetrability. A Brule Sioux (Lakota Nation, Great Plains, and prairies of North America) myth recalls how three out of four brothers turn into rattlesnakes (Erdoes, 405–7). Another Sioux myth recollects a band of warriors who turned into snakes, but remained friendly to humans (Spence, 274). A Tewa story (North American) recounts how Fish People failed in their prayer vigil, which caused a flood. After the flood, one of the Fish People turned into a snake; her friends delivered her, saying, "You are now a young lady snake, and with the help of the Great Spirit you will live among your own kind" (Erdoes, 416). They also spoke to the snake community: "I have brought you a sister; take her into your arms" (Erdoes, 416).

Indigenous traditions do not think about or speak of a species boundary. Instead, they see all animals as kin, and view a species similarly to how progressive human beings view skin color—it looks different, but what lies underneath is what matters, and under our skin, we are fundamentally the same. Consequently, indigenous myths speak of animals "changing skins,"—moving from one species to another.

Anymal Powers

Indigenous cultures usually demand respect for kin who are furry and scaly, for relatives who hop and fly, because they recognize these many individuals as exceptional, because they understand that anymals are part of their family, and because they know that they are dependent on the anymal people for survival. They also know that anymals are spiritual powers; they "possess consciousness, will, and other capacities...superior to those of humans" (Harrod, 159).

Anymals are understood to be exceptional in many ways. For example, indigenous myths portray anymals "as more sensitive and aware than their human counterparts" (Feinup-Riordan, 543). San Bushmen (Africa) "are quick to acknowledge that the sensory capacities of life-forms around them are far superior to their own" (Suzuki, 114).

Some indigenous peoples believe that anymals "mediate a variety of transcendent powers to humans" (Harrod, 128). For the peoples of the Great Plains, powers of the universe can be channeled through anymals to human beings (Harrod, 23). Many Great Plains peoples understand anymals not only to be capable of knowing the future, but also to be willing to provide warnings to humans, when necessary, concerning future events (Harrod, 128). Blackfoot mythology teaches humans to listen to anymals, to allow these other individuals and communities to guide them, and to obey anymals that come to them in dreams, bringing instructions and guidance. Anymals' knowledge and powers are so important to the Blackfoot (Western Montana, and north into Canada) that, no matter which "animal answers your prayer, you must listen" (Grinnell, 141). Because anymals sometimes hold special and miraculous powers, indigenous peoples often turn to other species in a time of need.

Many myths describe the special powers of particular anymals. Blackfeet (northwestern Montana) believe Lizard controls the coming and going of the rains (Harrod, 119). They also associate Beaver with tremendous sacred power, which humans can gain if a woman unites with Beaver, creating mixed-species children (who must be treated with much kindness) (Harrod, 78). African myths of Matabeleland tell of compassionate crocodiles who bring a poor girl back to life for the sake of her family (A. Smith, 30). A Brule Sioux (North America, Great Plains) myth explains how people visited rattlesnake relatives, beseeching Rattlesnake to bestow on them the ability to strike quickly and "wiggle out of bad situations" on the battlefield (Erdoes, 407). After a successful battle, the Brule Sioux return to thank the snakes; they continue to show their respect by never harming rattlesnakes (Erdoes, 405–7). An understanding of anymals as superior beings often dictates how indigenous peoples behave toward creatures.

As noted, indigenous mythology often credits anymals with creative powers. The special powers of anymals lend various species to critical roles in the creation of humankind. For example, Yup'ik myths sometimes portray anymals as models of instruction, able to teach people about matters that were extremely important, such as arts and crafts (Prabhu, 58). Crow cosmology holds that Coyote created earth, anymals, and human beings, and then brought culture to people (Harrod, 47). Northern Distant Time stories (Koyukon) describe Raven as "creator-trickster extraordinaire"; Raven "acts as a principal creative force and culture-bringer in the Koyukon cosmos" (Suzuki, 35). In the Brazilian highlands, Bat is credited with bringing laughter to humans (Bierhorst, 94), while Opossum shows people where to find corn (Bierhorst, 98–99). Creek mythology (Southeastern North America) credits Rabbit with stealing fire from weasels (D. Brown, 70–71). In the mythology of the Yaruro (Northwestern South America), Snake created bows and arrows, and showed the first person how to use weapons (Bierhorst, 182). A Yekuana myth from South America explains how Fish provides people with songs, rattles, and tobacco for shamanic rites (Bierhorst, 73–74).

Okanogan peoples (northern Washington State and British Columbia) remember that human beings were exceptionally helpless—the most helpless of all animals. The Creator sent Coyote to protect people, and to teach them how to live; Coyote, with his powers and wisdom, first made the people's lives possible, and then made their lives easier (Erdoes, 15).

According to their mythology, the Trio people of South America (Surinam and Brazil) are taught survival by a fish-woman. Her father, Alligator, brings plants for the Trio people to cultivate, and Fish-woman explains that they should "never eat all of the food" but should save some to replant, so that they will always have food to eat. She teaches them how to clear land and cultivate, and then returns to show the humans how to make necessary utensils and how to turn the yucca plant into bread (Rosenberg, 479). It is unlikely that many skills would compare in fundamental importance to those by which a people acquire food, and it is just these skills that Fish-woman taught the Trio people.

Not all myths are complimentary toward females—whether Fish-woman or Eve. Mythology is sometimes blatantly misogynistic, portraying women as deviant, dangerous, and uncivilized. A misogynistic Toba (South America) myth explains how a handful of various anymals were critical to the peaceful union of men and women. Men came up from the earth (in various forms), and women down from the sky (in human form). Anymals worked with men, in community, using their special abilities to control and tame women, who stole from men. First Rabbit, and then Parrot, were posted as guards to catch the thieves. Women, on seeing Parrot, began to fight over who would marry this fine bird, and in the fray, Parrot's mouth was broken so he could not speak. Hawk was then placed on guard, and the women again began fighting over who would marry Hawk, threatening his life with their combative ways. As a result, Hawk cut the rope on which women retreated back into the sky, and the women fell, sinking into the earth. Hawk then called the men back to camp, but only keen-hearing Iguana caught Hawk's message. Armadillo dug the women out of the earth, and Hawk warned men that women were not safe for intercourse. Fox (often the mythic trickster) was impatient, ignored Hawk, and lost his penis in the teeth of a woman's vagina. He perished. Hawk again came to the rescue, at least for men, throwing stones at women to break the teeth out of their vaginas, and make them safe for intercourse. Not long after, the first children were born (Bierhorst, 134–35).

Haida (British Columbia, Canada) myths also portray animals as critical benefactors of humanity. The west coast of Canada can be remarkably damp, and Raven is the hero and helper who brings sunlight to Earth. To do so, Raven uses special powers to transform himself into a seed to be swallowed by the chief's daughter, which allows him to be born into their loving home. His doting grandfather allows Raven to play with a bag of stars and a bag containing the moon. Raven, as if by accident, releases them through the smoke-hole into the universe until he has released all the sparkling "toys" into the world. Grandfather is somewhat chagrinned but still allows Raven to play with his final and most prized possession—the sun. Raven plays with the sun day after day, carefully watched by Grandfather, with the smoke-hole tightly closed. But humans are inclined to err, and Grandfather eventually neglects to close the smoke-hole, through which clever Raven carries off the sun, bringing light and warmth to Earth (Rosenberg, 519).

Navajo mythology includes a flood story in which Turkey—an anymal much maligned by Western humans—is given considerable credit. In this story, Turkey warns people of the coming flood, even instructing them to head for higher ground. Turkey also remembers not to leave without life-sustaining seeds for cultivation (which all of the humans have forgotten in their rush to escape the rising waters). With this important insight, Turkey assures the survival of those who have escaped the flood (Rosenberg, 502). Because Turkey returns to gather the forgotten seeds, she falls behind the others, and the flood waters lap at her tail as she waddles up the trail to safety, providing the characteristic white fringe on her otherwise shimmering black tail.

The same Navajo flood story includes a cast of other important anymal characters. Spider assists the many animals who are escaping the flood, weaving a ladder for them to climb into a tree for safety. Locust is the first to emerge from the tree's hollow after the flood, and claims lands for all *people*. (Each species is viewed as a community, a *people*, and each being is endowed with personhood.) Badger and Coyote enlarge the opening in the tree so that people can emerge from their protective hiding place into the present world (Rosenberg, 502–3). In this story, animals survive the flood by cooperating, by working together as one community; while humans are able to do little, they benefit much from the wisdom, strength, and special abilities of anymals.

Navajo (New Mexico/Arizona) myths explain how human beings sought a leader for their own community from among the anymals, due to their special knowledge and powers. Different people—Wolf, Bluebird, Mountain Lion, and Hummingbird—proposed different possibilities. Each anymal then brought something to the people to demonstrate their worthiness as a leader. Wolf brought spring rain, morning light, and young corn. Bluebird brought summer rain, blue sky, and soft corn. Mountain Lion brought autumn rain, evening light, and ripe corn. Hummingbird brought northern lights, winter nights, dried corn and beans, and the abalone storage bowl. These four anymals, Wolf, Bluebird, Mountain Lion, and Hummingbird, brought the beauty and bounty of the natural world, and "First People realized that they needed the gifts of all four leaders" (Rosenberg, 501).

One of the most powerful and important among Brule Sioux (Lakota Nation, great plains and prairies of North America) characters is White Buffalo Woman, both human and buffalo. White Buffalo mythology reveals the depths of anymal powers and the importance of what they know and can teach humanity. She visits the Brule Sioux, saying, "Good things I am bringing, something holy to your nation. A message I carry for your people from the buffalo nation" (Erdoes, 49). Humans immediately recognize her as powerful and holy. She shows the Brule people how to build an altar, gives them the sacred pipe, and instructs them in using this pipe. She also shows them how to pray, and reminds them of their kinship with all that exists and of the unity of all beings:

> "With this holy pipe," she says, "you will walk like a living prayer. With your feet resting upon the earth and the pipe stem reaching into the sky, your body forms a living bridge between the Sacred Beneath and the Sacred Above. Wakan Taka smiles upon us, because now we are as one: earth, sky, all living things, the two-legged, the four-legged, the winged ones, the trees, the grasses. Together with the people, they are all related, one family. The pipe holds them all together." (Erdoes, 50)

The feathers on the pipe represent sacred Spotted Eagle, who is the Great Spirit's messenger. The bowl of the pipe represents both Human People and Buffalo People; the buffalo also "represents the universe and the four directions" (Erdoes, 50). Spiritually powerful White Buffalo Woman reminds people, "You are joined to all things of the universe" (Erdoes, 50).

White Buffalo Woman also brings staples, corn and wild turnip, and shows the people how to make a hearth fire. As she departs, she rolls over four times, becoming a black buffalo, then a brown buffalo, a red buffalo, and finally a white female buffalo calf. For the Brule Sioux, "A white buffalo is the most sacred living thing you could ever encounter" (Erdoes, 52).

While indigenous religious traditions recognize animals as fundamentally the same under their skins, they grant extraordinary powers to many anymals—if not all anymals. Whether they are viewed as more sensitive and aware than humanity, as essential to reaching transcendent powers, or as critical to the creation of earth and/ or humanity, bats, beavers, and buffalo are likely to be viewed as holding exceptional powers—even dangerous powers.

Dependence and Fear

Indigenous peoples lived off of the land for thousands of years. They gathered, dug, hunted, climbed, fished, and planted. But the land that they dug up and the anymals that they killed were understood to be their kin. Morality required that these long-ago human beings show respect for the larger community of beings on which they depended, most of whom were understood to be more powerful than *Homo sapiens*.

Many indigenous peoples continue to believe that their greatest danger stems from dependence "on the taking of life from other beings" (J. Brown, 6). Indigenous peoples of the northern Philippines, for example, believe that their survival is dependent on honoring and respecting anymals. Myths remind humanity that we must not deviate from ancient ways, or alter long-established relationships with the natural world, unless we are willing to assume tremendous risk. Such changes are likely to upset an otherwise balanced existence (Cajete, 628). Most fundamentally, humans risk starvation if they deviate from long-established ritualized relations with anymals. Because there is so much at stake, many indigenous peoples live in fear of the powers of nature, and in fear of reprisal, should they somehow offend southern tamandua, black caiman, and other essential and powerful anymal kin.

The Guajiro, who live on the northernmost tip of South America, tell a myth about the "animal mother" who lives in an underground world. Deep within her underground home, she protects her earthly children from hunters, and exacts vengeance against killers. The mother of fish and sea turtles is no less protective or fierce: "Whoever 'steals' from her must outrun the surf, which she hurls after the thief with a terrifying sound" (Bierhorst, 185–86). Fear of animal mothers guides how the Guajiro treat anymals.

Similarly, the Inuit (Arctic) believe that the mother of the anymals, Sedna ("She Down There"), dwells deep within the sea, from which vantage point she decides whether or not her children will become food for humans—she decides whether or not humans will eat. Not surprisingly, Sedna is "the sole focus of Inuit myth and religious ritual and the supreme ruler of the Inuit supernatural world" (Rosenberg,

521). If the Inuit do not behave respectfully toward anymals, and toward Sedna, they understand that she will withhold her children, and they will starve (Rosenberg, 521). One Inuit hunter's remarks reveal that he is fearful because anymals not only have much power, but because they also have immortal souls:

> The greatest peril of life lies in the fact that human food consists entirely of souls. All the creatures that we have to kill and eat, all those that we have to strike down and destroy to make clothes for ourselves, have souls, like we have, souls that do not perish with the body, and which must therefore be propitiated lest they should revenge themselves on us for taking away their bodies. (Suzuki, 104)

Yup'ik (Northwestern Alaska) myths also remind people that they are dependent on and must be respectful of anymals. In the Yup'ik spiritual vision, anymals choose whether or not to maintain voluntary relations with human communities (Feinup-Riordan, 544). They understand that a lack of respect for anymals is likely to result in starvation, because musk oxen and willow ptarmigan can choose to leave the area if they are offended. "On the other hand, if they receive proper treatment, they will return in abundance," even though they are hunted (Feinup-Riordan, 544). The Cree believe that individuals from a scarce species "are angry with humans and will not make themselves available to be killed" (Kinsley, *Ecology*, 11). In response, out of respect, the Cree "desist from hunting in a given area until the animals' anger has dissipated" (Kinsley, *Ecology*, 11). This Cree understanding of the disappearance of species helps hunted anymals to recover, aiding their survival.

In the sacred lore of the Koyukon (interior Alaska), Raven created a world in which spiritual powers are pervasive—including anymals as spiritual powers. The Koyukon believe that humans and other natural entities share a "constant spiritual interchange that profoundly affects human behavior" (R. Nelson, *Make*, 229)—and human survival. Constant reverence is required if humans are to avoid misfortune brought on by insulted spirits (R. Nelson, *Make*, 240). In the Koyukon worldview, humans are at the mercy of red snappers and tundra swans; are anymals sacred and powerful—quite capable of preventing a hunter from having success (R. Nelson, *Make*, 231). "Each animal knows way more than you do.... [T]he old people ... told us never to bother anything unless we really needed it" (R. Nelson, *Make*, 225). When a hunter brings home food, there is no talk of skill, no place for boasting, only deep appreciation for Arctic ground squirrels and rock ptarmigan who choose to die so that the Koyukon might live.

The Warao (Orinoco Delta, Venezuela) show respect and exercise caution by rotating which ecological zone (aquatic, terrestrial, arboreal, or aerial) they target in their search for food (Wilbert, 396). Showing respect for hunted anymals—killing no more than is necessary (particularly from any one zone) and never allowing an anymal to suffer—is critical for the survival of their human community:

Whether he be hunting or fishing, he knows that his every action is monitored by the spirit guardians and the members of the communities he targets. To minimize the damage he inflicts on any one species, he hunts and fishes in various places. Should he abuse a species by overexploitation or by allowing a creature to die a slow and painful death, the spirit(s) of the victimized may target him and his kinfolk for…retribution. The worst imaginable scenario ensues when a guardian spirit, disgruntled over immoderation, gathers his or her community and moves away to another region, leaving the people of the abuser without food. (Wilbert, 396–97)

Rituals and Taboos

Because humans are dependent on anymals, and because anymals are powerful and might choose to shun human beings, allowing humans to starve, many indigenous communities maintain elaborate rituals as a method of showing respect for anymals. For example, sub-Saharan Africans maintain "numerous restrictions and taboos" to maintain harmonious relations with the "world around them" (Opoku, 351). The Cree show respect for anymals through a series of rituals, specifically directed toward the souls of anymals who were killed by hunters (Kinsley, *Ecology*, 13). The Kayapo of Brazil, who "have no question about their existence and future health being dependent upon plants and animals and the forces of nature," offer songs of appreciation to the spirits of anymals whom they have killed for food (Posey, 8). Inuit rituals that surround the return of a hunter reinforce a communal relationship with an anymal whom they believe has willingly given her or his life for the sake of a hungry human community—for the benefit of the larger community of beings (Cajete, 627).

Ritual actions permeate traditional Koyukon (interior Alaska) lifeways so thoroughly that almost every practical act is simultaneously worship—a religious act. Some anymals require absolute silence when their bodies are carried into the village, or are kept inside a Koyukon home before preparation. Others must be given a great feast, at which their recently acquired corpse is the guest of honor. Anymals are spiritual powers, and because they are critical to human survival, these spirits must be treated with great care and respect. Through such rituals, Koyukon people discover their Distant Time stories perpetually asserted in the world around them; life is a religious act ever renewed in the daily ritual of living (Jette, "On Ten'a").

Indigenous Traditions and Anymal Liberation

For most indigenous peoples, when interacting with the natural world, the "essential focus [is] relationship, [and] the guiding sentiment [is] respect" (Cajete, 626). This outlook results in an anymal-friendly philosophy that aligns with contemporary anymal liberation. For example, Chewong (Malaysia) sacred law controls proper attitudes toward anymals and "mandates that no animal whatsoever may be teased or laughed at" (Suzuki, 40).

> Openly laughing at or teasing an animal may be the most blatant human violation of the Chewong's *talaiden* [sacred law]. But more subtle transgressions against animals are also forbidden, including using ridiculous or demeaning images of animals for human entertainment, as most Western societies so routinely do. If the Chewong traveled abroad, they might well see worrisome breaches of *talaiden* in Hollywood's long legacy of buffoonish cartoon creatures.... They might justifiably invoke *talaiden* rules upon seeing Ringling Brothers circus bears astride bicycles or wide-eyed monkeys dressed up in clownish human attire.... To Chewong sensibilities, each of these would seem to represent a bonafide case, however unconscious, of direct human affront to the inherent dignity of a fellow animal. (Suzuki, 42)

Chewong *talaiden*, or sacred law, prohibits ridiculing anymals, and if followed, would close down circuses, and the anymal entertainment industry in general.

Enslaving anymals for entertainment seems a frivolous reason to breach core teachings and practices, but what of food industries? How have indigenous religious traditions informed anymal liberation in the larger spheres of anymal exploitation?

Indigenous beliefs and practices stem from a time when hunting, fishing, and trapping were essential for survival—they were not optional activities. Today, these activities are optional for almost all indigenous peoples in Western countries, and for many indigenous peoples in other areas of the world. What does it mean for Cree or Koyukon to "kill respectfully"—to show the required respect for the individual who is killed—when their sustenance need not depend on hunting, fishing, or trapping?

Because most peoples no longer need to hunt, trap, or fish for food, some indigenous peoples maintain historic traditions in contemporary times by *denouncing* such unnecessary killing, which not only saves the lives of anymals, but also prevents the environmentally destructive effects of these practices when modern methods are employed. For example, in January 2000, four indigenous groups in western Washington accepted 300 pounds of deer and elk flesh from alongside roadways. They gave up their legal right to hunt in exchange for subsisting on roadkill (Kelley). These indigenous people demonstrated that their ancient ethic of respect for nature, their commitment to kill only when necessary, and their vision of harmony and kinship are alive and well.

So did Barbara Aripa, a Colville elder in eastern Washington State, who "has taken it upon herself to preserve a way of life. She fought successfully to ban clear-cutting and herbicide spraying in the reservation's forests" (Associated Press, "Colville"). Aripa is currently fighting against plans for a gold mine that could leak cyanide into surrounding wilderness. She also teaches traditional beliefs and practices that do not involve killing, such as how to make shawls and dresses (Associated Press, "Colville").

Makah elders stood against a renewed whale hunt, planned by other members of their community. Isabell Ides (age 96), Harry Claplonhoo (78), Margaret Irving (80), Ruth Claplanhoo (94), Viola Johnson (88), Alberta N. Thompson (72), and Lena McGee (92) openly spoke against reestablishing the Makah whale hunt along the coast of Washington State on the grounds that such a hunt was billed as traditional and sacred, when it was neither. Makah elders expressed their concerns in the Peninsula Daily News:

> We are elders of the Makah Indian Nation (Ko-Ditch-ee-ot) which means People of the Cape. We oppose this Whale hunt our tribe is going to do....
>
> The Whale hunt issue has never been brought to the people to inform them and there is no spiritual training going on. We believe they, the Council, will just shoot the Whale, and we think the word "subsistence" is the wrong thing to say when our people haven't used or had Whale meat/blubber since the early 1900's.
>
> For these reasons we believe the hunt is only for the money. They can't say "Traditional, Spiritual and for Subsistence" in the same breath when no training is going on, just talk.
>
> Whale watching is an alternative we support. (Ides)

"It would be one thing if the whale meat were truly needed," Thompson added, "as in the times of the ancestors....But that is no longer true today" (Dunagan). Hunting when flesh is no longer necessary for survival, and defending such practices as central to indigenous spiritual traditions, is a bastardization of indigenous spiritual traditions.

It is not surprising that indigenous peoples have aligned with anymal liberation, working to free Earth and anymals from the clutches of capitalism and consumerism. Linda Fisher, who is Ojibway and Cherokee (Great Lakes region of North America), and is a tribal member of the Ojibway Nation, is also a professional artist and anymal liberationist.

As a little girl, Fisher's father took her fishing, but she was horrified by the suffering and fear she witnessed in the shimmering fish. She also remembers watching a man cut up a snake simply to demonstrate that creatures continue to twitch and move after death (Fisher, "Mother", 216–17). She was mortified, and could not understand why some people care so little for the lives of other creatures.

Fisher used to enjoy watching the birds in a shop in her hometown, but was thrown out by a security guard for shyly noting that a little budgie looked sick and needed special care. This act took great courage for a small, timid child, and was perhaps Fisher's first foray into speaking up on behalf of abused and neglected anymals.

Fisher now tends a houseful of rescued anymals, including birds, and remains especially fond of these feathered residents. She has dedicated much time to educating people about the suffering and death entailed in the capture, transport, and confinement of birds in the pet trade (Fisher, "Freeing", 114). Fisher is also quick to note that Native Americans traditionally ate very little meat:

> The conventional, Hollywood depiction of the Native American diet and lifestyle is false. The Americas were a rich and fertile land, providing plentiful berries, vegetables, nuts, beans, squash, roots, fruits, corn, and rice. Most tribal people survived comfortably eating meat sparingly, while thriving on the cornucopia of the land.
>
> European influence introduced Native people to commercial trade, and fire power, and buffalo began to be killed in great numbers. Only recently has meat become an important staple. Europeans and immigrants believe that meat is a critical part of the human diet, but ancient Native Americans had a much more varied diet. Europeans are carrying their meaty ways overseas to other lands, as well. In China today, meat is served much more heavily in restaurants where European/Americans eat, whereas locals have for centuries eaten a mostly vegetarian diet. It now appears that this introduced diet of "heavy meat" is harming native cultures and causing health problems such as diabetes, cancer, and heart disease. (Fisher, "Freeing", 115)

Fisher reminds people that hunting is no longer necessary. She is troubled by indigenous artistry that continues to use feathers, furs, teeth, and hides. She notes that decorations made from the body parts of anymals are no longer appropriate: We no longer need to kill anymals in order to live.

Fisher, devoted to the ancient ways of her people, is vegan:

> In modern Western culture, most of us, including the American Indian, no longer need to hunt to survive. However, we almost always associate the Indian—even today's Indian—with wearing and using animal hides, furs, and feathers. Yet I assure you, as a vegan, though I avoid hides and fur, my Indianness is critical to who I am. The same is true of my mother, who is both an elder of our Ojibway tribe, and a vegetarian. It is not our dark hair, dark eyes, or Indian features that speak for who we are, but something much deeper, something not visually apparent: our commitment to the teachings of our ancient Ojibway ancestors. (Fisher, "Freeing", 111)

Fisher avoids wearing leather and all other anymal products; she is proud that her indigenous heritage has taught her to be respectful of anymals, and she is happy that she has no reason to cause anymals harm (Fisher, "Mother", 221–22).

Fisher discovered early in life that she had an uncanny ability to communicate with anymals, to feel their emotions, and she was consequently inspired to tell their stories through art. Fisher now paints anymals, especially birds, in bright and lively colors, visually expressing the freedom and joy she wishes for all creatures. Her sensitivity and remarkable connection to anymals is visible on every canvas (http://www.lindagfisher.com); it is easy to see why Fisher's work has earned international recognition (Fisher, "Freeing", 116).

Rod Coronado, a Pasqua Yaqui from the Sonoran Desert of northern Mexico and southern Arizona, is also an anymal liberationist. For more than twenty years, he fought "corporate and government policies" which are harmful to earth and anymals ("AZ").

As a child, Coronado was horrified when he watched a documentary on the slaughter of harp seals in Canada; as a teenager, he joined the Sea Shepherd Conservation Society to protect sea creatures and the seas (Sprig, "Living"). Within a year he and a coconspirator had "sunk two illegal whaling ships off the coast of Iceland" (a nation that continues to hunt whales in spite of international laws that forbid such whaling). He and his coconspirator destroyed half of Iceland's whaling fleet, and paused long enough to cause $2 million worth of damage to their whaling station (Sprig, "Living").

Coronado continues to be much honored in the anymal liberation community for sinking ships on behalf of whales, and for his ongoing bravery on behalf of anymals. He joined the Animal Liberation Front, and in 1995 was jailed for a series of attacks on anymal-testing operations and fur facilities that caused $125,000 in damages to Michigan State University. He destroyed thirty-two years of research and freed many caged mink (Sprig, "Living"). More recently, Coronado was jailed for spreading lion urine to protect mountain lions from hunters (urine confuses hounds) and for dismantling a lion trap.

Coronado has been an effective activist for anymals for many years, and he has paid the price in a nation bent on exploiting and killing anymals. He was sentenced to a one-year sentence, which he served—in a country that claims to have free speech—"for answering a question after a talk in which an audience member asked him how incendiary devices were made" (Rosenfeld). Although his most recent incarceration flies in the face of the U.S. Constitution, Coronado's work to free anymals from the tyranny of humanity has simply been too effective, and law enforcement has been determined to keep him behind bars.

Coronado's battles to protect Earth and anymals are grounded in his indigenous spirituality and stem from the indigenous lifeways that he learned among his people:

> When I returned to the rez [reservation] and started hanging out with the
> elders, direct action, deep ecology, radical environmentalism—whatever

you want to call it—were all part of the sacred knowledge handed down orally....

Spirituality for me is not only about sustenance, but a kind of road map one uses to successfully navigate through life....When who you are and what you are is about the Earth, you learn that your own true power can only come from the Earth....It is power that comes not out of fear but through simply listening and learning the lessons of how to live harmoniously with the rhythms of nature....

As an indigenous person, I've had to relearn that fighting for the Earth...is a very old, sacred and honorable duty. (Sprig, "Living")

Summary

Indigenous religious traditions around the world continue to provide an ancient yet living vision of nature as sacred, requiring human respect and entailing human responsibilities. Anymals are understood to be "people" living in community as humans live in community—all of whom are part of a larger—community of living beings. Indigenous religious traditions teach people that we owe respect, responsibility, and compassion to our nonhuman kin, and remember a time of great peace, before predation began. Most indigenous peoples believe that all beings are endowed with souls. Anymals are generally thought to hold exceptional abilities and remarkable powers. Indigenous myths teach that anymals are Creators, and that they hold the power to decide whether or not they will die at the hands of a hungry hunter. Indigenous peoples often fear the power of nature, including the powers of anymals, should they offend their powerful kin, on whom they depend for survival.

‖ 2 ‖

Hindu Traditions

If there were no meat-eaters, there would be no killers. A meat-eating man is a killer indeed.

—Mahabharata

By the time Socrates was born, the people of India had accumulated more than one thousand years of religious practice, traditions, and knowledge, including a broad spectrum of sacred verses which continue to form the foundation of Hindu religious traditions. Hindu beliefs and practices emerged from Vedic religion, which in turn was a compilation of earlier beliefs and practices recorded in Vedic texts. The ancient story of Indian religions can most clearly be picked up on the banks of the Indus River around 1500 BCE.

Sacred Nature, Sacred Anymals

Roughly four thousand years ago, worship in the Indus Valley revolved around nature, as recorded in a series of compositions called the Vedas, which remain the most sacred scriptures of the Hindus. The earliest surviving hymns, contained in the *Rig Veda*, "express a sense of the vastness and brilliance of nature" (Embree, *Sources*, 7). In this ancient Indian civilization "God and nature were one and the same" (Dwivedi, 6); for Vedic peoples (as for Hindus later), all that exists *is* God (Dwivedi, 5).

Many Vedic deities are personified powers of nature. Ancient hymns honor dawn, storms, vegetation, fire, and the sun as divine elements of a spiritually charged world (Embree, *Hindu*, 9–20). The *Yajur Veda* beseeches, "To the heavens be peace, to the sky and the earth; to the waters be peace, to plants and all trees" (Subramuniyaswami, 204).

The *Aranyaka*, or "forest books" (part of the Vedas), contain religious wisdom accumulated during spiritual retreats in remote unsettled regions (Embree, *Sources*, 29). Vedic people viewed the natural world as a window to the spiritual world. Hindus continue to retreat to areas devoid of humanity to gain spiritual wisdom and seek the divine (Marshall, 25).

Hindus also undertake long pilgrimages to visit holy sites, such as sacred mountains and rivers. In most religions, mountains are viewed as an access point to the heavens because they reach up into the world of the gods (as do the high and pointed tops of many places of worship, mimicking mountain peaks; places of worship also tend to be cave-like, as if worshipers were entering the sacred mountain). Rivers are also important to Hindus because they represent passageways (*thirta*) to the divine, ways of "crossing over" into another realm. On the boat of devotion and/or practice, Hindus cross over the turbulent waters of life to the world beyond. The mighty Ganges River, sacred to the people of India for centuries, and a preferred place for spreading the ashes of the dead, is also a goddess—Ganga (Eck, 64).

Early archeological evidence indicates that anymals held religious significance in ancient India (Embree, *Sources*, 4). Excavations have unearthed clay seals containing images of bulls, unicorns, elephants, and tigers (Munsterberg, 18–19; Zimmer, plates 21–23). The titles of some of the oldest Vedic hymns are named after anymals, including "The Frogs," "The Cows," and "The Bird" (O'Flaherty, *Rig*, 8–9). "The Frogs" compares the croaking of frogs with the religious chanting of priests; both were viewed as critical to the advent of seasonal rain—essential to life (Maurer, 208).

The heroes of the *Mahabharata* (a sacred epic composed between 400 BCE and 400 CE) traverse deserts, mountains, and deep forests, finding both shelter and character-building challenges in the forests of India. This epic reveals a rich and spiritually important natural world, including the many and wondrous anymals of the planet. Those who composed the *Mahabharata* warmly describe the varied and beautiful lands and anymals of India, such as a lake "where elephants bathed and flocks of swans and wild red geese rested" (Buck, *Mahabharata*, 155). One of the best English retellings of this story (a shorter version of a very long epic) includes many meticulous descriptions of nature and anymals as part of the sacred landscape of the *Mahabharata*:

> The rain began to fall and all the Earth was peaceful. In the forests of Kailasa, while the rain fell day and night, the animals were talking—the yak and the deer, the monkeys and boars and bears, the elephants and oxen, lions and leopards, buffalo and tigers—and the frogs ran joyfully about, and the sparrows and cuckoos sang. (Buck, *Mahabharata*, 167)

In the *Mahabharata*, a great sage comments that "in every creature that is endued with the five senses live all the deities" (Chapple, "Ahimsa," 111).

In Hindu traditions, every being is envisioned as coming from the same source and as connected with the divine. Just as a goldsmith fashions many ornaments from gold, the Great Goldsmith "makes many ornaments—different souls—out of the one Universal Spirit" (Subramuniyaswami, 89). Each of these unique beings shares a common source and, in the process, shares "something of the divine"

(Coomaraswamy and Nivedita, 15–16); "all living beings have souls, and God resides as their inner soul" (Dwivedi, 5).

Because anymals hold something of God, "Hindus are called to give other species not only respect, but reverence" (Dwivedi, 6). The divine is in all that exists, and everything that exists is "meant for the benefit of all" (Dwivedi, 5). Human beings are not entitled to dominate. Each species is expected to live "as part of the system, in close relationship with other species" but without any one species dominating or exploiting others (Dwivedi, 5). Hindu sacred writings like the *Upanishads* (later texts in the Vedas) honor the many wondrous anymals and every aspect of earth— including every individual of every species—as indistinct from Brahman, the eternal, perhaps best translated as "God." The *Svetasvatara* Upanishad praises Brahman *as* sun, fire, wind, moon, stars, water, human, and so on: "Thou art the dark-blue bee, thou art the green parrot with red eyes, thou art the thunder-cloud, the seasons, the seas" (Müller, "Fourth Adhyana").

Early nature deities left an indelible mark on Hindu traditions; Indian sacred literature continues to regard the earth as a "fitting symbol for the deepest of religious impulses" (Embree, *Hindu*, 45). "To the Hindu the ground is sacred. The rivers are sacred. The sky is sacred. The sun is sacred" (Subramuniyaswami, 195). Indian religious traditions cultivate humility, reverence, and awe by "seeing God everywhere" (Subramuniyaswami, 183). For the Hindu, "all of nature, all of the universe, is sacred" (Kinsley, *Ecology*, 57).

Reverence for Cows

Perhaps the most renowned aspect of the Hindu religious traditions is reverence for cows—a species that Westerners tend to disparage as stupid and expendable.

Cows, whether deoni or gir, are praised and respected in Hindu traditions because they exemplify munificence and mother's love. "The cow is venerated as the great provider and is naturally therefore identified with the earth and regarded as too sacred to be killed" (Brockington, 205).

Indian reverence for cattle reaches clear back to the earliest days of Vedic religion in the Indus Valley. The Vedic hymn titled "The Cow" considers the well-being and happiness of cows: "Let them lie down in the cow-shed! Let them be pleased in us!" (Maurer, 291). This Vedic hymn, written sometime before 1000 BCE, also identifies cows with the entire universe (Embree, *Hindu*, 39–40), as do writings in both the *Artharva Veda* and the *Mahabharata*. Vedic texts reveal the historic shift from more barbaric times, when cows were killed, to a more enlightened time of "preserving their lives" (Doniger, 113). This critical historic text tells of a famine in which King Prithu pursues the earth, which was withholding stores, in order to secure food for his people. At some point in the chase, earth becomes a cow (a symbol of munificence) and begs for her life. The king grants the cow life in exchange for life-sustaining milk for his starving community. Ancient texts note that, through this act of animal liberation, "righteous kingship arose on earth" (Doniger, 112–13). At the end of the day, this king's decision can be recognized as common sense: Cows eat grass and produce milk; the people of India understood that *living* cows could carry them through famine much better than *dead* cows, especially in a land without freezers or refrigerators.

Indians speak of "mother-cow-love" as ideal love, and Indian literature often compares a good human mother to a cow mother: A good mother runs to those in need "as a cow runs to her calf" (Buck, *Mahabharata*, 58). Mythology recalling the life of the popular deity Krishna portrays tender affection between cows and calves, whom he spent much time with as a cowherd. These stories emphasize mother-cow-love (Gosvami, 157). Cows not only care for their own young tenderly, but can also provide life-sustaining milk when a human mother cannot breast-feed her off-spring. Indeed, cows are protective and dutiful mothers, and their distress is both audible and visible when their calves are in danger or when their calves are forcibly taken from them (as routinely happens in the dairy industry).

Hindu reverence for cows serves as a foundation for a more general human responsibility for anymals. Cows, whether Hallikar or Haryana, are generally docile. Protecting cows, whom we might easily harm or kill, is an expression of compassion that acknowledges both our power over other creatures and our own vulnerability before the gods—*our* need for protection from that which is more powerful and potentially deadly. We are also "related to and dependent on the whole creation," and on the munificence and compassion of powerful gods (Rao, 34).

When we protect those who are least able to protect themselves, we show an understanding of the vulnerability of life in general, and of our own vulnerability. In this sense, the Hindu attitude toward cattle is "symbolic of reverence and respect for all forms of life" (Kinsley, *Ecology*, 65). As the earth and gods nurture us, so must we nurture others who are in need—whether a Brahman cow or Barkudia skink (a leg-less lizard found only in India, now so rare as to be sighted only once in the last eighty-seven years).

Hindu Philosophy and Morality

Ahimsa

Ahimsa is "the first and foremost ethical principle of every Hindu," who is required to abstain "from causing hurt or harm to all beings" (Subramuniyaswami, 195). *Ahimsa* literally means "not to harm," or "noninjury," and carries an injunction for "non-injury toward all living beings" (Jacobsen, 287). *Ahimsa* is usually translated as "nonviolence," but *ahimsa* "is not simply a matter of refraining from actual, physical harm. *Ahimsa* is the absence of even a desire to do harm to any living being, in thought, word, or deed" (Long, 97). In Hindu traditions, the common Christian precept to "love thy neighbor as thyself" is enhanced so that "every living being is thy neighbor" (Kushner, 148).

The cardinal Hindu virtue is "compassion for all" (Subramuniyaswami, 183), and every Hindu is encouraged to practice nonviolence toward "the community of all beings" (Kinsley, *Ecology*, 65). The *Rig Veda* notes that those of faith must protect both the "two legged and four legged," and provide water and food for all creatures in need (Subramuniyaswami, 204). The *Yajur Veda* speaks on behalf of "God's creatures, whether they are human [or] animal," warning that no life is expendable (Subramuniyaswami, 204). The *Devikalottara Agama* (350 verses of dialogue between the deities Karttikeya and Shiva regarding the worship of Shiva) plainly states, "No pain should be caused to any created being" (Subramuniyaswami, 204). Later (second-century BCE) compositions present specific duties expected of Hindus (in this case, citizens of the Mauryan Empire), including both nonviolence and compassion toward anymals (James, 504). In the *Mahabharata*, the deity Brhaspati encourages devotees to understand all beings as like ourselves, and to treat them accordingly (Chapple, "Ahimsa," 113). The thirteenth-century Hindu poet Jnanadeva teaches the following: "Let universal friendship reign among all beings" (Embree, *Hindu*, 250).

Mahatma Gandhi, likely the most famous Hindu internationally, believed that *ahimsa* was not only a way of life, "but an eternal quality of truth itself" (Shinn, 219). According to Gandhi, if a man practices *ahimsa* as a religious commitment, "the spring of all his actions is compassion, [and] he shuns to the best of his ability the destruction of the tiniest creature, tries to save it, and thus incessantly strives to be free from the deadly coil of *himsa* [harm/violence]" (Gandhi, *Autobiography*, 349). Consequently, Gandhi shunned animal sacrifice, which not only kills, but kills the most vulnerable beings. He noted that sheep would surely have their own accounting of such deeds:

> To my mind the life of a lamb is no less precious than that of a human being. I should be unwilling to take the life of a lamb for the sake of the human body. I hold that, the more helpless a creature, the more entitled it is to protection by man from the cruelty of man. (Gandhi, *Autobiography*, 235).

While the Hindu worldview holds that people "have no special privilege or authority over other creatures," human beings "do have more obligations and duties" (Dwivedi, 6). This moral obligation is well represented in the *Mahabharata*, where concern for the lives and the well-being of anymals is central to Hindu heroes and beloved deities alike. In the *Mahabharata*, when a young woman meets an ascetic in the forest, she asks, "Is all well with your life here, and with your trees, and with the animals and birds that live with you?" (Buck, *Mahabharata*, 127). And when the fire god, Agni, is hungry and weak and desperately needs to consume a forest to regain his strength, he asks permission from the deity, Krishna, before torching his surroundings. Krishna answers Agni's urgent request with a question: Will any people, animals, birds, or trees be harmed? Agni replies that the anymals will run away, the birds will fly away, and "the trees have their roots beyond my reach" (Buck, *Mahabharata*, 81).

In the *Mahabharata*, the poetic voice of the deity Brhaspati reminds readers that there is no religious practice that surpasses that of nonviolence.

> Just as the tracks of a snake
> and the footprints of other animals
> are all covered over in the footprints of an elephant,
> so in all the world nonviolence
> is proclaimed to be the highest dharma. (Chapple, "Ahimsa," 114)

Hindu gods and heroes are praised for compassion in India's sacred literature; power over others is always to be used compassionately, and restraint with one's powers when dealing with the weak and vulnerable is the hallmark of a Hindu hero. In a dream near the end of the *Mahabharata*, Yudhishthira (one of five heroes termed the *Pandavas*, five brothers who in many ways exemplify the Hindu ideal) finds himself in a great desert, where he is befriended by a small brown dog. All of his beloved human companions die for want of water, while the dog somehow survives. When the god Indra arrives to rescue Yudhishthira from the "death-desert," Yudhishthira first inquires as to the whereabouts of his lost human companions. He is told that they have "gone before" (Buck, *Mahabharata*, 365). Indra then encourages Yudhishthira to climb into his chariot and join his fallen companions:

"Come, get in."

"Lord of the Past and Present," said Yudhishthira, "this little dog who is my last companion must also go."

"No," said Indra. "You cannot enter heaven with a dog at your heels...."

"He is devoted to me and looks to me for protection. Left alone he would die here."

"There is no place for dogs in heaven.... It cannot be."

Yudhishthira frowned. "It cannot be otherwise."

"Don't you understand: You have won heaven! Immortality and prosperity and happiness in all directions are yours. Only leave that animal and come with me; that will not be cruel...."

"I do not turn away my dog; I turn away you. I will not surrender a faithful dog to you...."

"But I can't take him! I'll put him to sleep; there will be no pain. No one will know."

"Lord of Heaven," said Yudhishthira, "you have my permission to go."

"Your splendor will fill the three worlds if you will but enter my car alone,"
said Indra. "You have left everyone else—why not this worthless dog?"
"I am decided," answered Yudhishthira. (Buck, *Mahabharata*, 365–66)

Here readers see the highest Hindu moral and spiritual champion, Yudhishthira, the
hero-son of the god of moral and cosmic law, turn away the great god Indra—and a
life in paradise with his loved ones—to fulfill his responsibility for a stray dog who
has befriended him, and whom he has had the heart to love in return. Seemingly in
desperation, Indra offers to put the dog painlessly into an eternal sleep, but
Yudhishthira will not sacrifice the dog's life, even painlessly—even for his own
eternal happiness.

Ultimately, the stray dog transforms into Yudhishthira's father, Dharma (the god
of moral and eternal law). Dharma praises Yudhishthira for his steadfast commitment to protect and accompany a small, common mutt in need—even against the
will of an extremely powerful god. While most people might consider Indra's advice
to be commonsensical—justifiable self-interest—Hindu moral law does not. *Ahimsa*
is a basic, essential, and unwavering moral law, critical to spirituality and salvation,
and the *Mahabharata*'s exemplary characters demonstrate that deities, kings, heroes,
and commoners are *expected* to be mindful and protective of all living beings.

Reincarnation

Reincarnation (transmigration) is the belief that after death, the imperishable *atman*
(generally and perhaps best translated as "soul") lodges in another body, whether in
an Indian striped hyena, Bengal river fish, Caucasian human, amrit mahal cow, or
whippet dog.

Indian philosophy holds that time has no beginning; reincarnation has been in
play for unending eons. Across incalculable ages, each *atman* has moved from birth
to birth, from body to body, dwelling in billions of individuals from innumerable
species. Each of us has been a Namdapha flying squirrel and an Andaman spiny
shrew. A banteng and a blue whale can house the same imperishable *atman* consec-
utively, or in two different centuries. One *atman* can be a capped leaf monkey one
moment, and an Indus River Dolphin the next. Indian philosophy of reincarnation
is well represented in the words of Ingrid Newkirk (Government), when she mentioned the relevance of suffering across species: "A dog is a pig is a rat is a boy."

Reincarnation creates bonds between every living being and diminishes our tendency to view ourselves as an individual, separate entity. Our present life is merely
"an infinitesimal part of a much larger picture that encompasses all of life" (Kinsley,
Ecology, 64). Every animal, whether primate or rodent, at some point across incalculable eons, has been reincarnated as our mother, brother, or best friend. How can the
choice to consume factory-farmed dairy products—a diet that causes remarkable
suffering—be spiritually or morally acceptable in a worldview in which one's deeds

are recorded in an eternal *atman* that has many times been housed in a sindhi cow, exploited for dairy products?

Reincarnation requires Hindus to see themselves in every living being, and to see every living being in Self, supporting and fostering *ahimsa*.

Karma

Karma means "action"; actions determine karma. Karma is an unavoidable force, like gravity. Karma is a force of justice whereby "every act carries with it an inevitable result" (Embree, *Hindu*, 51).

In the Hindu spiritual understanding, reincarnation and the condition of one's next life rests on karma. We are the rulers of our fate; we reap precisely what we sow. In the Hindu worldview, all living beings are in moral relationship with one another; we create our spiritual moral ledger via conduct toward other living beings and nature itself (Curtin, "Making," 71): Our treatment of the Indian rhinoceros and spotted redshank help to determine our future existences. Hindus understand that the "pain a human being causes other living beings . . . will have to be suffered by that human being later, either in this life or in a later rebirth" (Jacobsen, 289).

The Hindu *Shastras* (textbooks that expound on Hindu philosophy and practice) explain how humans might gain a favorable rebirth by practicing *ahimsa*: In seeking to cut the bonds of karma, one should do what "is good for all creatures" (O'Flaherty, *Textual*, 124). Those aspiring to relatively pain-free future existences must avoid even the accidental killing of other entities (Basham, 59). Harming others—any others—carries negative karma.

One might argue that karma does not encourage humanity to *care* about other creatures, but only about one's self—one's future lives. Such an outlook fails to note that for the ongole cow who is not killed for hamburger, the reason for her release from the death industry matters little to her. She will stand in the hot Indian sun and chew her cud, not minding that a Hindu may, ultimately, have had a selfish motive for sparing her life. That said, motive is critical in all great religious traditions, including Hindu traditions. Any "living being can be tainted" by violence in action, speech, *or thought* (Chapple, "Ahimsa," 115); compassion must be practiced not only in words and actions, but also in one's thoughts and intentions (Subramuniyaswami, 195). Inevitably, sincerity is important to spiritual practice, but for anymals who are either exploited (and likely slaughtered prematurely) or in the grip of anymal agriculture, human reasons are of little or no importance.

Oneness

The *Upanishads*, composed between 700 and 500 BCE, are some of the most fascinating and celebrated Hindu religious teachings. These sacred texts remind Hindus that the inner essence of each living being—*atman*—is identical with the inner essence of every other being. As a pinch of salt placed in water cannot be seen or touched, but makes freshwater salty, so the subtle essence of life runs through all, pervading the giant squid, the human being, the massasauga, and the endangered broad-nosed gentle lemur, though it cannot be perceived or touched (Müller, *Chandogya*, 104–5).

If we understand *atman*, we know that all things are unified by this shared, subtle essence. As all rivers join one great sea, which again rises into the atmosphere to become individual drops, so all living beings—whatever form they might take—are united through this shared "subtle essence" (Müller, *Chandogya*, 102). The ground of each individual's being "is identical with the ground of the universe," whether that individual is mollusk or bird (Embree, *Hindu*, 59). "As by one clod of clay all that is made of clay is known," so we can understand all living beings through this shared essence of life (Müller, *Chandogya*, 92): To know what it is to be human is to understand what it is to be a yellow wagtail or mugger crocodile.

The divine, the eternal—Brahman—dwells in the *atman* of every creature. The Brahman in every *atman* is identical. All animals have *atman*/Brahman, and through Brahman/*atman* each creature is linked to every other creature, and to Brahman. A holy person (too often assumed to be a man in the world's religious literature) "sees himself in the heart of all beings and he sees all beings in his heart" (Mascaro, *Bhagavad*, 71–72). Brahman lies behind and within each of us, as well as within all that we see and know (Embree, *Sources*, 30). In this spiritual vision, no individual is an island—each of us shares Brahman, the eternal, with every other animal. "This Great Being...dwells in the heart of all creatures as their innermost Self....His hands and feet are everywhere; his eyes and mouths are everywhere. His ears are everywhere. He pervades everything in the universe" (Prabhavananda, *Svetasvatara*). The *Upanishads* remind Hindus that each being *is* "the One that lies behind all" (Zaehner, 7).

In the most famous portion of the *Mahabharata*, the *Bhagavad Gita*, the divine asserts, "I am not lost to one who sees me in all things and sees all things in me" (Mascaro, *Bhagavad*, 6). The divine, in this case Krishna, then reveals himself as a form of the great God, Vishnu, and also as indwelling in every individual: "I am the life of all living beings....All beings have their rest in me....In all living beings I am the light of consciousness" (Mascaro, *Bhagavad*, 74, 80, 86). The *Mahabharata* notes that those who are spiritually learned behold all beings in Self, Self in all beings, and God in both.

Mahatma Gandhi accepted the "essential unity...of all that lives" and understood that shedding of any "blood means shedding of our own blood" (Gandhi, *Essential*, 264, 70). Brahman *is* the very life in *all* that lives, and Hindu religious traditions teach people to extend compassion to *all* fellow beings (L. Nelson, 67). The *Bhagavad Gita* explicitly connects oneness with *ahimsa* and karma:

> He who sees that the Lord of all is ever the same in all that is—immortal in
> the field of mortality—he sees the truth. And when a man sees that the

God in himself is the same God in all that is, he hurts not himself by hurting others. (Subramuniyaswami, 205)

Those who love God must have "love for all creation" (Mascaro, *Bhagavad*, 30). According to the *Bhagavad Gita*, an advanced spiritual practitioner "treats a cow, an elephant, a dog, and an outcaste" with the same high regard because *God is all*, and those who are spiritually advanced, those who are *true* devotees of the divine, find "in all creation the presence of God" (Dwivedi, 5). Speaking to Arjuna, Krishna notes the following:

> [When a man] sees me in all and he sees all in me, then I never leave him and he never leaves me. He who in this oneness of love, loves me in whatever he sees, wherever this man may live, in truth this man lives in me. And he is the greatest Yogi, he whose vision is ever one: when the pleasure and pain of others is his own pleasure and pain. (Mascaro, *Bhagavad*, 71–72)

The divine, the eternal, flows through all that exists, and this sense of oneness with the divine ought to guide our interactions with others—men and women, hispid hare and hoolock gibbon.

Diet

In the Hindu worldview, killing anymals for food is sacrilegious—perhaps best viewed as spiritual suicide. Flesh cannot be obtained without injury, and "injury to sentient beings is detrimental to the attainment of heavenly bliss," so we ought to "shun meat" (Subramuniyaswami, 205). Refusing flesh "is considered both appropriate conduct and one's *dharma*," or duty (Dwivedi, 7).

Eating cows is particularly base for Hindus, but flesh eating in general remains spiritually abhorrent. In light of reincarnation, eating hens and ducks, goats and Kangyam cattle is "foolish," for it is "like eating the flesh of one's own son" (Chapple, "Ahimsa," 114). Those who understand the oneness of all that exists, the "wise ones, who regard the life of [anymals] as their own breath," abstain from eating flesh and praise those who abstain from eating flesh (Chapple, "Ahimsa," 117). For many Hindus, "wanton killing of animals is little better than murder, and meat eating is little better than cannibalism" (Basham, 58).

The *Mahabharata* calls attention to the moral and spiritual importance of dietary choice. When the great warrior-sage Bhishma, one of the most respected heroes in this much-loved epic, learns of the spiritual importance of *ahimsa* from the deity Brhaspati, he extols nonviolence and renounces the eating of flesh:

> 25. Nonviolence is the highest dharma,
> nonviolence is the highest austerity,

nonviolence is the highest truth;
by this dharma [one's duty] is done
26. Meat is not born of grass, wood, or rock.
Meat arises from killing a living being.
Thus, in the enjoyment of meat there is fault.
27. The beloved, sincere, truthful gods
have in hand (for nourishment)
oblations, sacrificial offerings, and nectar.
(By contrast), consider the tortuous,
unrighteous ways of flesh-eating demons....
29. If there were no meat-eaters,
there would be no killers.
A meat-eating man is a killer indeed,
causing death for the purpose of food.
30. If meat were considered not to be food,
there would be no violence.
Violence is done to animals
for the sake of the meat-eater only.
31. Because the life of violent ones
is shortened as well (due to their deeds),
the one who wishes long life for himself
should refuse meat, O splendid one.
32. Those fierce ones who do violence to life
are not able to go for protection (when they need it).
They are to be feared by beings as beasts of prey. (Chapple, "Ahimsa," 118–19)

The *Mahabharata* notes that the "one who kills beings/for the sake of food is the lowest sort of person,/a maker of great sin" (Chapple, "Ahimsa," 120), and the butcher is not the only one who qualifies:

> The meat eater's desire for meat drives another to kill and provide that meat. The act of the butcher begins with the desire of the consumer. Meat-eating contributes to a mentality of violence.... India's greatest saints have confirmed that one cannot eat meat and live a peaceful, harmonious life. Man's appetite for meat inflicts devastating harm on the earth itself, stripping its precious forests to make way for pastures. The *Triukural* candidly states, "How can he practice true compassion who eats the flesh of an animal to fatten his own flesh?" (Subramuniyaswami, 201)

The farmer, rancher, butcher, *and* consumer who order, buy, or eat flesh are rightly considered killers, who fail to practice *ahimsa*:

The purchaser of flesh performs *himsa* (violence) by his wealth; he who eats flesh does so by enjoying its taste; the killer does *himsa* by actually tying and killing the animal. Thus, there are three forms of killing: he who brings flesh or sends for it, he who cuts off the limbs of an animal, and he who purchases, sells or cooks flesh and eats it—all of these are to be considered meat-eaters. (Subramuniyaswami, 205)

Eating flesh is recognized as a *choice* in the Hindu tradition—one with severe karmic consequences. The *Manu Smriti*, or *Laws of Manu*, one of the oldest and most important texts holding Hindu laws, warns that one "who kills an animal for meat will die of a violent death as many times as there are hairs on that killed animal" (Dwivedi, 7). In contrast, Manu refers to the vegetarian as a "friend of all living beings (Chapple, "Ahimsa," 113).

For most Hindus, the vegetarian diet is understood as "a way to live with a minimum of hurt to other beings, for to consume meat, fish, fowl or eggs is to participate indirectly in acts of cruelty and violence" (Subramuniyaswami, 201). True, the anymal is already dead, but it would not be if consumers did not pay the rancher and the butcher.

Gandhi was raised both vegetarian and without eggs (Gandhi, *Essential*, 12). As a young man, his dietary choices were based on health, but as time passed, "religion became the supreme motive" (Gandhi, *Autobiography*, 49). Gandhi recognized that people "have no right to destroy life that we cannot create" (Gandhi, *Essential*, 14). While studying in England, he read books on vegetarianism and was soon committed to the concept both religiously and intellectually. He noted that "in order to get meat, we have to kill" (Roberts, 117), and he felt that spiritual progress demands "at some stage that we should cease to kill our fellow creatures for the satisfaction of our bodily wants" (Roberts, 119). If we continue killing anymals for food, Gandhi understood that, through karma, we ultimately "kill ourselves, our body and soul" (Roberts, 124). He comments in his autobiography that spreading the word about the importance of a compassionate vegetarian diet "henceforward became my mission" (Gandhi, *Autobiography*, 48). On learning of "the tortures to which cows and buffaloes were subjected by their keepers," Gandhi also gave up cow's milk (Gandhi, *Autobiography*, 272–73, 328). The only anymal product that Gandhi consumed later in life was goat's milk, which he took only at his wife's insistence. Even this small concession troubled Gandhi; he understood that stealing the nursing milk of cows was *himsa*, a form of violence against gentle, munificent mothers. Why would goat's milk be any different?

In contemporary Indian society, despite hundreds of years of British influence followed by decades of American influence, Hindus remain overwhelmingly vegetarian. A diet with very few animal products—usually limited to milk and yogurt—has been standard among Hindus for centuries. Members of the International

Society for Krishna Consciousness ("Hare Krishnas") are strictly vegetarian. The Hindu diet is shaped by an understanding of reincarnation, and a sense of oneness backed by karma—and *ahimsa*, the Hindu commitment to a lifestyle that is "loving and kind" (Subramuniyaswami, 181).

Hunting

In Indian literature, anymals often express their desire to be left alone, without hunters terrorizing, wounding, and ultimately killing members of their communities. Hunters who kill without necessity and/or without compassion are mocked and despised.

In the *Mahabharata*, a king shoots a stag who is mating, and the stag, who "looked up at him and with tears in his eyes asked, 'Why have you done this?'" (Buck, *Mahabharata*, 31). As a result of the king's indifference and cruelty, the deer curses the king to die a similar fate: "Death will strike you down when you next make love" (Buck, *Mahabharata*, 31). Because of his cruel arrow and the deer's curse, the fool-hardy king must hand his kingdom over to his son and retreat to the forest and forced celibacy. The lusty and forgetful king ultimately dies in the arms of one of his wives. The story of the stag and the hunting king reminds readers that wildlife also live in communities; they enjoy their lives of freedom in the forest and would prefer not to be killed. With karma in the balance, hunters risk their own welfare by choosing to kill others for sport.

In the same epic, exiled into the forest, the Pandavas are forced to live by hunting and foraging. In one of many camps, a deer approaches Yudhishthira, one of the Pandavas, in a dream: "We are the deer of this forest. Majesty, now only very few of us remain, like seeds, like broken words; if you do not leave us we shall all perish for your food" (Buck, *Mahabharata*, 142). In the morning, Yudhishthira announces, "We must move on and let the forest animals recover" (Buck, *Mahabharata*, 142). Although humans may sometimes need to kill to survive, they may not decimate the critically endangered pygmy hog, the nearly extinct Sumatran rhinoceros, or any other community. Yudhishthira, the quintessential moral exemplar, bows willingly to the needs of anymals.

The *Pancatantra* (300–500 CE, compiled from stories told and retold for generations), composed to teach young princes moral lessons, also gives anymals a voice against hunting. In the chapter on friendship, a crow, pigeon, mouse, tortoise, and deer, all of whom are friends, work together to escape a cruel and greedy hunter. When Deer becomes caught in a hunter's trap, Crow quickly carries Mouse over to chew through the bindings. Tortoise comes along, slowly, to see if his friend is safe, but as Deer is released, the hunter arrives, taking the slow-moving Tortoise away in fresh binds. The remaining friends hatch a scheme to save Tortoise: Deer lies by a nearby lake, as if freshly dead, with Crow pretending to peck his eyes. The greedy hunter drops Tortoise and rushes over to claim the "dead" deer. Meanwhile, Mouse chews through the leather bindings to free Tortoise, who slips into the lake. Deer then leaps up and dashes off, as does Mouse, while Crow lifts onto the wind.

The *Pancatantra*, like most sacred Indian writings, assigns a high value to life and encourages nonviolence. In this *Pancatantra* story, the hunter is portrayed as opportunistic and cruel; he is thwarted at every turn by the friendly and noble anymals he seeks to kill. The ever bloodthirsty hunter is left empty-handed, and the anymals are granted at least a temporary reprieve from the dread of being captured and killed by hunters. This story of anymal friendships provides a vision of the effects of hunting through the eyes of hunted anymals: Hunting steals friends, threatens communities, and terrifies individuals. This story also mocks hunters as incompetent, greedy, and bloodthirsty, reminding readers that eating flesh is a *choice*, and those who make this choice are *not* models of moral virtue (Olivelle, 71–104). Mouse succinctly offers what seems the most important moral teaching in this sweet story of trial and friendship: "What's righteousness? Compassion on all beings" (Olivelle, 91).

Divine-Anymal Relations

Hindu gods often interact closely with anymals, and many deities are associated with specific anymals. Sometimes the gods take the form of anymals; other times they *are* anymals. Divine association inextricably links gods and goddesses with anymals: "The goat is Agni. The sheep is Varuna. The horse is Surya. The earth is the deity Virat. The cow and calf are Soma" (Chapple, "Ahimsa," 111).

Vehicles

Artists generally portray Hindu goddesses and gods in the company of their vehicles, or anymal associates and companions. These vehicles are powerful and distinguished in their own right (Coomaraswamy, 16–17), and inextricably connect the divine with anymals.

Brahma rides a goose (or swan), which is a symbol of knowledge in India (Danielou, 237). Geese and swans also migrate great distances, "a symbol to Hindus of the soul's quest for release" (Brockington, 195). Skanda, son of Shiva and Parvati/ Kali, flies through the air on a peacock with the rooster as his emblem (Danielou, 298). The peacock is the victor over time itself, symbolizing our ability to transcend the limits of our physical being (Danielou, 300). Ganesha keeps company with a rat (or mouse), the master of all things that are kept or contained inside—most notably, the *atman*. The mouse/rat is also a "thief," who slips through the smallest hole or crack and carries away treasures, demonstrating access to all things hidden, including the *atman*: "The all-pervading *Atman* is the mouse that lives in the hole called Intellect, within the heart of every being" (Danielou, 296, italics added).

The fierce goddess Durga wields a battery of weapons and rides gracefully atop a powerful lion (or tiger). A lion also helps Shiva to climb atop his great bull, Nandi (Danielou, 220). The powerful Shiva rides on his trusty white bull, the giver of life. Nandi is massive, with large brown eyes and a shoulder hump that "resembles the top of a snow-covered mountain" (Danielou, 219). The great bull represents unbridled sexual power, which Shiva, a great ascetic, rides with ease (Danielou, 219). Nandi is also associated with the lofty principles of justice and virtue. In temples dedicated to Shiva, Nandi is usually present, often standing at the entrance.

Vishnu "rides upon a bird, half vulture, half man, named 'Wings of Speech' (Garuda)" (Danielou, 160). In more ancient texts, Garuda is an independent deity; he becomes associated with Vishnu only in later writings (Brockington, 195). Vishnu's vehicle is "huge and fierce-looking; his color is that of molten gold. He has the head of an eagle, a red beak, and feathered wings, together with a large belly and two arms like a man" (Danielou, 162). Garuda is so swift that the wind from his wings can upset the rotation of the planets, and when he flies, the earth and its great mountains "seem dragged after him" (Danielou, 162). He represents the magical sounds of sacred scripture, the essence of knowledge, and his wings transport the dead to worlds beyond (Danielou, 220, 298, 288, 296, xxvii, 160, plate 20).

The vehicles of the Hindu gods are important and powerful. As with Garuda, many were once deities in their own right, in the days when zoomorphic deities reigned. These diverse and colorful anymals, vehicles of gods and goddesses, are among the oldest Indian religious powers.

Krishna and Cows

Stories of Krishna (an incarnation of Vishnu) would not be complete without images of his boyhood, cavorting with cattle and colorful peafowl in the countryside around his home (Dwivedi, 7). He shares milk with the calves, and plays both with and among the cattle; he struts with peafowl.

Most important, Krishna is associated with cattle. The youthful Krishna is often depicted in Indian art playing a flute beside a peaceful and contented cow. Stories tell of his childish delight as he grabs the tail of a cow to be pulled through mud and manure (O'Flaherty, *Hindu*, 219). As an infant, he is sometimes depicted suckling directly from a cow, with the cow's calf alongside. When little Krishna grows from babyhood to boyhood, he tends white, brown, and spotted cattle with the other boys of his village, keeping them from harm while they graze, as rural Indian children still do today. Krishna's youthful attention does lapse, and in one story the frightened cattle are threatened by a forest fire. Of course, Krishna comes to their rescue. He takes his duties as a cowherd seriously, and the gentle bovines are soon safe.

Partly as a devotion to Krishna, there are many sanctuaries in India specifically for cows. *Gaushalas* provide shelter to cows, largely catering "to the needs of non-lactating, weak, unproductive, and stray cattle" (Yadav). In the land of Krishna's childhood, contemporary devotees tend a herd of 300 needy cows at a sanctuary in Vrindavan (India), Care for Cows. Volunteers at this sanctuary provide "hay, flour, fresh grass, medical attention" and safe haven for "abandoned cows, bulls, retired oxen, and orphaned calves…in Krishna's holy land" (Care). The website for Care for Cows indicates that, although devoted to Krisha, they are also devoted to protecting and tending bovines, whether malvi cows or oxen:

> Unless they are protected they are destined to subsist on refuse and become plagued by various debilitating and often terminal diseases or suffer injury from careless motorists. However, the most immediate danger is that they become abducted for slaughter by cattle rustlers who are active in this area today. Our present facility is full and there is an urgent need to acquire more land for their protection. (Care)

Snakes/*Nagas*

Snakes are often used as a religious symbol either of great good or great evil. India has a healthy share of poisonous snakes, including kraits, cobras, and two species of vipers, yet Hindu traditions are overwhelmingly snake-friendly.

The great god Shiva is surrounded by snakes; a cobra often hangs from his neck. The cobra, though deadly, is a symbol of positive characteristics. Coiled before striking, the cobra represents latent energy, the source of spiritual endeavor and advancement, ready for action (Danielou, 217).

In the Indian religious traditions, *nagas* are semidivine serpents who are understood to be "superior to man" (Zimmer, 63). For centuries, South Indian royalty proudly claimed *nagas* in their ancestral lines. In ancient Indian myths, snakes guard the waters that are essential for life in the arid lands of India (Zimmer, 63).

There are Indian stories of naughty snakes, such as Kaliya who poisons villagers and gets into a battle with Krishna. Still, snakes are not generally hated or killed in India, but are revered, and even Kaliya's life is spared by Krishna for the sake of his pleading wives. Perhaps this is because violence and killing are not consistent with the spiritual life of most Hindus; for thousands of years, respect and compassion have prevented Hindus from inflicting violence on snakes—or on rats, cockroaches, or pretty much any other dangerous or "annoying" anymal. In India, snakes are yet more protected because of their association with *nagas*, and also because of their association with great deities such as Shiva and Vishnu.

In Hindu art, after devouring the universe at the end of an age, Vishnu often reclines on the cosmic sea in the coils of the cosmic serpent Sesha (Remainder), (Zimmer, 60–61; Danielou, 162): "The supreme God, having devoured all beings, sleeps on the lap of the serpent" (Danielou, 163). Sesha represents all that remains of the universe between creation cycles—the raw materials of the entire universe, the germ of the next creation, and the endless cycles of time (Danielou, 163). Remainder is understood to be the king of *Nagas,* the ruler of all serpents. Lakshmana, Rama's younger brother, is often viewed as a human incarnation of the Great Serpent in whose coils Vishnu rests in Hindu depictions of cyclical existence.

Hanuman

Hanuman, a great hero in the *Ramayana* (the other enormously popular sacred epic of the Hindu tradition, composed between 300 BCE and 300 CE), is a monkey and ultimately a god. He is mighty and powerful, can fly through the air, roar like thunder, and wreak havoc with his exceptional tail. Hanuman is commander in chief of the monkey army, fighting on the side of the gods, taking tremendous responsibility on behalf of Rama. He is essential to the victory of good over evil in the classic war story that is central to the unfolding of the *Ramayana.*

Hanuman has exceptional powers. Before the great battle, he turns into a cat to find Rama's wife, Sita (also understood to be an incarnation of a goddess). When he locates her, he returns to monkey form and offers Sita a token sent by Rama, thereby bringing Sita renewed hope. Hanuman then reveals himself to the enemy, Ravana (the wife-napper), who promptly lights the monkey's tail on fire. Hanuman simply assumes his gigantic form and rushes through the streets, setting the enemy city ablaze.

Hanuman is not only a fierce protagonist for the good (and a lively prankster), but ultimately a deity. At the outset of the *Ramayana,* Hanuman is ignorant of both the depths of his learning and the heights of his physical power, but his devotion to Rama—to God—is crystal clear. Hanuman is Rama's "perfect servant" and devotee (*Coomaraswamy,* 22).

> Hanuman is said to be present wherever Rama's name is even whispered. At a corner of any hall, unnoticed, he would be present whenever the story of Rama is narrated to an assembly. He can never tire of hearing about Rama, his mind having no room for any other object. The traditional narrator, at the beginning of his story-telling, will always pay a tribute to the unseen Hanuman, the god who had compressed within himself so much power, wisdom, and piety. Hanuman emerges in the *Ramayana* as one of the most important and worshipful characters; there is a belief that to meditate on him is to acquire immeasurable inner strength and freedom from fear. (Narayan, 170)

Indian art portrays Hanuman ripping open his chest to reveal Rama and Sita in the core of his body, where his heart should be. Hanuman models perfect devotion to God:

> It may be questioned whether there is in the whole of literature another apotheosis of loyalty and self-surrender like that of Hanuman. He is the Hindu ideal of the perfect servant, the servant who finds full realization of manhood, of faithfulness, of his obedience; the subordinate whose glory is in his own inferiority. (Coomaraswamy, 22)

Hanuman dedicates his life to the fight for goodness, to fight alongside Rama for the cause of God, in a humble and selfless manner. Hanuman is honored and worshipped by Hindus for this exemplary devotion to the divine: He is worshiped because of his perfect devotion to God. Through Hanuman's spiritual devotion, his imperfections dissipate, and he becomes a deity. In the perfect Hindu twist of circumstances, the one who worships perfectly—and in Hanuman's case it is a monkey—*becomes* a deity.

Hanuman's image is found in nearly every ancient fort in south India, and he remains a primary deity of northern India as well (Danielou, 173).

Human-Anymal Relations

Anymals as Individuals

Hindu literature often presents anymal characters alongside of and equal to human beings. Indian sacred writings portray anymals as lively, humorous, bold, honorable, wily, devoted—the gamut of possible human characteristics. Diverse Hindu texts present anymals as unique, each one being endowed with his or her own rich life of family, community, personal achievements, intelligence, culture, personality, soul, and spiritual life (Narayan, 128).

"Speaking animals appear in some of the most ancient texts of India, going back to the early first millennium BCE" (Olivelle, xi). Each anymal in the *Pancatantra* is endowed with personality (both good and bad), personal interest, desires, and inclinations to be just or unjust.

In the *Pancatantra*, any species can play the role of sage or villain for the purpose of teaching a moral lesson; anymals are treated as equal individuals in the vast and varied community of life. In the hunting story mentioned previously, a crow, pigeon, mouse, tortoise, and deer become fast friends through a host of engaging occurrences. In this same story, we learn that Deer was rescued in his youth by a "noble" man from "thoughtless people" who beat him because he spoke to human beings. The noble man, by way of calming violent humans, notes that "all species of animals…do indeed speak, but not in front of people" (Olivelle, 99). Anymals in Hindu myth are endowed with individuality, with the same range of abilities and tendencies familiar to humans, and they speak for themselves, clearly stating that they wish to remain alive and free, just as people wish to remain alive and free.

For those who are good to anymals, nonhumans often prove to be powerful allies. In the *Mahabharata*, a captured swan pleads, "Do not hurt me. Let me go" (Buck, *Mahabharata*, 120). The swan promises to help his captor in exchange for release, and the swan is as good as his word, helping the man to achieve that which he could never have achieved without the help of the swan (Buck, *Mahabharata*, 120–22).

Anymal soldiers are critical to Rama's success in the great battle that lies at the center of the *Ramayana*, which features Rama, an incarnation of the primary deity Vishnu. One day Rama is wandering the forest with his brothers in search of his wife, Sita, who has been abducted by the evil demon Ravana. Of course, there are many anymals in the forests. A tiny fawn informs Rama that Sita has been taken, sending the hero in hot pursuit of a wife-napper (Buck, *Mahabharata*, 176–77). Indeed, the demon Ravana has made off with Sita, and an eagle named Jatayu "nobly" fights to protect Rama's wife from the evil abductor. In the process, Jatayu loses his life (Narayan, 128), but by an "effort of will" he stays alive long enough to tell Rama what has happened (Narayan, 95). Jatayu's older brother, also a gigantic and noble bird, later joins the search and the battle to conquer the evil perpetrator, Ravana, and recover Sita (Narayan, 129).

During their prolonged journey to locate and rescue Sita, the heroes meet and conspire with forest communities. Rama's army is composed almost exclusively of bears and monkeys, who voluntarily and eagerly sign on to work with Rama on the side of the good. Aside from their service as brave and worthy warriors, the bears and monkeys do most of the work to build a bridge to the island where Rama's abducted wife is held hostage. Bears and monkeys then storm the demon fortress, and a great battle ensues, culminating in the rescue of Sita. Bears and monkeys are critical to Rama's success.

In a very popular English translation, Jambavan, the leader of the bear contingent, is described as "full of knowledge and wisdom" (Narayan, 98). But it is monkeys who shine most through the pages of the *Ramayana*. In this Indian epic, monkeys "have the power of speech and their intelligence is equal to that of humans" (Basham, 80). These clever and capable anymal warriors are described as "beings endowed with extraordinary intelligence, speech, immeasurable strength and nobility" who stem from "godly parentage" (Narayan, 98).

Hanuman, one of the most famous from among many anymals featured in Hindu writings, is central to the *Ramayana*. On meeting Hanuman, the general of the monkey army, Rama feels an "instinctive compassion" for this monkey and his community (*Ramayana*, 99). Later, as the battle draws near, Rama says to Hanuman, "Were I to lose any of you, then without you my life would be empty and worthless" (Buck, *Ramayana*, 315).

Hanuman also makes a noteworthy appearance in the other key Hindu religious epic, the *Mahabharata*. When the heroes, the Pandavas (five brothers), are wandering the forests, the mightiest of the brothers, Bhima, stumbles upon a monkey lying in the trail. Hanuman, who is both a monkey devoted to the gods and a god himself, slips into trickster mode and decides to teach at least one careless, bumbling human being how to behave respectfully toward other creatures. (It just so happens that the man he will teach is a brave, mighty, holy, and much-honored son of a powerful deity.) Note the trickster monkey's sarcasm, intelligence, and power as he speaks to Bhima in this lively retelling of the *Mahabharata*:

> "Out of my way monkey!" cried Bhima. "Get away!"
>
> The monkey only opened his sleepy red eyes a little and shut them again.
>
> "Go away and let me by!" said Bhima.
>
> The monkey looked at him for awhile, licked his sharp white teeth with his coppery tongue, and said, "I am ill, and was resting peacefully. We animals are ignorant, but why have you no better manners? And what is a dunce like you doing here anyway?"
>
> Bhima frowned and bit his lip. "Then who are you in the shape of a monkey?" he asked.
>
> "Why you simpleton, I am a monkey! Can't you see well? Please, go on home and learn to be a gentleman."
>
> "You're in my way," said Bhima, "so move."
>
> "Ah, great hero," sighed the monkey, "I am too sick to get up. I haven't even the strength to crawl away. It takes all my energy just to breathe. The unearthly honor of talking to you will probably kill me." (Buck, Mahabharata, 157)

After disobeying and insulting the mighty Bhima, the mouthy little monkey invites Bhima to simply move his tail for him, since he is ill:

> Bhima caught the monkey's tail in his left hand to push it away, but it would not move. He grabbed it with both hands and pulled and strained and rolled his eyes till he was exhausted. But for his life Bhima could not move that monkey's tail even the width of a barley corn. (Buck, Mahabharata, 159)

Score one for the little guy. Bhima, son of the wind-god, shares the strength of the deities—yet he cannot move Hanuman's tail. Bhima soon surmises that the ordinary-looking monkey is none other than Hanuman, a God who stands above the great Pandavas (mere mortals), and belatedly greets him with due respect.

Such stories remind Hindus that the divine sometimes appears as an anymal, and that sometimes an anymal *is* divine. Hindus are thereby reminded that it is best to make a habit of treating each individual anymal with respect—even if you are the mighty Bhima, son of the god of the wind.

Kinship and Community

> To this day in the Indian imagination there is a unique sympathy with
> animal expression. Man or boy, gentle and simple alike, telling some
> story of mouse or squirrel, will bring the tale to a climax with the very
> cries and movements of the creature he has watched. It is assumed
> instinctively that at least the fundamental feelings, if not the thoughts, of
> furred and feathered folk are even as our own. And it is here, surely in
> this swift interpretation, in this deep ignition of kinship, that we find the
> real traces of temper that went into the making long ago of... the gentle
> faiths. (Coomaraswamy, 14)

Hindu readers think nothing of a swan or spotted deer living in an organized society,
complete with nuclear family units and community rulers. Hindu texts recognize
anymals as part of the larger community of beings, and as part of one moral
universe.

Pancatantra stories often entail interspecies communities. In the chapter on
interspecies friendship mentioned previously, the anymals weather trials and tribulations, share personal histories, and rescue one another from hardship. True to core
Hindu teachings, "humans and others share the world equally in the *Pancatantra*,
and they are all governed by the same natural laws" (Rukmani, 107).

The *Ramayana* provides an excellent example of interspecies kinship and
community. Anymals are willing soldiers in Rama's interspecies army, fighting
on the side of the good alongside humanity; only hybrid monstrosities fight on
the side of evil (Narayan, 98). Rama respects his kindred soldiers, and is
concerned about their safety and welfare as they all approach a massive battle on
behalf of Rama and his wife. As the battle of the *Ramayana* draws near, Rama
urges the anymals to go home safely to their villages, not to fight the great war of
Lanka. Hanuman's response to Rama, however, shows both his loyalty and his
wisdom—he understands reincarnation and the deeper unity that underlies all
living beings:

> Dear Rama, we are indeed your old good friends from long ago, and your
> companions of ancient days come here to help you. We are your forefa-
> thers. We are your ancestors the animals, and you are our child, Man. As
> for our friendship, why we've known you a long long time, Rama, and the
> number of those days is lost in Silence. (Buck, 315)

As stated by Hanuman, reincarnation fosters an understanding of all species—
every individual of every species—as kin (Kinsley, *Ecology*, 64). In the Indian religious traditions, the ties that bind animals are ancient and deep, and Hanuman
intends to stand by his brother, Rama, to the bitter end.

Interpenetrability

Hanuman is a god who is also a monkey, and when it suits him, he takes the form of a cat to find Sita. No clear line divides human beings, gods, and anymals in the Hindu worldview; many characters are a mix of all three (Buck, *Mahabharata*, xix). Gods and goddesses can *be* anymals, or take any form they choose. Indeed, Shiva might take the form of

> men and women, … aquatic animals, … tortoises and fishes and conchs. …
> Indeed, the illustrious god assumes the forms of all creatures too that live
> in holes. He assumes the forms of tigers and lions and deer, of wolves and
> bears and birds, fowls and of jackals as well. He it is that assumes the forms
> of swans and crows and peacocks, of chameleons and lizards and storks.
> (Embree, *Hindu*, 235)

A story from the *Mahabharata* also provides an excellent example of species interpenetrability. A hunting and foolhardy king, angry that a deer escaped him, mindlessly strikes out to vent his fury, and mortally wounds "a serpent who meant him no harm" (Buck, *Mahabharata*, 11). The snake curses the king "for his cruelty," vowing that the ruler will be bitten by a snake, and die, within seven days. Though the king tries to secure his safety, the serpent morphs into a beetle, gains access to the king in his elevated hut, changes back into a snake, and then bites the terrified king.

As the story continues, the king's son seeks revenge against the *naga* who has now killed his father. He must use strong magic, because *nagas* are notoriously powerful. Fortuitously, a man arrives on the scene who is half *naga*. The newcomer willingly tells the king's son where he can find the offending serpent. For his assistance he is granted one wish, and of course he asks that the life of the *naga* be spared.

This short story includes a snake who becomes a beetle then returns to snake form, a man who is half serpent, a king who is cursed by a powerful naga, and a prince who is duped by a man-snake. ("A dog is a pig is a rat is a boy.") The story ends by encouraging snakes and people to live in peace with one another: "Have no fear of any serpent but think—*Serpents of good fortune, live in peace here with our dear ones*" (Buck, *Mahabharata*, 14). (For an interesting comparison, see Genesis 3:14–15.)

In another story told in the *Mahabharata*, a red deer gives birth to a boy who is half human and half deer. A holy man raises the mixed-species offspring in the forest, as an ascetic. When a great drought comes to the area, the king learns that only "a man with a pure heart" can bring rain (Buck, *Mahabharata*, 145). Purity is extremely important in Hindu religious traditions, and one who is half human and half deer is considered to be spiritually elevated above human beings—more pure and more spiritually powerful—especially when living in the forest as an ascetic. A few villagers had glimpsed the deer-man, and they surmised that he was "as innocent as a deer" (Buck, *Mahabharata*, 145). The deer-man is ultimately lured into the city by the king's daughter, bringing rains. He soon marries the king's daughter but chooses not to remain entirely civilized: He commutes between the world of his father and the forest and wild anymals, and the world of his wife and civilization.

Vishnu's Incarnations

Vishnu is reborn as the much-loved heroes Rama and Krishna, of the two great epics the *Ramayana* and the *Mahabharata*, and also as a fish, tortoise, boar, and man-lion (Danielou, 165). Each life is assumed by Vishnu for the purpose of restoring the balance of good over evil. Vishnu's incarnations not only demonstrate interpenetrability, but also stand as further examples of interesting divine-anymal relations.

Vishnu's incarnation as a fish, in which he saves many from the great flood, is explained in the *Matsya Purana* (the oldest of the post-Vedic texts, the *Puranas*, which record history, cosmology, and Hindu philosophy). In this story, Vishnu identifies a man who is worth saving (from the upcoming deluge) based on his compassion: On hearing of the great and inevitable flood, the man's only wish is to "be able to protect the multitude of all beings, moving and still" (O'Flaherty, *Hindu*, 182).

Because Vishnu has seen the man's goodness, Vishnu places a tiny fish in front of him while he is performing oblations. The man perceives the little swimmer's vulnerability and protects the fish in a small container, which the fish quickly outgrows. The fish then cries, "Save me! Save me! I have come to you for refuge!" (O'Flaherty, *Hindu*, 182). The man moves the fish from one container to another, until this Vishnu-fish becomes so gigantic that he must be turned loose in the sea. The god-fish (as opposed to, say, a codfish) then returns the favor, saving humanity from the great flood by telling the man how to build a large boat. When the flood comes, the fish pulls the man and his boat over the waters to safety. In this flood story, Vishnu (in the form of a fish) affirms a devout man's worthiness by witnessing his compassion for all living beings (O'Flaherty, *Hindu*, 182).

As a tortoise, Vishnu helps the gods to churn the ocean in order to obtain the nectar of immortality, with which they defeat demons and restore order to the universe (Embree, *Hindu*, 210). The cosmic snake also helps to obtain the nectar, allowing his long body to be used as a rope for agitating the land mass and thereby churning the ocean (O'Flaherty, *Hindu*, 275). As a result, precious anymals emerge from the churning waters, including a wish-cow, the divine horse, and an elephant—all of whom become important in the ongoing unfolding Hindu mythology and the Hindu universe (Danielou, 167).

In his incarnation as a boar, Vishnu again saves the world from a flood in a story that includes salvation from a flood and creation. He dives to the depths of the ocean to lift up the world, which has sunk under the seas (Danielou, 168). He then proceeds to flatten the earth and shape the mountains and continents, working as the world's "architect" (Danielou, 168).

Vishnu's incarnation as the man-lion provides a particularly excellent example of interpenetrability. In this story, a pious boy is persecuted by his powerful and cruel father. The evil father has received a boon from the gods so that he cannot "be killed by day or by night, by god, man, or beast, inside or outside his palace" (Danielou, 169). Vishnu is determined to rescue the boy, and so he arrives "at twilight (neither day nor night) as a lion-headed man (neither man nor beast)" among the pillars on the porch (neither inside nor outside the palace) (Danielou, 169). Vishnu, in the form of the man-lion—at once god and anymal, man and beast—saves the world from an overbearing evil demon by ripping out the evil father's guts.

Ganesha

Ganesha (son of Shiva/Parvati) has a short, squat body, a potbelly protruding beneath his four arms, and an elephant's head, complete with a broken tusk (Danielou, 293). While still young, Ganesha's head is severed by his fierce and powerful father, Shiva, in a case of mistaken identity (though there is, of course, more than one explanation). In order to bring the boy back to life, an elephant's head is secured to replace the original head (Embree, *Sources*, 330). And so Ganesha has an elephant's head atop his human frame. Neither Indian mythology nor contemporary Hindus envision Ganesha's unusual head as ghastly or problematic. Instead, his elephant head is understood to be "auspicious" (Embree, *Sources*, 329). Elephant-headed Ganesha is "gentle, calm, and friendly" (Coomaraswamy, 18), and he is extremely popular: "Not only is he worshiped at the beginning of every enterprise, his image is seen at the entrance of every house, of every sanctuary" (Danielou, 293). In the Indian vision of interspecies communities and interpenetrability, the boy-elephant-god, Ganesha, is not the least bit unusual.

Anymal Powers

Commenting on anymal powers in Hindu stories, a contemporary Indian writer wonders, "Who could tell what was the store of wisdom garnered behind the little old face of the grey ape out of the forest, or hoarded by the coiled snake in her hole beside the tree?" (Coomaraswamy, 16). Hindu compilations such as the *Ramayana*, *Mahabharata*, and *Pancatantra* include anymals that preach and teach, have special knowledge and powers, and are indispensable to the workings of both humanity and divinities. Indeed, with such powerful anymal characters as Hanuman, and with great Gods such as Vishnu incarnate in anymal form, the powers of anymals are unlimited.

Common, everyday anymals are often honored in Hindu stories as spiritual exemplars, as wise and pure. In the *Mahabharata*, Arjuna (one of the Padavas) visits the God of Wealth in "a castle of gold and crystal" where he finds "huge high walls of jewels and watery pearls...; and soaring towers and turrets of silver and ivory, with clear windows of diamond sheets and sharp roofs of turquoise and lapis lazuli...; and the gardens of flowers and trees outside the wall, where uncut piles of gems slept in the shade" (Buck, *Mahabharata*, 161). The God of Wealth assumes that this visitor, seeing such an opulent palace, will be smitten with greed, and will attempt to steal, so he prepares to kill Arjuna. But before he can strike, Arjuna reminds the weapon-wielding Treasure Lord, "All these things you have are overlooked by the birds and dismissed by the animals" (Buck, *Mahabharata*, 163). Anymals are not driven by greed for material wealth, and they stand as an excellent example of the simple life. Arjuna reminds the God of Wealth that anymals are excellent models by which we might live. Seeing that Arjuna understands and incorporates the lesson against material greed exemplified by the birds and beasts, his life is spared.

Nagas are always powerful; when a *naga* sinks fangs, he or she generally does so with reason and conviction. In the *Mahabharata*, for example, a *naga* bites a man for the "victim's" own good. The serpent's poison twists and deforms the man so that his pursuers cannot recognize him. This helpful *naga* even provides two pieces of silk and instructs the man as to how these might be used to regain his original appearance when the coast is clear (Buck, *Mahabharata*, 131).

Hanuman has extraordinary powers. He is not only a great and noble warrior, but also an individual of deep insight, tremendous physical power, and superhuman loyalty. When Rama's search party enters the monkeys' village, Hanuman alone recognizes Vishnu in the form of Rama (Narayan, 99). From the start, he feels an inseparable connection with Rama—with God. Hanuman is also able to detect goodness in human beings, even when humans themselves are unable to do so. When a soldier from Ravana's army defects, Hanuman alone perceives that the warrior is sincere and trustworthy. Thanks to Hanuman's insight, this "traitor to evil" becomes the new king of Lanka when the great battle is over.

Pancatantra

The purpose of the *Pancatantra* is to offer moral advice; instruction contained in the *Pancatantra* "is carried out by animals and the teaching is all about good or wise conduct" (Rukmani, 106). Characters in the *Pancatantra* include an array of species, such as crocodiles, owls, monkeys, bulls, fish, pigeons, snakes, mongooses, frogs, sparrows, tigers, jackals, cranes, crows, crabs, biting insects, cats, and many more. These anymals teach principles of good government and public policy, as well as critical values and morals, like simplicity, compassion, and respect for life.

In a story that speaks against covetous greed, a pigeon explains how a passerby ventured to take a golden bangle from a cunning tiger. The tiger waxed eloquent about his religious observances and his consequent benevolent nature. The covetous traveler decided to trust the tiger in order to gain the bangle. Needless to say, he became the tiger's dinner, and the golden bangle remained a lure for the next wayfarer who might be greedy enough to risk life and limb for material gain (Embree, *Hindu*, 177–78). In this story a pigeon stands as sage, warning readers and listeners alike against covetous greed.

Wise anymals in the *Pancatantra* teach human children that they must not exploit or harm other creatures. At different times, each character exemplifies foolishness or wisdom and compassion. For instance, in the chapter on friendship mentioned earlier, though Mouse saves Tortoise, his failings emerge earlier in the tale. When Mouse loses his wealth, and concurrently his followers and fortune, Crow benevolently carries his needy friend to safety. Thus Mouse learns that wealth is easily lost, while other aspects of existence, such as friendship, are more enduring and are therefore more worthy of pursuit.

Jain Philosophy and Morality

The world harbors only 4.2 million Jains, most of whom are Indian and live in India (Long, 13). Though their members are few in number, Jain religious traditions are of particular importance with regard to religiously sanctioned human-anymal relations. Jain religious traditions emerged from Vedic/Hindu religious traditions during the Upanishadic era, in the sixth century. Jains (like Buddhists) are deeply indebted to the earlier Indian beliefs and practices for such concepts as reincarnation, karma, and *ahimsa*.

Ahimsa in Jain traditions, as in Hindu (and Buddhist) traditions, requires "compassion for all living beings" (Long, 99). "*Ahimsa* is the central ethical principle of Jainism, embodied in the often-quoted statement *ahimsa paramo dharmah*—ahimsa is the highest duty"; the "centrality of *ahimsa* to Jainism is difficult to exaggerate" (Long, 99).

The Jain *Acaranga Sutra* acknowledges that "to all beings life is dear" and no being would prefer to be harmed or killed (Embree, *Sources*, 68). To practice ahimsa in Jain traditions is therefore "to wish to harm no living thing, either deliberately (which of course produces the worst karmic effects) or even through one's carelessness (which, though not as bad as intentional violence, is still regarded in Jainism as carrying a negative karmic affect)" (Long, 97).

In light of karma and reincarnation, "thoughts, words, and deeds that are harmful or that intend harm toward other beings will inevitably" have an undesirable affect (Long, 107). The *Acaranga Sutra* states this simply: "To do harm to others is to do harm to self" (1.5.5 in Long, 107); whether by snaring a bird or caging a sow, we enslave ourselves if we enslave others:

> Those who snare and keep encaged the partridge or the quail,
> Which dwell in the wilds where beetles hum around the flowers,

> Shall [in a later life] till black and hungry soil,
> Their legs in fetters, as slaves to alien lords. (Embree, *Sources*, 73)

Similarly, the *Sutrakrtanga* teaches that we should be cognizant of the innate similarities shared by all living beings, and behave accordingly. To do otherwise is to invite misery.

> Know that they all seek happiness.
> In hurting them men hurt themselves,
> And will be born again among them. (Embree, *Sources*, 63)

Some might argue that karma turns ahimsa into a selfish act, but as noted before, from an anymal's point of view, it matters little why freedom is granted, why their life is spared, so long as it *is* spared and freedom granted.

In the Jain worldview, acts of violence carry the worst karmic affects (Long, 99). Jains tend to avoid overt acts of violence, including work that requires violence and products that are linked with harm to other beings. Consequently, Jains are highly unlikely to choose occupations such as breeding anymals for agricultural purposes or selling anymal products (Dundas, 163).

For Jains, investing in anymal products is *himsa*—violence, or harm. It is also ignorance: "An ignorant man kills...and eats meat, thinking that this is the right thing to do" (Jacobi, "Fifth"). Basic restraint requires that "the Jaina must never partake of meat" (Jaini, 167). Eating flesh is *himsa*—entails the taking of life—and the Jain "taboo against eating animal flesh is enforced more strongly in the Jaina community than in any other" (Jaini, 168). This rule is for all Jains, not only monks—"under no circumstances may [laity] take meat" (Jaini, 168). This commitment to nonviolence does not permit hunting, even among kings. The *Uttarâdhyayana Sutras* tell the story of a king who enjoys the hunt, kills a deer, and nearly kills a monk in the process. He immediately feels the horror of killing more generally, and bows before the monk, seeking forgiveness. The monk satisfies the king's request for forgiveness, instructs the king to "grant safety to others also; in this transient world of living beings," and asks the hunter outright, "Why are you addicted to cruelty?" (Jacobi, "Eighteenth"). In the Jaina tradition, "one should not permit (or consent to) the killing of living beings" (Jacobi, "Eighth").

Jain compassion reaches beyond diet to touch every aspect of their lives. Some Jains walk with whisk brooms to brush away insects who might otherwise inadvertently be crushed underfoot, and they wear face masks to avoid inadvertently inhaling insects or microorganisms—"a practice of nonviolence so radical as to defy easy comprehension" among many Westerners (Long, 3). Despite these compassionate measures, at the end of their yearly calendar, Jains ask forgiveness for any harms they might have done, whether to human or nonhuman, whether purposefully or inadvertently (Embree, *Sources*, 56–57).

In the *Uttarâdhyayana Sutra*, when the crown prince, Balasrî, decides to become a monk, his royal parents question his ability to survive the ordeals that are inherent in the life of a monk. In response, he reveals Jain links to the larger Hindu tradition as he reflects on past lives:

> An infinite number of times have I suffered hopelessly from mallets and knives, forks and maces, which broke my limbs. (61)
>
> Ever so many times have I been slit, cut, mangled, and skinned with keen-edged razors, knives, and shears. (62)
>
> As an antelope I have, against my will, been caught, bound, and fastened in snares and traps, and frequently I have been killed. (63)
>
> As a fish I have, against my will, been caught with hooks and in bow-nets; I have therein been scraped, slit, and killed an infinite number of times. (64)
>
> As a bird I have been caught by hawks, trapped in nets, and bound with bird-lime, and I have been killed an infinite number of times.... (65)
>
> Always frightened, trembling, distressed, and suffering, I have experienced the most exquisite pain and misery.... (71)
>
> In every kind of existence I have undergone suffering which was not interrupted by a moment's reprieve. (74) (Jacobi, "Nineteenth")

In this world of pervasive suffering, Jains are called to provide "refuge for injured creatures, like an island that the waters cannot overwhelm" (Embree, *Sources*, 71). Jain population centers across India create and support *panjorapors*, sanctuaries where stray anymals (birds, camels, water buffalo, and cows) are "cared for, loved, and visited at least once a week by veterinarians" (Tobias).

Though a comparatively small religion in number of adherents, Jain religious traditions have had considerable influence. It was Jain "ideals of truth and nonviolence that, in the hands of Gandhi, were transformed into powerful tools for bringing about social justice" (Long, 182), and some would argue that Jains "contributed much to the eventual triumph of vegetarianism" throughout India (Jaini, 169).

Hindu Traditions and Anymal Liberation

Core Hindu teachings have created a civilization naturally inclined to anymal liberation. The first Westerners in India marveled at the degree to which Hindu spiritual teachings were realized in daily life (Jacobsen, 288). One surprised and frustrated imperialist, intent on using pesticides to kill insects, noted that "killing is anathema for Hindus," that, by nature,

> [the Hindu] agriculturist is generous, wanting to bestow on others what he reaps out of Mother Earth. He [*sic*] does not think that he alone should

enjoy the fruits of his labor... to kill those unseen and unknown lives... is foreign to his nature.... It takes some time for [Hindus]... to get acclimatized to the very conception of killing tiny helpless and unarmed creatures. (Curtin, "Making Peace," 71, from *Journal of the Indian Pesticide Industry*)

As a more recent visitor, I was similarly surprised by life-affirming practices in central India. My sister and I were walking through a temple complex, where we paused to watch two men pick up a cobra from the sidewalk, with a stick and a small bucket, determined to transport the snake to a safer location. Their methods were simple, yet their deft handling of this deadly poisonous snake—without any evidence of alarm or distaste—testified to centuries of peaceful snake relocation.

Hindu religious traditions teach followers to avoid occupations that harm anymals, to avoid eating flesh, and to speak out against anymal exploitation. The *Manu Smriti*, a critical and foundational Hindu text, rejects occupations in agriculture because they cause "injury to many beings" (Embree, *Hindu*, 94). In the Hindu traditions, there is "a profound opposition... to the institutionalized breeding and killing of animals, [including] birds and fish for human consumption.... [Such] abuse and exploitation of nature for selfish gain is considered unjust and sacrilegious" (Dwivedi, 6). The *Mahabharata* expects yet more of Hindus: "He who never eats meat but assents to it/is considered as having killed and is stained with fault" (Chapple, "Ahimsa," 119). It is not enough to choose a vegan diet for oneself; a Hindu ought to *speak out* to prevent others from harming anymals, including harm caused by eating anymal products.

Mohandas K. Gandhi (most often called Mahatma Gandhi), a devout Hindu, offered wisdom that aligns with anymal liberation, and has proven to be of great interest to many anymal liberationists. For Gandhi, spiritual life and truth entailed *ahimsa*, and he could not "intentionally hurt anything" (Gandhi, *Essential*, 225). Gandhi felt "an instinctive horror of killing living beings under any circumstances whatever" and taught that every human, bird, and beast "has an equal right to the necessaries of life" (Gandhi, *Essential*, 187, 247); he "respected the rights of all creatures to fulfill their lives" (Kinsley, *Ecology*, 65). He understood this core Hindu requirement as active, rigorous, and demanding (Easwaran, 53). He knew that how we live—what we *do*—is the best indicator of our morality, and of our religious convictions: "The act will speak unerringly" (Desai, 111–12).

Gandhi understood nonviolence to be "an extremely active force" (Easwaran, 87). In his autobiography, he states that "those who say that religion has nothing to do with politics do not know what religion means" (Gandhi, *Autobiography*, 504). He explains why he spent his adult life struggling against cruelty and injustice: "My soul refuses to be satisfied so long as it is a helpless witness of a single wrong or a single misery" (Gandhi, *Essential*, 271). As a Hindu, he noted that "all embodied life is in reality an incarnation of God" (Roberts, 30), and so, when faced with injustice, Gandhi felt that "patience... is not a virtue. It [ought to be] impossible to restrain ourselves. Patience with evil is really trifling with evil and with ourselves" (Gandhi, *Essential*, 219). Yet Gandhi redirected the anger that was stirred in him by injustice, and was thereby able to transform this negative energy "into a power which [could] move the world" (Easwaran, 74). Advocacy, to be effective, must be well planned and well executed.

Gandhi recognized civil disobedience as "the inherent right of a citizen.... [T]o put down civil disobedience is to attempt to imprison conscience" (Easwaran, 43). He exhibited unwavering diligence in the cause of social and political change to end oppression and exploitation. *Ahimsa* required Gandhi to break laws and challenge the highest political authorities. His understanding of *ahimsa* left "no room for cowardice or even weakness"; Gandhi felt that there was "hope for a violent man to be some day nonviolent, but there [was no hope] for a coward" (Easwaran, 87). Gandhi believed that a "nonviolent person will lay down his life" in the cause of justice, to prevent the powerful from harming the weak (Easwaran, 91). "Where there is a choice only between cowardice and violence," Gandhi said, "I would advise violence" (Gandhi, *Essential*, 137). He understood that abuse and injustice cannot persist without our cooperation, and he encouraged people to die opposing unjust laws and practices rather than tolerate injustice (Easwaran, 49, 43). "He who is a passive spectator of a crime," Gandhi noted, "is really, and in law, an active participator" (Gandhi, *Essential*, 220).

Though arrested numerous times, Gandhi was granted only one trial, and he seized this opportunity to highlight the injustices of the British government. In front of the audience provided by the spectacle of court, Gandhi noted that disobedience to injustice is "the highest duty of a citizen" (Easwaran, 62). Indeed, Gandhi "was at his very best when being persecuted" (Easwaran, 71). He challenged the judge—and all who were present—to find him guilty and punish him to the fullest extent of the law. But, he argued, if they could not find him guilty, they must join him in his struggle against injustice (Easwaran, 62). Small wonder he was never granted another trial in his long battle against Britain, though Gandhi courted prison sentences. He felt it was "wrong to be free under a government [that is] wholly bad....A Government that is evil has no room for good men and women except in its prisons" (Gandhi, *Essential*, 153–54).

Gandhi learned and taught that reformers generally work best alone, even though they often must work in the face of criticism and persecution, and that activists must persevere despite difficult challenges and setbacks:

> They cannot—must not—lose faith in themselves or in their mission because they may be in a minority. Indeed, all reform has been brought about by the actions of minorities in all countries and under all climes. Majorities simply follow minorities. (Gandhi, *Essential*, 82)

"Strength of numbers," Gandhi wrote, "is the delight of the timid. The valiant in spirit glory in fighting alone" (Easwaran, 92). Gandhi exemplified and encouraged unrelenting activism against the powerful to liberate the oppressed.

Dharmesh Solanki is a contemporary Hindu Vaishnavite, and a vegan. He grew up eating some flesh, but his grandmother was a more traditional Hindu, and therefore avoided both eggs and flesh. As Solanki became more religious, he realized that he must change his diet. In 1992, he gave up flesh, and in 1995, he made two more important changes: "I joined a one-week animal welfare officer's course organized by Bombay SPCA....And I joined the International Society for Krishna Consciousness (ISKCON)" (D. Solanki, pers. comm., December 21, 2008). The first change committed Solanki to anymal activism, while the second committed him to Hindu faith and practice. They fit well together, and transformed his life.

When Solanki began putting his faith into practice, he volunteered full time with Bombay SPCA and AHIMSA (an anymal advocacy group in Mumbai), worked with a website portal for anymals and served as managing trustee of People for Animals in Mumbai. Solanki was soon rescuing anymals, finding loving homes for needy dogs, filing cruelty complaints, organizing meetings and activities on behalf of anymals, functioning as group secretary, and taking on the difficult but essential tasks of fund-raising and filing income tax returns.

Solanki joined the staff of the Indian branch of People for the Ethical Treatment of Animals (PETA-India) in 2004 and was soon committed to a plant-based diet and lifestyle. Solanki was assigned to work with the Mumbai Zoo Project for two years before becoming PETA-India's senior vivisection campaign coordinator, where he was challenged to organize two Indian tours for the Physicians Committee for Responsible Medicine (PCRM) (2007 and 2008).

Solanki is also a voluntary member of the Committee for the Purpose of Control and Supervision of Experiments on Animals (CPCSEA) with India's Ministry of Environment and Forest. As a volunteer for CPCSEA, Solanki provided oversight for anymal research at Wockhardt Research Lab in Aurangabad, Lupin Laboratories and Bio-Ved Pharmaceuticals in Pune, and Reliance Life Sciences in Mumbai. He also initiates discourse on the topic of anymal experimentation with large labs in Mumbai (including Haffkine Bio-pharmaceutical Corporation Ltd., Haffkine Institute, Bombay Veterinary College, Nicholas Piramal India, Bombay College of Pharmacy, University Institute of Chemical Technology, Ethicon Institute of Surgical Education, and Bharat Serum & Vaccines Ltd. in Thane).

As a volunteer for CPCSEA, Solanki also joined a three-member team of experts to inspect laboratories in Maharashtra. He created the first photo album exposing the conditions of anymals who are trapped in and exploited by India's labs, and organized workshops on alternative methods of research for teachers and students on behalf of InterNICHE, WSPA, and People for Animals. He also helps train interested newcomers who are willing to provide oversight for anymal research in India. He continues to attend trainings in order to increase his effectiveness as an advocate for anymals who are trapped in research/pharmaceutical industries, even trainings set up by researchers themselves.

Solanki has taken to the streets on behalf of anymals. Outside the Ministry of Health and Family Welfare in New Delhi, Solanki demanded a ban on cosmetics testing on anymals. He organized street plays and student awareness programs, conducted raids to rescue anymals, organized demonstrations and flood relief camps for anymals, conducted surveys on anymal sacrifice at Karla Caves and Jivdani Temple, and directly rescued bears from street performers. Solanki continues to compile information, write letters, and demonstrate and lobby on behalf of anymals, with the ultimate goal of anymal liberation.

Solanki has even engaged in direct rescue on behalf of anymals who are exploited for science and product testing. He saved four dogs, thirteen pigeons, thirty hens, and ninety quails from Jai Research Foundation in Gujarat; fourteen dogs from Bombay Veterinary College in Mumbai; thirty-seven monkeys from National Institute of Virology; and ten horses from Haffkine Bio-pharmaceutical Corporation in Pune. He also helped to rescue nineteen monkeys from the National Institute of Research in Reproductive Health (NIRRH) in Mumbai, and he assisted Maharashtra Forest Department in rescuing two more monkeys who were illegally captured and imprisoned for experiments at NIRRH. Solanki even interfered with an illegal antivenom operation at Haffkine Bio-pharmaceutical Corporation, thereby securing the wild release of every single snake. For good measure, he helped close down this same corrupt lab's sheep brain antirabies vaccine production.

Finally, as coconvenor of the Committee for Preventing Cruelty and Illegal Trade of Birds and Animals (CPCITBA), an organization formed by the order of Honourable High Court of Bombay to combat the illegal exploitation of India's wildlife, Solanki has raided several pet shops, railway stations, and traffic joints to rescue birds and other anymals who had been illegally obtained or sold.

Solanki's Hindu philosophy and practice provides him with the commitment and strength necessary to face the horrors of anymal abuse and exploitation in laboratories, and on and around the streets of India. He comments, "When I started working for animals, I progressed rapidly in my Hindu devotional path" (D. Solanki, pers. comm., December 21, 2008).

Anuradha Sawhney is also a firm vegan, a Hindu, and an anymal activist. She was placed in charge of the Indian branch of People for the Ethical Treatment of Animals (PETA-India) in 2000; her work keeps her on call twenty-four hours a day, seven days a week. "This is not just a job, but a calling. I love animals, and now I fight for animals; I make a difference in their lives. Actually, my work is more than a profession; it is a fight for justice" (Sawhney, 154). Sawhney explains what motivates her to continue this difficult work:

> My heart cries out when I see an animal suffering. Abhorrence of injustice drives me. I hate knowing that, just because an animal is unable to

stand up for him or herself, human beings take advantage and cause harm. Have you ever looked into the eyes of a bull pulling a loaded cart all day long without rest? Have you looked into the eyes of a horse left to stand in the monsoon rain and tropical sun alike? Have you looked into the eyes of a dog who has been beaten by his human? Their incomprehension—their pain—drives me, makes me work harder in search of justice. (Sawhney, 157)

As a Hindu, Sawhney understands that each anymal has a soul, that each anymal is unique and precious, that each anymal *is* divine. She writes that anymals "are loyal, affectionate, inquisitive, playful—and more often than not they are taken for granted, as if they were created specifically for our enjoyment, to cater to our selfish whims" (Sawhney, 157).

Sawhney rescues bears and tigers from India's street entertainers. These unhappy individuals can never be returned to the wild but must be housed in sanctuaries. Their teeth have been removed, and of course they can never again live free in the wild without their teeth. Additionally, a hole large enough for a rope has been burned through their noses, allowing the street entertainers to control these understandably unwilling bears. No painkillers are used for breaking teeth or burning holes (Sawhney, 155).

Exploiting and damaging bears and tigers for entertainment is illegal in India. When Sawhney receives information on where to find misused bears, she must move quickly and carefully, coordinating her actions with officers of the law. She notifies appropriate authorities, then uses her years of experience and boundless determination to deftly snatch the bears while police arrest the offenders. Once rescued, are placed the bears in sanctuaries, where they live free of ropes—free from human contrivance—for the rest of their lives. PETA-India, under Sawhney's leadership, has rescued twelve bears and has helped to rescue over fifty-three tigers and lions (Sawhney, 155).

Sawhney also rescues cattle and chickens from India's factory farms. She notes that few people eat meat in India, but dairy consumption is common. In fact, after learning about the realities of the dairy industry, she became an anymal advocate:

I was unaware of the cruelty prevalent in the dairy industry. Through PETA, I learned how the dairy industry treats cows and their calves. Cattle, once revered partners in Hindu culture—part of our spirituality and considered part of our families—now endure dreadful lives and miserable deaths [in the dairy industry]. (Sawhney, 156)

Sawhney had no idea that yogurt, milk, and cheese were linked with such intense misery for these gentle and revered creatures—that consuming these products perpetuated and supported industries rooted in exploitation and anymal suffering. She notes that "going vegan was probably the best decision of my life" (Sawhney, 155).

Sawhney's compassion for anymals is rooted in her religious upbringing and her spiritual outlook:

> Our religion advocates compassion. Ahimsa teaches us not to harm others—any others. If people would only stop to think that animals are more like us than [not], more of us would extend our empathy to animals. We would speak out when animals are treated unkindly. Many Hindu Gods are animals. For example, Hanuman has the physical form of a monkey, and Ganesh has the head of an elephant. Hinduism advocates ahimsa, or nonviolence. Mahatma Gandhi showed the political power of ahimsa, how ahimsa can change our world, using this principle to force British imperialists to leave India.
>
> I have always believed that spirituality requires compassion; helping those who cannot help themselves forces us to find the courage to speak up. I believe that if I love my work and help another soul, I am living out good karma. I believe that every action in my life has taken me to this point, where I stand today. I have wound through many different avenues to get here, but I am finally doing what I love most, and I feel it would not have been possible without divine intervention. I believe that there is a higher power that is guiding and directing my actions. And it is all these actions, throughout my life, that are helping me to help animals. (Sawhney, 156–57)

Sawhney concludes:

> I am thankful that I am doing what I love. I am thankful that I can make a difference for animals. Many people join social causes because it makes *them* feel good. At the end of the day, though, working for animals is not about our own satisfaction, or making ourselves feel good. The needs of an exploited nonhuman must come first. (Sawhney, 157)

Swahney, motivated by core Hindu teachings, states that "being compassionate towards animals comes easy because I am a Hindu" (Sawhney, 156).

Summary

Hindu religious traditions hold nature to be sacred and offer a philosophy of *ahimsa*, karma, reincarnation, and oneness that leads Hindus to a vegan diet. Gods are associated with anymals as vehicles, and also through divine manifestations. Gods, humans, and anymals are sometimes indistinguishable: A Hindu god might manifest as human, tortoise, man-lion, or elephant-headed human; a small, playful monkey might turn out to be the powerful god Hanuman. As gods, and through their own special powers, anymals are spiritually powerful in the Hindu tradition, and provide innumerable lessons and worthy examples for human beings. Humans are obligated to live a life of *ahimsa*, which requires Hindus to speak up in defense of those who are exploited.

‖ 3 ‖

Buddhist Traditions

All beings fear before danger, life is dear to all. When a man considers
this, he does not kill or cause to kill.

—*Dhammapada*

Buddhism emerged in the sixth century BCE, on the outskirts of the Hindu world, in northeastern India. Not surprisingly, Buddhism inherited key concepts from dominant Hindu traditions, such as karma, reincarnation, *ahimsa*, and oneness. Buddhism traveled both north and south from India, carrying Indian philosophy and religions to new lands, where these ideas were enhanced and renewed under the influence of diverse cultures.

Buddhism is commonly divided into two branches, Theravada and Mahayana. The Theravada Buddhist tradition is slightly older. The Pali Canon contains the sacred writings of Theravada Buddhism, but these texts are also central to Mahayana schools—along with a plethora of additional texts. Novel Mahayana Buddhist traditions grew and flourished in China, then traveled to Korea, Japan, parts of Southeast Asia, and ultimately to North America (most notably in the forms of Zen and Tibetan Buddhism); Tibetan Buddhist traditions are sometimes collectively referred to as Vajrayana Buddhism.

Sacred Nature, Sacred Anymals

Buddhist monasteries often sit unobtrusively in remote settings, protecting and preserving surrounding habitat and wildlife. Buddhists, like Hindus, tend to associate wild places with spiritual growth and insight. For centuries, Buddhist monks have purposefully lived far from bustling population centers (Fung, 65), choosing a simple life. The *Dhammapada* (third century BCE) teaches Buddhists, "As the bee takes the essence of a flower and flies away without destroying its beauty and perfume, so let the sage wander in this life" (42).

Buddhist writings reveal "delight in the wooded and mountain heights" and in the wild anymals who share these secluded dwellings (Burtt, 73). In the seventh century, Buddhist poet Shantideva wrote of his desire to be a "homeless wanderer" with trees as companions, where he might "dwell in a deserted sanctuary, beneath a tree, or in a cave.... /dwell in spacious regions owned by no one" (Conze, *Buddhist Scriptures*, 102). The Pali Canon (Theragata and Therigata) contains a host of poems called "Psalms of the Brethren and Sisters" (or Hymns of the Elders), composed by monks and nuns in the first century BCE. These poems celebrate the beauty of nature, and the spiritual delight of remote regions:

> Those upland glades delightful to the soul,
> Where kareri [tree] spreads its wildering wreaths,
> Where sound the trumpet-calls of elephants:
> Those are the braes wherein my soul delights.
> Those rocky heights with hue of dark blue clouds,
> Where lies embosomed many a shining tarn
> Of crystal-clear, cool waters....
> Free from the crowds of citizens below,
> But thronged with flocks of many winged things,
> The home of herding creatures of the wild....
> Crags where clear waters lie, a rocky world,
> Haunted by black-faced apes and timid deer,
> Where 'neath bright blossoms run the silver streams:
> Such are the braes wherein my soul delights. (Burtt, 75–76)

When Buddhism traveled to Korea, Japan, and beyond, Buddhists maintained this vision of nature as spiritually significant. In nature, Buddhists tend to find a medium through which the highest spiritual truths might be learned. The following Chinese Buddhist poem, perhaps written by a poet whose name means "Cold Mountain" (Hanshan, who lived sometime before the ninth century), offers a vision of nature as providing a rough path leading beyond the material into the spiritual realms:

> I climb up the Way to Cold Mountain,
> But the Cold Mountain road is endless:
> Long valleys of boulders stacked stone upon stone,
> Broad streams thick with dense undergrowth.
> The mosses are slippery, though there's been no rain;
> Pines cry out, but it's not the wind.
> Who can get beyond worldly attachments
> And sit with me among the white clouds? (Sommer, 167)

The great Japanese Zen Buddhist Dogen (1200–1253) found that the splendors of nature hold the *essence* of enlightenment, and that spiritual ideas themselves are "the entire universe, mountains and rivers, and the great wide earth, plants and trees" (Curtin, "Dogen," 198; Swearer, "Moral," 15). Buddhists continue to retreat to the wilderness, and to respect and appreciate nature. Tae Heng Se Nim, a Korean Zen master, spent ten years wandering outside civilization during the Korean War. She writes that "nature accepted her with affection. The birds and animals, trees and rocks were her friends and teacher" (Nim, 133). Immersed in the natural world, Nim found the core and essence of her Buddhist practice, feeling "drunk with love for the earth and all sentient beings (Nim, 137).

Thich Nhat Hanh, perhaps the most renown Zen Buddhist, also finds much that is spiritual in the natural world. Hanh, a contemporary Vietnamese monk, recently wrote that the "trees, birds, violet bamboos, and yellow chrysanthemums are all preaching the same dharma that Shakyamuni taught 2,500 years ago" (Hanh, *For a Future*, 95). He reminds readers that both inner peace and world peace are "based on respect for life, the spirit of reverence for life. Not only do we have to respect the lives of human beings, but we have to respect the lives of animals, vegetables, and minerals" (Hanh, *Peace*, 113). In his recent books, Hanh continually reminds readers that the scope and vision of a practicing Buddhist must include every aspect of every ecosystem (Hanh, *For a Future*, 9).

Buddhist Philosophy and Morality

Buddha

According to biographies, anymals were important in the life of the Buddha. At his conception, his mother dreamed of a white elephant entering her body, a favorable premonition (Conze, *Buddhist Scriptures*, 35). Just after his birth, the Buddha announced his intent to help *all* living beings—the Vietnamese potbelly pig and the Beltsville small white turkey, the purple pit viper and the violet tarantula: "For enlightenment I was born, for the good of all that lives" (Conze, *Buddhist Scriptures*, 36). Just before the Buddha attains enlightenment, it is reported that a *naga* king (*nagaraja*)[1] sees the Buddha's bowl floating upstream and grasps the meaning of this incident; the serpent "knew that such a miracle could only be performed by someone destined to become a Buddha" (Swearer, *Becoming*, 132). When the Buddha attained enlightenment, anymals celebrated, maintaining respectful silence: There was great joy among all living beings, and "the herds of beasts, as well as the birds, made no noise at all" (Conze, *Buddhist Scriptures*, 48). The Buddha's achievement was for all, and all responded: "All living beings rejoiced" when they sensed that the Buddha had achieved his goal (Conze, *Buddhist Scriptures*, 51). After the Buddha attains enlightenment, he is asked to teach—not just for the sake of humanity, but in order to "rescue also the other living beings who have sunk so deep into suffering" (Conze, *Buddhist Scriptures*, 52).

---

[1] The concept of *nagas* was inherited from earlier Indian traditions. See previous chapter for more on *nagas*.

According to Buddhist literature, the Buddha held a depth of insight, and showed great compassion with regard to anymals. When the Buddha's jealous cousin turned loose a rampaging bull elephant to crush the Buddha, he felt no anger or ill will. Instead, the Buddha beseeched the elephant not to be violent, not to threaten his own future (through karma) by killing an enlightened being. The Buddha was not concerned for his own life, but for the likely negative karmic affects if the elephant were to be violent, and so the "Blessed One embraced the charging beast in a great field of lovingkindness" (Bercholz and Kohn, 39). The rampaging elephant was calmed by the Buddha's unexpected kindness and compassion, as the Buddha "stroked the elephant's head" (Conze, *Buddhist Scriptures*, 58).

Several important Buddhist writings teach of the Buddha's connection with anymals. Ashvaghosha, a second-century Indian Buddhist who wrote about the life of the Buddha in the *Buddhacarita* (*Acts of the Buddha*), notes that the Buddha spent much of his life in the wilds of India, where anymals figured prominently in his life. Most biographies of the Buddha include considerable portions about his interactions with anymals. *Jataka* tales ("Birth Stories") are also important for any understanding of the Buddha's connection with anymals. *Jataka* tales are in many ways similar to the Hindu *Pancatantra*—both collections stem from the same ancient sources. Like the *Pancatantra*, these entertaining stories teach morality, but *Jataka* tales teach by recalling the Buddha's past incarnations, many of which were in anymal forms.

Jataka stories feature animals of every kind, including such diverse creatures as a crow, jackal, snake, swan, quail, horse, goose, tortoise, boar, cuckoo, pigeon, woodpecker, chameleon, chicken, human, mongoose, mosquito, otter, shrew, beetle, osprey, and many more. Numerically, the most important *Jataka* anymals are monkeys, who appear in twenty-seven stories, followed by elephants (twenty-four), jackals (twenty), lions (nineteen), and crows (seventeen). There are seventy different anymals in the *Jataka*, many of whom act as central characters who are ultimately described as the Buddha-to-be (Chapple, "Animals," 134, 145–46).

One of the many *Jataka* stories that focuses on the life of the Buddha as an anymal tells of a patient water buffalo who is harassed by a mischievous monkey. The monkey dances on the buffalo's back and swings from his horns. He beats down the grass where the buffalo eats—flattening his meal—and irritates the gentle buffalo by tapping the great beast's ears while he chews. But the water buffalo, who could pierce the monkey with a horn or crush him with his hoofs, is never stirred to anger. When asked why he tolerates the insolent primate, the buffalo replies that "monkey is small,...and Nature has not given him much brain....Moreover, why should I make him suffer in order that I may be happy?" (Khan, 90). Needless to say, this very patient water buffalo is an exemplary citizen, and of course he is a previous incarnation of the Buddha-to-be.

Another *Jataka* tale tells of a monkey leader (and future Buddha) who saves his followers and community by using his body to form a bridge to create an escape route for his community. The monkey's back is broken in the process, but he holds firm through painful personal self-sacrifice, and thereby saves his companions. Witnessing his compassion, self-sacrifice, and perseverance, an observer tells the monkey, "It is not your sword which makes you a king; it is love alone" (Khan, 18). As with all great religions, love is a central moral principle, and Buddhist literature recognizes that anymals are also capable of deep and abiding love.

Incarnate as a wise, fast-flying golden gander in yet another *Jataka* tale, the goose (who is a Buddha-to-be) counsels two young geese not to chase after the sun, but being young and foolish, they ignore his advice. He understands youth, and is deeply compassionate. Rather than be angry, he is determined to be there in their time of need, to support and protect these foolish youth. He follows them, and as their strength wanes, he carries each young gander safely back to the flock. A neighboring human king notices the glory of the golden gander who saved the young fliers, and comes by to pay his respects. The gander responds in kind, and the two become friends.

The king-gander is often busy with his flock, and as a consequence cannot visit the human king, who longs for his feathered friend. But the king visits when he is able, and during one such visit, the human notices the gander's extraordinary speed, and inquires, "Can any speed be compared to yours?" (Khan, 129). In response, the goose provides the Buddhist dharma (law, wisdom, truth, teachings of the Buddha), reminding the king that our bodily strength will ultimately wane with the passing of time, and redirecting the king away from worldly gains and achievements, toward spiritual understanding: 'Yes,' replied the bird, 'there is a speed greater than mine. A hundred times faster, a thousand times, a hundred thousand times faster is the speed of Time. Pleasures, riches, palaces! Time takes them away faster than my fastest flight'" (Khan, 129). Whatever impresses us about worldly existence will soon pass; not so with regard to our investment in spiritual matters.

Jataka stories of self-sacrificing compassion—stories of the Buddha's previous lives—remind readers (and listeners—these stories are often told to children) that the Buddha has taken many physical forms, as have all living beings, and that anymals are capable of respectful and compassionate action. No anymal is so insignificant—each being is on their own spiritual path, and when we come into contact with these myriad creatures, our spiritual paths are linked. How we treat anymals matters not only to them, but to our future lives. *Jataka* stories remind that any living being might house the karmic presence of a future Buddha; no anymal is morally irrelevant.

Ahimsa

The Buddhist moral obligation to show concern for anymals is "a significant, indeed a radical message" (Waldau, *Specter*, 123). *Ahimsa* (not to harm) encompasses all living beings and is a central and foundational Buddhist precept both in the Pali Canon and in extracanonical Buddhist writings (Waldau, *Specter*, 149). *Ahimsa* "is an ethical goal" for every Buddhist (Shinn, 219); "indeed, Buddhists see this orientation to the suffering of others as a sine qua non of [an] ethical life" (Waldau, *Specter*, 138). Release from *samsara* (the ongoing cycle of life, death, and rebirth) is dependent on *ahimsa*; one who is cruel will not attain *nirvana*, which is achieved only by those who avoid causing any harm to living beings (Mascaro, *Dhammapada*, 68).

Buddhist philosophy indicates that no creature lies beyond the spiritual concern of a practicing Buddhist (Martin, 99). "There is never a hint in Buddhist teachings that intellectual ability, a sophisticated sense of self, or any characteristic beyond the ability to suffer is relevant to moral standing" (Phelps, *Great*, 40). The "Dhammika" (in the *Sutta Nipata*) states, "Let him not kill, nor cause to be killed any living being, nor let him approve of others killing, after having refrained from hurting all creatures, both those that are strong and those that tremble in the world (393)" (Fausböll, 66). The *Dhammapada*, attributed to one no less than the Buddha, remarks:

> All beings tremble before danger, all fear death. When a man considers this, he does not kill or cause to kill.
>
> All beings fear before danger, life is dear to all. When a man considers this, he does not kill or cause to kill. (Mascaro, *Dhammapada*, 54)

The Buddha was aware that nothing matters more to any one individual than general happiness, and he taught those who desire happiness to recognize this same wish in others, and thereby avoid causing harm (Conze, *Buddhist Thought*, 212). Consequently, confining and restricting anymals is contrary to Buddhist teachings; the *Dhammapada* laments that the captive elephant "remembers the elephant grove" (81). Just as we wish for freedom, "peace, happiness, and joy for ourselves, we know that all beings wish for these qualities" (Phelps, *Great*, 44). If we confine anymals in cages where they cannot move about, and cannot engage in their instinctive and natural behaviors, then we cause great harm. In the Buddhist view, animal agriculture causes great harm not only by confining anymals, but also through slaughter: Buddhist writings remind people that "even the tiniest creatures don't wish to die" and that we must "stop creating pain for others" (Kornfield, 99). Buddhists are instructed to remember of anymals that "all have the same sorrows, the same joys as I, and I must guard them like myself" (Burtt, 139). Whether a macaque in an anymal lab, or a male chick thrown into the grinder, each must be regarded as I regard myself: Would I wish to be treated in such a way? Buddhist traditions teach adherents that *ahimsa* applies to human beings and anymals alike (Kraft, 277), and Buddhists are encouraged to make choices, including diet and livelihood, to avoid causing harm to any living being (Rahula, 47).

Buddhist philosophy is sensitive to any and all pains and needs, whether those of a snow leopard, chiru, or kiang (protected for centuries by Tibetan Buddhists but now decimated by an influx of foreign hunters and trappers); this sensitivity is not peripheral, but stands at "the core of the tradition" forming "the foundation of Buddhist morality" (Waldau, *Specter*, 138). A Buddhist adept "hurts not any living being" (Mascaro, *Dhammapada*, 74).

Metta and Karuna

The Buddhist moral obligation to show concern for anymals requires humanity not only to avoid causing harm, but also to *prevent and/or alleviate* pain and suffering that is caused by others, and also *to overtly bring happiness* to other beings (Hanh, *For a Future*, 28): Buddhists are expected to foster and practice *metta* (lovingkindness) and *karuna* (compassion). *Metta* is the "intention and capacity to bring joy and happiness to another person or living being" (Hanh, *For a Future*, 16), whereas *karuna* is the "intention and capacity to relieve the suffering of another person or living being" (Hanh, *For a Future*, 16). The Buddha taught that both *metta* and *karuna* are essential aspects of Buddhist practice (Hanh, *For a Future*, 16). *Metta* and *karuna* constitute a Buddhist "condition of the heart" in which one wishes to avoid harming the Bengal slow loris and the Himalayan thar, just as one wishes to avoid harm to self (Conze, *Buddhist Thought*, 212).

Buddhist practice is "built on the vast conception of universal love and compassion for all living beings" (Rahula, 46). One set of Buddhist vows states, "With all am I a friend, comrade to all/And to all creatures kind and merciful" (Burtt, 79). The *Sutta Nipata* contains some of the oldest and most profound Buddhist writings, including the "Metta Sutta." This text includes an impassioned expression of the Buddhist teachings of *metta* and *karuna* (as well as *ahimsa*):

> May all beings be happy and secure, may they be happy-minded. (144)
>
> Whatever living beings there are, either feeble or strong, all either long or great, middle-sized, short, small or large. (145)
>
> Either seen or which are not seen, and which live far (or) near, either born or seeking birth, may all creatures be happy-minded. (146)
>
> Let no one deceive another, let him not despise (another) in any place, let him not out of anger or resentment wish harm to another. (147)
>
> As a mother at the risk of her life watches over her own child, her only child, so also let everyone cultivate a boundless (friendly) mind towards all beings. (148)
>
> And let him cultivate goodwill towards all the world, a boundless (friendly) mind, above and below and across, unobstructed, without hatred, without enmity. (149)
>
> Standing, walking or sitting or lying, as long as he be awake, let him devote himself to this mind; this (way of) living they say is the best in this world. (150) (Fausböll, 26)

Metta (lovingkindness) radiates outward from practicing Buddhists "in every direction, to reach every being in every corner of the world" (de Bary, 37). The *Dhammapada* (attributed to the Buddha and one of the oldest and most honored texts of Buddhism) teaches that those who follow the Buddha will "ever by night and day" "find joy in love for all beings" (Mascaro, *Dhammapada*, 78).

The Buddha was "compassionate towards all that lives" (Conze, *Buddhist Scriptures*, 58), and despite the constant presence of suffering in the world, Buddhists are expected to behold "all living beings with the eyes of compassion" (Hanh, *Peace*, 80). Inasmuch as we prefer to be treated kindly, we ought to extend compassion to all other beings (Dalai, 173). *Karuna,* or compassion, literally means "to suffer with" and entails putting ourselves "inside the skin" of other beings (Hanh, *Peace*, 82, 81). Buddhist compassion is a "feeling that suffers all the agonies and torments" of every sentient creature (Kushner, 148ff), and therefore "makes the heart tremble and quiver at the sight and thought of the sufferings of other beings" (Conze, *Buddhist Thought*, 86).

Buddhism requires, at its most fundamental level, "compassionate protection of all living beings" (Mizuno, 132). Buddhist morality entails "an unlimited selfgiving compassion flowing freely toward all creatures" (Burtt, 46), a life that is "compassionate and kind to all creatures" (Burtt, 104). A Tibetan Buddhist monk notes, "Compassion is the root of all Dharma [Buddhist teachings/law] and virtues" (Tashi). Indeed, compassion is "one of the indispensable conditions for deliverance" (Kushner, 148ff).

Buddhists are certainly known for compassionate action. A Chinese Buddhist emperor (T'ang, 759 CE), exemplifying *metta,* "donated a substantial sum toward the construction of eighty-one [fish] ponds...for the preservation of animal life" (Harris, 386). In China, Liang emperor Wu Ti (502–550), as part of his Buddhist devotions, fed the fish in a monastery pond (Harris, 386). While soldiers killed one another with great conviction in the Korean War, Zen master Tae Heng Se Nim fostered *karuna.* Wandering the wilds of Korea, she came upon a handful of tadpoles struggling in a small puddle. Feeling for the small beings, who were trapped in a shrinking bit of muddy water, she released them into the freedom of a larger pond (Nim, 133). Despite the war that raged all around her, Nim had the time and energy to save a few needy tadpoles from distress and slow death. In spite of her awareness that "all beings are suffering," she was moved "to assist and save all sentient beings," even a handful of stranded tadpoles (Nim, 133).

Tenzin Gyatso, the present Dalai Lama (Tibetan Buddhist leader), practices *karuna* and claims *metta,* or loving-kindness, *as his religion* (Gyatso, 8). He describes Buddhist love and compassion as "unconditional, undifferentiated, and universal in scope," a "feeling of intimacy toward all other sentient beings" (Dalai, 123). He encourages his followers to develop *nying je chenmo,* or "great compassion," which reaches across *all* imagined lines—race, gender, class, age, and species—extending our responsibilities of care to *all* beings (Dalai, 124, 125). The aging Dalai Lama, who has been studying Buddhism since he was a toddler, comments, "Through developing an attitude of responsibility toward others, we can begin to create the kinder, more compassionate world we all dream of" (Dalai, 173). Buddhism teaches that people are to "strive to be compassionate" in their daily actions: when deciding what they will purchase, wear, and eat (Dalai, 175).

Bodhicitta and *Bodhisattvas*: Selfless Service

In Mahayana Buddhist traditions, *bodhisattvas* are individuals who have gained enlightenment, yet instead of moving into *nirvana*, they return to be born again, taking on an embodied existence repeatedly with the specific intent to help save *all* creatures from the suffering that is inherent in the process of life, death, and rebirth (Conze, *Buddhist Scriptures*, 30; de Bary, 81–82):

> Compassion is given an especially prominent place in the Mahayana branch of the Buddhist tradition by virtue of its association with the central ideal of the bodhisattva, although concern for living things is conceptually no less central in the Theravadin branch. The bodhisattva is known, and even defined, by his or her commitment to the salvation of other beings. (Waldau, *Specter*, 138)

Mahayana Buddhist traditions refer to the highest mind as *bodhicitta*, the "intention or vow to practice and help countless living beings" (Hanh, *For a Future*, 92) to escape the suffering entailed in endless rebirths (Laumakis, 61). Bodhisattvas commit to *bodhicitta*. Again and again, they suffer the trials and tribulations of rebirth in a selfless act of service designed to help *every individual of every species* to escape from the painful cycle of life, death, and rebirth (de Bary, 81):

> A Bodhisattva resolves: I take upon myself the burden of all suffering, I am resolved to do so, I will endure it. I do not turn or run away, do not tremble, am not terrified, nor afraid, do not turn back or despond. And why? At all costs I must bear the burdens of all beings....I have made the vow to save all beings. All beings I must set free. The whole world of living beings I must rescue from the terrors of birth, of old age, of sickness, of death and rebirth, of all kinds of moral offence, of all states of woe, of the whole cycle of birth-and-death...from all these terrors I must rescue all beings....I must rescue all these beings from the stream of Samsara, which is so difficult to cross; I must pull them back from the great precipice, I must free them from all calamities, I must ferry them across the stream of Samsara. I myself must grapple with the whole mass of suffering of all beings. (Burtt, 133)

A bodhisattva, the embodiment of compassion, thinks, "As many beings as there are in the universe," with or without form, with or without perception, "all these I must lead to Nirvana" (Conze, *Buddhist Scriptures* 164). Filled with *metta* and *karuna*, the bodhisattva seeks to light the way to nirvana for "countless beings" just as the sun illuminates the earth for all (Burtt, 130–31). For the sake of all suffering beings, bodhisattvas vow unending service extending across untold lifetimes. They set an example of undying self-sacrifice on behalf of all living beings. Bodhisattvas carry "the flower and fruit of compassion,/And its name is service" to all living beings (de Bary, 121).

"Selfless service" is perhaps not an appropriate term. Buddhism "has no actual thought of another" (de Bary, 122). Through reincarnation (and other aspects of Buddhist philosophy), living beings are all related, and some Buddhist schools view all beings as one. In this view there can be no selfless service: To serve the black howler monkey is to serve self. To serve the mealy parrot is to serve your best friend. To serve the tharparkar cow is to simultaneously serve all living beings.

The First Precept: Do Not Kill

The Buddha taught humankind to live by five basic precepts (laws or rules). The first and most fundamental precept, featured prominently in Buddhist literature, requires that Buddhists "refrain from killing living beings" (Waldau, *Specter*, 136; Robinson, 77). This proscription against killing "is central to the Buddhist tradition. Indeed, it is in fact one of the few common features across the vast Buddhist tradition and its many sects, strands, and branches" (Waldau, *Specter*, 143).

The first precept is comprehensive and can be tricky to implement. For example, what if cockroaches overtake the kitchen? Does it make sense to repeatedly call in the exterminator to destroy a host of busy beetles? Clearly the solution does not lie in killing *or* in ignoring a high population of kitchen roaches. A reasonable response will remove the cause, rather than temporarily remove the effect. A thoughtful Buddhist will "keep the kitchen as clean as a Zen temple, so that the roaches must do their scavenging elsewhere. Then the occasional roach can be escorted outside" (Aitken, 28).

Buddhaghosa (early fifth century), one of the most famous translators and interpreters of Buddhist texts, delineates various factors that measure the weight of an offense against the first precept—against life. One need not kill to break this precept. It is enough to have "a thought" of killing," and this is only compounded by "the action of carrying it out, and the death as a result" (Conze, *Buddhist Scriptures*, 70–71). Buddhaghosa reminds Buddhists that intent matters, that what humans desire and envision affects karma and future lives, and can hinder the Buddhist path. According to the first precept, human beings must not kill, and even the thought of killing a critically endangered Himalayan wolf or one of the last remaining Saolas (a Southeast Asian wild cow, ancestor of domestic cattle, with only a few hundred individuals remaining) will carry a serious negative karmic affect.

Reincarnation

Eons of reincarnation (transmigration) has had a predictable yet remarkable affect on the Buddhist understanding of relations: Today's duck and dog are yesterday's human lovers, siblings, and best friends. The Lankavatara Sutra states:

> In the long course of *samsara,* there is not one among living beings ... who has not been mother, father, brother, sister, son, or daughter, or some other relative. Being connected with the process of taking birth, one is kin to all wild and domestic animals, birds, and beings born from the womb....Repeated birth generates an interconnected web of life which, according to the Buddhist precept of harmlessness, must be respected. (Chapple, "Animals," 143)

Many countries hold parents in great esteem—they are due much respect from their children. This respect does not end with death: Parents are due ongoing respect, and "there is not one among living beings" who has not been our mother and our spouse.

How do we respect our past parent and best friend now embodied as a sun bear, Kankrej cow, or yellowtail surgeonfish? Fundamentally, we must kill no living being. (Reincarnation encourages Buddhists to honor the first precept.) Any creature "could have been our mothers and fathers, and with this belief in mind, Buddhists abstain from killing animals" (Tashi). Each kosimewat cow and asil chicken was at some point our mother, and humans must not harm their mothers, who gave them life and protected them when they were weak and vulnerable.

The sense of extended familial relations fostered by an understanding of reincarnation reminds Buddhists that it is very important to avoid killing anymals, and encourages Buddhists to approach every living being with *metta* and *karuna,* as we ought to approach a beloved grandmother.

Karma and the Afterlife

In the Buddhist worldview, all species are subject to the same karmic laws (Waldau, *Specter* 140). Gray squirrels and caracaras, "like ourselves, make choices that govern both this immediate life and future experiences" (Chapple, "Animals," 144). The *Sutta Pitaka* (attributed to the Buddha or his close associates, and therefore foundational to Buddhism) notes that one's actions determine one's future as surely as "the wheel follows the foot of the ox that draws the carriage" (Burtt, 52). Karma is a law of the universe, like gravity. No one can avoid the affects of gravity or karma, whether the endangered black buck or eastern sarus crane.

Buddhist teachers remind practitioners that a firm devotion to Buddhist laws and practices is critical to our own well-being. The Dalai Lama reminds humans it is in our own best interest to bring greater happiness to all beings, to avoid any cause of suffering: Karma will carry the choices we make into our next life. The *Dhammapada* also reminds Buddhists of the following:

> He who for the sake of happiness hurts others who also want happiness, shall not hereafter find happiness.
> He who for the sake of happiness does not hurt others who also want happiness, shall hereafter find happiness. (Mascaro, *Dhammapada*, 54)

Buddhist philosophy teaches that our interests are "inextricably linked," yet "certain actions will lead to suffering while others lead to happiness" (Dalai, 47). Those who seek happiness in this life yet cause misery to others "will not find happiness after death" (Burtt, 59). Neither morality nor the cosmic process of justice is speciesist—Flipper and Queen Anne were both subject to the same effects of the same moral law. Karma determines the future lives of *all* animals without favoritism (Kraft, 277).

Many Buddhists foster a complicated vision of the afterlife that includes a host of hells. For many Buddhists, especially those influenced by Chinese Buddhism, the realms of hell entail punishment for cruelty to anymals, including a long look into the Terrace of Mirrors of the Wicked, where humans see in the glass all those they have harmed, including those they have eaten, enslaved, or otherwise exploited (Kwok, 47). Depictions of the Terrace of Mirrors often show cattle, pigs, dogs, and fish gazing back from the mirror's revealing glass, their premature deaths destined to affect all those who were responsible for their demise.

In the ancient Indic language of Theravada Buddhism (Pali), the word *peta* means "souls of the dead" (Fred Porta, pers. comm., March 20, 2004). The name of the organization People for the Ethical Treatment of Animals is most often identified with the acronym PETA. This acronym, when informed by an understanding of karma and reincarnation (and Pali) takes on a life of its own. The *peta* (souls) of humans who eat or wear the body parts of anymals, or who are indifferent to the plight of "lab" or "entertainment" anymals, are likely to face considerable future suffering because of their indifference and/or overt cruelty.

Anatta

Indian concepts (like reincarnation) led early Buddhist philosophers to conclude that there is no independent "self" (Robinson, 38): Individuals and species are mere name and form—outward vestiges and labels applied to something that is indistinct and transient—something that does not really exist. *Annata* reminds Buddhists that individual existence is a mirage: That which we understand to be *self* is mere matter in human form, soon to disintegrate physically, to be reborn in another temporary body. *Anatta* is consistent with a cosmos that perpetually changes, forming and reforming all beings.

Self-importance often lies behind our tendency to exploit earth and anymals. An understanding of *anatta* helps Buddhists to spend their short and ephemeral existence in their present body serving and loving other suffering beings, whether jackal, green sea turtle, or upland sandpiper. What can be the point of selfish ends when there is no self?

The Buddhist teaching of *anatta* helps diminish human pride while fostering self-sacrificing service. As noted, there is no such thing as "self"-sacrificing service in the Buddhist worldview. Not only do our actions ultimately affect both self and "other," but our conception of *self* exists only momentarily by way of common perception and language. Though all animals are devoid of self, what we do to or for other beings remains spiritually critical. Intent matters. People, though devoid of *self* in any ultimate sense, are wise to make choices that do not harm anymals, or the earth itself. While our temporary bodily existence is not important in and of itself, intent and actions, manifest in karma, are critical.

Oneness and Interdependence

Jataka tales remind Buddhists that anymals are an integral part of *our* spiritual lives; we are *all* subject to the *same* moral and spiritual laws, across eons; we have each lived in innumerable bodily forms (Waldau, *Specter*, 150). *Ahimsa, karuna, metta*, reincarnation, and *anatta* foster a Buddhist sense of oneness and interdependence rich with moral imperatives: Our habitual distinction between self and other evaporates.

Buddhist philosophers developed the concept of oneness, to reach what would appear to be this idea's logical conclusion. Buddhists thereby offered a vision of *radical* oneness, of interidentification, wherein all entities are identified with all other entities. Each "individual" *atman* (soul) has at some point in time been embodied as a pony, a woman, and a tick many times throughout the course of existence. How can these animals be different when they hold just one *atman*? What defines a being, the atman or the body? Buddhist philosophers concluded that oneness not only suggests that we are all "in this together," but also that we all *are* this, "rising and falling as one living body" (Cook, 229).

The *Bodhicharyavatara* of Shantideva (ca. 600 CE) notes that fellow creatures *are the same as* the practitioner. Similarly, Thich Nhat Hanh teaches that we "can see everything in the universe in one tangerine" (Hanh, *Peace*, 22). One who looks deeply into a tangerine sees the grocer who stored and sold the fruit, the truck drivers and transporters who carried the fruit to the grocer, the pickers and fields where the fruit ripened and was collected, the sun and rain that allowed the fruit to ripen, and the tiny seed, tree, and earth—all of which were required to bring the tangerine to the table (Hanh, *Peace*, 21–22).

Hanh calls this radical interconnection between a tangerine and the rest of the universe "interbeing." He points out the cloud in the paper on which this book is written. We see this cloud when we understand that rain is necessary for trees, which were necessary to make paper for this book. He concludes that a book and a cloud "inter-are" (Hanh, *Peace*, 95). All things coexist, are codependent, Hanh asserts, and being is better understood as inter-being.

Radical Buddhist oneness teaches that we do not, and cannot, exist independently. "We have to inter-be with every other thing" (Hanh, *Peace*, 96):

> I am one with the wonderful pattern of life which radiates out in all directions....I am the frog swimming in the pond and I am also the snake who needs the body of the frog to nourish [his or her] own body....I am the forest which is being cut down. I am the rivers and air which are being polluted. (Allendorf, 43–44)

Radical oneness does not identify any entity as "other"; we are not separate from anyone or anything.

Hanh encourages humans to meditate on other beings. Only through understanding what it is like to be a gharial, wild boar, or toad—feeling the fears and the hopes of these creatures "from within their own perspective"—do we foster compassion and plant the seeds of peace that will preserve both every other creature, and the ponds and forests that are necessary to nurture and sustain these beings (Hanh, *Peace*, 105). If we understand oneness, we see ourselves as the toad, and we and the toad inter-exist as one ever-changing unit (*Peace*, 106). Thich Nhat Hanh elucidates the Buddhist understanding of oneness:

> A human being is an animal, a part of nature. But we single ourselves out from the rest of nature. We classify other animals and living beings as nature, as if we ourselves are not part of it. Then we pose the question, "How should I deal with Nature?" We should deal with nature the way we deal with ourselves...! Harming nature is harming ourselves, and vice versa. (Hanh, "Individual," 41)

A Buddhist understanding of the oneness of all beings enriches the foundation moral teachings of *ahimsa*, *metta*, and *karuna* (Martin, 98). A Buddhist who understands oneness also understands that pain inflicted on any other being, whether a shikra, chousingha (the only four-horned antelope), rusty-spotted cat, or the critically endangered Ganges shark, may as well be inflicted on self (Conze, *Buddhist Thought*, 86).

Codependent Arising

The Buddhist concept of "codependent arising" adds yet one more twist to the Buddhist vision of the oneness of all beings. It holds that no individual or action can be separated from any other individual or action (Robinson, 23–29). In this way codependent arising does not allow for an independent entity, action, word, or thought; all things influence all other things. Each being and each act is critical to every other being and every other act. In the words of a contemporary Thai monk, "The entire cosmos is a cooperative. The sun, the moon and the stars live together as a cooperative. The same is true for humans and animals, trees and the Earth.... [T]he world is a mutual, interdependent, cooperative enterprise" (Swearer, "Moral," 5).

One of the most earth-embracing extant religious philosophies, Hua-yen, a school of Chinese Mahayana Buddhism that took shape around 600 CE, carried codependent arising to its logical extreme. In the Hua-yen worldview, all is reflected in all. The Hua-yen worldview is perhaps most easily grasped by imagining an infinitely regressing mirror that encompasses the entire universe in "simultaneous *mutual identity* and *mutual intercausality*" (Cook, 214, italics in original). Because mirrors reflect all that is around them, nothing is independent in this "vast web of interdependencies in which if one strand is disturbed, the whole web is shaken" (Cook, 213).

The Buddhist concept of interdependence is consistent with our commonsense understanding of existence. Without mechanical transport, we could not live as we now live. We could not expect to travel very far, generally not more than fifty miles in a day. Without cars, we would plan more carefully how to bring supplies to our kitchen and how to earn a living near our homes. The Internet is also critical to our current lifestyle. Without these modern devices, we could not know instantly what is occurring in Taiwan or New York unless we lived in or very near these places. Without modern communications, we would be aware only of what has occurred in our immediate vicinity, unless or until news spread slowly to neighboring villages and beyond.

Without fast transport or the Internet, our lives would change fundamentally, but Buddhist codependent arising teaches that we are affected by *any* change, even the slightest change in a faraway place. We cannot live *as we now live* even if a small flea is knocked from the tail of a mouse in a village in northern Malaysia. *All* is changed even by what seems to us a slight change; the ripple effect is unending and all-encompassing because all things are interconnected. If asked, the flea would most likely find the disappearance of cars to be irrelevant, just as you might feel unaffected by the dislodging of a flea, but change for one brings change to the universe, which affects all of us.

By applying codependent arising to a specific case we might explore the concept more fully. Consider a milk truck traveling south in North America toward Arizona. How might this affect the larger world? In the course of the trip, the truck is likely to run over at least one creature. In this case, let's say a roadrunner is squashed under the tires of the milk truck. The roadrunner had been sitting on eggs, which will now spoil and never hatch. But someone will consume the abandoned eggs, and will therefore be satiated, and will not eat someone or something else. That which was not consumed, say a shrew, will go on to affect other creatures and plants, perhaps even parenting several families. Meanwhile, back at the road, a magpie feasts on the dead roadrunner, but the new generation of roadrunners will never join the food chain, which means that either someone will go hungry or someone else must die. As for humans passing by in cars, some will be saddened to see the dead roadrunner, while others will be gladdened to see a feasting magpie. Maybe someone will swerve to miss the magpie, which could lead to another long set of actions and reactions.

And what of the milk carried in the truck that mowed down the roadrunner? To acquire the milk for human consumers in Arizona, a host of Holstein cows were perpetually impregnated, forced to give birth, and had their calves snatched. The cows would have been perpetually reimpregnated and milked until they were "spent" and sent to slaughter. Calves *not* earmarked for the same fate (males, for instance) would have became veal after six months of deprivation—kidnapped, confined, alone, deprived—never knowing their mother or their mother's milk. This milk equates to a lot of misery, and a lot of negative karma.

What of those who drink the calves' milk? Milk, designed to turn a tiny calf into a huge bovine in roughly one year, clogs human arteries and carries bovine growth hormone to little children...contributing to early puberty in girls. No doubt some of these very young girls will become pregnant at a time when they otherwise would not have been able to become pregnant, had they not consumed the milk delivered to Arizona loaded with bovine growth hormone. Their children, if carried to term, will feel the consequences of having very young mothers, or will perhaps be adopted, and so the effects go on endlessly rippling outward through the universe. This miniature analysis does not even touch on several key effects of factory farming to produce milk, such as the environmental effects (fossil fuel use, chemical fertilizer pollution, freshwater depletion waste disposal, and land use).

Buddhist philosophers understood that the cycle of cause and effect ultimately includes the entire cosmos. Radical Buddhist interdependence exposes the fact that cruelty and exploitation are counterproductive. All things *are* one another *in their very essence.* To harm another is to harm oneself, and a negative affect will ultimately touch all who exist.

Buddha Nature

There is yet one more Buddhist concept of radical oneness and interdependence that is worthy of note. The influential Chinese Mahayana Buddhist school T'ien T'ai developed a philosophy that recognizes all as contained in one moment and one moment as containing all. This combination of single and universal—encompassed simultaneously in every second—led to the development of the concept of "Buddha-Nature" (de Bary, 156–57).

Buddha Nature is Ultimate Being inherent in all living things (de Bary, 120). Buddha Nature provides a form of oneness that holds nirvana in *samsara*—perfection in the mundane—the Buddha in every olive baboon and Himalayan palm civet.

Buddha Nature speaks to the inherent perfection of each being *as it naturally is*. All things have Buddha Nature, and to acknowledge this is to acknowledge that *all creatures are perfect in their essence, just as they are.*

Buddha Nature, intermingled with radical interdependence, encouraged Buddhists to honor the Ganges soft smelt tortoise and Brahma chickens in and of themselves, *and* as integrally linked with all else—as anymals, perfection, and the ultimate goal. The dragonfly, bourbon red turkey, and alley cat—"everything is Buddha without exception" (de Bary, 121).

The Buddhist concept of Buddha Nature holds that each being has inherent value, spiritual value, and that we can learn important religious truths from every aspect of the natural world, just as we can from the Buddha. Snake birds and nilgai have Buddha Nature, as does the exquisite peafowl. Recognizing Buddha Nature in every living being brings attentive respect to each Indian pond heron and ghariyal crocodile, and might have brought rescue to the now-extinct black soft-shelled turtle (who desperately needed our attention and respect, and who now stands as perfection lost).

Diet

Across time, "many Buddhists have felt that meat-eating of any kind is out of harmony with the spirit of the Law of Righteousness, and have been vegetarians" (de Bary, 91). Buddhist philosophy teaches that, just as surely as one who throws dirt into the wind will have dust in their eyes, a flesh eater piles up negative karma.

Buddhist moral ideals require practitioners to make choices that reduce suffering; an enlightened Buddhist is one who "does not kill [or] cause slaughter" (Burtt, 71). The bodhisattva, "desirous of cultivating the virtue of love, should not eat meat, lest he [or she] cause terror to living beings" (de Bary, 92). The Mahayana *Lankavatara Sutra* (attributed to the Buddha) also notes that it is unacceptable for a bodhisattva to eat flesh. Moreover, the Enlightened One forbade flesh altogether among his disciples, though followers have since, due to selfish desires, misrepresented the Buddha's clear teachings:

> Here in this long journey of birth-and-death there is no living being who...has not at some time been your mother or father, brother or sister, son or daughter....So how can the bodhisattva, who wishes to treat all beings as though they were himself...eat the flesh of any living being?...Therefore, wherever living beings evolve, men should feel toward them as to their own kin, and, looking on all beings as their only child, should refrain from eating meat.
>
> It is not true...that meat is right and proper for the disciple when the animal was not killed by himself or by his orders, and when it was not killed specially for him....Pressed by a desire for the taste of meat people may

string together their sophistries in defense of meat-eating... and declare
that the Lord permitted meat as legitimate food, that it occurs in the list of
permitted foods, and that he himself ate it. But... it is nowhere allowed in
the sutras as a... legitimate food.... All meat-eating in any form or manner
and in any circumstance is prohibited, unconditionally and once and for
all. (de Bary, 92)

Flesh eating—as well as drinking the nursing milk of factory-farmed cattle, or eating
the eggs of factory-farmed hens—fosters massive amounts of misery (and premature death) for billions of farmed anymals. One who *buys* a dead bird or her eggs
causes a chicken to be slaughtered by the law of supply and demand, and has thereby
caused unnecessary suffering and premature death as surely as does the person
wielding the knife. For the Buddhist, good conduct requires "putting away the
killing of living things" and holding "aloof from the destruction of life" out of compassion for sentient beings (Burtt, 104):

> If we are fully and genuinely mindful in our eating, we will not allow our
> choice of foods to bring needless suffering and death to living beings.... The
> correct question is not, "Should I be a vegetarian?" but "Should I partici-
> pate in the unnecessary killing of sentient beings?" ... *It is not about us; it is
> about the animals.* A vegan lifestyle is not a dogma, it is an essential element
> of Buddhist compassion." (Phelps, *Great*, 127, 137, 141)

Jataka tales also speak to a vegan diet. In one story, a small quail refuses to eat worms
or insects, subsisting only on the grass seeds that his mother brings to the nest. He
does not grow as quickly as his siblings, since he has much less to eat. Yet when a fire
comes raging through the forest, and the little quail is too small to escape, it is he
who is unafraid. His special powers—the same powers that led him to a vegan
diet—allow him to speak to the fire, and calm the raging flames. This little quail
character is then exposed as the future Buddha, busy building up good karma that is
essential to his inevitable enlightenment (Khan, 115–16). A vegan diet maintained
for the sake of all living beings is good karma.

An especially sweet *Jataka* story involves an old woman who adopts and tends
two piglets as if they were "her own children," holding them in her lap and laughing
with delight at their antics (Khan, 81). But the evil flesh, "having eaten all the meat
that was in the village" and having become very drunk, attempt to buy the pigs from
the woman so they can kill and eat her beloved pigs (Khan, 81). " 'Nay,' she replies,
'I shall not give them to you. Does one give away one's children for money?' " (Khan,
82). But the evil flesh eaters conspire to give the mother enough liquor to make her
drunk and then talk her into handing over at least one of the pigs.

The pigs sense trouble, and the smaller one is terrified. The wise pig (and Buddha-
to-be) tries to comfort his brother, telling him that he must obey when his mother

calls, even if in fear of his life. But the wise pig also offers a Buddhist teaching, instructing his brother to bathe in a pool which leaves a never-fading fragrance. His words transform the environment: "The little flowers in the grass opened their hearts to listen, the trees bent over, the wind became silent, and the birds tarried in their flight. The men and the old woman were no longer drunk and the ropes fell from their hands" (Khan, 83).

The little pig is amazed, and asks his older brother to explain. The pool of water, the wise Buddha-pig explains, is love, "and love is the fragrance that never fades" (Khan, 84). The people are moved to compassion, the pig is spared, and a lasting reign of peace and justice comes over the land (Khan, 84–85). This *Jataka* tale makes it clear that flesh eating fosters terror and death, whereas a vegan diet is synonymous with life, justice, and an umbrella of peace. Moreover, the story allows readers to see the horror of flesh eating from the eyes of two little pigs who are terrified of being eaten; flesh eaters fill their lives with sorrow and dread.

Jataka stories honor both those who choose to starve rather than kill anymals for food and individuals who choose to give their bodies to those who are starving. One *Jataka* tale reveals the Buddha in a former life as Prince Mahasattva, a human who comes upon a hungry tigress who is too weak to hunt; she and her little ones are on the edge of death from starvation. Prince Mahasattva says, "Holy men are born of pity and compassion," and then offers his body that the tigress and her young might live (Conze, *Buddhist Scriptures*, 24–26). His is an act of radical and generous service to others who are in need, in this case a tiger family. Mahasattva is eventually reincarnated as the Buddha, due to good karma accumulated through his generous kindness.

Jataka tales indicate that eating bodies is acceptable only when the flesh is already absent of life and has not been killed specifically for food—and will not be replaced with another "eatable" corpse by someone who profits from selling flesh. In two *Jataka* scenarios that reverse species from those represented in the Mahasattva tale, a rabbit and elephant offer their bodies to starving humans. The rabbit flings himself into a fire to be cooked, while the elephant runs off a cliff to land at the feet of those in need (Khan, 46–47, 106–7). The Buddha is ultimately revealed to be the brave and generous rabbit and the courageous and self-sacrificing elephant. *Jataka* stories remind readers that there is a difference between those who have nothing to eat *except* anymals who are already dead and those who *choose* to kill for food, against the will of the anymal consumed. Eating roadkill is not morally objectionable.

A Tibetan Buddhist story in the *Abhidharmakosha* (Vasubandhu, fourth century) also speaks to the moral superiority of a vegan diet. In this story, an advanced Buddhist practitioner, Aryakatayana, is begging for food and happens into a home where the mother holds a small child on her lap while she eats fish curry, pausing only briefly to beat an unfortunate dog. Through his "power of intuitive knowledge," accumulated from years of Buddhist practice, Aryakatayana sees the relationships that existed previously between the four individuals, and marvels that this villager, in complete ignorance, is

> Eating the flesh of her father,
> Beating her mother's back,
> And nursing her enemy on her lap. (Tashi)

If we eat flesh, we are like the village woman and the hungry people who consumed the Buddha-rabbit. We have no idea who we are eating in this world of interconnected oneness. How many bodhisattvas—future enlightened souls—are among the chickens trapped in battery cages, or the cows held by their necks while the milk is stolen from their udders? Who would choose to cause extreme suffering or the death of a future Buddha out of ignorance? Who would wish to harm a being with Buddha Nature simply because they were unwilling to choose different foods?

Mahayana Buddhism teaches that all beings have Buddha Nature, that all beings will eventually reach Buddhahood. Mahayana Buddhists look to the self-sacrificing elephant of the *Jataka*, and then to the elephant in today's circus, or the pigs trapped in farrowing crates, knowing that we are surrounded by innumerable Buddhas-to-be—and each cow and hen has Buddha Nature. How is our spiritual journey affected if we willfully exploit or harm these beings? Moreover, Buddhist traditions teach *ahimsa*, *metta*, and *karuna* and hold as their very first precept: Do not kill. Only a plant-based diet honors core, foundational Buddhist teachings.

Hunting

As with Hindu religious traditions, Buddhist writings depict hunting as a cruel pastime, as a way of life that is inimical to spiritual progress.

The Prince Who Became a Cuckoo (1857), a Tibetan tale, tells how Prince Dharmananda becomes trapped in a cuckoo's form when he willingly enters the body of a dead cuckoo. His sly "friend" has hatched a plot, and soon steals Dharmananda's human form so that the evil friend might "become" the prince. With his own body no longer available, the real prince must remain embodied as a cuckoo.

While living as a bird, he provides dharma instruction to a tiger, at which time a friend from his (human) community comes through the forest hunting, and takes aim at the tiger. Dharmananda cries out against such cruelty and spiritual folly:

> My friend, do not shoot.
> What are you thinking about?
> You must have come under the influence of bad companions.
> Once you were my friend,
> Have you now gone mad?
> Even should you be in mortal danger,
> How could you kill an innocent beast? (Wangyal, 121)

During his time as a preaching cuckoo, the prince gathers a flock of roughly 5,000 feathered followers, as well as numerous other wild beasts, including lions and elephants. Soon another savage human hunter visits the realm, killing many of Dharmananda's flock and scattering the remainder. Again he beseeches and scolds the hunter:

> O hunter, though you have obtained
> A precious human life,
> Wise beings will consider you undeserving of it
> Because you perform such cruel actions.
> It is extremely sad.
> Your face is fierce and terrifying;
> Your sharp arrows again and again
> Cut short the lives, as precious to them as yours,
> Of innocent animals,
> Who have been your mothers in countless previous births
> And sustained you lovingly again and again.
> Merely to obtain food and skins, which will only increase your suffering—
> Which will bring you no lasting satisfaction, only discontent—
> You take the lives these creatures hold so dear.
> You cannot bear the pain of a thorn in your own flesh
> For even a moment,
> Yet you inflict endless pain upon others.
> Alas! How stupid and merciless. (Wangyal, 146)

Impressed with the prince's understanding of dharma, and his distaste for hunting, the great Lama Vimalasri promises that he and the prince will "aid countless beings" (Wangyal, 124).

Milarepa, one of the "most beloved figures in Tibetan history," spent his later years wandering the high Himalaya, meditating in caves (Robinson, 278). In art, he is often depicted as an ascetic protecting a deer from a passing hunter. The hunting hound is represented, too, taking refuge with the saint. The hunter, looking hideous and rough in the illustrations, offers a gesture of respect to the saint, even though Milarepa harbors both the deer he hoped to kill and his otherwise trusty hunting hound. Though prevented from satisfying his blood lust, the hunter pays obeisance, acknowledging the spiritual superiority of one who does not hunt or kill. In response, Milarepa sings Buddhist wisdom to the hunter: "There is plenty of time to shoot an arrow at a poor helpless deer, but not enough time to live forever. As you follow a deer to kill it, so...the Lord of Death (Yamaraksha) follows you" (Tashi). Milarepa reminds the hunter—and all who hear the story—that our time is short; therefore each act is critical, and killing (or causing to kill) is spiritually disastrous. Hunters store up bad karma, and suffer as a consequence of the misery and death they cause.

Jataka tales also expose hunting as an activity for those who are base and mindless. One *Jataka* story tells of a bloodthirsty king who is seized with desire to kill when his eyes fall upon a beautiful deer. He takes chase, shouting "furiously" that he will catch the deer—that his prey "cannot escape" (Khan, 93). He shoots arrows wildly in the direction of the deer as he rushes forward "in a fury," with only the prize of death on his mind. So single-minded and greedy is the king that he fails to notice an approaching chasm. His horse, however, sees the chasm and comes to a screeching halt. The king flies over the horse's head and down into a deep slit in the earth's surface.

The deer sees what has happened, and takes pity on the king, returning to help the man who pursued him with deadly intent. The deer speaks gently to the hunter, aware that both he and the king drink water, eat, sleep, and share the basic needs of all living beings. The king, locked into dualistic thinking, is unable to see unity, or even commonality, and marvels: "Is this not my enemy, who has come to help me?"

Ultimately, the small-minded king is ashamed when the one he hoped to slay saves his life. Not realizing that the forest is comparatively quiet, peaceful, and safe in his absence, the king invites the deer to his palace: "I cannot leave you here in the forest to be killed by hunters and wild animals" (Khan, 95). The deer (and future Buddha) replies: "Here is my country, in this forest; the trees are my palaces. But if you wish to make me happy, grant then this favour, I pray. Hunt no more in the forest, that those who live beneath the trees may be happy and free" (Khan, 96). In response, the king sent out a decree that no one should hunt in the forest, and "the King and his people and the animals in the forest all lived happily ever after" (Khan, 96).

Another *Jataka* tale tells how deer were terrorized by a king who loved to hunt, descending on the quiet forest every day with flying arrows, chasing the deer through thick forests with intent to kill, and wounding many in the process. The deer decide that it is better to volunteer death than to be hunted, so they draw straws each day to determine who must go to the palace to be killed and consumed. From then on, a deer goes willingly to the king to be killed each day for his feast.

One day a doe with a tiny fawn draws the short stick. She pleads with the leader not to send her off to the chopping block, knowing that her fawn cannot survive without her. He sends her back to nurse her little one, granting reprieve, then turns toward the palace to offer his own life in exchange. The king, impressed by the generous gift of the stag—one the king would not likely offer his subjects—spares the stag's life. But instead of hastening back to the hills with his life, the stag remains to speak with the king. First he inquires after the lives of the *other* deer—might they also be spared? Might they live safely not only today, but also tomorrow?

The king, moved to compassion once again, grants the entire herd reprieve—but the stag still does not leave. He next asks about the many other creatures of the forest—the wild boar and mountain sheep, Himalayan black bear, and Hanuman langur—might they also be spared? The king is amazed at the depth of the stag's compassion and is moved to yet greater kindness. He agrees not to pursue or kill any of the creatures of the forest. Still the stag does not leave, but remains standing before the king, this time asking after the birds of the air, noting that the spot-billed duck and painted wood grouse also have families, community, and prefer to live. The king, seeing that the stag is right, agrees not to slaughter those who are busy on the wing. Now, at last, the king believes that the deer must take his leave, but he does not. The remarkable stag awaits the answer to one final question before disappearing back into the forest: "What of the fish?"

The stag's willingness to die for others, and to speak up on behalf of all sentient beings, moves the king to compassion. He ultimately agrees to stop killing *all* creatures; the four-footed, the birds, and the fish. Because of the stag, "Love had entered into the heart of the King," and he ceased to kill anymals so that "all the living creatures in his realm were happy ever after" (Khan, 33). The stag is, of course, the Buddha in one of his innumerable future lives, teaching against the deadly horrors of hunting.

Divine-Anymal Relations

Perhaps you have noticed that there has been no mention of goddesses, gods, or deities of any kind with regard to Buddhism. The Western conception of a divine being does not transfer easily to the Buddhist world. Buddhism certainly contains beings with supernatural powers, but supernatural powers are not innate in Buddhist traditions; such powers are earned over many lives, through Buddhist practice. For this reason, the notion of "divine-anymal" relations is meaningless in Buddhist traditions.

That said, stories in this chapter from the life of the Buddha, or from the lives of bodhisattvas, offer examples of relations between the *supernatural*—those who have gained special powers through Buddhist practice—and anymals. In all instances, kindness and compassion are central and fundamental.

Human-Anymal Relations
Anymals as Individuals

Anymals are revealed as individuals in Buddhists literature, pleading for their lives, learning the dharma, and helping others in need. Whether taking shelter with Milarepa or bowing to the Buddha's compassionate touch, anymals are always presented as individuals in Buddhist literature, especially in the *Jataka*.

Like the Hindu *Pancatantra*, Buddhist *Jataka* stories focus on individual anymals, complete with their own personality, volition, fears, hopes, flaws, and moral or immoral inclinations. Anymals are not incidental to these birth stories; they are primary, and every creature is "presented with remarkable detail and accuracy" (Chapple, "Animals," 143). In *Jataka* stories,

> animals have their own lives, their own karma, tests, purposes, and aspirations. And, as often brief and painful as their lives may be, they are also graced with a purity and a clarity which we can only humbly respect, and perhaps even occasionally envy. (Martin, 100)

Buddhists are often introduced to *Jataka* tales at a young age, and these stories remind Buddhists of the significance of each individual of every species (Waldau, *Specter*, 153). Children, on hearing *Jataka* stories, learn *not* to view an elephant or a magpie as an alien other—a thing. Instead, they learn to see anymals as moral individuals, as members of an anymal community, and also as members of a larger community that includes human beings. A contemporary Buddhist, reflecting on the *Jataka*, notes the following:

> Was not the Buddha a hare? a quail? a monkey, a lion, a deer or ox? Who is to say that the dog guarding our porch or the cat twining around our legs is not a Bodhisattva...? Entering the market one sees live rabbits and chickens and turkeys for sale. And one wonders..."Should I buy them all? How can I save them?" For in the *Jatakas* one has seen that their inner life is the same as our own. (Martin, 100)

By presenting anymals as individuals, *Jataka* tales encourage aspirants to recognize dusky eagle owls and barking deer as individuals who are inherently worthy of compassion and respect. These individuals are bodhisattvas and future Buddhas, and every last being holds Buddha Nature. *Jataka* tales reveal anymals as spiritually important both in and of themselves—they also have karma and a life to live—and also as spiritually important to any being who chooses to bring them harm or help, to cause them suffering or joy.

Kinship and Community

The Buddhist vision of family, friendship, and community includes all living beings. This is especially remarkable because India is home to such anymals as Indian cobras, Russell's vipers, saw-scaled vipers, common kraits, Bengal tigers, leopards, and Asiatic lions—and each of these poses a very real threat to human life. Nonetheless, Buddhist philosophies of reincarnation, oneness, and inter-being have created a sense of kinship and community across all species.

Reincarnation stands at the core of the Buddhist sense of kinship between all beings—we are kin through eons of transmigration. At some point, across eons of reincarnation, our *atman* (soul) has been embodied as both worm and eagle—as every other creature on the planet—and has been in familiar relations with every other *atman* that exists. Consequently, interspecies kinship and community are taken for granted: We are just one birth away from the life of a mountain bluebird or desert toad.

In Buddhist literature, anymals are also aware of kinship, including a kinship with all other animals. For example, *Jataka* tales reveal a flock of quails working together to dodge the cruel nets of bird catchers, and a lion struggling to convince his friends of many species that the sky is not falling (Khan, 111, 119–22). *Jataka* stories present anymals of all sorts speaking with one another, sharing familiar concerns and joys, and also interacting, living, and working with human beings. Anymals are viewed as neighbors—just like human neighbors—in *Jataka* tales.

One such story tells of a parrot who grows up to assume the responsibility of caring for his aging parents. Every day he flies off to a farmer's field, eats some of the grain, then carries some food back for his mother and father. The farmer, hearing of this parrot's exceptional beauty and his strange habit of carrying grain from the field, asks field workers to catch the parrot. The parrot is snared and brought before the farmer, who asks the colorful bird why he is hoarding grain. The parrot replies, "A duty I fulfill each day, A treasure do I store away" (Khan, 59).

Intrigued, the farmer asks about the duty and the treasure, and the Buddha-parrot replies, "My duty," said the parrot, "is to bring food to my parents who are old and cannot fly; and my treasure is a forest of love. In that forest, those who are weak are helped by stronger ones, and those who hunger are given food" (Khan, 59). The parrot is ultimately released to return to his worried and waiting bird community—and he is encouraged to return to the fields each day to fulfill his rightful and important duty to his mother and father.

The Prince Who Became a Cuckoo highlights interspecies kinship and community among birds, humans, snakes, and bodhisattvas—including the great bodhisattva Avalokitesvara (now understood to be incarnate as His Holiness, the Dalai Lama). In this story, as noted, a young man becomes trapped in a cuckoo's body; bodhisattvas, supernatural emanations, and reincarnated soldiers are also embodied as cuckoos. Cuckoo-Prince Dharmananda accepts his fate, settles into bird life, and promptly begins transmitting the dharma to a willing parrot, Buddhadhara. As the story unfolds, the prince's "two most trusted companions [are] the parrot, Buddhadhara, and a kalapidaka bird, Prakasavan, who [is] a supernatural emanation of Avalokitesvara" (Wangyal, 117), unbeknownst to Dharmananda. His parrot friend, Buddhadhara, is left to teach the dharma while the prince flies into the forest to meditate, where a bodhisattva eventually comes to the prince's rescue—in bird form. Avalokitesvara, the bodhisattva of compassion, becomes a "Bodhisattva bird"—a cuckoo—in order to help Prince Dharmananda regain his rightful body and his rightful inheritance (Wangyal, 110).

The Prince Who Became a Cuckoo clearly indicates that, through the process of birth and rebirth, the prince and the bodhisattva have each been in the form of a cuckoo many times: As they sit together high in the trees, the Bodhisattva reminds the prince, "I have been your protector throughout beginningless time" (Wangyal, 92). Similarly, the bodhisattva would have protected the prince when he was born as a stray dog, a wild turkey, and a little black ant. Their ongoing relationship transcends species, and because the bodhisattva is a supernatural being, it even transcends earthly existence in embodied forms.

In light of *atman* and reincarnation, Buddhist kinship reaches across both lifetimes and species. In light of inter-being and *anatta*, Buddhist kinship becomes so all-encompassing that it is submerged into a great oneness of being.

Interpenetrability

Buddhism arose "during a time and in a place where the boundaries between humans and animals were far more fluid than in contemporary industrialized societies" (Chapple, "Animals," 143). Consequently, Buddhism postulates "no essential distinction between humans and animals" (Phelps, *Great*, 33), and in many Buddhist stories individuals morph from one species to another.

For example, one *Jataka* story tells of a poor man who could not provide for his family, and so wandered off into the forest, where he became a gander graced with golden feathers. He returned to his poverty-ridden family each time the family needed money, donating a feather. Unfortunately, fearing that the goose might one day disappear, his wife captured him and greedily plucked all of his golden feathers. Because she imprisoned and exploited the gander—due to a lack of gratitude as well as a dearth of compassion—the bird became a common, ordinary, white-feathered gander. Perhaps eager to leave such a wife behind, the man remained a gander, and when his ordinary feathers grew back, he flew "far away to the forest where every bird [is] happy," far from human greed and exploitation (Khan, 53).

A particularly charming Tibetan folktale, "The Frog," exemplifies interpenetrability along with a host of other core teachings from Buddhist philosophy and morality, such as oneness, inter-being, *metta*, *karuna*, and Buddha Nature. In this tale, a frog begs an old widow to adopt him as her son. After several days, she finally agrees and quickly comes to love the frog, who is now overtly her kin. Eventually Frog hops away to secure the most beautiful young woman in the area, who happens to be an only child. The young woman's family is mortified at the thought of their only child, their beloved daughter, marrying a frog. Frog reminds the reticent people, "Human beings, animals, birds, even frogs" are all "of the same spiritual force" (Hyde-Chambers, 177). Nonetheless, a frog son-in-law is a hard sell, and the parents offer the frog *anything* else in place of their daughter. He again presents Buddhist philosophy: "Can you not see that all beings, human or animal, are the same?" (Hyde-Chambers, 180).

Apparently they cannot, and Frog resorts to a series of disruptive events to demonstrate his powers and convince the parents to let him marry their daughter. Finally, he is able to pressure the parents to consent—but he still must gain the young woman's heart, and she is equally disenchanted with this web-toed marital match. Under her father's instruction, she makes three attempts on Frog's life as they travel from her home toward his. Each time the frog patiently returns her weapon, reminding her "that we are all one" (Hyde-Chambers, 180).

Eventually Frog does win her heart and, consistent with Western folklore, she discovers him to be a handsome young man, but there are noteworthy differences between the European and Asian outcomes. In the Tibetan tale, the "frog" is wearing a magic frog-skin, and the moral of the Buddhist story bears no resemblance to that of similar Western stories, which focus on *inner* qualities of *human* beings. The moral of the Tibetan folktale centers on Buddhist philosophy, reminding people of the oneness of all beings encouraging interspecies compassion: "All things differ only in their 'skin.' ... [A]ll are really one nature" (Hyde-Chambers, 186). Whether we are born with frog skin or human skin, we are essentially one. (Pity that the man who composed this story failed to realize that the physical appearance of the young woman matters as little as the skin of the frog.)

Anymal Powers

In the above story, Frog has considerable power and is able to outsmart and outmaneuver humans to achieve his ends. True, he is a man—or is he really a frog? Anyway, *atman* (soul) ultimately has no body, and therefore no species affiliation, and Buddhism teaches that there is no "self" (*anatta*). In this sense, it is somewhat meaningless to speak of the powers of anymals as opposed to those of humans—many of the powers held by an anymal will likely hold across reincarnations, across species.

In Buddhist traditions, every individual is infused with spiritual possibilities. For Mahayana Buddhists in particular, with their understanding of Buddha Nature and the ultimate enlightenment of all creatures, *every* being *is* Buddha—every being holds the powers of the Buddha, if they would but discover their true nature. In Buddhist stories, these inherent Buddha powers are frequently manifest in anymals.

In *Jataka* tales, a host of anymals "set an example" for humans (Chapple, "Animals," 135, 144), exhibiting "compassionate and often heroic self-giving" (Martin, 97). They speak out against killing for sacrifice, food, pleasure, and profit (Chapple, "Animals," 135–38); they are both humble and noble. Each pre-Buddha anymal in the *Jataka* tales exemplifies the all-important spiritual qualities of the Buddha, including self-sacrificing generosity "for the benefit of all living beings" (Martin, 98). Even the tiniest of heroic *Jataka* anymals has special and remarkable powers: A small vegan quail is able to stop a raging fire, and a young pig teaches the dharma, asking his brother to become immersed in love, thereby transforming a violent situation into one of enduring peace.

In *The Prince Who Became a Cuckoo*, birds have lofty spiritual aspirations, meditate, and teach and learn dharma: "Owing to their good karma and prayers, the birds understood clearly what they had heard and resolved to keep it always in mind" (Wangyal, 119). The story notes that, in learning the dharma, birds "become the equal of a human being" (Wangyal, 103). In fact, as it turns out, they are in a better spiritual position than many humans, who are more likely to turn their powers toward harming other life forms, for example, by hunting, eating flesh, or working as soldiers. Prince Dharmananda soon learns that some of the birds in the forest were previously soldiers in the prince's battalions but were not reborn as humans due to their acceptance of a violent occupation. In contrast, the birds gain good karma, through Dharmananda's teachings, and some of the birds and beasts gained enough spiritual merit to attain release without rebirth. The prince thereby learns, as do all who hear the story, that it is *not* essential to be born a human being to attain release from samsara, so long as one is able to receive and practice the dharma.

While dwelling with the birds, Dharmananda learns that he will one day be reborn a semidivine serpent, a *naga*, and will worship a future Buddha (enlightened being) and "bring much happiness to the world" (Wangyal, 126). The prince ponders the lives of birds, *nagas*, and humans, and notes that the life of a human is spiritually preferable to that of a bird *only* because it is more conducive to learning and practicing the dharma. A bird's life is not lower, or of less value, but is merely less likely to be conducive to Buddhist knowledge and practice. Dharmananda notes that birds can easily learn dharma, if feathered teachers are willing and able to teach, and that his life as a bird is one of simplicity and contentment—a perfect Buddhist life (Wangyal, 178). In fact, Dharmananda's life as a cuckoo provides significant advancement on his bodhisattva path.

In Buddhist traditions, especially in Mahayana Buddhist traditions, every creature holds special powers, and all such powers are inherent, contained in our Buddha Nature—each living being is a Buddha awaiting realization. In addition to these inherent powers (shared by all creatures), anymals hold spiritual power *over* humans. Our interactions with those who currently moo, croak, or meow are critical to our own self-realization, to our own spiritual path. How we treat a flower snake is evidence of our spiritual past, and also determines what will lie ahead for our *atman*. Through the process of reincarnation, in conjunction with karma, in light of our personal decisions, anymals might be said to have tremendous power and influence over the future lives of human beings.

Buddhist Traditions and Anymal Liberation

To live a spiritual life, Buddhist teachings must be applied in "everyday human affairs" (Mizuno, 131); the *Dhammapada* explicitly identifies enlightened human beings by their actions. Tenzin Gyatso, the fourteenth Dalai Lama and present

Tibetan Buddhist spiritual leader, teaches that Buddhists ought to foster a sense of "universal responsibility" and live up to those convictions (Dalai, 174). Similarly, contemporary Vietnamese Zen Buddhist Thich Nhat Hanh notes that feeling compassion "is not enough. We have to learn to express it.... Understanding and insight show us how to *act*" (Hanh, *For a Future*, 14, italics added). Hanh adds, "We can realize peace right in the present moment with... our actions. Peace work is not a means. Each step we make should be peace" (Hanh, *Peace*, 42).

At least some Buddhist kings have exemplified, and continue to exemplify, Buddhism in *action* through a personal commitment to anymal liberation. For example, King Ashoka (268–233 BCE) converted to Buddhism, became the first Buddhist emperor, and ruled India "according to the precepts of Buddhism" (Embree, *Sources*, 141). King Ashoka was greatly concerned for the welfare of anymals in his kingdom (Burtt, 23; Harris, 386), and "famously attempted to integrate the First Precept" (not to kill), both in his own life and among the people over whom he ruled (Waldau, *Specter*, 143). He gave up hunting, one of the traditional pleasures of an Indian king, and he "banned animal sacrifice at least in his capital, introduced virtual vegetarianism in the royal household, and limited the slaughter of certain animals" (Embree, *Sources*, 144).

On behalf of anymals, Ashoka engraved edicts (first on large rocks and later on pillars) that encouraged citizens to feel empathy with all creatures (Embree, *Sources*, 143). These engraved writings reminded citizens that the king's munificence necessarily extended to all living beings, providing both humans and anymals in his realm not only with shade and watering holes, but also with medicines (Embree, *Sources*, 144–45). His Fourth Rock Edict called for "abstention from killing animals and from cruelty to living beings" (Thurman, 113). In his Seventh Pillar Edict, King Ashoka reminded citizens that "the greatest progress of righteousness among men comes from exhortation in favor of noninjury to life and abstention from killing living beings" (Embree, *Sources*, 148–49). Some of Ashoka's edicts still stand, testifying across centuries to the first Buddhist king's commitment to compassionate service toward all sentient beings (Waldau, *Specter*, 143).

Buddhist commoners have also exemplified, and continue to exemplify, Buddhism in *action* through a personal commitment to anymal liberation. For example, in Sri Lanka Buddhism has been central to everyday life for centuries. Buddhist compassion created "a paradigm of public administration and justice in pre-colonial Sri Lanka," in which the power of the state extended to protect anymals (Weeraratna). In fact, Sri Lankan citizens sometimes *insisted* that the government fulfill its obligation to protect all creatures. Around 300 BCE, an adept Buddhist practitioner (Arahant Mahinda) petitioned King Devanampiyatissa on behalf of anymals, to remind the emperor of his Buddhist obligation to protect, represent, and defend all creatures in his realm: "Great King, the birds of the air and the beasts have an equal right to live and move about in any part of this land as thou. The land belongs to the peoples and all other beings and thou art only the guardian"

(Weeraratna). As a result of long-term Buddhist piety in Sri Lanka, "extensive state protection was granted to animals and the slaughter of cows was strictly prohibited" before the interference of Europeans (Weeraratna).

In late thirteenth-century Japan, by order of the Shogun, citizens honored national "animal day." Rooted in Buddhist texts and supported by basic Buddhist philosophy (such as *ahimsa*, *metta*, and *karuna*), this annual celebration encouraged practitioners to "work for the liberation of living beings,... practice liberation of living beings,... and cause others to do so" (*Bommyokyo*, in Williams, 150). Buddhists who witnessed anymals being exploited on "animal day" were required to "save and protect them from misery and danger" (*Bommyokyo*, in Williams, 150). Consequently, the most common practice on this particular day was to release captive anymals, such as fish or birds (Williams, 149). Records from 1017 report that a courtier found two men fishing along the Kamo River on "animal day" and promptly purchased and released the fish (Williams, 156). In Japan, into the mid-1930s, the National Buddhist Association continued to broadcast radio lectures to inform citizens of the importance of protecting anymals from harm, and many Japanese Buddhists continue to honor "animal day" (Harris, 386).

Early accounts from visitors to Tibet also reveal Buddhist compassion in action, and a strong reverence for life:

> A traveler is invited to tea by Tibetan monks; a fly falls into his cup; there is a big ado, until the fly has been fished out, safely placed on a dry spot and gently blown upon so that its wings may dry quickly; [then] the cup is courteously returned to the guest. Similarly there was the Chinese abbot who was asked for his views on an antimalarial scheme which involved the draining of a lake. He finally turned it down with the words, "but what will happen to the dragons and fishes?" (Conze, *Buddhist Thought*, 212)

In a Tibetan Buddhist restaurant in Dharamsala, India, I observed this same pervasive commitment to *ahimsa* and the first Buddhist precept. In this instance, the owner live-trapped a rat in his restaurant, then dutifully carried the large rodent out the door and away to a new life in the thick forests of Northern India.

In some of his writings, the Dalai Lama remembers his early life in Buddhist Tibet before Chinese occupation. Tibet was then a place where anymals were "rarely hunted, except in the remotest areas where crops could not be grown" (Dalai, 188). He remembers Buddhist leaders issuing a "proclamation protecting wildlife: 'Nobody,' it read, 'however humble or noble, shall harm or do violence to the creatures of the waters or the wild'" (Dalai, 18). Based on Buddhist philosophy and practice, the Dalai Lama's Government of Tibet in Exile provides teachings on the Buddhist doctrine, which simultaneously provide a Buddhist rationale for anymal liberation:

According to Buddhist doctrine, we should protect not only wildlife, but also the whole range of sentient beings for three reasons:
1. All sentient beings have feeling.
2. We believe that all sentient beings [have] been our mother in one of our infinite previous lives.
3. A spontaneous feeling of compassion arise[s] in us on observing all suffering living beings. (Tashi)

Thich Nhat Hanh encourages anymal liberation in his Buddhist message of "reverence for life" (Hanh, *For a Future*, 14). He writes that violence can be manifest in our daily choices, in "the way we develop our industries, build up our society, and consume goods" (Hanh, *Peace* 115). He encourages Buddhists to practice mindfulness concerning "eating, drinking, and consuming" in general (Hanh, *For a Future*, 7). Hanh's teachings require adherents to think about their consumption, including diet (*For a Future*, 7); he asks people to speak with their lives, and not merely through words (Hanh, *Peace*, 120). Hanh encourages his followers to "ingest only items that preserve peace" and notes that moving away from anymal products is an action that speaks of nonviolence and is an important part of mindful eating (Hanh, *For a Future*, 7, 13). He concludes that those interested in nonviolence should choose to be vegetarians (Hanh, *Love*, 65).

In fact, Hanh's teachings—consistent with Buddhist philosophy—require a plant-based diet. He offers fourteen precepts by which to live, three of which require not only a vegan lifestyle, but animal advocacy on behalf of anymal liberation:

- Do not live with a vocation that is harmful to humans and nature. *Do not invest in companies that deprive others of their chance to live.* Select a vocation that helps realize your ideal of compassion.
- *Do not kill. Do not let others kill. Find whatever means possible to protect life....*
- *Possess nothing that should belong to others.* Respect the property of others but *prevent others from enriching themselves from human suffering or the suffering of other beings.* (Hanh, *Peace*, 129, italics added)

If one is not a vegan, one cannot avoid investing "in companies that deprive others of their chance to live"; only a vegan might possess "nothing that should belong to others." A pig's flesh, a cow's nursing milk, and chicken's eggs rightly belong to the anymals from which they have been stolen; anymal industries perpetually deprive other beings of "their chance to live."

In these three precepts, Hanh also urges Buddhists to "prevent others from enriching themselves from human suffering or the suffering of other beings" and reminds his followers that "we can kill by our inaction or our silence"; we must "become ahimsa" (Hanh, *Love*, 69–70). Hanh teaches people to moderate their lifestyle "for the protection of all beings" and also to "speak out decisively with like-minded friends" (Aitken, 29). The Buddhist Eightfold Path calls for "right speech," which includes "criticizing compassionately" when necessary (Mizuno, 132). Hanh requires adherents to engage in compassionate confrontation with those who kill or harm, whether their victim is a human being, a hezuo hog, or a great Indian horned owl.

Thich Nhat Hanh's first training in mindfulness states, "I am committed to cultivating compassion and learning ways to protect the lives of people, animals, plants, and minerals. I am determined not to kill, *not to let others kill*, and not to condone an act of killing in the world, in my thinking, and in my way of life" (Hanh, *For a Future*, 5, italics added). Similarly, Hanh's fourteen precepts demand not only that we "not kill," but that we also "not let others kill." He teaches his followers that Buddhist practice *requires direct action*—including overt confrontation—on behalf of anymals: "We cannot support any act of killing; no killing can be justified. But not to kill is not enough. We must also learn ways to *prevent others from killing*" (Hanh, *For a Future*, 10, italics added). Hanh's teachings rally his followers to overtly oppose all forms of anymal exploitation and to politely but firmly confront those who exploit anymals, as well as those who support the exploitation of anymals.

Hanh also encourages his followers to "find whatever means possible to protect life" (Hanh, *Peace*, 129). This is precisely what anymal liberationists do when they jam slaughterhouse machinery, spring traps set along pathways, destroy computers in anymal labs, ram whaling ships, and burn feedlots and transport trucks. In so doing, anymal liberationists destroy *property* on behalf of *life*. It is therefore not surprising that Hanh balances the protection of life with a requirement that people "respect the property of others" (Hanh, *Peace*, 129). Nonetheless, life takes precedent over property in Buddhist religious traditions, which is consistent with the behavior of anymal liberationists who destroy property only to save anymals. Cattle, chinchillas, and cats *are* property *by law* in Western nations, as slaves once were. If we must respect property at the expense of life, then we must respect both the rancher's right to buy, sell, and kill Black Angus cattle *and* the slave owner's right to buy, sell, and kill human slaves.

Hanh's Buddhist teachings are consistent with (and require) anymal liberation— vigorous and unrelenting protests against anymal testing facilities and fur shops, destruction of machinery and equipment in vivisection labs and breeding facilities, informing the public about the cruelties of marine parks and zoos, and boycotting companies that exploit anymals—most obviously, those who profit from flesh, dairy, or eggs. Hanh reminds us that if "we appreciate and honor the beauty of life, we will do everything in our power to protect all life"—*everything in our power* (Hanh, *For a Future*, 14). Hanh teaches Buddhist philosophy, and in the process, he supports and encourages anymal liberation.

Phaik Kee Lim, raised a Buddhist in Malaysia, has always been sensitive to the needs and sufferings of anymals. She vividly remembers a neglected dog from her childhood and the suffering of numerous stray anymals in her neighborhood. She also remembers the cruelty of circus men who performed in her town, overtly punishing their "circus" anymals, and creating a horrifying experience for little Lim (Lim, 119).

As an adult, Lim was determined to help liberate anymals from human cruelty, greed, ignorance, and indifference. For twenty-five years, she has worked for Friends of the Earth Malaysia, a group that protects wildlife and habitat, and promotes and enforces conservation laws. She notes that Malaysian wildlife has been decimated by "human encroachment, greed, ignorance, and indifference" and is in severe need of protection and advocacy (Lim, 117).

In her long-term job with Friends of the Earth Malaysia, Lim networks with other earth and anymal activists in order to seek out and disclose illegal acts, whether local or international. She works to enforce laws that protect anymals and their habitat, and demands that justice be brought to bear on those who break laws. Lim is determined to stop others from harming and killing anymals; she practices what Hanh teaches:

> I will continue to work to educate others about . . . Malaysia's wildlife, and about any other exploited or abused nonhuman. I have found that the pen is mightier than the sword. We must all refuse to support industries that exploit nonhumans, and be willing to write letters and protest when nonhumans are treated cruelly. . . . If we do not understand what we cause with our money, if we do not understand the power of our support through entrance fees, through buying animal products, and through what we choose to eat and wear, then animal exploitation will continue. . . . (Lim, 121–22)

Lim understands that others have *not* seen what she has seen, so she spends hours writing articles to educate the public, and writing letters to encourage those in power to enforce legislation designed to protect anymals.

Lim's work has been a sweet blessing to many anymals trapped under the unscrupulous power of humanity. On more than one occasion, Lim has been instrumental in forcing criminals to return helpless captives to their lands of origin, thereby sparing anymals from miserable lives in shoddy circuses and poorly maintained zoos. For example, on learning that orangutans at the Kuala Lumpur Bird Park were forced to perform tricks to entertain humans—at risk of physical punishment if they should fail—Lim was determined to help these unfortunate primates escape their cruel exploiters. She knew that orangutans were protected—by law—from wild capture, and she used this law to secure their release. Indeed, after she discovered that at least some of the orangutans had been illegally obtained, she

> brought this to the attention of the office of Trade Record Analysis for Flora and Fauna in Commerce 9TRAFFIC) in Petaling Jaya. Consequently,

the Wildlife Department was forced to investigate how these primates were obtained. They conducted DNA tests, and as a result, the smuggled orangutans were seized and they were sent back to their country of origin—Indonesia. The show at the Kuala Lumpur bird park has since stopped. (Lim, 119–20)

Lim often feels overwhelmed by the injustices she actively seeks out and battles every day on behalf of anymals, while most of humanity remains oblivious—and even contributes to cruel injustice: "Defenseless creatures are always at the mercy of humans. Some countries eat dogs, or hunt wildlife or train animals for the circus; people everywhere brutalize defenseless creatures" (Lim, 119). Lim understands that anymal suffering is perpetuated by consumer ignorance:

Animal acts are neither entertaining nor educational; they devalue both the unfortunate nonhumans and the mindless viewers, who fail to recognize or see the deprivation that these nonhumans suffer. These practices continue because of human indifference and ignorance. (Lim, 120)

Aware of the connection between human ignorance and anymal suffering, Lim has spent much of her adult life educating humans in the hope of bringing change for anymals. If consumers demand cruel products, capitalists will be sure that those products remain available. Lim encourages consumers to use their buying power to protect and release anymals who are cruelly exploited: "The killing will only end if we stop buying." (Lim, 122)

Though Lim is often disappointed, frustrated, and almost always overwhelmed, she finds strength and solace in Buddhist philosophy, and in her Buddhist practice:

In this difficult work, I am often motivated by one of the sayings of the Buddha, which I read in a magazine, *Animal Citizen*: "As much as you value your own life you must also value the lives of others."

I am a Buddhist, and I believe in the Buddha's teachings. Therefore I believe that animals should not be killed for human vanity, for food, for luxury or decorative items, for aphrodisiacs, or for entertainment. They value their life and freedom as much as we value our own life and freedom. I detest angling for pleasure because fish suffer for such mindless sport. Birds should never be caged for our pleasure. I strongly discourage people from buying nonhumans from pet shops. Buying from pet shops contributes to the trade in wild-caught nonhumans. (Lim, 119)

Buddhism helps Lim to confront anymal suffering day after day. Buddhism provides a moral and spiritual framework that moves Lim to continue working on behalf of anymal liberation.

Norm Phelps in not only an anymal liberationist and vegan (since 1985), but also an American Tibetan Buddhist. Phelps's Buddhist compassion is evident in his anymal advocacy and in his writing. He has published several major books in the area of anymals, ethics, and religion, including *The Longest Struggle, The Dominion of Love*, and *The Great Compassion* (on the Buddhist imperative for a vegan diet). He writes, "Compassion becomes real when it becomes active in the world" (Phelps, *Great*, 162).

I met Phelps at a conference in 2003. He approached me after I spoke, and he thanked me for reminding him to refocus his upcoming books on compassion. Any attempt to argue for an act that fundamentally lacks compassion (whether eating flesh or wearing leather) is inherently against Buddhist religious traditions—or any of the most prominent religious traditions. Why focus on short passages of scripture when the core of the religion is ahimsa, or love?

Phelps has long been practicing Buddhist compassion, fighting from the front lines on behalf of anymals. He has protested against fur, vivisection, hunting, and anymal agriculture. He worked for the Fund for Animals for eleven years, tabling at conferences and events in and around Washington DC, and every Labor Day he protested the Hegins Pigeon Shoot.

At this annual pigeon shoot, which took place in Hegins, Pennsylvania, human beings exploited 7,000 pigeons as targets. For nearly ten years, Phelps protested alongside other dedicated activists until this insidious event was finally shut down in 1998. Phelps also worked as a team leader for the Peacekeepers at the Hegins Pigeon Shoot. The Peacekeepers were a group of activists who took responsibility for preventing violence between shooters and anymal activists.

In the late eighties and early nineties, Phelps participated in a number of hunt sabotages at the McKee-Beshers Wildlife Management Area in Maryland. He was twice cited for violating Maryland's hunter harassment law, but in both instances the charges were dropped. In 1994, at a gun club in Pennsylvania, Phelps ran in front of a tractor that was hauling pigeons to a private pigeon shoot, forcing the tractor to a halt. He and other protesters were then able to swarm around the bird cages and release some 200 pigeons. Phelps was arrested and jailed; bail was set at $5,000. He was convicted of criminal trespass and malicious mischief, and placed on probation for one year. But the pigeons were free, and for Phelps, the risks and punishment entailed in anymal liberation are an essential part of his Buddhist practice.

"Activism—speaking and acting against any form of exploitation that may cause suffering or death for sentient beings," Phelps explains, is in the "guidelines for attaining enlightenment called the *perfections*" (Phelps, *Great*, 160). There are two lists of perfections, and *dana*, or "giving," is at the top of both lists. Phelps notes that *dana* includes three types of gifts, one of which is "fearlessness" (Phelps, *Great*, 160). Phelps has learned that anymal liberation requires a measure of fearlessness. He also recognizes fearless acts on behalf of others as part of his Buddhist practice, part of "compassion at work in the world" (Phelps, *Great*, 161). For Norm Phelps, social activism—and more specifically, the struggle for anymal liberation—is the greatest expression of *dana,* and is essential for attaining enlightenment (Phelps, *Great,* 161).

Anymal liberation has focused and shaped Phelps's life and labor. Anymal liberation is rightly the *primary* focus of Phelps's Buddhist practice: "For sheer scope and depth of suffering," Phelps explains, "there is no social injustice that can begin to compare with human oppression of nonhuman animals. There are none who need the gift of fearlessness more desperately than the animals" (Phelps, *Great,* 164).

Summary

The Buddha lived close to nature and anymals, and exemplified compassion. Buddhist practice is rooted in *ahimsa, metta,* and *karuna,* and the first Buddhist precept prohibits killing. Buddhist philosophy teaches that harming other living beings is inimical to the spiritual life because we cannot avoid harming our own future through acts of cruelty due to reincarnation and karma. Buddhist philosophy also teaches that there is no independent self; we are part of an interconnected and interdependent universe. Anymals are inherently worthy of our respect and care; in light of years of reincarnation, they *are* our loved ones. Buddhist morality and practice requires human beings to actively strive to help anymals, and to fearlessly protect every sentient and suffering being.

4

Chinese Traditions

So is the superior man affected towards animals, that, having seen them
alive, he cannot bear to see them die; having heard their dying cries, he
cannot bear to eat their flesh.

—Confucian, Mencius

Give wisely to the birds and beasts, to all species of living creatures. Take
from your own mouth to feed them, let there be none left unloved or not
cherished.

—Daoist, *Great Precepts of the Highest Ranks*

Outside of the Judeo-Christian-Islamic faiths, notions of the *one* right way, the *only*
truth, are generally viewed as peculiar, narrow, and shortsighted. People in China,
for example, tend to believe that adhering to one religion does not preclude "adher-
ence to another—or several others" (Blofeld, *Taoism*, 90). Chinese people who are
inclined toward spirituality are likely to view all of the world's collective spiritual
wisdom as worthy of consideration. Chinese religious traditions are therefore
not exclusive: Chinese people have traditionally been Daoist, Confucian, *and*
Buddhist.

This inclusive vision is ancient in China, and runs deep in Chinese philosophy
and religions. For example, Zhuangzi, a Daoist mystic—second only to the pseudo-
historical Laozi, who is considered the founder of Daoism—and the assumed
author of the *Zhuangzi* (fourth century BCE), comments that categories (which
have a tendency to divide and separate) are best avoided and, in any event, are irrelevant: When we define a particular category, we also define those items or beings
that are outside of that particular category, thereby demonstrating the irrelevance of
dualistic divisions.

So I say, "that" comes out of "this" and "this" depends on "that"—which is
to say that "this" and "that" give birth to each other. But where there is
birth there must be death; where there is death there must be birth. Where
there is acceptability there must be unacceptability; where there is unacceptability there must be acceptability. Where there is recognition of right

there must be recognition of wrong; where there is recognition of wrong
there must be recognition of right. (B. Watson)

Indeed, China is home to a handful of great philosophies and religious traditions
that were traditionally practice simultaneously.

Chinese belief and practice are therefore an amalgam of philosophies and religions. "Chinese philosophy and culture tend to be 'Taoist' [Daoist] in a broad sense,
since the idea of Tao [Dao] is, in one form or another, central to traditional Chinese
thinking" (Merton, 20). But Chinese social mores and family structure are deeply
Confucian, and because of this primary focus, Confucian traditions have generally
had less to say about nature and anymals than have Daoist traditions, though this
changed somewhat with the advent of Neo-Confucian traditions. There are other
schools of thought in China, equally ancient and foundational, that have deeply
affected both Confucian and Daoist traditions. These schools of thought have
shaped core aspects of the more well-known Chinese religious traditions. For
example, yin-yang cosmology and the Book of Changes (Yi Jing) are deeply
embedded in the Chinese conscience, critically shaping the Chinese understanding
of nature and the cosmos—without their influence, the Confucian and Daoist traditions would not be what they are. In keeping with Chinese practice, I do not dis-
cuss these schools independently, but note only that they are essential to both the
Confucian and Daoist traditions as discussed in this chapter.

Buddhist belief and practice are also well represented in China. Indian philosophies and practices traveled north from India, over the mountains and plateaus,
merging with Chinese religious traditions to create unique and fascinating schools
of Buddhism. Buddhism also helped to shape Neo-Confucian traditions and
Daoism. For example, Daoist traditions accepted the philosophy of karma, which
transformed the Chinese understanding of death, the afterlife, and ancestors.
Buddhism and Daoism, in turn, helped to shape Neo-Confucianism.

Chinese people tend to be influenced by and practice several religions, and are
therefore bound not only by anymal-friendly teachings in one religion, but also by
parallel teachings in a handful of religions. Chinese religions include Buddhist religious traditions—indeed, Chinese Buddhism is fascinating, diverse, and overwhelmingly anymal-friendly, as evidenced in the previous chapter. But because
Buddhism was covered in the previous chapter, only those aspects of Buddhism that
are particularly important to Daoism are discussed here. This chapter focuses on the
Confucian and Daoist religious traditions.

Sacred Nature, Sacred Anymals

The natural world plays an important spiritual role in Chinese religious traditions
(L. Thompson, Chinese Way, 29). The Daoist and Confucian traditions complement

one another. While the Confucian tradition holds no disregard for nature, it is the Daoist tradition that emphasizes the sacred nature.

Confucian scholar Wang Yang-ming writes of the equanimity that comes with the wild beauty of the natural world:

Under the cliff lives an ancient recluse;
Pine and bamboo encompass his dwelling.
Birds sing at dawn and at evening is heard
The companionable roar of a cliff-dwelling tiger. (Blofeld, *Taoism*, 65–66)

Writers in the Confucian classics tend to focus on human civilization—proper roles in the family and community. In contrast, the Daoist philosophers focus on nature—landscapes, plants, and anymals.

The Dao infuses all that exists, and Daoist morality explicitly protects the natural world—including anymals—from human domination and exploitation. When asked where the Dao might be found, Zhuangzi reportedly replied that the Dao could not be found in any distinct place (B. Watson). The Dao permeates all that exists—all of life and all that is natural are part of the Dao, and all of nature is therefore sacred.

In China, spiritual wisdom has long been associated with those who live close to nature, particularly Daoist and Buddhist monks (L. Thompson, *Chinese Religion*, 81, 107). Beautiful Daoist poems were inspired by a love of nature and "convey the spirit of mountain-dwelling recluses" (Blofeld, *Taoism*, 55). For example, Li Po's (eighth century) poetic lines reflect deep appreciation for the spiritual beauty and peace of nature:

You ask me why I dwell
Amidst these jade-green hills?
I smile. No words can tell
The stillness in my heart.
The peach-bloom on the water,
How enchantingly it drifts!
I live in another realm here
Beyond the world of men. (Blofeld, *Taoism*, 56)

Le Feng Lao-jen describes nature to convey the bliss of meditation:

Faintly upon the breeze
Come the scents of cassia and pine.
The moon's cold radiance
Bathes the temple hall.
Lapped in stillness,

The hermit sits
And flies beyond the world.
To him, all sounds are silence
And there is nothing else at all—
Just all-pervading coolness. (Blofeld, *Taoism*, 59)

Daoist adept Meng Haoran (ca. 700 CE) depicts the natural world as a religious retreat, as a place of spiritual insight and ultimate transcendence:

All my life I have respected true reclusion
For days on end sought spiritual mysteries....
There are many pure notes in pines and streams;
These moss-grown walls are wrapped in a feeling of antiquity.
How I would like to retire to this very mountain,
"Casting off both self and world alike." (Mair, *Columbia*, 194)

In a poem titled "Oxhead Temple," Sikong Tu (ca. ninth century) offers similar sentiments, weaving imagery of monks into the poetic landscape:

From my favorite place in the Chung-nan Mountains,
The chanting of the monks emerges into the dark sky.
Groves of trees stand out clearly in the somber solitude,
thin mist floats in the desolate void. (Mair, *Columbia*, 241)

Lu Yen encourages humanity to exchange their material wealth for the spiritual delights of nature if they wish to cultivate the Dao:

When one wanders on high peaks
Letting his gaze roam wide,
The universe seems vast,
Its people numberless.
Yet, alas, there are but few
Who win to true attainment....
Discard your jade and gold;
You'd best forget such dross.
Spring blossom, autumn frost
Are worthier of attention. (Blofeld, *Taoism*, 62–64)

In China, mountains are divinities (L. Thompson, *Chinese Way*, 179); "China has a very extensive set of sacred mountains, both real and imaginary"—a mountain need not exist physically to exist in the Daoist landscape (Kwok, 39). Until sometime after the Chinese revolution—until very recently—every village contained "a temple dedicated to the local mountain god" (Bernbaum, 24). Temples and monasteries have frequently been built on China's sacred mountains, far from civilization. Climbing sacred peaks and visiting temples along the way is still "believed to bestow great merit" (Kwok, 39), and people continue to travel—and walk—many miles to visit these sacred sites. Ch'uan Te-yu writes of his visit to the sacred mountain, Maoshan (Mao Mountain). He focuses on the importance of a place that is devoid of humanity and rich with other living beings:

> I hear amidst the silence
> The plash of a mountain rill.
> Birds sing and petals fall;
> Of men there is not a trace.
> The window of my hut
> Is curtained with white cloud. (Blofeld, *Taoism*, 57)

For centuries, Chinese poets and practitioners have described the spiritual wealth of nature, the important spiritual advances that can be found in the deep green among the high, rocky peaks, amid flocks of birds more likely to be heard than seen. Mythic legends hold that Taishan (Tai Mountain) was one of Laozi's favorite haunts; this mountain remains the center of the Daoist sacred world (Kwok, 41). Both Buddhist and Daoist monks continue to seek wild places to further their spiritual growth.

In the Daoist spiritual vision, that which is natural is preferred. Furthermore, if human beings wish to avoid bringing misery into their days, they ought to leave anymals and all of nature free and untamed: The Dao "operates wisely and reliably, without human assistance," and "any interventional activity by humans will inevitably interfere" with the proper functioning of Dao, resulting in tragedy (Kirkland, 294). The *Daode jing* (*Classic on the Way and Its Virtue*, attributed to pseudo-historical Laozi, ca. 500 BCE) specifically warns against the most common forms of human intervention, technology and population growth: "A small country has fewer people. Though there are machines that can work ten to a hundred times faster than man, they are not needed" (Tao Te Ching, #80). The Daoist ideal for a human community is a small group of people earning their living directly with their hands.

Daoist writings also warn against meddling with the natural world, including features of the landscape and individual plants. The Daoist *180 Precepts* (*Yibai bashi jie*, fifth century) specifically protects forests and waterways, and even such seemingly small aspects of nature as individual flowers and beaver dams:

14. Do not burn fields, wild lands, mountains, or forests....
18. Do not wantonly cut down trees.
19. Do not wantonly pick herbs or flowers....
47. Do not wantonly dig holes in the earth and thereby destroy mountains and rivers....

53. Do not drain waterways or marshes.

77. Do not landscape mountains....

100. Do not throw anything filthy or defiled into public wells.

101. Do not block up ponds or wells....

109. Do not light fires on the plains....

116. Do not urinate on living plants or into water....

134. Do not wantonly open up dammed-lakes.... (Kohn, *Cosmos*, 138–42)

Similarly, the medieval Daoist *Precepts of the Three Primes* (*Sanyuan pin jie*) denounce "burning fields, wild lands, mountains, or forests" (#86) and "cutting down trees or idly picking flowers and herbs" (#87) (Kohn, *Cosmos*, 190). Daoist precepts remind human beings that they ought to use discretion when their actions affect wild places. Daoists are instructed to live as companions to nature, never interfering or imposing their own personal will (Chan, 177).

Because the excessive wealth of a few often contributed to the misery of the masses, Chinese people long ago concluded that undesirable human behavior brings imbalance to the world at large, which in turn brings misery (Marshall, 20). The Chinese understanding of cause and affect did not stop with humanity; imbalance in human communities, particularly human corruption and domination, was believed to cause imbalance in nature. For example, human imbalance such as injustice or greed would likely lead to natural disasters such as famine or a severe earthquake. Consequently, an unobtrusive lifestyle was held as the ideal lifestyle.

> Simplicity without a name
> Is free from all external aim.
> With no desire, at rest and still,
> All things go right as of their will. (Lao-Tzu, #37)

In this passage, the *Daode jing* discourages striving and competition, growth and development. In the Daoist worldview, spiritual advancement is preferable to material advancement, and philosophical growth is preferred to technological growth (Marshall, 18).

Confucian Philosophy and Morality

Tian

Tian (Heaven) is the ultimate religious and moral authority in Confucian traditions: "Heaven is purposive and is the master of all things" (Chan, 16). Confucian traditions do not teach of an anthropocentric ruler in charge of the universe. Instead, deities must comply with *Tianli*, and it is the Principle of Heaven from which "the myriad creatures receive their life" (Ivanhoe 50).

Tianli is also the moral order of the Chinese universe. This moral order "permeates all living things, animals as well as humans, plants as well as animals" (Taylor, "Animals," 293). The same moral order pervades all living beings and the natural universe. In Confucian religious traditions, the "natural order is a moral order" (Taylor, "Animals," 293), and the natural force of *Tian* is ultimate. Confucius wrote that he studied "what is below in order to comprehend what is above" (Ivanhoe, 43).

Ren

The moral nature of the universe is reflected in humanity, which is by nature virtuous. Consequently, both "humanity" and "virtue" are indicated by a single Chinese term, *ren*. In the Confucian tradition, the importance of *ren* cannot be overstated: "*Ren* must come before any other consideration…; it is a supreme value more precious than one's own life and therefore an idea worth dying for" (Tu, *Confucian*, 88).

Ren is envisioned as both fundamental and critical to human nature. *Ren* is many-faceted, combining the concept of *human* with all of the best and most important virtues of humanity. In the Confucian understanding, *ren* must be fostered to perfection by any truly spiritual human being. The spiritual goal, as well as the natural outcome of a sound Confucian life, is *ren*.

Love is "a defining characteristic" of *ren* (Tu, *Confucian*, 81, 84). Love is "the tender aspect of human feelings" and entails "an altruistic concern" for others (Tu, *Confucian*, 84). Those who are *ren* are humane and benevolent. Tenderness and altruism, kindness and benevolence are central to humanity and to Confucian morality; gentle compassion is the ultimate Confucian virtue.

Junzi

A *junzi* is a moral (or noble) human being, a person who lives up to human moral responsibilities and is therefore sensitive to anymals (Taylor, "Animals," 296). In Confucian traditions, one who shows sensitivity to a brown-eared pheasant, Chinese alligator, endangered giant panda, and the takin (a goat-antelope in the Eastern Himalayas, and one of the rarest and most endangered anymals in the world), also expresses a moral nature, and simultaneously reflects *Tian* and *Tianli* (Heaven and the Principle of Heaven). "Thus sensitivity to animals is not only ethically suitable but also carries religious authority" (Taylor, "Animals," 294).

The majority of Confucian scholars—most significantly Mencius (ca. 300 BCE), second only to Confucius as a scholar and sage in the Confucian traditions—assume human nature to be good rather than evil; good people do not delight in suffering or premature, unnecessary death. The *junzi*, or noble person, exemplifies this central human characteristic, and "cannot bear to see the suffering of others," whether fellow humans or other sentient creatures (Taylor, "Animals," 297).

Confucian writings focus on relationships, and morally correct actions include "proper relations" with anymals (Taylor, "Animals," 294). The primary Confucian text, *Analects* (ca. 500 BCE), focuses on conversations between the master, Confucius, and his disciples. In these dialogues, Confucius teaches his pupils not to take unfair advantage of other creatures. He tells his pupils that the human mind, which is innately good, "cannot bear to see the suffering of others.... [T]he Confucian mind of compassion feels all suffering and every loss of life as its own moral responsibility" (Taylor, "Animals," 306).

Great Ultimate

Neo-Confucian traditions began to take shape around 1000 CE and have long since become mainstream. In fact, there is no longer any Confucian tradition outside of Neo-Confucianism.

Neo-Confucian scholars developed a sense of the original source, or creative power, "Great Ultimate" (Taylor, "Animals," 300). This fundamental conception of the origins of the universe has important implications for white-flag dolphins, blue slate turkey, golden-haired monkeys, and the South China tiger. In the Neo-Confucian vision—now simply the Confucian vision—all things stem from the Great Ultimate, and therefore no being is above or separate from any other. In light of the Great Ultimate, we are "organically connected with rocks, trees, and animals" (Tu, "Continuity," 74–75). Neo-Confucian Cheng Yi (1033–1107) draws a moral conclusion from this understanding of the Great Ultimate: the essential requirement of humanity, that we be kind and helpful rather than cruel and harmful, extends to all creatures.

Zhu Xi, also a Neo-Confucian, notes that all beings receive "mind" from this single source. When the Great Ultimate lodges mind in a particular being, that endowment *becomes* the thoughts and motivations of that creature, so that each animal's mind is "simply the one mind of Heaven and Earth" (Taylor, "Animals," 301). Every red-crowned crane, Cochin chicken, Middle Eastern human, and Bactrian camel receives mind from the same source—the Great Ultimate. Consequently, there is no fundamental difference between the mind of a red ibis and that of Jackie Chan.

Great Unity

Neo-Confucian scholars quickly surmised that, if all things stem from the Great Ultimate, then all things are interconnected, forming one Great Unity. Indeed, core Confucian teachings "affirm the fundamental similarity of all living things" (Taylor, "Animals," 293). As all clay pots are made of clay—though they take different shapes under the potter's hand—so we are of the same essence, stemming from the same Great Ultimate. Neo-Confucian scholar Cheng Hao (ca. 1050) notes that the human of understanding knows that he or she "forms one body with all things" (Taylor, "Animals," 301).

Cheng Hao's younger brother, Cheng Yi, expands on this Confucian sense of unity, adding an element of morality: "The humane man regards Heaven and earth and all things as one body. We are not overlords; we are not separate. There is nothing which is not part of his self" (Taylor, "Animals," 301). Yet more clearly, in the *Jinsilu* (*Reflections on Things at Hand*), renowned Neo-Confucian Zhu Xi (1130–1200) instructs people to regard all that exists as *equal to self* (Taylor, "Animals," 301). Whether sun bear, human being, or Fengjing hog, all creatures are equal in light of the Great Unity.

Benevolence

Benevolence is central to *ren*, and is therefore central to Confucian morality. Under the all-encompassing umbrella of Confucian teachings of the Great Unity, only "one body" exists. Benevolence is further fostered by this vision of interconnections:

> Everything from ruler, minister, husband, wife, and friends to mountains, rivers, spiritual beings, birds, animals, and plants should be truly loved in order to realize my humanity that forms one body with them, and then my clear character will be completely manifested, and I will form one body with Heaven, Earth, and the myriad things. (Wang, 302)

Understanding Great Unity, Neo-Confucian Cheng Yi asks, "Where is the limit to our expression of benevolence?" (Taylor, "Animals," 301).

Diet

Confucian religious traditions teach of a moral universe and view the nature of humanity as benevolent, compassionate, humane, and sensitive to the needs and wants of anymals. Confucian religious traditions teach of a Great Ultimate that lies behind all, providing mind to all beings, and of a Great Unity that underlies all that exists. Confucian religious traditions teach that the sufferings of anymals, and their lives, are morally important, and that the innate goodness of humanity recoils at the thought of harming fellow creatures, who are equal, sharing the Great Unity.

Consequently, the Confucian tradition teaches against consuming anymal products which cause pain and suffering to other creatures. When an ox is spared sacrifice at the alter, it is therefore not surprising that Mencius comments that "the superior man [is] *affected* towards animals, [so] that, having seen them alive, he cannot bear to see them die; having heard their dying cries, he cannot bear to eat their flesh" (Taylor, "Animals," 297). He goes on to note that those who eat flesh will need to remain ignorant both of the individuals who are slain and the process that is inherent in turning individuals into consumable body parts (Ivanhoe, 119–20).

Daoist Philosophy and Morality

Chinese religions and philosophies share critical, fundamental similarities with Buddhist religions and philosophies. For example, Chinese philosophies of Great Unity and benevolence dovetail with Indian concepts of oneness and ahimsa. Daoism in particular shares core philosophical concepts with Buddhism, and ultimately paved the way for Indian Buddhism to penetrate the borders of China and enter into the hearts of the Chinese people. Core similarities between Daoism and Buddhism facilitated the travels of this fundamentally Indian religion on to the protected soils of China, where Buddhism took root and flourished. Over time, Buddhism helped to shape Daoist religious traditions.

Dao

The concept of Dao, or the Way, is central to Chinese religious traditions. This core concept is mentioned in the texts of each important Chinese religious tradition, and in the texts of many of the more obscure Chinese religious traditions. Confucius and Mencius both wrote of the Dao. But it was the Daoist religious tradition that placed this concept front and center.

Dao is not just a path, as "the Way" might suggest. In the Daoist tradition, Dao "abides in all" (Jochim, 8); Dao permeates all that exists. Dao is infinite, eternally changeless, nonbeing (Wu, 26–27). Dao is ultimate reality (Henricks, xviii). Dao is also critical to the formation of every individual.

> [The Dao (or Way) is] that reality, or that level of reality, that exists prior to and gave rise to all other things, the physical universe (Heaven and Earth), and all things in it.... The Way in a sense is like a great womb: it is empty and devoid in itself of differentiation, one in essence; yet somehow it contains all things in seed-like or embryo form, and all things "emerge" from the [D]ao...as babies emerge from their mothers....

> But the Way does not simply give birth to all things. Having done so, it continues in some way to be present in each individual thing as an energy or power, a power that is not static but constantly on the move, inwardly pushing each thing to develop and grow in a certain way, in a way that is in accord with its true nature (Henricks, xviii–xix).

Despite the importance of Dao, and the many words that have been put to paper to explain this concept, the full extent of Dao lies beyond our comprehension. The first lines of the most important Daoist compilation, *Daode jing*, remind readers: "The [D]ao (Way) that can be told is not the eternal [D]ao; the name that can be named is not the eternal name" (Chan, 139). Similarly, the *Zhuangzi* notes that even Zhuangzi, a great sage, found only the beginning of the realm of Dao and did not know where it might end (Waley, *Three*, 52–53). Humans are limited, and our grasp of the eternal is limited. The Dao represents that which we cannot know, that which lies outside of and beyond our understanding, that which maintains the order of the universe and permeates all that exists (Xiaogan, 323).

That said, there is much that we can and do understand about the Dao. Dao is "a natural force that is not only utterly benign but continuously at work" in the world (Kirkland, 296). The Dao encompasses all living beings and humbles humanity. According to the *Zhuangzi*, Dao is everywhere: in the ant, in the weeds, in "excrement and urine" (Chan, 203). Zhuangzi writes, "The Way [Dao] has never known boundaries" (B. Watson). Dao resides in every long-tailed shrike and Chinese sturgeon, every eld deer and crested ibis (one of the most endangered birds in the world). Each creature shares Dao—the ultimate reality—and is shaped by Dao, moved by Dao. Dao thereby offers a measure of perfection and perfectibility to everything that exists, every skink and Chinese paddlefish (though apparently now extinct).

The Daoist mind, which apparently delights in paradoxes, finds expression in this inexpressible Dao. Zhuangzi writes of Dao:

> The Way has its reality and its signs but is without action or form. You can hand it down but you cannot receive it; you can get it but you cannot see it. It is its own source, its own root. Before Heaven and earth existed it was there, firm from ancient times. It gave spirituality to the spirits and to God; it gave birth to Heaven and to earth. It exists beyond the highest point, and yet you cannot call it lofty; it exists beneath the limit of the six directions, and yet you cannot call it deep. It was born before Heaven and earth, and yet you cannot say it has been there for long; it is earlier than the earliest time, and yet you cannot call it old. (B. Watson)

Daoism postulates no definitive, personal Creator, no teleological goal, no intelligent design, and no judge to plan, punish, or even favor one activity over another. Instead, Daoists write of "a natural force that is not only utterly benign but continuously at work" in the world (Kirkland, 296). This natural force, Dao, simply "abides in all things" (Jochim, 8).

> [Dao is] the final source and ground of the universe. . . . Dao runs through the whole universe and human life and is both the transcendent and the

immanent. Therefore, as the model for human behavior and as the object of the ultimate concern of human beings, Dao is similar to God. The difference is that Dao has nothing to do with will, feelings, and purposes. (Xiaogan, 322–23)

Ci, Jian, and Bugan Wei Tianxia Xian

Daoist philosophy is built around three central moral treasures: ci (compassion or deep love), jian (restraint or frugality), and bugan wei tianxia xian ("not daring to be at the forefront of the world") (Kirkland, 294; Xiaogan, 330). All three of these concepts are deeply interconnected, and together they provide powerful protection both for nature generally and for anymals specifically.

Ci

While the basic meaning of ci is love, "ci is deeper, gentler, and broader than love" (Xiaogan, 330). Ci manifests as "gentleness, motherly love, commiseration" and is not limited to one's own species (Xiaogan, 330).

Ci requires "fostering life," a concept that is central to Daoist morality. "Fostering life" requires human beings to avoid harming any living being, even the wriggling worm. Daoism teaches respect for nature, requiring human beings to maintain habitat where the channel catfish and the Chinese water dragon might continue to live. The second to the last sentence in the Daode jing reminds readers, "The Way of Heaven is to benefit others and not to injure" (Chan, 176).

Daoist literature "abounds in stories of exemplary men and women who earned recognition—even 'transcendence'—by secretly performing compassionate acts, particularly for creatures disdained by others" (Kirkland, 293). In the famous novel, Monkey, when a good man releases a fish back into the river, his aging mother comments, "To release living things... is an act of piety. I am very glad you did it" (Ch'eng-en, 87). Monkey, and other Chinese stories that include Guanyin, are rich with anecdotes reminding people of the spiritual importance of ci.

Guanyin, a Daoist/Buddhist supernatural being (who has several well-known forms), is the most worshipped and popular of all Chinese spiritual beings (Kinsley, Goddesses', 26). Both a Daoist goddess and a bodhisattva of compassion, Guanyin is the "essence of mercy and compassion" (Kinsley, Goddesses', 26); she is ci itself (Graham, 21). Guanyin embodies and exemplifies both wisdom and deep, abiding love—moral and spiritual perfection (Graham 21; Kinsley, Goddesses', 51).

Guanyin, "She Who Listens to the World's Sounds," listens to the many sounds of the world and responds to those who cry out for help (Kinsley, Goddesses', 35). She strives to free all sentient beings from suffering and as a bodhisattva, strives to help "all beings on earth to attain enlightenment" (Sommer, 127; Storm, 194). Her central role as the "protector of all creatures" is repeatedly stressed in theater, song, myth, and literature (Palmer, 41).

Guanyin is central to the Chinese novel *Monkey* (*Hsi-yu chi*, most often translated as "Journey to the West," written by Ch'eng-en in the sixteenth century). *Monkey*, a fictional tale of adventure, utilizing popular conceptions of "Daoism" and peppered with characters from Daoist and Buddhist religious traditions, is one of China's most popular and beloved novels.

Monkey centers around the historic journey of Xuanzang (Tripitaka in the novel), a seventh-century Buddhist monk who traveled to India to acquire scriptures. His journey took seventeen years (Mair, *Columbia*, 966). Xuanzang's travels have been embellished with fantastic adventures (many of which have been adapted for lively stage productions) and transformed into a uniquely Chinese allegorical tale riddled with spiritual lessons (Hu, 5; Waley, 7–8). This "book of good humor, profound nonsense, good-natured satire and delightful entertainment" is peppered with religious satire and spiritual insights from core Chinese religious traditions that reach across Daoist, Buddhist, and even Confucian lines (Waley, "Preface," 7; Sommer, 239, 240).

Guanyin is the "guardian and protector" for the main characters in *Monkey*: a pig, a horse, a monkey, and a human who is also a Buddhist monk (Kinsley, *Goddesses'*, 37). At the outset, Guanyin gathers the various anymals who will travel with Tripitaka (the human), each of whom is important to the success of the monk's long journey west, to India. She gives to each traveler what they need, whether headache or helping hand, aiding pig and human alike in their quintessential *spiritual* journey.

Guanyin shows magnanimous generosity of heart "every day to all living beings" (Palmer, 67), and compassion is a central theme in many Guanyin myths, including *Monkey*s. For example, evil characters in *Monkey* are commonly portrayed as those who destroy the lives of others. In the most popular English rendition of *Monkey*, before converting a monster to righteous ways, Guanyin admonishes him for "adding sin to sin, slaying living creatures" (Ch'eng-en, 80). Another story of Guanyin, this time as the princess Miao Shan, tells of the bodhisattva saving a cicada from certain death, scaling a wall and falling to the ground in the process. When she alights with a bleeding wound, she remarks that both a wound and a scar are "a small price to pay for the life of a cicada" (Palmer, 67). In another story revealing an act of kindness, Guanyin purchases a carp who has been caught by fishers, and then releases him back into the sea (Palmer, 74). The carp happens to be the son of a dragon king who lives deep in nearby waters (Kinsley, *Goddesses'*, 48). He handsomely rewards her for saving his son's life from the cruel jaws of fish eaters.

Always, in all forms, toward all creatures, Guanyin shows mercy and compassion—*ci* (Blofeld, *Bodhisattva*, 80). Colorful Daoist tales such as *Monkey* repeatedly remind readers that those who are spiritually enlightened are also compassionate; cruelty is spiritual ignorance. Children, hearing these stories, are likely to understand the importance of *ci*—that their treatment of a five-toed pygmy jerboa, yellow cattle, and the critically endangered Kozlov's shrew are all matters of considerable spiritual importance.

Jian

Jian (restraint, frugality) holds out the ideal of simplicity, of living lightly on the earth. Humanity, to practice *jian*, must avoid destroying habitat, and must not exploit Manchurian hares, Yangtze giant softshell turtles, or Fengjing pigs when such exploitation is entirely unnecessary.

For Daoists, the natural state is the ideal state; therefore, humans ought to behave in a way that is harmonious with the natural world (Marshall, 19). *Jian* discourages human beings from striving or grasping at material wealth, while encouraging humanity to live gently, causing little disturbance. While humans tend to squander their short lives grasping after businesses and books, nature shows the folly of such wild bursts of mindless energy:

> A violent wind does not last for a whole morning; a
> sudden rain does not last for the whole day....
> If Heaven and Earth
> cannot make such (spasmodic) actings last long, how much less can man!
>   (Lao-Tzu, #23)

Nature shows us how to live—the preferred way to live, and the folly of alternative behavior. For those who are paying attention, nature—including anymals—teaches *jian*.

The author of the *Zhuangzi* encourages the simple life. When combined with *ci*, *jian* encourages human beings to live simply *for the sake of compassion*—so that other creatures might also live without being harmed or crowded from the planet. Human beings who practice *jian* will engage in only that which is necessary to existence and will leave by the wayside those many unnecessary activities that use resources and destroy habitat (Anderson, "Daoism," 278). For example, Daoists living with restraint and practicing frugality will avoid anymal products, and will thereby greatly reduce their harm to anymals, living simply and showing compassion.

Bugan Wei Tianxia Xian

Ci and *jian* stem from *bugan wei tianxia xian*. In other words, compassion for other creatures and a life of restraint and frugality both stem from "not daring to be at the forefront of the world."

When we place ourselves in the forefront, we push other creatures to the back. If we imagine that our needs are more important than the needs of any other species, or any other individual, then our lives become cruel and exploitative. If we imagine ourselves to be superior to other creatures, we are likely to consider other creatures expendable and to exploit them for our purposes. *Bugan wei tianxia xian* reminds humanity that we are not the center of the universe and should not behave in an exploitative, arrogant manner.

Cryptic stories in the *Zhuangzi* emphasize maintaining humility in our interactions with other individuals, particularly individuals of other species. The *Zhuangzi* reminds humanity that to "insist that one's view of things is universally valid and true for all others and all species is simply wrongheaded" (Kinsley, *Ecology*, 81). The *Zhuangzi* mocks "our tendency to view reality as if it were constructed especially for human beings," reminding that "there is more to the world than can be imagined. One should not try to conform the world to one's limited perspective" (Kinsley, *Ecology*, 81). For Daoists, *bugan wei tianxia xian* helps work against the human tendency to be arrogant, and encourages us to take our humble place in the universe, allowing other creatures to do the same.

Transformation

Daoism holds that individuals are neither isolated nor enduring; everything that exists is part of a great and ongoing transformation (L. Thompson, *Chinese Religion*, 6). Every aspect of this great cosmos interacts and participates in a self-generating process of constant fluctuation (Tu, "Continuity" 67). No one stands outside of the great process of transformation; all of us are bits and pieces of everything else. "Now a dragon, now a snake,/You transform together with the times,/And never consent to be one thing alone" (from *Zhuangzi*, in Parkes, 92).

Our bodies are recycled, after death, back into the world of matter and life. The "chain of being is never broken," and a link therefore exists between each entity and every other entity, whether agamid lizard, Euploea, Inuit human, or red-headed vulture (Tu, "Continuity," 70). All things—all beings—are bound together by this transformation process, by coming and going from the same matter, from one Great Unity (Parkes, 91).

We may prefer not to see ourselves in nose-picking children and squabbling apes, we may prefer to envision ourselves as civilized, educated, mature, or highly intelligent, but at the end of the day, we are animals. As creatures of the earth, we decompose to become yet other elements of this ever-transforming cosmos. I am this particular individual only for a handful of decades, and like all other beings who exist at this point in time, or who have existed before, my current existence as this particular being is only a momentary happenstance in an ever-transforming universe.

Unity of Being

The ongoing, endless transformations of the Daoist universe cause Unity of Being. Every part "of the entire cosmos belongs to one organic whole" that interacts as "one self-generating life process" (Tu, *Confucian*, 35). Every link in this web of life is criti-cal to every other link; everything that exists in the universe is "intrinsically related to and thus constitutive of 'self'" (Ames, 120). In words attributed to Zhuangzi, "Although the myriad things are many, their order is one" (Chan, 204). Humans, rivers, shrubs, lizards, fungi, and all other aspects of this universe, are part of a much larger whole (Tu, "Continuity," 74–75). Ultimately, the "universe and I exist together, and all things and I are one" (Chan, 186).

Daoism fosters a sense of "self" as an intimate part of a larger whole, a whole in which human beings are of no greater importance than any other species (L. Thompson, *Chinese Religion*, 6). The constant flux of the universe ties each individual to all other beings, binding "all things into one, equalizing all things" (Chan, 177). Everything that exists benefits all else, and no particular species or individual is favored in the impersonal process of transformation (Tu, "Continuity," 71–73). Consequently, the author of the *Zhuangzi* presented anymals as "equivalent to human beings" (Anderson, "Flowering," 165).

In the Daoist worldview, humans are "one of the myriad kinds of beings" (Wu, 37)—*only one* of the myriad kinds of beings. Each bar-tailed tree creeper and black-spined toad is but part of this larger whole, the Great Unity of Being (Tu, "Continuity," 71). A human being and the mountain bamboo-partridge can exist *only* as part of this larger whole. As *Zhuangzi* notes, "Heaven and earth are one attribute; the ten thousand things are one horse.... For this reason, whether you point to a little stalk or a great pillar, a leper or the beautiful Hsi-shih, things ribald and shady or things grotesque and strange, the Way [Dao] makes them all into one" (B. Watson).

Death

The Daoists, with their inclusive approach to philosophies, have a sense of death as a scattering of body parts, and as a journey through various hells.

Daoist transformations cause body parts to be scattered back into the universe after death. Transformation carries flesh and fluids back into the Great Unity, back to become parts for other individuals living as the myriad species, and back to the earth itself.

The *Zhuangzi* describes the human body as mere bits and pieces of the universe. The author explains death and decay as the physical mixing of matter. In the *Zhuangzi*, a man who is described lying on his deathbed (Master Lai) speaking with a visitor (Master Li), offers insight into the Daoist vision of death and dying. Master Lai comments:

> "I received life because the time had come; I will lose it because the order of things passes on...."
> Suddenly Master Lai grew ill. Gasping and wheezing, he lay at the point of death. His wife and children gathered round in a circle and began to cry.

Master Li, who had come to ask how he was, said, "Shoo! Get back! Don't disturb the process of change!"

Then he leaned against the doorway and talked to Master Lai. "How marvelous the Creator is! What is he going to make of you next? Where is he going to send you? Will he make you into a rat's liver? Will he make you into a bug's arm?"

Master Lai said, "A child, obeying his father and mother, goes wherever he is told, east or west, south or north. And the yin and yang—how much more are they to a man than father or mother! Now that they have brought me to the verge of death, if I should refuse to obey them, how perverse I would be! What fault is it of theirs? The Great Clod burdens me with form, labors me with life, eases me in old age, and rests me in death. So if I think well of my life, for the same reason I must think well of my death. When a skilled smith is casting metal, if the metal should leap up and say, 'I insist upon being made into a Mo-yeh!' he would surely regard it as very inauspicious metal indeed. Now, having had the audacity to take on human form once, if I should say, 'I don't want to be anything but a man! Nothing but a man!,' the Creator would surely regard me as a most inauspicious sort of person. So now I think of heaven and earth as a great furnace, and the Creator as a skilled smith. Where could he send me that would not be all right? I will go off to sleep peacefully, and then with a start I will wake up."
(B. Watson)

After Master Lai's death, Confucius is reported to have sent a messenger carrying condolences. In this quintessentially Daoist telling of the story, his messenger finds the corpse still lying on the deathbed, with a man weaving nearby, and another playing a lute and singing. He is at first horrified, but reportedly realized his mistake:

> They look upon life as a swelling tumor...and upon death as the draining of a sore or the bursting of a boil. To men such as these, how could there be any question of putting life first or death last? They borrow the forms of different creatures and house them in the same body. They forget liver and gall, cast aside ears and eyes, turning and revolving, ending and beginning again, unaware of where they start or finish. (B. Watson)

The onlooker came to see that there was no cause for solemn rights of mourning. The dead had merely been scattered back into the universe, "to wander in the single breath of heaven and earth" (B. Watson). In the Chinese worldview, all that exists is connected through the Great Transformation. Whether spotted linsang or Yunnan golden monkey (of which only about 2,000 remain, decimated by logging and hunting), we are all of one substance, all related through endless transformations.

Daoists, like Buddhists, foster a complicated vision of the afterlife that includes a host of hells. These many hells provide a window into "the structure and values" of the Chinese people (Kwok, 48). In the Daoist view of the realms to which we go after death, the second realm of hell is envisioned as a punishment for "those who have deliberately caused pain to animals" (Kwok, 48), while the first realm of hell forces the deceased to face the dreaded Terrace of Mirrors of the Wicked. The Terrace of Mirrors forces humans to "look into a mirror and see all those whom [they] have harmed in any way" (Kwok, 47)—*any* being "who has suffered for your sake" (Kwok, 47). Depictions of human beings looking into the Terrace of Mirrors often show cattle, pigs, dogs, and fish gazing back from the mirror's revealing glass, their premature deaths destined to affect all those who were responsible.

Chinese Buddhist hells where human beings suffer for indifference and cruelty to anymals further encourage compassion for all living beings. Visions of transformation and the Great Unity, combined with a healthy fear of hells, foster compassion for all beings.

Harmony, Ultimate Integrity, and Peace

Harmony is core and central to Daoism—to the Chinese worldview more broadly. The well-known "yin-yang" image, rooted in the yin-yang school of philosophy, perhaps most clearly conveys the ancient and well-developed Chinese idea of balance and reciprocity—harmony—in a vast and varied universe.

The Daoist universe is ordered—harmonious—so that "alternating forces and phases" shape "rhythms of life" (Kleeman, 67). Daoism portrays discord as shallow, like the waves that skim across a great ocean. Waves are part of the ocean—they *are* the ocean—they only *appear* separate. The turbulence of waves is likened to disharmony. Waves are turbulent, but the great body of water on which they travel, and of which they are ultimately part, is quiet and still. Waves ultimately break onto the shore and retreat back into the ocean, once again absorbed into a vast body of water that is both moving and still, dark and light, one and many. The wave is soon spent and again becomes indistinct from the larger body of water.

Harmony is a Chinese ideal to be realized in the lives of human beings, but humans sometimes get caught up in their personal lives, like waves tearing across the ocean; Daoism discourages this shortsighted approach to existence and encourages *bugan wei tianxia xian*—not daring to stand apart, as if we were something noteworthy or miraculous, when we are merely momentary primates. Daoism fosters the harmonious life, and choices that are mindful of our short existence. Daoists are encouraged to maintain an outlook and lifestyle that speaks to deeper realities. Spiritual advancement requires people to *know* and *act* on this understanding of harmony. It is our duty to live "for the fulfillment of the health and harmony of all living things" (Kirkland, 296).

Harmony pervades the cosmos, which *is* union, integration, and synthesis, rather than exclusivity, individuality, and separation. Shallow, human disharmony arises from the error of forgetting, or neglecting to notice, our deeper, shared unity with the larger world. In contrast with this shallow lifestyle, harmony is envisioned as reaching the depths of quietude that stretch down to the ocean floor. However much we might behave like an independent wave, we are the ocean, the Great Unity, along with the rest of nature, all of which functions in and through harmony.

Daoist writing, like most sacred writings, envisions a time of harmony (often considered a time of great peace in other traditions). In this ideal time of harmony, which exists somewhere in the future, communities of varied species will live together in peace. The *Zhuangzi* explains that, "left to their own devises, human beings and animals would form harmonious natural communities" (Mair, *Wandering*, 80). When people stop exploiting and terrorizing anymals, we will live in a golden age of "ultimate integrity"—side by side, together and separate. In this world, anymals will not fear humans—but they will not be domesticated. Writings attributed to Zhuangzi state the following about this flourishing land of harmony, untrammeled by humanity, a world that can only be realized when we live into our true nature:

> In a time of Perfect Virtue the gait of men is slow and ambling; their gaze is steady and mild. In such an age mountains have no paths or trails, lakes no boats or bridges. The ten thousand things live species by species, one group settled close to another. Birds and beasts form their flocks and herds, grass and trees grow to fullest height. So it happens that you can tie a cord to the birds and beasts and lead them about, or bend down the limb and peer into the nest of the crow and the magpie. In this age of Perfect Virtue men live the same as birds and beasts, group themselves side by side with the ten thousand things. . . . In uncarved simplicity the people attain their true nature. (B. Watson)

Wuwei

The Daoist concept of *wuwei* dovetails with *jian* (restraint, frugality), *bugan wei tianxia xian* (not daring to be at the forefront of the world), and the Daoist conception of harmony. *Wei* refers to "human action intending to achieve results"—results thought to be "superior to what would result if nature were simply allowed to take its own course" (Kirkland, 295). *Wu* is a prefix that negates whatever comes after. Therefore, *wuwei* means "not to engage in human action intending to achieve results superior to those that would naturally occur." *Wuwei* is generally translated as nonstriving, acting without acting, nonaction, or perhaps most appropriately, "action as non-action" (Xiaogan, 316).

Wuwei does not demand *no* action. In fact, it is impossible to be alive and refrain from action, since we must at least breathe to live. *Wuwei* "refers to a higher standard of human actions and their results" (Xiaogan, 315–16). *Wuwei* requires that practitioners abandon human intrigue and live "in accordance with nature" without attempting to control or change our surroundings or other creatures (Po-Keung, "Taoism," 334).

Wuwei is consistent with the humble place of human beings in a much larger universe. *Wuwei* is consistent with keeping a low profile and maintaining harmony. The *Zuangzi* encourages humanity to practice *wuwei* to avoid "corrupting the inborn nature of the world":

> I have heard of letting the world be, of leaving it alone; I have never heard of governing the world. You let it be for fear of corrupting the inborn nature of the world; you leave it alone for fear of distracting the Virtue of the world. If the nature of the world is not corrupted, if the Virtue of the world is not distracted, why should there be any governing of the world? (B. Watson)

Daoist religious traditions encourage people to practice *wuwei* so that nature can takes its course, with the understanding that nature operates exactly as it should because it is moved "by a force [Dao] that is like a loving mother" (Kirkland, 298). Extraneous human actions can only cause disturbance because "there actually is a benign natural force at work in the world," (Kirkland, 297). Therefore, in the *Daode jing*, the greatest accomplishment is no accomplishment:

> He who acts does harm; he who takes hold
> of a thing loses his hold. The sage does not act,
> and therefore does no harm; he does not lay hold, and
> therefore does not lose his hold....
> The sage desires to have no desire....
> He learns to be unlearned, and returns to what the multitude has missed ([D]ao).
> Thus he supports all things in their natural state but does not take any action.
>   (Lao-Tzu, #64)

The *Daode jing* reminds Daoists to keep "hands off the processes at work in the world" because the world is a "spiritual vessel, and one cannot act upon it; one who acts upon it destroys it" (Kirkland, 296).

> Dao represents forever the unknown final reason of the world surrounding us, reminding human beings of their limitations. As average members of the...universe, humans have no power to do what they wish without

facing unexpected consequences. Therefore, prudent behavior and action, namely [*wuwei*] are important and beneficial. (Xiaogan, 232–34)

Wuwei is central to the Daoist life. *Wuwei* encourages simplicity. Those who live a simple life are not driven to action by desires. *Wuwei* also allows humans to live "in harmony with…all other creatures" (Kinsley, *Ecology*, 79). Acting without action embodies "the spirit of naturalness," which coincides with harmony and is "directed toward the realization of natural harmony both among human societies and between humans and nature" (Xiaogan, 321). Consistent with the larger Daoist vision, *wuwei* reminds humans that they are not to dominate or control. *Wuwei* discourages "movements exercised intensively, coercively, dramatically, and on a large scale" (Xiaogan, 217). The author of the *Zhuangzi* writes the following:

"What do you mean by Nature and what do you mean by man?"…
"A horse or a cow has four feet. That is Nature. Put a halter around the horse's head and put a string through the cow's nose, that is man. Therefore it is said, "Do not let man destroy Nature." (Chan, 207)

Controlling horses or cows is a form of interference. Horses and cattle are not here to satisfy our whims. Horses and cattle should be allowed to go about their own lives, consistent with their own natures. Controlling actions (*wei*) are likely to turn happy equines into "brigands" and ultimately destroy their lives (Mair, *Wandering*, 82):

Horses' hooves are made for treading frost and snow, their coats for keeping out wind and cold. To munch grass, drink from the stream, lift up their feet and gallop, this is the true nature of horses. Though they might possess great terraces and fine halls, they would have no use for them.
Then along comes Po Lo. "I'm good at handling horses!" he announces, and proceeds to singe them, shave them, pare them, brand them, bind them with martingale and crupper, tie them up in stable and stall. By this time two or three out of ten horses have died. He goes on to starve them, make them go thirsty, race them, prance them, pull them into line, force them to run side by side, in front of them the worry of bit and rein, behind them the terror of whip and crop. By this time over half the horses have died. (B. Watson)

Wuwei reminds people that nature requires no change or refinements, no human control or alterations, and that any such attempts will only lead to ruin (Kinsley, *Ecology*, 80). Daoist writings remind human beings not to force anymals to fulfill our needs or satisfy our whims.

In the Daoist view, tampering with the lives of anymals demonstrates a lack of spiritual understanding. Breeding to acquire fatter cattle, debeaking, artificial insemination, and genetic manipulation are all examples of *wei*—"human action intending to achieve results," thought to be "superior to what would result if nature were simply allowed to take its own course" (Kirkland, 295). Rather than support factory farming, the Daoist practitioner ought to allow for the ongoing harmonious unfolding of the universe, where "everything develops or is accomplished naturally" (Xiaogan, 321). Daoist traditions teach that what is natural is ideal; anymals (like people) are best left in their natural state (Anderson, "Daoism," 279).

This is no less true of wild animals than it is of animals that humans have domesticated. Humans sometimes imagine that wild anymals are better off in human care, where food and water are abundant. On this subject, Zhuangzi is credited with writing that the "swamp pheasant has to walk ten paces for one peck and a hundred paces for one drink, but [he] doesn't want to be kept in a cage. Though you treat [him] like a king, [his] spirit won't be content" (B. Watson). Though the wild pheasant must work for water and food, such menial tasks are natural—they are the pheasant's life, the pheasant's special way of being, or *te*—the pheasant's Dao. The wilds are where such fowl belong, where the pheasant will always prefer to remain, and in Daoist philosophy, where we ought to leave the pheasant—and all other creatures. The *Daode jing* notes, "Fish should not be taken away from the water" (#36) (Chan, 157). Even if we imagine that we improve the lives of anymals, meddling in their lives is harmful.

Wuwei speaks against development, against interfering with the lives of wild anymals—especially to benefit human interests, such as the interests of hunters or ranchers. Our interferences are ultimately self-defeating. (The *Daode jing* notes, "Racing and hunting cause one's mind to be mad" (#12) (Chan, 145).) *Wuwei* requires human beings to leave other creatures alone (Kinsley, *Ecology*, 79), and *wuwei* reminds people that the only "wise and beneficent behavior" for humans— the only way to achieve harmony—is *bugan wei tianxia xian* and *jian*, "humble and enlightened self-restraint," which leads to *wuwei* and which is essential to the natural and proper functioning of Dao (Kirkland, 296).

> Attain complete vacuity,
> Maintain steadfast quietude....
> Being one with Nature [is to be] in accord with [D]ao. (Henricks, #16)

Daoist wisdom reminds people of their limitations, and instructs human beings to be mindful (if not leery) of factory farming—or any other methods of interfering with the planet and anymals (Xiaogan, 232). What do we know of the unfolding universe? How often have humans discovered—too late—the ill effects of well-intentioned manipulations?

Dao operates by *wuwei*: "Dao invariably takes no action, and yet there is nothing left undone" (Henricks, #37). The *Zhuangzi* notes that the Dao is "without action or form" and that "The Perfect Man uses his mind like a mirror—going after nothing, welcoming nothing, responding but not storing" (B. Watson). To practice *wuwei* is therefore to behave according to Dao (Xiaogan, 323).

Daoist Precepts: Do Not Kill or Harm

Daoist precepts specifically promote "compassion, empathy, and kindness" toward anymals (Kohn, *Cosmos*, 71). Daoism speaks clearly against killing and provides a compassionate "universalistic ethic" that extends "not only to all humanity, but to the wider domain of all living things" (Kirkland, 284).

Anymals are explicitly protected by a multitude of Daoist precepts (lists of rules) that define "who Daoists [are] and where they fit into the greater network of society, world, and cosmos" (Kohn, *Cosmos*, 135). The *Record of Purgations of Precepts* (Zhaijie lu, eighth century), for example, teaches Daoists to be compassionate, nurturing, caring, and selfless "for the sake of all beings" (Kohn, *Cosmos*, 68). Similarly, the first precept of *The Scripture of the Ten Precepts* (*Shijie jing*, fifth century) requires Daoists to "always be mindful of the host of living beings" (Kohn, *Cosmos*, 185).

The many lists of Daoist precepts that reach modern readers across history are generally similar, usually containing five foundational precepts, the first of which is an injunction not to kill (Kohn, *Cosmos*, 67). *The 180 Precepts of Lord Lao* (Laojun yibai bashi jie, fifth century), one of the oldest Daoist compositions (and one that contains a compilation that is foundational to Daoism), is often recapitulated in community moral codes and in more recent Daoist lists of precepts (Kohn, *Cosmos*, 137). The Daoist injunction against killing is repeated frequently in *The 180 Precepts*, in varied forms, including warnings against "killing in general, killing birds, killing animals, [and] eating meat" (Kohn, *Cosmos*, 136). Additionally, *The 180 Precepts* warn against harming anymals, whether insects, birds, or mammals, whether by disrupting their homes, destroying their families, or through abuse such as overwork (Schipper, 84–85):

  1. Do not keep many animals....
  4. Do not kill or harm any being....
  8. Do not raise pigs or sheep....
  24. Do not...eat meat....
  39. Do not engage in killing....
  40. Do not encourage others to kill....
  49. Do not step on or kick...domestic animals....
  79. Do not fish or hunt and thereby harm and kill the host of living beings....
  95. Do not in winter dig up insects hibernating in the earth....
  97. Do not wantonly climb trees or plunder nests and destroy birds' eggs....
  98. Do not catch birds or beasts in cages or nets.

129. Do not wantonly whip the six domestic animals.

130. Do not ride a horse or drive a carriage without good reason....

132. Do not startle birds or beasts....

142. Always be mindful of purity and remember the divine law, honor the pure and wise, and [sparingly] eat like a deer and drink like cattle....

150. Always diligently avoid being cruel....

172. If someone kills birds and beasts, fish or other living beings for you, do not eat them.

173. If something has been killed for food, do not eat it....

176. To be able to cut out all meat of living beings and the six domestic animals is best; without doing this, you will violate the precepts.

180. Practice these precepts without violation, and if you violate one make sure you repent properly. Then change your behavior.... [W]idely pursue the salvation of all beings. (Kohn, *Cosmos*, 137–44)

Precepts of the Highest Lord Lao (*Taishang Laojun jiejing*, sixth century) clarify that all beings are included in the first precept: "The precept to abstain from killing means that you must not kill any living being,...be it flying or merely wriggling" (Kohn, *Cosmos*, 148). *Great Precepts of Self-Observation* (*Guanshen dajie*, sixth century) forbid harming anymals and offer a specific list of examples, including harm caused by raising domestic anymals (#33), destroying small creatures by burning (#39), riding horses or using carriages (#138), startling anymals or digging them out of the earth (#146), or capturing wild anymals or birds in cages (#153) (Kohn, *Cosmos*, 205–211). This same text contains equally clear prohibitions against harming wild lands—against destroying habitat.

Chinese precepts, like many religious precepts, tend to be stated as prohibitions, but *The Great Precepts of the Highest Ranks* (*Shangpin dajie*, fifth century) offer a list of affirmative actions under the title of "The Highest Precepts of Wisdom for the Salvation of All Living Beings." Three out of six of these precepts focus on *munificence* in our interactions with anymals:

4. Give wisely to the birds and beasts, to all species of living creatures. Take from your own mouth to feed them, let there be none left unloved or not cherished. May they be full and satisfied generation after generation. May they always be born in the realm of blessedness.

5. Save all that wriggles and runs, all the multitude of living beings. Allow them all to reach fulfillment and prevent them from suffering an early death. May they all have lives in prosperity and plenty. May they never step into the multiple adversities.

6. Always practice compassion in your heart, commiserating with all. Liberate living beings from captivity and rescue them from danger. (Kohn, *Cosmos*, 175)

The explicit goal of affirmative actions listed in *The Great Precepts of the Highest Ranks* is to "help all living beings realize the Dao" (Kohn, *Cosmos*, 168). Similarly, the previously mentioned *Great Precepts of Self-Observation* require adherents to "place the myriad beings first and not... attain the Dao only for" oneself (Kohn, *Cosmos*, 215).

The Daoist school of Complete Perfection (Quanzhen) gained state sanction under the rule of the Mongol, Genghis Khan, in the thirteenth century, and soon became the leading branch of Daoism. Complete Perfection has remained China's "major monastic organization" ever since (Kohn, *Cosmos*, 134). This Daoist order maintains "strong continuity" with earlier "Daoist ethics and behavior models" and exemplifies core Daoist teachings, most importantly, requiring adherents to nourish and protect the natural world, including anymals (Kohn, *Cosmos*, 134).

Wang Kunyang (1622–1680) of the Complete Perfection branch of Daoism, compiled manuals and precepts that remain "an indispensable means to enlightenment and an important element in the education of the Daoist clergy" (Kohn, *Cosmos*, 253). In traditional Daoist style, the initial precept in his *Precepts of Initial Perfection* (*Chuzhen jie*) requires that members "not kill any living being" (Kohn, *Cosmos*, 255). The precepts that follow in the *Precepts of Initial Perfection* reiterate this principal requirement: "Do not kill or harm anything that lives in order to satisfy your own appetites [22a]. Always behave with compassion and grace to all, even insects and worms" (Kohn, *Cosmos*, 255, 256).

Diet

While the first precept clearly requires a plant-based diet, many Daoist precepts explicitly denounce eating flesh under any circumstance. For example, the *Ten Precepts of Initial Perfection* (contained in the work of Wang Kunyang) forbid monks from consuming flesh (Kohn, *Cosmos*, 256). In *The Great Precepts of Self-Observation*, among thoughts that one ought to cultivate, the first is a commitment to vegetarian food (Kohn, *Cosmos*, 214). The *Precepts of the Three Primes* (medieval) specifically denounce slaughtering domestic anymals (#68), shooting wild anymals or birds (#69), setting traps to catch fish (#71), and setting fires to hunt (#70) (Kohn, *Cosmos*, 137–144). *Great Precepts of Self-Observation* (*Guanshen dajie*, sixth century) similarly forbid harm caused by hunting or raising domestic anymals (#33) (Kohn, *Cosmos*, 205–211). Finally, *The 180 Precepts* (listed above) specify "particular situations in which killing might be indicated but should not be pursued" (Kohn, *Cosmos*, 36). For example, precepts #172 and #173 indicate that eating flesh is inadmissible *even if*, as a guest, one is served the wings of a hen or part of a pig's leg. To eat flesh is to "violate the precepts" (Kohn, *Cosmos*, 144).

Guanyin, in the form of the princess Miao Shan, refused the riches of the palace in preference for "a bowl of rice and vegetables" (Palmer, 66). Devotees of Guanyin, the protector of all life, often take up a "purely vegetarian diet" (Palmer, 40). The most popular English translation of *Monkey* explains that Monkey's breath is pure because he consumes only plant foods, while the breath of flesh eaters is defiled (Ch'eng-en, 199). In this same novel, the Chinese Buddhist monk, Tripitaka, dwelling with hunters, explains that he has never and does not eat flesh. The hunter apologizes for giving him food that "his conscience forbids" him to eat (Ch'eng-en, 123).

Like Buddhist monastic practice, Daoist monastic practice does not allow for violence of any kind, including killing anymals and consuming their flesh (Kohn, *Cosmos*, 50). Ko Hung (fourth century) wrote that practitioners ought to "entirely abstain from flesh" (L. Thompson, *Chinese Religions*, 85). It is therefore not surprising that Daoist monks continue to enjoy a peaceful life fueled by a fleshless diet. In fact, because dairy products are not part of the traditional Chinese diet, many "vegetarians" in China are actually much closer to vegan. They do not partake of any anymal products, with the possible exception of eggs. Monastery meals consist "largely of rice, wheat, and barley, combined with various vegetables and tofu. In Daoist religious literature, meat is not even mentioned among the five main food groups" (Kohn, *Cosmos*, 51). A Daoist priest comments on temple food:

> Generally speaking, the dishes tend to be simple combinations of vegetables with minimal amounts of seasoning, supplemented with rice, millet, or *mantou* (steamed buns). At times, one also finds *doufu* (Tofu). Generally speaking, monastic meals go beyond modern conceptions of "vegetarianism"; they are vegan (no eggs or dairy products). Until quite recently, dairy products were not consumed in China, so the avoidance of eggs is most noteworthy. (Komjathy, 97)

Members and leaders of the school of Complete Perfection continue to live in wild places, embracing Daoist simplicity and celibacy, and subsisting on a vegan diet. As a consequence, wildlife and landscapes are preserved in areas around Complete Perfection monasteries; no humans are engendered to flood across the earth, consuming everything in their wake, and no living beings are slaughtered to fatten the monks. Additionally, Daoist ritual purity "requires the avoidance of animal slaughter and blood sacrifice"—not just on the altar, but on the kitchen counter, and in one's own body (Komjathy, 101).

Daoists view living beings as sacred vessels, and the concept of cosmic harmony and salvation includes "all sentient beings" such that any sacred space "is simultaneously in the world and in the self" (Komjathy, 101). Daoism teaches of a "subtle" or energetic body that resides "within the body"; this subtle body requires "attentiveness to what one ingests," which requires that human beings avoid consuming impurities (Komjathy, 101) such as flesh and blood, pus (which is always present in factory-farmed dairy products), and antibiotics and hormones (also always present in factory-farmed products).

What one ingests is what one is. To consume the meat of slaughtered animals is to make suffering, injury, and violent death part of oneself. Meat
eating is not the practice of priest or immortal; such is not the practice of
"adepts *of* the Dao" or realized beings. (Komjathy, 101)

Daoist purity requires a plant-based diet—not just a vegetarian diet—because dairy
and eggs are created in industries that slaughter cattle and hens when they no longer
produce milk or eggs. Furthermore, both male calves and chicks are destroyed at
birth or shortly thereafter for the sake of milk and egg production. Anymal products, including dairy and eggs, are inevitably linked with slaughter in contemporary
markets. Because bloodshed is spiritually impure, and because both the internal
physical body and the physical universe are sacred, Daoist practice requires a vegan
diet.

Divine-Anymal Relations

Guanyin is often depicted with a peacock, reminding devotees both of her role in
creation, and of the original peace that existed among all living beings:

At the beginning of time, when the world was young and all the creatures
of the world but newly made, Kuan Yin dwelt with all the creatures upon
Earth. At first she taught them how to live, each according to their own
ways. She taught them how to treat others and how to show kindness to
their young. Under her tutelage, the animals, birds and insects lived happily together. If a disagreement broke out, they came to her for advice.
Thus was all peaceful in the world and every creature loved and adored
[Guanyin]. (Palmer, 58)

The peace of the original world is broken every time Guanyin returns to the realms
of the divine, and as a consequence she repeatedly returns to the earth to help anymals settle disputes, and once again teach them to live peacefully with one another.
Finally, she establishes the peacock as her proud helpmate, leaving him in charge in
her absence. She gives the peacock many eyes in his tail and leaves him to guard and
watch over the anymals when she is away. She tells the anymals, "When you see the
peacock's 100 eyes you will know that I care for all of you.... [A]nd know that I look
after you" (Palmer, 61). To this day, the peacock, with his proud strut and many-
eyed tail, reminds all beings that Guanyin "watches over them" (Palmer, 62).

Another Chinese myth that reveals the spiritual importance of anymals focuses
on the teachings of a highly respected heavenly ruler, the Yellow Emperor (considered the source of all human knowledge). He teaches one of the famed immortals
(part divinity, part human being) "that every person, animal and plant is important

no matter how small it is" and that we should "not be critical" of the natural world (Kwok, 136). In many Chinese myths, a sage's exceptional spiritual accomplishments can be demonstrated, or revealed, by a visit from a wild beast (Anderson, "Daoism," 283).

More commonly, Chinese deities are associated with specific anymals. For example, the popular Chinese god of long life is associated with the crane, stag, and tortoise (Storm, 231).

The most distinctive feature of Zhang Guolao (an immortal) is that he is often atop his donkey, riding backward—this is how he first landed on the donkey, and so he remained. One story tells how he was united with this donkey, and also with immortality, through the help of a rabbit, who later turns into a wolf. The wolf loses his life helping Zhang, but the fleet-footed donkey, who flies through the air in pursuit of immortality, becomes his friend across lifetimes (Kwok, 122–27). Another tale of Zhang Guolao explains how he stumbled across a wonderful lunch that had been left to cook in an abandoned temple, and shared it with his companion donkey. The potent herbs turned both into immortals (Kwok, 118–19). Yet a third myth explains how the donkey prevented Zhang Guolao from being kidnapped by a band of marauding sea crabs.

The mythology of the bodhisattva Guanyin is extensive, and perhaps best exemplifies divine-anymal relations. Her associates involve a considerable list of anymals, including the peacock mentioned above. In many stories, anymals assist her in critical times of need. In the story of Miao Shan, for example, she is aided by an earth God who takes the form of a gigantic tiger and, when she is toiling in a monastery kitchen, "gods summoned to her service" tigers and birds, to help her out (Palmer, 70). Anymals freely serve the benevolent Guanyin, and she helps each of them in his or her time of need. She cares for anymals, and they care for her.

Human-Anymal Relations

Neither Neo-Confucian nor Daoist traditions are rooted in a hierarchy of being (Hall, 109). All creatures are part of the Great Unity/Unity of Being, and what is natural—each being as he or she stands—is understood to be good. This appreciation for the whole and its parts sets the tone for amiable equality among animals.

Anymals as Individuals

In Daoist traditions, each entity is just as it should be; each anymal is just as acceptable as any human. Each has her or his special way of being, a *te*, and this *te* is to be honored both in self and in others—all others—whether Chinese serow, dhole, or dice snake (Hall, 110). Preferences, ways, and the personal experiences of other creatures are therefore to be acknowledged and respected.

The *Zhuangzi*, presents anymals as independent individuals, mentioning roughly seventy-five anymals, including the tortoise, fish, butterfly, rat, fly, gibbon, yak, frog, snake, centipede, dog, rooster, ant, calf, dragonflies, sea birds, white horned owl, pigeons, marsh pheasant, ox, and wildcat (Anderson, "Flowering," 165; Anderson, "Daoism," 276; Merton). The author does not use anymals as mere metaphors; he relates personally to each individual. Under his pen, even "insect transformations are recorded in exquisite . . . detail" (Anderson, "Daoism," 276). He presents even the smallest creature vibrantly, as a colorful individual.

According to writings attributed to Zhuangzi, if we fail to adopt the point of view of anymals—if we fail to understand their individuality—we fail in our empathy, and we lose something central to our humanity. In mystical musings, the *Zhuangzi* notes that our attitudes and opinions are just that—our attitudes and opinions. These human understandings cannot touch the real world, which is beyond our judgments, just as it should be:

> People suppose that words are different from the peeps of baby birds, but is there any difference, or isn't there? . . .
>
> What is acceptable we call acceptable; what is unacceptable we call unacceptable. A road is made by people walking on it; things are so because they are called so. What makes them so? Making them so makes them so. What makes them not so? Making them not so makes them not so. Things all must have that which is so; things all must have that which is acceptable. There is nothing that is not so, nothing that is not acceptable. (B. Watson)

As spiritual human beings, we ought to recognize our limited perspective, the many ways in which our viewpoint prevents us from seeing what other creatures might see—or be. This insight is expressed in other stories in the *Zhuangzi*, such as the author's recollection of a pompous official's monologue while visiting a pigpen (here referred to as the "shambles"):

> The Grand Augur, in his ceremonial robes, approached the shambles and thus addressed the pigs: "How can you object to die? I shall fatten you for three months. I shall discipline myself for ten days and fast for three. I shall strew fine grass, and place you bodily upon a carved sacrificial dish. Does not this satisfy you?"
>
> Then, speaking from the pigs' point of view, he continued: "It is better, perhaps, after all, to live on bran and escape the shambles. . . ."
>
> "But then," added he, speaking from his own point of view, "to enjoy honour when alive one would readily die on a warshield or in the headsman's basket."

So he rejected the pigs' point of view and adopted his own point of view.
In what sense, then, was he different from the pigs? (Giles, 60–61)

The author of the *Zhuangzi* encourages human beings to recognize our tendency to
view the world from our own perspective, and the importance of moving beyond
this limited perspective to see the individuality of each creature. In this way, we gain
a more realistic view of the larger universe, and in the process, we empathize with
other creatures, gaining the ability to view the world from their perspective. This
ability to see the world through another's eyes is presented as a critical requirement
of mature, enlightened human beings. The pompous Grand Augur, like a three-year-
old, is unable to understand another's perspective. He imagines that honor in war is
as important to a pig as it is to him, that an honorable death is preferable to life itself.
The *Zhuangzi* suggests that those who assume that an anymal is too dumb and
senseless to prefer life best demonstrate their own shortcomings.

While the ability to take the point of view of other individuals—including other
creatures—is critical, the *Zhuangzi* cautions, noting that we should not assume that
our experiences and the experiences of others (especially when dealing with other
species) are identical. All beings are individuals—unique. We should therefore be
reticent to draw firm conclusions as to what others prefer:

> If a man sleeps in a damp place, he will have a pain in his loins and will dry
> up and die. Is that true of eels? If a man lives up in a tree he will be fright-
> ened and tremble. Is that true of monkeys? Which of the three knows the
> right place to live? Men eat vegetables and flesh, and deer eat tender grass.
> Centipedes enjoy snakes, and owls and crows like mice. Which of the four
> knows the right taste? (Chan, 187)

We are not eels or owls; they are unique individuals with their own *te*, their own
Dao. No two species are identical, and even within one species, no two individuals
are identical. Each living being is unique and ought to be understood as a unique
individual. Only someone as small-minded as the Grand Augur imagines that anymals prefer our manipulations to the natural unfolding of their own fate.

Along the same lines, the *Zhuangzi* relates a poignant tale of a seabird blown
ashore, for whom the foolish marquis of Lu offers fine dining and musical perfor-
mances, but the "bird only looked dazed and forlorn" and after three days, died
(B. Watson). The author admonishes such foolishness—attempting to nourish a
bird with human dainties—and suggests that a bird be given what a bird prefers, not
what Lu prefers:

> If you want to nourish a bird with what nourishes a bird, then you should
> let it roost in the deep forest, play among the banks and islands, float on the
> rivers and lakes, eat mudfish and minnows, follow the rest of the flock in

flight and rest, and live any way it chooses. A bird hates to hear even the sound of human voices, much less all that hubbub and to-do. Try performing the Hsien-ch'ih and Nine Shao music in the wilds around Lake Tung-t'ing; when the birds hear it they will fly off, when the animals hear it they will run away, when the fish hear it they will dive to the bottom. Only the people who hear it will gather around to listen. Fish live in water and thrive, but if men tried to live in water they would die. Creatures differ because they have different likes and dislikes. Therefore the former sages never required the same ability from all creatures or made them all do the same thing. (B. Watson)

Our pleasures and preferences should not be forced on anymals; each creature is unique. Human beings who understand *te* understand the importance of approaching anymals from *their* perspective, not ours. Just because we like symphonies does not mean that a sea bird will also like symphonies. Just because some humans might prefer to "die on a warshield" does not mean that a Ningxiang pig prefers to die "upon a carved sacrificial dish." If we honor the individuality of anymals, we will not imagine human joys to be perch joys, or human pains to be hummingbird pains.

The *Zhuangzi* walks a fine line, honoring individuality while accepting commonality, expecting humans to empathize with anymals but insisting that we not transfer our agenda onto the lives of individuals from other species. Although Daoism requires empathy—taking the position of another—the *Zhuangzi* cautions against making hard and fast determinations about what is best for others based on what we imagine we would choose for ourselves, as did the self-serving and pompous Grand Augur.

The fictional novel *Monkey* provides an excellent example of anymals as independent individuals with well-developed personalities. While entertaining and lighthearted, the anymal characters are intended to inspire humanity, and allow human beings to see themselves, struggling along on their own difficult and often halting spiritual paths. Along with the monk and the monkey, both discussed previously, the main characters in this story are a pig and a horse—both of whom have "been banished to horrid existences on earth" because of inappropriate behavior in the heavenly realms (Jochim, 106). Pigsy, who "drunkenly dallied with the moon goddess" (Jochim, 106), represents "physical appetites, brute strength, and a kind of cumbrous patience" (Waley, *Monkey*, 8). Sandy, the white horse, was transformed from dragon prince to fierce dragon after he broke a crystal dish at a heavenly banquet (Ch'eng-en, 80; Mair, *Columbia*, 966). Both were banished to lives of bloodshed, which would only further distance them from their ultimate spiritual goals (Jochim, 106). Each character in *Monkey* is critical to the journey, and no player is either perfect or perfectly awful—each is a "delinquent convert" (Jochim, 106). Tripitaka, ostensibly the main character, similarly represents a very mixed bag of traits—just like his anymal companions. Though Tripitaka is a monk on a great pilgrimage, he exemplifies "the ordinary man, blundering anxiously through the difficulties of life" (Waley, *Monkey*, 8). Tripitaka sometimes sits by the side of the road, reduced to helpless tears in the face of life's difficulties. The human character is not distinct from the other characters—ultimately he is no better, and no worse. Each is portrayed as blundering along their own spiritual path, sometimes with a measure of grace and determination, other times falling victim to weakness and uncertainty. Each character is important; each plays a key role in the exciting adventures that unfold as this unusual foursome travels westward in tandem; each is under the careful watch of Guanyin as they walk together and alone through the unfolding of their spiritual journeys.

When reading *Monkey*, it is easy to see how this story came to be named after just one character. Monkey, the most vibrant and interesting character in the novel, "represents the human mind and, as such, is resourceful and intelligent, but at the same time is unbridled and wild unless controlled" (Mair, *Columbia*, 967). In this entertaining novel, Monkey outwits or defies some of the most famed spiritual powers of Chinese religious traditions, including "Heaven, the Court, Lao Tzu [Laozi] and the Jade Emperor himself" (Kwok, 43). He combines "beauty with absurdity" and "profundity with nonsense," sporting "the restless instability of genius" (Waley, *Monkey*, 7–8).

Those who work across religious traditions cannot help but compare this boisterous primate to Hanuman in the Hindu *Ramayana*. Both are powerful and likable, though the Chinese monkey has a much more questionable character. In the Chinese tale, for example, Monkey causes so much trouble in the Halls of Heaven that he must be contained and controlled—and punished. So he is entrapped in a stone for five hundred years. He is released by the bodhisattva Guanyin only for the purpose of helping Tripitaka on his journey to India. Desperate to escape, the difficult monkey promises to fulfill this task faithfully, if released, but soon kills a handful of thieves. Tripitaka, bent on honoring at least the first and most fundamental Buddhist precept—not to take life—scolds Monkey. In the face of Tripitaka's criticism, the undisciplined primate neglects his promise and abandons his responsibilities. Only with help from the bodhisattva, Guanyin, can Monkey be recalled to the tasks at hand.

To assure Monkey's compliance, Guanyin provides a cap and jacket that Monkey impulsively dons, not knowing of the cap's powers and always inclined to act before pausing to think. He is vexed when he finds that the cap is impossible to remove and capable of delivering a splitting headache. Thereafter, whenever Tripitaka recites a certain spell, the cap reminds Monkey of his promise, and his obligations (Ch'eng-en, 133–37). In this way, Monkey is forced to focus on accomplishing the spiritual task at hand—the journey west. Of no less importance, Guanyin thereby helps Monkey—and each of the other travelers—to progress on his own personal spiritual journey.

Kinship and Community

Animals are kindred spirits in the Daoist tradition. They form one spiritual community. They are kin not in the sense of relatives, but in the sense of a shared source, of core attributes, and of a common individuality. Animals are kin because of "the numinous presence of the Dao" and because of the Great Unity, both of which we share equally (Komjathy, 103). In the first century CE, Wang Chong, recounting "Daoist Truths," noted, "Man is a creature ...; his nature cannot be different from that of other creatures" (Mair, *Columbia*, 65–66). A thousand years later, on pondering the Great Unity, Zhang Zai (Neo-Confucian, ca. 1050) wrote, "All things are my companions" (Taylor, "Animals," 301; Tu, *Confucian*, 43).

In Daoist writings, kinship and community are expressed in typical Chinese style, emphasizing paradoxes and stretching our assumptions as to what is outrageous. For example, writings attributed to Zhuangzi grant a specific experience involved with being a butterfly, and also with being human, yet the author also notes that there is, in addition, a *shared* experience *between* species. Because we are all animals, because of constant transformations, there is a certain ambiguity regarding personal, individual existence. This means that we might be kept guessing as to who we are at any one moment. The example offered in the *Zhuangzi* involves a butterfly: Is the butterfly who dreams she is a human really a human dreaming that she is a butterfly dreaming she is a human? How can we know?

The *Zhuangzi* indicates that there is an important advantage in this shared animalian existence. This shared commonality—this kinship—provides human beings with a strong sense of how other creatures feel and what they might prefer (Anderson, "Daoism," 278). For example, love of freedom and love of life reach across species, and this shared interest is an excellent guide for understanding the preferences of all individuals. While we cannot assume that a bird likes music, we can be absolutely certain that a bird, as kindred creature, prefers life to death, freedom to confinement, and health and welfare to injury and illness. Northern snakehead fish, human beings, hill mynas, and water deer are kindred spirits—they share our preference for remaining alive, free from pain, and in a state that is natural to their species—natural to their highly individualized *te*. Subduing or training anymals is therefore inherently harmful and cruel, as it would be cruel to treat another human being in this manner. Freedom—the ability to live one's life without disturbance or under the control of another—is understood to be no less ideal for horses than it is for human beings (Anderson, "Daoism," 278). Confinement and training turns healthy, happy horses first into brigands, and eventually saps their health and their life. Through our love of freedom and autonomy, in our need to actualize our personal *te*, animals are all kin. Each creature, whether cochin or amur hedgehog, prefers to be what he or she is born to be—what is natural, to follow Dao—and not to be exploited for the purposes of others.

The author of the *Zhuangzi* expresses this understanding of kinship with characteristic humor, explaining how he refused an invitation to become a powerful administrator. He knew that this post would bring fame and notoriety, but not happiness. In the explanation for his refusal, which he provides the two officials who deliver the message, the author compares himself to a long dead but much venerated tortoise:

> Without turning his head, [Zhuangzi] said, "I have heard that there is a sacred tortoise in Ch'u that has been dead for three thousand years. The king keeps it wrapped in cloth and boxed, and stores it in the ancestral temple. Now would this tortoise rather be dead and have its bones left behind and honored? Or would it rather be alive and dragging its tail in the mud?"
>
> "It would rather be alive and dragging its tail in the mud," said the two officials.
>
> [Zhuangzi] said, "Go away! I'll drag my tail in the mud!" (B. Watson)

The officials readily understand that anymals share fundamental qualities, such as the love of one's own life, lived in one's own natural habitat. The author of the *Zhuangzi* compares his freedom from official duty to a tortoise's life in the mud—it may not seem particularly glamorous compared with life as a powerful administrator, but it is a life that is far more natural to one's *te*. Pomp and circumstance, power and prestige, are not a reasonable trade for freedom to realize one's *te*, or for any creature's life.

The *Zhuangzi* explores this shared experience of individual *te* in another example of Chinese paradox and wit. In this story, Zhuangzi (Chuang Tzu) and a disciple are standing on the bridge over the river Hao, observing fishes:

> Chuang Tzu and Hui Tzu were strolling along the dam of the Hao River when Chuang Tzu said, "See how the minnows come out and dart around where they please! That's what fish really enjoy!"
>
> Hui Tzu said, "You're not a fish—how do you know what fish enjoy?"
>
> Chuang Tzu said, "You're not I, so how do you know I don't know what fish enjoy?"
>
> Hui Tzu said, "I'm not you, so I certainly don't know what you know. On the other hand, you're certainly not a fish—so that still proves you don't know what fish enjoy!"
>
> Chuang Tzu said, "Let's go back to your original question, please. You asked me how I know what fish enjoy—so you already knew I knew it when you asked the question. I know it by standing here beside the Hao." (B. Watson)

In this story, the *Zhuangzi's* amusing writing highlights shared creatureliness (Anderson, "Daoism," 278). This tricky bit of writing suggests that "people and fish share enough basic similarity that humans can understand" fish (Anderson, "Daoism," 278). This fleeting interaction, recorded hundreds of years ago near the river Hao, reminds readers that there is something odd about challenging anything as obvious as someone else's ability to understand or relate to another individual, whether that individual is a Chinese trumpetfish or a Chengdu brown goat. Indeed, many of the writings attributed to Zhuangzi encourage people to take the point of view of others, including anymals. The author even goes so far as to note that those who lack this ability, or doubt this ability in others, are lacking qualities so basic as to define what it is to be human.

Anymals often play important roles in Chinese sacred literature. In many stories, as in the Zhuangzi, anymals are understood to be similar enough for human beings to draw meaningful parallels across species (Anderson, "Flowering," 165–66). Just as the main characters in *Monkey* are fellow comrades on a great spiritual journey, so are all creatures understood to be fellow sojourners on planet Earth. Daoist traditions do not postulate a "barrier between people and animals, or, more generally, between humanity and nature.... In a deep and basic sense, *Dao* unites humans and animals," and teaches human beings to treat anymals with respect (Anderson, "Daoism," 286). In the Daoist worldview, human beings "experience nature from within" (Tu, "Continuity," 77).

Interpenetrability

The Daoist world is in a constant state of transformation. A wolf becomes a rabbit, a carp is the son of a dragon king, and Guanyin manifests as a noble horse (Blofeld, *Bodhisattva*, 69, 75). After death, there are yet more transformation possibilities: "Now a dragon, now a snake,/You transform together with the times,/And never consent to be one thing alone" (*Zhuangzi*, in Parkes, 92). Who knows what we become after death, when a human ear might become a catfish fin.

In the Daoist worldview, only the great Unity of Being and the pervasive presence of Dao remain constant. We are mixed in the bowl of transformation, thereby sharing a jumbled material existence that complements our shared spiritual existence (the ubiquitous presence of the Dao). The *Zhuangzi* pushes humans to see the world from this Daoist perspective, to abandon our tendency to view the world from an isolated, separatist, anthropocentric point of reference (Parkes, 91), and to mingle in the lives of black-bellied hamsters and binturongs. Writings attributed to Zhuangzi are filled with this "numinous aspect of the human-animal interface" (Anderson, "Daoism," 278). The author likens himself to a turtle, relates personally to a minnow, and in one of his most famous passages, cannot distinguish himself from a butterfly (Chuang Tzu, 66, 67, 26).

Once Chuang Chou dreamt he was a butterfly, a butterfly flitting and fluttering around, happy with himself and doing as he pleased. He didn't know
he was Chuang Chou. Suddenly he woke up and there he was, solid and
unmistakable Chuang Chou. But he didn't know if he was Chuang Chou
who had dreamt he was a butterfly, or a butterfly dreaming he was Chuang
Chou. (B. Watson)

Anymal Powers

Daoist writers often use anymals as good examples—role models—when teaching
Daoist philosophy (Anderson, "Daoism," 278). For example, many Daoist stories
emphasize the excellent spontaneity of anymals, and their ability to live in harmony
with the natural world (Anderson, "Daoism," 278). Anymals also demonstrate "how
to move in powerful, natural, spontaneous, and healthy ways" (Anderson, "Daoism,"
277). Animals are neither wasteful nor extravagant—they practice simplicity:
"When the tailorbird builds her nest in the deep wood, she uses no more than one
branch. When the mole drinks at the river, he takes no more than a bellyful"
(B. Watson). Anymals also exemplify *wuwei*. What human practices *wuwei* as well as
the Chinese monal; what human maintains harmony with nature more easily than a
corsac fox?

   In many ancient Chinese stories, anymals are endowed with "varying degrees of
spiritual or numinous power" (Anderson, "Daoism," 277). Zhang Guolao's donkey
is immortal, and a rabbit transforms into a wolf to help Zhang. Anymals are a critical
and powerful force on the side of the good in Guanyin mythology. A gigantic Earth
God tiger rescues her (as Miao Shan) from an execution arranged by her angry
father. Tigers bring firewood to help Guanyin as she toils over the stove, while birds
collect vegetables for the meals she must prepare. Anymals use their miraculous
powers to help Guanyin to work toward her lofty goal of alleviating suffering
throughout the world, and these powerful anymals are "summoned to her service"
by forces no less than the gods (Palmer, 70).

Chinese Traditions and Anymal Liberation

In Confucian religious traditions, ethics are "a way of thinking that leads to a way of
living" (Taylor, "Animals," 303). Neo-Confucian Wang Yangming emphasized *zhix-
ing heyi*, or "unity of knowledge and action" (Taylor, "Animals," 302). He noted that
knowledge and action are mutually interdependent: "To speak of knowledge
without action is empty talk, ... while to speak of action not motivated by knowledge
is to speak of action of no consequence" (Taylor, "Animals," 302).

Mencius noted that humanity (*ren*) is compassionate (*ren*), reflecting Heaven. Followers of Confucius were therefore expected to have knowledge of *ren* and to act with benevolence. Humans, who are part of the "basic ethical goodness of nature," should thereby behave with "loving kindness" (Taylor, "Animals," 303). Consequently, one who is *ren*, who has realized humanity, "cannot bear to see [anymals] die" or to "eat their flesh" (Taylor "Animals," 297). *Ren* and knowledge of the Great Unity prevent cruelty and indifference, including factory farming and anymal experimentation.

As in the Confucian tradition, Dao directs how people ought to *live* (Parkes, 81). Dao is "an abstract, universal principle in the realm of ethics" (Merton, 21) that encourages people to live in a particular way (simply and gently), to make certain choices (ones that are compatible with the health of the natural world), and to exemplify compassion toward all creatures (Schipper, 81–85). Daoism is a way of life rooted in "weakness and humility," "openness and emptiness," living so as to cause no harm (Chan, 137). Daoism encourages benevolence toward all living beings (Chan, 143). For a Daoist, "to be human is to be humane. A lack of concern for suffering and dying reveals a loss of humanity" (Komjathy, 99).

Guanyin is not only an embodiment of the abstract concept of *ci* or a helpful bodhisattva. *Guanyin represents what humans are meant to become*—her way of being ought to be mirrored by devotees. Practitioners are meant to follow in her steps, living lives of compassion, mercy, and selfless service to those in need—all those in need (Kinsley, *Goddesses'*, 51). Anyone who calls on Guanyin—she who listens to the cries of those in need—is also expected to listen, and, when needed, to provide assistance to others who need help, whether a stray dog, a factory-farmed hog, or a clouded leopard (whose families have been hunted nearly to extinction in the last few decades).

In the Chinese worldview, human greed and cruelty upset balance and harmony, and cause to natural disasters. In this way, Chinese religions speak against the veal industry and battery cages, gestation crates and factory fishing. Such massive suffering and exploitation, such uncounted premature deaths, such a gross imbalance of power is not only contrary to *ren*, but represents imbalance, injustice, and a lack of harmony, which will be reflected in natural disasters, including such inauspicious happenings as global climate change. Chinese religions call for a vegan diet (L. Thompson, *Chinese Religion*, 116).

Like many Chinese people living in Beijing, Jie Ding (who goes by Hanyue) practices more than one religion. She remembers how her grandma paid homage to images of the Buddha in dim light, sending her out with homemade corn cakes for beggars. Now that she has had a chance to read more of the Confucian classics, she also realizes that her grandmother fostered *ren* in her granddaughter when Hanyue was very young (S. Zhou, pers. comm., February 25, 2010). Hanyue now turns to the Confucian teachings for much of her core morality. Here she learned of humanity's innate goodness and compassion, the seed of our innate goodness. As a

Confucian, she believes that the primary task in the course of our lives is to realize our innate nature and express human goodness through kindness. Through the Confucian classics, she has learned that humans ought to be "friends to everything in the world," because "all dwell in one, all are equal"; the classics have taught her to foster and nurture universal love (S. Zhou, pers. comm., February 25, 2010).

As an expression of benevolence and love, Hanyue does not eat anymals. Because anymals are too often considered more expendable than humans, she devotes her time to anymal activism. Previously a teacher, Hanyue rescues stray cats and takes advantage of every opportunity to educate people about issues involving anymal suffering, including the meat industry and the benefits of giving up flesh (S. Zhou, pers. comm., February 25, 2010).

Another Confucian anymal activist, Youshui Lin, is an outspoken person who speaks up whenever he sees humans engaged in thoughtless acts of cruelty. For example, he feels compelled to remind strangers of an inconvenient truth when he must sit next to those who consume flesh. Rather than mince words, he states a fact: "You're eating a corpse" (S. Zhou, pers. comm., February 13, 2010).

Lin, an electrical engineer in Belgium, also bristles at sentimental "animal lovers" who love their dog and squirm at the sight of blood, yet consume flesh and wear leather. As a point of honesty, he asserts that such people ought to admit that they are either indifferent—or downright hostile—toward every creature they consume or whose skins and fur they buy. They may love their dog, or most cats, but they most certainly do not love anymals generally. One who loves pigs does not eat them. One who loves chickens does not eat their reproductive eggs.

Lin is also put off by people who speak much of their love for anymals while buying cats, birds, snakes, lizards, or dogs at pet stores. Anymals around the world suffer from such shortsighted, irresponsible humans, who pay for anymal breeding while hundreds of millions of anymals around the world are homeless. For many, the answer to their need is dictated with gas or a needle. Lin pleads, "Please don't buy pets! Please stop supporting the capitalistic market to satisfy your personal desires!" (S. Zhou, pers. comm., February 13, 2010).

As an outspoken activist, Lin also encourages wealthy human beings—especially Americans—to change their consumption patterns to protect and aid anymals and the earth. In particular, he asks that people living in the United States "try to use less than 60 litres of water every day" (S. Zhou, pers. comm., February 13, 2010). He notes that Americans generally use more than 900 liters of water per person, per day; Europeans use more than 300 liters and also need to reduce consumption. Many of us waste water washing cars and watering lawns despite the inevitability of serious future water shortages. Lin notes that "every life on the planet relies on water" and every living being requires water "to sustain life" (S. Zhou, pers. comm., February 13, 2010).

Lin finds much of value in Mencius's comment, "A true gentleman cannot bear to see an animal being killed. If he hears the sound of slaughter, he'll not eat meat"

(S. Zhou, pers. comm., February 16, 2010, from "Liang Hui Wang I"). He notes that *ren* requires a vegan diet. Lin also takes religious inspiration from "The Counsels of Great Yu" (in *Shang Shu*, or "Book of History"), much of which is likely 2,500 years old. These Chinese classics record that Meng Tse writes to those who hold power: "Rather than wrong and kill an innocent, let the suspicious go even if that means you'll be punished for negligence. If you love your people, they'll be inspired by your compassion and leniency" and peace will reign (S. Zhou, pers. comm., February 13, 2010). Lin notes that Meng's quote "stresses compassion" as the key to good rulership and peaceful coexistence (S. Zhou, pers. comm., February 16, 2010).

Louis Komjathy, a contemporary Daoist scholar and practitioner of fifteen years, is also an ordained Complete Perfection priest. He notes that "for *anyone* who claims to have ecological commitments or environmental concerns, vegetarianism is a *minimal* requirement" and that " 'animal industries' ought to be systematically undermined and eventually extinguished through a shift in consumption" (Komjathy, 99).

> Anyone who understands the realities of modern slaughterhouses ("meat-packing plants") and still has access to the core goodness of innate nature— the Dao made manifest in/as/through us—will accept the responsibility of vegetarianism. The consumption of meat enmeshes an individual in an interconnected system of suffering, exploitation, and murder—such are the perils of domination and domestication. A lack of direct killing does not lessen one's karmic involvement for one who eats animal products. The personal consequences of that involvement may differ with each person, but the consequences for the animals (human and non-human), for society, and for the world are quite clear.
>
> One important consequence is suffering. This suffering is clearly audible, as is the inner call to relieve suffering. (Komjathy, 102)

Komjathy views "all of life as a 'ritual process,' as a form of *communitas* and as an expression of reverence for the sacred" (Komjathy, 101). By choosing vegan foods, one frees not only anymals who are confined and prematurely killed, but also those people who confine and kill other creatures. Komjathy notes that dietary change is a spiritual process:

> Liberating oneself from a context of violence liberates those who inflict violence, and those upon whom the violence is inflicted. Through a dietary shift away from animal products, one becomes less material and more rar-ified. Through a process of cosmicization, a state of transpersonal intercon-nection develops; one abides in the primordial undifferentiation of the Dao in which personal selfhood and selfish desires disappear, and beings are able to abide in their own natural places. (Komjathy, 101)

While this transformation has many personal benefits for the spiritual life, this change benefits not only anymals, but also other human beings, who are similarly struggling along their own personal journey.

> The choice of compassion for sentient beings, especially those who are unheard and unseen, has other effects: One begins to free oneself from karma; one becomes part of a different community, lineage, and reality, a community in which reverence, sacred presence, and energetic aliveness are nourished and expressed. One's decision to rectify detrimental patterns and to cultivate beneficial patterns may also exert a transformative effect on one's family, community, and society. (Komjathy, 102)

Komjathy spends time among other Daoist practitioners who practice *ci* (compassion or deep love), *jian* (restraint or frugality), and *bugan wei tianxia xian* ("not daring to be at the forefront of the world"). Spending time with Chinese associates, Komjathy has had a chance to see, first hand, Daoism expressed in direct action on behalf of anymals:

> I personally witnessed Complete Perfection monks on various occasions express and embody compassion and affinity with non-human beings: a daily appreciation for the grace and carefree movements of fish and birds, patterns of wind and water through local forests and valleys, and "activism" on the part of birds and dogs. With respect to the latter, some monks requested and secured the release of captured song-birds, owls, and monkeys, while others reprimanded young boys for abusing dogs. (Komjathy, 98)

Spiritually, Komjathy feels personally responsible to make choices that will alleviate suffering. His vision is expansive, including the suffering of anymals, the suffering of those caught in the dreadful work of anymal slaughter, and his own spiritual journey:

> As a Daoist, I am responsible to relieve suffering among sentient beings, especially those suffering and helpless under human hands: those in distant forests, rivers, and mountains; those experimented on for "human benefit"; those abused and neglected domesticated animals; and those raised for consumption.
>
> I endeavor to follow a Daoist way of life, a life based in attentiveness, reverence, and connection. Energetic sensitivity, observation, and deep listening reveal vast suffering. And yet, beneath this, there is the numinous presence of the Dao. We must cultivate the ability to recognize both suffering and the Dao in all beings. We may begin with a commitment to

inquiry: What are we cultivating? What are we listening to? From a Daoist perspective, we may ask a perennial question: What does it mean to be fully human? (Komjathy, 102–3)

Daoist Zheng Xie (English name, Shay) is a rock star and anymal liberationist in Beijing. He tends thirteen rescued cats and four rescued dogs, assists with spay-neuter programs, helps place needy companion anymals in dependable homes, and supports animal advocacy with the money he generates at concerts (S. Zhou, pers. comm., January 26, 2010). He notes that "real animal protection" (encompassing *all* anymals—not just cats and dogs) has just arrived in China.

As an activist and a Daoist, Xie comments that he will always "incorporate traditional Chinese culture into his activism" (S. Zhou, pers. comm., February 13, 2010). He finds inspiration to nurture and foster compassion in works attributed to Laozi, and, like ancient Daoist sages, Xie retreats to the mountains as part of his religious practice (S. Zhou, pers. comm., February 13, 2010).

The Daoist view of harmony has also been particularly important to Xie: "*Tian ren he yi.*" A literal translation of this phrase produces "heaven and man in one," which is perhaps best translated as Unity of Being. Xie quotes from the works of Zhuangzi: "*Tian di yi zhi, wan wu yi ma.*" Zhuangzi teaches that the universe is singular, including the myriad beings, though they have individual forms (S. Zhou, pers. comm., January 26, 2010). While we perceive individuality, we are all part of one Great Unity: The many are one.

Xie comments that we have taken too much from nature—that we have upset the natural balance and forgotten the Great Unity—and we must change our ways. Toward this end, he practices Daoist simplicity, and when he does need to purchase something, he picks it up from a secondhand store (S. Zhou, pers. comm., January 26, 2010). Whether buying used goods or new items, food or clothing, Xie will not invest in anymal products (S. Zhou, pers. comm., January 26, 2010). He believes that anymal exploitation is "absolutely unnatural"—as is any form of exploitation in a unified system.

Xie has held twenty-eight benefit concerts since 2006, donating all revenues to anymal advocacy. Xie writes that he would "rather pursue Dao and compassion than make a living" (S. Zhou, pers. comm., January 26, 2010). He has sent a remarkable $3,000 to Animals Asia Foundation—a great deal of money in China, *especially* as a donation from a young artist. He also contributes to the International Fund for Animal Welfare and a handful of local/Chinese anymal advocacy organizations.

Xie is not content to give away all that he earns—he also invests his time. He leaflets at his own concerts and makes a point of educating his fans. Whenever possible, he exposes cruelties, such as those that are inherent in the flesh and fur industries, and advocates for consumer-based change.

Soon Xie will release his first collection of recordings. Every song on this new CD is an expression of Xie's Daoist vision. Every song is an expression of Great Unity, harmony, and *ci*, and stands as a Daoist's commitment to anymal advocacy (S. Zhou, pers. comm., January 26, 2010).

Summary

Confucian traditions teach that all beings stem from one source, the Great Ultimate, and participate in the Great Unity. *Ren* (love or benevolence) is the essence of all that is good in humanity, and extends across species, as exemplified in the noble person (*junzi*). Daoism also encourages people to love deeply and live compassionately (*ci*), to exercise restraint and frugality (*jian*), to seek harmony, and to practice *wuwei* (action as nonaction). Daoist precepts speak often and strongly against harming any creature, whether by disturbing their homes or eating their bodies. Guanyin, the most popular Chinese deity, exemplifies deep compassion for all beings. The *Zhuangzi* highlights basic similarities between humans and anymals, and encourages people to treat all beings with care and respect.

5

Jewish Traditions

Man has no superiority over beast.
—*Ecclesiastes* 3:19[1]

Judaism emerged from earlier, Middle Eastern religious traditions in the first millennium BCE, distinguishing itself from previous traditions by requiring followers
to focus on just one deity. In Jewish religious traditions, the one God of the Jewish
people has created and continues to sustain the universe, and is the author and judge
of a moral code, both for humanity generally and for Jews specifically. The Tanakh
(often referred to as the Old Testament among Christians), is the most sacred book
of Judaism, and is also sacred for Muslims.[2]

Sacred Nature, Sacred Anymals

The Tanakh celebrates the power and glory of a single deity who acts as Creator,
who "fashions the hearts" "of all the inhabitants of the earth" and brings forth the
spiny tail lizard, Nubian ibex, and starling with the breath of life (Ps. 33:15, 14).

> How many are your works, O LORD;
> In wisdom, you have made them all;
> the earth is full of your creatures. (Ps. 104:24)

Jewish religious traditions teach humanity that all of the created world belongs to
God. "The earth is the LORD's, and all that it holds, the world and its inhabitants"

---

[1] Offset passages from the *Tanakh* have been translated from the Hebrew by Samantha Joo, Ph.D
(Old Testament Studies). In-text translations are from the *Tanakh: The Holy Scriptures: Torah, Nevi'im,
Kethuvim, The New JPS Translation* (Jerusalem: Jewish Publication Society, 1985).

[2] The meaning of scriptural passages from the Tanakh discussed in this chapter, compared with the
same passages in the Christian Old Testament, is the same. Therefore, explorations of the *Tanakh* in
this chapter are applicable to both Christian and Islamic traditions, but will not be repeated in
subsequent chapters.

(Ps. 24:1). The "heavens to their uttermost reaches belong to the LORD your God, the earth and all that is on it!" (Deut. 10:14).

> For every animal of the forest is mine,
> the cattle on a thousand hills.
> I know every bird of the hills,
> the creatures of the field are mine. (Ps. 50:10–11)

Jewish religious traditions teach people to "respect and preserve the manifold species which God created"—and the earth itself—because they are good, and because they are God's (Schwartz, 23).

Jewish scriptures remind readers that anymals have been important in the unfolding of the universe. For example, in verses covering the great flood (Gen. 6–8), God preserves all species. God remembers not only humanity, but also "all the beasts and all the cattle" that are bobbing on the swollen waters (Gen. 8:1). Scriptures reveal that the earth was created for *all* creatures, or, perhaps more accurately, for *each* creature. The Jewish deity provides for wild creatures, causing the heavens

> To bring rain on land where no man dwells,
> A desert where no human exists,
> To saturate the desolate wasteland,
> And make the crop of grass sprout forth. (Job 38:26–27)

The wild boar roots in the hills for her food; and the rains bring greenery for the white oryx (though the white oryx has been driven nearly to extinction by hunters). And human beings are to maintain this diversity. The Tanakh requires Jews to allow fields to lie fallow, to be given "a complete rest," every seventh year, during which time human, domestic anymals, and every other creature of the land "may eat all its yield" (Lev. 25:4–7; Exod. 23:11). Persian fallow deer and field mice may freely eat whatever springs up on the land as it rests every seventh year, land that humans would otherwise cultivate strictly for their own benefit.

The Tanakh informs human beings that the deity expects all creatures to prosper. After creating sea creatures and birds, the Creator commands them: "Be fertile and increase, fill the waters in the seas, and let the birds increase on the earth" (Gen. 1:22). If anymal populations are to increase, then people must leave space for the many natural splendors; if anymals are to flourish, then humans must not cover every space of the earth with homes and fields and factories. The Tanakh specifically cautions against our tendency to "add house to house/And join field to field,/Till there is room for none but you" (Isa. 5:8). The leopard and Syrian onagers (fleet-footed asses of the desert, now extinct) were also given the divine command to reproduce and prosper.

According to scriptures, the Jewish deity created a good universe, with many good creatures. Six times before humans are created, God declares creation to be good, revealing the "intrinsic worth of species...'*kol tov*—and it was good.'" Jewish traditions find nothing wanting in the natural world, or a marsh harrier, or an endangered Israeli painted frog—every species was declared "good" in and of itself before humankind was created.

When dealing with the natural world and wild anymals, Jews are to be mindful of the Creator. Throughout the Old Testament, people are told of the "reverence humans should have toward the land" (Regenstein, 19). In scripture, God reminds the faithful, "The land is Mine; you are but strangers resident with Me" (Lev. 25:23). The Tanakh unveils a God who is personally invested in creation and does not wish the land—the Creator's land—to be despoiled or wrongfully claimed by human beings. God commands: You "shall not pollute the land" or "defile the land in which you live, in which I Myself abide" (Num. 35:33–34).

Jews are expected to find "God in and through" nature (Cobb, 506–7). The Jewish deity manifests in burning bushes and whirlwinds (Exod. 3:2, Job 38:1 and 40:6), and speaks through a laboring burro (Num. 22:28). "Jews have often depicted God through His handiwork" (Schwartz, 84): inanimate objects, plants, and all living beings (Schochet, 248). Hasidic Jews (flourishing largely in Poland and the Ukraine), mindful of scripture, see the entire universe as the dwelling place of God. Hasidic rabbis (Jewish scholars) such as Shneur Zalman hear the voice of God in the chirping of birds (Schochet, 248).

Jewish religious traditions hold nature to be sacred. The Jewish God is invested in the world; the Creator is present in date palms and daisies, blind worm snakes and mountain gazelles. The Tanakh reminds readers of "God's unfathomable power and wisdom and humankind's obligation to respect the natural world" (Regenstein, 32).

Jewish Philosophy and Morality

Mercy and Compassion

Leviticus states simply, "Love your fellow as yourself" (19:18). "Fellow" has been an expanding concept for centuries. For many people, this once narrow term (referring largely to one's religious community) has moved from fellow/neighbor Jew to fellow/neighbor race or nation, and on to fellow/neighbor human beings. Jewish religious traditions include anymals in this increasingly expansive view, and teach human beings to demonstrate compassion and mercy for anymals.

Compassion for anymals is a requirement in the Jewish religious traditions (Kalechofsky, 93). Isaac Bashevis Singer comments, "Early in my life I came to the conclusion that there was no basic difference between man and animals. If man has the heart to cut the throat of a chicken or a calf, there's no reason he should not be willing to cut the throat of a man" (Schochet, 297). If human beings take life lightly, then all life is at risk—why would any sentient being be excluded from the Jewish moral community? "Throughout its long history, Judaism has emphasized that the animal kingdom is to be respected and dealt with kindly"; Judaism carries "a profound moral commitment to respect" anymals (Cohn-Sherbok, 90). Abraham Ibn Ezra, one of the most distinguished Jewish writers and thinkers of the Middle Ages (referred to as "Wise", "Great", and "Admirable Doctor") understood neighborly love as extending to anymals (Schochet, 263). The creatures of the earth are God's, they are good, and they are due human kindness.

> It is not enough to say that kindness to animals is mentioned in the Hebrew Bible. The fact that the welfare of animals is mentioned in the Ten Commandments and that compassion toward animals is the topic of passages in a number of books of the Bible, justifies the statement that compassion toward animals is an important theme of the Hebrew Bible. (Berman, 3)

Jewish anymal stories remind readers that anymals are sentient, and that we have a moral and spiritual obligation to be thoughtful of these myriad beings. Fish fear and dread the fisher's net, and caged birds know the coldness of surrounding bars; domestic and captured anymals live at the mercy of their captors (Schochet, 122). Zussya of Anapole (Hasidic Jew), while on a mission to collect money to free human captives, came upon a host of caged birds "beating their wings against the bars" (Schochet, 250). He recognized that these birds were also captives, in need of release, and promptly freed the birds. Oppression harms not only humans, but also the lesser sand plover and the endangered Dorcas gazelle. In the words of Rabbi Hirsch, a highly regarded German neo-Orthodox Torah commentator (*Torah* refers to the first five books of the Tanakh: Genesis, Exodus, Leviticus, Numbers, and Deuteronomy), compassion should cause human heartstrings to "vibrate sympathetically with any cry of distress sounding anywhere in creation.

Many well-respected Jewish authors instruct readers to be merciful and kind to all that God has created (Schochet, 246). Rabbi Sherira Gaon of the tenth century wrote that anymals were created so that "good should be done to them" (Kalechofsky, 95), and Jewish spiritual leaders exemplify this understanding. Hasidic Rabbi Moshe Leib of Sassov willingly tended another man's neglected cattle (Schochet, 250). In *Sefer Hasidim* ("Book of the Pious," an account of the daily life of pious medieval German Jews known as Hasidim, or "Pious Ones"), Rabbi Judah heHasid retells the story of a Jewish holy man who refused to surrender a terrified dog to her abusive caretaker. Instead, he allowed the dog to hide in his protective cloak (Schochet, 246). *Midrash Tehillim* perhaps holds the most remarkable testimony to the sensitivity of rabbis to the needs of anymals in the words of Rabbi Tanhum b. Hiyya: "The falling of rain is greater than the giving of the Law, for the giving of the Law was a joy only to Israel, while the falling of rain is a rejoicing for all the world, including the cattle and the wild beasts and the birds" (Schochet, 146).

In the Jewish religious traditions, creatures of the earth are God's, they are good, and they are due the mercy and compassion of the faithful: Anymals are "to be respected, loved, and helped to attain their purpose according to God's will" (Hirsch, "Letter"). Jewish writings therefore honor those who fulfill obligations of compassion toward other creatures, such as Noah and Joseph. Rabbis praise Noah for his care of animals on the ark, and he is one of only two biblical characters honored with the term *zadik*, "one who practices charity." Rabbis note that with so many different anymals on the ark, Noah's duties of caretaking were extensive and complicated. "He is pictured as being unable to sleep, neither by day nor night, owing to his perpetual preoccupation with the proper care of his 'passengers'" (Schochet, 148). Joseph is the only other character honored with the title *zadik*: Like Noah, he cared for anymals in times of hardship (*Midrash Tanhuma*, in Schochet, 148).

Other much-respected scriptural characters also exemplify compassion toward anymals. Rebekah's watering of camels is noted as "evidence of a tender heart…a virtue upon which Judaism lays stress" (Hertz, 83). When Rebekah's people prepare for the arrival of guests—people *and* camels—the camels are unburdened, bedded down, and fed *before* human guests are similarly cared for (Gen. 24:32). In Jewish religious traditions, a "kind man first feeds his beasts before sitting down to the table" (Regenstein, 183); rabbis continue to teach people to feed and water anymals—to tend to the needs of dependent or needy anymals—even before tending to their own needs (Schochet, 155).

Key biblical characters are morally elevated *because* they show concern for animals, and their moral concern for anymals "is not merely a nice sentiment"; kindness toward other animals "points to historic destiny" (Kalechofsky, 95). Rabbis note that God determines human leadership capabilities through an individual's treatment of anymals (most often sheep). Moses was rewarded with a spouse for providing water to thirsty animals (Exod. 2:16–21), as was Rebekah (Gen. 24:15–19, 51). Those chosen as leaders (such as Moses and David) first prove their suitability through their gentle attentiveness to helpless lambs (Schochet, 150). Similarly, the uncle of Haakov Yitzhak of Pshiskha predicted that his nephew would be a "worthy leader of his people" because he was so tender toward anymals (Schochet, 251).

Anymal care supersedes other religious requirements in Jewish religious traditions. For example, Rabbi David of Lelov is credited with missing the sounding of the *shofar* for Rosh Hashanah (New Year) because he paused to feed a horse whose thoughtless and irresponsible caretaker had rushed off to the synagogue (Schochet, 250). In the Tanakh, Proverbs 12:10 warns, "The righteous man knows the needs of his beast, but the compassion of the wicked is cruel." The righteous care about and for anymals; the wicked do not.

Mercy toward anymals is central to the Jewish moral life (Cohn-Sherbok, 83), and cruelty and kindness toward anymals are linked with divine punishment and reward. Humans are *expected* to be compassionate, to work to secure the well-being of anymals (Schochet, 144). Jewish mystical traditions have passed down anymal stories that encourage compassion and mercy, and which link mercilessness with misfortune and unhappiness. The *Kav haYashar* (*The Just Measure*, Rabbi Tzvi Hirsch Kaidanover, 1750) contains a story of a woman who, by removing a ladder, deprived thirsty young birds of water. For her indifference to the young birds, God sealed her womb. Her ability to have children was restored only after she returned the ladder to its original position, permitting the thirsty fledglings to drink (Schochet, 247).

Rabbi Judah haNasi, redactor of the *Mishna* (ca. 200 CE, the first written compendium of oral law, contained in the Talmud), connects personal hardships brought on by God directly with his failure to show mercy. The rabbi failed to help a calf who was about to be slaughtered, who was pleading for mercy. He writes that God inflicted him with pains because of his failure to rescue this calf—because of the rabbi's hardness of heart. When faced with another scenario in which anymals required mercy and compassion, the rabbi demonstrated that he had learned his lesson—he rose to the defense of weasels who were at risk of being driven from their home, which also happened to be a human home. Though the slaughter of calves was an accepted practice in the rabbi's community, and though ridding one's house of weasels might seem perfectly normal in most any community, the rabbi notes that God punished him for accepting the former, and rewarded him for rejecting the latter.

Jewish religious traditions teach that personal "punishment and absolution are clearly contingent upon compassion toward animals" (Schochet, 165), even if one must swim against the currents of convention in the process. "It is our duty to relieve the pain of any creature" (Ganzfried, 84; Schwartz, 19; Cohn-Sherbok, 83). Human beings are obligated to defend the bawling calf and release the caged bird—and failure to do so, a lack of moral courage, can bring retribution from the Creator: "God condemns and harshly punishes cruelty to animals" (Regenstein, 21), as well as neglect or indifference. Human well-being "rests on God's grace"; our lives are worthy of God in relation to our ability to live the moral life, "particularly with respect to animals," for they are at our mercy (Kalechofsky, 95).

Tsa'ar Ba'alei Chayim (Not to Harm)

The "Hebrew phrase *tsa'ar ba'alei chayim* provides a biblical mandate not to cause 'pain to any living creature'" (Schwartz, 15). The *Shulchan Aruch* (*Code of Jewish Law*) clearly states that humans have an obligation not to harm anymals: "It is forbidden, according to the law of the Torah, to inflict pain upon any living creature" (Ganzfried, 84; Schwartz, 19; Cohn-Sherbok, 83).

The Jewish mandate not to cause harm to anymals requires Jews to consider the needs of anymals over personal profit, and also above personal desires and self-interests. Rabbinical law comments: "A good man does not sell his beast to a cruel person" (Regenstein, 183). Judaism condemns pleasures motivated by bloodlust, such as "bullfights, dogfights, and cockfights" (Cohn-Sherbok, 88), as well as frivolous methods of exploitation that cause misery, such as circuses, in which anymals are forced into unnatural situations for the sake of human fascination or amusement (Schochet, 159).

Nesting birds, for example, are completely at the mercy of humans, and the Torah clearly indicates that it is cruel and therefore unacceptable to thwart the purposes of nesting birds—whether Narragansett turkey, Manx Rumpy chicken, or Rufous hummingbird. Deuteronomy 22:6–7 commands: "You shall not take the mother with the young. Let the mother go." Maimonides (1135–1204), one of the most influential Jewish theologians of all time, notes that this injunction is a *minimum* requirement; we ought to leave *both* young *and* mother, so that the mother will "not be pained by seeing that the young are taken" (Linzey, *After*, 46–47). Birds, too, were commanded to multiply. They, too are protected by the Jewish mandate not to cause pain to any living creature.

Maimonides also interpreted the repeated biblical injunction not to "boil a kid in its mother's milk" (Exod. 23:19 and 34:26, Deut. 14:21) as protection against cruel acts that harden the human heart (Linzey, *After*, 47). Many Jews have responded to this passage by separating dairy and flesh physically in the course of their meals, both on and in kitchenware and within the body. But Maimonides observed that it is cruel to boil a baby in milk produced by a protective mother for the purpose of nurturing and sustaining her offspring. Such a meal mocks the mother, the babe, and the deity who created both. Maimonides asserted that boiling young in their mother's nursing milk is cruel, and is therefore forbidden. This interpretation does not suggest the separation of dairy and flesh products, but rather conscientious rejection of both.

Scriptures also teach the devout not to cause frustration or disappointment to anymals. A Torah paragraph, consisting of one sentence, commands, "You shall not muzzle an ox while it is threshing" (Deut. 25:4). This passage reveals remarkable sensitivity to an ox's appetite while laboring, and also reveals a compassionate understanding of an ox's taste for grains: "At the time of threshing, when the ox is surrounded by the food" that he or she would enjoy eating, given the chance, he or she "should not be prevented from satisfying" this natural appetite (Schwartz, 19). Maimonides interpreted this biblical prohibition as requiring humans to justly compensate anymals for their labor, requiring that those who work with anymals be attentive to their needs (Schochet, 154).

Rabbinic traditions interpret "ox" in the above Deuteronomy passage to be "a generic phrase incorporating all animals" (Schochet, 58, 261). *No anymal* would like to be muzzled, especially when surrounded by tasty foods. Consequently, eighteenth-century rabbi Moses Sofer argued (in the *Chatam Sofer*) that muzzling anymals is always wrong (Schochet, 266). By extension, *any* behavior that causes an anymal frustration, unhappiness, or hunger pangs is against Jewish ethics, including factory farming, animal experimentation, fur farming, and the entertainment industry.

Whereas compassionate Torah characters are praised and rewarded, cruel characters are used as examples of what humans must *not* be. Genesis records Jacob speaking to his sons, whose cruelty was indiscriminate. He ostracizes his sons for their wanton indifference to life:

> Simeon and Levi are brothers,
> Their swords are weapons of violence.
> Let me not enter their council,
> Let me not join their assembly.
> For in their anger, they slew men,
> And at their whim, they hamstrung oxen. (Gen. 49:5–6)

In Numbers 22 of the Torah, Balak, king of Moab, commissions a professional seer named Balaam to curse the Israelites. En route to Moab, Balaam's donkey sees an angel with sword drawn, which her rider does not—cannot—perceive. Consequently, when she swerves around the angel into a nearby field, her harsh rider strikes her, and then turns her back onto the path. The angel returns, standing directly in the path that runs between two walls. The donkey swerves, but in the process, scrapes her rider's foot against the wall, for which he again strikes her. Finally, the angel stands so that the donkey simply cannot pass. As a consequence, the donkey simply lies down, again feeling the sting of her rider's staff.

After this third incident, "the Lord opened the mouth of the donkey, [who] said to Balaam, 'What have I done to you, that you have struck me these three times?'" (Num. 22:28). In response, the abuser offers a threatening, small-minded, selfish response—a response rooted in pride—which fails to honor the inherent value of the ass: "Because you have made a fool of me! I wish I had a sword in my hand! I would kill you right now!" (Num. 22:29).

The patient beast of burden, with the voice of the divine, proceeds to remind Balaam of their history, their *mutual* responsibility, and the amiable relationship that they have shared for many years: "Am I not your donkey, which you have ridden all your life to this day? Have I been in the habit of treating you this way?" (Num. 22:30). The donkey challenges her rider's cruel and exploitative ways, and reminds him of her own goodness—that she has been an honorable and dependable ass.

Balaam backs down, simply saying, "No." God then allows Balaam to see the angel, and the angel speaks to Balaam:

> Why have you struck your donkey these three times? I have come to oppose you because your path is perverse before me. The donkey saw me

and turned away from me these three times. If it had not turned away from me, I would certainly have killed you and let it live. (Num. 22: 32–33)

The angel reiterates the message that the divine has already sent through the donkey, challenging Balaam's violent cruelty against the little burro. The angel notes that Balaam's ways are "perverse"—as cruelty must be in the eye of a just and compassionate deity. The angel also reminds the violent man that, were it not for the donkey, Balaam would be dead by force of the angel—but the angel would not harm the innocent donkey. Balaam realizes his ignorant savagery and consequent disgrace. He abandons his journey and returns home.

This passage reveals a tender connection between divine and ass, and between human and equine (horse family), in which a faithful beast, with God's help, asks her rider why he treats her harshly—why he has so little understanding of her life and her feelings. In this passage, scripture reminds readers that every creature is an individual in her or his own right, with individual personality, needs, expectations, and hopes. Scripture reminds people that we establish relations with anymals, and that we must honor, respect, and in some way reciprocate the loyalty and protection of dogs, the relaxation and liveliness that cats bring to our homes, and the personal relationship and incredible power that we might share with horses. Each of these creatures can do us great harm with their jaws, claws, and hooves, but if we are good to them—and many times even when we are not—they do much to enhance our lives, for which we hold a debt of gratitude.

In the story of Balaam and the ass, an equine and an angel remind humanity that impatience, harshness, and cruelty have no place in our relations with anymals. Even when we do not understand or approve of their behaviors, anger and violence are unacceptable. In this story, *the ass's comment is really that of God*—God questions a man's abuse of the little burro who labors for him. Numbers 22 "contains a moving and eloquent plea on behalf of beasts of burden everywhere who are abused by their owners" (Regenstein, 24), from one no less than God.

Rulership in the Image of God

Genesis 1 and 2 (the first book in the Tanakh—and consequently the first book of the Torah) provide accounts of creation. Only these two chapters reveal the world as the Creator *preferred* and *intended* creation to be. After the fall, which occurs in Genesis 3, God's perfect creation has been changed. There is much to be learned about God, humanity, and anymals in these first two chapters of Genesis.

The order of creation that is described in Genesis 2 differs from that of Genesis 1: Genesis 1 culminates in the creation of humanity. Genesis 2 unfolds differently: basic earthly elements, man, vegetation, more complex inanimate matter, animals, and finally woman. This difference is critically important: The existence of two stories, with two completely different orders of creation, prevents a hierarchical interpretation of creation. How can any hierarchy of creation make sense to humanity in light of two completely different accounts? How can a hierarchy move from God to humanity to anymals, and finally to plants, when vegetation and anymals are created *between* man and woman in the Genesis 2 creation account?

No anymal can be considered lesser based on these two accounts of the order of creation. But there is much of importance in these two chapters with regard to rulership, responsibility, and accountability. In Genesis 1 the deity gives rulership to humans, and creates people in the image of God:

> God said, "Let the earth bring forth every kind of living creature according to its kind, cattle, creeping thing, and wild beasts according to their kind." And it was so. God made wild beasts according to their kind, cattle according to their kind, all the creeping things of the ground according to their kind. God saw that it was good. And God said, "Let us make humankind in our image according to our likeness so that they may rule over the fish of the sea, birds of the air, the cattle, all the earth, and all the creeping things that creep over the earth." So God created humankind in his image, in the image of God he created them; male and female he created them. (Gen. 1:24–27)

What could it mean to be created "in the image of God"? Clearly we do not look like the divine. Humans, made in the image (*slm* or *tzelem*) of God, have something of the divine within.

This shared attribute, this gift from God, is critical to our rulership. Human beings are to rule as the just and merciful Creator would rule (Kalechofsky, 98). We do not reign for our own profit, pleasure, and self-aggrandizement. Humans are charged with ruling *in God's stead*; we have "special responsibilities" toward the karakurt spider and the Ruddy Shelduck (Cobb, 506–7). This responsibility is to God, and therefore must mirror the Creator's compassion for anymals, as revealed in Psalm 145:

> The LORD is gracious and compassionate,
>   slow to anger and abounding in kindness.
> The LORD is good to all,
>   and his mercy is on all his works. (Ps. 145:8–9)

Humans, made in the image of God, are to rule in God's stead, and to reflect this divine compassion in their means and methods (Schochet, 144): "As God is compassionate,... so you should be compassionate" (Schwartz, 16). Jewish sages teach that human beings are capable of emulating Divine compassion for all living beings (Schwartz, 16). Indeed, if we are to live in the image of God, "we must love the world and take care of it" (DeWitt, "Behemoth," 306). As scripture indicates that

God tends a dependent and thankful creation, so ought humankind to tend God's beautiful world.

This interpretation of the Tanakh is supported historically and regionally; this wording was not unique to Israel. In ancient Egypt and Mesopotamia, kings were regarded as standing in "the image or likeness of the deity" in both "function and position"; the king was viewed as "the representative of the deity, with a divine mandate to rule" (Hiebert, 138). *Rule* means to "have dominion," "govern," or "have authority" and is generally used in Jewish scripture to indicate the authority of governments over citizens. Ideally, governments "use their authority for the benefit of the people" (Phelps, *Dominion*, 51).

Based on these passages from Genesis, human dominion can be practiced in such a way as to wrong the Creator (Kalechofsky, 95). Genesis gives humans rule, or dominion (*radha*), but human beings are charged with rule *as God would have us rule*, not for our own benefit. Scripture forbids cruelty and requires compassion and mercy. God did not create anymals for our purposes. Rulers who oppress the weak for the benefit of the powerful are "always considered unjust. There is no reason why humanity's dominion [over anymals]...should be judged by any other standard" (Phelps, *Dominion*, 52).

Indeed, Jewish traditions interpret dominion as "responsible stewardship." In this light, to be made "in the image of God" grants humans "a unique function...as God's representative in creation" (Hiebert, 138). To "image God is to image God's love and law...to be endowed with dignified responsibility to reflect God's goodness, righteousness, and holiness...to reflect the wisdom, love, and justice of God" (DeWitt, "Behemoth," 354). If people have a unique place in creation, it "is to be understood primarily in terms of special responsibility" (Kinsley, *Ecology*, 172).

Genesis 2 more clearly outlines our divinely ordained duties. God "took the man and placed him in the Garden of Eden, to till it and tend it," telling the man that he might eat of every tree but one (Gen. 2:15–16). Here we find the most explicit account of what human beings—or at least men—are to *do* as rulers. Unfortunately, the human role is obscured by poor English translations.

The Hebrew word most frequently translated in Genesis 2 as *tend* also appears in Numbers 6:24 (*shamar*), usually translated as "protect": "The Lord bless you and protect you" (DeWitt, "Three," 353). To *tend* requires vitality; it necessitates nurturance for "life-sustaining and life-fulfilling relationships.... [It indicates] a deeply penetrating meaning that evokes a loving, caring, sustaining" role (DeWitt, "Three," 353). "Protect" is a much more powerful, demanding—and accurate—translation.

Similarly, the Hebrew word most often translated as *till* in Genesis 2 (*'abad*), is translated as *serve* in other portions of the Bible, such as Joshua 24:15: "Choose this day which ones you are going to serve—the Gods that your forefathers served...or those of the Amorites" (DeWitt, "Behemoth," 204). The requirement of services is much more expansive than is indicated by the faulty translation of *'abad* as "till": Based on Genesis 2, Rabbi Hirsch comments that humans were created to "serve (work) and safeguard the Earth" (Hirsch, "Letter"; Schwartz, 16). Indeed, according to Genesis 2:15, humans are placed in the Garden of Eden to *protect* and *serve* that which God created. Genesis 2 reveals man "as the servant, not the master" of creation (Hiebert, 140).

Humility

Genesis 1 and 2 are just one example of the many ways in which the Tanakh speaks against human-centered utilitarian assessments of creation and explicitly humbles humanity. Jewish sacred writings seem to understand the human tendency toward arrogance, and the human tendency to see ourselves as above anymals—as superior and more important than fire salamanders, moody woody pigs, Chilumba fish, and the Greater Broad-Billed Moa, who has not been seen since 1640.

Though contemporary Western humans too often looked down their noses at anymals, Jewish religious traditions hold that we are "not distinguished from other forms of life but [are] identified with them" (Hiebert, 139). The Hebrew philosopher behind the writings in Ecclesiastes (Tanakh) notes that human beings are not "divine beings" and need to "face the fact that they are beasts" (Eccles. 3:18). Though created in the image of God, we are animals, and if we see animals as lowly and lesser, then we must also see ourselves in this way. However, if we see the beauty of the Creator in a Vladimir goose and a singing quail, then we can reasonably find the beauty of the Creator in Australian Aborigines and European Caucasians.

The Tanakh recognizes that humans are not much inclined to see anymals as their equals, and are much more apt to believe that they somehow stand closer to God than does the hula painted frog, who once filled Hula lake in Israel, and the laughing owl, who seems to have disappeared from Earth sometime around 1950. In the Book of Job (Tanakh), an arrogant and disappointed human (Job) laments, "I have become a brother of jackals,/A companion to ostriches" (Job 30:29). God asks the presumptuous human, "Where were you when I laid the earth's foundations?/Speak if you have understanding" (Job 38:4). Through visions of nature provided by the voice of God, Job comes to a new understanding of the magnificence of creation—and of the Creator—and of his creatureliness. Ultimately, the human learns that while created in the image of God, he is part of creation—he is, indeed, brother of jackal and companion to ostrich, including the now extinct Arabian ostrich. Upon recognizing himself as an animal, created from the earth and destined to return to the earth, he exclaims, "I recant and relent,/Being but dust and ashes" (Job 42:6).

In the Book of Job, through images of nature provided by God, a haughty man comes to understand the fullness of the divine and in the process comes to understand his smallness, his flesh-and-blood body, his mammalian primate existence. In Jewish religious traditions, humans are but another earthly creature—not exceptionally capable and not particularly bright—though quite conceited (and doubtless remarkably trying to the Creator as a consequence). Job ultimately repents of his arrogance, abandoning his false notion that he is more of God than creation. Indeed, the Psalmist asks, "What is man, that You have been mindful of him,/mortal man that You have taken note of him?" (Job 8:4). Only an arrogant interpretation of scripture, and one that fails to take Genesis and Job into account, would assert that this is a rhetorical question.

Many Jewish writings specifically humble humanity, lest we puff up like magic dragons. For example, an ant puts Solomon in his place in a Jewish fable, complaining that Solomon and his troops interrupt the insect's obligation to praise God. The ant also rebukes Solomon for sitting on his throne while speaking to the queen ant, who is standing on the earth nearby. Solomon scoops up the ant and, doubtless assuming himself to be superior not only to the ant but to all else within creation, inquires as to how she could make such a mistaken assumption regarding their respective places. She calmly notes that he, too, is created from dust, and that God has clearly sent the not-so-lofty Solomon to hold her in the palm of his hand. A humbled Solomon bows low before the little insect (Schochet, 117).

In Jewish traditions, any assumption that other creatures are of lesser importance to God, or that creation itself is not important to God, is likely rooted in the combined folly of human arrogance and spiritual ignorance.

The Peaceable Kingdom

Jews are intended to live in a way that furthers God's ends, and God's ends are peaceful—the "whole Torah was given for the sake of peace" (Schwartz, 95).

Jewish sacred writings indicate that we have come from a world of perfect earthly peace and are headed into yet another perfect earthly peace (Berman, 8). Violence is not chronic; there will be "reconciliation, concord, and trust" (Guthrie, 598).

The prophet Isaiah promises that God's peaceable kingdom will eventually return to earth, transforming life as we know it, bringing a time of "perfect peace among people as well as between human beings and the animal kingdom" (R. S. Y. Cohen, xix). This future Peaceable Kingdom is described in the Tanakh as a place of harmony among the many species. In fact, this future "state of peace and well-being" is "symbolized by the idyllic picture of powerful animals and poisonous reptiles in harmonious companionship with domesticated animals and truly spiritual human children" (Buttrick, 5: 249):

> The wolf shall dwell with the lamb,
> the leopard shall lie down with the kid,
> the calf and the lion and the fatling together,
> and a little child will herd them.
> The cow and the bear shall graze,
> their young will lie down together,
> and the lion, like the ox, shall eat straw.

The nursing child shall play
over the hole of the cobra,
and the weaned child shall put his hand
into the viper's nest.
They will not hurt or destroy
on all my holy mountain
for all the earth shall be filled with the knowledge of YHWH [God]
as the waters cover the sea. (Isa. 11:6–9)

A vision of this Peaceful Kingdom is offered in Isaiah, Hosea, and Job. Hosea prophecies a future covenant "with the beasts of the field, the birds of the air, and the creeping things of the ground," a time when God "will also banish bow, sword, and war from the land. Thus [God] will let them lie down in safety" (Hosea 2:20). The Book of Job also anticipates a time when people will neither kill nor fear beasts, but "the beasts of the field will be your allies" (Job 5:23).

Jewish religious traditions indicate that human beings are not merely to imagine and hope for this day, but are to *work* to bring about God's Peaceable Kingdom: "Seek amity [peace], and pursue it" (Ps. 34:15).

Jewish visions of the created universe begin and end with a peaceful world, a world where people and anymals live together harmoniously, without exploitation and bloodshed. Jewish sacred writings remind human beings that wisdom is precious and "all her paths, peaceful" (Prov. 3:17).

Afterlife

Jewish scriptures teach humanity that the Creator did not grant human beings a soul or spirit that is different from what was given anymals. Nowhere in the Tanakh does the Creator provide humans with an essentially different nature or substance, nor does God offer human beings an afterlife that is denied anymals.

Perhaps of most importance, the Torah indicates that animals are all given the breath of life in the act of creation. In the Torah, *nefesh chaya* (or *nephesh chayah* or *hayyah*) (Gen. 1:21, 24) means "living soul" (or living "being," or "creature"). This breath of life animates red poll cattle, African humans, bala sharks, and Israel's common tree frog (Schwartz, 15).

Given our shared breath of life as animals, we have every reason to believe that the afterlife is similarly shared by all animals. Indeed, the sage philosopher of Ecclesiastes notes that animals share the same prospect after death:

For the fate of humans and the fate of animals is the same. As one dies, so does the other. They have the same breath, and humans have no advantage over the animal; for all is meaningless. All go to one place; all come from dust and all return to dust. Who knows if the spirit of humans goes upward and the spirit of the animal goes downward to the earth? (Eccles. 3:19–21)

An egocentric humanity has sometimes objected to our lack of prestige: The author of Psalm 49 *laments* that humanity "is like the beasts that perish" (49:13). Human beings are given extra responsibilities only as caretakers in God's stead—not specific privileges, a distinct categorization, or a separate afterlife. (Thank goodness—how uninspiring existence would seem for many human beings without toads and tarantulas!)

Hasidic Jews hold a different and interesting understanding of "afterlife." In their view, souls transmigrate. This vision of what happens after death connects all living beings with one another both in this life and in the next—for all eternity (Schochet, 251–53).

Jewish Law

Judaism is rich with laws that regulate human relations with anymals (Kalechofsky, 93), protecting and benefiting the latter (Schochet, 259). Biblical, Talmudic, and medieval law reflect "a coherent system of humane legislation" designed to foster humane communities and to protect anymals (N. Cohen, 105).

Under Jewish law, anymals have legal standing. Mosaic law protects the interests of anymals, demonstrating that anymals are both morally considerable and endowed with rights (James Gaffney, cited in Kalechofsky, 96).

> Mosaic law laid down in the Books of Exodus and Deuteronomy clearly teaches compassion and kindness toward animals. Numerous passages forbid the overworking of animals and require that stray and lost creatures be helped. The law handed down by God makes it clear that these injunctions to help animals were intended for the sake of these creatures, and not that of the owner. One was required to help animals that belonged to enemies to whom no obligation was owed, as well as those of friends; one could not 'pass by' an animal in distress.
>
> Even the most holy of the laws—the Ten Commandments—specifically mention[s] that livestock must not be worked on the Sabbath. (Regenstein, 21)

Jewish law requires that anymals be allowed to rest (*yanuah*) on the Sabbath. This law is repeated several times in the Tanakh, and, as noted in the above quote, is included in the most fundamental Jewish laws, the Ten Commandments: "the seventh day is a Sabbath of the LORD your God; you shall not do any work—you, your son or your daughter, your male or female slave, your ox or your ass, or any of your cattle" (Deut. 5:14, Exod. 20:10 and 23:12). The ox, ass, and cattle are mentioned along with human members of an extended, working household: All are granted a day of rest.

While keeping the Sabbath—not working on the Sabbath—is a critical aspect of Judaism, scripture indicates that the well-being of anymals is yet more important (Kalechofsky, 93). An anymal's discomfort is sufficient cause to break Sabbath rules that might prevent freeing or aiding an anymal in distress, such as the prohibition against untying knots or blanketing an anymal. It is, of course, expected that those who keep anymals will tend to their basic needs on the Sabbath (Schochet, 156). Sabbath requirements do not permit human beings to rest at the expense of anymals, or to neglect the needs of anymals. As our dependents, their needs must be met, even on the Sabbath.

Ancient Jewish regulations, defended by rabbis down through the centuries, "bespeak an eloquent awareness of the status of animals as ends in themselves" (Rollin, 52). Scripture, and the rabbis who interpret scripture, agree that human beings are obligated to see to the needs of anymals, and to treat them with attentiveness and consideration. Rashi, an outstanding biblical commentator from the Middle Ages (and famed author of the first comprehensive commentaries on the Talmud, Torah, and Tanakh), interpreted the commandment to rest animals as requiring considerably more than a mere break from work. He asserted that "rest" includes *satisfaction*, such that those who "rest" anymals must make sure that anymals are contented, satisfied, and at ease (Schochet, 263).

Diet

Genesis 1 and 2 provide the Jewish account of creation, including indications as to what the deity intended.

Based on the Torah, it would seem that the Creator suspected that people might lose sight of their rightful place and responsibilities. Scripture clearly prohibits human actions that are likely to endanger the lives or welfare of anymals. Most important, immediately after we are given rulership, human beings are told that they may not eat anymals.

The Jewish God offered humans an overlordship that "does not include the right to kill animals for food" (Allen 1: 132). Genesis 2 explains that people were permitted to eat of every tree but one—a plant-based diet (Gen. 2:15–16). Genesis 1 also ordains a vegan diet:

> God said, "See, I give you every seed-bearing plant that is upon the face of all the earth, and every tree that has seed-bearing fruit. They will be yours for food. And to all the beasts of the earth, all the birds of the air, and all the creatures that creep on earth—everything that has the breath of life—I give all the green plant for food." And it was so. And God saw all that he had made, and it was very good. (Gen. 1:29–31)

Only after the deity explains what we are to eat—that we are to be vegan—is creation complete, and *only then* does God note that creation is "very good." The Torah establishes peaceful relations between humans and other animals, and describes "the pleasure and the delight of the divine viewer" in beholding this peaceful world (Allen, 1: 132). According to the Tanakh, preying on one another is contrary to the deity's preference for how we ought to live; the vegan world is "as God wanted it, in complete harmony, with nothing superfluous or lacking" (Schwartz, 2). Isaac Arama, a fifteenth-century Spanish rabbi and scholar, extols the highest ideal to be abstinence from flesh because vegetarians "elevate themselves above crass bodily appetites" in order "to live in keeping with god's initial blueprint for mankind" (Schochet, 289–90). Genesis 1 reveals the divine preference for a world without bloodshed, without fear and suffering, without predators and prey. God notes that the created world—plant-based and peaceful—is "very good."

This divinely ordained diet reminds people (yet again) that we are given a dominion of mercy and compassion. People are granted a vegan rulership, sustenance compatible with a Peaceable Kingdom, a diet that does not permit of tyranny or exploitation. A plant-based diet makes perfect sense in light of the Jewish expectation that human beings demonstrate mercy and compassion, and avoid causing harm or pain. A vegan diet is also consistent with the expectation of a compassionate Creator: Scripture records "six things the LORD hates," of which "Seven are an abomination"; third among these is "Hands that shed innocent blood" (Prov. 6:16–17). Anymals, especially farmed anymals, are innocent and helpless in the face of human oppression and exploitation. Jewish religious traditions uphold a vegan diet as "the high ideal of God...an ultimate goal toward which all people should strive" (Schwartz, 13).

Not surprisingly, many Jews have spoken out against eating anymals. Isaac Luria of Egypt, a well-known sixteenth-century Jewish mystic, spoke against the killing and eating of flesh (Schochet, 288). Joseph Albo of Spain, a fifteenth-century rabbi and philosopher, concludes that those who understand their spiritual essence will not dominate or destroy other life forms, or consume flesh, all of which are "dangerous" habits (Schochet, 292). Today, eating dairy products and eggs is just as rooted in the cruel domination of anymals as is eating flesh; under the current system of anymal agriculture, consuming any anymal products supports cruelty and premature death.

Many people overlook Genesis 1, and turn to Genesis 9, in which God accepts that a violent humanity is determined to eat flesh. Rav Kook, the first Ashkenazi chief rabbi of pre-state Israel, a Torah scholar, and a "highly respected and beloved Jewish spiritual leader," reminded Jews that eating flesh is but a temporary concession in the Bible. Kook taught that a merciful God could not prefer that humans continue eating flesh, and so he advocated a vegetarian diet (Schwartz, 3, 175; R. S. Y. Cohen, xix). Rabbi Cohen (Ashkenazi chief rabbi) writes, "We look at the vegetarian way of life as a special path of worship and as a step forward toward the 'Great

Day,' i.e., the coming of the Messiah, the day where 'Nation shall not lift up sword against nation, neither shall they learn war any more' (Isa. 2:4). Bloodshed will cease" (R. S. Y. Cohen, xix). Committing to a plant-based diet anticipates and participates in the return of God's Peaceful Kingdom.

Other distinguished vegetarian or vegan rabbis include David Cohen (the *nazir of Jerusalem*), Shear Yashuv Cohen (Ashkenazi chief rabbi of Haifa), David Rosen (former chief rabbi of Ireland), Shlomo Goren (former Ashkenazi chief rabbi of Israel), and such Jewish literary giants as Shmuel Yosef Agnon and Isaac Bashevis Singer (Schochet, 296–97). Singer writes of his vegetarian diet:

> The longer I am a vegetarian, the more I feel how wrong it is to kill animals and eat them. I think that eating meat or fish is a denial of all ideals, even of all religions. How can we pray to God for mercy if we ourselves have no mercy? How can we speak of right and justice if we take an innocent creature and shed its blood? Every kind of killing seems to me savage and I find no justification for it.
>
> I believe that the religion of the future will be based on vegetarianism. As long as people will shed the blood of innocent creatures there can be no peace, no liberty, no harmony between people. Slaughter and justice cannot dwell together. (Schochet, 297)

Hunting and Bloodlust

Rabbis have long recognized hunting as a cruel pastime. In their eyes, the only thing more deplorable than hunting for pleasure is hunting for both pleasure and profit. Italian rabbi Samson Morpurgo (1681) was reportedly shocked to hear of Jews hunting for profit (Schochet, 269).

Hunting, because it is often a form of pleasure rather than a necessary method of survival, and because this form of pleasure causes great suffering and premature death, is recognized as particularly irksome in Jewish religious literature. Maimonides, perhaps the most noteworthy of all Jewish theologians, condemned bird hunting as wanton destruction of God's creation (Schochet, 267). The Talmud (rabbinic discussions pertaining to Jewish law, ethics, customs, and history) forbids the faithful to associate with hunters who are so cruel as to set dogs on the trail of hunted anymals (Cohn-Sherbok, 88). The *Piske Tosafot* (medieval commentaries on the Talmud) and *Sefer haHinnukh* (thirteenth-century "Book of Education") forbid causing unnecessary pain, which includes hunting for sport (as well as the exploitation of anymals for food, entertainment, clothing, or science, at least among most citizens of industrialized nations) (Schochet, 267).

The Tanakh also speaks against consuming anymals. "In the Torah the sport of hunting is imputed only to fierce characters like Nimrod, who was known for brute strength as a warrior and hunter (Gen. 10:9), and Esau, who lived by his sword (Gen. 27:40), never to any of the patriarchs and their descendants" (Schwartz, 25). But perhaps the best story from the Tanakh revealing hunting and anymal products as unnecessary, and therefore cruel and base, is when the Jews were wandering in the desert. God provided manna, which is described as like coriander seed with a taste like wafers (Exod. 16:31), and is referred to as "bread from heaven" (Exod. 16:4). But some of the desert wanderers were not satisfied (Exod. 16; Num. 16), and rabbis who comment on this story note that Israelites angered God by demanding meat when given *manna*. The connotation is one of humans "lusting" after meat when we are well provided with plant-based foods (Schochet, 158). Those who seek anymal products when we have plenty of vegan foods are like the desert wanderers, nurtured by the hand of God yet complaining bitterly, always wanting something they do not have.

Most contemporary Jews generally have plenty of nonanymal options for nutritious food. Consequently, hunting is understood to be a "sport" that is unnecessary, cruel, and disrespectful toward God's creatures. When Rabbi Yechezkel Landau was asked about hunting, he responded, "I cannot comprehend how a Jew could even dream of killing animals merely for the pleasure of hunting"; such trivializations of life are "downright cruelty" (Schwartz, 25).

Divine-Anymal Relations

Scripture provides a rich understanding of the deity's relationship with anymals as intimate, caring, compassionate, sustaining, and personal. God is both constant provider and attentive sustainer for all creatures (Schochet, 144):

There is the sea, vast and spacious, with creatures beyond number, living things both small and great...

> All of them look to you to give them their food at the proper time.
> When you give it to them, they gather it up;
> when you open your hand, they are satisfied with good things;
> when you hide your face, they are terrified;
> when you take away their breath, they perish and return to dust;
> when you send your breath, they are created, and you renew the face of the
>   earth. (Ps. 104: 25–30)

Based on Tanakh passages such as this one, rabbis through the ages have viewed God as the benefactor of all life: "The Holy One, blessed be He, sits and sustains [all life], from the horns of the wild oryx to the eggs of lice" (*Shab.* 107b, in Schochet, 57).

The eyes of all look to you expectantly,
and you give them their food at the proper time.
You open your hand and satisfy the desires of every creature. (Ps.
     145:15–16).

Anymals, like humans, turn to God in times of need, crying out with hunger or in
fear (Joel 1:20). Anymals are aware of God's munificence, and they are thankful
when basic needs are met. "Throughout Psalms and elsewhere in the Hebrew Bible,
God is portrayed as...providing for the needs of animals, which in turn express
their gratitude to the Lord" (Regenstein, 33). Anymals lift up their voices in prayer
in the *Mishna* (*Perek Shira*, an ancient *Baraita*, Jewish oral law not included in the
Mishna): "All creation is a single hymn of praise in which humans, animals and
nature as a whole praise God with one voice" (Vischer, 5). Many rabbinical teachings are preserved in the *Midrash* (interpretations, studies, commentary, or exegesis
of Jewish scripture); the *Midrash* depicts anymals chanting scriptural passages,
"exhorting one another to greater piety and religious devotion" (Schochet, 134).
Psalms encourage all of creation to praise God:

Praise him, sun and moon;
Praise him, all you shining stars...
mountains and all hills,
fruit trees and all cedars,
wild animals and all cattle,
creeping things and winged birds...
Let them praise the name of the LORD. (Ps. 148:3–13)
The long collection of Psalms concludes: "Let all that breathes praise the
     LORD" (150:6).

The Creator is essential to the daily and ongoing survival of anymals, and they, in
turn, not only praise, but also assist God. Rabbinic stories tell how anymals serve
God both through ritual and as moral agents (Schochet, 135). Rabbi Aha notes that
God oversees the planet "with the help of all," including serpents, frogs, scorpions,
and mosquitoes (Schochet, 133). For example, in the *Targum Yonatan*, David questions God's wisdom in creating such "useless" creatures as spiders and wasps. David's
life is soon saved by an obliging spider, who builds her web across a cave where he
hides from his pursuers. Seeing the web, and assuming no one has passed through
the entrance, the soldiers pass by and David is spared (Schochet, 133).

According to Jewish texts, God calls on anymals to dispense divine justice
(Schochet, 129), and anymals demonstrate both willingness and considerable
ability in this capacity. A deer brings about Zedekiah's capture (Ginzberg).
Discerning lions do not harm Daniel, yet they devour his enemies (Dan. 6:10–28).
Snakes and scorpions do not harm the Israelites in the desert (Deut. 8:15). A dove

warns Abishai that David is in danger ("Og, King"). A serpent kills a deceitful priest beneath the altar of Baal. Ants (or worms) swarm the stored *manna* to expose those who are guilty of hoarding (Exod. 16:20), while mice swarm the Philistines, who capture the ark (1 Sam. 6:5). Ants also rescue the Israelites from the king of Bashan (Buchwald). Hornets help the Israelites defeat the Amorites (Josh. 24:12). Frogs plague the Egyptians—the frogs even endure oven time—but they are protected by the divine because they are engaged in God's work, so they can take the heat, and they survive to return to the river. In Exodus 8, gnats and flies create the third and fourth plagues (Schochet, 129, 130, 138, 139).

The rabbis whose teachings created the *Midrash*, demonstrate their understanding that anymals have a personal relationship with God and that the anymals are personally and individually important to the Creator. The *Midrash Tanhuma* notes that rain comes to earth—preserving *all* living beings—*because* of the "merit of the small cattle" (Schochet, 147). The *Midrash* attributes God's sparing the city of Nineveh to the Creator's concern for anymals: The people of Nineveh threatened to "show no compassion toward the animals" if God did not spare their lives, so God spared Nineveh to spare the anymals (Schochet, 147).

Covenant

The covenant of Genesis 9 reveals the centrality of God's concern for anymals. Scripture is no less than redundant in explicitly stating that God's covenant is with "every living creature on earth"—and with the earth itself:

> Then God said to Noah and to his sons with him, "I now establish my covenant with you and your descendants after you, and with every living creature that is with you—the birds, the cattle, and all the creature of the earth with you, all that comes out from the ark—every living creature on earth. I establish my covenant with you: Never again will all flesh be cut off by the waters of a flood, and never again will there be a flood to destroy the earth."
>
> God said, "This is the sign of the covenant that I make between me and you and between all the living creatures which are with you for all future generations. I have set my bow in the clouds and it will be a sign of the covenant between me and the earth. When I bring clouds over the earth and the bow appears in the clouds, I will remember my covenant between me and you and between all the living creatures of all flesh and the waters will never again become a flood to destroy all flesh. When the bow is in the clouds, I will see it and remember the everlasting covenant between God and all the living creatures of all flesh that is on the earth." God said to Noah, "This is the sign of the covenant that I establish between me and all the flesh upon the earth." (Gen. 9:8–17)

Seven times this biblical passage asserts that God's covenant includes much more than humanity; God's covenant includes not only every anymal, but the earth itself.

In this covenant, humans are categorized with "all flesh." The covenant is explicitly between the deity and "all the living creatures of all flesh that is on the earth," it is unambiguously established between God, "and all flesh that is on the earth" (Gen. 9:16–17). In these lines, the Creator reveals humans as part of the larger category of fleshy beings: This covenant admits of no separation between humans and anymals (Linzey, *After*, 22). God makes the rainbow covenant with White Holland turkeys, banded knife fish, Italian humans, Holando-Argentino cattle, endangered desert tortoises, and the hirola (of which only about 600 remain, largely due to hunting and human encroachment)—all are included in the Genesis 9 covenant with the Creator.

Human-Anymal Relations

Anymals as Individuals

Sacred Jewish literature includes a host of anymals, many of whom speak with humans to offer moral guidance, or simply to share in the unfolding of Jewish mythological history. Anymal personalities and individuality come alive in these entertaining and memorable stories.

The Torah includes the voices of two important anymal individuals, an ass and a snake. In the story of Balaam (Num. 22, discussed earlier), a patient and trustworthy beast of burden reminds Balaam of their history, their mutual responsibility, and the relationship that they have shared over the years. As an honorable and dependable ass, and an independent creation, she challenges his cruel and exploitative domination with the help of a voice that no one can reasonably challenge—the voice of the Creator.

The snake in Genesis 3 also speaks, and this time God does not assist. The snake's words reveal an individual who is independent, intelligent, and informed. Genesis offers a vision of the snake as a neighbor, not unlike any neighbor who might pause to chat in a shared garden behind cozy homes. But in this instance, the conversation focuses on God's rules regarding eating from the trees that stand in the garden. The human reports that God has prohibited the consumption of any fruits from a specific tree, lest they die (Gen 3:3). The snake understands more than the human being, and sets them straight: "You will not die; for God knows that when you eat of it your eyes will be opened, and you will be like God, knowing good and evil" (Gen. 3:4–5). The woman believes her neighbor, decides that she would like to know good and evil, becoming more like God, and samples the forbidden fruit, simultaneously offering a taste to a silent, apathetic Adam.

As the story unfolds, we find that the snake was right: Adam and Eve do not die. We also find the humans blaming the snake for their decision to feast on the forbidden fruits. A silent and seemingly listless Adam shrugs off his responsibility first, blaming Eve, who then blames the serpent: "The serpent tricked me, and I ate" (Gen. 3:13).

But any halfway capable reader can see that the snake did not trick the human beings. In spite of centuries of mislaid blame, despite thousands of sermons that have passed the buck first to the woman and then to the serpent, the snake merely corrected human ignorance—the people believed that they would die if they ate of the forbidden fruit, and the snake informed them that they would not. Indeed, they survived to begin the process of human production and reproduction.

It is important to note that the serpent does not say one way or the other whether humans ought to eat of the prohibited fruit. This goes to the much-maligned character of the snake. The serpent simply speaks the truth: By eating the illicit fruits, the people would "be like God, knowing good and evil" (Gen. 3:5). Apparently this appeals to Eve, so she takes the fruit, and then shares with the inert Adam. Indeed, when they eat the fruit, they become a little more like God, aware of nakedness, which they did not previously perceive. Though the final outcome of the snake's interaction with human beings is negative, and despite many harsh human-centered interpretations, the serpent in Genesis 3 is wise, speaks the truth, and does no obvious wrong.

Scripture indicates that God is displeased with humans eating the forbidden fruit, and curses the serpent. The snake cannot reasonably be held accountable for the choices of foolish, willful, irresponsible humans *unless the snake understood much more than did the human beings*, suggesting serious shortcomings of humanity in relation to the snake's superior grasp of the situation. The snake did not deceive, trick, or even tempt the human beings, but God's anger at the serpent indicates that perhaps the snake was guilty of failing to explain more fully that which the first humans were unable to grasp—the likely consequences of knowing good and evil.

Anymals appear in other places in the Tanakh. Proverbs 30 refers to anymals as "folk." In a patriarchal celebration of individual creatures who are bold and assertive, humans are placed alongside other proud and strutting males:

> There are three things that are stately in their stride,
> Four that carry themselves well:
> A lion, mighty among beasts, does not retreat before anything,
> A strutting rooster, a he-goat,
> And a king striding before his people. (Prov. 30: 29–31)

Other Jewish stories also provide an abundance of anymal characters with distinctive voices and individual personalities. "Rabbinic literature contains thirty-six animal tales known as 'fox tales'" (though the fox is featured in less than a third of these alluring stories) (Schochet, 115). Such well-known Jewish storytellers as Hillel and Johanan ben Zakkai were "acknowledged masters of the animal tale, and Rabbi Meir was reputed to have had a repertoire of three hundred fox fables, as was Bar Kappara" (Schochet, 115).

Rabbinic stories tend to feature anymals who teach or explain. For example, one story explicates why the mouse appears to have seams along her mouth, and another favorite tells why the steer's nose has a bald spot. (The latter yet again honors the importance of anymals: A kiss from Joshua left a bald spot—a kiss given to the bovine who carried him through the long siege of Jericho; Schochet, 118.) Another touching rabbinic story features a she-wolf. Jacob demands that his sons produce this wild creature because they claim that she has devoured his favored son, Joseph. The aggrieved father is determined to avenge his son's death. But the devious boys have actually disposed of their brother themselves. In order to continue the ruse, they capture a random wolf and present her to their father. In her time of need, God endows the canine tongue with human speech, and she eloquently proclaims her innocence. She also empathizes with Jacob, for she is missing a cub, and fears that her young one has come to harm. Jacob promptly frees the mother wolf to search for her lost pup (*Yasher Wa-Yesheb*, an ancient collection of oral traditions) (Schochet, 149).

Anymals as Independent

In the Jewish religious traditions, wild creatures are created splendid in both form and function, perfect in their own right, happy about their existence, and intentionally *independent*—wild anymals are not to be altered, exploited, dominated, or controlled by human beings.

Scripture reminds humans that "certain areas of God's creation are outside human control," *beyond* acceptable and proper realms of human influence (Vischer, 9). Jewish scriptures celebrate the independence and ferocity of wild anymals. For example, the she-bear is admired for her fierceness in protecting her young (2 Sam. 17:8, Prov. 17:12, and Hos. 13:8). In the Book of Job, the Jewish deity praises the mighty Hippopotamus (Eiselen, 507):

> Look at the behemoth, whom I made just like you;
> He eats grass like cattle.
> His strength is in his loins,
> His might in the muscles of his belly...
> His bones are tubes of bronze,
> His limbs are like bars of iron.
> He is first of God's work,
> Only his maker can approach him with his sword.
> The hills yield him produce,
> Where all the beasts of the field play.
> Under the lotus plants he lies,
> In the cover of the reeds and the marsh...
> Can his nose be pierced by hooks?

> Can you draw out Leviathan with a fishhook,
> Or press down his tongue with a rope?
> Can you put a ring in his nose,
> Or pierce his jaw with a hook? (Job 40: 15–26)

Perhaps modern humans *can* do all of the above to the great hippopotamus, but scripture reminds that this is not what God intended; the Creator, who made the hippopotamus "as I made you," asserts that these creatures' lives are rightly controlled only by God.

The above passage from the Book of Job also comments on how "all the beasts of the field play" in the mountains. The deity created hippos, and the myriad creatures, to enjoy the playground of the natural world. Whether beasts of the prairies and deserts, oceans and lakes, or mountains and forests, anymals are provided with their own splendid playground in which to romp, rest, and live out their natural lives. Anymals are here not to satisfy human needs, but for their own sake and for the sake of their Creator. Just as hippos were created to lie among lily pads and swamp reeds—praising God with their magnificence—so kingfishers were created to swoop down over the waters (also praising God with their magnificence), and ploughshare tortoises were created to amble across the Madagascar landscape (now only about 400 tortoises remain to praise God with their magnificence). Our purposes are not their purposes, and vice versa. The Tanakh reminds us that wild anymals are independent of human beings, that they were *purposefully created* independent of human beings, and that *they* wish to remain independent of human beings.

Finally, the passages describing a hippopotamus in the Book of Job point out that "the fearsome hippo, so mighty as to be outside of the power of human rulership, does not consume flesh, but dines on grass provided by God." So much for the manly powers of a fleshy diet.

Because anymals are intended to live on their own, God provided them with homes in the steppes and salt land where they might live free of human control and exploitation, far from domineering drivers who shout at laboring burros, safely away from exploitative breeders and herders. In the Book of Job, the Creator asks,

> Do you know when the mountain goats give birth?
> Do you observe the calving of the deer?...
> Who let the wild donkey go free?
> Who loosens the bonds of the onager,
> To which I have given the wilderness as its dwelling,
> The salt land as its habitat?
> It laughs at the tumult of the city,
> It does not hear the shouts of the driver.
> It roams the hills for its pasture...

Will the wild ox consent to serve you?
Will it spend the night by your crib?
Can you hold it by ropes to the furrow?
Will it till the valleys behind you? (Job 39:1–10)

Wild asses and oxen would scorn to bear human burdens or feed in the barnyard because "the great creatures of land and sea were not made to serve as our pets or playthings" (Goodman, 11). God *purposefully* created nature outside the domain of human beings—even beyond our comprehension. We are given no place or power in wild lands, and scripture reminds that people are not given license to destroy or tame the mighty beasts who dwell in wild places. The Creator's voice in Job makes it clear that anymals were not created for human beings, and that we must not treat them like means to our ends, as if they were nothing more than a source of human labor, profit, or a source of food.

Both wild and domestic anymals are presented in Jewish literature as rightfully independent of human exploitation and conniving, and in the *Iggeret Baalei Hayyim* they are portrayed as quite capable of seeking justice against human perpetrators. The *Iggeret Baalei Hayyim* (*The Book of Animals and Men*) first appeared in Hebrew in 1316, and quickly became a special favorite among medieval Jews. This book provides an opportunity to ponder anymal liberation through straightforward descriptions of human injustice. Anymals such as parrots and jackals complain of subjugation, question assumed human superiority, and give voice to "heartrending tales of suffering and torture endured at the hands of their human oppressors" (Schochet, 256). In the *Iggeret Baalei Hayyim*, the "best lines and most convincing arguments...are given to the animals" (Schochet, 256). This is likely because the power of justice *actually lies* on their side. For instance, a cock laments that humans slaughter him at their whim, and appeals to the Tanakh: "Have we not all one father? Has not one God created us all?" (Schochet, 256).

Kinship and Community

Indeed, all life has one creator in Jewish religious traditions—all life is a single, organic unity, including human beings, Caspian turtles, and the Sinai chameleon (Schochet, 53). Jewish religious traditions recognize a common bond that links humans with all other creatures and ties all creatures to God (Schochet, 245). Not one feather or tooth stands apart from the fundamental unity of creation.

Genesis 1 records God creating light, sky, water, land, vegetation, heavenly bodies, and living creatures in six days. On the sixth day, land animals (including human beings) were created. The Torah reveals what science has discovered only comparatively recently: We are land mammals, primates, great apes. Because we are animals, we are created with anymals on the sixth day. The Jewish creation story reminds that we are creatures of the earth, created along with jungle cats and mountain gazelles, insignificant but for God, stemming from the same hand and destined to the same end.

In the original Hebrew, when God notes that creation is *good*, those reading Hebrew recognize that the adjective is singular; "God views life in all its diversity as a fundamental unity" (Saperstein, 14). We are family—brothers and sisters—with one divine Creator, and our essential unity carries a moral imperative:

> As God is merciful, so you also be merciful. As He loves and cares for all His creatures because they are His creatures and His children and are related to Him, because He is their Father, so you also love all His creatures as your brethren. Let their joys be your joys, and their sorrows yours. Love them and with every power which God gives you, work for their welfare and benefit, because they are the children of your God, because they are your brothers and sisters. (Hirsch, *Horeb*, 72:482, as quoted in Schwartz, 24–25)

English translations sometimes obscure and distort our relationship with anymals. For example, as noted, *nefesh chaya* (Gen. 1:21, 24), or "living soul"—the breath of life—is given to all animals (Schwartz, 15), but translations fail to convey this critical message:

> According to Genesis, *the life force, the divine breath that brings will and consciousness, is the same in animals as it is in human beings.* Tragically, our English Bibles hide this fundamental truth by translating *nephesh* one way when it refers to animals and another when it refers to humans.
>
> The King James Version translates *nephesh chayah* in Genesis 1:21 and 24 as "living creature." Then in 2:7, where it refers to a human being, the KJV translates *nephesh chayah* as "living soul" [or "living being"]. But in 2:19, where it again refers to animals, *nephesh chayah* reverts to "living creature," obscuring the fact that the Bible makes no distinction between the nature of the living spirit with which God endowed humanity and that with which God endowed the animals.
>
> Unfortunately, most modern translators have followed suit. (Phelps, *Dominion*, 58)

In the Tanakh creation story, humans and anymals are *equally* "living beings" (Hiebert, 139): The breath of life given by God is the physical breath of *all* animate life.

Because all of creation is a single unity, creatures share the most fundamental and critical aspects of existence, including the "spirit of life" (*ruach hayyim*), the status of "living creature" (*nefesh hayyah*), and the frailty of "all flesh" (*kol basar*) (Schochet, 53). Perhaps most remarkably, all are intended to live together as companions and helpers in the task of serving and protecting creation:

The LORD God said, "It is not good for man to be alone. I will make a helper as his partner for him." And the LORD God formed out of the ground all the beasts of the field and all the birds of the air. He brought them to the man to see what he would call them; and whatever the man called every living creature, that was its name.... But for the man, no helper was found as his partner.... The LORD God made a woman from the rib he took from the man and he brought her to the man. (Gen. 2:18–22)

Anymals did not prove to be "fitting helpers," so woman was created *for the same purpose*. God intended that animals work together to till and tend, serve and protect creation (Gen. 2), both the bulbul and the critically endangered Mediterranean monk seal, both male and female *Homo sapiens*. The Creator never revokes or denounces this shared purpose. Anymals and women are fellow servants, helpmates alongside Adam in the God-given task of serving and protecting God's creations.

Given the unity of animals, and their shared, God-given duty, it is not surprising that Knesset member (Israeli legislator) Yoel Hasson recently commented that anymals "are also citizens of Israel, and they also deserve representatives who will speak for them" ("Pro-Animal").

Anymal Powers

Jewish literature portrays anymals as endowed with spiritual understanding, sometimes greater spiritual understanding than human beings, and the special and exemplary qualities of anymals are sometimes exalted "far above those of humans" (Schochet, 55).

For example, the Book of Job praises the wisdom of anymals:

> But ask the animals, and they will teach you,
> The birds of the air, and they will tell you,
> Or speak to the earth, and it will teach you,
> The fish of the sea, and they will inform you.
> Who among all these does not know
> That the hand of the LORD has done all this? (Job 12:7–9)

Anymals, and the earth itself, discern their Maker and Protector, and they sometimes understand this more readily than do human beings.

The story of Balaam atop his trusty ass (Num. 22) also reminds us that human beings are, in many ways, inferior to other creatures. The ass is aware of the angel while her rider is oblivious (Harrison, 300). In fact, Balaam is unable to interpret even the most basic anymal behaviors, while his burro can see angels. In this story, "an unprejudiced animal can see things to which a man in his willfulness is blind" (Noth, 178–79).

The Book of Proverbs also acknowledges wisdom in the anymal world, even in the smallest of creatures:

> Four things on earth are small,
> Yet they are the wisest of the wise:
> Ants are a people without strength,
> Yet they prepare their food in summer;
> Badgers are a people without power,
> Yet they make their home in the rocks;
> Locusts have no king,
> Yet they all march in formation;
> A lizard can be caught with the hand,
> Yet it is found in royal palaces. (Prov. 30: 24–28)

The Book of Proverbs advises people to observe and imitate anymals because they are wise, and have much that they might teach humanity:

> Go to the ant, you lazybones;
> Consider its ways and be wise.
> Without leaders, officers, or rulers,
> It stores its provision during summer,
> And gathers its food during harvest. (Prov. 6:6–8)

Anymals also carry moral authority: Rabbi Johanan, for example, notes that anymals teach morality in sacred Jewish writings (Schochet, 126). Anymals enter the ark without delay, peacefully and at the appropriate time, and are therefore celebrated in the *Midrash* for their compliance to divine command (Schochet, 131). The Tanakh compares the regular, dependable flights of migrating birds with the irregular, uncertain behavior of humans:

> And the turtledove, swift, and crane,
> observe the time of their coming;
> But my people do not know
> the justice of the LORD. (Jer. 8:7)

Even human beings sometimes come to see that anymals are better company than other humans. Job admits that he holds his herding dogs in higher esteem than he does certain humans, whom he "would have disdained to put among [his] sheep dogs" (Job 30:1).

Scriptures also praise anymals for their deep understanding and for maintaining rightful relations with the divine, which is sometimes quite challenging for humans, due to their arrogance:

> The ox knows its owner,
> An ass its master's crib,
> But Israel does not know,
> My people do not understand. (Isa. 1:3)

The *Pesikta Rabbati* (*Midrash*) includes the story of a spiritually informed heifer. Her thoughtless human has sold her to someone who does not keep the Sabbath, and her new, irreverent human requires her to work on the day of rest. Aware that she is due a day of rest on the Sabbath, a day protected by Jewish law, she refuses to work. Consequently, her previous owner, a devout Jew, is summoned. He whispers into the heifer's ear, admitting his error in selling her to someone who would work her seven days a week. He asks her to comply with her new owner's wishes, and she sets to work. The new owner, amazed by this turn of events, realizes that the young cow understands the Sabbath, and therefore knows of her Maker. As a consequence, he sets aside his irreligious ways and turns his life to scriptural study and religious observance (Schochet, 136), no doubt granting the young bovine her day of rest.

Rabbinic fables instruct and inspire humanity through good examples set by anymals (Schochet, 121). A locust sings joyfully to the heavens—even to the point of death—reminding us to live joyously and lovingly, to praise God mightily with each day, and to fulfill our duties to God diligently, though we will all soon perish (Schochet, 126). Sometimes anymals, including dogs and snakes, sacrifice their lives to protect others. Ants teach honesty; a cock reveals good manners; a cat demonstrates modesty; and a dove exemplifies chastity (along with a host of other admirable qualities) (Schochet, 126, 128).

Jewish Traditions and Anymal Liberation

Jewish Scripture is *centrally* concerned with "life on earth" (Berman, 43); Jewish law guides every aspect of day-to-day life. *Halakha* (Jewish law, including the collective corpus of religious, biblical, later Talmudic, and rabbinic law, as well as customs and traditions) stems from the Hebrew root "to go" or "walk." A more appropriate translation for Halakha might be "path" or "the way of walking."Scripture advises humans as to how we ought to *live*:

> He has told you...what is good,
> And what does the LORD require of you?
> To act justly, to love mercy, and to walk humbly before your God! (Mic. 6:8)

Jewish sacred writings indicate that justice does not admit of exploitation, goodness does not permit cruelty, and walking modestly with God does not allow humans to elevate themselves above other species, to exploit the earth and other living beings through such practices as factory farming, vivisection, or commercial or recreational fishing.

Most important among moral requirements, Jews are to be humane; cruelty to anymals is explicitly condemned in Jewish religious traditions and by Jewish leaders. Respected Lithuanian Orthodox rabbi Moshe Feinstein (twentieth century), for example, condemned the production and consumption of veal: "It is definitely forbidden to raise calves in such a manner because of the pain that is inflicted" (Kalechofsky, 96). Contemporary rabbis have also opposed the fur industry, which entails cruel and unnecessary acts of violence against anymals, such as "bone-crushing leghold traps," clubbing baby seals, and "hanging rabbits and raccoons by their tongues" to avoid scarring on the pelts (Cohn-Sherbok, 88). Based on Halakha, Rabbi David Ha-Levy (Israel, twentieth century) decreed that both manufacturing and wearing fur are a violation of the Jewish prohibition against harming other creatures (Kalechofsky, 97). Alternative varieties of clothing—much warmer varieties—are now available without the anymal suffering that is inherent in the taking of fur; wearing fur, like eating veal and attending circuses, is unnecessary. Because these choices harm anymals and are completely unnecessary, they conflict with the "merciful treatment of all living beings [which] has from time immemorial been a core value of Jewish views of the proper relationship between humans" and anymals (Cohn-Sherbok, 89).

Jewish prophets were also concerned with life on earth. They stood for truth; they stood against those with power who were corrupt and irreligious (Wink, 188). The prophets spoke on behalf of the downtrodden and beleaguered. Jewish prophets, who struggled to turn human minds, lives, and hearts back to God, have left an example of moral and spiritual courage. It is difficult to turn people away from customary behaviors; it is yet more difficult to bring about a deep spiritual change that permanently alters behavior—yet this is the hope of prophecy. Consequently, radical actions, sometimes motivated by righteous anger, are fundamental to prophecy, as revealed by Jewish scriptures. Prophecy often entails unusual behaviors:

> Prophecy is essentially eccentric, coming from the Greek, outside the center. The center is where conventions dwell. Prophecy pushes to the edges, to new horizons. Resistance to the dominant consciousness anchored in ill-gotten privilege is the essence of prophetic eccentricity. (Maguire, 420)

Jewish prophets were determined to call people away from worldly lives—by whatever means necessary.

Consequently, though "nakedness was taboo in Judaism" (Wink, 179), on behalf of God and on behalf of the wayward people of Israel, Isaiah wandered "naked and barefoot for three years" (Isa. 20:3), while Micah vowed to "lament and wail" and "go stripped and naked" (Mic. 1:8). Nudity was soon recognized as one of the indicators of prophecy so that when Saul "stripped off his clothes," and "lay naked" for a day and a night, people asked, "Is Saul also among the prophets?" (1 Sam. 19:24). Under divine instruction, Jeremiah harnessed himself to a yoke (Jer. 27:2) and was seen, understandably enough, as a "madman" (Jer. 29:26).

"The prophets intuited that only outrage speaks to outrage.... Only shock gets through" (Maguire, 420). Because of their behaviors, which not only stepped outside the center but threatened the established order, the prophets were persecuted. The prophets *lived* the moral expectations of Judaism and, on behalf of humanity and God, adopted bizarre behaviors with intent to bring people back to the divine.

Contemporary anymal liberationists sometimes walk a similar path to that of the prophets, employing outrageous methods with the hope of calling attention to the suffering and deaths entailed in factory farming, and ultimately with the hope of calling people back to rightful relations with anymals.

Not all anymal activists work outside the center. Lewis Gompertz (1779–1861) was a founding member and secretary for the Society for the Prevention of Cruelty to Animals (later renamed RSPCA). Gompertz was an anymal activist, a Jew, and an inventor with thirty-eight inventions to his name, "many designed to reduce animal suffering[;] he renounced flesh, eggs, milk, leather and silk, condemned vivisection and would not ride in a horse-drawn coach" (Gompertz, "Moral") because he was intensely aware of the suffering entailed in this form of transport ("History").

Gompertz questioned any "sport" rooted in pursuit and execution of the defenseless, and visited a slaughterhouse, afterward providing a graphic account of the horrors within(Gompertz). In *Moral Inquiries into the Situation of Man and of Brutes* (1824), Gompertz offers the following observations:

> The dreadful situation of the brute creation, particularly of those which have been domesticated, claims our strictest attention.
>
> Who can dispute the inhumanity of the sport of hunting—of pursuing a poor defenceless creature for mere amusement, till it becomes exhausted by terror and fatigue, and of then causing it to be torn to pieces by a pack of dogs? From what kind of instruction can men, and even women, imbibe such principles as these? How is it possible they can justify it? And what can their pleasure in it consist of? Is it not solely in the agony they produce to the animal? They will pretend that it is not, and try to make us believe so too—that it is merely in the pursuit. But what is the object of their pursuit? Is there any other than to torment and destroy? ("Gompertz")

Gompertz "devoted his life to the cause of kindness to animals" ("Gompertz")— and simultaneously devoted his life to God. Not only was he a founding member of the RSPCA, he also founded Animals' Friend Society in England (Gompertz, "Moral") and labored to end dogfighting, bullfighting, and bull baiting ("History"). Gompertz commented that he would never "do anything that would cause suffering to animals" ("History").

Richard Schwartz is a contemporary Jewish vegan, a member of Young Israel of Staten Island (Orthodox synagogue), and an anymal liberationist. He is also the author of *Judaism and Vegetarianism* and associate producer of the documentary *A Sacred Duty: Applying Jewish Values to Help Heal the World.* Additionally, he has written more than 130 articles (posted on http://www.jewishveg.com/schwartz/), many of which are about Judaism's requirement for a compassionate diet and anymal liberation. Schwartz also writes op-ed pieces, letters to editors, newsletters, and press releases, and frequently speaks on behalf of anymals, whether at conferences, as a guest speaker, or for radio and television interviews. Additionally, he takes to the streets; with the Farm Animal Rights Movement's AR2008 Conference, Schwartz recently demonstrated outside the Environmental Protection Agency's headquarters in Washington DC, urging this government agency to consider the impacts of anymal-based diets in the United States on global climate change.

Schwartz is the president of SERV (Society of Ethical and Religious Vegetarians) and the president and editor of the newsletter for the Jewish Vegetarians of North America (JVNA). JVNA maintains a website complete with vegan recipes, links to informative sites, and suggestions for political advocacy, and offers a ten-part online course called "Judaism and Vegetarianism," free of charge, developed by Richard Schwartz. The JVNA home page states the following:

> The Torah is full of commandments demanding humane treatment of animals, yet the modern factory farms that produce over 90% of the animal products we consume today raise their animals in unconscionable conditions of abject misery. The Torah reflects great concern for the land, yet as the primary cause of water pollution, water use, topsoil erosion, destruction of the world's rainforest, and other environmental harms, animal agriculture takes a devastating toll on the planet. Jewish teachings emphasize the grave importance of protecting human health, yet the consumption of animal products in the United States is responsible for numerous diseases including heart disease, America's number one killer. Judaism places great concern on providing for the poor and the hungry, yet while 800 million people do not have enough food to sustain themselves, our carnivorous diets are at least ten times as wasteful of food resources as a vegetarian [diet]. (JVNA)

The JVNA home page advocates a change of diet as *Kiddush hashem*—honoring God. Schwartz (and the JVNA) clearly indicates that only a dietary choice that protects planet, anymals, and human health, honors the Creator.

Schwartz's book can be purchased through Micah Publications (http://www.micahbooks.com), founded by Roberta Kalechofsky. Kalechofsky founded Micah Publications in order to put books into print on the topic of Jewish vegetarianism and anymal rights. She also founded Jews for Animal Rights (1985) and has been on the advisor's board for JVNA for many years. Kalechofsky provided financial support for the documentary *A Sacred Duty: Applying Jewish Values to Environmental Issues*, and was interviewed for this same film.

As a Jewish advocate for nonhumans, Kalechofsky writes letters, demonstrates, and offers presentations in the "hope of waking up the Jewish community to the atrocities that are taking place, particularly in the areas of animal experimentation and factory farming" (Kalechofsky, pers. comm., January 6, 2009). Most recently, she spoke on Jewish vegetarianism in Dresden, Germany, and on Genesis and veganism at the Minding Animals Conference in Newcastle, Australia. She is the author of many articles and a handful of books focusing on anymals and Judaism, including *Animal Suffering and the Holocaust; The Jewish Vegetarian Year Cookbook; The Vegetarian Pesach Cookbook; Judaism and Animal Rights*; and *A Boy, a Chicken, & the Lion of Judah: How Ari Became a Vegetarian*.

Nina Natelson's grandfathers were Orthodox Jews and immigrants to the United States, where her father attended a Conservative synagogue. When Natelson visited Israel, she was shocked to find a tremendous overpopulation of starving, diseased cats and dogs, and badly abused horses and donkeys, too often common sights on the streets of Israel.

On her return to the United States, Natelson decided to put conviction to action. She sought financial support for a program that would aid neglected and abused anymals in Israel. At first, she was unsure how to proceed—how does one find financial backing to begin the work that is required to help anymals? She met with success by networking with other activists: On a bus filled with people headed for a demonstration against steel jaw leghold traps, Natelson met a legislative assistant who suggested that she contact Congressman Tom Lantos and his wife, Annette. In 1984, the Lantoses—Hungarian Jews who had been rescued by Wallenberg—agreed to join the advisory board of Natelson's new group, along with a host of other high-powered anymal activists, including Isaac Bashevis Singer and Cleveland Amory of the Fund for Animals. With their generous support, Concern for Helping Animals in Israel (CHAI) was born.

CHAI has been active ever since, bringing the first anymal ambulance to Israel and the first mobile spay/neuter van, introducing humane education to schools, and sponsoring educational conferences for government ministries. CHAI has also been instrumental in establishing a group of legislators to help Israel's anymals.

One of CHAI's focuses has been Israel's horses, who are cruelly exploited and often treated with indifference on the streets of even the most holy cities. CHAI volunteers rescue and rehabilitate horses from the drudgery of endless labor on crowded streets, and from working all day without adequate rest, food, water, or medical care ("Cart").

CHAI also informs people of the pains, injuries, and casualties inherent in horse racing, and has helped to prevent this form of abuse from entering Israel. Rabbi Shlomo Amar, the Sephardic chief rabbi of Israel, recently noted that horse racing "involves slaughtering many horses, and this violates the Jewish law against wanton destruction" ("Ruling"). He also noted, "Whoever shows compassion is shown compassion," and horse racing "is unnecessary" ("Ruling"). Rabbi Shlomo Amar made it clear that "cruelty involved, only for the purpose of making some rich people richer, is prohibited" ("Ruling").

CHAI also works with pounds and shelters, and has sponsored the first Israeli conference on animal shelter management, held at the Koret School of Veterinary Medicine. Attendees at this conference, once trained, visited shelters and pounds around Israel to work with people who were already on site, sharing what they had learned at the conference on animal shelter management (Veterinarian).

During emergencies, CHAI hotlines remain open so that concerned citizens can report abandoned anymals. When calls come in, CHAI volunteers will enter war zones with bags of food and canisters of water to help distraught, lost, or needy companions. CHAI has entered the West Bank under protection of tanks to rescue a host of anymal companions, including chickens, geese, lizards, parakeets, dogs, and cats. When possible, these anymals are returned to their original homes. But when their people cannot be found, CHAI seeks out new homes for these lost or abandoned companions. Before adoption, cats and dogs are spayed or neutered to avoid the ongoing problem of human irresponsibility concerning dog and cat reproduction. In the past, when there were more dogs than placement homes, CHAI shipped needy companion anymals to waiting homes oversees. Thirty-nine warzone puppies were recently welcomed into the homes of compassionate people in the United States.

The exploitation of anymals who are exploited for food is also high on CHAI's list of concerns. CHAI lobbies on behalf of farmed anymals, and recently encouraged the chief rabbi to phase out the practice of shackling and hoisting live anymals in kosher slaughterhouses in both Israel and South America—and he did ("Israel's").

Natelson, initially shocked by the condition of many anymals in Israel, expects better from those who are bound by the Tanakh. Inasmuch as Jews keep the Sabbath, she notes they also ought to protect and care for anymals:

> I thought then and still think now that in Israel, of all places, the treatment of animals should be better than in countries that have no religious tradition of concern for animals. I also think the Jewish community worldwide should be involved in improving the condition of animals, as the religion dictates. Rabbis should be telling their congregations about Jewish teachings regarding the treatment of animals and should be encouraging them to strive for the ideal—to become vegetarian. As the Chief Rabbi of Haifa said,... the importance of demonstrating compassion for the suffering of

animals is "*de oraita*," which means it has the force of the Torah and is, therefore, not less important than keeping the Sabbath or being kosher or any other Jewish teaching. (N. Natelson, pers. comm., November 25, 2008)

Summary

The Torah teaches that God created all beings, all creatures are good in and of themselves, and that the Creator remains personally invested in creation. Scriptures also indicate that human beings were created "in the image of God" by a deity who is munificent and compassionate toward all creatures. The Creator assigned human beings the task of protecting and serving creation with the help of anymals. Jews are to be compassionate, to avoid harming anymals, and Jewish law specifically protects anymals as ends in themselves. Jewish religious traditions honor anymals as individuals, and as our kin. God created a vegan world, peaceful and without bloodshed, and the Tanakh encourages people to work to create a path back to this original Peaceable Kingdom.

‖ 6 ‖

Christian Traditions

God is love.
—1 John 4:8, 4:16

Christianity emerged from Judaism. Christian religious traditions hold the Tanakh to be sacred, though the texts are slightly altered, come in a variety of translations, and are referred to as the Old Testament (or Hebrew scriptures). Christians have also compiled their own sacred writings, called the New Testament, but the Old Testament continues to be of fundamental importance in Christian traditions, and *all* of the Tanakh passages discussed in the previous chapter are also important to Christians. Of most importance for this chapter, "the Old Testament point of view on animals was taken as valid in Judaism at the time of Jesus, and in the New Testament is considered as self-evident" (Vischer, 15). While this chapter only briefly returns to some of the many critical passages and messages from the Tanakh/ Old Testament, it is important to remember that all of the aforementioned passages from the Tanakh that were discussed in the previous chapter also constitute sacred literature in Christian traditions.

Sacred Nature, Sacred Anymals

All of nature is sacred in Christian religious traditions because all of nature is from and of God. Christian scriptures honor a God who created anymals "before man, and pronounces them good without man (Gen. 1:24–25)" (Griffiths, 8). "To affirm the blessedness of creation is to affirm an independent source of its worth....*All* creation has an irreducible value" (Linzey, *Christianity*, 8).

For Jews and Christians, who share the same creation accounts held in Genesis 1 and 2, the value of nature lies with God, "who made all things good and precious in his sight" (Linzey, *After*, 13). St. John of the Cross noted that anymals "are all clothed with marvelous natural beauty," reflecting the image of God (Linzey, *After*, 79). The influential monk Thomas à Kempis commented, "If your heart were right, then every creature would be a mirror of life and a book of holy doctrine. There is no creature so small and mean that it does not put forth the goodness of God" (69).

German Christian theologian Meister Eckhart writes that God is "present in all things and places. He knows God rightly who knows Him everywhere" ("Nearness"). Eckhart clarifies this point, explicitly including anymals: "God is equally near in all creatures. The wise man saith, 'God hath spread out His net over all creatures, so that whosoever wishes to discover Him may find and recognize Him in each one.' Another saith, 'He knows God rightly who recognizes Him alike in all things'" (Eckhart, "Nearnesss"). Eckhart goes so far as to say that those who are attentive to anymals and live in their midst can learn about God from the creatures, and need not attend church or read scriptures: "A man who would know nothing but creatures would never need to attend to any sermon, for every creature is full of God and is a book [about God]" (Eckhart, sermon, Walshe 67, p. 345: Quint 9, p. 156).[1]

As noted in the previous chapter, through covenant God enters into a special relationship with every living thing and the earth itself. God's covenant demonstrates that the Creator cares for all that exists, not just the miniscule fraction of life that has been born in human form. All of "creation, large and small, intelligent and unintelligent, sentient and non-sentient has worth because God values" every living being and the Earth itself (Linzey, *Christianity*, 9). Every Dermantsi pied pig sent to slaughter, every little male Rhode Island red chick thrown into the trash—each belongs to God. How can Christian nations permit citizens to treat God's creatures with such cruelty and indifference?

Christian exemplars (most frequently Catholic saints) have long spoken of and demonstrated love for the natural world as servants of God. Many saints viewed dwelling close to nature as dwelling close to God, and chose a life in which they shared space and time with anymals. For example, St. Kevin of Ireland (sixth century) preferred to dwell where "the wild things of the mountains and the woods came and kept him company, and would drink water, like domestic creatures, from his hands" (Waddell, 129). He did not consume these fellow creatures, or their body fluids and eggs, but only "nuts of the forest" and "herbs of the earth" (Sellner, 160). Blackbirds, which he befriended, helped to secure his hut against the frequent rains of Ireland (Zarin, 66), and a doe willingly provided milk for St. Kevin's adopted infant (Sellner, 164).

---

[1] Many thanks to Mr. Ashley Young, secretary and trustee of the Eckhart Society (http://www.eckhartsociety.org) for securing the help of Professor Loris Sturlese (University of Salento, patron of the Eckhart Society) to locate the source of these verses commonly attributed to Eckhart: "Apprehend God in all things, / For God is in all things. / Every single creature is full of God / And is a book about God. / Every creature is a word of God. / If I spent enough time with the tiniest creature / Even a caterpillar / I would never have to prepare a sermon. / So full of God / Is every creature." This poem holds the essence of what Eckhart is saying, but it is not a good translation, making it difficult to discover the Eckhart source of this commonly reproduced poem. Apparently this English poem (attributed to Eckhart) stems from Eckhart's comment (not in verse form): Der niht dan die crêatûren bekante, der endörfte niemer gedenken ûf keine predige, wan ein ieglîchiu crêatûre ist vol gotes und ist ein buoch (Predigt 9 Quint, Deutsche Werke, Vol. I, Stuttgart, Kohlhammer, 1958, p. 156).

Kevin's life, immersed in nature, was rooted in faith, and hagiographies report that angels visited Kevin to reward him for a well-lived life, telling him that God would grant any wish to such a faithful servant, even leveling the mountains to create rich meadows on Kevin's behalf. Kevin takes these figurative matters of speech literally, and seems troubled by the angel's suggestion that God would willingly level mountains, destroying the homes of many creatures on his behalf. He replies, "I have no wish that the creatures of God should be moved because of me....And moreover, all the wild creatures on these mountains are my house mates, gentle and familiar with me, and they would be sad" if their mountain homes were leveled (Waddell, 136). The one who created mountains and wild anymals—one who is personally invested in every living being—could not help but be pleased with Kevin's response.

Christian saints frequently exemplify kindness and demonstrate a strong connection with anymals. Saint Francis of Assisi, who lived in Italy from 1181–1226, is perhaps most famous among Catholics for personal relations with anymals. He "valued every species and was drawn into wonder and prayer by individual creatures" (Hughes, 315, 316). Saint Francis "was always very kind and wonderfully compassionate, especially toward gentle animals and little birds" (R. Brown, 91). For this well-known Christian saint, the natural world—and every creature—led back to the Creator; his love extended to the entirety of creation, exemplifying Christian humility in his daily life, which stood as testimony to his understanding of the inherent value of creation (White, 1206–7).

Pope John Paul II also seemed to understand God's love for all creatures of the earth, each one lovingly sustained (Englebert, 134). He noted that St. Francis recognized in creation "the marvelous work of the hand of God" (Scully, 24). Francis was drawn into worship by "the beauty of the world" and extended love outward to every big brown bat and bighorn sheep, to every long fin angelfish and English saddleback goose (Englebert, 135). Francis taught his followers to handle all beings compassionately, and it was his deepest hope that kindness might flow outward from people to touch every niche of the great expanse of the created world.

Emphasizing the spiritual importance of anymals, the Catholic Christian tradition holds patron saints for a handful of anymals, particularly domestic anymals likely to need protection from exploitative humans: St. Beuvon for cattle; St. George, St. Lewis [Louis] IX of France, St. Eusebius, and St. Eloy (Eligius) for horses; St. Anthony the Great and St. Wendelin for pigs; St. Hubert for deer; St. Agricolus for storks; and perhaps St. Germanus of Auxerre for donkeys, because "he so preferred his own humble beast to the splendid horse offered him by the Empress Placida" and because, "though it was in a dying condition, he raised [his donkey] again to perfect health" (Gumbley).

The function of the Christian church is as "guardian of creation" (Daneel, 535). The ministry of Jesus, which focuses on the oppressed, must in contemporary times "include the deteriorating planet" and anymals like North America's endangered Florida black bear, the rare Irish Moiled cow, Israel's highly endangered sand cat, and South America's endangered cactus ferruginous pygmy owl (McFague, 35). Unfortunately, there is nothing we can do for the hundreds of anymals we have already driven from the planet—except show our remorse and change our ways. Christian religious traditions indicate that we are obligated to help those who suffer—the more so if they are suffering because of human indifference, excessive breeding, and/or exploitation. Our domination of nature has allowed us to exploit the comparatively defenseless and innocent, and has placed human beings over and against creation as a whole, causing extinctions, soil erosion, pollution, deforestation, and climate change. Our current way of life brings "carnage and many casualties, as in any war...highlighting the need for the moral equivalent of planetary peacemaking" (French, 487).

The Christian Bible teaches human beings that the time will come to destroy those who "destroy the earth" (Rev. 11:18). According to Christian scripture—including the Old Testament (discussed in the previous chapter as the Tanakh)—and according to historic moral exemplars, human beings are to find God in the natural world, and to love and care for anymals. Christians have been given "an important role to play in the pursuit of sustainable community" (Hallman, 467), calling industrialized Christians to fundamentally change the way they live.

Christian Philosophy and Morality

Jesus

Christian religious traditions hold that Jesus had both divine and human attributes. In common (sexist) vernacular, Jesus was both God and man (human). To be human is to be animal, mammal, primate. God in the form of Jesus was born human, which means that he was simultaneously born animal, mammal, primate.

Christians give great importance to Jesus as a man, born bodily into the world of humanity, and inasmuch as Jesus was born man, it is no less true that Jesus was born human, mammal, and primate—animal. "All bodies matter because God became embodied and Jesus rose as a body from the grave" (Webb, 162). Many Christians recognize the importance of Jesus's humanity, but few seem to appreciate that, inasmuch as his humanity is important, so is his primate, mammalian, and animalian existence. God took the form of an animal, and to "know the Word made flesh requires that we honor *all* flesh" (Linzey, *After*, 103). Christians generally recognize that Jesus, though a Middle Eastern man, did not just live and die for Middle Eastern men, but also for Malaysian children and Arctic women. We have been slower to recognize that all flesh is spiritually united because Jesus took the form of animal flesh.

Jesus as Moral Exemplar

The Gospels, the first four books of the New Testament, record the life and teachings of Jesus. The Gospels are central to Christian religious traditions in many ways, including a general Christian understanding of the life of Jesus as exemplary, as the ideal Christian life—a life of gentle service to others, especially the downtrodden. Christians tend to hold that it is important to "remember, celebrate, and follow" the life exemplified by Jesus (Webb, 145); the Christian life should stand as "witness to Christ's love, compassion, and peace" (Kaufman, 48).

Though divine, Jesus took animal form. Though immortal in nature, Jesus suffered at the hands of cruel humans and died while yet fairly young (yet in comparable years, considerably older than most farmed anymals). Though a man, and therefore granted comparably greater social stature in his community, he spoke on behalf of the oppressed, including women and the poor. He empathized with those who were sick, dying, and/or suffering. God is redefined through the life of Jesus as a force of humble service to the sickly, the poor, and the oppressed. The life of Jesus, as recorded in the Gospels, reminds the faithful that Jesus exemplified the life of a humble servant working for God to help those who were in need—*all* those who were in need:

> God loves the whole world. What we see in Jesus is the revelation of an inclusive, all-embracing, generous loving. A loving that washes the feet of the world. A loving that heals individuals from oppression, both physical and spiritual. A loving that takes sides with the poor, vulnerable, diseased, hated, despised, and outcasts of his day. A loving that is summed up in his absolute commitment to love at all costs, even in extreme suffering and death. (Linzey, *Animal Gospel*, 23)

When Jesus's feet touched the earth, people walked or rode donkeys from place to place. Communications took place simply by word of mouth. People produced much of their own food, and often bartered for what they could not grow. The people of Jesus's day fished without mechanized equipment, and did not have the option of buying frozen vegetables or cans of soup at a corner shop. Jesus lived in times radically different from ours, prior to refrigerators and microwave ovens, before the advent of factory farming and anymal experimentation, but Christian traditions tend to view these radical surface changes as irrelevant with regard to scripture's core meanings and values: "Christians have always been shaped by the patterns of meaning in the gospel portraits, not by the particulars" (Young, 11).

One particularly important core meaning from the Gospels is that Jesus, the quintessential moral exemplar, lived a life devoted to the service of weak and imperfect beings. His overall message speaks of compassion and service of the strong for the weak, of the high for the lowly. The Gospels portray Jesus as engaged in self-sacrificing service to "the least of these" (Matt. 25:40); Jesus provides an excellent example of what we are meant to do on this earth, as stated in Genesis 2—protect and serve creation.

In Christian traditions, Jesus is the perfect moral exemplar. He taught and exemplified humility and self-sacrificing service: "Whoever wants to be first must be last of all and servant of all" (Mark 9:35); "Whoever wishes to become great among you must be your servant, and whoever wishes to be first among you must be slave of all. For the Son of Man came not to be served but to serve, and to give his life a ransom for many" (Mark 9:35, 10: 42–45). Christian traditions, through Genesis 1 and 2 and through the Gospels, which record the life of Jesus, teach human beings to love God by living a humble life of service. Christians are to serve the entirety of the suffering creation, whether bull snake, cotton mouse, human being, or Marsh Daisy chicken.

> The gospels teach—Jesus teaches—that we "love our neighbors by serving our neighbors, and the farther they stand below us in the hierarchy of power—the more they stand in need of our help—the greater is our moral obligation to serve them" (Phelps, *Dominion*, 150). Few are as desperately in need of Christian service as American Landrace pigs and White Holland turkeys, caught in the greed and indifference of anymal industries. "To stand with Jesus means to stand against the abuse of animals," including the California night snake and Hinterwald cattle (Linzey, *Animal Gospel*, 13). The Gospel as exemplified in Jesus Christ is about service to the sick, poor, disadvantaged, diseased, imprisoned, and all others who are regarded as the lowest of all, and not least to the whole world of suffering non-human creatures. . . . We cannot love God and be indifferent to suffering creatures. (Linzey, *Animal Gospel*, 94)

"If our power over animals confers upon us any rights, there is only one: the right to serve" (Linzey, *Animal Theology*, 38). Christian religious traditions generally hold that human beings find redemption by serving as Christ served, by helping the powerless, by sharing some of what Jesus suffered for the sake of humanity.

Jesus, the Christian moral exemplar, was most often associated not with powerful carnivores, but with "lambs, donkeys, and doves, animals that are gentle and easily abused" (Webb, 139). Though powerful in ways that humanity cannot even comprehend, Jesus was as meek as a lamb, never seeking "advantage through the suffering of another" (Phelps, *Dominion*, 151). Jesus taught, "Blessed are the meek, for they shall inherit the earth" (Matt. 5:5), and Christian poet William Blake wrote the following more than 200 years ago:

> Little Lamb, who made thee?
> Dost thou know who made thee?
> Gave thee life & bid thee feed

By the stream & o'er the mead;....
Little Lamb, I'll tell thee:
He is callèd by thy name,
For he calls himself a Lamb.
He is meek, & he is mild;
He became a little child....
Little Lamb, God bless thee!
Little Lamb, God bless thee!

Christian scriptures often compare Jesus to a sheep—an oft-exploited woolly mammal—because sheep are demure, and because "meekness is the child of love and compassion. As such, it is the quality that most clearly displays the image of God in our lives" (Phelps, *Dominion*, 151). Sheep, whether Damara or Dorper, are nonviolent, eating only plants.

Jesus as Liberationist

Although Jesus was gentle as a lamb, he was also proactive. Thomas Aquinas (Summa Theologiae 2.2.158.8) "noted that anger looks to the good of justice," and those who do not feel angry "in the face of injustice love justice too little. Thomas loved John Chrysostom's dictum: 'Whoever is not angry when there is cause for anger, sins!'" (Maguire, 419).

> Jesus did not teach an otherworldly religion; he did not tell his followers to accept the injustices of this world and piously look forward to an afterlife in which goodness and justice would rule. To the contrary, he told his followers that they were to behave in such a way that life on earth would be a reflection of the goodness of the heavenly kingdom. He told them to pray that God's "will be done, on earth as it is in heaven." (Mat. 6:10) (Hyland, *God's*, 85)

The Gospels indicate that Jesus "abhors both passivity and violence"—*but not all forms of violence* (Wink, 189). The Gospels reveal a man who "seeks out conflict, elicits conflict, exacerbates conflict" in order to move "against perceived injustice proactively with the same alacrity as the most hawkish militarist" (Wink, 192). Jesus modeled direct action, and encouraged others to be proactive: "Jesus does not propose armed revolution, but he lays the foundation for social revolution" (Wink, 183).

According to scripture, for example, when Jesus approached his community's temple he found people selling cattle, sheep, and doves, and money changers. Making a whip of cords, he drove all of them out of the temple. He also poured out the coins of the money changers and overturned their tables. He told those who were selling doves, "Stop making my Father's house a marketplace!" (John

2:14–16). He told the profiteers, "It is written, 'My house shall be called a house of prayer'; but you are making it a den of robbers" (Matt. 21:12). Jesus modeled direct action against economic corruption, against anymal enterprises, and he was willing to take vengeance against both the perpetrators and their property—driving out the businessmen and turning over their tables. As the last section reveals, at least some contemporary Christians now feel called to "turn over the tables"—to use physical force against property in defense of God's beautiful earth and the Creator's wondrous forms of life.

Jesus modeled direct action as a method of initiating change, and he modeled a life of service to the weakest and neediest of beings. Christians are called to model their lives after the life of Jesus. Human beings are called to lead humanity "out of the violence and selfishness that made a hell out of the paradise" (Hyland, *Slaughter*, 3). Because God was born Jesus, who died on behalf of earthlings, Christians are called to engage in costly, loving condescension toward a suffering, needy creation. Anymal activists follow in the footsteps of Jesus.

Love and Mercy

Jesus exemplified love, and called Christians to love. The New Testament informs readers that the "fruit of the Spirit is love" (Gal. 5:22–23). 1 John 4:8 and 1 John 4:16 state simply, "God is love." In this passage, love is not merely an attribute; love defines God's nature, "though in a practical rather than philosophic sense....God's nature is not exhausted by the quality of love, but love governs all its aspects and expressions" (Buttrick, 12:280). Christian scripture demands a life of sacrificial, Christ-like love, which originates in the munificence of God's love and connects Christians back to the Creator (Allen, 12:214). In Christian traditions, sensitivity to suffering is often understood to indicate fidelity to a compassionate Creator and is understood to originate in the munificence of divine love that connects each of us with the Almighty (Allen, 12:214).

Ten years ago, after I spoke at my first animal advocacy conference, author and activist Norm Phelps came forward to thank me for crystallizing the subject at hand: scripture, Christian ethics, and animal activism. My talk focused almost exclusively on love, asking those present to imagine Jesus walking through a slaughterhouse, a vivisection lab, or a poultry farm: "How would the Prince of Peace *feel* about contemporary exploitation of pigs, mice, and hens? Would he justify these institutions as readily as we do?"

Every other scriptural argument on behalf of anymal liberation pales when we turn our focus on the Christian responsibility to love. Phelps, one of the most respected authors on the topic of religion and anymals, thanked me for recalling his attention to the obvious. It is easy to get sidetracked. But rather than focus on many peripheral topics, Christians need to focus on only the core of their religious tradition: love. Not long afterward, Phelps published two strong books (on Christianity and Buddhism—please see the appendix for further readings) that repeatedly return attention to love and compassion—core religious values. Given the quantity of sacred literature behind any religious tradition, and the vested interests we humans carry to any given topic, it is easy to become entangled in lesser arguments and forget core teachings. While we might argue endlessly over scriptural minutia, Christians cannot reasonably ignore the fundamental scriptural and spiritual requirement of love and compassionate service, or the importance of these core teachings to anymal liberation. Contemporary anymal exploitation *is* indifference and cruelty; Christians are called to love. Is there any need for further discussion? Love is "the paramount scripture... essential to the Christian way of life" (Allen, 12:214). Christianity calls for an all-embracing and active love exemplified by Jesus—action on behalf of the needy and defenseless. "True Christian love reflects God's love in showing charity and compassion for all" (Young, 84)—even when love entails risk. "If we love nothing, we suffer little, if at all" (Linzey, *After*, 102).

In the Christian worldview, love is limitless. In the story of the Good Samaritan (as elsewhere in the Gospels), Christ expands the imperative to "love your neighbor" outward from a small circle of believers to a much larger circle of people, such as Samaritans and prostitutes. Saint Paul continued this process (Gal. 3:28), extending the circle of love to encompass gentiles.

> Love is not a "zero-sum game" or some sort of hydraulic fluid whose volume is perforce static. This is the argument of "compassion fatigue" and it only holds short-term. Long-term, all religions and especially Christianity, teach that one can expand one's capacity to love, and ought consciously to do so. (John Halley, pers. comm., May 6, 1999)

Any understanding of Christian love, or of God's love, that limits care and affection "is spiritually impoverished" (Linzey, *After*, 131). "God's love is free, generous and unlimited," and only a sadly wanting Christian theology would seek to limit love (Linzey, *Animal Gospel*, 24, 69). Conservative Christian Matthew Scully notes that "cruelty is not only a denial of the animal's nature but a betrayal of our own" (303). "*Cogito ergo sum:* 'I think, therefore I am'? Nonsense. *Amo ergo sum:* 'I love, therefore I am'" (Coffin, 11). Christian religious traditions are rooted in love. Love is their mainstay, and the "love of God is inclusive not only of humans *but also all creatures*" (Linzey, *Animal Gospel*, 24, italics in the original).

Where in scripture might we defend factory farms, anymal labs, or industrial fishing? The *Catechism of the Catholic Church*, a summary of basic Catholic doctrine, clearly states, "It is contrary to human dignity to cause animals to suffer or die needlessly" (2418). The *Catechism* also notes that God surrounds anymals with "providential care," and that the creatures of the earth bless God and bring glory to the Creator, and so we "owe them kindness" (2416). Catherine of Siena wrote that Christians ought to love all of God's creatures deeply because "they realize how deeply Christ loves them," and to love what is loved by God *because* it is loved by God is the essence of a Christian heart (Linzey, *After*, 74). Nothing suits the Christian heart as well as does munificent love.

Those who argue that love in the Christian religious traditions must first and foremost be directed toward humanity fail to understand core Christian teachings. They may as well argue that Christian love should first and foremost be directed toward Caucasians, Europeans, or the wealthy. Either the pain of other creatures "has moral value or it does not have moral value. Either there is a God or there isn't. Either [God] cares about animals or [God] doesn't. Either we have duties of kindness or we do not" (Scully, 310). Either human love is expansive or it is not *Christian* love. Christianity entails a vision of *limitless* love.

Hagiographies, which record the lives of Christian saints, demonstrate that holy people in the Catholic tradition, people known for their proximity to God and for living up to the Christian ideal, exemplify munificent love, and include anymals in their circle of love. "Indeed, one of the criteria for sainthood seems to be the compassionate treatment of animals" (Webb).

Stories of the saints remind Christians that to be in relationship with God is to be kind and attentive toward Dutch hookbill ducks, striped skunks, and African butter catfish. Saint Malo's heart "only had room for compassion" (Waddell, 53), and when a small wren laid an egg on his cloak, "he let his cloak lie there, till the eggs were hatched and the wren brought out her brood" for he understood that "God's care is not far from the birds" (Waddell, 55). Similarly, in the sixth century, St. Kevin of Ireland befriended a blackbird (as well as fish and dragonflies); the blackbird nested in his hand (Zarin, 64, 71). Kevin understood that one who loves God also loves and cares for creation—all of creation. Similarly, the gentleness of St. Godric's heart led him to "watch over the very reptiles and the creatures of the earth" (Waddell, 87).

> For in the winter when all about was frozen stiff in the cold, he would go out barefoot, and if he lighted on any animal helpless with misery of the cold, he would set it under his armpit or in his bosom to warm it. Many a time would the kind soul go spying under the thick hedges or tangled patches of briars, and if haply he found a creature that had lost its way, or cowed with the harshness of the weather, or tired, or half dead, he would recover it with all the healing art he had.... (Waddell, 87–88)

As part of his missionary work, St. Francis requested that captive animals be placed in his care. He tended them and/or released them, as was appropriate. When he came upon a boy destined for the market in Siena with a handful of turtle doves whom he had snared, he said to the boy, "Please give me those doves so that such innocent birds, which in Holy Scripture are symbols of pure, humble, and faithful souls, will not fall into the hands of cruel men who will kill them" (R. Brown,

91–92). The boy agreed, and Francis spoke gently to the captured doves: "I want to rescue you from death and make nests for you where you can lay your eggs and fulfill the Creator's commandment to multiply" (R. Brown, 92).

The lives of Christian saints are rooted in love. Christian traditions teach the faithful to model their lives after Jesus, who lived a life of love and mercy, who served the weak and vulnerable, helped those who were overlooked or overtly exploited. Jesus commanded people to help those in need—*whoever* "those" might be. The life of Jesus calls Christians to extend justice and compassion "from the human neighbor to 'otherkind' and the earth itself.... Solidarity with victims... and action on behalf of justice widen out to embrace life systems and other species" (Johnson, 15).

The Gospels record Jesus teaching, "Blessed are the merciful, for they will receive mercy" (Matt. 5:7). In Christian traditions, mercy extends to all "living souls who find themselves in our dominion" (Phelps, *Dominion*, 154). According to the conservative Christian Matthew Scully, within Christian traditions the question at stake regarding anymals and our choice of diet is "whether to side with the powerful and the comfortable or with the weak, afflicted, and forgotten. Whether, as... economic actor[s] in a free market, [those of faith] answer to the god of money or to the God of mercy" (Scully, 325). In his eloquent writing style, he clarifies this point:

> If, in a given situation, we have it in our power either to leave the creature there in his dark pen or let him out into the sun and breeze and feed him and let him play and sleep and cavort with his fellows—for me it's an easy call. Give him a break. Let him go. Let him enjoy his fleeting time on earth, and stop bringing his kind into the world solely to suffer and die. It doesn't seem like much to us, the creature's little lives of grazing and capering and raising their young and fleeing natural predators. Yet it is the life given them, not by breeder but by Creator. It is all they have. It is their part of the story, a beautiful part beyond the understanding of man, and who is anyone to treat it lightly? (Scully, 43)

The complete subjugation of anymals to the ever-growing power of human beings elicits—requires—Christian mercy and Christ-like protective tenderness (Polk, 185). Mercy is at the heart of Christian relations with God, and at the heart of Christian relations with anymals: As we require God's mercy, so they require our mercy. Christians "above all should hear the call to mercy.... They above all should be mindful of the little things, seeing, in the suffering of these creatures," a life that is God's, a life that is worthy of Christian care (Scully, 325).

The New Testament commands, "Be merciful just as your Father is merciful" (Luke 6:36). In Christian traditions, "sensitivity to suffering is a sign of grace and also a litmus test of our fidelity to the compassionate Creator God" (Linzey, *After*, 132). With regard to Christian mercy, anymals stand in a special place: The "more deeply someone can be damaged by our cruelty, the greater is our obligation to show mercy. And our cruelty damages no one more deeply than the defenseless animals on whom we turn our terrible power" (Phelps, *Dominion*, 152).

Service

As noted in the previous chapter, human dominion/rulership (bequeathed to humans in Genesis 1) carries heavy responsibilities (Hume, 6–7). Additionally, Jesus revealed "the sacrificial nature of lordship," calling human beings to a similar servitude (Webb, 97; Linzey, *Christianity*, 87, 96). Christian traditions, as exemplified by Jesus, indicate that human beings are to live a life of devotion to God through self-sacrificing service *in this world* (French, 488). And Christians are called to serve and protect all of creation. Nature is God's, and "we have an obligation to the Creator to respect what is created"; we "must never destroy without serious justification and without acknowledging that all life belongs not to us but to God" (Linzey, *After*, 49, 105).

It is not necessary for those of Christian faith to envision Mexican spotted owls and Hybridmaster cows (bred by humans for human exploitation) as endowed with rights to elicit a sense of spiritual obligation for anymals. Mexican spotted owls and Hybridmaster cows—even though we manipulated their genetics—are not ours: Because God is "sovereign Creator, all rights in an absolute sense are God's" (Linzey, *Animal Gospel*, 50), and we owe owls and cows our respect and caring through our respect and caring for their Creator.

> God loves and cares for creation and has the right to expect this loving care
> be replicated by humans. Creation exists, not for the glory of humanity,
> but for the glory of God....
>
> God's creatures have a derived right to live a natural life and to be loved,
> cared for, and protected against abuse and exploitation. Said another way,
> since God values and cares for all creation, creation has a derived right to
> be valued and cared for by humans for God's glory. (Young, 37)

Because human beings owe God respect, we owe respect and care to God's creation. Christians are expected to "conceptualize what is owed to animals as a matter of justice by virtue of their Creator's right—'theos-rights': Animals can be wronged because their Creator can be wronged" through creation (Linzey, *Animal Theology*, 27). Theos-rights require Christians to act on behalf of God, instead of making choices based on human interests (Linzey, *Christianity*, 87, 96, 98).

Christian traditions hold that all of creation is God's, and that humans are charged with rulership "as a wise king rules over and protects his subjects, or as God reigns over creation, sustaining, cherishing, and safeguarding every living thing" (Kowalski,

24). Humans are placed in a rulership position in which we are required to "take care of what God entrusts to us—our lives, our health, and all the world around us, including animals" (Braun, ix). If Christians "claim a lordship over creation, then it can only be a lordship of service" (Linzey, *Animal Gospel*, 43). Anglican priest Andrew Linzey explains our rightful place in the world:

> We need a conception of ourselves in the universe not as the master species but as the servant species.... We must move from the idea that the animals were given to us and made for us, to the idea that we were made for creation, to serve it and ensure its continuance. This actually is little more than the theology of Genesis chapter two. The garden is made beautiful and abounds with life; humans are created specifically to "take care of it" (Gen. 2:15). (Linzey, "Arrogance," 69)

Christianity teaches people that they are "the servant species: the species given power, opportunity and privilege to give themselves, nay sacrifice themselves, for the weaker, suffering creatures" (Linzey, *Animal Gospel*, 44).

All of creation is worthy of our attention and spiritual energy, but Christian traditions, through the life and teachings of Jesus, hold a *special* obligation to the poor and downtrodden. Christian traditions hold at their core the moral imperative to act on behalf of the downtrodden, and this imperative must now be "extended to nature: nature is the 'new poor'" (McFague, 30). Christian service should *not* be directed solely toward humans, or furry, large-eyed anymals; our attention should be to *all* creatures on behalf of the Creator—most specifically those who are endangered or distraught, exploited or overlooked. Christian scriptures indicate that those within Christian traditions ought to "have a sense of contributing to God's plan to reconcile all Creation" to a compassionate, peaceful, loving world (Kaufman, 48).

Christian exemplars provide many examples of such all-embracing caretaking. When individuals are in need of care, Christian saints rise to the occasion, no matter what the species. "Hares flew for refuge to Saints Cuthbert, Anselm, Francis, and Philip; St. Patrick saved a doe and a fawn" (Gumbley). Saint Martin de Porres, who fed rats and mice at the edge of his garden, also created a hospital for lost dogs and cats, where he lovingly tended his many needy patients. Similarly, Bernard of Corleone healed sick and injured anymals (Gumbley). St. Columba asked one of the brethren of the island monastery, Iona, to tend a "guest, a crane, wind tossed and driven far from her course" (Waddell, 44). Columba instructed him to treat the "bird tenderly and take it to some nearby house where you can kindly and carefully" nurse and feed the bird (Sellner, 94–95). Columba said, "May God bless thee, my son,... for thy kind tending of this pilgrim guest" (Waddell, 45).

Peace

Jesus taught, "Blessed are the peacemakers: for they will be called children of God" (Matt. 5:9). "At the heart of the Christian Gospel is the dream of universal peace," the dream of "a world where humans are no longer violent and cruel to other creatures" (Linzey, *Animal Gospel*, 81). Christian traditions promote peace with *all* creatures (Murti, 31, 100).

The Lord's Prayer, provided by Jesus in the Gospels, instructs the faithful to pray, including the following: "Your kingdom come. / Your will be done, on earth as it is in heaven" (Matt. 6:10). *The Lord's Prayer* demonstrates that Christians expect God's will and the coming kingdom (the Peaceable Kingdom of the Tanakh/Old Testament discussed in the previous chapter) to be realized on this very earth. Dutiful servants of God are obligated to help bring about this desirable end (Buttrick, 7: 312), to participate in the "final triumph of God's will" *through daily life* (Allen, 8: 115). Peace will not return to this beleaguered earth of its own accord; Christians are called to facilitate the process, and human beings "cannot be true ambassadors of Christ's peace nor agents for the world's reconciliation," unless we live a life of peace (Kaufman, 48). The fulfillment of God's plan can and will happen on this very earth, but it is meant to happen through the "work of all who believe in Jesus Christ and his kingdom" (Buttrick, 5: 250–51).

> Christian faith is to a large extent shaped by the hope of a radically new world. It finds its vitality through envisioning paradise restored, with no more suffering, oppression, sin, and death.... Faith in the resurrection of Christ opens up the future to seemingly incredible possibilities that lie beyond the normal expectation of history....
>
> What Jesus did was to shift the focus of the kingdom from something totally future to something now at hand and accessible. (Young, 143–44)

The New Testament teaches that a "harvest of righteousness is sown in peace for those who make peace" (James 3:17–18), and by working for universal peace in daily life, Christians "cooperate with God's Spirit in the work of wholeness and renewal" (Linzey, *After*, 109). Christian traditions teach human beings to live in a way that exemplifies peace and compassion, to live in a way that anticipates the return of peace promised in the Old Testament. This way of life, which requires choices that are loving, compassionate, and consistent with universal peace, is considered the actualization of "the knowledge of the Lord" (Isa. 11:9) (Guthrie, 598).

According to the scriptures, Christians look hopefully to the return of God's kingdom here on earth (Matt. 6:33), and this kingdom of God comes complete with peace and well-being not only for humanity, but also for anymals. Christian traditions call human beings to be peacemakers—not just between races, sexes, and nations—but peacemakers who strive to bring peace across the entirety of creation, to return earth to the peaceful paradise that God created. "The God who led the Israelites out of oppression and bondage in Egypt is the Creator God who is concerned with leading all creatures out of oppression, injustice, and bondage" (Young, 143).

Many Catholic saints have worked toward universal peace in their daily lives, returning "to paradisal relations with the animals, communing with them and curing them" (Sorabji, 203). Many exemplary Christians lived as if the peaceable kingdom had already arrived, as if the fall had never occurred. Saint Jerome, for example, was a vegetarian who lived with hens, sheep, and donkeys, as well as a lion whom he had healed (Hobgood-Oster, 15). Saint Moling lived with anymals "both wild and tame" who "would eat out of his hand" (Waddell, 107). Saint Colman "had in friendliness about him" a cock, a mouse, and a fly who offered "their kind service and company" (Waddell, 145, 147). The first disciple of St. Ciaran of Ireland was a wild boar, who was later joined by a fox, badger, wolf, and deer (Waddell, 104). Hagiographies record that St. Guthlac of Croyland and St. Godric lived with wild anymals, as did St. Columba (Ireland, sixth-century). Saint Columba lived peacefully among "wild" anymals so that they came to know him and responded to his call. He would "stroke them with his hand and caress them: and the wild things and the birds would leap and frisk about him for sheer happiness. . . . Even . . . the squirrel would come at his call from the high tree-tops" to run "in and out of the folds of his cowl" (Waddell, 51–52).

Scriptures indicate that Christians ought to be eagerly working toward a soon-to-come peace on earth. As Christian love is all-inclusive, so is the universal peace that will follow: "God is leading us toward a future where humans and animals coexist in peace, where justice, compassion, and love reign, and where oppression and exploitation are things of the past" (Young, 147).

Sharing

More than 70 percent of the United States grain crop is fed to animals who are bred for and raised in the food industry (Schwartz, 85). Cattle in feedlots require thirteen pounds of grain in exchange for one pound of flesh at the butcher's shop. Pig farms feed six pounds of grain for every pound of boneless flesh that reaches our tables; chickens eat three pounds of grain for every one pound of chicken flesh (Singer, "One"). Sixty-six percent of U.S. grains are fed to anymals who are killed for our consumption; animal agriculture wastes the vast majority of proteins and calories available in grains by feeding them to cattle, pigs, turkeys, and chickens. When we cycle grains through anymals and then eat anymal flesh, we waste a tremendous amount of food that humans could otherwise consume. In this way, meat-based diets contribute significantly to world hunger (Kaufman, 20).

Christian traditions offer a morality that is rooted in love and service, which is perhaps most easily exemplified through day-to-day sharing. When dietary preferences (like eating flesh) are more important than the well-being of others, people fail grievously in their obligation to fulfill Jesus' message of mercy, peace, and love. Love and service require those who care about cattle, *and those who care about people*, to quit breeding billions of cattle, hens, turkeys, and hogs, so that we can quit feeding billions of tons of available grains to anymals, and instead feed those grains to human beings who are chronically hungry—who are starving to death. If we care about those who are hungry, we will maintain a plant-based diet, eating grains directly. Our dollars decide what sort of industries will flourish. Our dollars decide where grains will go. Our dollars decide whether or not there will be enough food to go around.

Humility: A God-Centered Universe

Humanity is not the center of the Christian universe; this world was not created for human purposes. In Christian traditions, the value of creation, the value of a northern minke whale, ringtail, or the endangered diamondback terrapin "does not lie in whether it is beautiful (to us) or whether it serves or sustains our life and happiness.... Only God, and not man, is the measure of all" (Linzey, "Liberation," 513). If Christian traditions "neglect the place and significance of other creatures in God's good creation, Christian theology fundamentally weakens itself, and its claim to be... God centered" (Linzey, *After*, 119).

Humanism is human-centered; Christianity is God-centered. Human arrogance is contrary to a God-centered faith and tends toward humanism, a belief system in which people are the measure of all:

> Many of us seem to have lost all sense of restraint toward animals, an understanding of natural boundaries, a respect for them as beings with needs and wants and a place and purpose of their own. Too often, too casually, we assume that our interests always come first, and if it's profitable or expedient that is all we need to know. We assume that all these other creatures with whom we share the earth are here for us, and only for us. We assume, in effect, that we are everything and they are nothing. (Scully, xi)

Turning compassion toward anymals moves human beings away from our tendency to focus on ourselves and our families and our communities and our species and "thus opens a space for the return of God to the pinnacle of all our concerns" (Webb, 35). Remembering our responsibilities to other creatures—to God—can help "save theology from the distortions of human pride" (Webb, 35). Humility requires that human beings keep God—not humanity—at the center: "Kindness to animals is a small yet necessary part of a decent and holy life, essential if only as a check against human arrogance and our tendency to worship ourselves, our own works and appetites and desires instead of our Creator" (Scully, 99).

Habit and taste preference are not legitimate Christian explanations for factory farming. Profit is not a worthy Christian measure of a hen's value. The hope of scientific advancement is not an acceptable excuse to harm rabbits. Christian traditions do not focus on what humans might prefer, what profits humanity, or what pleases our palates—Christianity is a God-centered faith.

Robert Runcie, archbishop of Canterbury, notes that the concept of God "forbids the idea of a cheap creation, of a throw-away universe in which everything is expendable save human existence" because, in the Christian view, the "universe is a work of love" (Linzey, *After*, 13). Whether milk snake or pygmy shrew, whether Tyrolese grey cow or British lop piglet, even "that which seem[s] of little worth in human eyes [is] of value in the sight of God" (Hyland, *God's*, 47). Both the Old and New Testament "are united in their conviction that the world of living creatures exists because God loves them, and sustains them, and rejoices in them.... The central point is...the recognition of worth, of value, outside ourselves. Human beings are not the sum total of all value" (Linzey, *After*, 12). Christian traditions remind an egocentric humanity "that creation is not just a colorful backdrop for human actions" and simultaneously align us with more ultimate concerns, "with something good, permanent, and infinitely greater than any plan we could ever conceive or any profit we could ever gain" (Scully, 304).

Suffering

Christian traditions teach that Jesus suffered for our sake; Christian traditions are "centered on the divine vindication of innocent suffering" (Linzey, *After*, 132). Moved by the bombing of London in 1940, Edith Sitwell (who converted to Catholicism) wrote in "Still Falls the Rain" of "humanity's perennial culpability." She addresses the ongoing suffering of humanity, and the suffering of all life at the hands of humanity, including the suffering of Jesus. Sitwell describes human-induced miseries, the ugliness of human indifference and cruelty, and remembers that God "bears in His Heart all wounds," suffering with

> The wounds of the baited bear,—
> The blind and weeping bear whom the keepers beat
> On this helpless flesh...the tears of the hunted hare.

Inasmuch as Jesus is present in all love and life, he is present in all suffering (Linzey, *Animal Theology*, 48–52). When human beings cause suffering, they bring Jesus into that suffering: "If God is pre-eminently present in the suffering of the vulnerable, the undefended, the unprotected and the innocent, God's suffering presence is to be located...in the suffering of *all* the vulnerable, undefended, unprotected

and innocent in this world, including animals" (Linzey, *After*, 129). When we purchase products that stem from confinement of sows in gestation crates or hens
trapped in battery cages, or when we purchase items that exist only because Black
Angus and Hereford cattle have been forced forward into slaughterhouses thick
with the smell of blood or hens who have been dumped onto conveyor belts to be
hung upside down in shackles, we pay others to cause extreme suffering. Such
suffering is not irrelevant to the Prince of Peace, who is present in all life, and in all
suffering.

Afterlife

In Christian traditions, God is just and good; cruelty cannot be overlooked by a just
and good God. A loving God *must* remain morally responsible for and invested in
every sentient being, for "a redeeming God could not eschew the sighing and
suffering" of anymals, and to suggest otherwise "is to limit God and to deny the very
material reality of the resurrection" (Linzey, *Animal Gospel*, 34; Webb, 138). For
anymals, "as for us, if there is any hope at all then it is the same hope, and the same
love, and the same God" (Scully, 398).

The New Testament assures Christians that all creatures share in salvation:

> I consider that the sufferings of this present time are not worth comparing
> with the glory about to be revealed to us. For the creation waits with eager
> longing for the revealing of the children of God; for the creation was sub-
> jected to futility, not of its own will but by the will of the one who
> subjected it, in hope that the creation itself will be set free from its bondage
> to decay and will obtain the freedom of the glory of the children of God.
> We know that the whole creation has been groaning in labor pains until
> now; and not only the creation, but we ourselves. (Rom. 8:18–23)

Other scriptures also depict solidarity amid creation (Young, 145). Ephesians
teaches that the whole of creation is united in Jesus and awaits salvation:

> With all wisdom and insight he has made known to us the mystery of his
> will, according to his good pleasure which he set forth in Christ, as a plan
> for the fullness of time, to gather up all things in him, things in heaven and
> things on earth. (Eph. 1:9–10)

> For in him all things in heaven and on earth were created... all things have
> been created through him and for him. He himself is before all things, and
> in him all things hold together. He is the head of the body, the church; he
> is the beginning, the first-born from the dead, so that he might come to
> have first place in everything. For in him all the fullness of God was pleased

to dwell, and through him God was pleased to reconcile all things, whether on earth or in heaven, by making peace through the blood of his cross. (Col. 1:16–20)

All of creation is contained in Christ, and all things are reconciled through Christ; all creatures have eternal significance, and our actions toward Kerry cattle and La Fleche hens have moral and spiritual significance in Christian traditions. Christian salvation includes not only anymals, but all of nature: "God's good creation, a revealing pathway to the knowledge of God, and a partner in human salvation" (Johnson, 6). "In light of the resurrection hope, it is impossible to tolerate animal abuse, exploitation, and oppression" (Young, 149).

Significantly, the Christian (and Jewish) heaven is envisioned as a garden, while the Christian hell "has often been imagined as a carnivorous nightmare" (Webb, 176). In Christian traditions, a peaceful world, a world in which we do not exploit or harm other creatures, "corresponds to virtually every salvation text"; paradise is always portrayed as a "community without violence. Salvation would be an inconceivable paradox if killing of any kind" took place in paradise (Young, 21).

With or without human help, God will ultimately "gather up all things in him, things in heaven and things on earth" (Eph. 1:9–10). Christian traditions teach that paradise awaits the faithful. With or without the help of humanity, an all-inclusive world of peace will ultimately be reestablished.

Diet

Christians are to respect and care for creation. "How Christians relate to the rest of the world is determined, in part, by how they eat" (Webb, 144). Dietary choice has tremendous implications for the environment, world hunger, and anymals. From the Christian perspective, "the unexamined meal is not worth eating" (Webb, 17).

Christian religious traditions share the Jewish creation story and therefore worship a God who created a vegan world, a nonviolent world in which "no creature was to feed on another" (Hyland, *Slaughter*, 21). Christian traditions teach that humans are to assist God in reconciling creation to a peaceful, vegan world. The Christian commitment to end suffering is fundamental to Christian teachings, and the process is expected to be complex, varied, and costly (as is the expectation for Christian love). At a minimum, "regard for animals requires actually giving up a few things" (Scully, 107).

Stephen Kaufman, M.D., comments that a change of diet that eschews anymal products is neither a burden nor self-sacrifice, but part of a broader Christian life "manifesting core values such as love, compassion, and peace" (1). Christian author Richard Young agrees: "Because of the envisioned solidarity of creation in the peaceable kingdom, vegetarianism may be thought of as the quintessence of the kingdom, as it brings together humans and animals into a community of peace and harmony"

(Young, 145): A plant-based diet will help take "care of animals, the earth, and our bodies" and will also help to feed those who are malnourished with grains that will otherwise be fed to Hereford cattle, Duroc pigs, and Buff Orpington chickens (Braun, ix). Young asks, "How can one who is following the risen Christ any longer live a predatory lifestyle that reflects the pre-flood violence of a fallen race?" (51). A vegan diet provides "evidence of a total transformation—a conversion away from the values of this world and toward the world as God originally created it and will one day create it anew" (Webb, 25).

Not surprisingly, down through history, Christians have expressed attentiveness to God by abstaining from flesh. Chapter 39 of *The Rule of St. Benedict*, "The Measure of Food," establishes a vegetarian diet for healthy Benedictine brothers: "Let all abstain from the flesh of four-footed animals" ("In the Kitchens"). This trend began early on:

> James (Jesus' brother) was widely recognized as a vegetarian, and ancient sources also describe Matthew and all the apostles as abstaining from flesh. Many early church leaders practiced vegetarianism, including Clement of Alexandria, Origen, Basil, Gregory of Nazianzus, Arnobius, the Desert Fathers, John Chrysostom, Jerome, and Tertullian. St. Augustine... acknowledged in the fourth century that Christian vegetarians were "without number." (Kaufman, 8)

Beyond mercy, compassion, and our responsibility to restore the Peaceable Kingdom, human beings ought to rethink their current, fleshy diet for the sake of their own health. The New Testament teaches that the human body is "a temple of the Holy Spirit" (1 Cor. 6:19). A diet based on anymal products, such as the diet common to most of Europe and America, is linked with "a variety of human diseases, such as atherosclerosis, heart disease, stroke, adult-onset diabetes, various forms of cancer, and a host of other ailments, including kidney stones, osteoporosis, and obesity" (Young, 105). For example, colorectal cancers (colon and rectal cancers) are linked with a diet of flesh, and are the third largest cancer killers in the United States (second only to lung and breast cancer), afflicting nearly 150,000 citizens annually, and killing 50,000 people each year (Common). Similarly, obesity is now a critical problem for Americans, seriously harming even very young children (Nestle, 14).

Consuming flesh is also bringing new deadly diseases to humanity. Diseases that are common to cattle and poultry have been transmitted to humans with increasing frequency and with dreadful effects (Young, 106). E. coli, contracted from food sources contaminated by intestines in slaughterhouses, has become a serious threat to human health.

Factory-farmed anymals are crowded and unhealthy. Antibiotics are used to keep these exploited, miserable anymals alive in extremely unhealthy conditions. Flesh products are rich with "residues of antibiotics and hormones used on animals to combat diseases and promote growth" (Young, 106–7). According to the Union of Concerned Scientists, "Seventy percent of U.S. antibiotics are fed to anymals"; this practice contributes to "the rise of pathogens that defy antibiotics" (Krisotof).

Humans have long intestines, grinding molars, and bodies that are generally ill-suited for digesting a diet rich in animal products. This point is demonstrated by vegan athletes who excel at their highly competitive sports. Ironman triathlete Scott Jurek, for example, has won the Western States 100-Mile Endurance Run for the past seven years, holds the record for this race, and won the Badwater Ultramarathon just two weeks after completing the grueling Western States competition. By all counts, he is exceptionally healthy, and he is vegan. This should not surprise those within Christian traditions (or Jews): Genesis describes a world in which God created humans to consume a vegan diet (Gen. 1:29), suggesting that our biology is best suited to a plant-based diet.

Hagiographies report that many Catholic saints avoided flesh and even discouraged anymals from carnivory, anticipating the Peaceable Kingdom, and showing both mercy and compassion (Isa. 11:6–9). Some saints shared their meager stores with hungry carnivores to prevent them from hunting. Saint Macarius admonished a hyena who brought a sheep's skin to the door: "that which thou hast brought me comes of violence, I will not take it" (Waddell, 14). Saint Macarius manages to train the hyena "not to kill a creature alive" but only to eat that which is already deceased (Waddell, 14, italics removed). The saint, in turn, feeds the hyena when necessary: "If thou art distressed, seeking and finding none, come hither, and I will give thee bread. From this hour, do hurt to no creature" (Waddell, 14–15). Through observing the hyena's carnivory, and because he knew that God speaks through anymals, St. Macarius found "a reproach unto ourselves"—killing to eat is unnecessary and irreligious.

A vegan diet is good for *all* of creation and "expresses core Christian principles such as concern for human health and the environment, compassion for other people, and mercy toward all who suffer" (Kaufman, 11). In his book, *Is God a Vegetarian*, Richard Young asks and answers key questions:

> What is God like? Is not the God of the Bible a God of love, justice, and peace, who would never kill to satisfy selfish desires, who sides with the oppressed, and who would like us to live at peace without killing and war? If this is how we understand and experience God, then what metaphor best expresses that in today's context?... [V]egetarianism is more than diet. It is an orientation to life that encompasses love, justice, peace, and wholeness. (xii)

Catholic Stephen Webb, a Christian theologian who has been a member of many Christian communities, notes that the proper question for Christians to ask is not what Jesus ate, "but what Jesus would eat today" (Webb, 129). He further ponders what it represents to adopt a plant-based diet: "What would it say to the world about [Christian] willingness to put grace into practice and to witness to our own faith in God's love and our hope in God's ability to restore the world" to a place of peace? (Webb, 42).

Christian scriptures indicate that people of compassion can "serve the gospel" by changing to a plant-based diet (Webb, 29). A balanced vegan diet is nutritionally sound; anymal products are unnecessary to human health, so "why subject animals to unnecessary suffering, the environment to unnecessary degradation, and our own bodies to unnecessary health risks?" (Young, 163–64). A plant-based diet "is a celebration of life in which we permit our fellow creatures to experience the joy of existence that God graciously shared with us and our companions. It beckons us to a gentler, kinder way of life that exemplifies the Christian hope" (Young, 164).

Hunting

Christian stories recount the efforts of Catholic saints who protected anymals from deadly hunters. For example, a boar took shelter from the blasting guns in St. Kevin's oratory. When hunters arrived on the scene, they found Kevin praying under a tree with birds perched on his shoulders and flitting about "singing to the saint" (Waddell, 129). For the sake of the saint's blessing, the hunters left the boar under the saint's protection and turned home empty-handed (Waddell, 129). Similarly, St. Maedoc was in prayer when a stag came dashing into his hermitage for protection. He threw the corner of his cloak over the stag's antlers, and the hunting hounds ran past, leaving the deer in peace (Sellner, 169). Saint Godric also harbored a hunted stag in his forest hermitage, a stag who arrived "shivering and exhausted" (Waddell, 90). When the killers arrived, inquiring as to the stag's whereabouts, the saint "would not be the betrayer of his guest," and the stag thereafter returned to visit the hermitage regularly (Waddell, 91). Saint Godric did his best to protect all anymals who were terrified and endangered by hunters or trappers:

> And if anyone in his service had caught a bird or little beast in a snare or a trap or a noose, as soon as he found it he would snatch it from their hands and let it go free in the fields or the glades of the wood.... So, too, hares and other beasts fleeing from the huntsmen he would take in, and house them in his hut: and when the ravagers, their hope frustrated, would be gone, he would send them away to their familiar haunts. Many a time the dumb creatures of the wood would swerve aside from where the huntsmen lay in wait, and take shelter in the safety of his hut. (Waddell, 87–88)

In the West, many argue that hunting is essential in order to control populations. The *New Yorker* printed a comic in which two deer are asked why humans do not thin out their own burgeoning population. Why indeed? Do we really believe that overpopulation is best solved with bullets? Do we believe that deer, ducks, and pheasants are dangerously overpopulated in comparison with human beings? What is the most dangerously overpopulated species on the planet?

Divine-Anymal Relations

As noted in the previous chapter, the Old Testament explains that God considered every aspect of creation "good" (Genesis 1). Moreover, scriptures describe "animals as fellow creatures on their own terms" (Scully, 26), and all creatures are described as "dear to [God] for their own sakes" (Scully, 92). Scriptures even indicate that anymals know of God's munificence. Southern Rockhopper Penguins and Holland lops alike cry out to an attentive deity in their time of need (which is frequent for the Holland Lop, a domestic rabbit who has been inbred by human beings such that they have a tendency to dental problems). All beings are utterly dependent in relation to the Christian Creator, and not one fledgling lava heron or aging pit bull is "hidden from [the] Maker's sight" (Scully, 26). Every being has intrinsic value to the Creator, and God's love, mercy, justice, and protection extend to *all* of creation. The Christian worldview entails a loving and generous Creator, who created a world that can exist, and can *only* continue to exist, through the deity's attentive care.

Christian scriptures also indicate a vital relationship between Christ and creation: "In him all things in heaven and on earth were created... all things have been created through him and for him" and "through him God was pleased to reconcile all things, whether on earth or in heaven, by making peace through the blood of his cross." (Col. 1:16–20). Anymals, including the Kraienkoppe chicken, silver-haired bat, human being, and deer mouse, were created in, through, and for Christ, and all were reconciled through Christ. All that exists is intimately indebted and connected to Christ, including the Steppe polecat, the Bandicoot rat, Inuits, and the furry-eared dwarf lemur.

In their turn, anymals assist the Creator. Christian literature, especially hagiographies, portrays anymals as serving God in a host of different ways. They provide a locus for revelation, exemplify piety, act as martyrs, saints, sacraments, and servants, and demonstrate *agape*—the love of God. Their agency and power, "their action as subjects in their own right," is especially clear and prominent in Christian stories in which anymals are "bearers of God or *imitatio Christi*—imitators of Christ. In this role animals act, are acted upon, and enact the will of the divine" (Hobgood-Oster, 2, 5).

One such Christian story portrays a deer as God's servant, as the bearer of revelation. In this story, a hunter sees a beautiful stag and pursues him into a thicket with intent to kill. As the hunter draws near, he sees a cross in the stag's antlers, and the voice of God comes from the stag, both asking and telling, "Why are you pursuing me? For your sake I have appeared to you in this animal. I am the Christ, whom you worship without knowing it. Your alms have risen before me, and for this purpose I have come, that through this deer which you hunted, I myself might hunt you" (de Voragine, 266–67). The stag is spared, and like the New Testament fishermen who became fishers of men, this hunter of deer becomes a hunter of men— the proselytizing Saint Eustace (Hobgood-Oster, 15).

In another story in which anymals aid the divine, King Teudiric proclaims that he will not move until "my Lord Jesus Christ shall bear me hence." Two stags promptly appear, "yoked and ready" for transport (Waddell, 42). Whether lions who do not consume Daniel or an ass admonishes a wayward King, Christian scriptures indicate that anymals work with God to bring about God's desired and necessary ends. Christian "sacred history, though often obscured, suggests that animals may indeed be counted among the holy" (Hobgood-Oster, 16).

Human-Anymal Relations

Christian scripture teaches that God gave humans dominion so that we might tend and serve creation, and that humans are created in the "image of God," with "the capacity to reflect God's love and compassion" (Kaufman, 6). Human dominion, as given by the Creator in Genesis, is vegan. Human dominion requires responsibility and service, protection and nurturance, as exemplified by Christ: Our relationship with anymals is one of loving service to those who are at our mercy.

Genesis reminds Christians that humans are made in God's image, to care for creation in God's stead, as God would do. In Christian traditions, creation is God's, and the "abuse of animals—like the oppression of human beings—is opposed to the way of life that God has ordained" (Hyland, *Slaughter*, 1). How Christians treat anymals "is only one more way in which each one of us, every day, writes our own epitaph—bearing into the world a message of light and life or just more darkness and death, adding to the world's joy or to its despair" (Scully, 398). Scriptures encourage a life of love and service, especially to the weakest and neediest of beings.

We are one creation and were created to live together amiably. Many saints have exemplified this ideal human relationship with the world around them. For example, St. Godric shared company with a cow, whom he tended but never harmed, and the cow willingly complied with the saint's gentle voice commands. When a boy began to "harry and prod" the cow, she became "incensed," caught the boy "between her horns" and charged off "in a great heat of indignation" (Waddell, 78). How much more would the cows on factory farms react to their extreme frustration and pain! Like the boy, we are guilty of "boldness and presumption" in our relations with anymals—and with nature more generally. The story of St. Godric concludes that the cow rightly terrified the insensitive lad—she administered "well-deserved punishment" (Waddell, 78). God's creatures are owed respect and kindness from human beings—and they rightly object when mistreated by thoughtless, domineering, exploitative human beings.

Anymals as Individuals

Christian literature portrays a lively cast of anymal characters, from the noble lion to the spiritually challenged fox, with a full range of colorful personalities, just like human biblical characters. Hagiographies depict anymals as willful, spiritually challenged, spiritually gifted, devout, and gentle—each an individual, each sharing in the Christian spiritual life.

By pulling thorns from a lion's paw, St. Jerome gained a guardian for the cloister donkey; the lion and the ass lived at the monastery until the donkey was stolen. When the donkey turned up missing, St. Jerome assumed that the lion had devoured the donkey but did not wish to mistreat the lion "or make him wretched," so he did not overtly accuse the lion of wrongdoing (Waddell, 34). Instead, he instructed the brothers to treat the lion "as before, and offer him his food," and to make a harness so that the lion might do the donkey's labor (Waddell, 34). Meanwhile, the lion searched for his "comrade," the donkey, and ultimately retrieved his charge from the thieves, terrifying them in the process. They fled when they saw a lion approaching, abandoning their string of camels, which the lion delivered to the monastery along with the donkey, demonstrating his innocence.

Saint Moling shared company with a fox, who, unlike St. Jerome's lion, found discipleship challenging. First the fox consumed a monastery hen. Having been admonished for his bloodthirsty ways, the penitent fox snatched a hen from a nearby nunnery, bringing it alive to St. Moling as a replacement for the one he had already consumed. The patient St. Moling responded, "Thou hast offered rapine to atone for theft. Take back this hen to her ladies, and deliver her to them unharmed: and hereafter do thou live without stealing, like the rest of the animals" (Waddell, 108). Those closest to God are patient and loving toward the myriad creatures of God, helping them along their spiritual journey.

Perhaps the most famous story from the life of St. Francis is that of taming a dangerous wolf near the town of Gubbio. The townspeople were terrified of the wolf, and they ventured out only in fear and dread, fully armed, because the wolf was eating their community. Saint Francis was determined to stop the killing. He departed the city gates without safety of arms, headed for the wolf's den, and when the wolf spotted the saint, the great canine closed his mouth and lay down at the feet of St. Francis (R. Brown, 88–89). Francis said, "Brother wolf, you have ... committed horrible crimes by destroying God's creatures without any mercy" (R. Brown, 89). He created a "peace pact" between the wolf and the villagers. The wolf agreed to "never hurt any animal or man" (R. Brown, 89). The people of the town granted that neither their dogs nor they would harass the wolf, and they would feed the wild canine so that he would not need to kill. The townspeople then fed the wolf "courteously" until her passing, two years later, at which time they sincerely mourned the loss of their noble friend (R. Brown, 91).

Kinship and Community

All creatures are interconnected through the Creator, through creation, through the breath of life, and through our shared purpose as Adam's helpmates in serving God: "Scriptures depict a solidarity of all creation" (Young, 145). Christian "artwork, hagiography, oral traditions" (which were later recorded in written form), and legends "reveal a close connection between humans and the natural world. Stories and images of animals abound" (Hobgood-Oster, 2, 5).

Christian traditions have long demonstrated an understanding of the natural world as existing in "close relationship with humanity and God in their doctrinal and moral reflection" (Johnson, 17). Christian saints, in particular, have found little to separate humans from the rest of nature (Polk, 185), and they have often chosen mixed-species communities. Hagiographies reveal holy people who protected and served anymals, as ordained in Genesis 2, and anymals who willingly assisted monks in need.

Wild anymals sometimes delivered food to remote hermitages, providing the monks with much-needed sustenance: Saint Blaise and Paul the Hermit were fed by birds. Saint Giles was nursed by a lactating hind, whom he later protected from hunters (who mistakenly shot the protective saint) (Hobgood-Oster, 1, 16). Paralleling the Jewish story told in the previous chapter, Christian writers immortalize a spider who built a web to hide and protect Felix, a bishop (and saint) who was pursued by persecutors (Hobgood-Oster, 15). Domestic anymals also helped holy people. Dogs were protectors, companions, and faithful friends to Saint Philip and Saint Roch (Gumbley), and a cat was Julian of Norwich's companion in her long isolation.

Hagiographies include some very miraculous ways in which wild anymals have helped the devout. Celtic St. Brendan and his crew were rescued from a storm at sea by a whale who turned her body into an island shelter; a flock of birds brought a measure of peace to the stranded wayfarers (Zarin, 56–61). An eagle sheltered St. Medard from a rainstorm with her great wings (Zarin, 29). Crocodiles ferried St. Pachome and Abbot Helenus across a river (Waddell, 18); a wild ass helped Abbot Helenus carry a heavy load (Waddell, 19), and an ox helped a hermit in the desert to water his garden (by which both were fed) (Waddell, 3).

In Northern England in the seventh century, hagiographies report that St. Cuthbert stood neck-deep in water for his nighttime vigil, engaged in "chanting voiced like the sea," after which he was in the habit of falling onto his knees to pray on the beach. Each night, while he prayed, two otters emerged from the water to dry and warm his feet (Waddell, 60). When they had finished, they "received his blessing" and slipped back into their watery home (Sellner, 107).

Sixth-century St. Keneth (Cenydd in modern Welsh Cennydd, sometimes Kenneth in English, Kinède in French) of Wales was raised by wild anymals who were his family and community: He was abandoned by humanity because he was misshapen, but anymals took him in. He was housed and protected by gulls in his infancy; a deer provided nursing milk, and baby Keneth "lived happily in his nest. When the wind blew, the birds protected him with their outspread wings, and he grew strong, fed by the milk they brought him every day" (Zarin, 49). When grown, Keneth built a hut by the sea, and other human beings only occasionally caught glimpses of the young man, surrounded by his bird community, living in the wilds among the anymals.

Having heard of this deformed youth living among the anymals, a holy man visited and healed Keneth's misshapen body. Keneth explained that his infirmity was the source of his blessing: "Without it, [I] would not have come to live as [I] did with the creatures of the sea and the sky, and because of it [I] could be as one with those most beloved by God" (Zarin, 54). Keneth asks the holy man to restore his infirmity, and his request is granted.

Hagiographies report that anymals and humans sometimes live together as monastics. Saint Ciaran took on wild anymals as disciples. The fox was sorely challenged by discipleship, and slunk away to the wildlands to chew on the Bible, only to be pursued by hounds, which forced him back to St. Ciaran's cowl for penance (Sellner, 81). (A similar incident is attributed to St. Moling [Waddell, 107–9].) The fox again abandoned his vows, this time slinking away to chew the saint's shoe. Father Ciaran sent brother badger to bring brother fox back to his discipleship, noting that such thievery "becomes not monks" (Waddell, 104–5). Through thick and thin, St. Ciaran and his five anymal disciples lived together in community until the end of their days (Waddell, 106).

Exemplary Christians treat anymals as honored guests when they visit. In the above story of St. Jerome and the lion (and donkey), on seeing the camels that the innocent lion brought back with the stolen donkey, St. Jerome instructed his fellow Christians to "take the loads off these our guests" and feed them (Waddell, 34, 35). The camels are considered guests, just as human visitors would be. In a north island monastery, monks lived peacefully with seabirds who built their nests "beside the altar. No man presume[d] to molest them or touch the eggs" (Waddell, 93). When a chick fell into a rock crevice, St. Bartholomew noticed the distressed mother duck and followed her out to the rocks to rescue her duckling.

Most famously, St. Francis felt kinship with "animals, plants, the sea and the stars," acknowledging in daily life the bonds that link all creatures, and which link all creatures to God (Englebert, 133). When he heard a flock of larks singing, he paused on his journey to join them in praise of God (Englebert, 184). On another occasion, seeing a tree filled with birds and many birds in a neighboring field, he went out of his way to preach a sermon for his "sisters," the birds (Englebert, 134). (Perhaps, given our tendency to human hubris, in light of scriptural accounts of anymals praising God, St. Francis would have done just as well to listen and learn from the voices of his feathered sisters and brothers.)

In sacred literature, anymals often return to, or refuse to leave, their Christian protectors, thereby becoming a permanent part of the Christian community. For example, in a story similar to that of St. Jerome, Abbot Gerasimus pulled a reed from a lion's paw, and then drained and washed the wound, thereby gaining a loyal disciple. When Abbot Gerasimus died, the lion died of grief on the abbot's fresh grave (Waddell, 24–29). Similarly, when wild anymals were placed in the care of St. Francis, "he treated them gently and let them go. Often they sensed his friendship so strongly that they stayed near him instead of fleeing" (Hughes, 317). For instance, after this well-loved saint extricated a rabbit from a trap, the little creature was always nearby, and Francis had trouble convincing the rabbit to return to the wilds. Saint Bonaventure mentions a rabbit, dog, two birds, an insect, and a sheep with whom St. Francis shared company, remembering specifically

> the hare of Greccio which followed Francis like a little dog, the kingfisher and the fish in Lake Rieti which came regularly to ask his blessing, the pheasant of Siena that refused to eat for sorrow after its friend died, the cicada at the Portiuncula that came at his call and, lighting on his hand, sang God's praises with him, and finally the devoted sheep that also lived at St. Mary of the Angels. (Englebert, 135)

Stories of saints report that Christianity's spiritual giants have lived compatibly with anymals, sharing community, and that the myriad creatures did not fear these gentle, spiritual human beings. Instead, anymals looked to them for the service and protection that God has asked humanity to provide. The example of renowned saints who lovingly tended and lived among anymals is particularly important because we are all "called to be saints" (Webb, 29).

Anymal Powers

Anymals hold special powers in many Christian writings, and often these powers come directly from the Creator. Again, hagiographies hold many stories that elucidate these powers, crediting the myriad creatures with a spiritual understanding that humans often lack. For example, St. Columba's white horse "leaned his head against [the saint's] breast and began to mourn, knowing... from God Himself—for to God every animal is wise in the instinct his Maker hath given him—that his master was soon to go from him, and that he would see his face no more" (Waddell, 49). When an ignorant human being attempts to drive the horse away, St. Columba asks him to let it be: "Since [the horse] is so fond of me, let it shed its tears of grief on my chest" (Sellner, 97). The man knew nothing of the saint's imminent departure, but St. Columba noted that the divine had "evidently in some way revealed" to the horse that the saint was soon to depart (Sellner, 97). Saint Columba blessed the mourning horse.

Christian writings also present anymals as moral exemplars and teachers—even ministering to devout Christians. A talkative frog, for example, provides occasion for St. Benno to remember that all creatures praise God, and to consider whether or not the praises of anymals might be more precious than the sounds of human prayer:

> It was often the habit of the man of God [St. Benno] to go about the fields in meditation and prayer: and once as he passed by a certain marsh, a talk-ative frog was croaking in its slimy waters: and lest it should disturb his contemplation, he bade it to be [quiet].... But when he had gone on a little way he called to mind the saying in Daniel: "O ye whales and all that move in the waters, bless ye the Lord. O all ye beasts and cattle, bless ye the Lord." And fearing lest the singing of the frogs might perchance be more agree-able to God than his own praying, he again issued his command to them, that they should praise God in their accustomed fashion: and soon the air and the fields were vehement with their conversation. (Waddell, 71–72)

One of St. Kevin's brethren learns an important lesson from an otter, who kindly provided the struggling Irish monastery with food. This cold-hearted brother thought that the otter's "skin would be profitable to the monks and therefore decided to kill the otter" (Sellner, 163). The otter, sensing his cruel designs, ceased to bring food to the monks, causing a great scarcity that threatened the continuance of the monastery (Sellner, 163). Kevin prayed to God, who brought the brother to confess his evil intent; Kevin sent this cruel man away "to do penance for the evil intention that had caused so much harm" (Sellner, 163). The otter senses cruelty, knows the desperate needs of the brethren and willingly satisfies their hunger. In contrast, the human disciple had little understanding of the value of life.

Christian Traditions and Anymal Liberation

The Christian religious life includes "reflection and action, contemplation and prac-tice" (Mische, 591). Christians are to reflect, contemplate, ponder, study, and pray—they are also called to direct action—as exemplified by Jesus, who provided a paradigm for a way of life that ended on the cross, the ultimate sacrifice.

Contemporary anymal advocacy is indebted to ancient Christian ideals and practices. Jesus inspired many social reformers—slave abolitionists and anymal lib-erationists alike—with his bold acts of compassion and unending dedication to higher principles. Historic Christian documents testify to a host of "courageous

Christians: saints and seers, theologians and poets, mystics and writers who have championed the cause of animals" including two-thirds of all canonized saints from both the East and the West (Linzey, *Animal Gospel*, 27). Christian anymal liberationists who destroy property, sacrifice their time, and risk their freedom to protect and defend oppressed creation are following in the footsteps of the prophets, and walking a path prepared by Jesus.

Christianity "created a state of mind out of which the modern movement for the legal prohibition of cruelty to animals grew" (Hume, 3). With the exception of Lewis Gompertz (who was Jewish), the anymal protection movement was founded by Christians, largely Protestant clergy (Phelps, *Longest*, 85). Reverend Arthur Broome was among the founders of the Royal Society for the Prevention of Cruelty to Animals (1824). The English Society for the Prevention of Cruelty to Animals declared itself to be "conducted on exclusively Christian principles" (Preece, 257); for these early anymal activists, humanity and philanthropy "were united and could not be separated," and anymals were firmly *inside* the Christian moral circle (Li, 271).

It is not surprising that Dr. Humphrey Primatt, an eighteenth-century Anglican priest, offers what is likely the first theological argument for extending justice to anymals. In A Dissertation on the Duty of Mercy and the Sin of Cruelty to Brute Animals (1776), Primatt writes, "Love is the great Hinge upon which universal Nature turns. The Creation is a transcript of the divine Goodness; and every leaf in the book of Nature reads us a lecture on the wisdom and benevolence of its great Author.... [U]pon this principle, every creature of God is good in its kind; that is, it is such as it ought to be" (Murti, 74). Primatt noted that species differences are irrelevant to the primary Christian commandment to love—each creature is created exactly as God intended, whether with dark skin or light, whether gay or straight, whether cuckoo or louse:

> Now, if amongst men, the differences of their powers of the mind, and of their complexion, stature, and accidents of fortune, do not give any one man a right to abuse or insult any other man on account of these differences; for the same reason, a man can have no natural right to abuse and torment a beast, merely because a beast has not the mental powers of a man.
>
> For, such as the man is, he is but as God made him; and the very same is true of the beast.... And being such, neither more nor less than God made them, there is no more demerit in a beast being a beast, than there is merit in a man being a man....
>
> [T]he author and finisher of our faith, hath commanded us to be merciful, as our Father is also merciful, the obligation upon Christians becomes the stronger; and it is our bounded duty, in an especial manner, and above all other people, to extend the precept of mercy.... [A] cruel Christian is a

monster of ingratitude, a scandal to his profession and beareth the name of Christ in vain. (Murti, 75)

In light of Primatt's writing, justice among Christians is not simply "rendering to each their due," but is more profoundly understood as "rendering to each their dignity as a creation of God" (Martin-Schramm, 440). Perhaps Christian justice is ultimately about rendering to the Creator what is right and good through creation: "We may pretend to what religion we please," Primatt notes, "but cruelty is atheism. We may boast of Christianity; but cruelty is infidelity. We may trust to our orthodoxy; but cruelty is the worst of heresies" (Murti, 75). Primatt concludes, "Pain is pain, whether it be inflicted on man or on beast; and the creature that suffers it...suffers *evil*" (Primatt, 20–21).

In his later writings, Christian Russian writer and social activist Leo Tolstoy (1828–1910) offers reasoned spiritual justification for nonresistance, pacifism, and vegetarianism. In his early life, Tolstoy was a hunter and soldier, but as his faith grew in importance, he found it impossible to justify such violence and the unnecessary destruction of life.

Tolstoy's moral commitment to a fleshless diet, and to nonviolence more generally, was grounded in the Gospels. In "The First Step," Tolstoy explains the horrors he witnessed in a slaughterhouse. He notes that Christianity requires personal diligence toward spiritual goals, and concludes that such goals naturally lead to abstinence from flesh. If an individual "seriously and sincerely seeks a good life," he or she will abstain from consuming flesh because eating other creatures requires us to kill (407–8). "Tolstoy argues that killing for food is unnecessary, contrary to our moral sense, violates our deepest feelings of sympathy and compassion for all living creatures, and is provoked only by a selfish lust for 'good' eating" (Young, 42). Near the end of his life, in a letter to G. P. Degterenko, in which he reflected on his moral and spiritual choice to stop eating other animals, Tolstoy wrote that twenty years of vegetarianism never cost him "the slightest effort or deprivation" (*Tolstoy*, 622). (Today, with plentiful supermarkets offering a plethora of vegan options, this is even truer.)

Gandhi read Tolstoy's works when he was in Africa, just beginning his own struggles against oppression. These two great leaders exchanged a handful of letters in which Tolstoy helped shape Gandhi's philosophy of peaceful resistance. Gandhi, in turn, influenced Martin Luther King Jr., a Christian activist whose son and wife have turned to a plant-based diet (Church).

Stephen Kaufman, mentioned earlier, is a current member of the Protestant United Church of Christ and chair of the Christian Vegetarian Association. Kaufman tables, leaflets, discourses, and protests tirelessly on behalf of anymals, and has also written extensively on Christianity and anymal ethics, including two books: Good News for All Creation, and *Guided by the Faith of Christ*.

The Christian Vegetarian Association (CVA; http://www.all-creatures.org/cva/default.htm) is an international, nondenominational Christian ministry that advocates a plant-based diet, offering extensive information on faith and diet, advocating veganism, and actively campaigning to bring about change for anymals, humans, and the planet. CVA's website offers a host of informative links and provides a discussion group for Christian vegetarians. Through diet, CVA reveals "important ways Christians may positively impact our world for Christ, by caring for people, animals, and the environment" (Our).

The Christian Vegetarian Association was founded with intent "to actively participate in the 'reconciliation of Creation' that promises to result in the 'Peaceable Kingdom' foreshadowed by Scripture" (Our). Stephen Kaufman and the CVA encourage plant-based diets as "an effective, evangelistic witness to the gospel, as a contemporary response to Christ's command to 'go and make disciples of all nations.' (Matthew 28:19)" (Our).

Catholic Bruce Friedrich attends church just a few miles from where he lives with his wife and cat in Arlington, Virginia. He was raised in a Lutheran church, confirmed at age thirteen, and minored in religious studies at Grinnell College in Iowa, where he became a vegan (1987) after learning about links between a meat-based diet, environmental devastation, and global poverty (Pellisier). In his youth, he volunteered at a homeless shelter in Des Moines and organized fasts to raise money for Oxfam International. Friedrich spent more than six years working in a shelter for homeless families, and also worked for many years in the largest soup kitchen in Washington DC.

In 1996, motivated by his Christian faith, Friedrich took a job with People for the Ethical Treatment of Animals (PETA), where he is currently vice president for policy and government affairs. In his work for PETA, Friedrich organizes campaigns and coordinates protests both at home and abroad. He has been instrumental in forcing McDonald's to adopt groundbreaking animal welfare practices, paving the way for Burger King and Wendy's, who soon followed suit. Friedrich also produced the influential and well-circulated PETA film "Meet Your Meat," narrated by Alec Baldwin (which has been screened in the U.S. Capitol) (Friedrich).

Well versed in animal advocacy, Friedrich has debated meat, fur, and animal-experimentation representatives in mainstream media, including NBC's *Today*, CNN, Fox News, MSNBC, and Court TV. In an interview with the *San Francisco Chronicle*, Friedrich explained the following:

> God created every animal with needs, wants and a design for its life. God designed pigs to root around in the soil and play with each other. God designed chickens to make nests, lay eggs and raise their children. Jesus compared his love for humanity to a hen's love—not instinct, love—for her brood. God designed all animals with a desire for sunlight, fresh air, fresh water and so on, and he designed all animals to grow at a certain rate that won't tax their limbs and organs.

But all of these things are denied to animals who are turned into food by the meat industries. (Pellisier)

Friedrich's commitment to anymal liberation is very much a part of his faith:

> Jesus' message is about love and compassion, but there is nothing loving or compassionate [about] factory farms and slaughterhouses, where billions of animals endure miserable lives and die violent deaths. Jesus mandates kindness and mercy for all God's creatures. He'd be appalled by the suffering that we inflict on animals today to indulge our acquired taste for their flesh.
>
> Catholics, and all Christians, have a choice. When we sit down to eat, we can add to the violence, misery and death in the world, or we can respect God's creatures with a vegetarian diet. (Pellisier)

Anymal liberation is essential to Friedrich's faith. Through faith, he realized that he could not reconcile "Works of Mercy" and concern for the poor with meat consumption (Pellisier). He is now on the governing board of the Catholic Vegetarian Society and on the advisory board of the Christian Vegetarian Society, and he is a founding member of the Society of Ethical and Religious Vegetarians. Friedrich notes, "My concern for compassion is a product of my faith. That said, I agree with Gandhi—and the pope—that what's important is not your professed faith but how you live your life" (Pellisier).

Pelle Strindlund and Annika Spalde are Swedish anymal liberationists and faith-based social activists. Spalde is an ordained deacon in the Church of Sweden (Lutheran) and a founding member of the Swedish Christian Vegetarian Movement. Her commitment to nonviolence and social justice led her to participate in the Trident Ploughshares campaign to abolish the British nuclear arsenal. *Because* she is a Christian, she organized protests against the Swedish arms industry, served as an ecumenical accompanier in Israel/Palestine, worked as an assistant nurse in Paraguay, and lived with the homeless at a Catholic worker house in Duluth, Minnesota.

Strindlund holds an M.A. in religious studies and is a founding member of Räddningstjänsten (The Rescue Service) (http://www.raddningstjansten.org/english/), a Swedish organization using "non-violent civil disobedience for the liberation of all animals" ("Welcome"). Strindlund's commitment to justice and peace—a Christian commitment—has carried him to various continents. He volunteered as a social worker in Tyler, Texas, lived with threatened indigenous villagers in Guatemala, and accompanied harassed children to and from school in Palestine.

More recently, these two dedicated Christian activists have been campaigning to end Swedish weapons exports to the U.S. military in Iraq, and they published two books on faith and practice. One, published in Swedish, focuses on Christian nonviolence—nonviolence as theory and practice; the other, in English, is a book on Christianity and anymal liberation: *Every Creature a Word of God*. Strindlund and Spalde continue to work with the Rescue Service, engaging in direct action on behalf of anymals in danger and providing "them with loving homes in which they will be able to live for their own sake and avoid further suffering" ("Welcome").

As anymal liberationists and Christians, Strindlund and Spalde encourage human beings to

> reflect God's nature in our dealings with others, particularly when we are in a position of power. This ties in with the Bible's account of the earth's creation... [;] God asks human beings to relate to animals in the same way that God relates to us: with nurturing and protective care. (Spalde, 5)

Exemplifying the Christian practice of nurturance and protective care, Strindlund rescued a beagle pup from a laboratory, and has rescued dozens of hens (on different occasions) from several egg production plants. Spalde writes of one such rescue, in which activists openly broke human laws in order to uphold God's laws, which require people of faith to defend the weak and exploited:

> With some effort we worked the door open and Rønnaug walked in, opened one of the cages, and started to lift the hens out and place them in the cardboard boxes that we had brought with us. The hens flapped their wings. They were probably frightened even though we handled them carefully. I made sure that they didn't hop out of the boxes. Then we carried them, four hens to a box, out to the car. When they had all been loaded into the trunk, I pulled out the potted plant—a gift to the owner of the farm— and a letter explaining our action. I placed them both in a visible location near the empty cages. The letter included our names and telephone numbers. (Spalde, 4)

Strindlund and Spalde do not wish to offend or anger those who persist in exploitative lifestyles; they want only to rescue the needy, and to work in the hope that "creation itself will be set free from its bondage to decay and will obtain the freedom of the glory of the children of God" (Rom. 8:18–23) (Spalde, 55). They find in rescued hens a glimpse of renewal, and a vision of the Peaceable Kingdom for which all Christians are to strive:

> All was quiet when I approached the hen house and peeked inside.... We brought in the first box and slowly opened it. We lifted the freed hens out of the box and set them in the hay. They took small steps and looked around at their new home. It was lovely to see. (Spalde, 10)

Recently, Strindlund and two other activists participated in "the disarmament of slaughterhouse equipment and machinery" ("Welcome"). Afterward, the activists "remained on site to claim responsibility for their actions and to explain their moral duty to disarm equipment used for the purposes of animal abuse" ("Welcome"). Strindlund writes about this experience in "Butchers' Knives into Pruning Hooks: Civil Disobedience for Animals," noting that "illegal" actions "involve risks," but in light of his strong faith, these bold acts "simply seemed to be possible, normal, and undramatic" (Strindlund, 169). He describes disarmament actions in a slaughterhouse:

> Ida-Lovisa put on her goggles and set about disabling a circle saw. I took a sledgehammer and started pounding on a steering lever—hesitantly at first, then with greater authority. In an adjoining room, there were butchers' knives hanging on the wall. Fredric set to work in there, hammer in hand; when I finished my first task, I started helping him with his. Soon broken-off knife-tips were scattered over the tile floor. . . .
>
> After about an hour we felt we had finished. There was not much left to disarm. We set out raspberry sodapop and peanut-butter cookies for the employees, together with a letter in which we explained who we were, and assured them we were working *for* the pigs and the cows, and not *against* the employees.
>
> I rang Johan, press spokesman for our support group, and asked him to send out a press release. Ida-Lovisa put in a call to a somewhat bewildered policeman, and asked that the results of our efforts be inspected.
>
> "But do you work there?" [the officer] asked.
>
> In a way we did. An important job needed doing, and the three of us had—to the best of our ability—done it.
>
> While we were waiting for the police, we shoved open the door to a small cold-storage room. There the bodies of three slaughtered pigs were hanging low from the ceiling. The vibrations from the door prompted the bodies to twirl slightly. (Strindlund, 170–71)

Spalde and Strindlund are Christian anymal liberationists motivated to act on behalf of politically voiceless and powerless anymals. They hope that their faith in action will "inspire other people to take action against the uncivilized slaughter industry" a form of exploitation that is "barbaric and unnecessary" ("Bye"):

> When animals are set free and slaughterhouse equipment is rendered useless, the iniquitous violence against animals is made visible, while our utopia—a society that takes hens and pigs seriously—is rendered clear and concrete, albeit on a small scale. When we act in this way, our means and our ends coincide. (Strindlund, 172)

Strindlund received eight months in prison for disarming the slaughterhouse equipment and machinery as described above, and the activists were ordered to collectively pay damages: $25,000. But paying for damages to rekindle a slaughterhouse would support exploitation and bloodshed, two things that Spalde and Strindlund, as sincere Christians, will not do.

Summary

The Tanakh, slightly altered and referred to as the Old Testament, is sacred among Christians, who are therefore bound by Tanakh passages discussed in the previous chapter. The Christian spiritual life is modeled on the life of Jesus, champion of the oppressed, servant to those in need, protector of the abused, and humble defender of the downtrodden—a man who was not afraid to destroy the property of capitalists who willfully defiled that which God had made sacred. Exemplary Christians, especially saints, reveal that those who are close to God are compassionate and merciful servants, living close to nature and tending anymals. Most fundamentally, Christians are called to love.

|| 7 ||

Islamic Traditions

All the beasts that roam the earth and all the birds that wing their flight
are communities like your own.
                                                            —Qur'an 6:38

The root of Islamic religious traditions lies in Saudi Arabia, in the seventh century. The Qur'an, the word of Allah (God)[1] recited by the Prophet Muhammad, is the most sacred and foundational Islamic text. Islamic sacred literature also includes the Tanakh/Old Testament and the New Testament. "Islam accepts, and incorporates into itself, all antecedent prophets" from the Jewish tradition, as described in the Tankh, as well as Jesus and his mother, Mary, from the Christian tradition (Stoddart, 34). Islamic traditions hold Jesus and his mother to be prophets and moral exemplars. Just as much of the chapter on Judaism holds true for Christians, *both* of the previous chapters contain much that is morally relevant for Islamic religious traditions. Islamic sacred writings add a host of moral exemplars and anymal-friendly religious teachings to this already rich body of sacred writings that have their roots in the Middle East.

Sacred Nature, Sacred Anymals

For those within Islamic religious traditions—Muslims—all that exists has come from, and belongs exclusively to, the Creator: The universe is here by divine power and is "the personal creation" of Allah (Marshall, 128). The natural world is thereby endowed with "intrinsic value" (Ozdemir, 21); all that has been created has inherent value *because* it is inseparable from the Creator (Stoddart, 42).

The Qur'an describes nature as a masterpiece of the deity's "creative effort" (Ozdemir, 21), providing a vision of Allah's splendor: "Whichever way you turn there is the face of Allah" (Qur'an 2:115). The Qur'an therefore invites people of faith to ponder nature and the universe so that we might "have an idea about

---

[1] The word *Allah* simply means "God"; when Arabic-speaking Christians pray, they also use the Arabic word *Allah* (Kimball).

God's existence and His presence" (Ozdemir, 10). Muslims are invited to see and hear Allah in the natural world: "There are signs, too—for those with a mind to understand—in the alternation of night and day, and in the gracious rain God sends from heaven to renew the face of the parched earth, and in the veering of the winds" (Qur'an 45:1–6). The Qur'an exclaims, "Surely in the heavens and the earth there are signs for the faithful; in your own creation, and in the beasts that are scattered far and near, signs for true believers... signs for men of understanding" (45:1–8).

As in other religious traditions, devout Muslims have often turned to wild places where they could live among wild anymals and nature, where they could experience Allah through creation. Living among anymals "often led to an increased appreciation for the marvels of God's creation" and simultaneously brought the hearts of the faithful closer to anymals (Foltz, *Animals*, 81). Most of these Islamic ascetics were Sufis; they were Islamic mystics. Sufism is "an expression of Islamic spirituality"— not a separate faith (Stoddart, 61). Sufi traditions permeate "everything Islamic— philosophy, Qur'an commentary, economic life, and popular institutions" (Cragg, *House*, 64). Sufi traditions have helped shape Muslim faiths, including—especially— Muslim understandings of the natural world and of human relations with the natural world.

The most well-known Sufi in the Western world, the Persian (Iranian) poet Jalal al-Din Rumi (1207–73), expresses his commitment to Islam: "I am the servant of the Qur'an as long as I have life. I am the dust on the path of Muhammad" (*Divan-I*, quatrain 1173, quoted in Seker, 4). Rumi prolifically composed poems filled with imagery of nature, revealing his connection to Allah through the natural world. His *Mathnawi* states that all of the "forms and the creatures have a purpose" because they make Allah known to us (*Mathnawi*, IV, 3028).

Sufis find "beauty and wisdom" in every aspect of creation, as well as "a revelation of God" (Marshall, 135). German scholar Annemarie Schimmel wrote more than 100 books on the subject of Islam and specialized in Sufi traditions. She observes that among Sufis the "whole creation is one great mirror, or a large number of mirrors, reflecting God's overwhelming beauty" (Schimmel, 382). Egyptian mystic Omar Ibn al-Farid (1181) sought the divine in "valleys filled with beautiful gazelles,/In the freshness of dawn and dusk,/In the pearly dews, dropped on flowers" (Ullah, 158). Eighteenth-century Sufi poet Mir Taki Mir (Northern India) writes, "Rose and mirror and sun and moon—what are they?/Wherever we looked, there was always Thy face" (Schimmel, 289). Palm trees and cacti, the little worm snake and the Egyptian vulture—all point back to their Creator.

Other sacred writings also connect nature directly to the Creator. *Hadith qudsi* offers the voice of Allah: "I was a Hidden Treasure, and I wished to be known, so I created the world" (Stoddart, 80). In the words of renowned contemporary Muslim Turkish scholar Ibrahim Ozdemir, "Muslim thinkers regard nature as a sacred book... [J]ust like the Qur'an, the universe reveals to us the existence of a Sustainer and Creator" (Ozdemir, 21). Turkish Sufi master Bediuzzaman Said Nursi (d. 1960) "emphasized in his teachings that nature is most importantly a form of divine revelation" (Foltz, *Animals*, 96).

Because nature is inextricably linked with Allah, it is infused both with religious meaning and moral obligations. The Qur'an overtly teaches human beings to "have a moral feeling of obligation" toward the surrounding universe, and teaches that the primary duty of humanity is to "infuse the natural world" with moral obligations and imperatives provided by Allah (Ozdemir, 10).

> The Qur'an invited the pagan Arabs, who were illiterate, to ponder nature and the universe for at least two purposes: first, to have an idea about God's existence and His presence through whatever He creates; and second, to have a moral feeling of obligation toward a transcendental being.... To infuse the natural world with transcendent (revealed) ethics is the main purpose of man according to the Qur'an. (Ozdemir, 10)

Because Muslims are able to find Allah in every sprig and insect, the natural world is an avenue of both sacred experience and sacred responsibilities—nature has rights that must be respected, rights that are due the Creator. Any privileges that humans have been given by Allah "follow and do not precede responsibilities" (Nasr, 97).

As part of the Creator's work, anymals "are explicitly included among God's miraculous signs" (Foltz, *Animals*, 15). Numerous passages in the Qur'an reveal that every creature, including the endangered peregrine falcon and African butter catfish, have their own interests and a value all their own—a noninstrumental value. Allah is "Lord of All creatures" (Qur'an 69:28–52), and the Creator did not bring the universe into existence specifically for human beings: "And the earth has He spread out for all living beings" (Qur'an 55:10). Anymals have as their "birthright" a share in the natural world—a right to a habitat in which they can find clean water and sustenance (Masri, *Animal*, 21, 15).

Because Allah is invested in the lilt of every aspen leaf and the song of every katydid, Islamic traditions carry a moral imperative to protect the natural world and anymals. Islamic traditions contain "strong directives" for caretaking the planet, species, and individual anymals of every speckle and stripe (Foltz, *Animals*, 121). Because creation points back to Allah, it is due "watchfulness, gratefulness, and respect" (Ozdemir, 21). Every individual comes from Allah, *matters* to Allah, and has value through the Creator; every individual, whether dung beetle, dromedary, or Arabian angelfish, is a creature of Allah, and human beings will be held accountable. For Muslims, "the preservation of species is of paramount importance"—it is a religious duty (Masri, *Animal*, 21, 15). Richard Foltz, author of *Animals in Islamic Tradition and Muslim Cultures*, notes that "when we destroy habitats and species, it is like burning the pages of the divine texts by which God makes it possible for us to know Him" (Foltz, *Animals*, 96). Damaging the earth or any creature of the earth without necessity is disrespectful toward the Creator, and disobedient.

Given that the Nile River, a mountain goat, and a herd of Arabian horses are Allah's, who are we to despoil the river, "cull" and "harvest" mountain goats, or enslave and slaughter the horses? The Qur'an beseeches, "Do not defile the good earth, hallowed as it has been" (Qur'an 7:55–56). If we eat a kurgan cow or white leghorn chicken for supper—when we could as easily eat date and walnut bread with pineapple salad—we defile the individuals that we eat. Because we have other options, and because of the cruelty of factory farming, we also defile the cow, her calf, and the natural relations of mother and offspring when we buy and consume dairy products.

Islamic Philosophy and Morality
Prophet Muhammad

Muslim scholars collected and compared recorded accounts of the words and deeds of the Prophet Muhammad to be used as a supplementary guide for the faithful. *Hadith* ("tradition"), which preserve the life and words of Muhammad as remembered by his followers and collected by scholars, are the most authoritative Muslim texts after the Qur'an.

Muhammad is the moral and spiritual exemplar for the Muslim world; people of faith are encouraged to imitate the life of Muhammad (J. Smith, 403). The Qur'an assures Muslims that they have a "beautiful model (*uswa hasana*)" in the Prophet (Foltz, *Animals*, 18). Contemporary Iranian-American Shi'ite Muslim philosopher Seyyed Hossein Nasr notes that Muhammad is the "first and surest guide for the understanding of the Qur'an" (Nasr, 97).

Muhammad lived in a community where a few were wealthy while most were poor, and "social justice is one of the major themes of the Qur'an" (Foltz, *Animals*, 120). In fact, he lived at a time when life in general—including the lives of any- mals—lacked value. Accounts of Muhammad's life demonstrate that he is "one of history's most influential social reformers," compassionate not only toward suffering and downtrodden people, but also toward suffering and downtrodden anymals (Berry, 244–45).

Hadith qudsi states, "The heart of man is the throne of God" (Stoddart, 19, 81); it is through the *heart* that Allah touches the human soul (Stoddart, 46–51). Muhammad is reported to have said, "He who is devoid of kindness is devoid of good" (Friedlander, 65). It is therefore not surprising that Muhammad "loved ani- mals and displayed great kindness to them, and encouraged other Muslims to do likewise" (Nasr, 97). *Hadith* emphasize "compassion toward animals" as a religious requirement (Foltz, "Islamic," 254). For example, when wiping the mouth of his horse with his own personal cloth, Muhammad's followers asked what he was doing. The Prophet admitted that Allah had reprimanded him for having neglected the same horse (Masri, *Animal*, 36). Later, on seeing a man treating his camel roughly, the Prophet Muhammad reminded the man that "it behooves you to treat the animals gently" (*Sahih Muslim*, 4:2593, quoted in Foltz, *Animal*, 20; Masri, *Animal*, 35).

Muhammad's words and deeds often were designed to mitigate anymal suffering and death at the hands of human beings (Haq, 147). He encouraged riders to allow their camels to stop as needed, and to travel in the cool of night, so that the journey might be made more quickly (*Muwatta Malik*, 54:15:38). He spoke against the use of wild animals' skins, target practice on living creatures, and inciting animals to fight for human entertainment (Masri, *Animal*, 46). He forbade either branding or hitting an anymal in the face (*Sahih Bukhari*, 67:449); records indicate that the Prophet did not even allow the collection of eggs, because such theft distressed a mother bird (*Sahih Bukhari* referenced on *Jamaat*).

When the Muhammad was asked whether there was a heavenly reward for good deeds done for anymals, he duly noted that how we live, how we treat anymals, *matters* (Haq, 150). *Hadith* teach that killing anymals without justification is "one of the major sins" and that acts of kindness and charity to anymals will be rewarded by Allah: Muhammad recalled both a woman condemned for cruelty to a cat and a man blessed for saving a dog's life (Masri, *Animal*, 46). In the *Mishkat* (a secondary source of *hadith*), the Prophet states, "If anyone wrongfully kills [even] a sparrow, ... he will face God's interrogation" (Haq, 149). The Prophet taught that a good deed done for an anymal "is as good as doing good to a human being; while an act of cruelty to a beast is as bad as an act of cruelty to a human being" (*Mishkat al-Masabih*, bk. 6, ch. 7, 8:178.).

Muhammad taught his followers that all creatures matter in their own right, and that our interactions with other creatures are of moral and spiritual importance. *Hadith* indicate that Muhammad viewed anymals as members of their own communities, and also as individuals in their own right, due proper care and respect. The Prophet encouraged kindness and compassion, and taught his followers that how we treat anymals—how we invest our time and money—are noted by Allah and will be a matter of considerable importance on the day of judgment.

Love and Compassion

Allah created the universe with the "breath of compassion" (Bakhtiar, 16–17), and "Islamic teachings have gone to great lengths to instill a sense of love, respect and compassion for animals" (Masri, *Animal*, 45); "the overriding ethos enjoined upon humans is one of compassionate consideration" (Foltz, *Animals*, 27).

Islam shares the Judeo-Christian belief in a benevolent, all-powerful Creator who placed people "in dominion on the earth" (Qur'an 7:10). Allah personally beseeches followers to demonstrate patience and mercy (Qur'an 90:18–19), and notes that any "act of cruelty toward animals is strongly forbidden" (Siddiq, 455). Muslims are expected to treat this world, and all that has been created, with love. "Prevention of physical cruelty is not enough"—much more is required of Muslims (Masri, *Animal*, 48). We must also consider the emotional needs of other creatures; "mental cruelty is equally" forbidden (Masri, *Animal*, 48).

Love is equally important in Sufi traditions. Twentieth-century Turkish political activist Ziya Gökalp (born Mehmet Ziya) expresses his understanding of love as the core of Allah, reaching from the divine to touch humanity, and infusing the world. He concludes, "I do not worship God but for his love" (Ullah, 411). The prolific mystic Ibn 'Arabi, born in Spain in 1165, wrote of his love for all creatures, noting that love is the core of his faith—love *is* his faith: "My heart has opened unto every form: it is a pasture for gazelles, a cloister for Christian monks, a temple for idols, the Ka'ba of the pilgrim, the tables of the Torah and the book of the Qur'an. I practice the religion of Love" (Stoddart, 51).

For Sufis, "love is kindness" (Grisell, 33), which is to say, love is manifest in human actions. Islamic stories of saints, mystics, and holy people reveal that those who are closest to God are also close to anymals, sharing compassionate, companionable, and peaceful relations with the many creatures of Allah. The Sufi saint Sofyan al-Thauri (eighth century, Iraq) was filled with love, which he "showed to all God's creatures" (Attar, 132). Stories of the life of the well-known Sufi Sahl ibn Abd Allah al-Tostari (ninth century, died in Iraq) report that "lions and other wild beasts" came to him as visitors, and he would "feed and tend them" (Attar, 158).

One day a dog had pups in the cabin of the Muslim saint al-Termedhi (ninth–tenth centuries, southern Uzbekistan). The gentle mystic waited patiently for the dog to leave, coming and going eighty times before she finally moved her new family elsewhere, returning the small cabin to al-Termedhi. Not long afterward, in a dream, the Prophet spoke to an ascetic who had repeatedly criticized al-Termedhi: "If you desire eternal happiness," serve the mystic, al-Termedhi, who "brought succor to a dog" (Attar, 246). The embarrassed critic soon became the servant of the saint *because* al-Termedhi had shown compassion to a mother dog.

Rumi tells of a man who failed to show love for anymals—who kept but did not feed a dog. When the dog starved to death, the man wailed loudly, calling attention to his loss. When questioned by his neighbor, he admitted that he was too stingy to feed the dog, and the "neighbor, on hearing this, rebuked him for his hypocrisy." To claim to be a Muslim while starving a dog, Rumi notes, might cause even "the infidels [to] strike thee down with their very looks when they hear the reading of the Koran" (Rumi, "Story II," 228).

Many stories of Islamic saints recall holy people helping anymals in need. When the compassionate Sufi saint Sofyan al-Thauri (eighth century, Iraq) came upon a bird who was trapped in a cage, "fluttering and making a pitiful sound," he bought the bird and set her free (Attar, 132). After the death of the saint, a voice issued from the tomb: "God has forgiven Sofyan" on account of "the compassion he showed to

His creatures" (Attar, 132). When Ebrahim al-Khauwas (ninth century, Iraq) noticed that a great lion was limping toward him in the desert, he helped the lion, who rolled over at the ascetic's feet, presenting a paw that was "swollen and gangrenous" (Attar, 273). The saint lanced, drained, and bandaged the paw. The lion went his way but soon returned with a cub, showing appreciation to the man who had relieved his suffering (Attar, 273).

Well-known *hadith* remind believers that Muslims are *required* to provide for anymals and to treat them decently (Haq, 148). In the world of Islam, few acts of devotion carry the moral and spiritual weight of compassion. No matter how far one might have fallen from the straight path outlined by the Qur'an, *hadith* teach that one with a heart filled with compassion and tenderness is likely to be spared (Schuon, 9). In one story, a woman is *condemned* for cruelty because she confines and starves a cat, while a prostitute who "saw a dog panting, dying of thirst, on top of a well...removed her boot, tied it to her headcovering and drew water for the dog"—she "was forgiven on this account" (Friedlander, 63). The Prophet encouraged caretaking across species, and noted that those who give food from the heart—whether to a pink-backed pelican or a fire-bellied toad—"will enter paradise with peace" (Friedlander, 72).

Allah is aware not only of every scarab beetle, but also of our actions toward every scarab beetle: "He observes all things" (Qur'an 67:16–24). The human heart, by moving humanity to compassionate acts, provides a means through which Muslims might please Allah (Foltz, *Animals*, 80). Consequently, the Qur'an reminds of those who are lost to Allah: "It is not their eyes that are blind, but their hearts" (22:46). According to Islamic sacred texts and the lives of great Muslim exemplars—including the Prophet—a good heart acts with love and compassion in daily life, inspiring choices that demonstrate compassion toward all sentient beings.

Humility and Submission

Contemporary Syrian-born Islamic scholar Abdul Aziz Said notes that a Muslim's approach to the natural world is a spiritual matter. The power and splendor of Allah, the marvel of creation, the intricacies of a date palm, and the spiritual importance of every endangered Arabian jird help to remind us of our own insignificance in relation to the Creator (Schuon, 21). Many human beings are perhaps more intelligent than most other species; many human beings can overpower most anymals—but a puffed-up sense of our intelligence and power do not win favor with the Creator: Muslims are called to humility. Seeing the divine in all that exists, people ought to be humbled, to respect creation; we certainly must not damage or alter the perfect world that Allah has created. The Qur'an reminds people that we are Allah's servants, a role that requires "commensurate humility and sensitivity, predicated upon respect and reverence for the divine purpose in every created thing" (Said, 164).

The word *Islam* literally means submission—"surrender to God's law" (Esposito, 69). Humans may be "ecologically dominant," but we are fundamentally "an instrument of Allah's Will" (Zaid, 46–47). Many Muslims assert that "humankind has no rights, only duties" (Denny, 8). Our place in the universe is best understood in light of our obligatory submission to Allah: The correct relationship between humanity and Allah "is that of slaves to master" (Denny, 8). We are to tend rather than exploit, to assist rather than dominate—and our very salvation is dependent on an attitude and actions that demonstrate submission to Allah.

Vice-Regency

As Allah's servants, we are charged with vice-regency. As Allah's caretakers, humans are "accountable before God" (Haq, 129–30), and "the proper human role is that of conscientious steward" (Foltz, *Animals*, 15).

The Muslim deity is righteous and compassionate, and has created the earth for "just purposes" (Denny, 8). The Qur'an teaches that the earth, and all that exists herein, has been designed and created for the benefit of all—not just for humanity (Ozdemir, 23). Therefore, as vice-regents, Muslims must make choices that benefit creation as a whole; Muslims are to avoid decisions that merely satisfy human whims or self-interest (Dutton, 329); we are obligated to attend to the needs of Indonesian Aceh cattle and the Syrian spadefoot toad, not just our own needs and wants. We are not Allah's children in a playground, or God's beneficiaries in a gold mine: We are responsible to care for creation. By tending the world *for Allah*, and not for personal profit, we express a spiritual understanding of our proper place and role with regard to the larger world, and with regard to the Creator. Tending anymals as Allah's vice-regents is an act of religious devotion, an act of submission to Allah.

Allah has given humans the responsibility of looking after creation on behalf of the Creator. As vice-regents, humans will be held accountable. If we are cruel or indifferent to Turkish Grey Steppe cattle or stray cats, we must answer to Allah. If we harm marsh frogs or fast-disappearing Kemp's ridley turtles, Allah will hold us accountable. Anymals are not lesser, lower, or even very different from human beings—and they are certainly not expendable. In the turmoil of the great flood, Allah saved every species (Qur'an 11:38–40), and humans are now obligated to tend, protect, and preserve these anymals—maintaining the bounty that Allah has created—and to restore species that we have driven to the brink of extinction.

Zakat (Almsgiving) and Service

Islam carries a sense of "communal ownership of what is vital to common life" (Cragg, *House*, 45). Among Muslims, the "community has not only a stake in, but also a claim on," every individual's material wealth (Cragg, *House*, 45). Consequently, one of the fundamental pillars of the Islamic faith is *zakat* (almsgiving). *Zakat*, "an institution which undergirds a whole philosophy of social responsibility" is considered "an act performed for God," an act that purifies those who share wealth, resources, or time with those in need (Cragg, *House*, 44–45).

Almsgiving is obligatory, and it is not limited to care for human beings. The Prophet commented that planting a tree or cultivating land that provides "food for a bird, animal, or man" is charity, and satisfies the requirement of *zakat* (Friedlander, 100). Those who provide food for anymals give a "charitable gift" that yields great rewards from above (Haq, 145).

Many exemplary Muslims, including the Prophet Muhammad, demonstrated an understanding that the Islamic requirement of *zakat* (and service more generally) includes anymals. Muhammad is reported to have indicated that anyone who plants a tree that benefits a hamerkop, a yellow-lemon tree frog, or a little girl provides "a charitable gift" (*Sahih Bukhari* 3:39:513, *Guided Ways*). With regard to *zakat*, Rumi understood that our religious life originates in the heart, but must move outward, reaching *through the experienced world to Allah*. Rumi longed to be close to Allah, and so he lived a life of love, discipline, and self-sacrificing service in *this* world (Rumi, *Mathnawi* III, 3435), as expressed in his writings:

> A good man seeks in the world only pains to cure.
> Wherever there is a pain there goes the remedy,
> Wherever there is poverty there goes relief. (Rumi, "Story II," 86)

Whatever Rumi saw, whomever he helped, his actions stemmed from love for the Creator.

The great eighth-century mystic Ma'ruf al-Karkhi (Iraq), known both for generosity and devoutness, similarly expressed his religious duties through kindness and generosity to the needy—whoever the needy might be. When he shared his bread with a hungry dog, his uncle asked, "Are you not ashamed to eat bread with a dog?" (Attar, 164). Ma'ruf replied, "It is out of shame that I am giving bread to the poor" (Attar, 164).

Islamic religious traditions teach that those who limit their attentive hand to human beings also limit their heavenly rewards. *Zakat* requires us to tend and serve all who are in need, not just humanity.

Unity

There can be no "demarcation between human and nature as disconnected entities or objects"; all that is on the earth is interconnected and interdependent (Ozdemir, 22).

The Islamic universe is connected through creation, through a common Creator; all that exists comes from Allah, and all beings return to Allah. Islam teaches that we are each part of Allah, and Allah is part of all that exists—everything that exists is "one homogeneous organism" interconnected and interdependent—not just some creatures and the Creator, but *all* of creation *and* the Creator (Masri, *Animal*, 11, 10).

Consistent with this Islamic vision of unity, the "central doctrine of Sufism" is "oneness of being" (Stoddart, 43–44). For Muslim mystics, the very process of existence "binds the whole of creation to the Creator" (Stoddart, 62). Through the hand of the Creator, the slender-horned gazelle and the striped hyena (both of whom are now endangered) were placed in the arid regions of the Middle East, along with many other creatures of the sky, sea, and land whom Allah brought into being as species, but also in the form of myriad individuals. These individuals and endangered species exist only through Allah, just as we exist only through the One who brought All. Dhu'n-Nun, an Egyptian Sufi, writes:

> Oh God, I never hearken to the voices of the beasts or the rustle of the trees, the splashing of the waters or the song of the birds, the whistling of the wind or the rumble of the thunder, but I sense in them a testimony to Thy Unity, and a proof of Thy incomparability, that Thou art the All-Prevailing, and All-Knowing, the All-True. (Schimmel, 46)

Rumi's most famous work, the *Mathnawi*, contains 26,000 couplets that focus on mystical subjects presented as anecdotes (Ullah, 284). In this poetic master-piece, Rumi expresses oneness across lifetimes, culminating in oneness with the Creator:

> I died a plant and rose an animal.
> I died an animal and I was a man....
> "To Him we shall return." (*Mathnawi* III 3901–6)

In this same composition, Rumi similarly writes,

> Bread-giver, bread-taker, bread.
> The categories dissolve
> into One water. (Rumi, *Mathnawi* VI, 73)

The Sufi worldview does not envision physical matter as distinct from the divine; the essential nature of the earth is that of Allah (Stoddart, 49). Because Islamic traditions teach the devout to see all that exists in each beetle and bovine, because Muslims learn to view the universe as one unity, they are able to experience the divine in a mongoose, jerboa, and flamingo. Contemporary Islamic scholar Leila Ahmed reports that she learned this from her mother: "He who kills one being...kills all of humanity, and he who revives, or gives life to, one being revives all of humanity" (Ahmed, 13).

Afterlife

In Islamic traditions, anymals "possess an eschatological significance" (Nasr, 96)—
"they, too, will return to their Lord" (Said, 163). The Qur'an reminds readers that
anymals participate in both judgment and resurrection. Allah has created every
entity with his or her own destiny, and at the end of their time "they shall all be gathered before their Lord" (Qur'an 6:37–42). From Allah all come, and "to Him shall
all things return" (Qur'an 3:105–10, 24:36–43): "There is none in the heavens or on
earth but shall return to Him in utter submission" (Qur'an 19:88–98).

Islamic religious traditions allow that anymals have souls (*nafs*) (Foltz, "This," 5).
Turkish Sufi master Nursi taught that all souls are eternal (Foltz, *Animals*, 95):
"Islamic paradise is full of animals and plants.... Creatures will speak directly to God
on the Day of Judgment" (Nasr, 96). Nasr's understanding is consistent with the
Qur'an: "He has kept strict count of all His creatures, and one by one they shall
approach Him on the Day of Resurrection" (Qur'an 19:88–98).

Perhaps there will be more anymals than human beings in paradise: The ninth-
century Mu'tazilite theologian Abu Ishaq al-Nazzam noted that anymals are inherently good and innocent, and so "*all* animals [will] go to heaven" (Foltz, *Animals*,
6–7). All come from Allah; all return to the divine at the end of their days, and the
Islamic paradise is likely to be alive with geckos, Arabian waxbills, fat-tailed sheep,
and endangered Sind bats (which have become scarce in this present world). Allah
created a spectacular menagerie of living beings, and human beings will not be lonely
in paradise.

Islamic Law and Anymal Rights

Islamic anymal rights are rooted in one no less than the Creator, who "desires no
injustice to His creatures" (Qur'an 3:105–10). The Qur'an regulates human behavior
toward Allah's dependent creatures (Ozdemir, 22), providing a basis for anymal
rights: Human vice-regency requires "due regard for the rights of nature" (Said,
163). Muslims are therefore expected to "respect and pay what is due to each
creature," because "each creature has its rights accordingly" (Nasr, 97).

> Islam recognizes and accentuates the interdependence of humankind and
> creation, and their mutual dependence upon God. These relationships of
> interdependence and dependence have moral corollaries, requiring on the
> part of humans due regard for the rights of nature, understood in light of
> the rights and purposes of God. (Said, 163)

Well-known *hadith* remind believers that they are *required* to provide for anymals
(Haq, 148). One of the Prophet's companions noted as he crumbled bread for ants:
"They are our neighbors and have rights over us" (Haq, 149).

The Qur'an and *hadith* are foundational for Islamic law, which is compiled in bodies of written law called *shari'a*. *Shari'a* reveals the path that parallels the will of the divine, and comes from an Arabic word meaning "way," as in "direction" to a certain destination (such as "the *way* to a swimming hole"). *Shari'a* originally referred to a path taken by a camel to reach water and eventually came to be understood as the path of Allah—the guidelines for daily life laid down by Allah (Foltz, *Animals*, 29). *Shari'a* offers "the ideal social blueprint for the 'good society'" (Esposito, 75), informing Muslims of what they may and may not do. *Shari'a* is "God's ordaining of the right way for his faithful creatures," providing guidelines that have regulated day-to-day Muslim life for centuries (Denny, 8).

Islamic law tends to be lenient toward human inclinations, controlling rather than forbidding. "The spirit of *shari'a* law is one of acknowledgement, concession, and restraint," beginning with the assumption that humans are apt to engage in certain activities that must be controlled and limited. *Shari'a* therefore spells out the conditions under which these expected actions will be tolerated; few behaviors are forbidden outright (Foltz, *Animals*, 29–30).

Shari'a provides anymals with *legal* rights and explicitly outlines that which humans *owe* anymals. When asked about anymal rights, Muslim scholars are usually quick to note that Islam is anymal-friendly (Foltz, *Animals*, 88): "Each being exists by virtue of the truth" and is "owed its due" (Nasr, 97). *Shari'a* instruction and guidance on animal rights and human obligations "are so comprehensive that we need not go elsewhere for any guidance" (Masri, *Animal*, xi). Contemporary Egyptian cleric Yusuf al-Qaradawi comments on *Shari'a*:

> The protection of animals' rights found its realization in *shari'a* as represented in legal textbooks.... [T]he idea of animals' rights occupied the minds of medieval Muslim jurists. It is a distinctive characteristic of the *shari'a* that all animals have legal rights which must be enforced by the state. (Foltz, *Animals*, 88)

Based on Islamic law, the "Pure Brethren," a group of tenth-century Muslim philosophers from Basra, Iraq, wrote a story (*The Case of the Animals versus Man before the King of the Jinn*, their best known work) in which anymals accuse humans of abuse in an Islamic court of law. The anymals point out that they roamed the earth in peace and harmony before the creation of humans, and complain that people exploit and destroy the earth and anymals, and that they seem to "lack any sense of justice" (Foltz, *Animals*, 50):

> We were fully occupied in caring for our broods and rearing our young with all the good food and water God had allotted us, secure and unmolested in our own lands. Night and day we praised and sanctified God, and God alone.

Ages passed and God created Adam, father of mankind, and made him his vice-regent on earth. His offspring reproduced, and his seed multiplied. They spread over the earth—land and sea, mountain and plain. Men encroached on our ancestral lands. They captured sheep, cows, horses, mules, and asses from among us and enslaved them, subjecting them to the exhausting toil and drudgery of hauling, being ridden, plowing, drawing water, and turning mills. They forced us to these things under duress, with beatings, bludgeonings, and every kind of torture and chastisement our whole lives long. Some of us fled to deserts, wastelands, or mountaintops, but the Adamites pressed after us, hunting us with every kind of wile and device. Whomever fell into their hands was yoked, haltered, and fettered. They slaughtered and flayed him, ripped open his belly, cut off his limbs and broke his bones, tore out his eyes; plucked his feathers or sheared off his hair or fleece, and put him into the fire to be cooked, or on the spit to be roasted, or subjected him to even more dire tortures, whose full extent is beyond description. (Foltz, *Animals*, 50–51)

In response to this indictment, humans malign the furry and feathered plaintiffs, who ably defend themselves, vividly describing their fine qualities and special merits (Foltz, *Animals*, 52, 51). "In every case the animals are the ones providing the rational arguments, in contrast to the humans' arrogant, self-serving and unjustified claims" (Foltz, *Animals*, 51). *The Case of the Animals versus Man* reveals Allah's original munificence, and suggests that humans have failed to understand or live up to their rightful relations with other species. This story "is probably the most extensive critique of mainstream human attitudes towards animals in the entire vast corpus of Muslim literature" (Foltz, *Animals*, 50). Moreover, the Muslim philosophers who composed this text show remarkable empathy for exploited and slaughtered anymals—and an understanding that humans often breach Islamic law in their relations with nonhumans. This is yet truer with the passing of a thousand years, and with the advent of factory farming, fur farms, anymals in entertainment, and anymal experimentation.

Indeed, most contemporary human beings continue to ignore Allah's clearly stated protective measures on behalf of anymals as outlined in the Qur'an and expounded in *hadith* and *Shari'a*. Wild anymals "should be allowed to live their lives unmolested. . . . Birds should be allowed to fly free and not kept in cages" (Foltz, *Animals*, 33). These requirements speak against sport hunting and trapping, as well as factory farming (or caging in any way) chickens and turkeys. Numerous *hadiths* denounce hunting and/or killing for sport or amusement, as well as killing for "vanity," such as for ivory, fur, or feathers (Tomek). Muslims are also forbidden from keeping wild anymals as pets, and from orchestrating anymal fights, such as dog- or cockfights, for human entertainment (Llewellyn, 194). Islamic theologian Al-Hafiz Basheer Ahmad Masri, a twenty-first-century Muslim, likens such cruel exploitation to pre-Islamic Arab traditions and asserts that Islamic law should be brought to bear on such unholy acts (Foltz, *Animals*, 93). Most fundamentally, Islamic law protects the earth's varied creatures from cruelty and exploitation at the hand of humanity (Llewellyn, 233), whether in factory farms or circuses.

Al-Azhar jurists work at "the most prestigious institution of Sunni learning in the world," Cairo's venerable Al-Azhar seminary, which was founded over a thousand years ago (Foltz, *Animals*, 44). These jurists have tremendous power and authority in the Sunni world, which constitutes the vast majority of the Muslim population. In 2004, this venerable institution demonstrated the importance of the subject by hosting a conference on anymal rights, at which "scholars of Islamic law, history and philosophy, government officials, veterinarians, and animal rescue workers" determined that serious improvements were needed in our treatment of anymals, most notably in the areas of scientific research and food production, and they encouraged "further elaboration of concern for animals from an Islamic perspective" (Foltz, *Animals*, 45).

This recent Al-Azhar conference is part of an ancient yet ongoing Islamic tradition of respect for anymals that is rooted in submission to Allah, who provided anymals with legal rights in the Qur'an, which were expressed and exemplified by the Prophet Muhammad. Islamic peoples are expected to treat anymals with kindness and respect, and these requirements are written into Islamic law—*shari'a*.

Anymal Care

Islamic law requires Muslims to satisfy the basic needs of domestic anymals. Contemporary Shi'ite jurist Hashem Najy Jazayery notes that Muslims are required to feed and water anymals in their care even before they satisfy their own hunger or thirst (Foltz, *Animals*, 34–35). They are also required to offer clean, ample space to domestic anymals.

The Qur'an tells the story of a people in famine who had been neglecting the anymals who lived among them due to a scarcity of food. They were duly visited by a prophet who chose a representative camel and instructed the people to give her a fair share in whatever stores remained. The people promised to do so, but instead they killed her to satisfy their own needs, and as "retribution, the tribe was annihilated" (Masri, *Animal*, 25, Qur'an 7:73, 11:64, 26:155, 54:27–31). Islamic theologian Masri comments: "This historic incident sets forth the essence of the Islamic teachings on 'Animal Rights': Depriving them of their fair share in the resources of nature is so serious a sin in the eyes of God that it is punishable by punitive retribution" including the annihilation of an entire tribe (*Animal* 25).

Because Islamic law extends across species, anymals in Muslim societies sometimes enjoy protections and guarantees that amaze European visitors (Foltz, *Animals*, 5). For example, French essayist Michel de Montaigne (sixteenth century) noted with astonishment that "the Turks have alms and hospitals for animals" (Foltz, *Animals*, 5). Yusuf al-Qaradawi notes that organized Islamic efforts on behalf of needy anymals predate animal welfare societies in Europe by 1,300 years, making compassionate action an ancient—indeed, original—part of the Islamic faith (Foltz, *Animals*, 88).

A *shari'a* jurist of the thirteenth century wrote a legal treatise, titled *Rules for Judgment in the Cases of Living Beings*, in which he reminds humans of their obligations to anymals: Muslims must tend domestic anymals even when their days of service have ended, and provide for retired anymals exactly as they provide for younger beasts. He further notes that Islamic law requires anymals to be housed such that they cannot harm one another. Contemporary factory farms do not honor this requirement, but merely cut off tails and beaks to prevent the worst of physical injuries. Under Islamic law, human beings may not simply cut off beaks or horns, or castrate anymals to reduce the inevitable harm caused by crowding too many animals into a small space. Nor do factory farms satisfy basic requirements for lodging domestic anymals. *Shari'a* forbids Muslims from "imprisoning animals in unsuitably cramped conditions," such as sows in furrowing crates or calves in veal crates. *Rules for Judgment* notes that anymals must be kept in quarters that are cleaned regularly, and that offer "different resting shelters and watering places" (Foltz, *Animals*, 34).

Islamic jurists are now beginning to apply Islamic law to contemporary factory farming practices. In the 1960s, a committee of Al-Azhar jurists reached a unanimous decision: Modern methods of stunning before slaughter ought to be accepted in Islamic slaughterhouses because they are more humane than traditional slaughter (Foltz, *Animals*, 45). Such ongoing interpretation and application of Islamic law follows the original tendencies of guiding rather than forbidding, of pushing humans toward more humane choices. Not surprisingly, many contemporary Muslims aspire to more than the minimum, choosing to live up to the highest moral standards indicated in the Qur'an, *hadith*, and Islamic law itself—including a vegan diet.

Wartime Protections

Universally, when times are difficult, anymals under the care of humans often suffer disproportionately. When there is famine, anymals are the first to go unfed. When there is a flood, anymals are the last to be transported to safety. When there is war, anymals too quickly become chattel or targets, their lives expendable amid the overarching violence. This last injustice is addressed directly in Islamic law, which indicates that "our wars are our own problems and that we have no right to make the animals suffer" in the course of our violence (Masri, *Animal*, 37).

The Prophet Muhammad as recorded in *hadith*, instructed Muslims to spare those not engaged in combat. Commenting on this, an Islamic environmental planner in Saudi Arabia's National Commission for Wildlife Conservation and Development explains the inviolability of anymals caught in human conflicts:

> Muslim legal scholars have ruled that God's creatures possess inviolability (*hurma*) which pertains even in war: "The Prophet...forbade the killing of bees and any captured livestock, for killing them is a form of corruption included in what God has prohibited in His saying, "And when he turns away, he hastens through the land to cause corruption therein and to destroy the tilth and herds: And God loves not corruption" (Qur'an 2:205).
>
> For they are animals with the spirit of life, so it is not lawful to kill them...They are animals possessing inviolability just as do women and children. (Llewellyn, 236)

Islamic law requires Muslims to respect creation even while in combat. Those wielding guns and swords must spare girls and ponies and chickens from the horrors of battle—let them go their way. Anymals are not party to human conflict, and their lives are to be respected—like all lives—for each life is a gift from Allah.

Diet and Hunting

Muslims draw close to Allah by *becoming* compassion and mercy, "thus a true Muslim is one who honors, sustains, and protects the lives of creatures of God and does not kill them for her own food" (Foltz, *Animals*, 111). In the Islamic world, a plant-based diet is therefore ideal, one in which anymals are "allowed to live their natural lives" without cruel exploitation, and without "having their throats slit" (Masri, *Animal*, 56). It is therefore not surprising that Muslims abstain from flesh "for spiritual reasons" (Foltz, *Animals*, 109).

Killing is a grave sin for Muslims, and can be justified only when one is in great danger (Foltz, *Animals*, 93). Islamic law reminds Muslims that

> killing in general is essentially a bad thing. Muslims are not allowed to kill any living thing while in a state of ritual purity (*ihram*), for example while praying or on pilgrimage. This would seem to indicate that killing itself is seen as an impure act, to be avoided if possible. (Foltz, *Animals*, 33, 125)

The Qur'an forbids people to consume blood. All flesh contains blood, and is therefore technically forbidden unless essential for survival.

Some Muslims recognize that a plant-based diet is natural for human beings: Vegan bounty was provided when Allah "laid the earth for all living creatures, with its fruits, palm-trees, and their fruiting dates, the grain in the blade and herbs of fragrance" (Qur'an 55:1–17): While not every passage in the Qur'an is consistent with a vegan diet, many are:

We have spread out the earth and set upon it immovable mountains. We have planted it with every seasonable fruit, thus providing sustenance for man and beast. We hold the store of every blessing and send it down in appropriate measure. We let loose the fertilizing winds and bring down water from the sky for you to drink; its stores are beyond your reach. (Qur'an 15:9–32)

Sufi stories of saints and mystics are filled with lessons encouraging compassion and a fleshless diet. Twelfth century 'Abd al-Karim al-Qushayri tells of the awakening of Ibrahim ibn Adham, a Sufi who enjoyed killing (in the form of hunting):

Four times he heard a voice crying, "Awake!" but he steadfastly ignored it. At the fourth cry he spied a deer and prepared to give chase. However, the deer turned around and spoke to him, "You cannot hunt me; I have been sent to hunt you. Was it for this that you were created, and is this what you have been commanded?" At this last revelation Ibrahim ... gave a great cry and made sincere repentance. ("Hazrat")

Many Sufis advocate "harmlessness as a principle of faith" and are therefore apt to abstain from anymal products (Said, 174). A neighborhood in Istanbul, Turkey, known as *Etyemecz* ("Non-meat-eater"), is named after a local Sufi community where people live without consuming flesh.

Rumi's writings suggest that he recognized eating flesh as unnecessary and harmful—even emotionally harmful—to anymals. He tells the story of a handful of lost travelers who had to decide whether or not to kill an elephant to satisfy their hunger. A sage informed them that there was a plump young elephant in the area that they might eat, but added that if they did so, that youth's "parents would in all probability track them out and be revenged on them for killing their offspring" (Rumi, "Story II," 111). Nonetheless, on sighting the young elephant, the hungry travelers slew the beast. All but one traveler ate of the little pachyderm, "but no sooner were they fast asleep than a huge elephant made his appearance and proceeded to smell the breath of each one of the sleepers in turn. Those whom he perceived to have eaten of the young elephant's flesh he slew without mercy," and so only one traveler remained (Rumi, "Story II," 111). In this story, Rumi indicates that it is better to be hungry and merciful than well-fed and condemned.

Many Sufi stories teach that we ought to regard all lives as we regard our own life, all communities and families as we regard our own community and family, and that we ought to empathize with the suffering of other creatures. For example, Sa'di of Shiraz, who often wrote on themes of ethics and humanitarianism (Ullah, 296), recalls a man who "freed a lamb from the mouth and the claws of a wolf. But the same night he put a knife to the throat of the lamb/And the lamb's soul cried out: ... you are my wolf" (Ullah, 300). Similarly, seven hundred years later, Jenabe

Shehabuddin wrote, "Whoever has pity for his lamb does not eat the roast" (Ullah, 407).

The medieval Sufi poet Farid al-din'Attar speaks on behalf of wild anymals when telling of the gentle eighth-century saint and mystic Rabi'a. Rabi'a ventured into the mountains for a day, and was "soon surrounded by a flock of deer and mountain goats, ibexes, and wild asses" (Attar, 44–45). When Hasan of Basra (Iraq) approached, the anymals fled, causing him to feel "dismayed" (Attar, 45). He asked Rabi'a, "Why did they run away from me and associate so tamely with you?" (Attar, 45). Rabi'a minces neither flesh nor words: "What have you eaten today?" (Attar, 45). In contrast, Hasan does both, but Rabi'a knows that he has been feeding on bits of anymal bodies, and asks a second direct question: "Why then should they not flee from you?" (Attar, 45).

Dr. Rehana Hamid is a contemporary Sufi and a vegetarian. She grew up in New York City under the careful watch of a Jewish mother and Muslim father, and currently worships at the Bawa Muhaiyaddeen mosque. As a Muslim, she believes that compassion and empathy prevent her from participating in any way in unnecessary slaughter, including the consumption of flesh (Hamid, 259).

Similarly, followers of the late Sri Lankan Sufi teacher M. R. Bawa Muhaiyaddeen (twentieth century) are also vegetarians. Muhaiyaddeen asks those who would eat flesh to kill the anymal themselves, while looking into the animal's eyes, watching the last spark of life fade. He believed that a good heart cannot stand to see the cost of consuming flesh—life giving way to death. If people killed in this way, Muhaiyaddeen concludes, there would be few eating flesh (Hamid, 246). Muslims who continue to eat flesh under such circumstances will either have no other choice or no conscience.

Muhaiyaddeen wrote, "We must be aware of everything we do. All young animals have love and compassion. And if we remember that every creation was young once, we will never kill another life. We will not harm or attack any living creature" (Muhaiyaddeen, "Hunter," 28). He also emphasizes the importance of diet for flesh eaters with regard to justice and judgment:

> All your life you have been drinking the blood and eating the flesh of animals without realizing what you have been doing. You love flesh and enjoy murder. If you had any conscience or any sense of justice, if you were born as a true human being, you would think about this. God is looking at me and you. Tomorrow his truth and justice will inquire into this. You must realize this. (Muhaiyaddeen, "Hunter," 26)

In short, the required compassionate choice is to eat without slaughter—even *halal* slaughter (Foltz, "Is Vegetarianism," 12).

Halal, or "permissible" flesh, is taken from the body of an anymal who has been kept, tended, killed, and prepared according to the requirements laid out by Islamic

law. Accordingly, *halal* regulations include a number of specific slaughter requirements, and also outline how an anymal ought to be treated throughout his or her
lifetime. *Halal* flesh can come only from those who have been kept and tended
according to "clearly established Islamic principles of compassion toward animals"
(Foltz, *Animals*, 126). Muslims must therefore be certain that any flesh consumed—
and that any dairy or egg products consumed—meet this requirement. The Islamic
Food and Nutrition Council notes that *any* foods about which there is *any* question
regarding whether or not they are *halal* "should be avoided" (Foltz, *Animals*,
116–17).

Halal flesh comes from an anymal that has been killed humanely (Llewellyn,
233), but undercover footage has demonstrated repeatedly that "humane" does not
apply to factory farms or mechanized slaughterhouses, which now exist around the
world. Additionally, mainstream flesh and dairy products entail confinement in
unconscionably crowded quarters, miserable transport conditions, the cutting off of
beaks and tails from sentient anymals, and the presence of bovine growth hormone
and antibiotics fed to farmed anymals, all of which violate the Prophet's example
and the teachings of the Qur'an. Compassion and mercy are due anymals—including farmed anymals.

Knowing this, Islamic theologian Al-Hafiz Basheer Ahmad Masr (a twenty-first-
century Indian-born Muslim educated in Cairo) hopes for the day when "average,
simple and God-fearing Muslim consumers" are informed of "the gruesome details"
of anymal industries in Islamic countries; he is sure that these consumers will
"become vegetarians rather than eat such sacrilegious meat" (Masri, *Animal*, 45).
Some contemporary Muslims already have, noting that *"halal"* meat producers regularly buy anymals "from farms that do not treat animals in accordance with Islamic
rules....In other words, even *'halal* meat' is not really *halal*," and Muslims must
therefore choose other food options (Foltz, *Animals*, 119). Contemporary Muslim
scholar Tariq Ramadan agrees: "Islamic teachings on respect for animal life are
clear," and the way that anymals are treated in contemporary food industries "is
unacceptable" (Foltz, *Animals*, 118).

Masri further supports the vegan dietary option by looking to the Prophet
Muhammad:

> The basic moral question is,—how right is it to deny these creatures of god
> their natural instincts so that we may eat the end product? For Muslims
> these questions pose the additional question of a fundamental moral per-
> tinence—would our Holy Prophet Muhammad have approved of the
> modern methods of intensive farming systems if he were alive today? His
> overwhelming concern for animal rights and their general welfare would
> certainly have condemned (*La 'ana*) those who practice such methods, in
> the same way as he condemned similar other cruelties in his day. He would
> have declared that there is no grace or blessing (*Barakah*)—neither in the

consumption of such food nor in the profits from such trades. These are not just hypothetical questions. The cruel and inhumane methods of intensive farming are being practised in most Islamic countries these days, even in countries where indigence is no excuse. (Masri, *Animal*, 44)

Masri asserts that Muslims would refuse to eat flesh *on religious grounds* if they knew the horrors entailed in contemporary factory farming (Berry, 245–46). By extension, Muslims in industrialized nations would also refuse dairy and eggs if they understood the suffering and ecological degradation inherent in *all* mainstream anymal industries. Especially in light of industrial agriculture, a plant-based diet is most consistent with the teachings of Islamic religious traditions.

Choosing a diet that unnecessarily harms anymals and leads to their premature death is neither consistent with a life modeled on that of Muhammad, nor a life of submission and service to a deity who remains invested in—and is the rightful owner of—each created individual, whether that individual is a small Surabaya Babi pig, a handsome Sumatra hen, a shimmering royal palm turkey, a slick phantom goby, or a shy Delaine Merino sheep. To spare the lives of sentient individuals—to choose a vegan diet—Muslims need only bend to the will of Allah and the model of compassion set by the Prophet (Muttaqi, 2).

In light of the multitude of severe health problems associated with a diet rooted in animal products, it's of particular importance that, according to the Qur'an, Muslims are instructed to eat only foods that are both *halal and tayyib*:

> Tayyib means wholesome, pure, nutritious and safe. Traditionally, Muslims in North America have emphasized the Halal over the Tayyib when it comes to meat consumption....
>
> For instance, great emphasis is placed on ensuring that animals slaughtered for consumption are done so in the Islamic manner.... However, little to no attention is given to whether or not the animal itself is healthy, free of disease, hormones, antibiotics, and chemicals at the time of slaughter. Also, what kind of food [the animal] consumes is not taken into consideration. ("Halal V/s")

Overall, nonhuman animal products are neither as safe nor as nutritious as other food options. Anymal products are associated with the most common health problems linked with premature death in industrial nations, and according to Islamic food requirements, "unless proven to be safe," items sold for consumption "should be kept out of halal food chain" (Halal-Into). Muslims gain both physical and spiritual benefits when they commit to a plant-based diet (Foltz, *Animals*, 116).

Anymal-based diets should also be avoided because the consumption of flesh, dairy, and eggs contributes to chronic hunger in poorer nations. While we feed grains to cattle and chickens, hunger is a serious threat "for 20 percent of the world's human population, a disproportionate number of whom are Muslims. Even while so many human beings go permanently malnourished, more than half of all land under cultivation is given over to crops destined for livestock consumption" (Foltz, *Animals*, 120). Raising farmed anymals is wasteful and inefficient (Masri, *Animal*, 64, 65), and is therefore inconsistent with the social justice agenda put forward by Muhammad. In short, "for the vast majority of Muslims the eating of meat is not only unnecessary but is also directly responsible for causing grave ecological and social harm, as well as being less healthful than a balanced vegetarian regime" (Foltz, "Is Vegetarianism," 11):

> The reality of meat production today is that it entails severe environ-
> mental degradation and inefficiently diverts food resources that could be
> used to nourish hungry humans instead of doomed livestock—even
> apart from the fact that it condemns millions of innocent creatures to a
> life-time of unimaginable torture. Most Muslims, like people every-
> where, support this immoral system out of ignorance. (Foltz, *Animals*,
> 126–27)

When the facts are placed on the table, it would seem difficult for sincere Muslims to place anymal products on the table.

Divine-Anymal Relations

A Muslim from a small community in upstate New York, when asked if he didn't feel a little isolated, asked, "What do you mean?" Then, sweeping his hand outward toward the open landscape, he remarked, "Just look at all these cows!" (Foltz, *Animals*, 6).

Islamic religious traditions hold that every creature is Muslim; no creature is isolated from his or her Creator. Allah "takes care of the needs of all living things: 'There is no moving creature on earth, but Allah provides for [his or her] sustenance'" (Qur'an 11:6).

Allah's Ongoing Commitment

Six chapters of the Qur'an bear the names of anymals: Cow, Bee, Ant, Spider, Cattle, and Elephant. Anymals have a direct relationship with Allah (Nasr, 96). The Qur'an teaches that the Creator is the "merciful lord of mercy" (Qur'an 59:22): "To Him belongs all that is, in the heavens and in the earth, each and all subservient to His will. He it is who initiates creation and continually renews it" (Qur'an 30:26–27).

The Qur'an indicates that Allah is aware of each creature's folly and hardship, and sustains each individual and every aspect of creation: "Allah controls the destiny of every living entity" and attends to the needs of the entire earthly multitude (Qur'an 11:56). In the *Mathnawi*, Rumi describes Allah's caretaking role:

> Yea, all the fish in the seas,
> And all feathered fowl in the air above,
> All elephants, wolves, and lions of the forest,
> All dragons and snakes, and even little ants,
> Yea, even air, water, earth, and fire,
> Draw their sustenance from Him, both winter and summer.
> Every moment this heaven cries to Him, saying,
> "O Lord, quit not Thy hold of me for a moment!
> The pillar of my being is Thy aid and protection;
> The whole is folded up in that right hand of Thine."
> And earth cries, "O keep me fixed and steadfast,
> Thou who hast placed me on the top of waters!"
> All of them are waiting and expecting His aid,
> All have learned of Him to represent their needs. (Rumi, "Story II")

Renowned ninth-century Egyptian mystic Dho 'l-Nun al-Msri depicts Allah's attentiveness to every creature in his story of a small, blind bird, who taught the mystic to trust Allah:

> I saw a blind little bird perched in a tree. It fluttered down from the tree.
> "Where will this helpless creature get food and water?" I cried.
> The bird dug the earth with its beak and two saucers appeared, one of gold containing grain and the other of sliver full of rosewater. The bird ate its fill, then it flew up into the tree and the saucers vanished.
> Utterly dumbfounded, Dho 'l-Nun thenceforward put his trust in God completely, and was truly converted. (Attar, 89)

We are but one of many creatures fed by the hand of the Creator. The Qur'an reminds humanity, "Countless are the beasts that cannot fend for themselves. Allah provides for them, as He provides for you" (Qur'an 29:56–62).

The entire natural world worships Allah (Masri, *Animal*, 20). Creation offers an ongoing "song of praise," carried out by every aspect of the universe. Anymals, sustained by the Creator, know of Allah and pay "obeisance to Him by adoration and worship" (Masri, *Animal*, 19). "All in the heavens and the earth give praise to God" (Qur'an 61:1); to Allah "bow all the creatures of the heavens and the earth" (Qur'an 16:48–56): "The sun and the moon and the stars, the mountains and the trees, the beasts, and countless men—all prostrate themselves before Him" (Qur'an 22:18).

Sufis, like most mystics, are drawn by a strong "longing for God," and are likely to feel this same tendency in anymals. Yunus Emre of Turkey (early fourteenth century) pens a message to Allah in which he expresses his desire to join the voices of anymals and the natural world, praising Allah:

> I wish to call you in the mountains
> Amidst the rocks,
> With the birds in the cities,
> With the fish in the depth of the seas,
> With the gazelles in the plains....
> With the doves which sing,
> In the songs of nightingales,
> And through the voices
> Of those who love you and call you,
> I want to call you God. (Ullah, 377)

But most human beings do not notice the praises of a purple heron or a Cheesman's gerbil. The Qur'an indicates that every aspect of creation praises God, though "this praise is not expressed in human language" (Qur'an 17:44; 22:18; 24:41) (Foltz, "This," 5): "The seven heavens, and the earth, and all who dwell in them give glory to Him. All creatures celebrate His praises. Yet you cannot understand their praises" (Qur'an 17:44). Anymals "have their own forms of prayer" (Said, 163), though humans often fail to see the natural world's unending, abounding praise for Allah. The Qur'an asks, "Do you not see how Allah is praised by those in heaven and earth?" (Qur'an 24:41). Though we generally do not see the devotion of a small sand rat, a busy bulbul, or a graceful saluki, the Qur'an reminds those of faith that every part of creation stands in praise of Allah, and "Allah notes the prayers and praises of all His creatures, and has knowledge of all their actions" (Qur'an 24:36–43).

To kill a broad-toothed field mouse, a Hamadryas baboon, or an idmi (a gazelle that has been crowded and hunted out of the mountainous areas of the Middle East) is therefore to diminish Allah's praise. The Prophet rebuked a man who burned an entire anthill simply because he was stung by one ant, saying, "Because an ant stung you, you have destroyed a whole nation that celebrates God's glory" (Llewellyn, 230–31). Contemporary Muslims have many reasons to be concerned about our ongoing rampage of destruction in light of the Prophet's response. Contemporary scholar Seyyed Nasr notes, "In destroying a species, we are in reality silencing a whole class of God's worshippers," and for a Muslim, it would seem difficult to find a more compelling reason than this to protect habitat, species, and individual anymals—including farmed anymals (Foltz, *Animals*, 103).

Stories of saints, mystics, and ascetics include anymals who have done the bidding of Allah. With a swift kick from a passing camel, Allah punished the disciple of

Abu Bakr Al-Kattani (eighth–ninth centuries, Iraq) for inappropriate behavior (Attar, 255). When one of Allah's servants, an ascetic and renunciate, refused to eat anything "that involved the acquisition of material possessions," Allah sent "a cloud of bees to hover around him and give him honey" (Attar, 89). When Dho 'l-Nun (who pitied and learned from the blind bird) is accused of stealing a jewel while aboard a ship, thousands of fishes "put their heads out of the water, each with a jewel" in his or her mouth (Attar, 91). Dho 'l-Nun then takes a jewel from the mouth of one fish, giving it to the man who has lost his jewel, and is thereafter called Dho 'l-Nun: "The Man of the Fish" (Attar, 91).

Anymals do the bidding of Allah every day, all day. Whether or not humans understand a honey badger's adoration of the divine, the personal fears and anxieties of a burro, or the many ways in which anymals are part of the divine plan, Allah is attentive to all: "He alone hears all and knows all" (Qur'an 29:56–62).

Human-Anymal Relations

Islamic writings describe humans as similar to anymals in almost all respects, and as included in the moral community (Foltz, *Animals*, 27). Interspecies morality is rooted in two shared characteristics between humans and anymals: individuality and membership in communities.

Anymals as Individuals

The Qur'an notes, "Men, beasts, and cattle have their different colors"—their individuality (Qur'an 35:27–30). Anymals are given proper names in Islamic sacred writings, and this "individuation effectively admits a unique identity on the part of each and every member of a given animal species" (Haq, 148). Consequently, well-known contemporary Middle Eastern scholar Nomanul S. Haq asserts that "each animal is to be considered *as an individual*" in the Muslim world (Haq 148).

Anymals are understood to be unique individuals in Islamic traditions. Islamic sacred writings present anymals as "having feelings and interests of their own" (Foltz, *Animals*, 27): "Animals communicate among themselves, understand each other, and even worship Allah in their own unique way…, which Allah has given them" (Siddiq, 454–55).

The individuality of anymals has moral implications. Each species is unique, but all of Allah's creatures share certain fundamental qualities, and these shared attributes carry moral imperatives. Just as humans are harmed when their communities are disrupted, so Sahiwal cattle, Sultan chickens, red deer, and field mice are harmed when we manipulate their family lives and tear apart their communities—pulling family members and friends from one another for our own purposes. While some anymals live happily among humans, no anymal is happy when enslaved or entrapped by another. Humans are to treat every individual with the kindness and respect that all sentient beings deserve.

Famous Sufis have been known for their willingness to honor the individual nature of each anymal, to wholeheartedly include anymals in their moral community by establishing personal relationships through acts of kindness. Rumi often included anymals in his writings—mouse, frog, fox, lion, parrot, peacock, duck, elephant, bear, camel, jackal, snake, gnat, or donkey. In his mystical writing, anymals are not merely metaphorical—they have their own natures, "their own metaphysical truth *qua* animals" (Clarke, 47). Rumi's writings indicate that he recognized anymals as Allah's creatures—like ourselves—and interacted with them accordingly.

There are many stories of personal relations between Sufi saints and individual anymals. For example, a tragic story tells of a strong bond formed between a man and a bird. After the compassionate Sufi saint Sofyan al-Thauri released a bird who was trapped in a cage, the bird stayed near the saint, observing him while he prayed, and sometimes perching on his arms or shoulders. After Sofyan died, the forlorn bird joined the funeral procession, wailing pitifully with the rest of the mourners. Afterward, not wishing to live without the saint, the bird dashed herself to the ground (Attar, 132).

Kinship and Community

Muslim religious traditions teach that "there is no clear-cut distinction between humans and nonhumans;" we are all "creatures of the same Creator" (Ozdemir, 24). Most important, the Qur'an teaches that "the beasts that roam the earth and all the birds that wing their flight are communities like your own" (Qur'an 6:38). Anymals

> live a life, individual and social, like members of a human commune. In other words, they are communities in their own right and not in relation to human species or its values.... [E]ven those species which are generally considered as insignificant or even dangerous, deserve to be treated as communities; that their intrinsic and not perceptible values should be recognized, irrespective of their usefulness or apparent harmfulness. (Masri, *Animal*, 8)

Through the Qur'an, Muslims are taught to accept "all species as communities like us in their own right" and not to judge anymals "according to our human norms and values" (Masri, *Animal* xi).

Consequently, Islamic writings reveal anymals, whether porcupine or veiled chameleon, living much like humans in human communities. For example, Rumi writes of a parrot, unhappily exploited by a merchant, trapped in a cage, intelligent, and very much remembering his previous and now distant bird community.

When the man who held the bird captive planned a trip to the parrot's homeland, he asked his prisoner if he had any message for his kin back home. The parrot asked the merchant to tell them that "he was kept confined in a cage" (Rumi, "Story II," 28).

When the selfish man delivered this message, a parrot immediately fell down dead, and "the merchant was annoyed with his own parrot for having sent such a fatal message" (Rumi, "Story II," 28). As a result, he returned to rebuke the caged bird, but no sooner had he told the little trapped bird what had happened than his prisoner fell onto the cage floor. The merchant "after lamenting his death, took his corpse out of the cage and threw it away; but, to his surprise, the corpse immediately recovered life, and flew away" (Rumi, "Story II," 28). As the bird lifted up into the skies, free from human bars, he explained to the self-centered man how his relative and friend from afar—his original and rightful community—had "feigned death to suggest this way of escaping from confinement" (Rumi, "Story II," 28). This story reveals an individual bird's desire to be autonomous, to live out his or her natural life with his own community, and the flock's ability to reason and communicate.

The Islamic philosophical treatise *Alive, Son of Awake*, recalls a human baby, alone on an island, adopted and tended by a deer who had recently lost her fawn. She nurses the small human, who "grows up among the animals of the island and lives as one of them" (Foltz, *Animals*, 53). The author notes the tender, self-sacrificing diligence of the doe, describing how she would run to the boy when he cried out. This philosophical treatise presents animals living peacefully in one community on an island devoid of predators. The Muslim philosophers who wrote this text used this peaceful community "as an example of the perfection of God's creation" (Foltz, *Animals*, 54). Islamic philosophers encourage cooperation and harmony over predation and bloodshed, as is consistent with Islamic teachings.

The Qur'an teaches that anymals live in communities, as do humans (Qur'an 16:68). The Qur'an also states that Islamic communities are always provided with prophets. Ahmad ibn Thabit (ninth century) understood that prophets must therefore *necessarily* be provided to anymal communities (Foltz, *Animals*, 17). While anymal revelations and prophets likely lie outside what humans might readily identify, the Qur'an informs humanity that the African caracal, the Egyptian tomb bat, and the goitered gazelle have their prophets just as we have ours. Providing prophets to *all* communities testifies to interspecies equality in the eye of the Creator, and to the worthiness of anymal communities in the eye of the Creator. The insights of anymal prophets are likely impenetrable to human beings, as is likely for human revelation with regard to anymals, "but it is surely arrogant to imagine that they are less important or less divine" (Foltz, *Animals*, 149).

Allah created each creature as a unique individual, yet the Creator also provided *fundamental* similarities for all living beings: Every living being is a fellow creation, both sentient and dependent. Perhaps because Islamic traditions describe humans "as similar to non-human animals in almost all respects" (Foltz, "This," 5), Islamic traditions take human-anymal relations "quite seriously" (Foltz, *Animals*, 27). Allah expects humanity to include all creatures in their moral community, extending compassion and generosity across species. The "Qur'an repeatedly hammers home the fact that food and other resources of nature are there to be shared equitably with other creatures" (Masri, *Animal*, 23). Islamic ethics and law, derived from the Qur'an and *hadith*, teach that the "animal world should be treated as a silent partner...of humankind" (Siddiq, 454–55).

Anymal Powers

Islamic literature acknowledges the special powers that Allah has gifted other species, and also praises anymals for being superior to humans in many ways.

Anymals have much to teach humanity: Muslims have "often been advised by their mentors to learn lessons" from anymals (Masri, *Animal*, 7). In one story, presented by Rumi, a captured bird offers three bits of wisdom to his captor in exchange for release. First the bird notes that the man has "eaten many oxen and sheep" and yet has "never become satisfied with their meat"—so how will he be satisfied by consuming a little bird's flesh? (Rumi, "Story II," 200–201). The man sees sense in what the bird has said, agrees, and so the bird offers her first two bits of wisdom: "Believe not foolish assertions" and "Do not grieve for what is past" (Rumi, "Story II," 200–201). The bird, then safely out of reach, tells the man that she carries an incredibly heavy and precious jewel inside her body, which he might have had if he had kept and consumed her. On hearing this, the man falls into "lamentations and weeping," and the bird reminds the man of her first two bits of wisdom. She first chides the man: Did I not just counsel you not to grieve "over what is past and gone" and not to "believe foolish assertions?" (Rumi, "Story II," 200–201). The bird believes that the man is either daft or deaf—she does not weigh enough to carry a heavy jewel in her small frame. The man consequently recovers, and asks for her third bit of wisdom:

> The bird replied, "You have made a fine use of the others,
> That I should waste my third counsel upon you.
> To give counsel to a sleepy ignoramus
> Is to sow seeds upon salt land." (Rumi, "Story II")

In this story, Rumi mocks the exploitative flesh eater's insatiability and ignorance, while showing the bird's ingenuity and wit. Rumi's writings often present anymals as worthy of respect, as perfect creations of Allah with many admirable qualities, including considerable wisdom. Rumi found in anymals a "natural, God-given instinct," unobscured by human "intellect and false imaginings"

(Clarke, 47). Most important, Rumi attributes to anymals the critical ability to love intuitively, without confusion (Clarke, 47), to feel and express "loving devotion"—a trait that Sufis admire greatly (Foltz, *Animals*, 79). In this way, Rumi presents anymals as standing closer to Allah than do most humans, and therefore as holding special knowledge of the divine: "If only creatures had tongues (here below),/They could lift the veil from the Divine mysteries" (Nasr, 96).

Even saints have much to learn from the wisdom of anymals. Through the example set by a deer, a Persian (Iranian) saint learns to trust in divine munificence rather than traipse through the desert toting a bucket and rope. In this story, Ibn Khafif (tenth century) remembers that he was full of conceit when he noticed a deer drinking from a desert well—a deer that had much to teach the arrogant youth. Having walked miles without water, he eagerly approached the well with his bucket and rope, but as he drew near, both the deer and the water retreated. The arrogant Ibn Khafif objected, asking Allah if he were indeed "of less worth than this deer" (Attar, 258). Allah patiently explained that the deer trusted in Allah, while the young Ibn Khafif carried both bucket and rope. From that day on, he "flung away the bucket and rope," taking the example of the deer, and trusting only Allah to provide for his needs (Attar, 258).

Another story contrasts the ignorance of humans with the understanding of a pigeon, who suddenly drops to the ground of a mosque, apparently from heat exhaustion. Sahl ibn Abd Allah al-Tostari (whose home is referred to as "the house of the wild beasts") understands, and explains that the distressed bird bears witness to the fact that the saint, Shah-e Kermani, just passed on (Attar, 158). The failing bird knew that which the humans did not, and through her sensitivity to the death of Kermani, she carried this message to a saint, the only human being who was able to understand her distress.

In another Sufi story of anymal wisdom and spiritual sensitivity, a dove shows devotion to a saint while dull humans mar the moment. After the death of the renowned Sufi Abo 'l-Qasem al-Jonaid (tenth century, Iraq), his followers lift his body onto a bier, where a dove soon comes to perch. Those attending the body try to drive the bird away, causing a ruckus in an otherwise solemn ceremony. At last the dove speaks, both explaining and admonishing the unfriendly, ignorant humans:

> My claws have been fastened to the corner of the bier by the nail of Love.
> That is why I am perched here. Do not trouble yourselves; today his body
> passes to the care of the cherubim. Were it not for your clamour, his body
> would have flown with us in the sky like a white falcon. (Attar, 213)

Humans are often ignorant regarding the spiritual lessons and subtle messages that anymals provide, but human ignorance serves only to highlight the special insights and spiritual power of anymals in the Islamic religious traditions.

Islamic Traditions and Anymal Liberation

Islam is not merely a system of belief, but "a way of living and being" (Ahmed, 14). For Muslims, the truth cannot be merely spoken, or simply brought to mental awareness—the teachings of Islam must be "fully 'known' through realization in action" (Denny, 12).

Muhammad said that Allah looks to and values both our "hearts and deeds" (Friedlander, 123). The Prophet noted that each of us "is a vendor of his [or her] soul, either freeing it or bringing about its ruin" through our daily choices (An-Nawawis, #23). In *Hadith qudsi*, Muhammad is credited with saying, "It is but your deeds that I reckon up for you, so let him who finds good praise Allah and let him who finds other than that blame no one but himself" (An-Nawawis, #24). For Muslims, understanding morally right actions, and not bothering to *act* on this knowledge, is vanity, futility, and folly.

Indeed, Muslims advocating on behalf of anymals have assembled "all over the Muslim world, from Egypt, Jordan, and Syria to Turkey, Iran, Pakistan, Malaysia, and Indonesia," as well as North America and Europe (Foltz, *Animals*, 111). PETA member Ali Robert Tappan, now a graduate student in Islamic studies, introduced a website on Islam and vegetarianism in 1998 with the following statement:

> The purpose of this site is to show what many Muslims have long suspected: eating meat, dairy products, and eggs conflicts with Islamic teachings of kindness to animals. Not only that, animal industries are responsible for vast environmental pollution and destruction and also contribute to many deadly human diseases. ("Islamic")

This much-frequented website, now called Islamic Concern for Animals (http://islamicconcern.com), has expanded to cover a plethora of anymal concerns (vivisection, fur, and *halal* slaughter, for example) and now contains articles posted by Muslim scholars and activists, offering insights into contemporary dilemmas and recommending further reading. For example, Hakim Archuletta posted a lecture commenting on the irreligious nature of vivisection: Muslims "cannot torture an animal with the idea that we will find some medicine in the process"; such an act is "a denial of the immediacy of Allah's mercy" (Foltz, *Animals*, 98). The Animal Rights in Islam website also contributes significantly to the ongoing Islamic dialogue on anymal liberation, welfare, and rights. "If the internet is any indication of where things are heading," writes scholar and author Richard Foltz, it is clear that religious concern for anymals, "especially among young Muslims living in the West, is on the rise" (Foltz, *Animals*, 99).

With more and more Muslims concerned about our treatment of anymals, much impassioned dialogue has centered on diet, both on websites and in the larger Islamic community. There have even been several *fatwas*—or scholarly opinions—offered on the "permissibility" of the vegetarian diet (http://www.islamicconcern.com/ fatwas.asp). Enlightened Islamic doctors support vegetarianism, even noting that "Our Prophet was mostly vegetarian" (Athar). For example, Dr. Moneim A. Fadali, author of *Animal Experimentation: A Harvest of Shame*, writes:

> Islam, a religion of compassion and moderation, acknowledges animals' rights and emphasizes humans' responsibility for their welfare. A vegan vegetarian diet is healthful, promotes mental and physical well-being, and is cruelty-free. It does not include animal parts or products such as eggs and dairy products. I urge every Moslem and nonMoslem to become a vegan vegetarian. (Fadali)

Concern for anymals is not new to Islam, and the late Islamic theologian Al-Hafiz Basheer Ahmad Masri is "unquestionably the most prominent contemporary voice in articulating Islamic concern for non-human animals" (Foltz, *Animals*, 89). Masri (1914–1992) spent most of his later years in England tending toward anymal liberation before this social justice movement had gained much strength. He was born into a Muslim family in India, graduated from the University of the Punjab, and then proceeded to al-Azhar University, Cairo. In 1961 he settled in England and became coeditor of the *Islamic Review*. In 1964, Masri was the first Sunni *imam* (spiritual leader) of the Shah Jehan Mosque in Woking, which was then the European Centre of Islam.

Masri worked with both the World Society for the Protection of Animals (WPSA) and Compassion in World Farming (CIWF) until his death in 1992. He was well known for his radio and television broadcasts, lectures, and writings on the subject of anymals and Islam. Between 1984 and 1992, Masri wrote *Islamic Concern for Animals* (1987), a pioneering and groundbreaking philosophical book, followed by his more comprehensive *Animal Welfare in Islam*, and then he produced a powerful video, *Creatures of God* (1993).

In *Islamic Concern for Animals*, Masri notes that cruelty to animals has existed throughout the ages in various forms, from trapping and wearing fur to hunting and overworking domestic anymals. He also notes a recent change in the "nature and extent" of cruelty, which is now practiced on a much wider scale, often blocked from the public eye (Masri, *Islamic*, 1). He further notes that such practices are completely unnecessary, though they are often "justified in the name of human needs and spurious science," while alternative, humane products are readily available (Masri, *Islamic*, 1). He reminds those of faith that harming and killing anymals without necessity is unacceptable to Allah (Masri, *Islamic*, 17).

One of Masri's strongest complaints in *Animal Welfare in Islam* is against anymal experimentation, about which he writes:

> Think of the millions of animals killed in the name of commercial enterprises in order to supply a complacent public with trinkets and products

they do not really need. And why? Because people are too lazy or self-indulgent to find substitutes. Or do without. (Masri, *Animal,* 27)

He notes that we now have a host of preferable options with which to replace anymal models. He reminds readers that life is not ours, but Allah's, and scientific research "that is unlawful on humans" ought to be "unlawful on animals" (Masri, *Animal,* 29–30).

Masri notes that laboratories that exploit anymals break basic Islamic moral requirements because Islam includes a prohibition against cutting or injuring live anymals, which applies to vivisection (Masri, *Animal,* 37). Additionally, an Islamic Juristic Rule (*qa'ida fiqhiyyah*) states, "One's interest or need does not annul [an] other's right," which suggests that we may not use the bodies of anymals to satisfy our interests or needs (Masri, *Animal,* 30)—even if alternatives are not available. This is unambiguously the case with regard to anymal exploitation, whether for pleasure or profit, including animal experimentation:

> [Islamic rules] leave no excuse for Muslims to remain complacent about the current killings of animals in their millions for their furs, tusks, oils, and various other commodities. The excuse that such things are essential for human needs is no longer valid. Modern technology has produced all these things in synthetic materials and they are easily available all over the world, in some cases at a cheaper price....
>
> According to the spirit and the overall teachings of Islam, causing avoidable pain and suffering to the defenceless and innocent creatures of God is not justifiable under any circumstances. No advantages and no urgency of human needs would justify the kind of calculated violence...done these days against animals, especially through international trade of livestock and meat. One of the sayings of the Holy Prophet Muhammad tells us: "if you must kill, kill without torture." While pronouncing this dictum, he did not name any animals as an exception. (Masri, *Animal,* 32, 34)

Masri also asserts that farmed anymals have "certain basic rights" that industrialized agriculture fails to honor:

> For instance, the right to the companionship of their own kind, the right to an appropriate diet to keep them in health, and the right to a natural life and painless death. If their Divine Creator gave them legs, is it not a blasphemy to shut them in crates where they are unable to walk? Are we perhaps...becoming more bestial ourselves, unable to know right from wrong? (Masri, *Islamic,* 27)

"On the subject of factory farming, Masri is categorical: it is not compatible with Islamic ethics toward animals" (Foltz, *Animals,* 91).

Masri collaborated with his grandson Nadeem Haque to create a comprehensive treatise on Islam and the environment. In "Foundations of Advocacy and Compassion for Animals in Islam," Haque offers philosophical justification for anymal advocacy: Anymals are a trust from God, live in communities like our own, and possess personhood (Haque). Haque argues that anymals "have each been assigned a role on earth," that Allah created equilibrium, and it is our duty to maintain this divine balance (Foltz, *Animals*, 150). Islamic traditions teach human beings that justice *requires* us to allow each creature his or her place, life, and function in the larger universe.

Egyptian Muslim Nadia Montasser works with a handful of different organizations on behalf of anymal liberation: PETA, Egyptian Society for Animal Friends (ESAF), Society for Protection of Animal Rights in Egypt (SPARE), and Egyptian Society for Mercy on Animals (ESMA). She explains her dedication to anymal liberation through her Islamic faith:

> If we have dominion over animals, surely it is to protect them, not to use them for our own ends. There is nothing in [the Qur'an] nor in the Bible that would justify our modern-day programs that desecrate the environment, destroy entire species of wildlife, and inflict torment and death on billions of animals. A loving God could not help but be appalled at the way animals are being treated. (Montasser, "Animal," 37)

In light of contemporary anymal industries and the sad plight of many exploited and neglected anymals, Montasser feels that one of her tasks as a Muslim "is to make [this] a better place for all beings and to alleviate suffering" (Montasser, "Animal," 36).

Montasser is busy on behalf of Allah, working to alleviate suffering. She writes articles to expose the horrors of fur farms and anymal experimentation, and explains the importance of spay-neuter programs. She urges Middle Eastern governments to stop importing live sheep from Australia (Landais) and fights for anymal-friendly legislation, including improved and enforced Islamic slaughter laws.

She notes that a commitment to Islamic teachings would eliminate much of the current abuse in slaughterhouses. For example, she reminds those of faith that Muhammad forbade people from harming an anymal if there is "even a flicker of life" within that anymal's body (Montasser, "Australia"). Honoring the compassion of Muhammad would prevent much of the cruelty and egregious suffering now prevalent in slaughterhouses:

> The Holy Prophet once said to a man who was sharpening his knife in the presence of the animal: "Do you intend inflicting death on the animal twice—once by sharpening the knife within its sight; and once by cutting its throat?" (6:230).

When Muhammad migrated from Mecca to Medina, people there used to cut off camels' humps and fat tails of sheep. They used to eat those while the animals remained alive for future use. He ordered them to stop these barbaric actions. (Montasser, "Australia")

When Montasser learned of a new publication called "PetPost," she offered to write a column on behalf of anymal liberation. In this column, she reminded Muslims that only flesh from *halal* slaughter is acceptable for a Muslim (Masri, *Animal*, 145), and she adds that it is virtually impossible to be sure that any given product is *halal:*

> We [Muslims] tend to ignore the rules that govern whether meat is Halal or not, simply because we want to eat meat and we've been accustomed to eating meat .... [We need to ask ourselves] whether this meat is Halal or not:
> 1. Has your sheep been cruelly transported or handled or dragged before slaughter?
> 2. Has your sheep been starving or thirsty before slaughter?
> 3. Has your sheep been blindfolded before or during slaughter?
> 4. Has any other animal been slaughtered in the presence of your sheep?
> 5. Has there been blood of other animals in the place of slaughter?
> 6. Did your butcher sharpen his knife in the presence of your sheep?
> 7. Did the butcher slaughter your sheep slowly such that it felt pain?
> 8. Did the butcher skin or dismember any organ off the body of your sheep while there was still movement in its body after slaughter?
>   If your answer to any of the previous questions is YES, then ... this meat is not Halal according to Islamic [Shari'a]. (Montasser, "So")

Montasser's point is clear: Muslims who wish to comply with *halal* requirements will need to do some extensive research into where their food comes from, and/or choose a vegan diet.

Montasser reminds her fellow Muslims that we must be mindful of anymals— and that people will ultimately be held accountable for their choices. "Islamic concern [for] animals is so great," she notes, that "the infliction of any unnecessary and avoidable pain, even to a sparrow or any creature smaller than that, [is] a sin for which the culprit [is] answerable to God on Judgment Day" (Montasser, "Australia"). On the flip side, Montasser adds, quoting from the *hadith,* that people will be rewarded "for acts of charity to every beast alive" (Montasser, "Australia").

Montasser notes that Egypt has a long history of concern and care for anymals, reaching back to pre-Islamic times under the rule of the Pharaohs (Montasser, "Animal," 37). She recognizes that Islam has the power to enhance this ancient trend: Egypt "should have been the first country to have a law protecting animal rights," Montasser notes, "but better late than never" (Montasser, "Animal," 37). She views human and anymal suffering as "equally important" and expects Muslims fighting for human rights to "encourage those who fight for animal rights," and vice versa: "If we all encourage each other...we will definitely make this world a better place" (Montasser, "Animal," 36).

India's government-run Animal Welfare Board established a program designed to train citizens to assist in the process of protecting anymals. India's Animal Welfare Board's policy states the following:

> B. In order to increase the number of groups working in the field of animal welfare and generate awareness...the Board shall:
> 1. Make official master trainers/representatives of the Board whose duties will include monitoring all animal welfare activities and organizations working in the district, which is allotted to them and to conduct regular programmes of training and awareness generation for potential NGOs. They will also be put in charge of inspections....
> 4. To conduct training programmes of people already in the animal welfare movement in order to increase their effectiveness. (Policy)

On the basis of his dedication and years of experience protecting and defending anymals, Azam Siddiqui, a Muslim from northeastern India, was selected as a candidate for master trainer in animal welfare for the Animal Welfare Board of India (AWBI). He was then invited to attend a twenty-two-day workshop in New Delhi, where experts taught sixty carefully selected candidates a host of important facts and skills concerning anymals in India, including anymal law and wildlife crimes, rescue shelters and basic anymal aid, and disaster relief management. At the end of the training, candidates first passed a written exam, and, if successful, were assigned responsibilities in their respective districts:

- Start and run a Society for the Prevention of Cruelty to Animals (SPCAs), including shelter work, anymal rescue, fund-raising, lobbying, patrolling markets for anymal abuse, and giving legal help on behalf of anymals, as needed.
- Stop euthanasia of stray dogs by municipal authorities, and start animal birth control (ABC) programs.
- Remove *kalandars* (bear charmers) and *madaris* (monkey charmers), and rescue their exploited victims.
- Protest local anymal cruelty issues with intent to bring awareness and change.
- Inspect existing shelters and make recommendations for improvements.
- Inform local police of laws protecting anymals that must be enforced.
- Work toward shifting antiquated bullock yokes and carts to more modern and humane alternatives.
- Detect and discourage any form of local animal sacrifice.
- Network with local administrators and anymal organizations on all matters relevant to anymal care and protection.

Siddiqui has thrived as a master trainer in animal welfare. He acts as a watchdog against those who would sell or slaughter dogs for meat, educates against dog sacrifice in indigenous Indian rituals, and informs others about the exploitation of India's bulbul bird for sport fighting. He writes letters to protest the abuse and neglect of indigenous Manipuri ponies for the lucrative sport of polo, and joins let- ter-writing campaigns against the transport system, which too often results in anymals (most notably, elephants) lying maimed or dead along India's railroad tracks and roadways. He advocates for anymal rights and educates about infringe- ments of anymal laws, such as poaching or smuggling bullfrogs, elephants, endangered birds, or any other protected wildlife.

Siddiqui was an animal advocate for more than a decade before he became a master trainer in animal welfare—this ongoing interest and activity was critical to the job he ultimately earned as a master trainer in animal welfare. In the many years he has advocated for anymals, Siddiqui exposed cruelty and neglect in Indian zoos, including gross violations of housing regulations, thereby forcing zoos to relocate imprisoned anymals to more amenable quarters. He revealed entertainment injus- tices, forcing festivals to cancel bullfights in Assam and Meghalaya. He also called police to investigate the death of a homeless dog, killed by a group of adolescents. He notes that he owes much of his long-term success in anymal advocacy to net- working with a host of organizations, including People for Animals and PETA-India (with which he holds permanent membership).

Perhaps because he lives in India, Siddiqui has done considerable work on behalf of elephants. Under the guidance and supervision of Dr. Dame Daphne Sheldrick, Siddiqui acted as a surrogate mother to orphaned baby elephants, and took part in de-snaring operations at Nairobi and Tsavo East National Parks of Kenya. Siddiqui has closed down elephant races, elephant mock fights, elephant tug-of-wars, and elephant "football" at the prestigious Kaziranga Centenary Celebrations in Assam (India). He continues to educate and organize protests to stop elephant "polo," not only in India, but throughout Asia.

Siddiqui's ongoing work for anymals is an essential part of his religious life. Not only does he advocate for many different species in a host of different ways, but he also makes personal choices that are consistent with the teachings of the Qur'an, and the example set by a compassionate Prophet, with regard to anymals. He would not think of sacrificing the lives of anymals for his sustenance, even on Islamic feast days. He recognizes ritual sacrifice as an ancient tradition—and a deadly tradition— and as a practice that is not prescribed as a duty in the Qur'an. Instead of maintain- ing bloody traditions that bring about much suffering and death, he works to bring justice to Allah's many communities of beings, especially those most exploited and vulnerable:

> I raise my voice when I see injustice happening to any species. Humans can demonstrate, shout, and make others understand mistreatment meted against them, but animals unfortunately cannot. It is this weakness of the

animals that perhaps has allowed me to focus more on animal rights than human rights. (Siddiqui)

Summary

Islamic religious traditions hold much of what is recorded in Jewish and Christian scriptures as sacred. Islamic sacred writings reveal all of nature—all anymals—as created and tended by Allah, and destined to be drawn back to the divine. Sacred writings reveal a compassionate Creator; Muhammad models kindness; as vice-regents, Muslims are expected to be merciful and compassionate. In Islamic religious traditions, the role of Muslims is one of submission and service to Allah—of tending creation on behalf of the Creator. Each living being is an individual in the Islamic worldview, a devoted servant of Allah, living in her or his separate yet similar community. While we have no rights over other creatures, anymals are granted rights under Islamic law, such as freedom from cruelty and protection during times of war.

Conclusion

Across traditions and back to the beginning of recorded history, religious traditions around the world have established, recorded, and presented preferred human behaviors, including rightful relations with Earth and anymals. This book has examined anymal-friendly teachings in a host of indigenous traditions and seven major religions (Hindu, Buddhist, Confucian, Daoist, Jewish, Christian, and Islamic). (I refer specifically to these religions and their teachings and texts in this conclusion, since these are the religions discussed in the text.) By way of a conclusion, what might be said about religions, human morality, and nonhumans?

Review

Exploring sacred teachings from around the world demonstrates that nature, including anymals, is sacred, that anymals are central to our spiritual landscape, and that we owe them respect, justice, and compassion. Religious texts remind us that we share a fundamental kinship with tabby cats, rose-ringed parakeets, and slender pygmy swordtails, and that anymals are understood to be remarkable and marvelous—superior to humans in many ways—in the world's religious traditions. Sacred literature indicates that nonhumans and humans share the same fate after death; faiths that have a Creator teach human beings that the divine is personally invested in the life of every anymal, from the large flightless common rhea to each critically endangered Jenkin's shrew, from a factory-farmed chicken to each bovine trucked to slaughter. Religious exemplars remind us that all species have personality and intellect—other creatures, whether insects, fish, reptiles, mammals, or birds, can offer much-needed spiritual wisdom for the betterment of humanity. Religions teach of a deep and fundamental unity on planet Earth. Interestingly, consistent with Darwin, the world's dominant religions teach people that there is much more continuity than separation across species.

This fresh understanding of human-anymal relations must be viewed in light of the focus and limitations of this book, as stated in the introduction:

- This book focuses on aspects of religious traditions that protect and value any-mals because
  - religions are, overall, *radically* friendly toward anymals;
  - people tend to be ignorant of these prevalent teachings; and
  - our current economic choices (bolstered by our collective spiritual ignorance) perpetuate anymal industries that profit from untold misery and billions of premature deaths.
- This book focuses on *core* religious teachings in each of the world's largest reli-gious traditions. Although there are tremendous differences in the particular expressions of any one branch within each religion, core teachings tend to remain central to all branches of a given religion—each branch generally shares the same core texts, teachings, saints, and/or founders. For example, love is a core value among the many Christian traditions, *ahimsa* is central to each Hindu tradition, *zakat* is obligatory in all Muslim traditions, and the list goes on.
- In light of religious diversity down through the ages and across continents, almost any behavior or belief might be defended or sanctioned if one leans on an isolated phrase, sentence, or story from sacred texts, or an obscure religious document. Therefore, when assessing the importance of religious assertions, it is important to determine whether or not the basis for a given assertion is found in primary or secondary texts, whether the teachings are credited to an individual who carries little or much weight within the religious tradition, and whether or not the assertion is an anomaly in a tradition that overwhelmingly supports an opposing point of view. It is also important to scrutinize transla-tions when assessing critical passages. I have employed all of these processes in writing this book.
- Most people are raised with the belief that anymal exploitation is religiously sanctioned, and they will readily defend this point of view. Consequently, argu-ments in favor of anymal exploitation—including religious arguments—are easy to come by. On closer examination, most of these arguments do not defend any-mal exploitation in general; they merely defend particular habits and practices, most often dietary habits and farming practices. People who identify with a given religious tradition often use sacred writings to defend personal habits, but such arguments tend to be both shallow and specific, *contradicting* core and founda-tional teachings. Those who pose such arguments, when questioned, often agree readily that their religion does not teach or tolerate cruel exploitation, particu-larly when such cruel exploitation is entirely unnecessary.
- Those who defend animal exploitation from a religious point of view usually lack information in three critical areas:
  - First, they often have no idea what goes on in breeding facilities, on factory farms, in feedlots, on transport trucks, in slaughterhouses, and so on.
  - Second, they lack an understanding of—have usually not even heard about—speciesism, and therefore have no idea how our treatment of anymals is

    connected with social justice issues more broadly, such as racism, sexism, poverty, and world hunger.

- Third, they have often neglected to study sacred teachings or the lives of spiritual exemplars, and even if they have engaged in this important endeavor, they usually have not recognized the implications of religious ideals with regard to anymals or the effect of these teachings on such simple choices as what we eat.

- Religious *ideals* are the focus of this book. *This book makes no claim about actual practices or common religious understandings.* Anymal exploiters may or may not be religious, and those who are religious are likely to lack information in three critical areas just mentioned. Perhaps most fundamentally, religious people tend to be unaware that chewing on a chicken's body purchased at a grocery store contradicts the core religious ideals of every major religious tradition. Still other religious people do not take their religious commitment seriously and therefore do not care one way or the other about anymal suffering and slaughter. *This book is about what religions teach, not about what religious people believe or how they live.* There is often shamefully little correlation between the two.

Denial, Welfare, and Liberation

In a weekly journal (*Young India*), Gandhi noted, "The soul of religions is one, but encased in a multitude of forms" (Roberts, xiv). Indeed, although the world's religious traditions differ in many critical ways, there is much of commonality in core moral teachings with regard to nature generally and anymals specifically. Religiously sanctioned morals around the world encourage a gentle, benevolent, service-oriented relationship with anymals: "All the major religions have taught compassionate and humane treatment of animals" (Masri, *Animal*, 4). The sages who composed and compiled moral codes that are now encased in the world's major religions, "preached a spirituality of empathy and compassion" that includes all living beings, and the earth itself (Armstrong, xiv).

    Each of the world's dominant religious traditions agree that what we choose to *do* is spiritually critical (Armstrong, xiii); religions teach us who we should *be* (Armstrong, xii). Great ascetics like Milarepa, prophets such as Muhammad, and holy people like St. Godric demonstrate that those who take their religion seriously also take anymal suffering seriously. Consequently, religious adepts tend to extend their compassion beyond their species. Perhaps more important, when anymal- and earth-friendly teachings are taken seriously, sacred traditions favor (or overtly require) a plant-based diet. In short, religious traditions understand that compassion, a core religious value, requires religious adherents to modify their behavior accordingly, and at a minimum, this means that human beings must avoid purchasing or consuming anymal products from contemporary anymal industries.

Rightful relations between humans and anymals are spiritually significant in *every* major religion. *Core* religious teachings from around the world require humans to protect and respect all that is natural, to show compassion for all who are sentient, and in contemporary times, to rethink our relations with anymals—especially what we eat.

When religious adherents understand contemporary anymal industries and the values and morals that are central to sacred texts, they are faced with critical, life-defining decisions. I have identified three possible reactions:

- *Denial:* Some people simply reaffirm the status quo; they believe—in spite of overwhelming evidence to the contrary—that all is well in feedlots and slaughterhouses, chicken sheds and farrowing crates, laboratories, circuses, and zoos, and that contemporary anymal industry practices are therefore religiously acceptable.
- *Welfarist:* Others acknowledge problems in contemporary anymal experimentation and the food industries but insist that the *idea* of anymal exploitation is not *itself* irreligious. Welfarists understand that current anymal industry practices are religiously unacceptable, and therefore favor reforms such as anesthesia before vivisection, larger gestation crates, and better methods of stunning before slaughter. In order to remain consistent with their religious convictions, welfarists must not continue to support anymal industries (such as factory farms) with their consumer dollars while waiting—or ideally advocating and lobbying—for reforms.
- *Liberationist (or abolitionist):* Still others come to understand that exploiting anymals is *inherently* irreligious when it is not essential for our survival; anymals do not exist to satisfy *our* desires and pleasures. Liberationists do not accept larger gestation crates because crates of any kind are oppressive and exploitative, and are therefore inconsistent with compassionate action. They do not accept slaughter, even with improved stunning methods, because there is no need for slaughterhouses or factory farms—we can easily feed ourselves without slaughtering anymals—and because slaughtering without necessity lacks compassion and reverence for life. Even if we raise and slaughter anymals with a minimum of pain and misery, farmed anymals are killed when they are mere adolescents— lives nipped in the bud to satisfy habitual tastes and preferences. Such practices also demonstrate a lack of reverence for human life and are contrary to social justice: We can feed more of the world's many hungry people if we stop producing anymal products. Similarly, vivisection is a selfish exploitation of other creatures—and nonhumans are not here to live and die on behalf of our hopes. Anymal liberationists avoid consuming anymal products, and often actively lobby to close down exploitative anymal industries and to bring an end to human-anymal relationships that fail to honor each anymal's physical and emotional health and well-being.

Denial is not a mature, responsible, or even reasonable option, which leaves two other possibilities. Do the religious texts and exemplars support anymal welfare or anymal liberation? What do religions teach us to *be* with regard to anymals?

Rightful Relations

A concise formal argument, using deductive logic, rooted in three well-established premises, can help us to answer these questions about rightful relations between human beings and anymals.

> *Premise 1*: The world's dominant religious traditions teach human beings to avoid causing harm to anymals.
> *Premise 2*: Contemporary industries that exploit anymals—including food, clothing, pharmaceutical, and/or entertainment industries—harm anymals.
> *Premise 3*: Supporting industries that exploit anymals (most obviously by purchasing their products) perpetuates these industries and their harm to anymals.
> *Conclusion*: The world's dominant religious traditions indicate that human beings should avoid supporting industries that harm anymals, including food, clothing, pharmaceutical, and/or entertainment industries.

It is instructive to consider an additional deductive argument rooted in two well-established premises:

> *Premise 1*: The world's dominant religious traditions teach people to assist and defend anymals who are suffering.
> *Premise 2*: Anymals suffer when they are exploited in laboratories and the entertainment, food, or clothing industries.
> *Conclusion*: The world's dominant religious traditions teach people to assist and defend anymals when they are exploited in laboratories, entertainment, food, and clothing industries.

If these premises are correct—and they are supported by abundant evidence—the world's dominant religions teach adherents

- *to avoid purchasing products from industries that exploit anymals*, and
- *to assist and defend anymals who are exploited* in laboratories and the entertainment, food, and clothing industries.

Such industries include, but are not limited to, those that overtly sell or use products that include chicken's reproductive eggs, cow's nursing milk, or anymal flesh or hides (fur and leather), as well as industries that engage in or are linked with anymal experimentation of any kind, and entertainment industries such as zoos, circuses, and aquariums.

We have our answer: *The world's great religions provide a moral foundation for anymal liberation.* Those who stand within one of the world's largest religious traditions, if they are sincere in their religious commitment, must not buy flesh, nursing milk products, or hen's reproductive eggs in any form, or support *any* industry that profits at the expense of anymals, including zoos, circuses, aquariums, horse and dog racing, rodeos, and movies. Furthermore, those who stand within one of the world's largest religious traditions must *assist and defend* anymals who are exploited in any of these industries, as well as anymals who are exploited to gather or disseminate information, whether for medicine, biology, pharmaceuticals, veterinary science, pathology, psychology, sociology, anymal behavior, or weaponry, to name just a few. These requirements are not particularly stringent when we realize that these products and activities not only harm anymals, but also have been proven to harm human health and prevent us from gathering more pertinent information from willing and needy human subjects (for example, see *A Critical Look at Animal Experimentation*, http://www.mrmc-med.org/Critical_Look.pdf).

At a minimum, it is clear that human beings who claim a religious tradition that is rooted in compassion and/or respect for the natural world must adopt a plant-based diet. We might begin by removing certain products (for example, dairy products) at certain times (maybe two or three days a week). This allows us to adapt favorite recipes and to learn new ways of cooking. We can then progress, quickly reaching a completely vegan diet.

Such fundamental changes in diet may initially seem prohibitive, until we realize that not a single meal need be skipped—there is no weakness or hunger involved. We may eat delicious and nutritious foods—or junk food—to our heart's content at any time of day or night. Then we come to understand that *these changes do not require much of us, and a vegan diet is central to any sincere religious expression because either we make choices that cause tremendous suffering and the endless slaughter of adolescent farmed anymals or we do not.*

Corporate Capitalism, Profits, and Power

Those who are guided by core religious commitments in one of the world's most popular religions are rightly anymal liberationists. Why, then, do most religious people denounce anymal liberationists, complaining that these courageous activists break laws—even destroy property? Why do so many Christians and Buddhists assume that such activists ought to be harshly punished and imprisoned for long periods of time, as if they were dangerous terrorists?

Large industries now have tremendous power and influence over democratic political and legal systems. Consequently, contemporary Western laws tend to support industry (profits) over life. In contrast, most human beings (whether religious or not) recognize that life is more important than profits—that the lives of many trump the personal profits of a few (no matter how great those profits might be). Nonetheless, our taxes and legal system currently support large industries over social justice activists—especially earth and anymal activists.

Anymal liberationists who release fox or chinchillas from fur farms, free veal calves from chains in abysmal crates, destroy transport trucks that haul terrified turkeys and sheep to their premature deaths, burn slaughterhouses that dismember pigs and chickens, or destroy computers in research facilities are not dangerous terrorists. Anymal liberationists simply believe that life is precious, and that an industry designed to manipulate and destroy life for the sake of profits is ethically and spiritually unacceptable. They do not target the lives of random citizens—or the lives of *any* citizens. Anymal liberationists do not target life—they target industries (and profits) that flourish at the expense of life—and they attempt to rescue the exploited. Terrorists kill randomly; anymal liberationists have never killed anyone. Anymal liberationists exemplify what it is to live into the core teachings of every major religion concerning rightful relations between human beings and anymals.

On reflection, most of us recognize that we would rather protect citizens than corporations—human rights rather than corporate capitalism. On reflection, most of us recognize that anymal advocates who defend life against exploitative industries hold the high moral ground—their compassionate motivation and social justice actions are supported by core teachings in every major religion. Anymal liberationists demonstrate self-sacrificing service on behalf of the exploited. They risk long-term imprisonment on behalf of the defenseless and downtrodden, the maimed and condemned. Those who take core religious teachings seriously will respect anymal liberationists because these dedicated activists treasure life above property and profits, and risk their freedom on behalf of those who cannot help themselves. Anymal liberationists exemplify religious commitment in action, most notably compassionate, self-sacrificing service to those who are most in need.

Human Suffering/Anymal Suffering

If one focuses on foundational religious texts and core teachings from any of the world's major religions, it is much easier to defend anymal liberation than it is to defend anymal exploitation. Moreover, it is easier to champion anymal liberation than to defend other oft-claimed religious ideals, such as human rights or equality between the sexes. This is understandable when we realize that *anymals tend to be extremely vulnerable when compared with human beings.* Children, women, and minorities are vulnerable, but even children can (and might) destroy a healthy chicken, while it is rather preposterous to imagine a chicken destroying a healthy child.

Laws in industrialized nations tend to protect profits over life. Just a glimpse of anymals in our food industries (please see the appendix) can help readers to understand why religious teachings focus on respect for and protection of anymals. A hen is fated, from the day she hatches, to a pubescent death on a dismemberment belt. Calves are purposefully kept anemic and perpetually restrained to create veal. Turkeys are genetically manipulated to be too large to walk or breed naturally. Female anymals are perpetually impregnated, and their young taken from them, until they are "spent" and trucked to slaughter. Routine treatment of anymals through industrialized agriculture is, quite frankly, a moral and religious outrage.

Humans who are in positions of power make the rules, and therefore their interests almost always come first—no matter what the cost to anymals and less powerful human beings.

Certain humans suffer lamentably at the hands of powerful human beings, and billions of cattle, chickens, turkeys, and pigs suffer and die from manipulated birth to pubescent death because of decisions made by these same powerful human beings. Numbers and comparisons are often held to be irrelevant with regard to suffering and premature death—all suffering and premature death are lamentable. But in the case of anymals, the numbers and extent of suffering and premature death are so extreme as to require mention. For example, the combined total of gypsies, Jews, and homosexuals killed in Auschwitz *does not even approach* numbers killed *just* in the food industry, in *just* one day, *just* in the United States. The number of individuals enslaved and slaughtered on factory farms every year exponentially surpasses—by trillions—any form of exploitation of human beings anywhere, at any time: "According to recently published data from the U.S. Department of Agriculture and several other official sources, 59 billion animals died to feed Americans in 2009" ("59"). American meat eaters were responsible for about 198 deaths per person in 2009, which accumulates to about 15,000 animals in the course of one individual's lifetime ("59").

Cruelly exploiting and slaughtering human beings is widely recognized as spiritually problematic, but the veal industry is not, battery cages are not, *foie gras* and the use of farrowing crates are not, debeaking and slaughter lines are not. How can this be? Anymal suffering is extreme on factory farms, massive numbers of premature deaths are the expected end, and both are sanctioned not only by the government but also by the masses—including those who affiliate with a particular religious tradition and take their religious commitments seriously. The reason for this cruelty and indifference is obvious: With human beings creating the rules, anymals are the last to be noticed and the most likely to be discarded or exploited. Consequently, wherever humanity suffers, anymals suffer yet more.

It is a dangerous business to compare sufferings, and generally an unproductive enterprise. Yet compare we must, because *most people assume that anymal suffering is somehow lesser—or of less importance—than the suffering of human beings.* Why would human suffering be of greater moral or spiritual importance than anymal suffering? Not one of the world's largest religious traditions teaches that anymals are of lesser importance, or that their suffering might be overlooked while we remedy problems that are more central to human needs and wants. On the contrary—religious traditions hold human beings accountable for their actions with regard to anymals. Nonetheless, the assumption that it is right for humanity to focus social justice energy first and foremost on human beings persists in at least some religious communities. As a result, people turn a blind eye to factory farming and other horrendously cruel, life-destroying industries, and even continue to support these industries with their consumer dollars.

On reflection, it is clear why the world's great religions specifically and clearly protect anymals from cruelty at the hands of humanity—we are more powerful, and human beings have demonstrated across time that we are likely to exploit and abuse anymals for our purposes. Anymals *depend on* special religious protections to protect them against an often self-absorbed humanity. Indeed, even in light of this strong collection of core religious teachings on behalf of anymals, they remain the most cruelly abused and widely exploited individuals throughout the industrialized world, and beyond.

Diet and the Larger Picture

That said, *protecting anymals protects human beings:* There are four other critical reasons that the world's largest religions rightly pay particular attention to anymals— and particular attention to what we eat. Aside from respect for life and compassion for anymals, we ought to choose a vegan diet for the sake of the environment, to alleviate world hunger, to protect laborers, and on behalf of our own health. *The consequences of our dietary choices are monumental.*

The world's most celebrated religions teach people that the world around us, our environment, is sacred. A diet rooted in anymal products is exponentially more harmful to the earth than is a plant-based diet (see "Environmental Degradation" in the appendix, and/or read the United Nations report *Livestock's Long Shadow* [Steinfield, et al., 267]). Seventy percent more land must be cultivated in order to raise anymals for food than would be necessary for a vegan diet. This means that 70 percent more land is taken away from natural ecosystems to produce flesh, nursing milk, and bird's reproductive eggs for consumption, and this land that is necessary for a diet rich in anymal products will be sprayed with pesticides and earth-damaging fertilizers. These additional crops—70 percent more—also need to be irrigated, using exponentially more water. Anymals exploited by food industries also drink millions of gallons of water and drop millions of tons of manure. Finally, raising animals for flesh contributes significantly to carbon dioxide, nitrous oxides, chlorofluorocarbons, and methane—global climate change. The Food and Agriculture Organization of the United Nations noted "the very substantial contribution of animal agriculture to climate change and air pollution, to land, soil, and water degradation, and to the reduction of biodiversity" (Steinfield, et al. iii).

If one cares about the earth—if one respects nature—it is better to consume vegetables, fruits, nuts, and grains. If you care about the planet and wish to adopt an earth-friendly lifestyle, it is advisable to focus only secondarily on the car that you drive, or recycling, or turning off lights and turning down heat, and *primarily* on what you buy at the grocery store. *What we eat has a much greater impact on the environment than what we drive or any of these other factors.*

Another critical religious motivation for reconsidering diet is concern for *human suffering*—out of compassion—in light of poverty, malnutrition, and starvation. Each day, 18,000 children die "from hunger and related causes" (L. Brown, 46). Not only do we damage the environment with our choice of cheese and cutlets—burdening future populations with pollutants, dead zones, and global climate change—but we also feed tons of precious grains to hundreds of thousands of cattle, pigs, chickens, and turkeys *while fellow human beings go without food.* Food energy is wasted when we cycle grains through anymals. Rather than breed hungry cattle and chickens to consume grains, we should *stop breeding anymals* and feed precious grains to those who are already starving. *If we did not breed and consume anymals, billions of tons of grains could be redirected to feed hungry human beings, alleviating and/ or preventing starvation worldwide.*

At the end of Gail Eisnitz's book *Slaughterhouse*, she exposes unjust and cruel exploitation of laborers in anymal agriculture industries. Those working in slaughterhouses, for example, are often underpaid and overworked, lack insurance, and are required to use dangerous equipment without adequate training. Turnover and rates of injury for jobs in anymal industries are among the highest in the United States. Slaughterhouse employees are almost always poor, they are often immigrants, and they are inevitably viewed by their employers as expendable. Moreover, *if we would not like to kill pigs, hens, or cattle all day long, then we should not make food choices that require others to do so.* Our dietary choices determine where others work. Will our poorest laborers work in fields of green or in buildings of blood? Fieldwork is difficult, but I worked in the fields as a child, and I am very glad that I never worked in a slaughterhouse.

Health provides an important, final reason to adopt a plant-based diet. Westerners are choking their arteries, fattening themselves up, and fostering cancers by consuming anymal products. How many people who live on bean salad and vegetable soup are obese? How often do those with a steady diet of vegetables and rice suffer from colon cancer? How many people living on broccoli and tofu suffer heart attacks in their middle years? Obesity, heart disease, and cancers are just three common health problems that are linked with the consumption of anymal products. To look after both our spiritual and physical health, we must adopt a vegan diet.

Given these five compelling reasons to reconsider dietary choice—anymal suffering and premature death, environmental degradation, world hunger, labor injustices, and our own health—it is not surprising that the world's most commonly celebrated religions require and/or encourage a diet of greens, grains, fruits, and legumes, while simultaneously forbidding and/or discouraging the slaughter of anymals and the consumption of anymal products.

The Vitality of the World's Great Religions

Religious communities have the power to bring anymal industries to their knees. If religious adherents collectively change what they buy to fill their cupboards and closets, cabinets and refrigerators, and which forms of entertainment they support with their dollars—or tolerate with their silence—anymal exploitation as we know it will grind to a halt. If religious adherents change their consumer habits, anymal exploitation will cease to be profitable, and anymal mega-industries will rapidly decline and disappear. In a capitalist world of supply and demand, *we* decide which products will be offered in supermarkets, pharmacies, and entertainment centers.

What strikes me about these necessary changes—changes that would drive anymal exploiters out of business—is how paltry they are. Perhaps these changes seem cumbersome when one ponders "giving up" cheese, for example, but vegans need not simply "give up" foods like starving ascetics. Vegans *replace* cheese with other tasty foods, or with similar plant-based foods (such as Daiya cheese). We need not go without food even for one hour. Core anymal-friendly teachings require only that human beings make life-affirming choices—and they do *require* that our choices be life-affirming.

How have factory farming and anymal experimentation come to exist—even flourish—among a religious humanity whose core religious teachings center on compassion and respect for the natural world? Religious people and religious institutions have turned a blind eye, a deaf ear, and a numb heart to egregious problems facing anymals on factory farms and in research laboratories. When fighting racism in America, Martin Luther King, Jr., commented, "In the midst of blatant injustices..., I have watched...churchmen stand on the sideline and mouth pious irrelevancies and sanctimonious trivialities" (M. King, 408). Religious leaders "have been more cautious than courageous and have remained silent behind the anesthetizing security of stained-glass windows" (M. King, 408). Organized religion too often extends a "weak and ineffectual voice with an uncertain sound. So often it is an arch-defender of the status quo" (M. King, 409).

What does it mean when core religious teachings do not determine how we live? Of what moral relevance are contemporary religious organizations if they have nothing to say about the most egregious sufferings ever—both in quality and quantity? How can we call ourselves Buddhists, Native Americans, or Muslims if we fail to rebel against factory farming and anymal experimentation? Are religious traditions too "inextricably bound to the status quo" to save anymals from egregious exploitation (M. King, 409)?

Our complicity is not the fault of religious teachings, but of humanity: "Scriptures of all religions contain expostulations on all kinds of cruelty to animals, but they have ceased to be taken seriously—either by theologians or the public" (Masri, *Animal*, 3–4). As individuals, we must now call religious leaders and religious institutions to live up to the most fundamental moral teachings of our religious traditions. We must demand that our religious leaders speak out against anymal exploitation in laboratories and on factory farms. If we stand within one of the world's great religions, *and if we have integrity in our religious commitments*, we can and must reject anymal exploitation in all of its insidious forms. *What person who is firmly committed to one of the world's largest religion traditions can reasonably suggest that it is morally or spiritually irrelevant whether or not their purchases cause more or less suffering and premature death?* Indigenous peoples, Hindus, Buddhists, Daoists, Confucians, Jews, Christians, and Muslims are *obligated* to either change basic habits of consumption or admit that they don't care about the most fundamental teachings of their religion—that they aren't religious after all.

Islamic theologian Al-Hafiz Basheer Ahmad Masri writes, "Let us hope a day will dawn when the great religious teachings may at last begin to bear fruit; when we shall see the start of a new era when [humanity] accords to animals the respect and status they have long deserved and for so long have been denied" (Masri, *Animal*, 3–4). This change depends on us—on those who belong to mosques and churches, temples and shrines. Whatever we may *say* about compassion, service to the needy, respect for the natural world, humility, and other core religious commitments, what we *do* speaks unerringly. What we buy in local markets and grocery stores has either caused tremendous suffering and exploitation or it has not. What we serve for lunch is either linked with unnecessary suffering and pubescent death or it is not. Our choice of clothing, food, and entertainment either complies with core religious teachings or it does not.

If the world's religions are correct, our decisions with regard to anymals affect our relations with the Ultimate (however it might be envisioned), and our treatment of anymals is part of what determines our fate beyond the grave. As religious beings, we cannot use religious practices—prayers and rituals—to gloss over the damage we cause. Religious convictions "must translate into genuine caring behavior for other living beings.... Saying a prayer before you kill an animal is no more acceptable than saying a prayer before you rape" (Kheel, 111). If you stand within one of the world's many indigenous traditions, or if you are Hindu, Buddhist, Confucian, Daoist, Jewish, Christian, or Muslim, then what you eat and what you wear—whether or not you support anymal exploitation—*is critically religiously important.*

Core teachings in the world's great religions have the power to expand justice and ethics to end massive, horrific anymal exploitation. It is time for those who claim one of the world's largest religions to honor core religious teachings that delineate our rightful relations with anymals. Religious institutions, and people of faith who are serious about their religious affiliation, must reject, denounce, and work to end extant, common egregious anymal exploitation.

Complying with this religious requirement need not be difficult: We need not be without invigorating entertainment, delicious foods, fashionable and warm clothing, or effective pharmaceuticals. In fact, this shift in consumption habits will greatly improve to our health and longevity, our natural environment, and our spiritual lives. As religious beings, we are called to recognize that the most important benefits of this shift in our consumer habits are not those we gain for ourselves: nonetheless this shift ought to be undertaken as a commitment to core religious teachings, to protect anymals from painful, deadly, unjust exploitation.

In our day-to-day lives, we too often act without thinking, behave without conviction, and live without thoughtful intent. Our religious lives—including those of our spiritual leaders—too often take a back seat to selfish desires, convention, habit, and convenience. Given that the world's religions align with anymal liberation, it is time for those who have committed to a particular religion to put their personal religious convictions into practice: The vitality of a particular religion can be assessed by the way adherents treat anymals—by what we eat and wear.

It should not surprise us that the world's dominant religious traditions speak boldly and decisively against selfish, life-destroying exploitation of anymals. In fact, would it not be extremely disappointing to discover, at the end of our extensive study, of anymals and world religions that the egregious suffering and perpetual slaughter of industrial anymal agriculture, that the frivolous cruelties of the clothing industry, and the cruel exploitation of anymal experimentation *align* with religious teachings? Would it not be much more troubling to discover that the world's great religions *fail* to protect anymals from the overwhelming and often unjust power of humanity?

Personally, my faith in religions has been affirmed in the course of this study, and I hope that those who stand behind the world's great religions will begin to commit to core religious teachings that require human beings to protect and assist anymals. The world's great religions have tremendous potential to transform individuals and societies, and to fight injustice and alleviate suffering, but religions are ultimately only as powerful as the people they inspire.

APPENDIX: FACTORY FARMING AND FISHING

Anymal Agriculture

While practices in any of today's anymal industries (laboratories, fur farms, factory farming and fishing, circuses, zoos, and aquariums) would likely horrify those of us who are unaccustomed to their methods, this appendix explores just one area of production—food industries. The point of this appendix is to provide just one clear example of why the choices we make as consumers are a critical moral and spiritual matter. (If you have not viewed undercover footage of factory farms from websites such as those listed in the introduction, please do so now.)

Many people believe that anymals are generally well cared for in animal industries, that laws protect sentient beings, and that it is in a rancher's or farmer's best interest to provide good care to those whom they exploit. Furthermore, many people believe that consuming dairy products and eggs is preferable to eating flesh. All of these assumptions are incorrect. This appendix focuses on farmed anymals and fishing, with special attention to "laying" hens and "dairy" cows.

No federal laws regulate the treatment of anymals who are raised for flesh, eggs, or dairy products, and almost all customary anymal agriculture practices, no matter how painful, are exempt from extant animal cruelty statutes. The most basic interests of anymals take a back seat to the economic interests of human beings. Anymals are not individuals on factory farms; they are units of production—"live-stock." The cost of veterinary care, the cost of housing, and the cost of feed are all weighed against profits; as with any other industry, profits are the guiding principle.

With the advent of anymal activism, it has become almost impossible to gain access to slaughterhouses or factory farms; as a result, it is increasingly easy to find undercover footage on websites, in libraries, and on DVDs (sold at cost, sometimes even given away) by anymal advocacy organizations. At the end of this appendix, I include a handful of websites that offer undercover footage from factory farms.

I strongly encourage readers to view some of this undercover footage—a picture speaks a thousand words. Many of us have absolutely no idea what factory farming entails.

Cattle

Every year, thirty-five million cattle are destroyed for beef, nine million cows are exploited for milk (and soon destroyed), and one million calves are destroyed for veal.

"Dairy" Cattle and the Veal Industry

Cows, like humans and other mammals, lactate only after they have given birth. In order to produce milk, cows must be repeatedly, forcibly, artificially impregnated. Each time they are impregnated, cows carry their young for ten months, but their calves are stolen shortly after birth (though they try desperately to defend and protect their young). Cows, like most mammals, have a strong mothering instinct, but how can they protect newborns against exploitative human oppressors? They invariably lose their babies, and then bawl for days.

The motherless calves are then sold for veal: The veal industry exists because people buy yogurt and ice cream, cheese and milk. The veal industry was created to take advantage of an abundant supply of calves who are merely by-products of the dairy industry. "Dairy" calves are either killed shortly after birth, and sold as "bob" veal for low-quality dishes (like frozen TV dinners), or they are chained by the neck in a two-by-five-foot wooden crate, where they are unable to turn, and where they can neither stretch nor lie down comfortably. While we drink their mother's milk, these miserable little beings are given a milk substitute that is deficient in iron and fiber. This creates an anemic, light-colored flesh that is prized by those who purchase veal.

These unfortunate calves are usually slaughtered when they are four months old. The veal industry confines and kills one million calves every year.

Life is no better for calves who are bred to produce dairy products. "Dairy" calves' tails are "docked" to prevent swishing around those profitable udders and the expensive equipment. But tails are a cow's best defense against annoying insects, swishing into areas cattle can't otherwise reach. Nonetheless, their tails are docked. "Bladed clamps" are secured to a one-month-old calf's tail for docking; the blades cut through flesh, vertebrae, and tendons. These calves are also "disbudded"—the buds from which their horns would normally grow are seared from their skulls. An undercover investigator (Mercy for Animals) who witnessed this procedure noted that the calves were muzzled with cable and their heads were tied to steel fencing. Once the calves were immobilized, "workers used a smoking iron to burn out their nascent horns, searing through flesh and bone and leaving behind molten, bloody cavities" ("Dairy's," 11). Despite their bound mouths, the calves bellowed, "wheezed, frothed and strained" ("Dairy's," 11).

When they are old enough to be impregnated, to bear young (only to have both their calf and their milk stolen), they endure mechanized milking for ten out of twelve months per year (including seven months of their nine-month pregnancies). To be milked, cows are herded into a milking parlor with the help of electrified gates, which presumably keep the herd moving, but which only shock the cattle who are at the back of the herd. These unfortunate cows are perpetually shocked when they become trapped behind other cattle in clogged passageways.

Once in the parlor (a name that elicits images of soft chairs, tea, and books), a cow is locked into place via metal bars on each side of her neck. Milking machines are roughly and hurriedly attached to the cow's teats, and she stands there while her nursing milk, which she generates to feed her calf, is extracted. This process is repeated two or three times each day.

Genetic manipulation and dietary controls cause extraordinary and unnatural milk output—fifty pounds of milk per day. Cows naturally produce just over two tons of milk per year, but recombinant bovine growth hormone (rBGH) and recombinant bovine somatotropin (rBST)—synthetic human-created hormones— have increased milk flow so that cows now provide as much as thirty tons of milk annually, enough for *ten* calves. In this unhealthy and unhappy existence, one in five factory-farmed "dairy" cows secretes pus from her udders (which invariably mixes with her milk).

Most cows who are shipped out from the dairy industry are pregnant when they are slaughtered. Cows are so exhausted by the dairy process that they are "spent" and sent to slaughter after just four or five years of repeated impregnation, birth, hormone doses, and machine milking. (Those few cows who find their way to sanctuaries can live upward of twenty years.) "Dairy" cattle are much older than cattle who are slaughtered to produce beef, so their flesh is considered low quality, and is used for soup, burgers, or processed foods.

Many people become vegetarians to avoid supporting cruelty and premature death, but purchasing dairy products causes the slaughter of cattle just as surely as does eating a hamburger: When we buy the nursing milk of mother cows in our local supermarkets, we support the oppression and premature death of both cows and their calves. It is not financially feasible for dairy farms to keep millions of cattle—who are too young to produce milk, who are males, or who can no longer continue to produce extraordinary quantities of nursing milk. People who avoid flesh for moral reasons must remember that "dairy" cows are invasively impregnated, their young are stolen, and for months afterward their nursing milk is mined—again and again—because people buy dairy products. While most calves born into the dairy industry live a short but horrific life, mother cows endure exploitation year after year. People who are willing to adapt their diet to avoid supporting extreme cruelty and premature death must not shift to a vegetarian diet that increases consumption of dairy products. To reduce extreme suffering and premature death, we must cut back on *all* anymal products.

Dairy farmers control, manipulate, and capitalize on a cow's reproductive abilities—her nursing milk and her calf—and finally her flesh. To add insult to injury, the dairy industry has convinced consumers that cows' nursing milk is essential for good health. If milk is essential to human health, how have people in China lived so long without dairy products—and with much lower incidences of osteoporosis?

Slaughter

Four corporations slaughter more than 80 percent of the thirty-five million cattle who are killed annually in the United States. A standard slaughterhouse kills 250 cattle *every hour*, a rate at which it is impossible for workers to assure a quick or relatively painless death. In any event, killing cattle all day at high speeds does not create an attitude of caring or compassion. Hidden videos testify to the many anymals who are hoisted onto the slaughter dis-assembly line kicking, struggling, and fully conscious. An article in the *Washington Post* (April 2001) reported the experiences of one slaughterhouse employee and his friend Moreno:

> The cattle were supposed to be dead before they got to Moreno. But too often they weren't.
> "They blink. They make noises," he said softly. "The head moves, the eyes are wide and looking around." Still Moreno would cut. On bad days, he says, dozens of animals reached his station clearly alive and conscious. Some would survive as far as the tail cutter, the belly ripper, the hide puller. "They die," said Moreno, "piece by piece." (quoted in "Factory Beef")

Legislation offers only minimal protection for anymals sent to slaughter. Mammals are supposed to be "stunned" (rendered unconscious) before they are killed (Humane Slaughter Act, 1958), but slaughter (like most contemporary businesses) is shaped and driven by economic factors: In the slaughterhouse, the quicker each anymal is killed, the higher the profit margin. Time is money. Workers must be paid for their time, and while one anymal's body is on the dismemberment line, no other body can be processed. Consequently, economics encourages speed, which works against effective stunning. Not surprisingly, a USDA survey concluded that stunning was either "unacceptable" or a "serious problem" in 36 percent of sheep and pig slaughterhouses and 64 percent of cattle slaughterhouses.

There are several slaughterhouse stunning methods: captive bolt pistol (cattle, most calves, and some sheep); electric stunner (pigs, most sheep, and some calves); and, though not required—and not adequate to render the victims unconscious— an electrified water basin for birds. Although 90 percent of those killed in U.S. slaughterhouses are birds (chickens, turkeys, ducks), poultry are exempt from the Humane Slaughter Act, and there are no federal humane regulations for poultry slaughter.

Electric Stunner

When an anymal enters the slaughterhouse, a worker clamps the electric stunner (imagine earphones on an insulated handle) onto the victim's head, and then triggers an electric shock. As with all high-speed assembly-line operations, human and mechanical errors are common, and many pigs, calves, and sheep emerge conscious and fully sentient.

Making matters worse, there is currently no way to determine exactly how much electricity is required to properly stun a large pig or sheep versus a small pig or sheep—or any size in between. Insufficient current will paralyze the victim but not prevent sensation. Too much current will result in "blown loins": bruising caused by capillaries that have burst. Blown loins reduce the value of flesh, so managers often lower the electric current, which means that many anymals who are improperly stunned—especially larger anymals—go to slaughter fully conscious and sentient, able to witness and feel everything that happens to them along the assembly line until, at some point, they perish.

Captive Bolt Pistol

A captive bolt pistol is placed against a cow's or calf's forehead, and then fired, driving a rod through the skull and into the brain. If done properly, the anymal will immediately lose consciousness. However, poor aim, a hurried shot, or a sudden movement from the cow will cause tremendous pain and damage, but will not stun the victim. Nonetheless, the assembly line keeps moving—workers are pressured to process anymals as quickly as possible. Consequently, improperly stunned anymals are pushed forward, bellowing and struggling as they travel down the line, fully conscious, wounded, and frightened, to be disassembled. (Undercover videos expose this sordid truth.)

Religious Exemptions

In the United States, Jews and Muslims are exempt from "humane" stunning laws. Anymals killed to provide *kosher* (Jewish) or *halal* (Muslim) flesh go to the knife fully conscious. While religiously sanctioned methods of slaughter were once an improvement over earlier methods, these religious techniques are now even more primitive—and even more painful and frightening to the anymal—than are other contemporary slaughter methods.

In Jewish *shechita* slaughter, a cow's body is supported while the head is raised and extended to expose the jugular, which is then slit. The cow is supposed to die after a single cut, but the reality is very different, as undercover footage shows. (One undercover investigator watched a slaughterhouse worker saw across a cow's throat thirteen times while the cow struggled frantically for her life.) Even when the cut is performed correctly, cattle are sometimes conscious for several minutes, and are fully conscious and aware while they are hoisted onto an overhead rail to bleed out.

Downers

Transporting anymals to slaughter is a rough business. Like every aspect of the any-mal industries, transport methods are dictated by cost-benefit analysis, but what is cheapest is rarely best for anymals (or consumers). As a result, anymals arrive at slaughter exhausted, thirsty, hungry, and terrified; many arrive injured, and some are unable to stand or walk.

Slaughterhouse workers refer to arrivals who cannot or will not rise or move as "downers." Every year 100,000 factory-farmed cattle arrive at slaughter injured, or too dispirited to walk (Kirchheimer); undercover investigators have repeatedly documented downed anymals being kicked, beaten, pushed with bulldozers, and dragged from transport trucks with ropes or chains. These anymals are often fully conscious, in pain, and bellowing pitifully.

"Beef" Cattle

Motorists who see cattle grazing in wide open fields have no idea what cattle raised for the flesh industry have already suffered, how short their days of grazing, or what lies ahead for these doomed individuals. Cattle are bred to give birth early in the spring, to suit a rancher's schedule. Consequently, some calves do not survive the spring cold. A few weeks after birth, "beef" cattle are marked and identified; their ears are cut or pierced, and/or they are branded, which causes third-degree burns that ooze and fester. The males are castrated, either by slicing off the testicles with a knife or by cutting off the blood supply with a rubber band, causing the testicles to eventually fall off. (When I wander the prairies of Montana in the spring, I find little, withered testicles among the sage, with a hardy rubber band still attached.) Each of these invasive procedures is performed without anesthesia.

Cattle are then left to face whatever nature brings. Sometimes cattle are fried in fierce lighting storms or drowned in floods. In 1997, thousands of calves froze to death in a cold snap in New Mexico. Other cattle die slowly when they become stuck in mud or soft sand. (I sometimes find cattle hopelessly mired in saturated soils on the Montana prairie, exhausted from struggling, having sustained serious leg injuries in the process—all while their hungry calves look on.) Others suffer disease, illness, or injury from rattlesnake bites to broken bones, from puncture wounds to foot problems—without veterinary care. (I have seen cows die slowly from snakebite or grow thin from some unknown ailment. If they are discovered, they will be shot. Otherwise, they die slowly, day by day, and so does their calf.)

Calves are forcibly transported from vast, quiet grazing lands, where they have lived in community since birth, to a world of people, vehicles, and close confine-ment at roughly seven months of age. Cattle are not watered or fed during transport, even across hundreds of sweltering miles, including overnights in which they remain standing in crowded trucks.

Adolescent cattle destined for the beef industry are delivered to feedlots, where they are crowded into manure-packed pens with as many as 10,000 other cattle. They are given growth-promoting hormones and unnaturally rich diets, causing them to double their weight in just a few months; they are assessed by the pound. Their lives end at the slaughterhouses, on the dis-assembly lines described in the above section titled "slaughter."

Pigs

Pigs are intelligent and social, in many ways similar to dogs. They are also very tidy: When pigs have sufficient space, they do not defecate in areas where they sleep or eat. More than 95 percent of today's pigs are factory-farmed, spending their entire lives crowded in small, concrete, indoor pens. On factory farms, where a few extra feet of cage space reduces profit margins, pigs must live in their own feces, urine, vomit—even amid the corpses of other pigs (as discovered by many undercover agents).

One hundred million pigs are raised and slaughtered every year. Among these unfortunate pigs, breeding sows are the most unfortunate. Like cattle in the dairy industry, sows suffer a continuous cycle of artificial impregnation, controlled birth, forced nursing, and the stealing of their young. During four months of pregnancy, breeding sows are isolated in gestation crates—small metal pens just two feet wide—where they stand on cement floors. Lack of space prevents them from turning, or even lying down comfortably, and the sides of larger sows perpetually rub on surrounding bars.

When it is time to give birth, sows are transferred to similarly cramped farrowing crates, with concrete or metal floors, and bars that prevent mothers from reaching their piglets—while allowing the young to reach their mother's teats. Short chains or rubber straps are sometimes used to immobilize the mother, allowing for perpetual nursing (in order to fatten the piglets for slaughter). This intense, unlimited nursing frequently causes lacerations and painful infections on sows' udders, but they have no choice—they are unable to move.

Normally piglets nurse for about fifteen weeks, but factory-farmed piglets are taken from their mothers at just two or three weeks of age. These piglets are weaned in crowded, concrete "nursery" pens surrounded by metal bars, with little more than one square yard of floor space per pig. They are slaughtered at about six months of age, though pigs lucky enough to find a home in a sanctuary can easily live beyond fifteen years.

Five days after her piglets have been taken, a sow is again forcibly, artificially impregnated. Sows endure at least two pregnancies, births, and nursing stints per year, generally giving birth to more than twenty piglets annually. When a sow is no longer considered productive (after birthing four to seven times), she is sent to slaughter, usually at about four years of age.

As with cattle, the lucky ones are slaughtered young. Factory-farmed sows, who are repeatedly impregnated and perpetually confined, have weak bones and muscles, heart problems, and frequent urinary tract infections. The concrete that they stand on causes crippling leg disorders, which leads to arthritis, and a lack of exercise causes obesity—which farmers *strive* to create, breeding and feeding pigs so that they will grow as quickly as possible. (Transgenic pigs have recently been bred to grow even faster.) With barely enough room to stand or lie down, and no bedding to speak of, many sows have chronic sores on their shoulders and knees. Respiratory diseases are also common: Seventy percent of factory-farmed pigs suffer from pneumonia. Despite these common problems, throughout the course of a year, one in four commercial pig operations never summon a veterinarian.

Deprivation, chronic pain, and frustration cause sows to adopt neurotic coping behaviors. Sows would normally build a nest of leaves or straw before giving birth. In their barren cells, sows repeatedly and desperately try to build a nest, and often fall to moving their heads backward and forward pointlessly in a rhythmic fashion, gnawing on surrounding metal bars. Overcrowding and boredom also cause aggression, which is why pigs' tails are chopped off and their teeth cut at birth (without anesthesia). Giving pigs more space would allow them to create nests, root, and wallow—normal pig behaviors—which would also prevent neurotic behaviors and aggression. But from an economic point of view, it is cheaper to dock tails and cut teeth than it is to provide pigs with adequate space; pig psychosis does not affect a pig farmer's bottom line.

As with all factory-farmed anymals, pigs are not provided with food, water, or protection from extreme weather when they are transported to slaughter. Each year, 80,000 pigs die in transit. At the slaughterhouse, "downer" pigs are dragged from transport trucks. Survivors face questionable stunning methods before they are shackled and hoisted by their hind leg onto a belt that moves them to the "blood pit," where a worker cuts the pig's throat, sometimes at the remarkable rate of 900 pigs per hour. Needless to say, at such speeds, throat slitting cannot be achieved with any precision. Undercover video shows conscious pigs moving along the processing line kicking and struggling, hanging upside down by one leg, while workers try to "stick" the terrified victim. Sometimes the unfortunate pig remains conscious all the way to the scalding tank, where she or he is boiled alive.

Sheep

Those who buy wool, like those who consume dairy products, often believe that they do not support death and misery. But wool, like cheese and ice cream, is linked with considerable suffering, and routine, premature death. Sheep are raised to produce wool for clothing and lambs for slaughter, but all sheep are ultimately slaughtered for the flesh industry at a comparatively young age. About 33 percent of U.S.

sheep profits stem from wool; most of the remaining profit comes from the slaughter of lambs. Sometimes skins and nursing milk are also sold.

Genetic manipulation has produced sheep with excessive, unhealthy amounts of wool, such that skin folds are now routinely cut from sheep to avoid medical complications. Much wool sold in North America is imported from Australia or New Zealand, nations that permit tail docking, castration, and slicing off of skin folds; each of these surgeries is performed without anesthesia. Shearing also causes bruises and cuts, and brings traumatic and life-threatening change for sheep, who suffer greatly when their wooly coat is suddenly removed; some become ill and/or die from exposure.

Left to their own devices, ewes give birth to one or two lambs in warm, spring conditions. Lured by inflated Easter prices, farmers manipulate breeding cycles to bring lambs early into the world, and early to slaughter. As a result, 20 percent of U.S. lambs die before they reach two months of age, usually from exposure. In the United States, as many as 100,000 sheep and lambs perish in the spring because they are ill equipped to survive early spring weather. Survivors are slaughtered between the ages of one week and six months and marketed for religious feasts, especially Easter. How did the most important Christian holiday—the celebration of eternal life through a loving savior—become mired in bloodshed? How did Christians come to celebrate the resurrection of the Lamb of God with the slaughter of millions of God's defenseless lambs?

When a mother sheep's production declines, she is sent to slaughter, usually between four and eight years of age, though sheep who are allowed to live out their natural lives can live up to and even beyond fifteen years. Meat from these "older" sheep (mutton), who were first exploited for their reproductive abilities, is considered less desirable, and is used for processed foods.

Muslims also continue to sully their holy days with bloodletting, and Islamic ritual slaughter (*halal*) is exempt from stunning laws. *Halal* slaughter requires that fully conscious sheep (or goats) be placed on their backs in a metal cradle, where their throats are slit. Alternatively, they are hoisted up by a back leg, fully conscious, to have their throat slit.

Poultry

Nearly ten billion chickens are hatched annually in the United States. More than 95 percent of U.S. hens are factory-farmed. These hens are raised in giant warehouses, where they live out their short lives in confinement and deprivation.

"Laying" Hens
Factory farmers exploit thirty million "laying hens" each year. Shortly after hatching, without anesthesia, female chicks are "debeaked"—the tips of their sensitive

beaks are sliced off with a hot blade, cutting through bone, cartilage, and soft tissue. This procedure is intended to reduce injuries caused by stressed birds in over-crowded conditions, but it comes with a price: Debeaking causes many fragile little chicks to bleed to death or die of shock—newly hatched chickens are considered expendable in the poultry industry.

When they are just eighteen weeks old, four or more young hens are placed in crowded 1.5-square-foot cages (slightly bigger than your average microwave oven), even though one hen's wing span is roughly 2.5 feet. In these crowded conditions, their wings constantly rub against wire, causing featherless sore spots. Nonetheless, these cages are piled one on top of the other in giant sheds, where the hens remain until they are sent to slaughter.

Hens lay eggs (and cow's produce milk) as part of their basic, biological func-tioning, and they do so in excessive quantities due to biological manipulation—not because they are well cared for or contented. Even the most miserable human, if provided with adequate food, is likely to ovulate (pass eggs) and lactate (produce milk) after birth. Common sense tells us that the same is true for chickens (and cows). When hens ovulate, they feel a strong nesting urge, which they cannot satisfy in such cramped cages. Hens are forced to lay their eggs under their crowded feet, on wire, and their eggs roll onto a conveyor belt, to be taken away and boxed. Though each hen annually produces upward of 250 eggs (while their wild counterparts lay roughly twenty eggs per year), factory-farmed hens are never permitted to build a nest, sit on their eggs, or tend young—or even step out onto grass or feel the sunshine.

When a hen's egg production goes into a natural decline (after a few months), they are put through "forced molt," in which they are starved and kept in total dark-ness for as long as eighteen days. This shocks the hens' exhausted bodies into yet another egg cycle, and simultaneously causes hens to lose a great deal of weight. Some lose more than 25 percent of their body weight, and 5 to 10 percent of the hens die during that time—all of the hens suffer terribly. But this cruel practice increases profits by immediately bringing on another cycle of ovulation. Hens who die during forced molt are considered no loss whatsoever to the industry because their egg production had already declined, and factory farmers will quickly rid themselves of such birds in any case.

Due to forced ovulation, factory-farmed hens sometimes suffer from "cage-layer fatigue," a condition in which they become "egg bound" and die because they are too weak to expel yet one more egg. Factory-farmed hens also suffer from prolapse (the uterus is expelled along with an egg), egg peritonitis (an inflammation), can-cers, severe liver and kidney disease, and infectious bronchitis (caused by living in their own excrement). Because a tremendous amount of calcium is required to pro-duce eggshells, hens commonly suffer from calcium deficiencies, and often endure broken bones and paralysis.

Chickens at sanctuaries can live up to fifteen years, but factory-farmed hens are destroyed roughly one year after they hatch. "Egg-laying" chickens are bred for egg production; they don't grow fast or large enough to bring a profit in the flesh market, so it is not cost-effective to send these birds to slaughter. Consequently, millions of spent hens are thrown into wood chippers alive. Undercover investigators documented Ward Egg Ranch (California) throwing more than 15,000 live, "spent" laying hens into a wood-chipping machine. Despite tremendous outcry from a newly informed and horrified public, the district attorney declined to prosecute, noting that disposing of live hens in a wood-chipper is legal, and is recognized as a "common industry practice" ("Factory" Poultry).

Roughly half of a hen's offspring are males. Like veal calves, male chicks are an expendable by-product of poultry industries. Two hundred million newly hatched male chicks are discarded every year. These chicks are of no economic value to the egg industry (or to the flesh industry, because roosters are too aggressive to be kept in cramped factory-farm conditions); these little fellows are gassed, crushed, or simply thrown into garbage bins, where they dehydrate or asphyxiate, or they are tossed into a grinder or chipper (like spent hens). Eyewitness accounts describe struggling, peeping chicks dismembered by metal blades. Their little fluffy bodies, when ground to oblivion, are sold as fertilizer, or as feed for other farmed anymals— even those who would naturally eat only grass and grains.

When laying hens are sent to slaughter, though they are just beyond adolescence, they are much older than "broilers," who are raised for flesh. The flesh of "laying" hens is therefore of lesser market value, and their "spent" bodies are shredded to create soups, baby food, stock cubes, school dinners, pot pies, the restaurant trade, anymal food, or other low-grade products.

Please know that we pay for extreme suffering if we purchase skim milk, omelets, peach yogurt, mozzarella cheese, egg salad sandwiches, and strawberry ice cream (even if we purchase "cage-free" or "free-range"—discussed below). Egg and dairy industries cause extreme, prolonged suffering, and massive premature death. One individual cannot shut down the entire industry, but every dollar spent on dairy and eggs is a vote in favor of these cruel industries.

"Broiler" Hens

More and more people are moving from "red" flesh to "white" flesh in the hope of staving off heart attacks, strokes, and cancers linked with the consumption of cow flesh. This change in demand has provided a considerable boost to the "broiler" industry.

Hens are exploited not only for their reproductive abilities, but also for their flesh. Hens in the broiler industry are crowded by the thousands into warehouses that hold up to 100,000 birds. Roosters are far too aggressive to live in these unbearably crowded conditions. Consequently, like hens who are exploited for their eggs, "broilers" are sexed, and females are debeaked just after they hatch, while males are cast into a bin to suffocate, or into a chopper, where they are ground to bits.

Chickens have natural sleep rhythms that are determined by daylight and darkness. Light deters hens from sleeping, which encourages them to eat...too much of which causes them to gain weight rapidly. Most of the windowless sheds that are typical for battery hens are therefore equipped with artificial lighting, which remains on for most of a twenty-four hour period, perpetually disturbing and manipulating the hens' sleep patterns. Can you imagine being kept awake most of your life—rarely being allowed to sleep soundly, comfortably, or for a full night?

Not only is light manipulated to fatten hens, but they are also given high-protein feed and growth-promoting antibiotics, and they are genetically altered so that they grow twice as fast, and twice as large, as their recent ancestors. "Broiler" hens reach four pounds—slaughter weight—in just six weeks. But their immature bones cannot possibly support such unnatural weight gain, and these hens live in chronic pain for the last weeks of their short lives. Factory-farmed hens do not move much "because it hurts" (John Webster, *Guardian*, October 14, 1991, quoted in An HSUS). But those who are motivated by profit see this as a benefit—a hen who does not attempt to move about freely is likely to gain yet more weight.

Hens trapped in the broiler industry are handled with the expectation that their lives will be very short, and significant losses are expected—individual hens have very little market value. The floors of these giant, crowded sheds are quickly covered with excrement, creating lung-damaging air. Broilers stand and lie in their own heaped droppings, developing blisters, ulcers, and burns on their feet, legs, and breasts from their own nutrient-rich manure. Because hens in broiler sheds are confined in crowded, unsanitary conditions, thousands succumb to heat prostration, infectious diseases, and cancers. They also die frequently of heart failure because their hearts and lungs cannot sustain such fast and excessive growth (*Feedstuffs*, quoted in "Viva!USA").

"Broiler" hens reach "market weight" just forty-five days after they hatch, at which time workers enter the dismal sheds, grabbing the frightened, overweight birds by a wing, leg, or head—whatever they can grab—and cramming them into crates stacked on trucks. The terror-stricken, plump birds, with weak hearts and fragile bones, dislocate and break hips, legs, and wings, hemorrhage internally, and suffer heart attacks as they try desperately to escape. The end, like their lives in general, is a testament to human cruelty and indifference.

As with other factory-farmed anymals, it is cheaper to absorb high-transportation mortality rates than to pay for enclosed transport trucks. Though they travel as much as eighty miles per hour in all weather conditions, hens travel in open cages or crates stacked on open trucks, without food, water, or protection from rain, snow, or sun. Some birds inevitably freeze to death, while others die from heat stress or suffocation during their prolonged transport.

At the slaughterhouse, hens are dumped onto a conveyor belt, but some flapping and frightened birds inevitably miss the belt and fall onto the ground, where they are generally crushed by machinery, but also may die of starvation or exposure. Hens who land on the belt are quickly hung upside down by their legs, in metal shackles. For the sake of efficiency, most slaughterhouses attempt to stun birds—it is much easier to kill a bird who is not struggling. As the birds move along the assembly line, hanging upside down, turning their heads to see what might befall them, their heads are supposed to touch an electrified basin of water. Some birds, particularly smaller ones, raise their heads to avoid the water and are therefore not stunned. Furthermore, even if they touch the water basin, the shock is likely of no help to the hens. Like the electric tongs used on cattle, the amount of current needed to properly stun birds is uncertain. As noted, U.S. laws do not regulate the slaughter of fowl (though 90 percent of the anymals killed for food in the United States are birds). Too much electrical power damages the flesh, reducing profits, inclining managers to err on the side of too little electric current. As a result, birds are usually immobilized by the electric basin but remain fully sentient.

After they pass the electric water basin, a hen's throat is cut, either by hand or with a mechanical blade. Slaughter lines run up to 8,400 chickens *per hour*, so accuracy is the exception rather than the rule. Foster Farms' Livingston plant (California) kills nearly 600,000 chickens daily (Morrissey, 12). After the throat-slitting procedure—whether successful or not—birds are submerged in scalding water (with intent to loosen their feathers); those whose throats were not slit, or were not slit properly—millions annually—are boiled alive.

Roughly one million factory-farmed hens are killed each hour for human consumption. (Did those staggering numbers register as you read?) When adjusting one's diet on behalf of anymals, please do not reject red flesh in preference for white flesh. Also, please do not buy eggs—compassion does not permit us to become vegetarians who consume yet more dairy and eggs. Compassion must guide us away from poultry products in light of the sheer numbers of hens affected, in light of the intense suffering forced on hens and chicks, and because of their premature, unregulated demise. Compassion requires us to *cut back on all anymal products or eliminate anymal products entirely.*

Turkeys

Two hundred and fifty million turkeys are slaughtered for flesh each year. Forty-five million turkeys are killed each year for Thanksgiving alone. More than a quarter billion turkeys are hatched in the United States annually, though almost all of the males are quickly discarded. Most of the remaining turkeys are slaughtered after just four months, when they reach market weight, (though turkeys who live in sanctuaries can live up to fifteen years).

Poultry Press, a publication of United Poultry Concerns, published an account from an eyewitness who described what happens to a newborn turkey on a factory farm:

The newborn turkeys were dumped out of metal trays, jostled onto con-
veyer belts after being mechanically separated from cracked eggshells, then
sorted, sexed, debeaked and detoed, all without anesthetic. Countless baby
turkeys were "mangled from the machinery," suffocated in plastic bags, and
dumped into the "same disposal system as the discarded egg shells they
were separated from hours earlier." (Davis, 6)

Like chickens, turkey chicks are placed in large sheds with as many as 25,000 other
birds; they are allotted less than three square feet per turkey. Also like their smaller
cousins, turkeys suffer from burns and ulcers because they live in their own
excrement.

Turkeys are debeaked by removing half of the upper beak, and a little less of the
lower beak, making it extremely difficult to peck food. The last section of their toes
is also clipped off. Toe clipping removes the toenail, which reduces the danger of
fights among overcrowded, bored, stressed turkeys. All surgeries are performed
without anesthesia.

Like chickens, factory-farmed turkeys are genetically manipulated: They are
selectively bred for extremely large breasts so that neither their bone structure nor
their internal organs can withstand such rapid, excessive growth. Consequently,
millions of baby turkeys die prematurely from heart attacks and many turkeys have
problems standing upright. When they fall amid the grossly overcrowded flock,
they are trampled. It is more profitable for factory farmers to absorb this loss of life
than it is to allow turkeys to grow more proportionally, or to send smaller turkeys to
market. Losses caused by stress or trampling are easier to absorb than the cost of
providing poultry with adequate space.

Male turkeys now grow so large that they cannot mount hens, and therefore
cannot reproduce naturally. Consequently, turkeys are artificially inseminated,
known in the turkey industry as "breaking the hens" (Davis, 7). To "break" a
turkey, these large and cumbersome females are tipped upside down and
injected with semen that has been stripped from males. Turkeys who are
exploited for their semen and eggs continue to grow long after their peers have
been shipped off to slaughter, reaching such massive weights as twenty-five
pounds before they are worn out, at which time they are transported to slaughter
in crowded, open trucks, for low-grade products like turkey "ham" and turkey
"sausages."

Geese and Ducks

Like all factory-farmed anymals, the lives of water fowl are short and restricted,
stressful and monotonous. They are kept without bathing water, in small, dirty cages
that do not permit these unhappy prisoners to spread their wings; they often cannot
even turn around. The cruelty of exploitation is nowhere more evident than in the
production of *foie gras*.

Foie gras is created by force-feeding ducks and geese. To do this, employees shove a metal tube down the bird's throats, and into their stomachs; this process is repeated two or three times each day. The metal tubes cause painful bruising, lacerations, sores, and can even rupture organs. This forced feeding swells the livers of ducks and geese to reach a size that is ten times that of a normal liver. (Again, did you catch that statistic?) Needless to say, this predicament—both the feeding and the condition— is extremely painful.

"Free-Range," "Cruelty-Free," "Organic," and "Natural Foods" Products

Some people seek to avoid supporting the excessive cruelty of factory farms by purchasing products with special labels, but *these labels do not satisfy even the most basic requirements of a compassionate consumer.* "Free-range," "cruelty-free," "organic," and "natural foods" industries exploit farmed anymals for flesh, nursing milk, and reproductive eggs almost exactly as do other factory farms.

"Organic" labels protect farmed anymals in only one, meager way: Organic labels indicate that farmers feed only organic foods—no hormones—to their victims. Organic guidelines provide no further protections for farmed anymals. Therefore, *anymals who are exploited for "organic" foods are raised, maintained, transported, and slaughtered just like their "nonorganic" counterparts:* They are debeaked, dehorned, detoed, castrated, and/or branded, and they are kept, transported, and slaughtered in the same deplorable conditions.

"Organic" labels do *nothing* for a cow who is perpetually impregnated and milked, who loses her calf to the veal industry—or to protect her calf, who is sold at birth to the veal industry to be slaughtered. "Organic" products are designed to optimize human health and reduce environmental degradation. Those who invest in organic products are not making a choice that promotes the well-being of farmed anymals.

Despite the ugly truth of organic products, it is increasingly common for those touting "organic" products to claim that their label includes "rules about the humane treatment of animals" (What Does). (I suppose they justify this because they do have one rule that benefits their imprisoned, exploited farmed anymals—they receive organic feed.) One need only look up the Organic Foods Production Act of 1990—today's organic guidelines (http://www.ams.usda.gov/AMSv1.0/getfile?d DocName=STELPRDC5060370&acct=nopgeninf) to see that organic industries are not designed for the sake of farmed anymals. Organic regulations are not designed to alleviate the prolonged, extreme suffering of factory-farmed anymals, and they certainly do not do so.

Nor do we vote against cruel anymal exploitation if we buy "natural" or "all-natural" products. In fact, these labels don't even protect consumers—these labels are blatantly deceptive. "Natural" labels merely indicate that a product has no "artificial flavors, colors, or chemical preservatives" (NC State). There is no requirement that cows, pigs, or hens who were exploited to create "natural" products be treated any different from how other factory-farmed anymals are treated. Farmed anymals who are exploited for "natural" products are not allowed to live in natural conditions—they are not even allowed to satisfy their most basic natural behaviors. Despite reasonable consumer assumptions about what "natural" means, the USDA's "natural" food labels regulate *only* "the presence of artificial additives and the degree of processing" ("Farm").

"Free-range," "cage-free," and "certified humane" labels are just as meaningless for farmed anymals as are "all natural" labels. Just like farmed anymals who are enslaved by organic industries, farmed anymals exploited by "free-range," "cage-free," and "certified humane" producers are routinely debeaked, disbudded, detoed, castrated, their tails are docked, and/or they are branded (depending on the species). Nor do "free-range" and "certified humane" labels protect cows from perpetual impregnation, pregnancy, birth, calf snatching, transport, or dismemberment (slaughter) at a very young age. Finally, "free-range," "cage-free," and "certified humane" labels fail to protect "spent" hens, who are sent to slaughter at the same youthful age.

Eggs and chicken flesh marketed as "free-range" very rarely have more space than hens crowded into battery cages, and they may or may not be able to step outside. *If* they can step outside, their outdoor pen is likely tiny, crowded, and barren—it is simply not profitable to keep fewer hens on more land; it *is* profitable to keep a greater number of hens on less land. It is perfectly legal to keep 20,000 or more "free-range" hens in captivity such that each hen is allotted no more space than is encompassed in an average size sheet of paper, "with little or no access to the outdoors. If the hens can go outside, the exit is often very small, allowing only the closest hens to get out" ("Free-Range"). For those few who might be able to access the small doorway that leads to the outside world, much-touted "free-range" may be "nothing more than a mudyard saturated with manure" ("Free-Range").

Facilities that bill their eggs as "cage-free" are equally uninspiring:

> "Cage-free" means that, while the hens are not squeezed into small wire cages, they never go outside. "Cage-free" hens are typically confined in dark, crowded buildings filled with toxic gases and disease microbes the same as their battery-caged sisters. And like their battery-caged sisters, they are painfully debeaked at the hatchery. ("Cage-Free")

Visitors arriving expectantly at an organic egg farm were surprised to find that, despite "certified humane" and "free-range" logos, "100,000 debeaked hens [were] crowded into five 400 foot long sheds, each holding 'a sea of 20,000 brown hens,' so densely crowded the floor was invisible.... The 'range,' even if the hens had been outside, was just 'a bare patch of dirt between the sheds'" ("Organic"). Given that these institutions don't even live up to the most basic consumer expectations, I wonder how long it will be until free range and organic industries are as difficult to visit as are slaughterhouses.

In our capitalistic system, farmed anymals are merely units of production—live "stock." It is therefore inevitable that millions of farmed anymals raised for profit will be viewed—and treated—as if they were expendable, especially in the poultry and dairy industries. Male "dairy" calves have no reason to exist on dairy farms, and male chicks have no reason to exist on egg-producing farms. Yet male calves and male chicks are produced by the millions in these industries. How might "free-range," "certified humane," "organic," and "natural" labels protect male calves in the dairy industry, when these calves have no economic value except through a veal industry that developed as a response to a plethora of unwanted "dairy" calves? Similarly, "free-range," "cage-free," "certified humane," and "natural" labels do nothing to protect male chicks, who are a natural and constant by-product of poultry industries, yet are economically useless. What exactly do concerned consumers imagine that a business might do with millions of anymals who are born/hatched every year on their premises, who must be fed, watered, and housed, but who are of no economic value?

Farmed anymals who are exploited for "free-range," "cage-free," "certified humane," "organic," and "natural" products are also sent through an identical transport and slaughterhouse process as other factory-farmed anymals, at the same youthful age. "Free-range," "cage-free," "certified humane," "organic," and "natural" labels cannot satisfy the compassionate (or ethical) consumer.

For the sake of farmed anymals, who suffer terribly in their artificially short lives, please do not reject red flesh in preference for poultry flesh. Please do not replace flesh with eggs or dairy products. Please do not buy anymal products that try to disguise cruel exploitation behind meaningless feel-good labels such as "free-range," "cage-free," "cruelty free," "organic," and "natural." For the sake of your own health, and for the sake of farmed anymals, please eliminate (or at least reduce) your consumption of all anymal products.

Environmental Degradation

The most important choice you make with regard to the environment is the choice of what you will eat. Factory farming anymals consumes huge quantities of precious resources and destroys forests, soils, and waterways.

We raise many more tons of grain to feed farmed anymals than we would need to raise if we fed grains *directly* to humans. Grains that we cycle through anymals (pigs, cattle, chickens, and turkeys) require extra farming lands, which require hundreds of thousands of gallons of extra fossil fuels, water, and pesticides (pesticide use has increased 400 percent in the last fifty years).

Roughly sixty million acres of agricultural land is devoted to growing grain, and 70 percent of our grain crop is consumed by anymal agriculture. Farming anymals requires 70 percent more cropland because we must grow 70 percent more grain in order to feed cattle, pigs, hens, and turkeys; We could feed about twenty times as many people if we used our agricultural land to grow grains and greens only for human consumption (Schwartz, 86). Instead, we continue to destroy prairies, forests, and wetlands (the earth's purifiers) to grow grains to feed cattle, pigs, and chickens (Rice, "Environmental," 4).

In addition to the extra 70 percent of croplands created to sustain anymal industries, some 40 percent of United States lands, or about 800 million acres, are devoted directly to grazing farmed anymals. More than 60 percent of these lands are overgrazed, causing billions of tons of soil loss annually. Cattle graze on open range lands, trample sensitive streambeds, contaminate water, and destroy the natural flora and fauna of the area. More plant species have been lost because of overgrazing than for any other reason (Schwartz, 88). Public lands—mountains and prairies that ought to be preserved for all of us to enjoy—are rented to ranchers for a pittance as part of the government's generous meat industry subsidies. (Rice, "Subsidies," 9).

The primary cause of tropical deforestation is converting forests to croplands and pastures (Earth). Between 1960 and 1990, while meat consumption was on the rise, 13 percent of the world's forests were destroyed (Connor, 9). Currently, somewhere on this planet, a section of forest equal to twenty football fields is lost every minute; twelve million hectares of forests are cleared annually (Collins). Fifty-five feet of tropical forests are destroyed for each quarter-pound of flesh imported by the United States (Schwartz, 88). Between 1990 and 2005, Brazil was the unfortunate world leader in both beef exports and deforestation; Brazil tripled beef production exports and lost a patch of trees roughly the size of California in the process (HSUS).

We have now destroyed half of the world's rainforests—forests known to hold more than half of the world's life forms (Schwartz, 88), including Brazil's critically endangered capuchin and little blue macaw (of which only a handful remain). Scientists estimate that "a 90 percent decrease in the area of natural vegetation will result in the loss of between 30 and 55 percent of species" (Connor, 9). At our current rate, pretty much all tropical forests will be gone by the year 2050, along with the many anymals who depend on these forests for their survival (Collins).

Even if forests are not destroyed, such as in prairie lands, ecosystems (and individuals within ecosystems) are harmed by an influx of great herds of farmed anymals. Ranchers graze cattle on lands that once supported a multitude of wild anymals—great herds of bison, gazelle, deer, elk, or quagga. In South Africa, for example, ranchers drove the once-abundant quagga from the plains—and from the planet—to secure grasslands for their cattle. If you could have gone your whole life without ever eating any part of a cow's body in order to secure the existence of the quagga, would you have done so? It is too late for the quagga, but not for other anymals who are threatened by anymal agriculture. We vote with our teeth.

The U.S. federal agency euphemistically known as Wildlife Services (a branch previously—and more aptly—named "Animal Damage Control") is in charge of "resolving" wildlife conflicts. More specifically, they "protect American agriculture, including livestock such as cattle and sheep, a diversity of crops, and other agricultural resources" (Wildlife), usually by destroying any "problematic" anymals. In this manner millions of U.S. tax dollars are spent on "predator control," to protect the profits of anymal industries; Wildlife Services perpetually poison, trap, and shoot coyotes, bears, mountain lions, bobcats, prairie dogs, skunks, and many other anymals on behalf of rancher "investments." In 2007, Wildlife Services killed 1.6 million anymals for ranchers (M. Brown). Footloose Montana, an organization fighting to end trapping on Montana's public lands (trapping that is largely justified under the guise of protecting ranchers' investments), reported that U.S. tax dollars, through Wildlife Services, killed "252 gray wolves, 72,816 coyotes, 1.2 million starlings, 6,832 skunks, 330 mountain lions, 2,172 red foxes, 33,469 beavers, 356 black bears, three bald eagles and two grizzly bears" in 2007 (McQuillan, 1).

> Methods used to kill these animals include shooting from helicopters and fixed-wing aircraft, trapping, poisoning, and denning (killing pups in their dens with a fumigant). Used extensively at the behest of ranchers in some western states, aerial gunning accounts for the greatest percentage of predator "take" by Wildlife Services (33% of deaths in 1999)....Trapping is used almost as much (28%), generally in the form of leghold traps and neck snares—both of which can cause significant suffering to trapped animals. In addition, both types of traps routinely injure or kill "non-target" animals such as deer, birds, and pets. ("Lethal")

These are ugly, unnecessary deaths that manipulate and destroy natural ecosystems.

Raising anymals for flesh also contributes significantly to carbon dioxide, nitrous oxides, chlorofluorocarbons, and methane—global warming (Schwartz, 89). In fact, anymal agriculture causes more greenhouse gases than all transportation methods—automobiles, jets, and so on—combined. For example, one calorie of protein from feedlot beef requires about seventy-eight calories of fossil fuels, while one calorie of protein from soybeans requires only about two calories of fossil fuels (Schwartz, 87). For every two pounds of flesh, cattle produce roughly one pound of methane, a greenhouse gas that is twenty-five times as potent as carbon dioxide (Rice, "Environmental," 7).

A diet based on anymal agriculture also requires exponentially more water than does a plant-based diet. As noted, a diet based on anymal products requires 70 percent more grain, much of which requires irrigation. Water is also necessary to clean dairies and slaughterhouses, and to satisfy the water needs of *large* numbers of *large* anymals. Producing one pound of cow's flesh requires 100 times more water than does the production of one pound of potatoes. Americans who consume anymal products also unwittingly "consume" roughly 4,200 gallons of water on a daily basis. In contrast, a vegan diet requires only about 300 gallons of water per day. In semiarid regions like California, even more water is required: One pound of California beef requires roughly 5,200 gallons of water, whereas one pound of California vegetables requires only 25 gallons of water (Schwartz, 86).

We are using groundwater 25 percent faster than we are replenishing it. Some of our key sources of irrigation water are not from sources that replenish. For example, the Ogallala Aquifer, which formed over millions of years, is now "cut off from its original natural sources," and therefore has no refilling source (BBC). "About 27 percent of the irrigated land in the United States overlies this aquifer system, which yields about 30 percent of the nation's irrigation. In addition, the aquifer system provides drinking water to 82 percent of the people who live within the aquifer boundary" (High). Those dependent on this water source would do well to feel a bit nervous: "The great Ogallala Aquifer beneath America's Midwestern breadbasket is believed to be more than half gone" (Rice, "Environmental," 5). What will this region do when the Ogallala is drained? We are depleting this aquifer "at a rate of 12 billion cubic metres a year—amounting to a total depletion to date of a volume equal to the annual flow of 18 Colorado Rivers. Some estimate that the Ogallala Aquifer will dry up in as little as 25 years" (BBC).

On land, manure releases ammonia that damages leaves and forests, and the soil itself (Rice, "Environmental," 6), but manure causes the most damage when it is washed from lands to seas. "Factory farms generate 500 million tons of manure annually" (Sierra Club). Anymal waste in the U.S. has reached 1.4 billion tons of wet manure per year, or 89,000 pounds per second—130 times that produced by humans (Schwartz, 87). "But, unlike cities that must treat their sewage before discharging it to the environment, CAFOs store their liquefied excrement in large dirt cesspits called lagoons, or in piles of solids called 'litter,' then spread the raw wastes on surrounding cropland" (Sierra Club).

In the United States, anymals in anymal agriculture create five times as much water pollution as do human beings, and twice as much as do other industries (Schwartz, 87). Anymal waste is stored in large slurries on many pig farms; these slurries sometimes leak or spill, carrying E. coli into the water system and causing "massive fish kills and dangerous bacterial water contamination" (Sierra Club).

Anymal agriculture also causes dead zones, areas of the ocean where oxygen levels "are too low to support marine life" (Sierra Club). Dead zones develop in waters where phosphorus and nitrogen are abundant; manure is rich in both. Phosphorus and nitrogen provide nutrients that create algae blooms (excessive growth of algae) (Carlisle), which create microscopic phytoplankton that sink to the bottom of the ocean, where they are eliminated by oxygen-consuming bacteria—which also consume the oxygen, leaving little of this vital element for oxygen-dependent sea creatures (Roach). Oxygen-starved sea life soon falls unconscious, and then perishes. Those sea anymals who move slowly, like clams, crabs, shrimp, lobsters, and oysters, as well as many species of fish, have no hope of escape. While some escape, many die, and soon there is no life left in the area—now a dead zone.

The magnitude of the devastation of the Dead Zone is huge. The environmental impacts of low oxygen levels in water, or hypoxia, include: noxious algal blooms that choke out fish, shrimp and crabs; altered coastal phytoplankton food webs—the lowest rung of the ocean food chain upon which most sea life depends; altered stream-side ecosystems … massive fish kills, altered migration patterns for species like shrimp, and loss of suitable habitat for the spawning of fish, shrimp and crabs. (Sierra Club)

Dead zones are becoming both more numerous and more expansive. Anymal agriculture in the United States has created a gigantic dead zone in the Gulf of Mexico. Some 52 percent of U.S. farms are located along the Mississippi River, and waste from these farms drains into the Gulf of Mexico: "The dead zone in the Gulf of Mexico is one of the largest in the world, affecting some 6,000–7,000 square miles" (Sierra Club). Nitrogen input has at least doubled from the Mississippi River basin, and in some places it has increased sevenfold in the past century. Human beings have also created dead zones in the Baltic Sea, Black Sea, Chesapeake Bay, off the coast of Oregon (300 sq. miles)—even in Lake Erie. The UN Environment Programme reported 146 dead zones caused by a proliferation of nutrients in the water, caused by a proliferation of manure from animal agriculture (E. Buck, 2, 4).

Fishing

Sometimes people switch to chicken and fish when they learn of serious health problems associated with red meat. This change in diet results in more anymal suffering and death because fish and chicken are smaller than cattle and pigs—more anymals must be killed to provide the same amount of flesh. For example, one might feed a small village by killing a single cow, but one cannot even feed a large family with an average-sized chicken or salmon.

Humans currently consume roughly 100 million tons of "seafood" each year; some ten billion aquatic anymals are captured by the fishing industry annually. Over the latter half of the twentieth century, wild fish catches increased by 500 percent. The fish that we consume are rarely bred and reared for human consumption; they are stolen from the seas. Our tendency toward fish affects billions of sea creatures and the health of the sea's ecosystems: As a result of increased fish consumption, a "quarter of the world's commercially important ocean fish populations are depleted or slowly recovering from over-exploitation; another 47 percent are fished to the full extent of their capacity" (Singer, *Eating*, 111). The Atlantic salmon is commercially extinct, and the adult Atlantic cod population along Cape Cod is only 1.1 percent of what it was in the 1960s (Singer, *Eating*, 111, 114). Many other fish populations—such as sturgeon, grouper, red snapper, bluefin tuna, swordfish, sharks,

Chilean sea bass, and Pacific salmon—have been devastated by our hooks and jaws (Kher, 56).

Industrial fishing methods are wasteful and environmentally destructive. Miles of fishing line, laced with baited hooks that attract sea life indiscriminately, are lowered into the salty waters. Trawlers grind up and destroy everything in their path, leaving a devastated wasteland behind; for every edible pound, trawlers pull five inedible pounds from the suffering seas (Singer, *Eating*, 126). Nets are towed beneath the surface or float across many miles of water, entangling sea creatures indiscriminately, many of whom drown when they cannot reach the surface for air. More than 100,000 marine mammals are killed inadvertently each year by U.S. commercial fisheries alone.

One quarter of the sea life captured by fishing industries is *bycatch*. Bycatch refers to the many inedible and therefore unprofitable anymals who are mistakenly pulled from the sea when we fish for "seafood." Those who ply the world's seas throw one in four anymals—maimed, wounded, dead, or dying—back into the ocean as bycatch, whether small crabs, shellfish, turtles, dolphins, porpoises, small whales, rays, sharks, or diving seabirds. Worldwide, roughly seven million metric tons of wild-caught fish are hauled in annually and then discarded as bycatch (Singer, *Eating*, 112)—destroyed for no purpose. Bycatch is by nature indiscriminate, and therefore further threatens already diminished populations of endangered species. The worst bycatch offender is the shrimp industry, which brings in 2 percent of "edible" sea life and 30 percent of bycatch.

We also pull 80–100 million tons of marketable fish from the oceans, mostly herrings, cod, jacks, redfish, and mackerel. Like all vertebrates, fish have a central nervous system, including a brain, spinal cord, and nerves—yet we inevitably deny or ignore their suffering. When deep sea fish are brought to the surface, they suffer from decompression, just as we would; sometimes their organs burst. Billions of fish suffocate on boat decks; suffocation is the standard, slow death that awaits most individuals who have been pulled from the water by human hands.

Humans who persist in eating creatures from the seas are directly responsible for the starvation of individuals from a host of other species. Wild-caught fish and bycatch, if left in the water, would breed and/or be consumed by other creatures— pelicans, fishers, bears, seals, and larger fish. For example, pollock, a fish commonly consumed by humans, is a main food source for the endangered Stellar sea lion (Singer, *Eating*, 115). Hundreds of young penguins were recently washed up onto Brazil's shores, most likely as a result of overfishing (Associated Press, "Hundreds"). With so many humans eating so many fish, how will other creatures find what they need to survive? Ninety percent of big sea predators are now struggling to survive.

Not only are others starving because *we* are consuming so many fish, but they are also being *shot* so that we can consume fish. The Marine Mammal Protection Act was amended in 1994 to allow sea lions to be shot *because they eat fish*—"our" fish. In the same year, the Canadian government and the province of Nova Scotia also proposed killing thousands of seals to protect fishing interests ("What About," 2). Along the Columbia River, the government spent upward of $3 million to protect the profits of salmon fishers, and vacillates between a policy of killing sea lions on behalf of fisheries and standing by the federal Endangered Species Act (Questions). Namibia is one of the few remaining nations with a commercial seal kill; they justify the slaughter, noting that "seals consume 900,000 tons of fish each year," and claim that seal-killing is important "to protect fisheries" (Theriault). This year 90,000 seals were clubbed to death in Namibia, including 85,000 pups, "to protect fish stocks" (Theriault). Seals and sea lions are not our only victims. In the Gulf of Mexico, bottlenose dolphins (think Flipper) learned to snatch fish from the lines of fishermen, and have stirred greedy fishers to throw pipe bombs and shoot dolphins, even though these marine mammals are protected by federal law. Dolphins wash ashore with bullet wounds, adding to the forty-some dolphins who die annually because they are caught in fishing lines or because they swallow fishing gear (Reeves).

Aquaculture—factory farms for fish—is the fastest growing agricultural industry in the world; 30–40 percent of extant salmon (800 million pounds) live in captivity. Aquaculture is environmentally problematic and of course devastating for the lives and welfare of fish. Farmed salmon are transferred from freshwater to saltwater abruptly, causing a 50 percent mortality rate. Confinement itself is questionable, since wild salmon normally cover hundreds of miles while they feed, and also as they migrate to and from breeding grounds. Typically, fish farms "put 50,000 to 90,000 fish in a pen that is only 100 feet by 100 feet," raising from 400,000 to one million fish at a time (Los Angeles Times, December 9, 2002, quoted in An HSUS).

The best way to protect the seas, sea life, and wild anymals who are dependent on sea creatures for their sustenance is to stop eating fish.

Summary

North American flesh eaters generally consume more than 35 nonhumans each year, amounting to 2,600 individuals over a seventy-five-year lifetime, including some 2,460 chickens, 96 turkeys, 32 pigs, and 12 cattle/calves. This loss of youthful lives is only one aspect of the sordid truths behind our consumption of anymal products.

Factory-farmed anymals—whether cattle, chickens, pigs, turkeys, sheep, or ducks—are habitually deprived of fresh air, sunlight, mobility, their young, and the fulfillment of their most basic tendencies and urges. They are genetically manipulated, warehoused, and transported as if they were commodities—stock—rather than sentient individuals. Anymals exploited for their nursing milk, reproductive eggs, and flesh are routinely maintained, transported, and slaughtered in ways that maximize misery. Factory farms are designed and managed for profit; they are not conducive to the health, let alone happiness, of the individuals they exploit. Uninformed humans are now buying yet more fish and poultry, believing that such a diet is healthful; due to the smaller size of these individuals, this trend has exponentially increased the numbers of sentient and suffering anymals who are exploited by food industries.

Consuming anymals significantly increases our environmental footprint: It requires much more cleared land, consumes much more fresh water, and introduces many more pesticides, greenhouse gases, and anymal wastes into the environment than does a plant-based diet. Additionally, our taste for "seafood" has seriously depleted fish populations, simultaneously contributing to the starvation and disappearance of wild anymals who depend on sea life for their sustenance. If we care about the earth—if we consider the earth sacred—we are obligated to stop consuming anymal products, or at least to radically cut back our consumption of anymal products—all anymal products. (We must not move to a vegetarian diet that increases consumption of dairy and eggs, or replace factory-farmed flesh with fish, as both of these options exponentially enhance anymal suffering and environmental degradation.)

Understanding factory farming and fishing helps us to understand why our relationship with anymals is spiritually important. Our dietary choices intimately affect the lives of other creatures—and the earth itself. Whether or not we eat cattle, chickens, pigs, turkeys, sheep, ducks, salmon, cod, and shrimp is just one more daily expression of how we understand our place and responsibilities in the universe.

References

The above information on factory farming, and much more, can be viewed on the following websites:

- Farm Sanctuary (http://www.farmsanctuary.org/mediacenter/videos.html)
- Humane Society of the United States (http://video.hsus.org/)
- People for the Ethical Treatment of Animals (http://www.petatv.com/)
- Physicians Committee for Responsible Medicine (http://www.pcrm.org/resources/)
- Vegan Outreach (http://www.veganoutreach.org/whyvegan/animals.html)
- VIVA! USA (http://www.vivausa.org/visualmedia/index.html)

Information specifically on dairy cattle and laying hens can be found at the following sites:

- Farm Sanctuary's FactoryFarming.com (http://www.farmsanctuary.org/issues/factoryfarming/)

- Humane Society of the United States, *Overlooked: The Lives of Animals Raised for Food* (http://video.humanesociety.org/video/629262638001/Channels/729780768001/Factory-Farming/775249327001/Overlooked-The-Lives-of-Animals-Raised-for-Food/)
- VIVA! USA Guides (http://www.vivausa.org/activistresources/guides/murdershewrote1.htm#)

Undercover footage can be viewed on many websites. Here are some worthy suggestions:

- For U.S. footage, visit Mercy for Animals (http://www.mercyforanimals.org/) and Compassion Over Killing (http://www.cok.net/).
- For Canadian footage, see Canadians for Ethical Treatment of Farm Animals (http://www.cetfa.com).
- For Australian footage, visit Animals Australia (http://www.animalsaustralia.org/).
- For European footage, see Vief Pfoten (Four Paws) (http://www.vier-pfoten.org/website/output.php).
- For footage from France, see Éthique Animaux (http://www.l214.com/), Eyes on Animals (http://eyesonanimals.com/) and Varkens in Nood (Pigs in Peril) (http://www.varkensinnood.nl/english_.htm).
- For excellent footage from the Netherlands (and for an overall view), see Compassion in World Farming (http://www.ciwf.org.uk/).

These two short online videos are highly recommended:

- *Do They Know It's Christmas?* (http://www.youtube.com/watch?v=vCX7f_s1CA4)
- *Alec Baldwin Narrates Revised "Eat Your Meat"* (http://www.petatv.com/tvpopup/Prefs.asp?video=mym2002)

For more general information about factory farming, also visit these sites:

- Farm Sanctuary (http://www.farmsanctuary.org/mediacenter/videos.html)
- HSUS (http://video.hsus.org/)
- PETA (http://www.petatv.com/)
- PCRM (http://www.pcrm.org/resources/)
- Vegan Outreach (http://www.veganoutreach.org/whyvegan/animals.html)
- VIVA! USA (http://www.vivausa.org/visualmedia/index.html) or VIVA! UK (http://www.viva.org.uk/)

REFERENCES

Adams, Carol J. "Foreword." In *Animal Equality: Language and Liberation*, by Joan Dunayer. Derwood, MD: Ryce, 2001.

———. *The Pornography of Meat*. New York: Continuum, 2003.

Agarwal, Anil. "Can Hindu Beliefs and Values Help India Meet Its Ecological Crisis?" In *Hinduism and Ecology: The Intersection of Earth, Sky, and Water*, edited by Christopher Key Chapple and Mary Evelyn Tucker, 165–79. Cambridge, MA: Harvard University Press, 2000.

Ahmed, Leila. "The Heard Word: Passing on the Message of Islam, Woman to Woman." *Harvard Divinity Bulletin* 28.2–3 (1999): 13–14.

Aitken, Robert. *The Practice of Perfection: Paramitas from a Zen Buddhist Perspective*. New York: Pantheon, 1994.

Allen, Clifton J. *Broadman Bible Commentary*. 12 vols. Nashville: Broadman Press, 1971.

Allendorf, F. S., and B. Byers. "Salmon in the Net of Indra: A Buddhist View of Nature and Communities." *Worldviews: Environment, Culture, Religion* 2 (1998): 37–52.

Ames, Roger T. "Putting the *Te* Back in Taoism." In *Nature in Asian Traditions of Thought: Essays in Environmental Philosophy*, edited by J. Baird Callicott and Roger T. Ames, 113–44. Albany: State University of New York Press, 1989.

Anderegg, Christopher, et al. *A Critical Look at Animal Experimentation*. Shaker Heights, OH: Medical Research Modernization Committee, 2006.

Anderson, E. N. "Flowering Apricot: Environmental Practice, Folk Religion, and Daoism." In *Daoism and Ecology: Ways within a Cosmic Landscape*, edited by N. J. Girardot et al., 157–84. Cambridge, MA: Harvard University Press, 2001.

Anderson, E. N., and Lisa Raphals. "Daoism and Animals." In *A Communion of Subjects: Animals in Religion, Science, and Ethics*, edited by Paul Waldau and Kimberley Patton, 275–90. New York: Columbia University Press, 2006.

Andrae, Tor. *Mohammed: The Man and His Faith*. Translated by Theophil Menzel. New York: Dover, 2000.

An-Nawawis. *Forty Hadith: An Anthology of the Sayings of the Prophet Muhammad*. Translated by Saut-Ul-Islam. New York: Holy Koran Publishing House, 1979. http://www.witness-pioneer.org/vil/hadeeth/hadithnawawi.html (accessed February 2008).

Armstrong, Karen. *The Great Transformation: The Beginnings of Our Religious Traditions*. New York: Alfred A. Knopf, 2006.

Associated Free Press. "Egypt-Animal-Protest: Giant Chicken Loses Head Outside Cairo KFC." *PETA vs. KFC in Cairo*, (accessed February 18, 2007) http://arabist.net/archives/2007/02/18/peta-vs-kfc-in-cairo/.

Associated Press. "Colville Tribal Elder Shows Herself to Be a 'Natural' Resource." *Skagit Valley Herald*, December 28, 1999, C5.

Associated Press. "Hundreds of Dead Penguins Wash up on Brazil Beaches." *FoxNews.com*, July 19, 2008. http://www.foxnews.com/story/0,2933,386578,00.html (accessed March 9, 2009).

Associated Press. "Judge Favors Killing Sea Lions at Bonneville Dam." *Seattle Times*, September 3, 2008. http://seattletimes.nwsource.com/html/localnews/2008157130_websealions03.html (accessed March 9, 2009).

Athar, Shahid. "Muslim Vegetarians." http://groups.yahoo.com/group/Muslim-Vegetarians/ (accessed September 6, 2010).

Attar, Farid Al-Din. *Muslim Saints and Mystics: Episodes from the Tadhkirat al-Auliya'*. Translated by A. J. Arberry. New York: Arkana, 1990.

Az Here's the Deal—Ltr from Rod." Rod Coronado. December 15.2007. http://www.veggieboards.com/newvb/showthread.php?75047-AZ-Here-s-the-Deal-ltr-from-Rod&s=993e38a38b2e6 82c04fed78a2ceb0db (accessed Aprial 8, 2011).

Bakhtiar, Laleh. *Sufi: Expressions of the Mystic Quest*. New York: Thames and Hudson, 1987.

Basham, A. L. *The Origins and Development of Classical Hinduism*. Oxford: Oxford University Press, 1989.

BBC News. "Ogallala Aquifer." *BBC News: Water Hotspots*. http://news.bbc.co.uk/1/shared/spl/hi/world/03/world_forum/water/html/ogallala_aquifer.stm (accessed July 21, 2008).

Bercholz, Samuel, and Sherab Chodzin Kohn. *Entering the Stream: An Introduction to the Buddha and His Teachings*. Boston: Shambhala, 1993.

Berman, Louis A. *Vegetarianism and the Jewish Tradition*. New York: KTAV, 1982.

Bernbaum, Edwin. *Sacred Mountains of the World*. Berkeley: University of California Press, 1997.

Berry, Rynn. *Food for the Gods: Vegetarianism and the World's Religions*. New York: Pythagorean, 1998.

Bierhorst, John. *The Mythology of South America*. New York: William Morrow, 1988.

Bierlein, J. F. *Parallel Myths*. New York: Ballantine, 1994.

Blake, William. "The Lamb." *Songs of Innocence*. 1789. http://en.wikisource.org/wiki/The_Lamb (accessed September 6, 2010).

Blofeld, John. *Bodhisattva of Compassion: The Mystical Tradition of Kuan Yin*. Boulder, CO: Shambhala, 1978.

———. *Taoism: The Road to Immortality*. Boston: Shambhala, 1985.

Braun, Nathan. "Preface: Nathan Braun." In *Good News for All Creation: Vegetarianism as Christian Stewardship*, by Stephen R. Kaufman and Nathan Braun. Cleveland, OH: Vegetarian Advocates Press, 2002.

Brockington, J. L. *The Sacred Thread*. Edinburgh: Edinburgh University Press, 1996.

Brown, Dee. *Folktales of the Native American: Retold for Our Times*. New York: Henry Holt, 1979.

Brown, Joseph Epes. *The Spiritual Legacy of the American Indian*. New York: Crossroad, 1991.

Brown, Lester R. *Plan B 3.0: Mobilizing to Save Civilization*. New York: W. W. Norton, 2008.

Brown, Matthew. "Agents Killed 1.6 Million Animals in '06." http://www.mail-archive.com/helpthe-animals@yahoogroups.com/msg01347.html.

Brown, Raphael, trans. *The Little Flowers of St. Francis*. New York: Image, 1958.

Bruckner, Monica. "The Gulf of Mexico Dead Zone." *Microbial Life: Educational Resources*. http://serc.carleton.edu/microbelife/topics/deadzone/ (accessed October 28, 2007).

Buchwald, Rabbi Ephraim. "Og Stands Tall on the Stage of History." *National Jewish Outreach Program, Devarim 5769–2009*. http://www.njop.org/html/Devarim%205769-2009.html (accessed February 5, 2010).

Buck, Eugene H. CRS *Report for Congress: Marine Dead Zones: Understanding the Problem*. http://www.cnie.org/NLE/CRSreports/06Oct/98-869.pdf (accessed May 3, 2011.)

Buck, William, trans. *Mahabharata*. Berkeley: University of California Press, 1973.

———. *Ramayana*. Berkeley: University of California Press, 1976.

Buege, Douglas J. "The Ecologically Noble Savage Revisited." *Environmental Ethics* 18 (1996): 71–88.

Burtt, E. A., ed. *The Teachings of the Compassionate Buddha: Early Discourses, the Dhammapada, and Later Basic Writings*. New York: New American Library, 1955.

Buttrick, George Arthur, ed. and trans. *The Interpreter's Bible.* 12 vols. New York: Abingdon, 1956.

"Bye Bye Meat Industry: Civil Disobedience in Sweden." http://www.raddningstjansten.org/bye-byemeat/index_engelska.htm (accessed November 24, 2008).

"Cage-Free Hens Kept for Eggs: Free-Range Poultry and Eggs." UPC(United Poultry Concerns). http://www.upc-online.org/freerange.html (accessed February 16, 2011).

Cajete, Gregory. "Indigenous Education and Ecology: Perspectives of an American Indian Educator." In *Indigenous Traditions and Ecology: The Interbeing of Cosmology and Community,* edited by John A. Grim, 619–38. Cambridge, MA: Harvard University Press. 2001.

Cameron, Deborah. *Verbal Hygiene.* New York: Routledge, 1995.

Care for Cows in Vrindavana. http://www.careforcows.org/ (accessed January 23, 2010).

Carlisle, Elizabeth. "The Louisiana Environment: The Gulf of Mexico Dead Zone and Red Tides." http://www.tulane.edu/~bfleury/envirobio/enviroweb/DeadZone.htm (accessed October 31, 2007).

Cart Horses and Donkeys: Abuse and Rescue." CHAI (Concern for Helping Animals in Israel). http://www.chai.online.org/en/campaigns/horses/campaigns_horses-i.htm (accessed April 8, 2011).

Cassuto, Umberto. *A Commentary on the Book of Genesis.* 2 vols. Jerusalem: Magnes, 1961, 1964.

Catechism of the Catholic Church. Liguori, MO: Liguori, 1994.

CBC News. "Deadly Water: The Lessons of Walkerton." *CBC News in Review: September 2000.* http://www.cbc.ca/newsinreview/Sep2000/walkerton/facts.htm (accessed October 25, 2007).

Chan Wing-tsit, ed. and trans. *A Source Book in Chinese Philosophy.* Princeton, NJ: Princeton University Press, 1963.

Chapple, Christopher Key. "Ahimsa in the *Mahabharata:* A Story, a Philosophical Perspective, and an Admonishment." *Journal of Vaishnava Studies* 4.3 (Summer 1996): 109–25.

———. "Animals and Environment in the Buddhist Birth Stories." In *Buddhism and Ecology: The Interconnection of Dharma and Deeds,* edited by Mary Evelyn Tucker and Duncan Ryuken Williams, 131–48. Cambridge, MA: Harvard University Press, 1997.

Ch'en, Kenneth. *Buddhism in China: A Historical Survey.* Princeton, NJ: Princeton University Press, 1964.

Ch'eng-en, Wu. *Monkey: Folk Novel of China.* Translated by Arthur Waley. New York: Grove Press, 1943.

Chuang Tzu. *Teachings and Sayings of Chuang Tzu.* Translated by H. A. Giles. New York: Dover, 2001.

Church, Jill Howard. "A King among Men: Martin Luther King Jr.'s Son Blazes His Own Trail—Dexter Scott King." *Vegetarian Times.* http://findarticles.com/p/articles/mi_m0820/is_n218/ai_17444897/ (accessed February 5, 2010).

Clark, Wissler. *Indians of the United States.* New York: Anchor, 1966.

Clarke, L. "The Universe Alive: Nature in the *Masnavi* of Jalal al-Din Rumi." In *Islam and Ecology: A Bestowed Trust,* edited by Richard C. Foltz et al., 39–65. Cambridge, MA: Harvard University Press, 2003.

Cobb, John B, Jr. "Christianity, Economics, and Ecology." In *Christianity and Ecology: Seeking the Well-Being of Earth and Humans,* edited by Dieter T. Hessel and Rosemary Radford Ruether, 497–511. Cambridge, MA: Harvard University Press. 2000.

Coffin, Sloane. "The Politics of Compassion: The Heart Is a Little to the Left." *Harvard Divinity Bulletin* 28.2–3 (1999): 11–12.

Cohen, Noah. *Tsa'ar Ba'alei Hayim: The Prevention of Cruelty to Animals—Its Bases, Development, and Legislation Hebrew Literature.* New York: Feldheim, 1976.

Cohen, Rabbi Shear Yashuv. "Rabbinic Endorsement." In *Judaism and Vegetarianism,* by Richard H. Schwartz, xix–xx. New York: Lantern, 2001.

Cohn-Sherbok, Dan. "Hope for the Animal Kingdom." In *A Communion of Subjects: Animals in Religion, Science, and Ethics,* edited by Paul Waldau and Kimberley Patton, 81–90. New York: Columbia University Press, 2006.

Collins, Jocelyn. "Deforestation." *WWC Envirofacts*. http://www.bcb.uwc.ac.za/Envfacts/facts/deforestation.htm (accessed July 22, 2007).

"Common Cancer Types." National Cancer Institute. http://www.cancer.gov/cancertopics/commoncancers (accessed July 21, 2008).

Connor, Steve. "Going before Their Time." *Independent*, March 5, 1999, 9.

Conze, Edward, trans. *Buddhist Scriptures*. New York: Penguin, 1959.

———. *Buddhist Thought in India*. Ann Arbor: University of Michigan Press, 1962.

Cook, F. H. *Hua-yen Buddhism*. University Park, PA: Penn State University Press, 1977.

Coomaraswamy, Ananda K., and Sister Nivedita. *Myths of the Hindus and Buddhists*. New York: Dover, 1967.

Cragg, Kenneth, ed. *Readings in the Qur'an*. London: Collins Religious, 1988.

Cragg, Kenneth, and R. Marston Speight. *The House of Islam*. Belmont, CA: Wadsworth, 1988.

———. *Islam from Within: Anthology of a Religion*. Belmont, CA: Wadsworth, 1980.

Curtin, Deane. "Dogen, Deep Ecology, and the Ecological Self." *Environmental Ethics* 16 (1994): 195–213.

———. "Making Peace with the Earth: Indigenous Agriculture and the Green Revolution." *Environmental Ethics* 17 (1995): 59–73.

"Dairy's Dark Side: The Sour Truth behind Milk." *Compassionate Living: The Magazine of Mercy for Animals* 10.6 (Spring–Summer 2010): 10–14.

Dalai Lama, His Holiness the. *Ethics for the New Millennium*. New York: Riverhead, 1999.

Daneel, Marthinus L. "Earthkeeping Churches at the African Grass Roots." In *Christianity and Ecology: Seeking the Well-Being of Earth and Humans*, edited by Dieter T. Hessel and Rosemary Radford Ruether, 531–52. Cambridge, MA: Harvard University Press, 2000.

Danielou, Alain. *Myths and Gods of India*. Rochester, VT: Inner Traditions, 1985.

Davis, Karen. "The Mother Turkey and Her Young." *Poultry Press*, Winter 2008–09, 6–7.

Dawood, N. J., trans. *Qur'an*. Harmondsworth, UK: Penguin, 1956.

Dear, John. Quoted in "Bruce Friedrich."

de Bary, William Theodore, ed. *The Buddhist Tradition in India, China, and Japan*. New York: Vintage, 1972.

Denny, Frederick M. *Islam and the Muslim Community*. San Francisco: HarperSanFrancisco, 1987.

de Voragine, Jacobus. *The Golden Legend Readings on the Saints*, vol. 2. Princeton, NJ: Princeton University Press, 1993.

Desai, Mahadev. *Day to Day with Gandhi*, vol. 7. Varanasi, India: Navajivan, 1968–72. Quoted in Paul Waldau, "Guest Editor's Introduction, Religion and Other Animals: Ancient Themes, Contemporary Challenges." *Society & Animals Journal of Human-Animal Studies* 8:3 (2000): 227–44.

DeWitt, Calvin. "Behemoth and Batrachians in the Eye of God." In *Christianity and Ecology: Seeking the Well-Being of Earth and Humans*, edited by Dieter T. Hessel and Rosemary Radford Ruether, 291–310. Cambridge, MA: Harvard University Press, 2000.

———. "The Three Big Questions." In *Worldviews, Religion, and the Environment: A Global Anthology*, edited by Richard C. Foltz, 349–55. Belmont, CA: Wadsworth, 2003.

Doniger, Wendy. *The Hindus: An Alternative History*. New York: Penguin, 2009.

Douglas, Mary. *Purity and Danger*. Baltimore: Penguin, 1966.

Dunagan, Christopher. "Whale Watch: Tribal Views on Whaling." *Sun*, October 4, 1998. *Sunlink*, http://web.kitsapsun.com/packages/whalehunt/story30.html (accessed August 20, 2000).

Dunayer, Joan. *Animal Equality: Language and Liberation*. Derwood, MD: Ryce, 2001.

Dundas, Paul. *The Jains*. New York: Routledge, 1992.

Dutton, Yasin. "The Environmental Crisis of Our Time: A Muslim Response." In *Islam and Ecology: A Bestowed Trust*, edited by Richard C. Foltz et al., 323–40. Cambridge, MD: Harvard University Press, 2003.

Dwivedi, O. P. "Dharmic Ecology." In *Hinduism and Ecology: The Intersection of Earth, Sky, and Water*, edited by Christopher Key Chapple and Mary Evelyn Tucker, 3–22. Cambridge, MD: Harvard University Press, 2000.

"Earth Observatory: Causes of Deforestatio." NASA. http://earthobservatory.nass.gov/Library/Deforestation/deforestation_update3.html (accessed July 22, 2007).

Easwaran, Eknath. *Gandhi the Man: The Story of His Transformation.* Berkeley, CA: Nilgiri, 1997.

Eck, Diana. *Darsan: Seeing the Divine Image in India.* Chambersburg, PA: Anima, 1981.

Eckhart, Meister. "The Nearness of the Kingdom." *Eckhart's Sermons.* http://www.catholicprimer.org/eckhart/eckhart_sermons.pdf (accessed September 7, 2010).

———. *The Complete Mystical Works of Meister Eckhart.* Translated by Maurice O'C Walshe. New York: Herder & Herder, Crossroad, 2009.

Eiselen, Frederick Carl, Lewis Edwin, and David G. Downey. *The Abingdon Bible Commentary.* New York: Abingdon-Cokesbury, 1929.

Eisnitz, Gail. *Slaughterhouse: The Shocking Story of Greed, Neglect, and Inhumane Treatment Inside the U.S. Meat Industry.* New York: Prometheus, 1997.

Embree, Ainslie T., ed. *The Hindu Tradition: Readings in Oriental Thought.* New York: Vintage, 1972.

———. *Sources of Indian Tradition: From the Beginning to 1800.* New York: Columbia University Press, 1988.

Englebert, Omer. *St. Francis of Assisi: A Biography.* Ann Arbor, MI: Servant, 1979.

Erdoes, Richard, and Alfonso Ortiz, eds. *American Indian Myths and Legends.* New York: Pantheon, 1984.

Esposito, John L. *Islam: The Straight Path.* Oxford: Oxford University Press, 1988.

"Factory Beef Production." Farm Sanctuary. *FactoryFarming.Com.* http://www.farmsanctuary.org/issues/factoryfarming/beef/ (accessed August 9, 2008).

"Factory Poultry Production." Farm Sanctuary. *FactoryFarming.Com.* http://www.farmsanctuary.org/issues/factoryfarming/poultry/ (accessed August 9, 2008).

Fadali, Moneim A. "Muslim Vegetarians." http://www.vegetablekillers.net/forums/veg-food/34578-muslim-vegetarians.html (accessed September 6, 2010).

Fairclough, Norman, ed., *Critical Language Awareness.* New York: Longman, 1992.

———. *Language and Power.* London: Longman, 1989.

"Farm Sanctuary Challenges USDA's 'Natural' Labeling Standards." *Sanctuary: Farm Sanctuary's Compassionate Quarterly* (Winter 2010): 14.

Fausböll, V., trans. "MettaSutta" and "Uragasutta" (in "Uragavagga"). *The Sutta-Nipâta, The Sacred Books of the East, Vol. 10.* Oxford, UK: Clarendon Press, 1881.

Feinup-Riordan, Ann. "A Guest on the Table: Ecology from the Yup'ik Eskimo Point of View." In *Indigenous Traditions and Ecology: The Interbeing of Cosmology and Community,* edited by John A. Grim, 541–58. Cambridge, MA: Harvard University Press, 2001.

Feit, Harvey A. "Hunting, Nature, and Metaphor: Political and Discursive Strategies in James Bay Cree Resistance and Autonomy." In *Indigenous Traditions and Ecology: The Interbeing of Cosmology and Community,* edited by John A. Grim, 411–52. Cambridge, MA: Harvard University Press. 2001.

"59 Billion Land and Sea Animals Killed for Food in the US in 2009." *Free From Harm: Make Your Food Choices Matter.* http://freefromharm.org/farm-animal-welfare/59-billion-land-and-sea-animals-killed-for-food-in-the-us-in-2009/ (accessed April 27, 2011).

Fischer, Louis. *Gandhi: His Life and Message for the World.* New York: Mentor, 1982.

Fisher, Linda. "Freeing Feathered Spirits." In *Sister Species: Women, Animals and Social Justice,* 110–116. U. of Illinois Press, 2011 edited by Lisa Kemmerer. St. Paul, MN: Paradigm, forthcoming.

———. "Mother Earth and All Her Children." In *Call to Compassion: Religious Perspectives on Animal Advocacy,* edited by Lisa Kemmerer and Anthony J. Nocella II, 215–223. New York: Lantern, 2011.

Foltz, Richard C. *Animals in Islamic Tradition and Muslim Cultures.* Oxford, UK: Oneworld, 2005.

———. "Islamic Environmentalism: A Matter of Interpretation." In *Islam and Ecology: A Bestowed Trust,* edited by Richard C. Foltz et al., 249–80. Cambridge, MA: Harvard University Press, 2003.

————. "Is Vegetarianism Un-Islamic?" In *Food for Thought: The Debate on Vegetarianism*, edited by Steven Sapontzis, 209–22. Amherst, NY: Prometheus, 2004.

————. "'This She-Camel of God Is a Sign to You': Dimensions of Animals in Islamic Tradition and Muslim Culture." In *A Communion of Subjects: Animals in Religion and Ethics*, edited by Paul Waldau and Kimberley Patton, 149–59. New York: Columbia University Press, 2006.

Forbes, Jack D. "Nature and Culture: Problematic Concepts for Native Americans." In *Indigenous Traditions and Ecology: The Interbeing of Cosmology and Community*, edited by John A. Grim, 103–24. Cambridge, MA: Harvard University Press, 2001.

"'Free-Range' Hens Kept for Eggs: Free Range Poultry and Eggs." UPC (Uniter Poultry Concerns). http://www.upc-online.org/freerange.html (accessed February 16, 2011).

French, William C. "Against Biospherical Egalitarianism." *Environmental Ethics* 17 (1995): 39–57.

Friedrich, Bruce. "Bruce Friedrich." Biographical information. http://www.eviltwinbooking.org/events.cfm?view=speakers&artist_id=133 (accessed December 5, 2008).

Friedlander, Shems. *Submission: Sayings of the Prophet Muhammad*. New York: Harper Colophon, 1977.

Fung, Yu-lan. *A Short History of Chinese Philosophy*. New York: Free Press, 1948.

Gaard, Greta. "Tools for a Cross-Cultural Feminist Ethics: Exploring Ethical Contexts and Contents in the Makah Whale Hunt." *Hypatia* 16.1 (2001): 1–27. http//:proquest.umi.com/pqdweb?index=21&did=000000066871044&SrchMode=3&sid=1 (accessed August 7, 2004).

Gandhi, Mohandas K. *An Autobiography: The Story of My Experiments with Truth*. Boston: Beacon, 1993.

————. *The Essential Gandhi: An Anthology of His Writings on His Life, Work, and Ideas*. Edited by Louis Fischer. New York: Vintage, 2002.

Ganzfried, Rabbi Solomon. *Code of Jewish Law*, bk. 4, ch. 191. New York: Hebrew Publishing, 1961.

Gergen, Kenneth J. *An Invitation to Social Construction*. London: Sage, 1999.

Gill, Sam D. *Native American Religions, an Introduction*. Belmont, CA: Wadsworth, 1982.

————. *Native American Traditions, Sources and Interpretations*. Belmont, CA: Wadsworth, 1983.

Ginzberg, Louis. "Zedekiah." *Legends of the Jews*. http://ancienthistory.about.com/library/bl/bl_text_jewslegends4j.htm#_ednZedekiah (accessed February 6, 2010) (accessed October 17, 2010).

"Gompertz, Lewis." *JewishEncyclopedia.com*. http://www.jewishencyclopedia.com/view.jsp?letter=G&artid=355 (accessed November 27, 2008).

Gompertz, Lewis. *Moral Inquiries on the Situation of Man and of Brutes*. Borders. http://www.borders.co.uk/book/moral-inquiries-on-the-situation-of-man-and-of-brutes-(kinship-library)/389125/ (accessed November 27, 2008).

Gonzales, Tirso A., and Melissa K. Nelson. "Contemporary Native American Responses to Environmental Threats in Indian Country." In *Indigenous Traditions and Ecology: The Interbeing of Cosmology and Community*, edited by John A. Grim, 495–538. Cambridge, MA: Harvard University Press, 2001.

Goodman, Lenn E. "The Moral Case for Saving Species: Thirteen Prominent Thinkers Explain Why Society Should Give High Priority to the Purpose of the Endangered Species Act." *Defenders* (Summer 1998): 11.

Gosvami, Satsvarupa dasa. *Readings in Vedic Literature: The Tradition Speaks for Itself*. New York: Bhaktivedanta, 1977.

"Government-Required Animal Testing: Overview." PETA (People for the Ethical Treatment of Animals). http://www.peta.org/mc/factssheet_display.asp?ID=125(accessed August 14, 2008).

Graham, Lanier. *Goddesses in Art*. New York: Abbeville, 1997.

Griffiths, Richard. *The Human Use of Animals*. Cambridge, UK: Grove, 1982.

Grinnell, George Bird. *Blackfoot Lodge Tales*. Lincoln: University of Nebraska Press, 1962.

Grisell, Ronald. *Sufism*. Berkeley, CA: Ross, 1983.

Gumbley, Walter. "Saints and Animals." *Catholic-Animals, The Ark: A Publication of Catholic Concern for Animals.* "Selections from the Ark Number 196—Spring 2004." http://www.all-creatures.org/ca/ark-196-saints.html (accessed September 23, 2008).

Gunn, Alastair S. "Traditional Ethics and the Moral Status of Animals." *Environmental Ethics* 5 (1983): 133–53.

Guthrie, D., and J. A. Motyer, eds. *The New Bible Commentary.* Rev. ed. Leicester, UK: Inter-Varsity, 1970.

Gyatso, Tenzin. "Hope for the Future." In *The Path of Compassion: Writings on Socially Engaged Buddhism,* edited by Fred Eppsteiner, 3–8. Berkeley, CA: Parallax, 1985.

"Halal—Into the Future." Halal Food Authority. http://www.halalfoodauthority.co.uk/seminar-shalalfoodexhibit.html (accessed October 19, 2010).

"Halal V/s Haraam Food in a Non-Muslim Country." *ShiaChat.com: Forums.* http://www.shiachat.com/forum/index.php?/topic/234916013-halal-vs-haraam-food-in-a-non-muslim-country/#top (accessed October 19, 2010).

Hall, David L. "On Seeking a Change of Environment." In *Nature in Asian Traditions of Thought: Essays in Environmental Philosophy,* edited by J. Baird Callicott and Roger T. Ames, 99–111. Albany: State University of New York Press, 1989.

Hallman, David G. "Climate Change: Ethics, Justice, and Sustainable Community." In *Christianity and Ecology: Seeking the Well-Being of Earth and Humans,* edited by Dieter T. Hessel and Rosemary Radford Ruether, 453–71. Cambridge, MA: Harvard University Press, 2000.

Hamid, Rehana. "Conversation/Islam: Dr. Rehana Hamid." In *Food for the Gods: Vegetarianism and the World's Religions,* edited by Rynn Berry, 256–69. New York: Pythagorean, 1998.

Hanh, Thich Nhat. *For a Future to Be Possible: Buddhist Ethics for Everyday Life.* Berkeley, CA: Parallax, 2007.

———. "The Individual, Society, and Nature." In *The Path of Compassion: Writings on Socially Engaged Buddhism,* edited by Fred Eppsteiner, 40–46. Berkeley, CA: Parallax, 1985.

———. *Love in Action: Writings on Nonviolent Social Change.* Berkeley, CA: Parallax, 1993.

———. *Peace Is Every Step: The Path of Mindfulness in Everyday Life.* New York: Bantam, 1992.

Haq, S. Nomanul. "Islam and Ecology: Toward Retrieval and Reconstruction." In *Islam and Ecology: A Bestowed Trust,* edited by Richard C. Foltz et al., 121–54. Cambridge, MA: Harvard University Press, 2003.

Haque, Nadeem. "The Principles of Animal Advocacy in Islam: Four Integrated Cognitions." In *Society & Animals.* Vol. 19, no. 3 pages 279–290.

Harris, Ian. "Buddhism and the Discourse of Environmental Concern: Some Methodological Problems Considered." In *Buddhism and Ecology: The Interconnection of Dharma and Deeds,* edited by Mary Evelyn Tucker and Duncan Ryuken Williams, 377–402. Cambridge, MA: Harvard University Press, 1997.

Harrison, R. K. *Numbers.* Chicago: Moody, 1990.

Harrod, Howard L. *Renewing the World: Plains Indian Religion and Morality.* Tucson: University of Arizona Press, 1987.

"Hazrat Ibrahim Bin Adham *Current Affairs.Com: Pakistan News and Current Events.* http://thecurrentaffairs.com/hazrat-ibrahim-bin-adham-ra.html (accessed October 19, 2010).

Henare, Manuka. "*Tapu, Mana, Mauri, Hau, Wairua*: A Maori Philosophy of Vitalism and Cosmos." In *Indigenous Traditions and Ecology: The Interbeing of Cosmology and Community,* edited by John A. Grim, 197–221. Cambridge, MA: Harvard University Press. 2001.

Henricks, Robert G. *Lao-Tzu Te-Tao Ching: A New Translation Based on the Recently Discovered Ma-wang-tui Texts.* New York: Ballantine, 1989.

Hertz, J. H. "The Penateuch and Haftorahs." In *The Trees' Birthday,* edited by Ellen Bernstein. Philadelphia: Turtle River, 1988.

Hiebert, Theodore. "The Human Vocation: Origins and Transformations in Christian Traditions." In *Christianity and Ecology: Seeking the Well-Being of Earth and Humans,* edited by Dieter

T. Hessel and Rosemary Radford Ruether, 135–54. Cambridge, MA: Harvard University Press, 2000.

"High Plains Regional Groundwater Study." USGS (U.S. Geological Survey). http://co.water.usgs. gov/nawqa/hpgw/factsheets/DENNEHYFS1.html (accessed July 21, 2008).

Hirsch, Rabbi Samson Rafael. *Horeb*, vol. 2 (72:482). Translated by Grunfeld Dayan. London: Soncino, 1962.

———. "Letter 4." *Nineteen Letters*. New York: Feldheim (Elias edition), 1969.

"The History of the RSPCA." *Animal Legal and Historical Center*. http://www.animallaw.info/historical/articles/arukrspcahist.htm (accessed November 12, 2008).

Hobgood-Oster, Laura. "Holy Dogs and Asses: Stories Told through Animal Saints." http://www. southwestern.edu/academic/bwp/pdf/2001bwp-Hobgood-Oster.pdf (accessed March 5, 2008) (accessed May, 2009).

Holy Bible: New Revised Standard Version. New York: American Bible Society, 1989.

Hughes, J. Donald. "Francis of Assisi and the Diversity of Creation." *Environmental Ethics* 18 (1996): 311–20.

"An HSUS Report: The Welfare of Animals in the Meat, Egg, and Dairy Industries." HSUS (Humane Society of the United States). http://www.humanesociety.org/assets/pdfs/farm/welfare_ overview.pdf (accessed April 1, 2011).

Hultkrantz, Ake. *The Study of American Indian Religions*. Edited by Christopher Vecsey. New York: Crossroads, 1983.

Hume, Major C. W. *The Status of Animals in the Christian Religion*. London: UFAW, 1957.

Hu Shih. "Introduction to the American Edition." In *Monkey*, by Wu Ch'eng-en, translated by Arthur Waley, 1–5. New York: Evergreen Books by Grove Weidenfeld, 1987.

Hutterman, Aloys. "Genesis 1—The Most Misunderstood Part of the Bible." In *Worldviews, Religion, and the Environment: A Global Anthology*, edited by Richard C. Foltz, 280–89. Belmont, CA: Wadsworth, 2003.

Hyde-Chambers, Fredrick, and Audrey Hyde-Chambers. *Tibetan Folk Tales*. Boulder, CA: Shambhala, 1981.

Hyland, J. R. *God's Covenant with Animals: A Biblical Basis for the Humane Treatment of All Creatures*. New York: Lantern, 2000.

———. *The Slaughter of Terrified Beasts: A Biblical Basis for the Humane Treatment of Animals*. Sarasota, FL: Viatoris Ministries, 1988.

Ides, Isabelle, et al. "Whale Hunt Issue," *Peninsula Daily News*, June 16, 2000.

"In the Kitchens of the Roq." http://www.outremer.co.uk/kitchen.html (accessed June 24, 2008).

Ip, Po-Keung. "Taoism and the Foundations of Environmental Ethics." *Environmental Ethics* 5 (1983): 335–43.

"Islamic Concern and Vegetarianism." *Health and Vegetarians*. http://www.purifymind.com/ IslamicConcern.htm (accessed September 6, 2010).

"Israel's Chief Rabbis Grant CHAI's Request to End Cruel Slaughter Method." CHAI (Concern for Helping Animals in Israel). http://www.chai-online.org/en/news/press_releases/pr_ judaism_shackle2.htm (accessed November 27, 2008).

Ivanhoe, Philip J., and Bryan W. Van Norden, trans. *Readings in Classical Chinese Philosophy*, 2nd ed. Indianapolis: Hackett, 2001.

Jacobi, Hermann, trans. "Eighteenth Lecture: Sangaya." In *Jaina Sutras, Part II: The Sacred Books of the East, Vol. 45*, 1895. *Internet Sacred Texts Archive*. http://www.sacred-texts.com/jai/sbe45/ sbe4510.htm (accessed August 22, 2010).

———. "Eighth Verse: Kapila's Verses." In *Jaina Sutras, Part II: The Sacred Books of the East, Vol. 45*, 1895. *Internet Sacred Texts Archive*. http://www.sacred-texts.com/jai/sbe45/sbe4510.htm (accessed August 22, 2010).

———. "Fifth Lecture: Death against One's Will." *Uttarâdhyayana Sutra*. In *Jaina Sutras, Part II: The Sacred Books of the East, Vol. 45*, 1895. *Internet Sacred Texts Archive*. http://www.sacred-texts.com/jai/sbe45/sbe4507.htm (accessed August 22, 2010).

————. "Nineteenth Lecture: The Son of Mriga." *Jaina Sutras, Part II: The Sacred Books of the East,* Vol. 45, 1895. *Internet Sacred Texts Archive.* http://www.sacred-texts.com/jai/sbe45/sbe4521. htm (accessed August 22, 2010).

Jacobsen, Knut. "The Institutionalization of the Ethics of 'Non-Injury' toward All 'Beings' in Ancient India." *Environmental Ethics* 16 (1994): 287–301.

Jaini, Padmanabh S. *The Jaina Path of Purification.* Delhi: Motilal Banarsidass, 1979.

James, George A. "Ethical and Religious Dimensions of Chipko Resistance." In *Hinduism and Ecology: The Intersection of Earth, Sky, and Water,* edited by Christopher Key Chapple and Mary Evelyn Tucker, 499–527. Cambridge, MA: Harvard University Press, 2000.

Jette, Jules. "On Superstitions of the Ten'a Indians (Middle Part of the Yukon Valley, Alaska)." *Journal of the Royal Anthropological Institute of Great Britain* (1895).

————. "On Ten'a Folk-Lore." *Journal of the Royal Anthropological Institute of Great Britain.* 38 (1908): 298–367.

JVNA (Jewish Vegetarians of North America). JewishVeg.com home page. http://www.jewishveg. com/ (accessed November 29, 2008).

Jochim, Christian. *Chinese Religions.* Englewood Cliffs, NJ: Prentice-Hall, 1986.

Johnson, Lawrence E. *A Morally Deep World: An Essay on Moral Significance and Environmental Ethics.* Cambridge: Cambridge University Press, 1991.

Kalechofsky, Roberta. "Hierarchy, Kinship, and Responsibility." In *A Communion of Subjects: Animals in Religion, Science, and Ethics,* edited by Paul Waldau and Kimberley Patton, 91–99. New York: Columbia University Press, 2006.

Kalu, Ogbu U. "The Sacred Egg: Worldview, Ecology, and Development in West Africa." In *Indigenous Traditions and Ecology: The Interbeing of Cosmology and Community,* edited by John A. Grim, 225–48. Cambridge, MA: Harvard University Press, 2001.

Kaufman, Stephen R., and Nathan Braun. *Good News for All Creation: Vegetarianism as Christian Stewardship.* Cleveland, OH: Vegetarian Advocates Press, 2004.

Kelley, Peter. "Reaching Out in Friendship." *Skagit Valley Herald,* January 28, 2000, A1.

Kempis, Thomas à. *The Imitation of Christ.* Springdale, PA: Whitaker House, 1981.

Khan, Noor Inayat, trans. *Twenty Jataka Tales.* New York: Inner Traditions, 1985.

Kheel, Marti. "License to Kill: An Ecofeminist Critique of a Hunters' Discourse." In *Women and Animals: Feminist Theoretical Explorations,* edited by Carol Adams and Josephine Donovan, 85–125. Durham, NC: Duke, 1995.

Kher, Unmesh. "Oceans of Nothing: Study Says Overfishing Will Soon Destroy the Seafood Supply." *Time,* November 13, 2006, 56–57.

Kimball, Charles. "When Religion Becomes Evil." Lecture at Rocky Mountain College, Billings, MT, September 27, 2004.

Kinsley, David. *Ecology and Religion: Ecological Spirituality in Cross-Cultural Perspective.* Englewood Cliffs, NJ: Prentice-Hall, 1995.

————. *The Goddesses' Mirror: Visions of the Divine from East and West.* Albany: State University of New York Press, 1989.

Kirchheimer, Gabe. "US Cows: Sacred or Mad?" *High Times,* July 1, 2001. *Organic Consumer's Association.* http://www.purefood.org/madcow/cows7101.cfm (accessed June 22, 2009).

Kirkland, Russell. "'Responsible Non-Action' in a Natural World: Perspectives from the Neiye, Zhuangzi, and Daode Jing." In *Daoism and Ecology: Ways within a Cosmic Landscape,* edited by N. J. Girardot et al., 283–304. Cambridge, MA: Harvard University Press, 2001.

Kleeman, Terry F. "Daoism and the Quest for Order." In *Daoism and Ecology: Ways within a Cosmic Landscape,* edited by N. J. Girardot et al., 61–70. Cambridge, MA: Harvard University Press, 2001.

Kohn, Livia, ed. *Daoism Handbook.* Leiden, The Netherlands: Brill, 2000.

————. *Cosmos and Community: The Ethical Dimensions of Daoism.* Cambridge, MA: Three Pines, 2004.

Komjathy, Louis. "Meat Avoidance in Daoism." In *Call to Compassion: Religious Perspectives on Animal Advocacy*, edited by Lisa Kemmerer and Anthony J. Nocella II, 83–103. New York: Lantern, 2011.

Kornfield, Jack. "Afterword: Happiness Comes from the Heart." In *For a Future to Be Possible: Buddhist Ethics for Everyday Life*, by Thich Nhat Hanh. Berkeley, CA: Parallax, 2007.

Kowalski, Gary. *The Bible According to Noah: Theology as if Animals Mattered*. New York: Lantern, 2001.

Kraft, Kenneth. "Nuclear Ecology and Engaged Buddhism." In *Buddhism and Ecology: The Interconnection of Dharma and Deeds*, edited by Mary Evelyn Tucker and Duncan Ryuken Williams, 269–91. Cambridge, MA: Harvard University Press, 1997.

Kristof, Nicholas B. "Pathogens in Our Pork." *New York Times*, March 14, 2009. http://www.nytimes.com/2009/03/15/opinion/15kristof.html?_r=1&emc=eta1 (accessed July 12, 2011).

Kushner, Thomasine. "Interpretations of Life and Prohibitions against Killing." *Environmental Ethics* 3 (1981): 147–54.

Kwiatkowska-Szatzscheider, Teresa. "From the Mexican Chiapas Crisis: A Different Perspective for Environmental Ethics." *Environmental Ethics* 19 (1997): 267–78.

Kwok, Man Ho and Joanne O'Brien, ed. and trans. *The Eight Immortals of Taoism: Legends and Fables of Popular Taoism*. NY: Meridian, 1990.

Landais, Emmanuelle. "Ban Sought on Import of Australian Sheep." *Gulf News*. http://gulfnews.com/news/gulf/uae/environment/ban-sought-on-import-of-australian-sheep-1.255661 (accessed September 19, 2006).

Lao-Tzu. *Tao Te Ching, The Sacred Books of the East, Vol. 39*. Translated by J. Legge, 1891. *Internet Sacred Texts Archive*. http://www.sacred-texts.com/tao/index.htm (accessed March 8, 2011).

Laumakis, Stephen J. *An Introduction to Buddhist Philosophy*. Cambridge: Cambridge University Press, 2008.

"Lethal Predator Control Courtesy of Wildlife Services." *Humane Society of the United States*. http://www.coyoterescue.org/article_lethalcontrol.html (accessed March 17, 2011).

"Lewis Gompertz (1779–1865)." http://www.purifymind.com/Lewis Gompertz.htm (accessed November 22, 2008).

Li, Chien-hui. "Uniting Christianity, Philanthropy, and Humanity to Animals." *Society & Animals Journal of Human-Animal Studies* 8:3 (2000): 265–86.

Lim, Phaik Kee. "The Pen Is Mightier than the Sword" In *Speaking Up for Animals: An Anthology of Women's Voices*, edited by Lisa Kemmerer, 117–22. St. Paul, MN: Paradigm, forthcoming.

Linden, Maya. "Nadia Montasser Has Conducted a Small Interview with PETA Campaign Co-ordinator, Maya Linden." *The Paper* 14 (May 2006): 14.

Linzey, Andrew. "Animals." In *A New Dictionary of Christian Ethics*, edited by James Childress and John Macquarrie, 28–33. London: SCM, 1967.

———. *Animal Gospel: A Christian Faith as though Animals Mattered*. London: Hodder and Stoughton, 1998.

———. "Animal Rights: A Religious Vision." In *Faiths and the Environment: Conference Papers*, edited by Christopher Lamb, 86–97. *Faith in Dialogue* 1. Middlesex UK: Centre for Interfaith Relations, 1996.

———. *Animal Theology*. Chicago: University of Illinois Press, 1995.

———. "The Arrogance of Humanism." In *Animal Welfare and the Environment*, edited by Richard D. Ryder, 68–72. Melksham, UK: Duckworth, 1992.

———. *Christianity and the Rights of Animals*. New York: Crossroad, 1987.

———. "Liberation Theology and the Oppression of Animals." *Scottish Journal of Theology* 46.4 (1993): 507–25.

Linzey, Andrew, and Dan Cohn-Sherbok. *After Noah: Animals and the Liberation of Theology*. London: Mowbray, 1997.

Llewellyn, Othman Abd-ar-Rahman. "The Basis for a Discipline of Islamic Environmental Law." In *Islam and Ecology: A Bestowed Trust*, edited by Richard C. Foltz et al., 185–248. Cambridge, MA: Harvard University Press, 2003.

Lo-Dro, Lama of Drepung. *The Prince Who Became a Cuckoo: A Tale of Liberation.* Translated by Lama Geshe Wangyal. New York: Theatre Arts, 1982.

Long, Jeffery D. *Jainism: An Introduction.* New York: I. B. Tauris, 2009.

Maguire, Daniel C. "Population, Consumption, Ecology: The Triple Problematic." In *Christianity and Ecology: Seeking the Well-Being of Earth and Humans*, edited by Dieter T. Hessel and Rosemary Radford Ruether, 403–27. Cambridge, MA: Harvard University Press, 2000.

Mair, Victor H., ed. *The Columbia Anthology of Traditional Chinese Literature.* New York: Columbia University Press, 1994.

———. *Wandering on the Way: Early Taoist Tales and Parables of Chuang Tzu.* New York: Bantam, 1994.

Marr, Carolyn, Lloyd Colfax, and Robert D. Monroe. *Portrait in Time: Photographs of the Makah by Samuel G. Morse, 1896–1903.* Seattle: Makah Cultural And Research Center, 1987.

Marshall, Peter. *Nature's Web: Rethinking Our Place on Earth.* London: Cassell, 1992.

Martin, Rafe. "Thoughts on the Jatakas." *The Path of Compassion: Writings on Socially Engaged Buddhism*, edited by Fred Eppsteiner, 97–102. Berkeley, CA: Parallax, 1985.

Martin-Schramm, James B. "Incentives, Consumption Patterns, and Population Policies: A Christian Ethical Perspective." In *Christianity and Ecology: Seeking the Well-Being of Earth and Humans*, edited by Dieter T. Hessel and Rosemary Radford Ruether, 439–52. Cambridge: Harvard University Press, 2000.

Mascaro, Juan, trans. *Bhagavad Gita.* Baltimore: Penguin, 1965.

———. *The Dhammapada: The Path of Perfection.* New York: Penguin, 1973.

Masri, Al-Hafiz Basheer Ahmad. *Animal Welfare in Islam.* Leicestershire, UK: Islamic Foundation, 2007.

———. *Islamic Concern for Animals.* Petersfield, UK: Athene Trust, 1987.

Maurer, Walter H., trans. *Pinnacles of India's Past: Selections from the Rgveda.* Amsterdam: Benjamins, 1986.

McFadyen, Clark. "Koyukon." *Handbook of North American Indians.* Vol. 6, *Subarctic*, edited by June Helm, 582-601. Washington, DC: Smithsonian Institution, 1981.

McFague, Sallie. "An Ecological Christology: Does Christianity Have It?" In *Christianity and Ecology: Seeking the Well-Being of Earth and Humans*, edited by Dieter T. Hessel and Rosemary Radford Ruether, 29–45. Cambridge, MA: Harvard University Press, 2000.

McGee, Mary. "State Responsibility for Environmental Management: Perspectives from Hindu Texts on Polity." In *Hinduism and Ecology: The Intersection of Earth, Sky, and Water*, edited by Christopher Key Chapple and Mary Evelyn Tucker, 59–100. Cambridge, MA: Harvard University Press, 2000.

McLuhan, T. C. *Touch the Earth.* New York: Promontory, 1971.

McQuillan, Jessie. "The Exterminators." *Missoula Independent*, Jun 7, 2007, 1.

Merton, Thomas. *The Way of Chuang Tzu.* New York: New Directions, 1965.

Mische, Patricia M. "The Integrity of Creation: Challenges and Opportunities for Praxis." In *Christianity and Ecology: Seeking the Well-Being of Earth and Humans*, edited by Dieter T. Hessel and Rosemary Radford Ruether, 591–602. Cambridge, MA: Harvard University Press, 2000.

Mishkat al-Masabih. "Animals in Islam II." *Islam, the Modern Religion.* http://www.themodernreligion.com/misc/an/an2.htm (accessed October 19, 2010).

Mizuno, Kogen. *Basic Buddhist Concepts.* Tokyo: Kosei, 1995.

Monigold, Glenn W. *Folktales from Vietnam.* New York: Peter Pauper, 1964.

Montejo, Victor D. "The Road to Heaven: Jakaltek Maya Beliefs, Religion, and the Ecology." In *Indigenous Traditions and Ecology: The Interbeing of Cosmology and Community*, edited by John A. Grim, 175–96. Cambridge: Harvard University Press, 2001.

328 References

Montasser, Nadia. "Animal Rights." *PetPost* 1 (September 2006): 36–37.

———. "Australia Suspends Live Exports to Egypt and I Backed Them Up!!!" *The Paper* 14 (May 2006): 14.

———. "From Human Being to Being Humane" (special feature). *SouthAsia Magazine*, July 2006, 56–58.

———. "So You Think Your Meat Is 'Halal'? Think Again!" *PetPost.* September 2006.

Moore, Michael S. *The Balaam Traditions: Their Character and Development.* Atlanta: Scholars, 1990.

Morrissey, Christine. "Christine Morrissey, Director of East Bay Animal Advocates." *Poultry Press: Promoting the Compassionate and Respectful Treatment of Domestic Fowl* 17.4. (Winter–Spring 2007–2008): 12.

Muhaiyaddeen, M. R. Bawa. *Islam and World Peace: Explanations of a Sufi.* Philadelphia: Fellowship, 1987.

———. "The Hunter Learns Compassion from the Fawn." In *Come to the Secret Garden: Sufi Tales of Wisdom,* 28. Philadelphia: Fellowship Press, 1985.

Müller, F. Max, trans. *Chandogya Upanishad.* In *The Upanishads, Part I,* 1–144. New York: Dover, 1962.

Müller, Max, trans. "Fourth Adhyana." *Svetâsvatara Upanishad.* In *The Upanishads, Part II: The Sacred Books of the East, Vol. 15,* 1884. *Internet Sacred Texts Archive.* http://www.sacred-texts.com/hin/sbe15/sbe15103.htm (accessed August 22, 2010).

Muwatta Malik. Guided Ways: Hadith. http://www.guidedways.com/book_display-book-54-translator-4-start-30-number-54.12.31.htm (accessed October 19, 2010).

Munsterberg, Hugo. *Art of India and Southeast Asia.* New York: Abrams, 1970.

Murti, Vasu. *They Shall Not Hurt or Destroy: Animal Rights and Vegetarianism in the Western Religious Traditions.* Cleveland, OH: Vegetarian Advocates, 1999.

Muttaqi, Shahid 'Ali. "The Sacrifice of 'Eid al-Adha': An Islamic Perspective against Animal Sacrifice." IslamicConcern.org. http://www.islamveg.com/sacrifice01.asp (accessed June 29, 2004).

Namunu, Simeon B. "Melanesian Religion, Ecology, and Modernization in Papua New Guinea." In *Indigenous Traditions and Ecology: The Interbeing of Cosmology and Community,* edited by John A. Grim, 249–80. Cambridge, MA: Harvard University Press. 2001.

Narayan, R. K., ed. *The Ramayana.* New York: Viking, 1972.

Nasr, Seyyed Hossein. "Islam, the Contemporary Islamic World, and the Environmental Crisis." In *Islam and Ecology: A Bestowed Trust,* edited by Richard C. Foltz et al., 85–106. Cambridge, MA: Harvard University Press, 2003.

Nelson, Lance E. "Reading the Bhagavadgita from an Ecological Perspective." In *Hinduism and Ecology: The Intersection of Earth, Sky, and Water,* edited by Christopher Key Chapple and Mary Evelyn Tucker, 127–64. Cambridge, MA: Harvard University Press, 2000.

Nelson, Richard K. *Make Prayers to Raven: A Koyukon View of the Northern Forest.* Chicago: University of Chicago Press, 1983.

———. "Passage of Gifts," Video #1. *Make Prayers to the Raven,* KUAC-TV. Fairbanks: University of Alaska, 1987.

Nestle, Marion. "One Thing to Do about Food." *Nation.* September 11, 2006, 14.

Nim, Tae Heng Se Nim. *Teachings of the Heart: Zen Teachings of Korean Woman Zen Master Tae Heng Se Nim.* Occidental, CA: Dai Shin Press, 1990.

Noske, Barbara. "Speciesism, Anthropocentrism, and Non-Western Cultures." *Anthrozoos* 10: 4 (1997): 183–90.

Noth, Martin. *Numbers.* Philadelphia: Westminster, 1968.

O'Flaherty, Wendy Doniger, ed. *Hindu Myths: A Sourcebook.* London: Penguin, 1975.

———, ed. *The Rig Veda.* New York: Penguin, 1981.

———, ed. *Textual Sources for the Study of Hinduism.* Chicago: University of Chicago Press, 1988.

"Og, King of Bashan." *JewishEncyclopedia.com.* http://www.jewishencyclopedia.com/view.jsp?artid=215&letter=G (accessed December 12, 2009).

Olivelle, Patrick, trans. *The Pancatantra: The Book of India's Folk Wisdom.* Oxford: Oxford University Press, 1997.

Olsen, Dennis T. *The Death of the Old and the Birth of the New: The Framework of the Book of Numbers and the Pentateuch*. Chico, CA: Scholars, 1985.

Opoku, Kofi. "Animals in African Mythology." In *A Communion of Subjects: Animals in Religion, Science, and Ethics*, edited by Paul Waldau and Kimberley Patton, 351–59. New York: Columbia University Press, 2006.

"'Organic' and 'Certified Humane' Eggs: Free-Range Poultry and Eggs." UPC (United Poultry Concerns). http://www.upconline.org/freerange.html (accessed February 16, 2011).

"Our Mission." CVA (Christian Vegetarian Association). http://www.all-creatures.org/cva/mission.htm (accessed November 27, 2008).

Oxford English Dictionary. "Politically Correct." http://dictionary.oed.com/cgi/entry/50182872/50182872se6?single=1&query_type=word&queryword=politically+correct&first=1&max_to_show=10&hilite=50182872se6 (accessed March 8, 2005).

Ozdemir, Ibrahim. "Toward an Understanding of Environmental Ethics from a Qur'anic Perspective." In *Islam and Ecology: A Bestowed Trust*, edited by Richard C. Foltz et al., 3–38. Cambridge, MA: Harvard University Press, 2003.

Palmer, Martin, et al. *Kuan Yin: Myths and Prophecies of the Chinese Goddess of Compassion*. London: Thorsons, 1995.

Parkes, Graham. "Human/Nature in Nietzsche and Taoism." *Nature in Asian Traditions of Thought: Essays in Environmental Philosophy*, edited by J. Baird Callicott and Roger T. Ames, 79–97. Albany: State University of New York Press, 1989.

Patton, Kimberley. "Animal Spirits: A Q&A with the Editors of a Remarkable New Book." *Best Friends*, July–August 2007, 30–33.

Pellisier, Hank. "Is Eating Meat a Catholic Sin?" http://www.sfgate.com/cgi-bin/article.cgi?f=/g/a/2004/02/02/urbananimal.DTL (accessed December 5, 2008).

Phelps, Norm. *The Dominion of Love*. New York: Lantern, 2002.

———. *The Great Compassion: Buddhism and Animal Rights*. New York: Lantern, 2004.

———. *The Longest Struggle: Animal Advocacy from Pythagoras to PETA*. New York: Lantern, 2007.

———. *Love for All Creatures: Frequently Asked Questions about the Bible and Animal Rights*. New York: Fund for Animals, 2003.

"Policy of the Animal Welfare Board of India." AWBI (Animal Welfare Board of India). http://www.awbi.org/policy.htm (accessed January 24, 2009).

Polk, Danne W. "Gabriel Marcel's Kinship to Ecophilosophy." *Environmental Ethics* 16 (1994): 173–86.

Posey, Darrell Addison. "Intellectual Property Rights and the Sacred Balance: Some Spiritual Consequences from the Commercialization of Traditional Resources." In *Indigenous Traditions and Ecology: The Interbeing of Cosmology and Community*, edited by John A. Grim, 3–24. Cambridge, MA: Harvard University Press. 2001.

Prabhavananda, Swami, and Frederick Manchester, trans. *Svetasvatara Upanishad*. In *The Upanishads: Breath of the Eternal*. New York: Mentor, 1948.

Prabhu, Pradip. "In the Eye of the Storm: Tribal Peoples of India." In *Indigenous Traditions and Ecology: The Interbeing of Cosmology and Community*, edited by John A. Grim, 47–70. Cambridge, MA: Harvard University Press. 2001.

Preece, Rod. *Animals and Nature: Cultural Myths, Cultural Realities*. Vancouver: UBC Press, 1999.

Preece, Rod, and David Fraser. "The Status of Animas in Biblical and Christian Thought: A Study in Colliding Values." *Society & Animals Journal of Human-Animal Studies* 8:3 (2000): 245–64.

Primatt, Humphrey. *The Duty of Mercy and the Sin of Cruelty to Brute Animals*. Edited by Richard D. Ryder. Fontwell, UK: Centaur, 1992. Originally published in 1776.

"Pro-Animal Caucus in the Knesset." CHAI (Concern for Helping Animals in Israel). http://www.chaionline.org/en/campaigns/knesset/campaigns_knesset_overview.htm (accessed November 27, 2008).

"Questions and Answers: Sea Lion Predation on Columbia River Salmon and Steelhead." WDFW (Washington Department of Fish and Wildlife), Columbia River Sea Lions Management. http://wdfw.wa.gov/conservation/sealions/questions.html (accessed March 8, 2009).

Rachels, James. *The Elements of Moral Philosophy*, 5th ed. New York: McGraw-Hill, 2007.

Rahula, Walpola. *What the Buddha Taught*. New York: Grove Weidenfeld, 1959.

Rao, K. L. Seshagiri. "The Five Great Elements (*Pancamahabhuta*): An Ecological Perspective." In *Hinduism and Ecology: The Intersection of Earth, Sky, and Water*, edited by Christopher Key Chapple and Mary Evelyn Tucker, 23–38. Cambridge, MA: Harvard University Press, 2000.

Reeves, Jay. "Fishermen Face off again Pesley Dolphins." ljworld.com. http://www2.ljworld.com/news/2009/jun/27/fishermen-face-against-pesky-dolphins/ (accessed February 16, 2011).

Regan, Tom. *Defending Animal Rights*. Urbana: University of Illinois Press, 2001.

Regenstein, Lewis G. *Replenish the Earth*. New York: Crossroad, 1991.

Rice, Pamela. "The Environmental Impact of the Meat-Centered Diet." *American Vegan* 2.2, (2002): 4–7.

———. "Subsidies to the Meat Industry; Separation of Meat and State!" *American Vegan* 2.2 (2002): 8–9.

Riley, Shamara Shantu. "Ecology Is a Sistah's Issue Too: The Politics of Emergent Afrocentric Ecowomanism. In *Worldviews, Religion, and the Environment: A Global Anthology*, edited by Richard C. Foltz, 472–81. Belmont, CA: Thompson, 2003.

Rippin, Andrew, and Jan Knappert. *Textual Sources for the Study of Islam*. Chicago: University of Chicago Press, 1986.

Roach, John. "Gulf of Mexico 'Dead Zone' Is Size of New Jersey." *National Geographic News*, http://news.nationalgeographic.com/news/2005/05/0525_050525_deadzone.html (accessed October 31, 2007).

Roberts, Holly. *The Vegetarian Philosophy of India: Hindu, Buddhist, and Jain Sacred Teachings*. New York: Anjeli, 2006.

Robinson, Richard H., and Willard L. Johnson. *The Buddhist Religion: A Historical Introduction*. Belmont, CA: Wadsworth, 1997.

Rollin, Bernard E. *Animal Rights and Human Morality*. Amherst, NY: Prometheus, 1981.

Rorty, Richard. *Contingency, Irony, and Solidarity*. Cambridge: Cambridge University Press, 1989.

Rosenberg, Donna. *World Mythology: An Anthology of the Great Myths and Epics*. Lincolnwood, IL: NTC, 1994.

Rosenfeld, Ben. "Update on Rod Coronado." *Earth First! Newswire*. http://earthfirstnews.wordpress.com/2010/08/21/update-on-rod-coronado/ (accessed April 6, 2011).

Rukmani, T. S. "Literary Foundations for an Ecological Aesthetic: *Dharma*, Ayurveda, the Arts, and *Abhijnanasakuntalam*." In *Hinduism and Ecology: The Intersection of Earth, Sky, and Water*, edited by Christopher Key Chapple and Mary Evelyn Tucker, 101–26. Cambridge, MA: Harvard University Press, 2000.

"Ruling of Chief Rabbi of Israel against Racing." CHAI (Concern for Helping Animals in Israel). http://www.chai-online.org/en/campaigns/racing/campaigns_racing_psak.htm (accessed November 27, 2008).

Rumi, Jelaluddin. *Mathnawi*. In *This Longing: Poetry, Teaching Stories, and Letters of Rumi*, translated by Coleman Barks and John Moyne. Putney, VT: Threshold, 1988.

———. "Story II: The Building of the 'Most Remote Temple' at Jerusalem." In *The Mathnawi: The Spiritual Couplets of Maulana Jalalu-'D-Din Muhammad Rumi, Book IV*, translated by E. H. Whinfield, 1898. *Internet Sacred Texts Archive*. http://www.sacred-texts.com/isl/masnavi/msn04.htm (accessed September 8, 2010).

Sa'di. *The Book of Love*. Translated by Edwin Arnold. North Fitzroy, Australia: New Humanity, 1990.

———. *Ghazals*. "Sa'di." *Books and Writers*. http://www.kirjasto.sci.fi/sadi.htm (accessed March 8, 2008).

Sahih Bukhari. *Guided Ways: Hadith*. http://www.guidedways.com/searchHadith.php (accessed October 19, 2010).

Sahih Bukhari, 67. *Guided Ways: Hadith*. http://www.guidedways.com/book_display-book-67-translator-1-start-60-number-442.htm (accessed October 19, 2010).

Sahih Bukhari referenced on *Jamaat e Islami Hind, Kerala.* "10. The Religion of Compassion." http://www.usc.edu/schools/college/crcc/engagement/resources/texts/muslim/hadith/bukhari/ (accessed October 19, 2010).

Said, Abdul Aziz, and Nathan C. Funk. "Peace in Islam: An Ecology of the Spirit." In *Islam and Ecology: A Bestowed Trust,* edited by Richard C. Foltz et al., 155–84. Cambridge, MA: Harvard University Press, 2003.

Saperstein, Rabbi David. "The Moral Case for Saving Species: Thirteen Prominent Thinkers Explain Why Society Should Give High Priority to the Purpose of the Endangered Species Act." *Defenders* Summer 1998, 14.

Sarna, Nahum M. *Understanding Genesis.* New York: McGraw Hill, 1966; Schocken, 1970.

Sawhney Anuradha. "A Fight for Justice" In *Speaking Up for Animals: An Anthology of Women's Voices,* edited by Lisa Kemmerer , 151–58. St. Paul, MN: Paradigm, forthcoming.

Schimmel, Annemarie. *Mystical Dimensions of Islam.* Chapel Hill: University of North Carolina Press, 1975.

Schipper, Kristofer. "Daoist Ecology: The Inner Transformation. A Study of the Precepts of the Early Daoist Ecclesia." In *Daoism and Ecology: Ways within a Cosmic Landscape,* edited by N. J. Girardot et al., 79–94. Cambridge, MA: Harvard, 2001.

Schochet, Elijah Judah. *Animal Life in Jewish Tradition: Attitudes and Relationships.* New York: KTAV, 1984.

Schuon, Frithjof. *Sufism: Veil and Quintessence.* Bloomington, IN: World Wisdom Books, 1979.

Schwartz, Richard H. *Judaism and Vegetarianism.* New York: Lantern, 2001.

Schwarz, Douglas O. "Indian Rights and Environmental Ethics: Changing Perspectives, and a Modest Proposal." *Environmental Ethics* 9 (1987): 291–302.

Scully, Matthew. *Dominion: The Power of Man, the Suffering of Animals, and the Call to Mercy.* New York: St. Martin's, 2002.

Seker, Mehmet. "Rumi's Path of Love and 'Being Freed' with the Sama." In *Rumi and His Sufi Path of Love,* edited by Fatih Citlak and Huseyin Bingul, 1–8. Somerset, NJ: Light Incorporated, 2007.

Sellner, Edward C. *Wisdom of the Celtic Saints.* Notre Dame IN: Ave Maria, 1993.

Serpell, James. "Animal Protection and Environmentalism: The Background." In *Animal Welfare and the Environment,* edited by Richard D. Ryder, 27–39. Melksham, UK: Duckworth, 1992.

Shinn, Larry D. "The Inner Logic of Gandhian Ecology." In *Hinduism and Ecology: The Intersection of Earth, Sky, and Water,* edited by Christopher Key Chapple and Mary Evelyn Tucker, 213–41. Cambridge, MA: Harvard University Press, 2000.

Siddiq, Mohammad Yusuf. "An Ecological Journey in Muslim Bengal." In *Islam and Ecology: A Bestowed Trust,* edited by Richard C. Foltz et al., 451–62. Cambridge, MA: Harvard University Press, 2003.

Siddiqui, Azam. "Azam for Animals: With Animals of Northeast India." http://www.freewebs.com/azamsiddiqui (accessed December 23, 2008).

Sierra Club. "Water Sentinels: Factory Farms." http://www.sierraclub.org/communities/factory-farms/default.aspx (accessed April 8, 2011).

Silva, Javier Galicia. "Religion, Ritual, and Agriculture among the Present-Day Nahua of Mesoamerica." In *Indigenous Traditions and Ecology: The Interbeing of Cosmology and Community,* edited by John A. Grim, 303–24. Cambridge, MA: Harvard University Press. 2001.

Singer, Peter. "Animals and the Value of Life." In *Matters of Life and Death,* edited by Tom Regan, 218–59. Philadelphia: Temple University Press, 1980.

———. "One Thing to Do about Food: A Forum." *Nation,* September 11, 2006, 18.

Singer, Peter, and Jim Mason. *Eating: What We Eat and Why It Matters.* London: Arrow, 2006.

Sitwell, Edith. "Still Falls the Rain." In *Collected Poems,* 272–73. London: Sinclair-Stevenson, 1993.

Smith, Alexander McCall. *Children of Wax: African Folks Tales.* New York: Interlink, 1991.

zSommer, Deborah, ed. *Chinese Religion: An Anthology of Sources.* Oxford: Oxford University Press, 1995.

Sorabji, Richard. *Animal Minds and Human Morals: The Origins of the Western Debate.* London: Duckworth, 1993.

Spalde, Annika, and Pelle Strindlund. *Every Creature a Word of God: Compassion for Animals as Christian Spirituality.* Cleveland: Vegetarian Advocates Press, 2008.

Spence, Lewis. *North American Indians: Myths and Legends.* London: Studio, 1985.

Sprig. "Living the Truth: An Interview with Rod Coronado." *Earth First! Journal,* March–April 2003. http://westgatehouse.com/art129.html (accessed July 11, 2011).

Steinfield, Henning, et al., eds. *Livestock's Long Shadow: Environmental Issues and Options.* Rome: Food and Agricultural Organization of the United Nations, 2006.

Stewart, Philip J. "Islamic Law as a Factor in Grazing Management: The Pilgrimage Sacrifice," In *Proceedings of the First International Rangeland Congress,* edited by D. N. Hyder, 119–20. Denver: Society for Range Management, 1978.

Stibbe, Arran. "Moving Away from Ecological 'Political Correctness.'" *Language & Ecology Online Journal* Vol. 1. No. 1 and 2 (2004). http://www.ecoling.net/feb3.htm (accessed April 1, 2011).

Stoddart, William. *Sufism: The Mystical Doctrines and Methods of Islam.* New York: Paragon Press, 1985.

Storm, Rachel. *Myths of the East: Dragons, Demons and Dybbuks: An Illustrated Encyclopedia of Eastern Mythology from Egypt to Asia.* New York: Southwater, 2002.

Strindlund, Pelle. "Butchers' Knives into Pruning Hooks: Civil Disobedience for Animals." In *In Defense of Animals: The Second Wave,* edited by Peter Singer, 167–73. Malden, MA: Blackwell, 2006.

Subramuniyaswami, Satguru Sivaya. *Dancing with Siva: Hinduism's Contemporary Catechism.* Concord, CA: Himalayan Academy, 1993.

Suzuki, David, and Peter Knudtson. *Wisdom of the Elders: Sacred Native Stories of Nature.* New York: Bantam, 1993.

Swearer, Donald K. *Becoming the Buddha: The Ritual of Image Consecration in Thailand.* Princeton, NJ: Princeton University Press, 2004.

———. "The Moral Case for Saving Species: Thirteen Prominent Thinkers Explain Why Society Should Give High Priority to the Purpose of the Endangered Species Act." *Defenders,* Summer 1998, 15.

Tanakh: The Holy Scriptures: Torah, Nevi'im, Kethuvim. The New JPS Translation. Jerusalem: Jewish Publication Society, 1985.

"Tao Te Ching - Lao Tzu - chapter 80." http://www.wussu.com/laotzu/laotzu80.html (accessed July 11, 2011).

Tashi, Khenpo Phuntsok. "Importance of Life Protection: A Tibetan Buddhist View." *The Government of Tibet in Exile.* http://www.tibet.com/Eco/eco5.html (accessed May 8, 2008).

Taulli-Corpuz, Victoria. "Interface between Traditional Religion and Ecology among the Igorots." In *Indigenous Traditions and Ecology: The Interbeing of Cosmology and Community,* edited by John A. Grim, 281–302. Cambridge, MA: Harvard University Press. 2001.

Taylor, Rodney L. "Companionship with the World: Roots and Branches of a Confucian Ecology." In *Confucianism and Ecology: The Interrelation of Heaven, Earth, and Humans,* edited by Mary Evelyn Tucker and Jon Berthrong, 37–58. Cambridge, MA: Harvard University Press, 1998.

———. "Of Animals and Humans." In *A Communion of Subjects: Animals in Religion, Science, and Ethics,* edited by Paul Waldau and Kimberley Patton, 293–307. New York: Columbia University Press, 2006.

Theriault, Michelle. "Namibian Seal Hunt to Go On, 90,000 to Be Clubbed." *U.S. News & World Report.* http://www.usnews.com/science/articles/2009/07/06/namibian-seal-hunt-to-go-on-90000-to-be-clubbed (accessed May 3, 2011).

Thompson, Chad, and Helen Thompson. *A Teacher's Guide to Bakkaatugh Ts'uhuniy: Stories We Live By.* Fairbanks: Yukon Koyukuk School District and Alaska Native Language Center, University of Alaska Press, 1989.

Thompson, Laurence G. *Chinese Religion: An Introduction.* Belmont, CA: Wadsworth, 1996.

———. *The Chinese Way in Religion.* Belmont, CA: Wadsworth, 1973.

Thurman, Robert A. F. "Edicts of Asoka." In *The Path of Compassion: Writings on Socially Engaged Buddhism,* edited by Fred Eppsteiner, 111–19. Berkeley, CA: Parallax, 1985.

Tibbs, Molly. "Review of *Moral Inquiries on the Situation of Man and of Brutes*." *Contemporary Review*, March, 1993. *BNET*. http://findarticles.com/p/articles/mi_m2242/is_n1526_v262/ai_13810569. (accessed July 11, 2011)

Tobias, Michael. *Life Force: The World of Jainism*. Berkeley, CA: Asian Humanities Press, 1991. http://www.criticalthink.info/Phil1301/jainism.htm (accessed January 25, 2009).

Tolstoy, Leo. "The First Step." In *The Complete Works of Count Tolstoy*, vol. 19, 367–409. Boston: Colonial, 1904.

———. *Tolstoy's Letters*. Edited and translated by R. F. Christian. New York: Charles Scribner's Sons, 1978.

Tomek, Vladimir. "Environmental Concerns, Muslim Responses." http://www.religioustolerance.org/tomek14.htm (accessed March 22, 2011).

Tu, Wei-ming. *Confucian Thought: Selfhood as Creative Transformation*. Albany: State University of New York Press, 1985.

———. "The Continuity of Being: Chinese Visions of Nature." In *Nature in Asian Traditions of Thought: Essays in Environmental Philosophy*, edited by J. Baird Callicott and Roger T. Ames, 67–78. Albany: State University of New York Press, 1989.

Ullah, Najib. *Islamic Literature: An Introductory History with Selections*. New York: Washington Square, 1963.

Valladolid, Julio, and Frederique Apffel-Marglin. "Andean Cosmovision and the Nurturing of Biodiversity." In *Indigenous Traditions and Ecology: The Interbeing of Cosmology and Community*, edited by John A. Grim, 639–70. Cambridge, MA: Harvard University Press. 2001.

Van Biema, David. "The Pope's Favorite Rabbi: How a Jewish Scholar Became a Muse for the No. 1 Catholic." *Time*, June 4, 2007, 46–47.

VanStone, James W. *Athapaskan Adaptations: Hunters and Fishermen of the Subarctic Forests*. Chicago: Aldine, 1974.

Vawter, Bruce. *On Genesis: A New Reading*. Garden City, NY: Doubleday, 1977.

"Veterinarian, & Shelter Staff Training 1999." CHAI (Concern for Helping Animals in Israel). http://www.chai-online.org/en/companion/vet_shelter_training/vet_shelter_training1.htm (accessed November 27, 2008).

Vischer, Lukas, and Charles Birch. *Living with the Animals*. Geneva: WCC, 1997.

"Viva! USA Guides: Murder She Wrote." *Viva! USA*. http://www.vivausa.org/activistresources/guides/murdershewrote1.htm# (accessed August 14, 2008).

Waddell, Helen, trans. *Beasts and Saints*. London: Constable, 1934.

Waldau, Paul. "Animal Spirits: A Q&A With the Editors of a Remarkable New Book." *Best Friends*, July–August 2007, 30–33.

———. "Guest Editor's Introduction: Religion and Other Animals: Ancient Themes, Contemporary Challenges." *Society & Animals Journal of Human-Animal Studies* 8.3 (2000): 227–44.

———. *The Specter of Speciesism: Buddhist and Christian Views of Animals*. New York: Oxford University Press, 2002.

Waley, Arthur. Preface to *Monkey: Folk Novel of China*, by Wu Ch'eng-en. Translated by Arthur Waley. New York: Grove, 1943.

———. *Three Ways of Thought in Ancient China*. Stanford, CA: Stanford University Press, 1982.

Wang, Yang-ming. *Instructions for Practical Living and Other Neo-Confucian Writings*. . Quoted in Rodney L. Taylor, "Of Animals and Humans." In *A Communion of Subjects: Animals in Religion, Science, and Ethics*, edited by Paul Waldau and Kimberley Patton, 293–307. New York: Columbia University Press, 2006.

Watson, Burton, trans. *The Complete Works of Chuang Tzu Translated by Burton Watson*. Terebess Asia Online (TAO). http://www.terebess.hu/english/chuangtzu.html (accessed January 12, 2009).

Watson, Paul. Captain's Log: 1998–99 "Gray Whale Protection Campaign, Part II: Bury My Heart at Neah Bay." *Sea Shepherd Log: Sea Shepherd Conservation Society* 52 (1999).

Webb, Stephen H. *Good Eating*. Grand Rapids, MI: Brazos, 2001.

Weeraratna, Senaka. "Animal Friendly Cultural Heritage and Royal Decrees in the Legal History of Sri Lanka." http://online.sfsu.edu/~rone/Buddhism/BuddhismAnimalsVegetarian/Animal FriendlySriLanka.htm (accessed June 17, 2008).

Weintraub, Eileen. "Life as a Vegetarian Tibetan Buddhist Practitioner: A Personal View." December 5, 2008. http://www.serv-online.org/Eileen-Weintraub.htm.

"Welcome to the Rescue Service!" *The Rescue Service*. http://www.raddningstjansten.org/english/ (accessed November 24, 2008).

"What about Fish?" Editorial. *Animal People: News for People Who Care About Animals* 3.7 (1994): 2.

White, Nicholas P. *A Companion to Plato's Republic*. Indianapolis: Hackett, 1979.

"What Does the 'Organic' Label Really Mean?" NC State University, Cooperative Extension. http://www.ces.ncsu.edu/successfulfamily/Nutrition%20&%20Wellness/organlab.htm (accessed December, 2010).

Wikipedia contributors. "Solomon." *Wikipedia, The Free Encyclopedia*. http://en.wikipedia.org/wiki/Solomon (accessed February 5, 2010).

Wilbert, Werner. "Warao Spiritual Ecology." In *Indigenous Traditions and Ecology: The Interbeing of Cosmology and Community*, edited by John A. Grim, 377–407. Cambridge: Harvard University Press, 2001.

"Wildlife Damage Management," USDA APHIS (United States Department of Agriculture, Animal Plant and Health Inspection Service). http://www.aphis.usda.gov/wildlife_damage/ (accessed October 31, 2007).

Williams, Duncan Ryuken. "Animal Liberation, Death, and the State: Rites to Release Animals in Medieval Japan." In *Buddhism and Ecology: The Interconnection of Dharma and Deeds*, edited by Mary Evelyn Tucker and Duncan Ryuken Williams, 149–62. Cambridge, MA: Harvard University Press, 1997.

Wink, Walter. *Engaging the Powers: Discernment and Resistance in a World of Domination*. Minneapolis, MN: Fortress, 1992.

Wittgenstein, Ludwig. *Philosophical Investigations*. New York: Macmillan, 1953.

Wolpert, Stanley. *A New History of India*. Oxford: Oxford University Press, 1977.

Wu, Yao-Yu. *The Taoist Tradition in Chinese Thought*. Los Angeles: Ethnographics, 1991.

Xiaogan, Liu. "Non-Action and the Environment Today: A Conceptual and Applied Study of Laozi's Philosophy." In *Daoism and Ecology: Ways within a Cosmic Landscape*, edited by N. J. Girardot et al., 315–40. Cambridge, MA: Harvard, 2001.

Yadav, Dinesh Kumar. "Ethno-veterinary Practices: A Boon for Improving Indigenous Cattle Productivity in Gaushalas." *Livestock Research for Rural Development* 19.6 (June 2007). http://www.lrrd.org/lrrd19/6/kuma19075.htm (accessed January 8, 2010).

Young, Richard Alan. *Is God a Vegetarian? Christianity, Vegetarianism, and Animal Rights*. Chicago: Open Court, 1999.

Zaehner, R. C. *Hinduism*. Oxford: Oxford University Press, 1962.

Zarin, Cynthia. *Saints among the Animals*. New York: Atheneum, 2006.

Zaid, Iqtidar H. "On the Ethics of Man's Interaction with the Environment: An Islamic Approach." *Environmental Ethics* 3 (1981): 35–47.

Zimmer, Heinrich. *Myths and Symbols in Indian Art and Civilization*. Princeton, NJ: Princeton University Press, 1946.

FURTHER READING

Adams, Carol J., ed. *Ecofeminism and the Sacred*. New York: Continuum International, 1993.
———. *The Inner Art of Vegetarianism: Spiritual Practices for Body and Soul*. New York: Lantern, 2000.
———. *Prayers for Animals*. New York: Continuum International, 2004.
Akers Keith. *The Lost Religion of Jesus: Simple Living and Nonviolence in Early Christianity*. New York: Lantern Books, 2000.
Armstrong, Karen. *The Great Transformation: The Beginnings of Our Religious Traditions*. New York: Alfred A. Knopf, 2006.
Attfield, Robin. "Christianity." In *A Companion to Environmental Philosophy*, edited by Dale Jamieson. Malden, MA: Blackwell, 2001.
Berman, Louis A. *Vegetarianism and the Jewish Tradition*. New York: Ktav, 1981.
Bernbaum, Edwin. *Sacred Mountains of the World*. Berkeley: University of California Press, 1997.
Berry, Rynn. *Food for the Gods: Vegetarianism and the World's Religions*. New York: Pythagorean, 1998.
Best, Steven, and Anthony J. Nocella II, eds. *Terrorists or Freedom Fighters?* New York: Lantern, 2004.
Birch, Charles, and Lukas Vischer. *Living with the Animals: The Community of God's Creatures*. Geneva: WCC, 1997.
Brown, Raphael, trans. *The Little Flowers of St. Francis*. New York: Image, 1958.
Callicott, J. Baird, and Roger T. Ames, eds. *Nature in Asian Traditions of Thought: Essays in Environmental Philosophy*. Albany: University of New York, 1989.
Carman, Judy. *Peace to All Beings: Veggie Soup for the Chicken's Soul*. New York: Lantern, 2003.
Chapple, Christopher Key. "Ahimsa in the *Mahabharata*: A Story, a Philosophical Perspective, and an Admonishment." *Journal of Vaishnava Studies* 4:3 (Summer 1996): 109–25.
———. *Nonviolence to Animals, Earth, and Self in Asian Traditions*. New York: State University of New York, 1993.
Chapple, Christopher Key, and Mary Evelyn Tucker, eds. *Hinduism and Ecology: The Intersection of Earth, Sky, and Water*. Cambridge, MA: Harvard University, 2000.
Cohen, Noah. *Tsa'ar Ba'alei Hayim: The Prevention of Cruelty to Animals—Its Bases, Development, and Legislation in Hebrew Literature*. New York: Feldheim, 1976.
Curtin, Deane. "Dogen, Deep Ecology, and the Ecological Self." *Environmental Ethics* 16 (1994): 195–213.
———. "Making Peace with the Earth: Indigenous Agriculture and the Green Revolution." *Environmental Ethics* 17 (1995): 59–73.
Dear, John. *Christianity and Vegetarianism: Pursuing the Nonviolence of Jesus*. PETA pamphlet, 1990.
Dunayer, Joan. *Animal Equality: Language and Liberation*. Derwood, MD: Ryce, 2001.

Eisnitz, Gail. *Slaughterhouse: The Shocking Story of Greed, Neglect, and Inhumane Treatment inside the U.S. Meat Industry.* Amherst, NY: Prometheus, 1997.

Foltz, Richard C. *Animals in Islamic Tradition and Muslim Cultures.* Oxford, UK: Oneworld, 2005.

———. "Is Vegetarianism Un-Islamic?" In *Food for Thought: The Debate on Vegetarianism,* edited by Steven Sapontzis, 209–22. Amherst, NY: Prometheus, 2004.

———, ed. *Worldviews, Religion, and the Environment: A Global Anthology.* Belmont, CA: Wadsworth, 2003.

Foltz, Richard C., et al., eds. *Islam and Ecology: A Bestowed Trust.* Cambridge, MA: Harvard University Press, 2003.

Girardot, N. J. et al., ed. *Daoism and Ecology: Ways within a Cosmic Landscape.* Cambridge, MA: Harvard University Press, 2001.

Grim, John A, ed. *Indigenous Traditions and Ecology: The Interbeing of Cosmology and Community.* Cambridge, MA: Harvard University Press, 2001.

Gumbley, Walter. "Saints and Animals." *Catholic-Animals, The Ark: A Publication of Catholic Concern for Animals.* "Selections from the Ark Number 196—Spring 2004." http://www.all-creatures.org/ca/ark-196-saints.html (accessed September 23, 2008).

Hessel, Dieter T., and Rosemary Radford Ruether, eds. *Christianity and Ecology: Seeking the Well-Being of Earth and Humans.* Cambridge, MA: Harvard University Press, 2000.

Hobgood-Oster, Laura. *"Holy Dogs and Asses: Animals in the Christian Tradition."* Champaign: University of Illinois, 2008.

Hyland, J. R. *God's Covenant with Animals: A Biblical Basis for the Humane Treatment of All Creatures.* New York: Lantern, 2000.

———. *The Slaughter of Terrified Beasts.* Sarasota, FL: Viatoris Ministries, 1988.

Jacobson, Knut. "The Institutionalization of the Ethics of 'Non-Injury' toward All 'Beings' in Ancient India." *Environmental Ethics* 16 (1994): 287–301.

Jaini, Padmanabh S. *The Jaina Path of Purification.* Delhi: Motilal Banarsidass, 1979.

Kalechofsky, Roberta. *A Boy, a Chicken, and the Lion of Judea—How Ari Became a Vegetarian.* Marblehead, MA: Micah, 1995.

———, ed. *Judaism and Animals Rights: Classical and Contemporary Responses.* Marblehead, MA: Micah, 1992.

———, ed. *Rabbis and Vegetarianism: An Evolving Tradition.* Marblehead, MA: Micah, 1995.

———. *Vegetarian Judaism.* Marblehead, MA: Micah, 1998.

Kapleau, Philip. *To Cherish All Life: A Buddhist Case for Becoming Vegetarian.* San Francisco: Harper & Row, 1981.

Kaufman, Stephen R., and Nathan Braun. *Good News for All Creation: Vegetarianism as Christian Stewardship.* Cleveland: Vegetarian Advocates Press, 2004.

———. *Guided by the Faith of Christ: Seeking to Stop Violence and Scapegoating.* Cleveland: Vegetarian Advocates Press, 2008.

Kemmerer, Lisa, and Anthony J. Nocella II, eds. *Call to Compassion: World Religions and Animal Advocacy.* New York: Lantern, 2010.

Kinsley, David. *Ecology and Religion: Ecological Spirituality in Cross-Cultural Perspective.* Englewood Cliffs, NJ: Prentice-Hall, 1995.

Kowalski, Gary. *The Bible According to Noah: Theology as if Animals Mattered.* New York: Lantern, 2001.

———. *The Souls of Animals.* Novato: New World Library, 2006.

Lappe, Frances Moore. *Diet for a Small Planet.* New York: Ballantine, 1991.

Linzey, Andrew. *Animal Gospel: Christian Faith as though Animals Mattered.* Louisville, KY: Westminster John Knox Press, 2004.

———. *Animal Rites: Liturgies of Animal Care.* Cleveland: Pilgrim Press, 2001.

———. *Animal Theology.* Chicago: University of Illinois Press, 1995.

———. *Christianity and the Rights of Animals.* New York: Crossroad, 1987.

———. *Creatures of the Same God: Explorations in Animal Theology.* New York: Lantern, 2009.

————. "Good Causes Do Not Need Exaggeration." *The Animals' Agenda* (January/February 2000): 24–25.

————. "Liberation Theology and the Oppression of Animals." *Scottish Journal of Theology* 46.4 (1993): 507–25.

Linzey, Andrew, and Dan Cohn-Sherbok. *After Noah: Animals and the Liberation of Theology.* London: Mowbray, 1997.

Linzey, Andrew, and Tom Regan, eds. *Animals and Christianity: A Book of Readings.* New York: Crossroad, 1988.

Linzey, Andrew, and Dorothy Yamamoto, eds. *Animals on the Agenda: Questions about Animals for Theology and Ethics.* Champaign: U of Ill., 1998

Masri, Al-Hafiz Basheer Ahmad. *Animals in Islam.* Petersfield, UK: Athene Trust, 1989.

————. *Animal Welfare in Islam.* Leicestershire: Islamic Foundation, 2007.

Muhaiyaddeen, M. R. Bawa. *Islam and World Peace: Explanations of a Sufi.* Philadelphia: Fellowship, 1987.

Murti, Vasu. *They Shall Not Hurt or Destroy: Animal Rights and Vegetarianism in the Western Religious Traditions.* Cleveland: Vegetarian Advocates, 2003.

Noske, Barbara. "Speciesism, Anthropocentrism, and Non-Western Cultures." *Anthrozoos* 10.4 (1997): 183–90.

Patterson, Charles. *Eternal Treblinka: Our Treatment of Animals and the Holocaust.* New York: Lantern, 2002.

Phelps, Norm. *The Dominion of Love: Animal Rights According to the Bible.* New York: Lantern, 2002.

————. *The Great Compassion: Buddhism and Animal Rights.* New York: Lantern, 2004.

————. *The Longest Struggle: Animal Advocacy from Pythagoras to PETA.* New York: Lantern, 2007.

————. *Love for All Creatures: Frequently Asked Questions about the Bible and Animal Rights.* New York: Fund for Animals, 2003.

Preece, Rod. *Animals and Nature: Cultural Myths, Cultural Realities.* Vancouver: UBC, 1999.

Primatt, Humphrey. *A Dissertation on the Duty of Mercy and Sin of Cruelty to Brute Animals.* Whitefish, MT: Kessinger, 2007.

Regan, Tom. *Animal Sacrifices: Religious Perspectives on the Use of Animals in Science.* Philadelphia: Temple University Press, 1986.

————. *The Case for Animal Rights.* Berkeley: University of California, 2004.

————. *Empty Cages: Facing the Challenge of Animal Rights.* New York: Rowman & Littlefield, 2004.

————. "Patterns of Resistance." In *Defending Animal Rights*, 106–38. Urbana: University of Illinois, 2001.

Robbins, John. *Diet for a New America.* Tiburon, CA: HJ Kramer, 1998.

Roberts, Holly. *The Vegetarian Philosophy of India: Hindu, Buddhist, and Jain Sacred Teachings.* New York: Anjeli, 2006.

Rosen, Steven. *Holy Cow: The Hare Krishna Contribution to Vegetarianism and Animal Rights,* New York: Lantern, 2004.

Ryder Richard D., ed. *Animal Welfare and the Environment.* Melksham, UK: Duckworth, 1992.

Schochet, Elijah Judah. *Animal Life in Jewish Tradition: Attitudes and Relationships.* New York: KTAV, 1984.

Schwartz, Richard H. *Judaism and Vegetarianism.* New York: Lantern, 2001.

Scully, Matthew. *Dominion: The Power of Man, the Suffering of Animals, and the Call to Mercy.* New York: St. Martin's, 2002.

Sears, David. *The Vision of Eden: Animal Welfare and Vegetarianism in Jewish Law and Mysticism.* Spring Valley, NY: Orot, 2003.

Singer, Peter. *Animal Liberation.* New York: Harper Perennial Modern Classics, 2009.

Singer, Peter, and Jim Mason. *Eating: What We Eat and Why It Matters.* London: Arrow, 2006.

Society & Animals Journal of Human-Animal Studies: Special Theme Issue: Religion and Animals. 8:3, 2000.

Spalde, Annika, and Pelle Strindlund. *Every Creature a Word of God: Compassion for Animals as Christian Spirituality.* Cleveland: Vegetarian Advocates Press, 2008.

Stefanatos, Joanne. *Animals and Man: A State of Blessedness.* Minneapolis: Light & Life, 1992.

Sterckx, Roel. 2002. *The Animal and the Daemon in Early China.* New York: State University of New York Press.

———, ed. 2005. *Of Tripod and Palate: Food, Politics, and Religion in Traditional China.* New York: Palgrave Macmillan.

Tolstoy, Leo. "The First Step." In *The Complete Works of Count Tolstoy,* vol. XIX, 367–409. Boston: Colonial, 1904.

Toperoff, Shlomo Pesach. *The Animal Kingdom in Jewish Thought.* Amsterdam: Jason Aronson, 1995.

Tucker, Mary Evelyn, and Duncan Ryuken Williams, eds. *Buddhism and Ecology: The Interconnection of Dharma and Deeds.* Cambridge, MA: Harvard University, 1997.

Vischer, Lukas, and Charles Birch. *Living with the Animals: The Community of God's Creatures.* Geneva: WCC, 1997.

Waddell, Helen, trans. *Beasts and Saints.* London: Constable, 1934.

Waldau, Paul. *The Specter of Speciesism: Buddhist and Christian Views of Animals.* New York: Oxford, 2002.

Waldau, Paul, and Kimberley Patton, eds. *A Communion of Subjects: Animals in Religion, Science, and Ethics.* New York: Columbia University Press, 2006.

Webb, Stephen. *Good Eating.* Grand Rapids: Brazos, 2001.

———. *On God and Dogs: A Christian Theology of Compassion for Animals.* Oxford: Oxford, 2002.

Young, Richard Alan. *Is God a Vegetarian? Christianity, Vegetarianism, and Animal Rights.* Chicago: Open Court, 1999.

INDEX